Spatial Analysis, Industry
and the Industrial Environment
Progress in Research and Applications

Volume 3

Regional Economies
and Industrial Systems

Edited by

F. E. Ian Hamilton
*Senior Lecturer in Social Studies
London School of Economics and Political Science
and School of Slavonic and East European Studies,
University of London*

and

G. J. R. Linge

*Professorial Fellow, Department of Human Geography,
Research School of Pacific Studies,
The Australian National University, Canberra, Australia*

JOHN WILEY & SONS
Chichester · New York · Brisbane · Toronto · Singapore

332591

_c̸_

British Library Cataloguing in Publication Data:
Spatial analysis, industry and the industrial
   environment.
   Vol. 3: Regional economies and industrial systems
   1. Industries, Location of
   I. Hamilton, F. E. Ian   II. Linge, G. J. R.
   338.6'042   HD58
ISBN 0 471 10271 7

Filmset and printed in Northern Ireland at The Universities Press (Belfast) Ltd,
and bound at the Pitman Press, Bath, Avon.

Regional Economies
and Industrial Systems

Acknowledgements

Brenton Barr acknowledges that the completion of the analysis in his chapter was facilitated by an award from the Killam Fellowships Committee of the University of Calgary.

Anthony Edwards acknowledges the support of a Social Science Research Council Grant and expresses thanks to Sheila Thompson and Dr John Dickenson for their encouragement.

David Gibbs acknowledges the support of a Social Science Research Council Grant and expresses thanks to Peter Dicken, University of Manchester, for his advice and encouragement and also to Janet C. East.

John Goddard notes that several parts of his chapter draw heavily on research completed or in progress in the Centre for Urban and Regional Studies at the University of Newcastle upon Tyne. The sections dealing with corporate organization, information flows and telecommunications are based on a research project entitled 'Telecommunications and office location' undertaken by Vicki James, Neill Marshall and Nigel Waters; those sections concerned with the location of significant product innovations and of product and process innovations in the scientific instruments, metal working, machine tools and electronic components are based on a research project entitled 'Industrial innovation and regional economic development' being conducted by Alfred Thwaites, Raymond Oakey and Peter Nash. Both projects were financed by the Department of the Environment and its support and the contributions of all these individuals are gratefully acknowledged.

Geoffrey Hewings and Breandan O'hUallachain appreciate the comments of Guy Steed, Morgan Thomas, Ed Malecki and Gerald Karaska on their chapter, and acknowledge the assistance of the Graduate College Research Board, University of Illinois.

Ray Hudson notes that his chapter draws on results of research supported financially by the Social Science Research Council, the Centre for Environmental Studies, the Manpower Services Commission, the European Economic Community and the European Cultural Foundation and expresses his thanks to the people involved in these projects. He expresses appreciation for the comments received from various people, notably members of the CSE Regionalism Group, and to Jim Lewis who commented on the present version.

Gijsbertus van der Knaap wishes to express gratitude to Dr Keeble of the Department of Geography, University of Cambridge, for allowing him to use data from his EEC study on centrality and peripherality.

v

James E. McConnell wishes to thank the National Science Foundation (Grant No. SOC 78-24398) for its financial assistance, and Mr Al Marfurt for his assistance in preparing data for this research.

T. D. Mandeville offers particular thanks to Dr Stuart Macdonald of the Department of Economics, University of Queensland, for detailed comments on an earlier draft of his chapter.

Ray P. Oakey wishes to acknowledge the contribution of his colleagues Alfred Thwaites and Peter Nash to the design and execution of the MLH 354 innovation survey which was part of a broader study of industrial innovation sponsored by the Department of the Environment.

Lennart Ohlsson is grateful to the Expert Group on Regional Studies (ERU), Stockholm, Sweden, and to the International Institute for Applied Systems Analysis (IIASA), Laxenberg, Austria, for supporting the research leading to his chapter, which is based on an early version in the IIASA working paper series (Ohlsson, 1979a).

Editors' Acknowledgement

We wish to thank Pauline Falconer, Ethlyn Long, Catherine Woodgate and Pat Christopher for their expert typing assistance. Patrya Kay and Judy Thorne of the Department of Human Geography at ANU deserve much credit for the tenacity and patience with which they checked the references listed at the end of this volume. Pam Millwood, also of the Department of Human Geography at ANU, contributed much to the final appearance of the line drawings. We wish to express our warm appreciation for the practical support and assistance of Jan Linge.

Contributors

Brenton M. Barr, B.A., M.A. (University of British Columbia), Ph.D. (Toronto), is Professor of Geography at the University of Calgary, Canada.

Maurice Daly, B.A., Ph.D. (Sydney), is Professor of Geography at the University of Sydney, New South Wales.

Anthony Edwards, B.A. (London), is Research Associate at the Centre for Urban and Regional Development Studies, University of Newcastle upon Tyne, England; in 1978–79 he undertook research in Brazil as part of his postgraduate studies at the University of Liverpool.

David C. Gibbs, B.A. (Hons.) (Manchester), is Research Associate at the Centre for Urban and Regional Development Studies, University of Newcastle upon Tyne, England.

John Goddard, B.A., Ph.D. (London), is Henry Daysh Professor of Regional Development Studies, University of Newcastle upon Tyne, England.

F. E. Ian Hamilton, B.Sc. (Econ.), Ph.D. (London) is Senior Lecturer in Social Studies, University of London, and Chairman of the International Geographical Union Commission on Industrial Systems.

Geoffrey J. D. Hewings, B.A. (Hons.) (University of Birmingham), M.A., Ph.D. (University of Washington), is Professor of Geography and Regional Science at the University of Illinois at Urbana-Champaign, Illinois.

Diana J. Hooper, B.E.S. (Waterloo), is completing an M.A. degree at the University of Toronto.

Ray Hudson, B.A., Ph.D. (Bristol), is Lecturer in Geography at the University of Durham; since 1978 he has been engaged in collaborative studies of regional change in several European countries.

Meliton B. Juanico, B.Sc. (Education), M.Sc (Geography) (University of the Philippines), is in the Department of Geology and Geography, College of Arts and Sciences, University of the Philippines System, Quezon City.

Gerald J. Karaska, Ph.D. (Pennsylvania State University), is Professor of Economic Geography, Clark University, Worcester, Massachusetts.

Baruch A. Kipnis, B.A., Ph.D. (Hebrew University of Jerusalem), M.Sc in City and Regional Planning (University of Southern California), is Senior Lecturer and Chairman, Department of Geography, University of Haifa, Israel.

Gijsbertus A. van der Knaap, Drs. (Geogr.) (Utrecht), Ph.D. (Econ.) (Rotterdam), is Senior Lecturer in Social and Economic Geography at the Economic Geography Institute, Erasmus University, Rotterdam.

Godfrey J. R. Linge, B.Sc. (Econ.) (London), Ph.D. (New Zealand), is Professorial Fellow, Department of Human Geography, Australian National University, Canberra, and Vice-Chairman, International Geographical Union Commission on Industrial Systems.

James E. McConnell, M.A. (Miami University of Ohio), Ph.D. (Ohio State University), is Associate Professor of Geography and Director of the International Trade Concentration at the State University of New York at Buffalo.

T. D. Mandeville, B.Sc. (Ag.) (University of Alberta), M.Ec. (University of New England), is Research Officer in the Department of Economics, University of Queensland.

Avinoam Meir, B.A. (Tel-Aviv University), M.A., Ph.D. (University of Cincinnati), is Senior Lecturer in the Department of Geography and Research Fellow in the Jacob Blustein Institute for Desert Research, Ben Gurion University of the Negaev, Israel.

Craig L. Moore, Ph.D. (Syracuse University), is Professor, School of Management, University of Massachusetts, Amherst, Massachusetts.

Ray P. Oakey, B.A. (C.N.A.A., Portsmouth), M.Sc., Ph.D. (London), is Research Associate at the Centre for Urban and Regional Development Studies, University of Newcastle upon Tyne, England.

Lennart Ohlsson received his licentiate and doctoral degrees, and his docent title, from the University of Uppsala; currently he is a Senior Research Economist, Economic Research Institute, Stockholm School of Economics.

Breandan O'hUallachain, B.A. (Hons.) (University College, Dublin), M.A. (Indiana University, Bloomington), Ph.D. (Illinois), is Associate Professor of Geography at Northwestern University, Evanston, Illinois.

S. K. Saha, B.A. (Hons.), M.A. (Patna, India), Ph.D. (Wales) is currently Director of Land Records and Surveys and Special Secretary in Revenue and Land Reforms Department, Government of Bihar, India.

Domingo C. Salita, B.Sc. (Civil Engineering) (National University), B.Sc. (Mining Engineering) (University of the Philippines), Ll.B. (Arellano University), M.Sc. (Geography) (University of the Philippines), Ph.D. (Economics) (University of Santo Tomás), is in the Department of Geology and Geography, College of Arts and Sciences, University of the Philippines System, Quezon City.

Suzane Savey, Docteur d'Etat (Montpellier), is Professor in the Teaching and Research Unit in Geography and Planning, Paul Valéry University, Montpellier, France; she is associated with the National Scientific Research Centre (GRECO No. 6).

Andrew Sayer, B.A. (London), M.A., D.Phil. (Sussex), is Lecturer in Human Geography in the School of Social Sciences, University of Sussex, England.

Victor F. S. Sit, B.A., M.A., Ph.D. (London), is Lecturer in the Department of Geography and Geology, University of Hong Kong.

Paul Susman, Ph.D. (Clark University), is Assistant Professor at Bucknell University.

Michael Taylor, B.Sc., Ph.D. (London), was formerly Senior Lecturer, University of Auckland, New Zealand, and is currently Research Fellow, Department of Human Geography, Australian National University, Canberra.

Nigel Thrift, B.A. (Wales), Ph.D. (Bristol), is Senior Research Fellow, Department of Human Geography, Australian National University; he is a co-editor of *Environment and Planning A* and a member of the Editorial Board of *Society and Space*.

David F. Walker, B.Sc. (Econ.) (London), M.A., Ph.D. (Toronto), is Professor in the Department of Geography and Director of the Economic Development Programme, Faculty of Environmental Studies, University of Waterloo, Ontario.

M. J. Webber, B. A., Diploma in Agricultural Science (Cantab.), Ph.D.

(Australian National University), is Professor and Chairman of the Department of Geography, McMaster University, Hamilton, Ontario, Canada.

Robert Orr Whyte, B.Sc. (New Zealand), Ph.D. (Cantab.), has held the posts of Director, Commonwealth Bureau of Pastures and Field Crops; Chief, Crop and Improvement Branch, FAO; FAO Adviser to the governments of India and Japan; Visiting Fellow, Institute of Southeast Asian Studies, Singapore; and Research Fellow, Centre of Asian Studies, University of Hong Kong.

Contents

Editors' Preface

This is the third volume in a series that attempts to disseminate progress in research and applications in the broad field called 'spatial analysis, industry and the industrial environment'. The focus here is mainly on regional economies and industrial systems although the range of the argument and content of the chapters at one and the same time point up the complexity and also the complementarity of the relationships between local, urban, regional, national and international industrial systems.

One of the basic aims of this series has been to encourage contributions that would provide viewpoints from countries at various stages of development and operating within diverse political, economic and social philosophies. It is regrettable, then, that for practical reasons several chapters being prepared by contributors in CMEA countries could not be finalized for this volume. In the preface to the previous volume we drew attention to the problems faced by authors in the developing world. The contributions from such countries are fewer than we sought but, as one potential author in South-East Asia explained, 'my government pays me to solve problems not to philosophise about them'.

The reduction in the level of support for universities and other educational and research institutions in most developed countries since the mid-1970s, along with the intensification of inter-regional stress and intra-regional disparities, also appear to be encouraging a greater emphasis on 'problem-solving' work. Indeed several of the chapters in this volume had their origins, directly or indirectly, in 'contract' research. Some may applaud this shift: Clark (1982, p. xi), for instance, asserts that 'there has been far too much theorising on the subjects of regional and urban location, and too little factual study'. Others would deplore any diminution in the effort to develop the new theoretical approaches that have begun to emerge, as Storper (1981, p. 17) has noted, 'in response to the conceptual deficiencies of conventional location theory and its inability to explain satisfactorily the dramatic changes taking place in the industrial landscapes of advanced capitalist nations'. Although we would argue that the 'dramatic changes' are not confined simply to 'advanced capitalist nations', there is no denying the need for improved paradigms; indeed, the review of traditional location theory is beginning to make useful and substantial progress. Yet if undue stress is placed on the differences between what Rees *et al.* (1981, pp. 4–5) have termed the 'old' and 'new' industrial geography there is a danger that some of the worthwhile attributes of the existing body of knowledge may be thrown out with the bathwater. While it is healthy and refreshing that several sets of ideas are emerging—the 'structuralist' and 'systems' approaches being but 2 of them—it would be unfortunate if such terminology were to become anything more than convenient shorthand 'labels'. In our view, workers in this general field have more in common than the labels they choose to wear may suggest.

None the less there is room for concern about the relationship between the conceptual and empirical approaches within industrial geography. The theoreticians—and especially (but not only) those who hold a 'conspiracy' view of the industrialization process—are, it seems, becoming more content with sweeping generalizations and less comfortable with real data; for their part the empiricists are seeking ever more refined and subtle data sets without perhaps recognizing the complexity and interdependence of the processes involved and the speed at which their relative importance may be changing. A major task for the 1980s is to encourage greater cross-fertilization between these approaches.

One of the healthiest developments in recent years has been the ever-widening range of literature being consulted by people with interests in the general field of industrial development. This diversity is well illustrated in the reference list at the end of this volume which in itself we believe forms an important aid to research. Yet in a world where political and economic strains are re-emerging—in the form, for instance, of increased protectionism and barriers to trade—it would be unfortunate if industrial geographers returned to the kind of insular thinking that dominated much of their work during the 1950s and 1960s.

We have used the expression 'regional economies' in the title of this volume because the term 'region' has particular connotations in some schools of geography around the world whereas our usage is more catholic and embraces analyses at a wide range of spatial scales. The 24 chapters can be divided into 7 groups although no such formal division has been made in the text itself because in practice there is considerable overlap between them.

The first 2 chapters present different viewpoints about the past, present and future focus of research on the industrial components of regional systems. For the most part, work since the Second World War has been conducted in a milieu of rapid economic expansion and thus the emerging concepts are not well tailored to cover the regional impacts of slow or even negative rates of development, the declining relative importance of manufacturing in post-industrial societies, and the greater exposure of local economies to circumstances and decisions over which they (and even national governments) have little control. For example, Volkswagen AG, which in April 1978 opened a plant in Pennsylvania to make its 'Rabbit' car (see Krumme's chapter in Volume 2 in this series), was being forced by early 1982 to cut its workforce and curtail production because diesel fuel had lost its price advantage against unleaded petrol and the strengthening of the US dollar had made imported Japanese vehicles more competitive. Both the rapidity with which circumstances like this change, as well as the speed and unevenness with which they are transmitted through all levels of the industrial system, make prognostication by regional analysts difficult. None the less the call by Hewings and O'hUallachain in Chapter 2 for a greater emphasis on research with predictive value needs support.

In the next group of 3 chapters, Sayer, Hudson and Savey adopt the structuralist argument. Sayer (Chapter 3) considers that the behavioural approach, by de-emphasizing economic explanations, has created misconceptions about the role of technological change in capitalist economies and, in particular, to wishful thinking by the advocates of innovation-orientated regional policies which can simply lead to the reproduction of uneven development. Instead of trying to find regular associations among empirical phenomena as a possible basis for generalization, Sayer advocates the adoption of the structuralist approach. Essentially, this argues that industry creates a specific demand for labour power which alters when macro-economic fluctuations initiate organizational restructuring and labour process changes; in turn, this leads to shifts in investment patterns to take advantage of more appropriate labour supplies. Technological innovation brings about changes in the types of jobs available, including both the de-skilling of some existing work and the creation of new skills and opportunities. Hudson (Chapter 4) argues that the restructuring of the economy of North East England since the Second World War must be understood both as the outcome of, and partly a pre-condition for, the process of accumulation—the driving force of the capitalist mode of production. The internalization of production and the emergence of a new international division of labour have reduced the central government's capacity to steer the national economy and to cope with regional problems. The failure of state intervention to prevent the continued deterioration of the local economy has the potential to develop into a socio-political crisis in which the legitimacy of the state, or even of the capitalist mode of production, is brought under serious challenge. While this has not yet occurred in North East England, Savey (Chapter 5) draws attention to the precarious situation that has been mounting in France during the last 15 years as a result both of the increasing ownership concentration of industry and capital and of the growing disparities between those parts of France which contain the decision-makers and the R & D facilities of the new conglomerates and the regions where unskilled low-paid workers carry out the actual manufacturing operations. In addition, new management attitudes have sapped the paternalistic attitude towards employees and engendered de-skilling. Savey points to the critical role of the state if the collapse of the social consensus is to be avoided: this warning has been underlined in the early 1980s by the reaction—sometimes violent—of Usinor and Sidelor employees when these nationalized steelmaking groups announced further workforce cuts.

The next 3 chapters illustrate analytical approaches at different spatial scales. Van der Knaap (Chapter 6) demonstrates the value of economic potential analysis to distinguish central and peripheral regions in the EEC and, in turn, to invoke speculation about the processes involved in perpetuating or reducing spatial inequalities. Webber (Chapter 7) examines the nature and utility of operational models designed to specify the changes that will occur over time from a known initial distribution of manufacturing within an urban area. Arguing that existing models are capable only of predicting short-run change, he proposes one that is consistent with a structuralist view of the way that cities work, embracing the ideas that production is for profit and profit is for expanded reproduction. Webber's contribution heralds the exciting prospect of a new and powerful predictive tool being developed as these early ideas are further researched and refined. In contrast, Mandeville (Chapter 8) reports how work at the University of Queensland has enabled the well known input-output technique to be developed from a somewhat 'academic' research tool to a ready means of providing information to entrepreneurs and bureaucrats within the time-span in which real world decisions have to be made. At the same time the case study used by Mandeville—the impact of an investment in an Austra-lian aluminium smelter—reinforces the point made earlier that international events can quickly be transmitted through other levels of the industrial system: since that chapter was completed expectations for increased world aluminium demand have not been realized so that 4 of the 6 new smelters planned or under construction in Australia have been deferred, mothballed or abandoned.

Chapters 9 to 14 consider various aspects of the problem of inducing or maintaining innovative industrial activity in peripheral regions. Hooper and Walker (Chapter 9) provide an historical perspective of ways in which contact between alert entrepreneurs can lead to ideas being translated into innovative products, the manufacture of which stimulates local economies. They develop the case that judicious 'engineering' by governments, research groups and business organizations can create a 'seed-bed' atmosphere that motivates innovators, especially relatively small locally based ones, to take advantage of latent business opportunities and hence help places break into a more successful development path. But Gibbs (Chapter 10) illustrates how in Manchester (and no doubt many other communities) clothing manufactur-ers have had to contend not only with international competition and fashion changes but also with local government inner city development and rede-velopment schemes which have changed both long-standing residence-work relationships and also reduced the amount of cheap inner area 'seed-bed' accommodation that facilitates the entry of new firms. He argues that factors like this, along with a failure to innovate to keep abreast of changing fashion and production methods, accounted for most of the job losses in the Manchester clothing industry during the 1966–75 period; contrary to popular belief the direct impact of competition from developing country imports was relatively slight.

Goddard (Chapter 11) wonders whether the growing disparity between regions in Great Britain stems in part from what appears to be a global 'innovation trough': while many electro-mechanical products are coming to the end of their life cycle the stimulus from micro-electronic based goods and services has yet to come. In Great Britain (echoing the picture Savey's chapter painted for France) lagging regions are managerially and technologically becoming ever more like puppets dancing on strings held by decision-makers and R & D centres in leading regions and turning out products near the end of their life in branch factories near the margins of corporate concern. Goddard makes a plea for national innovation policies to be given a spatial dimension and for more effort to be devoted to stimulating technological change in lagging regions especially by improving the availability and flow of information and expertise. Oakey's study in Chapter 12 of the British scientific instruments industry illustrates one of the dilemmas: the employment effects of diffusing *process* innovations to lagging regions are likely to be small, but the chances of diffusing *product* innovations—which could have a more significant impact—to such regions are reduced because of the shortage there of skilled development and production workers.

One of the themes that emerges from these chapters is that regional assistance policies appear to be more effective during periods of general economic buoyancy. But Ohlsson indicates in Chapter 13 that the partial smoothing out of differences between leading and lagging regions in Sweden may have cost that country dear. International market signals were not noticed or acted upon so that the Swedish economy has been slow to react and adapt to changing world circumstances. Thus, suggests Ohlsson, the relatively good adjustment performance in regions granted aid since the mid-1960s may be a reflection of the poor adaptability of the mix of economic activities in the metropolitan areas, 2 of which are themselves now receiving special assistance.

Chapter 14 by McConnell, the last in this group, adds a further dimension by examining the behaviour of foreign-owned firms establishing manufacturing facilities in the US. During the 1970s such foreign direct investment has mainly been in technology-intensive activities (entering for the most part through acquisitions rather than new construction) which tend to be located in a relatively few large metropolitan areas with high concentrations of R & D. The flow of direct investment *to* the US is a fairly recent phenomenon, however, so that foreign companies, still being in a 'learning situation', appear to be more cautious than US-owned ones about locating outside the traditional manufacturing belt. These chapters highlight the need for further attention to be focused on the relationships between processes occurring at various spatial scales. For example, the problem of inducing technology-intensive activity to locate in North East England cannot be divorced from the international circumstances that have encouraged British firms to use financial and managerial resources to acquire technology-intensive subsidiaries in the US. Simplistically, UK capital which might otherwise have been available for investment in Great Britain is being attracted instead to regions in the US where it is helping to offset some of the decline in employment opportunities resulting from the out-migration of US firms to the south and west.

The literature on industrial geography contains few studies of the sources of capital, perhaps—as Taylor and Thrift suggest in Chapter 15—because of an assumption inherited from classical partial equilibrium models that capital is both freely available and perfectly mobile. Yet, of course, the availability, cost and source of funds directly and indirectly impinge on almost every aspect of investment decision-making. Taylor and Thrift note that in the UK since the First World War institutions rather than individuals have become the main source of risk capital. One consequence is that investment funds have been redirected from small firms to large and less risky ones; another is that, as the control of finance has become concentrated in London, the outlying regions have been starved of funds from sources other than government. Karaska, Moore and Susman (Chapter 16) develop a 'financial flows' framework as a way of emphasizing the linkages between industry and other activities in a region and the mechanisms by which households, banks and governments influence the dynamics of the processes involved. Karaska *et al.* also note the high mobility of productive capital between regions in the US: on the basis of the Taylor-Thrift argument, as the US banking system becomes less regionally organized and orientated some regions—and especially the smaller businesses in them—may find it more difficult to obtain investment funds. Daly (Chapter 17) examines the implications of the increasing mobility of manufacturing activity and capital in the context of the 'growth centre' approach to regional development in Australia during the late 1960s and early 1970s. This attempt to reduce what was seen as the undue concentration of economic activities in Sydney and Melbourne was based on a *national* perception of space and failed to take account of the rapid trend towards the internationalization of industry and finance with investment decisions being made by corporations operating in a global context. Apart from multinationals engaged in manufacturing, the 1960s and 1970s saw a dramatic restructuring of the banking sector of the international financial community. Ironically, then, attempts by government to encourage industry to locate in growth areas were being negated by one set of factors while at the same time the upsurge in resource development in Australia was bringing Sydney into the forefront of world finance because local institutions had insufficient assets and experience to cope with very large mineral projects.

The contributions in this volume illustrate both the great diversity of spatial scales and also the wide diversity of organizational forms and underlying objectives that form the basis of regional economies. While the traditional concept of industrial regions like the 'Black Country' in the UK and the Ruhr in West Germany still retains some relevance, increasing attention is being given to events at smaller spatial scales, as illustrated by the discussion of problems in the inner areas of Sydney, Melbourne and Manchester by Webber and Gibbs in Chapters 7 and 10.

Most regional economies develop more or less organically but an increasing number of meso and micro-scale industrial nodes are being fashioned in a more deliberate and planned way. Thus Barr, in Chapter 18, draws attention to the rapid growth in the number of planned industrial parks (more usually known as industrial estates outside the US) which he suggests reduce risks for corporate and regional planners and provide an environment likely to foster innovative activities. A related, but rather different, form of industrial park is the export processing zone (also known as the free-trade zone), a phenomenon that has proliferated in developing countries during the 1960s and 1970s as Salita and Juanico explain in Chapter 19. By allowing firms to import and export materials and products free of duties and taxes, developing countries have encouraged overseas enterprises to make use of the abundant supplies of local labour and, to some extent, indigenous resources like timber and rubber. The costs and benefits to developing countries are far from clear and any such assessment is complicated by the fact that some of these zones are poorly sited, that some governments have failed to live up to their promises, and that fierce competition between zones has led firms to play off the inducements offered by one country against those offered by another. Almost the complete antithesis of the export processing zone concept is that described by Kipnis and Meir in Chapter 20. The Kibbutz movement in Israel tries to establish small production entities which are controlled by local owner-operators and aim to balance revenues and personal welfare. This chapter serves as a timely reminder of the impacts of industrialization on new and traditional societal mores.

The final set of 4 chapters considers various aspects of government intervention in the operation of regional economies in developing countries. Edwards (Chapter 21) shows how during the 1960s and 1970s in Brazil there was increasing centralization of economic control and greater government intervention in regional planning. Among other circumstances, rising energy prices and growing balance of payments problems led to a reorientation of industrial policies for the problematic Northeast Region so that it has become vulnerable to swings in the international trade in cotton textiles and more subject to head office investment decisions made in the Southeast. Yet a further problem has been an emphasis on capital-intensive technologies (especially in the textile industry to boost exports) whereas the Northeast is a low-wage economy in need of job creation programmes. In India, in contrast, one long-standing aim of industrial policy has been the promotion of small-scale industries and their dispersion among small towns and villages. But, as Saha (Chapter 22) points out, such a policy has little chance of success without an effective programme of redistribution of incomes and productive assets to overcome the extreme inequalities in the rural-urban as well as the inter-personal distribution of wealth. In a country where most non-subsistence production is geared to the needs of a small affluent section of the population, which is either located in or linked to the larger urban places, decentralization of small-scale industry does not make sense in the absence of more broadly based rural transformation programmes.

In India and other countries in South, South-East and East Asia, reviewed by Whyte in Chapter 23, manufacturers in the larger cities sub-contract work to small firms in the surrounding villages and, as in Taiwan, even further afield. Whyte suggests, however, that both benefits and costs may be involved in this transformation of rural settlements, including some of the intrinsic values of village life and society. In effect his chapter reinforces Saha's argument that the introduction of small-scale industry into rural areas would require either a massive programme of income redistribution or an impossibly high level of public sector investment in infrastructure. This is one reason, suggests Whyte, why the planners in these countries have turned to more cost-effective ways of providing facilities such as by establishing industrial estates and export processing zones. However, Sit (Chapter 24) provides a reminder of the importance of the informal (or, in one sense, non-planned) industrial sector in many Third World countries. In the People's Republic of China the informal sector contains 93 per cent of all industrial enterprises, employs 47 per cent of all industrial workers and contributes 25 per cent of the total value of industrial output. Even though for ideological reasons socialist countries do not favour the development of the informal sector, it is none the less helping to ease the conflict between the existence of large numbers of unemployed (especially in urban areas) and the promotion within the formal sector of large-scale production processes. As the small collectives in the People's Republic of China are not provided with financial or material support from the state they have to resort to a certain amount of ingenuity in procuring materials and markets, and this may make them a better vehicle to assist in the decentralization of industry. It is important to remember, however, that industrial policy in the People's Republic of China is under review and this may have an impact on the role of informal sector enterprises, since the priority previously given to heavy industry appears to have been reduced in favour of smaller-scale activities based on local resources.

Although the chapters in this volume vary greatly in approach and content, at least 3 themes run through them. One is the increasing disparity between 'core' and 'peripheral' regional economies along with the related division between ownership/control and major R & D functions on the one hand and the mass production functions on the other. But, second, when governments respond to calls to intervene, their actions may be constrained or overtaken by forces operating at a global level and therefore largely neutralized. Third, given these kinds of problems, a view appears to be emerging that smaller-scale and locally controlled enterprise may be a more reliable engine for promoting regional economies and that government intervention would be more effective if directed towards making the national and regional milieux more conducive to industrial development. This may involve, for example, income redistribution in India (Saha), greater regional autonomy in France (Savey), better communications/information systems in the UK (Goddard), or more thoughtful redevelopment of inner city areas (Gibbs).

It is significant that many of the contributors to this volume—all of whom wrote their chapters independently—are at pains to stress the importance of the environment in which industry operates, and this reinforces our editorial view (Hamilton and Linge, 1979) that the spatial analysis of industry cannot be considered in isolation from numerous political, social, technological and global imperatives.

No single volume can possibly hope to consider all aspects of this particular topic and, editorially, we are more than conscious of the gaps, especially as several of the planned chapters have had to be omitted. Many topics touched on throughout this collection of essays deserve fuller treatment. For example, if forces at the international level have such powerful impacts at the meso and micro-scales as many of the authors suggest, what future has regional planning, what role can (or should) national governments play, and to what extent can (or should) political, planning and administrative authority be devolved, and what are the problems and possibilities of selective regional 'closure' proposals to promote greater self-sufficiency?

The contributions, we must emphasize, represent the views of the author(s) concerned: all have been subjected to searching editorial questioning but the opinions expressed may not necessarily be shared by us or by the referees to whom we turned for advice.

G. J. R. Linge
Canberra, Australia

F. E. Ian Hamilton
London, England

Spatial Analysis, Industry and the Industrial Environment. Vol. 3 Regional Economies and Industrial Systems
Edited by F. E. I. Hamilton and G. J. R. Linge
© 1983 John Wiley & Sons Ltd.

Chapter 1

Regional Economies and Industrial Systems

F. E. Ian Hamilton and G. J. R. Linge

'The region' has been the bane and the banner of modern geography. Yet the region has not commanded the same methodological prominence nor generated as much controversy in the study of industrial patterns, processes and trends, except in the intense debates in the USSR about the identification of territorial production complexes and their relationships with energy-production cycles and with economic regions for planning purposes. Nevertheless, as reference to Miller and Miller (1978) shows, regions have provided a very important spatial framework, particularly in the more industrialized world, for numerous empirical time-space analyses of sequent occupance by industry and industry-related activities and for many studies using various techniques to define their spatial, functional and structural cohesiveness.

Indeed, for some industrial geographers the demise of regional study in geography was bypassed comparatively easily as the rise of regional science and of regional economics in the 1960s opened new opportunities in methods, theory and practical applications. This is not to say that industrial geographers remained 'comfortable' with the regional dimension. Far from it. The appropriate scale and proper delineation of regions have remained perennial problems. More importantly, organizational and technological changes, combined with recent deepening business cyclical fluctuations, have stimulated significant reassessments of the interactions between industry, regional economies and regional environments. In turn these have led to shifting interpretations of understanding and managing the nature and purpose of these interactions, and have also evoked more radical demands for 'industry with a human face'. Such trends have taxed the ingenuity, tested the inhibitions and tried the inertia of many geographers, but they have also revived studies in industrial geography.

This chapter begins by discussing the *raison d'être* of regional industrial study in the light of these challenges. It then sets regional systems of industry and industry-related functions into their global, international and national contexts since much regional industrial analysis has incorporated only partial views of national economic, social and political space and neglected the international forces at work in the region. A further aim is to examine selected processes operating in the dynamics of regional industrial systems such as state policies, technological and organizational changes and their impacts, thus setting the scene for issues considered in subsequent chapters as well as raising others still neglected.

THE REASONS FOR REGIONAL STUDY

The region is a useful analytical tool for identifying structure, stage and process; a framework for policy decisions involving resource allocation; and a convenient didactic way of generalizing real world complexity. Each of these roles clearly carries recipes for dissent and, while they should not be confused, their interrelationships should be recognized and understood. Yet very substantial convergence in these purposes, a marked tightening of their interaction and hence, a broader acceptance of the regional division of any national space, should result nowadays in the light of:

(a) experience from past controversies about the definition of regional systems;

(b) increased state intervention in economic and social affairs in most countries;

(c) the call for more 'relevance' and problem-orientation in education at all levels;

(d) a more urgent sense of a need for regional problem-solving in society at large.

Perhaps there should be less haggling over what is or is not a region since the *raison d'être* of very precise regional frameworks for analysis seems to have been severely eroded by recent economic forces.

An integral part of the debate over theory and concept (elaborated later) relating to industrial distributions and location is the role of the spatial variable. Neo-classical (and to an extent, behavioural) theories have been criticized for over-emphasizing the importance of physical distance in shaping decisions and for neglecting significant social-distance relations (although these have been recognized by the behaviouralists and brought to prominence by the Marxists). Social distance has been critically important ever since the beginnings of industrial, financial and trading contact systems but technological innovations since the early nineteenth century have progressively 'collapsed' physical distance for most industrial functions, apart from those still involving significant face-to-face contacts and teamwork. One result has been the undermining of the *raison d'être* of the region both as a 'real geographic' and as an analytical framework for very cohesive and integrated industrial structures, organizations and operations. Functional units, freight flows, information circulation and financial transactions have all become increasingly footloose and less tied to particular types of regions.

A growing, even dominant, proportion of them are organized in multi-locational patterns with interactions stretched over national and international space.

As a result, the need for the regional study of industry today resides far less in the definition, description and analysis of internally 'formal' and 'functional' industrial regions and far more in other considerations, including:

(a) the appreciation of the changing quantitative and qualitative relationships (and their consequences) between the increasingly footloose yet basic export-orientated larger production and service units managed in multi-regional organizations (often externally controlled) and the more inert regional factors and conditions, notably the non-basic, regional, locally orientated and smaller businesses; people; public consumption functions; and infrastructure;

(b) the role of industry and industry-related functions in the economic health, social well-being and development of the region;

(c) the ways in which regional environments might be improved, and by whom, to stimulate structural change and adjustment (whether or not involving industry) which would lead to sustained economic vitality and high social victualling;

(d) inter-regional relationships and changes within and across national frontiers, leading to a better understanding of, and capability to monitor, provide, contain and manage for, the inter-regional transmission of industrially or environmentally induced economic and social consequences;

(e) offering a statistically manageable laboratory for investigating and testing interactions of organizations as well as international and national forces with the local milieu.

These, it would seem, are the prime concerns of regional industrial study in terms of analysis, social objectives and policy orientation. Some are elaborated here and, from other perspectives, in the ensuing chapters.

THE GLOBAL CONTEXT

The world's intricate industrial economy can still be usefully 'regionalized' in several ways, for different purposes and at various spatial scales. At the most aggregated level, 2 *global regions* can be differentiated largely by the mode of ownership of their respective industrial organizations, with all that that implies in their initiation, management and dynamics. The larger, 'L-shaped', region of the 'West' (embracing the Americas and Western Europe) and the 'South' (comprising the whole of non-communist Asia, Africa and Australasia), generally has an interdependent, international and intercontinental imperialist industrial system resulting from the intricate competitive-cooperative inter and intra-organizational relationships of capitalist (and some state-owned or parastatal) corporations. The 'Northeast' region (the CMEA countries, socialist southeast Europe and the People's Republic of China) in contrast contains a rather independent continental group of socialistic national industrial systems—which some call 'social imperialistic' (Amin, 1976)—still typified by comparatively low foreign trade components, despite their spatial contiguity (apart from exclaves like Cuba and Yemen) and their seeking intensified mutual cooperation.

By another set of criteria, embracing levels of industrialization and structure, 3 broad types of *international regions* can be distinguished, each containing free-standing, single-country and grouped-nation components:

(a) the structurally advanced, integrated and very diversified industrial cores and control centres in the 'North';

(b) the recently industrialized and newly industrializing 'semi-peripheries', mostly in the world's 'middle regions' (eastward from Mexico, through the Mediterranean, to South-East and East Asia) or in parts of the southern hemisphere, where indigenous capitalism is (or has been) partially compensating for dependencies on the North; and

(c) the relatively thinly industrialized 'periphery' making up much of the South, in which at least one segment of the dualistic economy exhibits a considerable dependency on the North.

This division could be revised to incorporate the politico-economic elements from the first set of global regions. Within the North the capitalist-imperialist core industrial systems could be distinguished from the socialist-imperialist ones; within the newly industrializing group of countries and elsewhere in the South a distinction could be made between industrial systems firmly dependent within semi-peripheral and peripheral capitalism and those experiencing socialist transformation (Amin, 1976; Rogerson, 1981). These sets of international regions might be further differentiated into national and transnational sub-regions according to their economic growth, restructuring, stagnation or decline characteristics of the past 30 years and to their specific social formations, a notion which allows for socio-cultural and ethnic variations and also substitutes for the abstract formal 'mode of production' (Coraggio, 1977).

A Systems View of Industrial Location Paradigms

These global or international regions are not the focus of this volume *per se* but provide a fundamental framework for it. They are a spatial description or form enshrining specific assumptions rooted in the scientific analysis of processes and relationships. Hence they must be embedded in the wider debate concerning the conceptual and theoretical underpinnings of industrial systems, of which industrial and industry-related activity distribution and location are but a part.

Since the publication of Launhardt's (1882) pathbreaking conceptual approach to industrial distributions, there has been a succession of waves of innovation, at shortening intervals, of what in the West have tended to become somewhat 'fashionable' or bandwagon approaches, including the classical-neo-classical, the behavioural-organizational, the (rediscovery of the) Marxist, the structural, and the systems paradigms. As they were initiated and developed all have suffered from some partial—even erroneous—assumptions, methodological weaknesses and inadequate empirical evidence. Extreme abstraction in some has been paralleled by extreme empiricism in others. The assumption of rational economic man in an economically rationalized market world economy by the neo-classicists, for instance, has been as much a disservice to progress towards theory and concepts revealing the truth and relevance of industrial distributions and location as have the purely descriptive case studies by some behaviouralists and the preoccupation of the Marxist and structuralist schools with the deterministic omnipotence of economic structures. Insufficient attention has been paid to the merits of each approach and the additions to understanding and knowledge that it can provide about selected components of the industrial problems, processes and patterns of the real world. Serious gaps remain but their revelation by the systems approach can assist towards a more holistic view of industrial phenomena.

Political variation and value judgements in emphasis and interpretation as to what is or is not the most relevant explanation and for whom must be expected, but this does not mean that they cannot be accommodated within a holistic framework. There has been a tendency, not necessarily intentional, for the proponents of the various paradigms or selected components of them to fragment the explanation and prediction of the processes and patterns relevant in industrial studies. Each paradigm *per se* has tended to lead to a conceptual, methodological or factual cul-de-sac because its proponents have perceived *their* paradigm as providing the exclusive explanation of the *whole* industrial problem and all of the time.

This has led to the criticism or rejection of other paradigms on similar grounds of 'mono-causality' (such as minimum cost, maximum profit, product cycle, entrepreneurial behaviour, or the class struggle under capitalism) or because those other approaches appear to have ignored, or not stated, certain basic underlying assumptions. Misinterpretations thus abound in industrial geography: that the neo-classical approach is irrelevant to industrialists' behaviour or to capitalist (and socialist) production structures; that the behavioural approach abstracts industrial decisions from their environmental context (be it historical, organizational, spatial or structural); that the systems approach is 'technological determinism' (Storper, 1981, p. 34); that industrial systems do not embrace the totality of the production system and its environment; and that the Marxist approach is simply a political ploy. Theory and concept would be further advanced today had each paradigm not been frequently seen as both mutually exclusive of other paradigms and as being capable of explaining the totality of industrial and industry-related phenomena.

Interpretations and explanations of the industrial system—past, present and future—can be better achieved by adopting a holistic industrial systems approach which, in part, has been expounded through the volumes in this series. The various paradigms to an extent complement each other, though collectively they also illuminate real world conflicts or contradictions involved in structures, goals, viewpoints, decisions and actions. Each paradigm is more pertinent to a specific level, time, or type of decision, operation and analysis than to others. The nature and dynamics of industrial systems *at any level* (urban, regional, national or international) can only be fully understood through the interaction and interlocking of all paradigms. It is this that confounds views such as those of Wood who states (1981, p. 416) that 'if [the message of Sayer, 1980 and Taylor and Thrift, 1980] is that we must study the whole world economic order as a prelude to the explanation of any specific location problem, it may not result in very much progress in the field!'. A 'new' paradigm may, of course, be developed to refine even more our understanding and conceptualization of reality.

Real world industrial systems are shaped by many interacting processes and forces (and may be seen from various angles such as those of entrepreneurs, workers, consumers, investors and governments), but not by methodological approaches. Anyway, the processes and forces *tend* to exhibit certain, even marked, hierarchical features and can be treated generally, therefore, as sets of dominant macro-level and subordinated meso and micro-level processes which are reflected partially by the various paradigms. Their relationships are unlikely to be static and are liable to some modification in time, structure and place; nor does dominance and subordination imply that there are not necessarily also significant 'bottom-up' influences in operation.

Generally, therefore, the world's industrial systems are dominantly shaped within the 2 global regions by capitalism or by socialism which set the key structural parameters (e.g. rate of profit under capitalism; improved social conditions under socialism) for constraints of the macro-environments. Within these the decision-makers performing the strategic control functions in organizations of both social systems operate at the meso-scale to set in train commonly aspatial actions such as innovations, investments, disinvestments or take-overs with implicit or explicit spatial attributes. In so doing they generate variety in organizational and entrepreneurial sub-processes and behaviour for a wide range of economic, ethnic, historical, national, organizational, political, social and temporal reasons. The micro-level solution of each specific set of problems or choice of project alternatives will involve some use of the neo-classical types of economic and/or social evaluation of production factors and comparative advantages (with deliberate or derived assessment of place-specific advantages and disadvantages). Such cost-benefit calculations are the specific (time-place) means towards realizing the meso-level decision strategy which in turn should fulfil the requirements of the system dynamic at the macro-level.

This system view of the essential, though not static, relationship of the paradigms—the 'nesting' of the neo-classical in the behavioural in the structuralist frameworks within both capitalist and socialist structures—merits elaboration far beyond the scope of this chapter, yet some further comment is relevant to the regional scale.

First, recognition that industrial capitalism leads to increased dichotomization between large corporations and small firms has spawned ideas that the former operate in what Watts (1980, 1981) unfortunately terms a 'planning' system or an 'industrial system' best interpreted in a more behavioural framework while the latter comprise a market system which can be treated in the neo-classical framework (Hayter and Watts, forthcoming). The systems view, set out in Hamilton and Linge (1979), rejects such ideas because in most cases

(a) small firms are directly dependent on large corporations (for inputs, sales outlets) or indirectly on the business and political environments manipulated by large organizations or by the state and hence they are an integral part of any industrial system;

(b) entrepreneurs in small firms are as much responsive to, or constrained by, the system dynamic as are managers of large corporations and their financiers, although, under socialism, handicrafts—generally the only sector with small industrial firms—may operate in a more market-orientated and informal environment (see Sit, Chapter 24 in this volume);

(c) the small firm exhibits *par excellence* the problem of choice of product or service from a fixed location, if not a fixed site (Hamilton, 1974), though neo-classical frameworks are relevant to the entrepreneurs' behavioural adjustment of the firm's spatial-functional relationships through time.

Thus, although *emphasis* will differ, the same relationship of the paradigms or 'nesting' applies to large and small firms and both belong, within capitalism and within socialism, to the *same* system.

Second, recent attempts to integrate the behaviour of multi-plant firms within neo-classical models are steps in the right 'integrative' direction. The interaction of organizational strategy, business information environments and entrepreneurial or decision-maker perception with the neo-classical type of cost-benefit analysis is often complex. Yet neo-classical analysis, which is more mechanistic or normative, is unlikely to do more than modify specific organizational perceptions, goals and behaviour and will not determine them: hence neo-classical models nest in the behavioural ones.

Third, the sharp division between the global capitalist and global socialist regions might also be challenged on at least 2 grounds. The rise of East-West and East-West-South industrial cooperation and credit dependency (Linge and Hamilton, 1981)—even though currently dampened by recession and political tension—can be seen both as diffusing essentially capitalist para-meters and imperatives into the socialist region and as disseminating more socialist parameters globally. Supporting the former idea has been the need for management attitudes and techniques to be reconsidered in socialist enterprises as a result of the introduction of turn-key factories using Western technology and production methods or as a result of movement towards 'market socialism' as has occurred in Yugoslavia and, more recently, in Hungary. Supporting the latter idea, state intervention in capitalist societies—however imperfect and constrained by the capitalist dynamic—is often motivated by social goals (employment protection currently being uppermost) and distorts competitive business environments through overt or covert subsidies in ways allegedly like socialist economies. For instance, Canadian government subsidization of underground rail-car production threatens to substitute, within North America, Toronto for Chicago (where the Budd Corporation would lose US orders) and so modify regional struc-ture and relations. Yet the socialist dynamic is sufficiently distinctive to merit its own global region even though practical Soviet-inspired socialism deviates from most of the officially propagated descriptions of it in ways not dissimilar from the deviation between real capitalism and neo-classical economic idealism; socialism also varies between socialist countries and underlines the importance of social formations.

Social Formation and Reproduction

The significance of 'social formation' requires further elaboration. While recognizing the basic distinction between societies shaped respectively by capitalist and by socialist structures, the concept also embraces variations within both structures which result from the interaction of their stages and processes of development with local, regional and national inherited ethnic, historical and social milieux. It incorporates interdependencies between class (under capitalism), status and occupation (under socialism) on the one hand and ethnicity on the other. This permits readier understanding, for instance, that attitudes and behaviour can vary, say, between American, various European and Japanese capitalists and workers under Hungarian, Polish,

Soviet or Yugoslav socialism. It would also go some way towards removing the 'congruence' (Seers, 1978) between Marxist and neo-classical economic doctrine.

Understood this way, 'social formation' becomes relevant to other recent debates, 2 of which can be briefly touched on here. During the 1970s, before the world economic recession deepened, Castells (1974) argued that the process structuring space in advanced capitalist economies was the simple and enlarged reproduction of labour, while Coraggio (1977) underscored the continued importance of the production and reproduction of capital in backward capitalist economies. Clearly these 2 processes are interdependent. They are broadly rooted in (a) the growth-induced labour shortage in the advanced economies in the 1960s, which raised wages *vis-à-vis* productivity and lowered profit rates, thus requiring labour immigration from less developed countries; and (b) the ensuing need for firms to maintain their profit rates insofar as such immigration failed to reduce the home-market labour shortage sufficiently, and so to search for compensating increases in capital accumulation by locating in less developed countries to employ much cheaper labour per unit output.

Severe economic recession in the late 1970s and early 1980s might well have altered this apparent dichotomy of process between developed and developing countries. Capitalists in some newly industrializing countries (NICs) now face the same need to reproduce labour in their core regions while capitalists in advanced economies are under less pressure to do so with present high unemployment rates and opportunities to raise productivity sufficiently to stress again the significance of the capital reproduction process.

Another recent debate is intra-national and is about the definition and occurrence of 'internal colonialism', which is seen essentially as the exploitation of culturally and ethnically distinct groups of people in a nation by the dominant group in the nation (Stavenhagan, 1965). Internal colonialism has been perceived to exist in a wide range of environments, some of which are more 'regional' than others: Blauner (1969), for instance, examined its association with the inner-city ghettos of US cities. Clearly it may describe the inner cities of many urban-industrial zones and metropolitan areas throughout the world in which industrial growth or survival depended upon migrant or immigrant labour in the 1960s and early 1970s: West Indians and Asians in areas of Great Britain, Turks in West Germany, Ghanaians in Nigeria, Samoans in New Zealand and Puerto Ricans in the US, can all be cited as examples. Hechter (1975) and Rees and Rees (1980) point to internal colonialism in the peripheral regions of advanced economies, the 'Celtic fringe' of the UK generally and Wales in particular, while Hartwig (1978) and Drakakis-Smith (1981) examine it in Aboriginal areas and reservations in Australia. Frank (1969), Wolpe (1975) and Rogerson (1980,

1981) expose internal colonialism in the world semi-periphery and periphery, respectively Latin America and Africa.

The 2 processes seen by Castells (1974) and Coraggio (1977), among others, as operating in the capitalist global region—and distinguishing its 2 international component areas—really operate simultaneously and inter-dependently at every geographic scale. The actual occurrence, strength and dominance (or subordinance) of the one process or the other in any particular place at any particular time will depend upon structure and stage interacting with the local milieu. Both processes, therefore, can also be integral to internal colonialism. Yet as the processes are structural, the dichotomy between a dominance of labour reproduction in cores and a dominance of capital reproduction in peripheries at any scale suggests that this may also be the aggregate product of an analogous dichotomy between (a) a prevalence of labour-reproduction processes in large and lead firms, in leading industrial sectors, in the earlier stages of product cycles, and in the critically expanding functions of any kind (but especially control, R & D, and innovation activities) of multi-functional organizations; and (b) a preva-lence of capital production-reproduction processes in small firms, lagging firms and sectors, later stages of product cycles, and in the mature, stagnant or component-supplying functions of large multi-functional organizations.

While undoubtedly this is a gross simplification and does not differentiate particular types of capital restructuring, some credence is given to this dichotomy by Andreff (1976). From research in France he established 'a hierarchy of rates of profit' between the 'integrated sectors' (which had high levels of organizational interdependence, of technological innovation, of 'conglomeration' within firms manufacturing both capital and consumer goods, and of international accumulation by multinational firms) and other sectors comprising mostly smaller, lagging firms and 'fragmented' organiza-tions. Similar support comes from data on the rates of profit in various Italian industries in the 1951–77 period (Onofri and Stagni, 1979).

REGION AND NATION

There is, of course, nothing specifically regional in any of these processes. Rather they operate through spatially coincident and spatially associated populations of industrial and industry-related organizations and production units of diverse scale, function and performance to manifest themselves in the dynamics and segmentation of labour markets and in the associated household systems. Labour markets tend, because of the journey to work, to be regional in scale.

'The region' is defined for present purposes as a sub-national unit of space, many types and scales of which are illustrated by the chapters in this volume. Scale contrasts, however, are largely of secondary concern from the viewpoints both of the organization and operation of the industrial system and of the economic and social well-being of the people. For, as Owen (1968, p. xii) generalized from his research into Indian development, 'there is the same relation between economic progress and the capacity to move men, materials, and ideas'. The inverse should be emphasized in the current world politico-economic environment: that the same relationship always exists between economic decline (stagnation and underdevelopment) and the incapacity of an economy to move men, materials and ideas.

One implication is that any region within a country is first and foremost a component of the economy of the nation in which it is located and, as such, its structural characteristics and its progress or decline are substantially influenced or conditioned, if not largely determined, by the nature and extent of national structure and policy. Another reason for emphasizing here the international context has been to draw attention to the fact that the nation—any nation—is merely an intermediary between region and globe. The ability of the state varies, both in time and space, to filter international forces into its industrial system and into its regions or to act as a sufficiently powerful force to generate influences on the international environment of other countries. A significant number of industrial geographers in the older West European economies (especially in the UK) has been preoccupied with the effects of national policies, to the extent that they have assumed that the state has substantial ability to steer industrial location and regional develop- ment and so to manage spatial structural change. Until recently they have ignored or underestimated the international forces powerfully shaping cer- tain components of—if not entire—regional systems beyond the willingness, capacity and the capability of the national government to manage them. This major research field, outside the central focus of this volume, involves both the whole range of overt and covert policies to improve national efficiency, equality, location or employment and also the accuracy of governmental perception of international constraints, possibilities and trends and of national problems as well as the appropriateness of government policy responses. Central to these issues are the autonomy of the state and the segmentation or cohesion of state management of policies and productive organizations. In reality the world's nations range from the few in which the state has substantial ability to the majority with limited ability to control or filter international input and output constraints. Researchers in developing countries have emphasized the *overseas* dependency of the most important regional economies making up the national economy.

Hence the dynamic interaction of nation and world is significant for the region. In the capitalist global region in particular the capacity of an economy to move men, materials, money and ideas depends on the interac- tion of states and capitalist organizations. The capacity of firms or corpora- tions to move their essential ingredients across national frontiers has vastly grown in scale, not least encouraged by decolonization and the proliferation of independent states. In this context, therefore, the region is dependent on the ability or willingness of the state of which it is part to influence both the national and the regional comparative advantages with which to retain, expand or drive out locally based productive organizations and to attract or deter investments by foreign-owned organizations from their international resource allocations. It is also dependent on the performance, efficiency and goodwill of the organizations located in the region.

Regions do not necessarily have passive relationships with either the nation or with the international economy. Those possessing active economies and a high proportion of lead firms can be given sufficient scale, innovativeness, efficiency and dynamism, both to lead a national economy and to provide capacity for reallocation to other less active or passive regions if required by national policy (see Ohlsson's chapter in this volume). Such regions can also exert some competitive displacing or growth multiplier generating influences on regions elsewhere in the world. For instance, the rapid and large-scale growth and development in the 1960s and 1970s of very efficient and innovative steel, shipbuilding, vehicles and electrical/electronics industries in the Tokyo-centred Keihin region of Japan (Murata, 1980) has had 2 types of effect overseas. On the one hand, through competition in foreign markets it has directly displaced growth from, and then helped to create surplus capacity, job loss and even plant closure, in these industries located in such areas as Lorraine, the Ruhr, the peripheral northern and western regions of Britain and in Appalachian and Midwestern USA (with feedback effects on coal-mining and iron-ore mining), as well as in 'core' regions like the northeastern USA, London and Paris. On the other, it has generated growth and development effects through demand in raw materials regions around the Pacific and Indian Oceans such as the Pilbara area of northwestern Western Australia. Furthermore, as a result of inflationary effects on labour costs in the Keihin region itself, it has diffused the more labour-intensive sections of Japanese industrial production chains into nearby peripheral areas of Japan and into South Korea, Taiwan, Hong Kong, and the Philippines.

Regions with passive economies, with a high level of dependent activities, can be strongly under the influence of active regions. In any case, various components of each region's economy anywhere in the world operate under a range of forces, some being subject to dominantly international pressures, others to mainly national or regional ones. The balance of these interactions varies between regions and can change through time. Since the beginning of the twentieth century more components have become subject to international organization, control and competition; thus more regions are directly or indirectly in competition with each other internationally and are open to substitution for each other in the same organization. This also means that regional economies may contain both active and passive components and that the balance of these determines at any one time the competitive position and economic health of the particular region concerned.

The interrelationships of the industrial and industry-related functions in the regions with the national economy of which they are part thus range from the very simple to the very complex. Yet some broad generalizations can be formulated.

(a) Regional and urban economies are usually much more 'open' than national economies, the exceptions being areas with very poor transport access and subsistence economies essentially unaffected by industry in any form.

(b) At one extreme the system of regions that makes up a particular national space could in theory form an operational planning and management system for organizing industrial development and change at a subnational scale as an integral component of that country's economic and social policy (of which industry policy is but a part). At the other, the system of regions (historic administrative areas, functional or formal regions perceived or considered to be objectively defined) may merely act as the passive recipient of either nationally directed (in centrally managed economies) or nationally uncontrolled (in *laissez-faire* capitalist economies) industrialization.

(c) Regional economies will usually exhibit closer and more intensive inter-regional interdependencies within the same national space the more closed is the national economy (i.e. with a low foreign trade component in per capita GNP).

(d) Focusing on the region as a component of national space should not obscure the real world importance of cross-frontier, transnational and international linkages between regions that are facilitated by low degrees of national economic closure or conversely by high levels of international integration and openness and furnished by the transnational or multinational control and organization of production, banking, finance, wholesaling, communications and other activities.

A national economy and its regional components are interrelated in 2 essential ways. One is through the willingness and the ability of the nation to influence, manage or control regional and urban economic and social change and development. The nation in this context comprises the indirect policies of the national (in federal systems, State) government with regional and urban implications; direct state intervention in production and infrastructure provision; and the non-governmental organizations, corporations or enterprises controlled by capital dominantly from within the nation (e.g. General

Motors Corporation in the US, Nestlé Alimentana SA in Switzerland) or by workers.

The other is through the contribution that the region can (or is perceived to be able to) make to the national economy or to the national system of the corporation through its physical environment and resources, its human resources including entrepreneurial spirit and skill, and its locational advantages for fulfilling nationally determined or conditioned objectives and for enabling organizations to satisfy their goals and system dynamic (e.g. profitability or long-term access to materials or markets).

This interrelationship implies that regions with a preponderance of active sectors and organizations contribute most to national growth and development through earnings from inter-regional and international exports of goods and services, while the regions with a predominance of passive functions are in need of national (federal or state) assistance to enable them to participate more effectively in long-term national development or to share more equally in the benefits accruing from such development.

Internal Colonialism and the Regional Problem

A flood of publications since the mid-1970s (Williams, 1981, from a total of 60 references, cites 45 dated 1974 or later) underscores the recent 'discovery' of internal colonialism. This is surprising for it is merely another expression of the 'natural order' of capitalist-imperialist economic stratification resulting from the general process of capital accumulation (as elaborated by Marx, Engels and Lenin a century ago) which manifests itself at *all* spatial (neighbourhood, city, regional, national and international) scales. The difference is that it occurs in association with particular ethnic groups inhabiting certain zones, areas or regions rather than in class differentiation within the same ethnic group.

There is as yet little work to illuminate the problem within the social-imperialist system. While Lenin used internal colonialism to describe the effects of capitalist development in Tsarist Russia (Lenin, 1952), some researchers would argue that the USSR, with its 51 per cent Russian majority, offers fertile ground for attempting to discover the phenomenon in the system of ethnically defined non-Russian Soviet Socialist Republics outside, and Autonomous Soviet Socialist Republics, Autonomous Districts and National Districts mostly inside, the dominant Russian Soviet Federated Socialist Republic. Others might point today to the 'internal colony' of the Hungarian-inhabited parts of Transylvania within Romania. In contrast, the consistently high priority accorded since 1950 to the industrialization and broader development of Slovakia, formerly the most backward area of Czechoslovakia, testifies to the capability of centrally managed socialist economies to eradicate internal colonialism (Mihailović, 1972).

Interest in internal colonialism in the developed West, however, has had to be 'imported' via students of the problems of the semi-periphery and periphery (like Frank, 1969, in Latin America) where, often, the European dominance was more overt. Concern for internal colonialism has also emerged from the shift in social science from an over-emphasis on economic determinism towards a growing recognition of the real relevance of 'social formations' as the dialectic interaction through time of structural forces and specific urban, regional, national and international social milieux. Thus recent research (e.g. Carney *et al.*, 1980) has emphasized the significance for people and society of the appearance at local, urban and regional levels of problems resulting from real world changes. The impacts of industrial decline and restructuring and of some government attempts to cope with them are major explanations. Two such impacts should be noted here.

First, considerably above average rates of unemployment have been created amongst, in particular but not only, the 1960s and 1970s immigrants to inner city areas by the flight of manufacturing from these zones (e.g. Linge, 1979); the wider diffusion of unrest in British and to a degree other West European cities recently has underlined the broader relevance of Blauner's (1969) work.

Second, some significant 'nationalist' and 'regionalist' separatist movements have emerged which express people's conviction that they live in an 'internal colony'. Such views have proliferated in parts of the 'old' industrialized world in the wake of the global economic crisis that followed oil price inflation by OPEC after 1973, but their emergence may be more generally associated with the appearance and timing of substantial structural problems in the economies of regions inhabited by ethnically distinct minorities. Most regions in which such movements have become active share certain common features. Peripheral location in the national geographic, social and economic space distinguishes such 'troubled regions' as Quebec in Canada, Wales, Scotland and Northern Ireland in the UK, Brittany and Corsica in France, the Basque and Catalan areas of Spain, and the Alto Adige in Italy. Physical distance from the capital region has combined with social distance from the centre of power created by limited (or no) access for the ethnic minority to jobs in administration and government to give a sense of remoteness and neglect. Distinctive language and culture (as in Quebec, Catalonia or Alto Adige) sometimes 'lengthens' this social distance, while past sovereignty rent by international division (e.g. Basques from France, Germans in Alto Adige from Austria) and suppression of the native language have generated resentment. Feeling has often lain dormant while people seemed to enjoy a sufficient measure of economic prosperity, particularly from flourishing local enterprise. Tension mounted, protests erupted and calls for (more) regional autonomy were unleashed when the people perceived that they were not receiving or being substantially denied their proper slice of the national cake. Such perceptions have been rooted, however, both in economic adversity and in success, though in at least one region (Scotland) they were sharpened by the perceived failure to use success to overcome adversity.

Most commonly charges of internal colonialism are nurtured by unfavourable and worsening economic conditions. Usually these take the forms of regional concentrations and urban dominance of above average, persistent and rising unemployment, declining incomes, and broader pauperization of the regional environment. The principal industrial components of such deterioration are several.

(a) Accelerated closures or severe contraction of firms and plant in the older and more labour-intensive industries. High rates of job loss in various combinations of the coal-mining, steel, shipbuilding, heavy engineering, textiles and clothing industries have contributed to the social tensions in urban centres in Northern Ireland, Clydeside in Scotland and Wallonia in Belgium.

(b) Closures or contraction of plant attracted into these peripheral regions mostly after 1960 by government policies designed to offset job decline in older industries. In these cases job losses have occurred in a wide range of newer, footloose industries, such as vehicles (Scotland) and household appliances (Wales) serving national markets which are stagnating or being eroded by import penetration, or synthetic fibres supplying a disappearing regional industrial market in textiles and clothing (Northern Ireland: Harrison, 1982). Closure has generally emaciated the more labour-intensive production stages or facilities within those multi-locational firms facing severest international competition.

(c) Organizational changes, particularly the growth of external control which is a fundamental variable also in (b) above, and associated with creating regional 'branch-plant' economies, may also generate contention of internal colonialism (and, insofar as foreign-based multinationals may be involved, colonialism *per se*). External control, or 'integration-domination' as Lipietz (1980b) also calls it, becomes a most sensitive issue when decisions are threatened or made to close or run down facilities in ethnically distinct areas. In the UK acquisitions and mergers have been instrumental in bringing firms in Scotland, Wales and Northern Ireland under the management of firms based in southeast England while, as mentioned under (b) above, government policy also played a role in encouraging firms based in the Midlands and southern England to diffuse branches into the 'Celtic fringe'. Nationalization of basic sectors, like coal, steel, shipbuilding and gas also preceded or paralleled such trends, and often shifted local control and key decision-making to headquarters in London. Organizational change has resulted in more centralized financial control and investment/disinvestment decision-making which facilitated or demanded greater selectivity and substitutibility between regions with competing resources and locational advantages. The entry of foreign-based multinational firms into such regions as Flanders, Wallonia, Wales and Scotland has added a new dimension to these problems but this lies outside the realms of internal colonialism.

(d) External domination of natural resources is often perceived as a major form of internal colonialism. Scotland provides a good example. The rise of the nationalist-separatist movement there in the 1970s expressed the strong desire to control and manage the use of North Sea oil (from fields located offshore to the northeast of Aberdeen) and its large predicted revenues for fear that profits, jobs and other multiplier effects would be mainly exported to other regions of the UK or abroad.

These 4 processes, of course, also operate in other less developed or depressed regions such as northern England, Yorkshire-Humberside (Watts, 1981) or Lorraine without generating either the same level of, or any, separatist movement. The key variable is the lack of a cohesive ethnic bond or social formation to articulate such movements.

Charges of internal colonialism are not only made by ethnic minorities living in underprivileged regions. More than half the largest Spanish firms have major plants or headquarters in the Basque country (e.g. in Bilbao) and Catalonia (e.g. in Barcelona), while in Belgium Flanders has been the main region of industrial growth and development since 1960. Yet complaints often emanate from these regions that local enterprise and capital could industrialize, develop or restructure the regional economy faster and more effectively were the central government, dominated by a different ethnic majority, not to 'milk' it through financial redistribution to support development in other, more backward regions. Perhaps this can be termed 'internal colonialism inverted'. Similar arguments were commonplace among Slovenes and Croats in Yugoslavia in the late 1950s and early 1960s; their pressure on the federal government succeeded in decentralizing economic management and in introducing market socialism after 1964. That the gap in the indices of national income per capita (Yugoslavia = 100) between the northwestern 'developed' republics (Slovenia 198.5, Croatia 121.3 in 1962; 195.3 and 129.2 respectively in 1978) and the underdeveloped republics and areas (Bosnia-Herzegovina 72.7, Montenegro 66.3, Macedonia 57.7 and Kosovo 34.0 in 1962; 66.1, 6.7, 62.2 and 26.8 respectively in 1978) supports the prediction of Hamilton (1968, p. 113) that while

the reforms may thus accelerate overall growth. . . they also jeopardise the policy of developing the backward areas and encourage greater regional imbalances, for the greater the dependence for economic growth upon autonomous [republic] funds, the greater is the advantage to the developed areas.

It is precisely this situation that, despite some federal efforts to the contrary, led to real—and locally sensitively perceived—underinvestment in particular in Albanian minority-inhabited Kosovo and created the environment for the disturbances there in the late 1970s. Under Yugoslav socialism, however, this cannot be termed internal colonialism, yet the example points to the difficulties that arise from very substantial regional autonomy and autarky in countries with very marked inter-regional disparities.

INDUSTRY AND REGION

Industry-region interrelationships can vary enormously between regions during any one period and through time within any single region.

First, there are the interrelationships with the regional environment, made up of opportunities, constraints and needs in material, human and capital resources and their comparative national and international advantages and disadvantages for use in various industries. Second, there are those with the industrial system which include:

(a) the importance of industry and related functions for the regional economy as expressed in jobs, occupations, incomes, inter-sectoral multipliers, export earnings and land uses relative to other economic activities;

(b) the dynamics of the system, evidenced in growth, development, stagnation, decline and restructuring which may be brought about by a combination of births, in-migration, closures, out-migration or other changes to existing firms and enterprises;

(c) the organization of the system in terms of ownership, source of control, scale, technology, capitalization, and intra and inter-organization linkages;

(d) the type of industry as expressed in sectors, functions within the production chains of these sectors, and their place in the national and international division of labour.

Third, there are the impacts of the industrial system and its dynamics on the quality of the economic, social, physical and built components of the people's regional environment, especially labour market conditions, real incomes, welfare and cultural provision, and atmosphere.

While the variety in these relationships is encouraging some current trends in analysis—particularly those which stress the importance of the specificity of time, place and social formation—to err on the side of 'uniqueness', it is essential that work be continued within a regional systems framework (Grigg, 1965, 1967). As long as regional case studies test, discover or do not lose sight of general processes and variables, and help predict the types of

changes and impacts occurring or likely to occur in industrial spatial structure, there will not be a confrontation with what seems to be a widening
abyss between analysis and real world dynamics.

Traditionally, scant regard was paid either to organization (and hence to
non-manufacturing activities) before the rise of the geography of enterprise
or to impacts before the rise of 'environmental' or 'welfare' geography.
Areal differentiation in industry was mostly measured by sectoral specialization or diversification, scale, density, and linkage in material production.
Interest centred on industrial regions typified by large-scale mining and/or
manufacturing, a substantial degree of functional linkage between production stages and units and pockets of very concentrated industrial activities.
Metropolitan, port-centred, and coalfield-based industrial regions epito-
mized this analysis. Devotion to the regional method usually meant that
other areas were largely ignored from the industrial perspective as their
landscapes and functions were, or seemed to be, dominated by other
sectors, such as agriculture, forestry and fishing: the small amount of
industry there was usually explained in terms of Weberian location factors.

A modern systems approach encompasses all industry and industry-related
activities and embraces their interrelationships with society and environment, especially at the urban and regional scales. Industrial systems do not,
of course, exist everywhere at these levels. The industrial regions already
mentioned may be sufficiently large in economic terms, intricate in structure,
and integrated to merit being called 'regional industrial systems' in their own
right. None the less their existence has depended on a substantial degree of
regional closure and spatial monopoly, particularly in intermediate products,
though this was combined with significant comparative advantages in the
national and international division of labour in final products. The same
broadly applied to the 10 model regional industrial 'climaxes' and their
spatial structures developed by Hamilton (1967, pp. 406–10). These identified integrated systems of industries rooted in local resources and, where
sufficiently large, serving the demand for capital and consumer goods in
regions variously typified by isolated resources and sparse population;
forests; the production of hydroelectricity; livestock-rearing; mixed/arable
farming; coalfields; metal-ore fields; oil or gas fields; port facilities; and
metropolitan development. Similarly Khrushchev (1970), following Kolosovskiy (1947) and Saushkin (1967), differentiated 17 'energy-production cycles'
or industrial production chains which could make up regional industrial
structures (Linge *et al.*, 1978).

Since the 1960s the regional industrial systems or sub-systems in advanced
industrial economies appear to have lost some of their cohesion or have
even disintegrated. Many emerging or embryonic industrial systems in newly
industrializing and Third World regions have not evolved or developed in the

ways in which the model regional industrial climaxes originally suggested. The collapse of physical distance and the increased accessibility of all regions to capital and competition is clearly one explanation but there are others.

First, the role of industry seems to have weakened in the national and regional economies of advanced capitalist countries in North America, Western Europe, Japan and Australasia. Manufacturing employment began to decline there absolutely after the mid-1960s (late 1970s in Japan) while tertiary and quaternary jobs grew consistently until the mid-1970s. Similar trends have been discovered in Moscow, the leading industrial centre of the CMEA (Hamilton, 1976). This phenomenon was widely interpreted in the West to indicate that these societies had become 'post-industrial' (Kumar, 1978). Soviet research, however, has related it to the 'scientific-technical revolution'. Yet even under capitalism, the term post-industrial is misleading. Contraction of manufacturing employment, which began in the 1960s, has largely reflected fundamental underlying structural changes, notably the increasing substitution of newer 'growth' industries with higher capital intensities and labour productivities for more traditional labour-intensive ones; and the adoption of some of the products of those newer industries as process innovations by the existing industries, which thus shed labour more quickly. These changes have caused the culling of producers in the older, coalfield-based industrial regions which specialized in steel, metal products, textiles, clothing and shoes. At the same time they have strengthened chemicals, machinery and electronics industries in metropolitan or port regions and changed intra-regional linkages to inter-regional ones (e.g. by the substitution of plastics for previously locally supplied metals). The regional distribution and interaction of industry have thus been altered within industrialized nations.

Even a substantial trend towards complete 'robotization' of material production, manufacturing processes and warehousing will not necessarily reduce the regional and national importance of industry in advanced economies and may actually raise it because

(a) these countries will largely retain control over the introduction and use of these techniques and a significant monopoly of the skills and know-how to refine and apply them;

(b) industry is still by far the biggest source of value creation and capital accumulation, so fundamentally affecting the incomes and ability of the population to consume services and to fund infrastructure, welfare, and cultural activities;

(c) further sophistication of industry will increase the scale and diversity of R & D required and of new technology applications, raising yet further needs in technical, managerial and information-generating and processing functions and business services;

(d) research by Gershuny (1978) suggests that trends in employment and consumption in advanced economies since 1950 show an increased reliance of society on industrial products, especially consumer durables which have had, or are having, the effect of transferring to the 'self-service economy' in the household a growing number of services formerly purchased from labour-intensive service units outside the home;

(e) new ranges of automated and computerized business machinery coming on to the market now threaten to displace much labour from the more routine office and service jobs which were a major component of the 1950s–1980s service sector expansion in metropolitan and urban centres, but new office-machinery servicing and maintenance jobs will be created.

Overall, industry (including related service activities) will assume a different form in the most industrialized countries by the twenty-first century rather than becoming significantly less important. This may not be incompatible with the ability, within the capitalist global region, for multinational and transnational corporations to have shifted a substantial proportion of their labour-demanding manufacturing operations by the year 2000 to Third World countries to maintain profits and so to remit much of those profits to their 'old' industrial home countries. In this sense 'globalization' of corporate activities may ensure the continued importance to developed nations of wealth created by manufacturing, even though it may have largely disappeared from these countries. (A contrary view is that the apparent hiatus between the phasing out of electro-mechanical and the introduction of micro-electronic technologies [see Goddard's chapter in this volume] may— at least in the medium-term—lead to a reconcentration of production in international and national core areas near to head offices and, more particularly, R & D facilities.)

A second factor is the sharpened international competition which is making industrial systems and sub-systems at urban and regional level in developed countries either lose cohesion or disintegrate. Recession, inflated currencies in gas or oil-rich countries like the Netherlands or the UK, and the apparent profitability for international bankers of investments in some of the NICs have all encouraged the displacement and substitution on world markets of a widening range of intermediate and finished goods from producers in older industrial regions by producers in emerging industrial areas, centres and countries. So acute has this become that the 'Second Great Depression' has begun to 'de-industrialize' most UK regions (Martin, 1981; Moore and Rhodes, 1982), various areas of the northeast USA, Lorraine and the Ruhr, where unemployment rates now range from 15 to 30 per cent of the workforce and in some towns exceed 50 per cent. The downward spiralling multiplier effects are as yet hardly known let alone understood, but some of the broad impacts on regional industrial systems are clear:

(a) substantial contraction, if not the virtual disappearance, of major segments of intra-regional, vertically integrated production chains, such as coal-mining, ore-mining, steel production, marine engineering and ship-building, as in Western Europe;

(b) selective and often uncharted feedback effects on small sub-contracting firms and the stranding of many footloose industrial firms which must rapidly restructure product lines and production processes or find new buyers for their existing output in other regions;

(c) the disappearance of inefficient, more labour-intensive firms and sections of production chains (e.g. in textiles), leaving in the region only finishing, specialized and high-quality product lines (e.g. in clothing) which have now become dependent on backward linkages that are often 'stretched' overseas;

(d) the lateral effects of rising unemployment and falling incomes on regional demand which may sufficiently 'despoil' the business environment to jeopardize the profitability and operations of other industrial organiza-tions in various systematic and random ways.

The overall effect of competition, therefore, is to shrink and fragment the regional industrial system, decimate certain dominant industries in selected towns leaving their populations and small firms stranded, to enforce capital restructuring by remaining firms and to increase their backward and forward linkages outside the region.

Third, a global phenomenon particularly rising to prominence in the past 35 years is the presence of external control, if not ownership, in urban and regional industrial systems. Organizations based elsewhere have imported industry into many regions of the world and continue to do so. Multinational corporations initiated and still operate a significant proportion of industry in the regions of NICs and developing countries, but they seldom develop strong links with indigenous small business. Centrally managed state organ-izations have similarly introduced mining and manufacturing to extensive areas of Eastern Europe, the USSR, and the People's Republic of China. There, however, planning has attempted to create more integrated industrial complexes and territorial-production complexes, serving mainly national needs, and which exhibit today the features of regional industrial sub-systems in various stages of formation and adaptation.

In advanced capitalist economies, however, external control is most closely associated with the reorganization of industrial systems that results from the concentration of capital to create multi-locational firms. Destruc-tion or acquisition of competitors and backward and forward integration by merger or take-over are necessary means of maintaining market share, sustaining profits and enabling investment in new products and technology to achieve market lead or supremacy. There are 3 principal ways in which these firms have been able to spread their operations.

First, they have deconcentrated most of their manufacturing facilities from the central city to outer zones of, or beyond, metropolitan regions as costs rise while retaining their headquarters, R & D and some production facilities in or near the central city. As a result, many small and medium-size towns in the rural periphery of core regions are being drawn more into the web of metropolitan-based control.

Second, by taking over or acquiring firms in other regions they have usually been able to achieve a greater division of labour between the regions and more inter-regional interaction within corporate industrial systems.

Third, they have gained by setting up branch plants in other regions either in response to government inducements or to achieve some comparative advantage (such as lower labour costs) inherent to the region. Branches established tend to be 'linked' mainly by the sharing of common infrastructure or by the tapping of common local resources; production, service and control linkages tend to remain within separated corporate systems and are rarely developed significantly between branches set up by different firms in a single region.

In recent years, therefore, external control under capitalism or mixed enterprise has been setting up segmented or truncated industrial sub-systems in newly industrializing regions; maintaining such systems in infant, immature or adolescent conditions in regions in the international periphery; and fragmenting the industrial systems of already industrialized regions. These have replaced their former, dominantly intra-regional inter and intra-organizational transactions by more disparate entrepôt industrial and industry-related functions embedded in distinctive inter-regional/international but intra-corporate systems of transactions.

That cities and regions are being used increasingly as entrepôts or 'conveyor belts' in the various stages of the corporate production chain needs further elaboration. It indicates that the populations of production units making up industrial systems within regions are now linked less through the production chain *per se* and more through their competitive, cooperative or complementary relations with the infrastructure, labour markets, finance, resource and business opportunities and constraints which comprise the regional environment. This emphasizes why the shift from the study of production systems to the analysis, understanding and prediction of industry-environment relations is so essential, especially at the regional level.

This shift, however, raises more directly the questions of industrial 'impacts' and of the study of industry not for its own sake but for the contribution that industry can make to human welfare. Work by Lipietz (1980b) among others, suggests that the organizational changes outlined already create and cumulatively perpetuate a new spatial division of labour, a stratification of regions nationally and internationally into 3 broad types, namely those with a highly technological environment; those with a significant proportion of skilled personnel but lacking a diversified and modern industrial structure; and those with reserves of unskilled labour which is either surplus to farming and rural occupations or redundant from declining industries. Clearly this 3-fold division highlights the crucial importance of industry-labour relations and, in effect, generalizes the complex interrelationships underlying them between the segments of production chains in different industries, populations of active and passive enterprises, labour market segmentation and the reproduction of capital and labour.

The scale and structure of industrialization varies markedly from region to region and may do so in the same region through time. The progression from mainly unskilled labour-intensive through capital, raw material, machinery-intensive to knowledge-intensive industries suggested at the national scale has come about in only a few regions of the developed world. National economies comprise regions which range widely in their specialization, diversification, industrial scale and stage of development in this progression. External control, and the entrepôt functions associated with it, may only partially contribute to the dynamics of regional industrial systems. In some regions, despite externalization trends, significant parts of the industrial system may still be managed by small or medium-size locally owned firms. As Léo (1978) notes, it is these firms operating in intermediate manufacturing stages with high inter-organizational linkages, often dependent on sub-contracting regionally and for which spatial proximity may still be important, that give a regional system its cohesion. The machinery, electrical, vehicle and aerospace industries in the Rhône-Alpes region of France demonstrate just such a high degree of intra-regional financial transactions. Externalization of control of a major regional contractor may, however, force local firms to adapt their linkages. The aggregated capacity or incapacity of locally based firms to change by forging new links within or outside the region can be a key strength or weakness. Some comfort may be taken from recent experience in the West Midlands of England where, following negative feedback effects of vehicle industry recession and British deindustrialization through many local small and medium-size firms, some have been able to turn to supplying recent newly arriving overseas-owned robotic and computer firms with high-quality components.

Adaptability stems from a high capacity for enterprise managements, workforce and plant to innovate or to adopt innovations. This is sometimes seen as a major strength of the smaller firm—whence some governments' attempts, as in Sweden or the UK, to aid such firms is in part also designed to support technology and innovation policies. Not infrequently, however, small firms are born specifically to use and to adapt new technologies and innovations, sometimes in ways in which the large firms normally dominating their production and use cannot or will not do. Small firms can thus sometimes find or create niches in the industrial system and—at least in the short-run—enjoy quasi-monopolistic conditions. A regional economy with a wide range of large and small innovative firms is healthy and has a high growth and development potential. No less important is a diversity of industries which provides opportunities for varied innovations to be made and adopted more regularly through time, which become filters for different impacts of innovations to be diffused in the region and which yield incremental growth, development and change. Regions and cities narrowly specialized, by contrast, may experience more spasmodic, stepped innovation which could generate inflation or create bottlenecks followed by inertia: managerial complacency might then exacerbate the vulnerability to cyclical and structural changes in the dominant industry.

The dynamics of regional industrial systems emanate from births, deaths, growth, development and restructuring in the population of production units. Léo (1978) has classified the aggregate regional effects into 4 types. 'Recessive dynamism' describes industrial decline or stagnation which can only be offset by restructuring to raise labour productivity; this has become a dominant process throughout the older industrial areas of developed capitalist economies. 'Filtering' occurs particularly in the more rural or underprivileged peripheries of advanced economies: decentralization, usually of footloose industries with low capitalization from metropolitan areas, redistributes manufacturing even under conditions of stagnation. 'Normal evolution' is demonstrated by regions in which industry develops or expands at, or just above, the national average: investments are essential, however, if employment decline is not to occur. 'Dynamic' regional systems exist where there is rapid growth in many firms (activities) excepting those industries which are nationally in decline.

In a study of French and West German regional industrial systems Léo (1978) found the Paris region to be the most diversified and dynamic followed by Baden-Württemburg, Hesse, Lower Saxony, Bavaria and Alsace. Three other 'well structured regions', however, had only low-to-average potential because of problems of contraction in basic and resource-extracting industries (Ruhr, Saar-Rhine Palatinate, Rhône-Alpes). Lorraine and Nord in France showed a high degree of specialization and poor dynamic potential. Less industrialized regions with structural deficiencies ranged from good potentials (Schleswig-Holstein/Hamburg and Auvergne) through average ones (Provence, Bretagne-Loire) to poor ones (Aquitaine, Midi-Pyrenees). Languedoc-Roussillon and Limousin were classified as embryonic industrial regions.

STATE POLICIES AND REGIONAL IMPACTS

Even given the willingness of the state to intervene, the ability of a nation to redistribute development between regions depends on several factors.

(a) The rates of birth, growth and sustained development of enterprises and the scales of functions and capacities in the active core regions (a point elaborated by Ohlsson in this volume and long overlooked in many countries including Great Britain and Australia).

(b) The economic and social costs or savings involved which relate to the state's policies to counter congestion and inflation leadership in core regions while resources are unemployed and hence unproductive in others, and to achieve regional balance.

(c) The congruence or conflict of the objectives of state and non-state organizations.

(d) The maximum social redistribution of wealth, power and opportunity.

(e) The nation's ability to prevent international 'leakage' of economic development or development capacity, including the export of earnings and the international transfer of productive capacity and resources by national and foreign organizations.

Serious limitations on the availability, comprehensiveness and reliability of regional accounting data for both economic and social phenomena have in most countries stymied proper assessment of who is subsidizing or assisting whom and where. Indeed, many national governments still do not appreciate the need for such data, sometimes even in the face of the use or misuse of fragmentary information in extreme cases by regional or nationalist separatist movements. It may be that the latter represent an awakening reaction to long-term internal colonialism which central governments want to help cover up by not collecting or publishing all available data. Controversies surrounding the effectiveness in job creation or replacement of British regional policy because of inadequate data collection and publication especially, are a case in point: governments, political parties and civil servants alike are said to have used secrecy to block full impartial public evaluation of policy effectiveness. Such blocking can be exercised when government perceives failure or insufficient success of genuine policy measures and also when government wants to *seem* to be assisting less developed regions rather than actually doing so. Such a cosmetic approach may reflect a perception or conviction that regional aid may have only limited effects but it may also be an expression of a deep-seated ideological unwillingness to permit genuine assistance. Usually, however, information and political understanding of the functioning and dynamics of industrial and economic systems are not such that government can predict sufficiently well what *will* happen in future.

In this context research by Courbis (1975) in France is important. His team's oft-refined REGINA (regional-national) model permits fairly accurate assessment of the quantitative and qualitative impacts of

(a) regional and urban factors on national development to expose the consequences of regional imbalances on national economic performance;
(b) central government urban and regional policies on the development of each region and on national economic equilibria;
(c) national policies on the regions so as to identify regional components consistent with national objectives and which may be particularly amenable to decentralization instruments favouring regions.

On a significantly larger scale, for regional development within a command socialist economy, are the very intricate systems of interlocking models of inter-sectoral and inter-regional allocation, production structures and dynamics of economic regions and their component territorial production complexes. These are designed in the USSR by Soviet and Republic (e.g. Byelorussian, Estonian or Georgian) Gosplan organizations and also by the Institute of Economics and Organization of Industrial Production which is part of the Siberian Branch of the USSR Academy of Science at Novosibirsk.

Interactions between a national economy and its urban and regional components largely hinge on the existence, objectives, extent and types of institutional environments and policies fashioned by the state that can help shape regional development and change. One conceptualization of the range of possible public policy scenarios is set out in Hamilton (1979, pp. 5–10). In the absence of state policies, urban and regional economies can become entirely dependent on the ambitions of the indigenous and foreign capital controlling production organizations and on their performance in the market-place. Such *laissez-faire* conditions long pervaded the North American business environment.

Increased state intervention, especially after 1930, has assisted in diffusing more widely the acceptance of state involvement in decision-making, not least in the decolonized Third World, bringing virtually two-thirds of global industrial capacity under various forms of *mixed enterprise economy*. Typically, this combines broad national-level economic, social and military policies both with direct ministerial-level investments in infrastructure, new towns and industrial estates in selected places and with state-managed or state-supported parastatal industrial and business organizations in an attempt to fulfil a range of non-spatial and perhaps some spatial objectives. Often, however, the cyclical 5-year (or shorter) process of political democracy results in government vagueness about aims and vacillation about commitment to policies and instruments that shape the national and regional business environments. The mixed economy itself evinces contradictory and conflicting objectives, policies and processes. Governments frequently support—even laud—capitalism as an ideology and as the dynamic of their system, so restricting their autonomy. Simultaneously, however, they attempt to manage the impacts of capitalism by filtering or preventing the import penetration of its international operation and by shaping the thresholds and parameters of the export overseas of its own national, regional and urban capitalist processes. On the one hand, private and corporate capitals criticize—and use every possible means to evade, circumvent and reduce—state intervention whenever and wherever it is perceived to constrain their business activity, raise their costs or restrict profit rates. Yet, on the other, those same capitals avidly seek, expect or demand state aid or changes in policies wherever and whenever these can assist their survival or enhance performance and profitability in the market-place. In addition, the state in mixed enterprise economies applies myriad national, sectoral, social, fiscal and foreign policies, as well as ones that are specifically urban and regionally orientated. Not infrequently these embody conflicting aims or mechanisms and lead to contradictory decisions under the aegis of separate ministries and departments. In short, the regional environment in mixed enterprise economies is shaped in segmented fashion by different national level and regionally orientated state policies which interact with the actual and perceived role of each region within the corporate systems of business organizations.

In centrally managed economies the state may aspire, through its ownership of land and capital and a far wider range of direct and indirect instruments, to manage all regional and urban economies in the country as a planned system of complementary components to satisfy prescribed sets of economic, social and cultural goals at every spatial level. By analogy, the state tries to fit each urban and regional economy as a whole piece into the jigsaw puzzle of the national economy while controlling change in the picture shown by the jigsaw as if it were a movie film in slow motion. In reality, the socialist economies that manage one-third of the world's industrial capacity do not satisfy their aspirations; their component regional economies are normally subordinated to fragmented sets of central sectoral decisions which may not necessarily be in harmony and which may or may not take account of specific regional and urban interests and conditions.

Only time will tell if the late 1970s marked a more significant change, or just a passing phase, in state interventionalism. 'De-regulation', 'less government' or 'less bureaucracy' have become more than political slogans in an increasing number of advanced, newly industrializing and developing countries; they indicate attempts by the state to 'disentangle' itself from a morass of contradictory policies. One indication is the proliferation of export-processing zones, freeports, free-trade zones or enterprise zones. While these have potentially significant urban and regional implications, their national economic and social roles are of dubious value. Nevertheless their diffusion and wider acceptance symbolizes the extent to which state *non-intervention* has become sufficiently rare as to be deemed a competitive advantage in attracting multinational business in a global environment of ever more complex regulations, slower state bureaucracies and more stringent state financial control. Although the return or strengthening of more strongly right-wing ideological factions in some governments (as in the UK, USA, South Korea and the Philippines) has precipitated such policies, recessionary conditions have encouraged them: cities and regions are now facing far stiffer competition than at any time since the 1930s for a markedly decreasing supply of new or 'transferable' industrial and industry-related capacities.

Regional Policies

Past research by geographers in many countries has focused mainly, if not exclusively, on the effects of the overt regional and locational policies. These are more properly described as policies which are primarily intended to result in certain desired, spatially distributed urban and regional consequences. Normally policies involve various geographically selective improvements to economic, environmental, political and social conditions within the nation in an attempt to increase social justice through greater equality of access to jobs, welfare or public consumption goods and services and to redistribute income more equally between the regions to raise national economic efficiency or to strike a balance between them. Specific objectives which may be combined in several ways are to provide more and better jobs in areas of persistently high or above average urban-industrial unemployment or of rural overpopulation; to make fuller use of national resources; to reduce congestion in densely urbanized and industrialized areas both to relieve inflationary pressures or bottlenecks and to improve the environment; to preserve and to strengthen regional or local cultures and identities; and to maintain political unity.

The spatial redistribution of manufacturing has usually figured very prominently in such policies in the more advanced and the industrializing countries of both East and West. To achieve it, governments have used various administrative and fiscal instruments to steer the location of industrial capacity, though in socialist economies central or republic ministerial-level decisions involving location choices have been, and still are, a fundamental force in this process. In the West such instruments were usually intended in the 1960s and early 1970s to divert job creation by growth industries inter-regionally either into backward rural areas with an agrarian labour 'surplus', such as the Mezzogiorno in Italy (Rodgers, 1979), or into urbanized regions where localized declining industries shed workers on to labour markets already swelling with unemployed, as in the old coalfield-based industrial areas of northern and western Great Britain, and the Nord Pas-de-Calais and Borinage areas of the Franco-Belgian border.

Administrative measures have generally been applied negatively by governments to control, or even prohibit, new growth and development mostly in urbanized regions in an attempt to slow or reverse agglomeration tendencies in metropolitan areas with high densities of population, economic activity, traffic, pollution and with higher perceived social costs. An example of control by permit was the Industrial Development Certificate in the UK: this was required by manufacturers seeking either significant *in situ* plant expansions or places to locate new medium and large-size plants (over 50,000 square feet [4645 m^2]). In principle the Board of Trade (later the Department of Industry and Trade) refused permission for such industrial growth in Greater London and the West Midlands conurbations, but the system worked only imperfectly, particularly under right-wing governments: not infrequently controls were relaxed when firms seeking expansion were major exporters.

Similar restrictions have been imposed with varying degrees of effectiveness in Eastern Europe and the USSR—through the regional policies set out in the legally binding 5-year development plans—on the location of new industry and some expansions in or near capital cities and congested industrial areas such as Budapest, Warsaw, Łódź, the Upper Silesian Industrial District and such Soviet cities as Moscow, Leningrad, Kiev, Kharkov, Donetsk and Sverdlovsk. In some cases, especially in the USSR, these regulations have been reinforced by the use of work or residence permits to restrict the migration of labour into major cities. These usually serve 2 purposes. One is to ease the pressure on city and regional authorities trying to cope with serious housing, welfare service, retail, transport, infrastructure and other shortages which originated in priority resource allocations to large-scale capital-intensive industry. The other is to perpetuate labour shortages: since in many cases these would restrict production growth and hinder plan fulfilment, *ceteris paribus* they help 'persuade' ministries and departments seeking expansions or new plants to locate or relocate capacities elsewhere in labour-abundant areas. Support is thus given to the state's urban and regional policies which are designed in part to reduce inter-regional disparities. Environmental 'conditioning' of this sort has been deemed necessary in most of the centrally managed socialist economies, at least from the mid-1950s through the 1970s, because the ministries and departments are very powerful and often pursue their own sectoral policies to maximize production growth at least capital cost to the sector; are not primarily concerned about social or other costs; and are not subject in the planning and plan-implementation stages to adequate higher coordinating executive control, even including Gosplan, unless the Politburo (which may also contain certain, or all, of the industrial ministers) can insist on it.

While administrative controls usually impose restrictions in attractive regions, governments, mostly in capitalist economies, have also introduced various fiscal incentives to encourage the diversion of industrial growth and development into other selected regions or cities with backward or structurally maladjusted economies. These are designed to mitigate, eliminate or outweigh the medium and long-term perceived or real comparative disadvantages of such areas in attracting industry. Monetary measures are usually the main instruments of regional policy in the more *laissez-faire* economies since administrative controls are deemed undesirable or unworkable. In more mixed enterprises and state-interventionist economies, however, fiscal instruments are usually invoked as 'sticks and carrots' to complement as well as to enhance the success of administrative controls. Fiscal measures, despite their many forms, basically operate as environmental variables external to a firm which affect its profitability—positively if it chooses a location or is already operating in selected assisted areas, negatively if it operates in non-assisted areas of national space. Profitability of the organization is influenced by the effect the measures have in raising or lowering overheads or the operating costs. Interest-free or low-interest grants for plant construction and equipment and publicly financed 'advance factories', industrial estates or modernized small-industry premises offered at below market rates cut capital costs. Subsidized utilities (on or off industrial estates) and tax and profit remission concessions in selected areas, free-trade or enterprise zones lower operating costs. Employment incentives or penalties (e.g. payroll subsidies or tax) are sometimes applied to induce job creation or to encourage the substitution of capital for labour.

Not infrequently governments set up special funds to be spent only in less developed or underprivileged regions. The best known is the Italian Cassa per il Mezzogiorno (Rodgers, 1979) but parallels may be found in other countries such as the system of 'guaranteed investments' operated out of the General Investment Fund in Yugoslavia from 1957 to 1964 (Hamilton, 1968). Governments perceive that such funds would help ensure minimum or essential investment levels in less developed areas which would not normally be attracted there under free market conditions.

The application of these overt regional policies by government and the scientific analysis of their impacts have been dynamic. Governments have generally increased the range of policy instruments and the areas of national space to which they apply, moving from single measures with simple aims to quite complicated and graded packages of incentives. The history of UK experience from the industrial parks of the Special Areas in the 1930s to the myriad administrative and fiscal instruments applied to 'development areas' and 'intermediate areas' in the 1960s and early 1970s is a case in point. One reason for the change has been the appearance of unexpected side effects which have called policy into question. Many countries have found that capital cost-cutting incentives for the industrialization of less developed areas (e.g. the Italian Mezzogiorno) or for the re-industrialization or industrial restructuring of depressed areas (e.g. northern England, Wales, Scotland) encouraged the location of capital-intensive industries that hired skilled workers from other regions. Introduction of job-creation incentives also often proved ineffective because they perpetuated older outdated labour-intensive industry, protected lagging firms, or stimulated the in-movement of the less technologically sophisticated and more routine 'branch' industrial functions. These deficiences became apparent as scientific evaluation of the efficacy of state policies became more refined and more questioning. From measuring numbers of jobs created, a preoccupation especially of UK government and researchers, analysts have progressively moved towards more complex evaluations of both the quantitative and qualitative cost-effectiveness of policies.

Growth Poles

One of the most apparently regional of all government policies has been the establishment of growth poles or growth centres. Usually these have been promoted in less developed or structurally maladjusted areas to stimulate local and regional development and to counteract agglomeration tendencies elsewhere. The creation of growth poles has involved

(a) the building up of some vertically integrated industrial complexes;
(b) the provision of modern infrastructure and often the whole range of public expenditures embodied in new or substantially expanded towns;
(c) the construction of advance factories and the offer of generous fiscal inducements to encourage linked or symbiotic and other newer industries.

By the 1970s, however, it became increasingly recognized that the spatial diffusion of the effects generated by growth poles, their scale, character and direction, were still poorly understood. Hopes that they would generate significant intra-urban and intra-regional multipliers through integrated and accelerated transactions within their surrounding regions leading to the attraction of further growth and development were often dashed (see the chapter by Daly in this volume). Multi-locational organizations were tempted to set up branch plants in newly created estates or sites, a trend which coincided with the increasing spatial division of labour. Various manufacturing functions that were being automated, generating few new jobs, and locating in new poles were becoming separated from various non-manufacturing functions that were expanding their relative employment and occupational importance but remaining at or near metropolitan-based head-quarters.

Higgins (1977) argues that the assumption that the greatest multiplier effects are generated by new growth industries experiencing rapid innovation is not proven and may be false: for instance, it ignores their differential impacts. This raises queries about the effort currently being put into technologically orientated policies and their growth generating capacities. Growth pole policies and research have intended to neglect the spatial and temporal succession of leading industries, though recent work (discussed in Linge and Hamilton, 1981) takes up this issue in relation to the plans of the NICs.

Schumpeter's 'cluster of sectors' ideas have been neglected although, as Sallez (1975) notes, several initiatives were taken in France in the early 1960s to create 'bourses of sub-contracting' to raise regional productivity through linkages between regional firms using up-to-date equipment to achieve lower costs and higher quality. In many countries growth pole strategies were abandoned as rapidly as they had been incorporated in planning policies. For instance, Chile, Colombia and Bolivia soon dropped such strategies because they appeared likely to extend the capitalist system through 'concentrated decentralization' thus admitting further metropolitan dominance; to require a theoretical level of competition absent from the essentially monopolistic structures of Latin America; and to be associated with large-scale plants inappropriate to small national markets. Several of these issues are canvassed in Diamond (1982).

National Policies and Regional Impacts

Preoccupation with state policies for steering manufacturing as a regional instrument is justified. For example, in Northern Ireland (leaving aside law and order issues) the 'trade, industry and employment' programme showed the greatest inter-regional variation in UK public expenditure during the second half of the 1970s (Short, 1981). Yet since the early 1970s there has been a growing awareness that national-level policies and decisions—which were neither specifically intended nor even considered to have any significant locational or regional effects—may in fact have operated in powerfully selective ways over national space just as do corporate decisions. Several reasons explain the shift in research focus to national policy impacts. First, in most OECD countries government policies specifically designed to influence the regional allocation of capital and labour have weakened: by 1982 development areas in the UK outside Scotland had largely shrunk to a few major urban areas. Second, there has been a concomitant strengthening of national economic policies to support sectors or branches of industry, technological innovation, export promotion, small firms and energy conservation, but knowledge about the size, causes and effects of such measures has not grown at the same rate as the expansion of these measures. Third, a rise in interest in regional economics has combined with improved analytical techniques to facilitate better regional disaggregation of the effects of national policies. Fourth, there has been an increased awareness and revelation in the socialist economies, especially in the CMEA, of serious gaps in the coordination of national, regional and urban plans and decisions, and a growing recognition of the need to overcome the real subordination of urban and regional economic change to decisions made, but not necessarily coordinated, nationally. Fifth, the increased multinationalization of production systems has required sovereign states to adopt more nationally orientated policies.

The effects of state demand for military manufactures on the functions, scales and location of industrial organizations attracted early interest by geographers (Rees, 1979b). National and overseas government orders for military equipment and weaponry attracted publicity on account of the profitability or instability brought to a few firms specializing in high-technology (particularly aerospace) products: dependence on irregular government orders led to fluctuating levels of employment for highly skilled local labour. By contrast, purchases by national and local governments of products used in welfare and public consumption—education, medical care, security and housing—have been overlooked even though state purchasing behaviour undoubtedly operates selectively on the shape and flows of competing corporate systems.

Recently there has been an upsurge of research in capitalist economies into the regionally differentiated effects of 'blanket' national policies and decisions such as taxation, monetary control (Catsambas, 1978; Short, 1981) and tariff protection (Rama, 1979). The imposition of tariffs is almost invariably designed to protect jobs by weakening competitive import penetration. Not infrequently protection is called for because shorter or longer-term structural contraction of highly localized industries may seriously undermine regional economies or the small-town economic base. Tariffs may be combined with capital grants to facilitate modernization in the hope that firms will be able to survive and compete, but experience of the textile industries in the Netherlands, UK, Canada and Australia appears to indicate the long-term futility of such policies. Nevertheless, it is with national fiscal policies and 'packages' of national policy instruments that much of the novelty of research lies. Short (1981, p. 5) has observed that in the UK 'Despite the recommendations of the DEA [Department of Economic Affairs] . . . decisions on the distribution of public expenditure among the various programmes are not taken with a view to their regional incidence'. The main reason, he suggests, is that regional planning has never been an accepted fact of political life in the UK and that

> In practice ... regional policy ... relates to ... [an] aid to industry approach [which] is narrow and ... excludes ... expenditure on infrastructure ... [and] many programme areas ... [which have] a very definite regional impact (p. 107).

Government and research attention has been largely concerned with the direct state expenditure on the 'trade, industry and employment' programme, whereas the time-space effects of other state programmes on the regional environments for industry have been overlooked. These other state expenditures in the 11 regions of the UK are for agriculture, forestry and fisheries; roads and transport; housing; other environmental services (e.g. water); law, order and protective services; education, libraries, science and arts; health and social services; and social security (mostly benefits for the unemployed).

Given the brevity of the period covered by Short's study (the 4 financial years 1974–78), regional variations in state expenditures in the UK may be distorted by the timing of specific projects and may mask salient long-term trends, even allowing for significant regional differences noted in population age-structure, in specific local government priorities, in costs and in the taxation base. Nevertheless, the study showed a net transfer of resources broadly from the 5 southern, eastern and Midland regions of England, to the 6 northern and western peripheral ones, so supporting the hypothesis that government policies usually yield a negative relationship between public expenditure in a region and that region's per capita income. Similarly, Catsambas' (1978) study of federal expenditures in the USA in the early 1970s on such sectors as defence, space research, international affairs, government, sanitation, police and natural resources, concludes (pp. 97 and 100) that

> there is a clear pattern of net fiscal transfer from the more industrialized parts of the country—the East Coast and the Great Lakes—to the South and the Rocky Mountains. In this respect, the spatial activity of the federal government may be termed "progressive". . . [and] contributes to a more uniform income distribution across the states.

Yet alongside the UK regions receiving above average assistance—Northern Ireland, Northern England, Scotland and Wales—was also the most prosperous region, South East England. Above average public expenditure there suggests that population and business in the region also demanded more and higher-standard public services, which could be provided by local authorities with larger per capita tax bases. Short's data show this was particularly so in housing, transport, education, health and protection.

While these higher outlays undoubtedly reflected higher labour, land, housing and social costs in London, they also contributed to significant sophistication of the regional environment, an important factor for example in the emergence of an R & D corridor to the west of London. By contrast, a higher proportion of the above average expenditure in the 4 peripheral regions went into supporting unemployed labour and security (especially in Northern Ireland) and in upgrading environments which still remain poor by the standards of the South East.

INFERENCES AND ISSUES

Relationships between industry and region, and vice-versa, are multivariate and changeable as is their appraisal. Regions are located in capitalistic or socialistic economic systems which condition the objectives, mechanisms and dynamics of the industrial and industry-related organizations that can populate them. Some regions may become 'transitional' for a period following radical political change. The inference is clear. Capitalist organizations (including state ones in 'mixed' economies) will develop in a region in 'their' arena to profit from the region (see Sayer's chapter in this book). Under socialism, organizations ought to populate a region as vehicles for the development of the region's resources and environment to improve human welfare and to achieve cultural betterment; in addition they should also permit inter-regional cooperation and mutual assistance for the benefit of the whole society. The discussion of region-nation interaction specifically pinpointed doubts about the real interdependence of the national and the regional economy under capitalism. These fundamental differences generate contrasts in the reasons why and the ways in which the industrial sectors— common to both economic systems—are developed and linked at regional and national levels.

Regional economies and their workers under capitalism have become far more 'remotely controlled' from a diversity of metropolitan and international sources as corporate systems evolved towards being multi-regional in the pattern of labour market areas and sub-contractors tributary to them. Technological and economic processes have tended to equalize especially transport, and also capital, costs and access between regions, while in many developed countries the differentials between regional labour markets in productivity, costs and skills have widened. As a result, regional specialization in the form of major segments of, or even entire, production chains of a narrow range of industries is being displaced by specialization in limited segments of the production chains of a wide range of Standard Industrial Classification orders. Intra-regional labour market requirements are to some extent being homogenized while inter-regionally they are becoming more stratified. Thus, at any time, regions in the capitalist system and their industrial structures can be placed in a hierarchy which—as the discussion of the interrelated issues of active and passive functions, leading and lagging organizations, reproduction of labour and capital, segmented labour markets and social formations has shown—is rather more complex than Lipietz's 3-fold typology. That grouping itself broadly corresponds to core, semi-periphery and periphery. Yet all 3 types of region contain nested hierarchies or stratified sub-regions at different levels of development. Cores like Rio de Janeiro-São Paulo in Brazil occur in semi-peripheral areas and peripheral areas in developing countries just as semi-peripheries and peripheries exist in core nations and regions like the EEC or Japan. Regional disparities occur in most countries. Regions and metropolitan centres must thus be ranked and grouped according both to the scales of their various industrial and related functions and to their diversification or specialization in traditionally defined industrial sectors in addition to populations of leading and lagging firms; their dynamics; capital and labour reproduction processes; and labour market structures. There are, however, serious pitfalls in exaggerating the regional or spatial aspects of these structural processes.

Work still remains to be done on core and periphery under socialism; yet there is evidence (Hamilton, 1976; French and Hamilton, 1979) that the main metropolitan areas in the CMEA are also experiencing greater specialization in knowledge and skill-intensive activities (control, R & D, higher-technology manufacturing) and decentralization of existing, or steering of new, routine industrial functions into rural areas. The lesson of Yugoslavia, however, is that workers' self-management of production units and strongly decentralized regional government do not provide the answer to regional inequality in an environment of ethnic division and an economic and social legacy of a serious north-south rift.

Governments intervene in national interests and may or may not be concerned with regional or urban objectives. There is closer coincidence of identity between the goals and mechanisms of government and industrial organizations under socialism than under capitalism, though in autocratic states ruling classes may identify themselves with the business aims of indigenous and foreign firms. More democratic states seek to modify corporate behaviour in the 'social interest' which in part may be regional and urban in expression. Too few governments have realized, though, how much their national tariff, taxation, public expenditure and various industrial policies can assist, retard or neutralize specific regionally orientated policies: regional economies distil these policies in their effects on the behaviour and performance of regional populations of industrial organizations.

The regional significance of state policies can be volatile. Shifts in developing countries from import substitution to export orientation may simply alter the industrial structures of port-centred regions; yet the economic effects of the technological changes involved and of new linkages forged with populations of firms elsewhere in these countries can be quite striking. In several OECD countries the recent partial substitution of regional aid by measures to assist selected industries and firms is essential to reduce rising unemployment consequent upon localized or widely diffused deindustrialization. These include innovations-based and labour retraining policies designed to foster quantitative and qualitative changes in the national industrial system in order to generate new job-creating and diffusing industries. Rarely are the regional impacts coincident. Moreover, competition between governments themselves is growing fiercer. Peripheral or declining regions concentrating protected industries are being drawn into international politics over surplus capacity. Intermediate and core regions find their international competitiveness is simply re-established at a higher parity as governments race to raise labour productivity and to hasten the rise of a new set of Kondratiev waves. State policies to invigorate inner city areas seem to be running into a new difficulty, namely the feedback multiplier effects of recent and planned moves of headquarters and key divisional offices from large-city centres to smaller towns in the metropolitan periphery. Relocation of Union Carbide's headquarters from downtown Manhattan, New York, to Danbury, Connecticut and Imperial Chemical Industries' recent announcement to move out of London are but 2 instances among many which suggest that a new era is dawning of decentralized headquarters and offices using the more standardized computer, telecommunications and office-automation machinery. Yet another trend is to change the shape and form of control and business services and of their labour market requirements in the world's core regions.

The diffusion of job-replacing technologies, being encouraged by many governments to reduce national inflation and as a short cut to hoped-for job-creating competitive growth in future, provides little comfort to clusters and concentrations of workers made redundant in the prime of life, to long-term unemployed school-leavers in urban-industrial areas, or to the many unemployed and underemployed people in the world's developing regions.

Even more depressing is that those same governments seem content to allow big business to shape society through its innovations and technological applications; spend more money on the parasitic and uncertain armaments sector; reduce investment in people's education and retraining; lack ideas or objectives about the future volume, character and distribution of work and use of time between people; and hence show little concern for, or no conception of, the kind of society people should enjoy in the twenty-first century. Reinvigoration of declining regional economies either by direct investment or indirect support from dynamic regional economies, and proper development of the world's semi-peripheral and peripheral regions requires a fundamental shift in social values. This includes a reduction in the importance of pseudo-values (status goods) and parasitic demand (weapons) and a new role for use-values (Sachs, 1981). By producing for the real needs of society, the advanced economies could provide a lead with new industries which would enable the developing regions to play a much greater part in global industry.

Spatial Analysis, Industry and the Industrial Environment. Vol. 3 Regional Economies and Industrial Systems
Edited by F. E. I. Hamilton and G. J. R. Linge
© 1983 John Wiley & Sons Ltd.

Chapter 2

Industrial Factors in the Development of Regional Systems

GEOFFREY J. D. HEWINGS AND BREANDAN O'HUALLACHAIN

Just as the structure of developed economies has changed over the last several decades, so has the composition, content and focus of studies of the industrial components of regional systems. While, at first glance, little discernible continuity is apparent in the changing research foci since the Second World War, several major trends can be noted, especially in the development of analytical techniques used to describe the structure and dynamics of regional systems. The review and evaluation here is topical rather than temporal, although the latter perspective is an important component of many of the factors discussed, and is largely biased towards North American and West European economic experiences.

MAJOR FACTORS

At this stage no attempt is made to rank factors according to their importance: rather, the major components of the industrial system which influence the direction, magnitude and rate of growth of regional systems are discussed.

Overriding all industrial factors is the onmipresent influence of structural change in Western economies. Until recently, manufacturing activity was the dominating source of employment: even critics of 'economic take-off' were impressed by its contribution in fostering sustained growth. The richness and variety of experience embodied in the industrial development dominance period has left a legacy—in varying regional economic landscapes—which has simultaneously provided a basis for continued growth and for continued no growth. One of the first recognitions of the importance of structural change in industrial systems was provided by Thomas (1964). Drawing upon many generally accepted economic principles, he was able to postulate the likely impacts of structural change on regional economies through both technological innovation and changes in consumer tastes which were themselves partially induced by technological change (through raising per capita incomes).

This research enquiry has led to many important studies of the impacts of components of structural change: these include the importance of scale (both internal economies of scale and spatial scale of analysis), the concepts of lead and lagging industries, the diffusion and adoption of technological innovations, the identification and measurement of regional and inter-regional business cycles, the location of R & D activities, and the import-ance of product cycles to regional economic health. These and many other avenues of research have provided a wealth of detail and analytical capabili-ties leading to the articulation of a body of truly 'regional theory'.

Very closely related is research into the 'industrial milieu' which continues a long tradition in economic geography, namely, the study of individual industries and their specific location patterns. Whereas the traditional con-cern was with determinants of location (particularly the importance of production factors), recent investigation casts the industrial system more broadly into the economic environment of supply and demand and considers the entrepreneurial skills involved, the decision-making structures, and the collection and use of information in location decision-making. Recent work has examined issues related to the birth, death and survival of firms in various environments and tried to link these studies with the product cycle concept and diffusion of operations within multi-plant and multinational enterprises.

Early regional science analysis stimulated interest in the proselytizing of Leontief's input-output analysis to the sub-national level. The first regional input-output models and Isard's inter-regional model of the US economy provided a new view of the structuring of interrelationships within an economic system which, hitherto, had been limited to specific industry studies. These models have mostly been for impact analysis, focusing on the extent to which regional economies are self-sufficient or, more appropriate-ly, dependent upon other regional economies. However, this is one major field in which conceptual development has far exceeded empirical imple-mentation and represents a rich source for continued development. The work of Pred (1974) and others provided a multi-dimensional view of the nature of information flows, contact linkage systems and, most importantly, ownership linkage patterns. But regional economic theory has failed to keep pace with the rapid growth in understanding the workings of regional systems: this represents a major focus in the whole spectrum of regional industrial analysis.

Once the impact of industrialization was better understood, particularly its asymmetric influence upon spatial development, the contribution of industry to articulated goals associated with regional development was soon to become embodied in the policy formulation of central governments in Western economies. The Royal Commission on the Distribution of the Industrial Population (the Barlow Report) (1940), reporting on the impact of industrial development in Britain prior to the Second World War, made many important suggestions about the role of government policy in moving the industrial pattern of activity closer to one deemed 'better' from the perspective of the broader goals of society rather than the narrow view of profit-maximizing entrepreneurs. As a result, industrial development policy became an important and generally accepted component of regional development strategies in post-war Europe and subsequently, to a lesser extent, in North America. Research has focused upon many aspects of this problem, one of them being the relative advantages and disadvantages of moving jobs to unemployed workers and moving workers to locations with better job opportunities. The theme of 'place versus people' prosperity has been dominant in general regional development debates. The problem of structure reappears again in policy analysis: research has been directed towards identifying the causes of industrial decline, the problems of dependence upon a narrow range of industries (the diversification argument), and the appropriate mechanisms that should be used to effect a better distribution of economic activities (the dispute over 'carrot' and 'stick' regional development policies). More recently, discussion has focused on the issues of capital versus labour intensity in development and on the inter-regional impacts of central government development and expenditure policies. Many policies were enacted as though regional economies were viewed as separable, black-box entities having little interaction. Significant inter-regional feedback effects and spillovers have necessitated a more thorough evaluation and monitoring of government policies and programmes.

Evaluation, particularly of government-initiated industrial development, has attracted much recent research, especially in the UK. The initial work has created many difficult and sometimes embarrassing questions about the efficacy of regional development policies. Nevertheless, it has also provided some measure of justification for programmes which were often viewed as little more than marginal tampering with the regional economic system.

The change in the employment structure of the whole economic system, with increased dependence on the tertiary and quaternary sectors, has raised fundamental questions about the validity of regional economic models developed on the premise of industrial dominance. Furthermore, the character of the industrial system itself has changed, with greater integration of the economy at the macro-level. The structural changes have also created major differences in the composition of the workforce as participation rates from the secondary labour force (especially females) have risen dramatically over the last decade, particularly in the United States.

Since the oil crisis of 1973, concern about energy supply and cost has begun to dominate industrial development issues and their influence on regional systems. While the environmental concerns of the late 1960s had begun to make an impression on research needs, the energy crisis provided a focus for research which will have many far-reaching implications in the future. The concept of key or critical sectors in a regional economy now takes on a totally different meaning: 'classical' location factors once thought to be superfluous in the 'ubiquitous' economic space of the 1960s have again begun to be considered seriously. The energy crisis has changed the connotation of 'footloose industry', created some uncertainty about the development of certain regions and, at a more local scale, the long-term shape, form and development of metropolitan areas.

These exciting aspects to the role of industrial systems in regional development must now be discussed in more detail.

STRUCTURAL CHANGE IN INDUSTRY AND ITS EFFECT ON REGIONAL SYSTEMS

The recognition that the economic structure of society had changed dramatically was acknowledged in various publications which charted the percentage of the labour force engaged in primary, secondary, tertiary and quaternary activities. None the less, there persisted a view that manufacturing activity would continue to be associated with the success of the industrial sectors. Non-manufacturing and non-primary activity were seen as dependent on, or induced by, manufacturing and primary industrial growth: the theoretical underpinnings of the economic base model created on these premises proved difficult to modify. While Tiebout and Lane (1966) pointed out that US manufacturing activity since the Second World War had barely grown in absolute terms and had declined relatively, the idea of service activities providing some independent (in a relative sense) driving mechanism to a regional economy was not conceded. Although Thompson (1965, 1966, 1968) recognized that urban economies could mature to such a stage that the export of non-manufacturing activities was possible, this view was not shared by many researchers and certainly not by central governments concerned with regional development planning. For example, the British government did not appreciate until the mid-1960s that its regional development policy, primarily focused on industrial growth, had overlooked the 15,000 office jobs being created in central London each year: service activity was continuing to locate in traditionally prosperous areas, thus reducing the impact of policies designed to improve the economic health of the less prosperous regions (see Manners et al., 1972).

The implications of these shifts in employment were very dramatic since they came just when structural change within certain industries (technological change) and the impact of international competition combined to produce an overall economic environment which proved to be devastating for certain regional economies. As Brown and Burrows (1977) point out, these regions tended to be dominated by traditional industrial activity the demand for which, as Thomas (1964) noted, was becoming increasingly inelastic as incomes per capita were rising sharply in real terms. Thus regions dominated by textile industries were unable to adjust to a new era of synthetic fabrics and foreign competition and regions heavily dependent on coal production have faced declining absolute demand once the post-war boom subsided.

At the same time, the industrial system was refocusing on a set of activities which was, for the most part, more market-orientated than its predecessors and no longer tied to primary resources. The direct and indirect impacts of these changes were cumulative and far-reaching. For instance, declining demand for coal in the Appalachian region provided the first major signs of foreboding for the railways in the midwest and northeast of the United States (the Penn-Central railway system, for example, derived much of its total and staple revenue from coal haulage). A further technological change, the ability to transmit electricity efficiently over long distances, led to a further decline in the demand for transport services because many new power plants were being located at the mines.

In the US structural change was also accompanied by large-scale movements of population and industrial activity to the southern and western States with far-reaching impacts on economic activity in the old industrial heartland, although not as great as in some European nations. Even so, there is increasing recognition that the new population distribution and the concomitant restructuring of political districts will diminish the influence of elected officials from the midwest and northeast because numbers in the US House of Representatives are based, for the most part, on population size; and since the hegemony of the federal government in controlling the magnitude of expenditures over space has continued to grow, there is also concern about the impacts that the cumulative processes of structural change and population movement will have on the future economic health of these older regions.

ORGANIZATION OF INDUSTRIAL ACTIVITY

Studies of the location of industrial activity for many years derived their theoretical inputs from the models of Weber (1909), Palander (1935), Lösch (1954 edn.) and others (see Isard, 1956). The major limiting assumption was the use of *homo economicus*, an entrepreneur whose omniscience transcended in incredulity the assumptions embodied in the nature of the uniform plane and transport surface on which he operated his activity. Very little attention was paid to forms of firm organization, although there were many attempts to examine the importance of firm size and a recognition that the size distribution of firms was anything but normal. More recently spatial industrial analysis has examined the effect of corporate structure on locational behaviour, the extent of competition and control exercised by individual firms, and the way uncertainty has been handled. While the literature has been voluminous the richness of the insights and contributions to theory and the resulting formulation of regional development policy have been very uneven. In part this may be because this field is so new, a major problem being that, released from the bounds of conventional micro-economic theory, the analyst often finds the behavioural approach offers almost too much flexibility. Often the research has been an *ex post* rationalization of past decision-making rather than a conscious attempt to build towards a theory of firm behaviour in economic space; only selected studies are reviewed here.

Krumme (1969a,b), tracing the reluctance of geographers to examine the unit of operation of firms (rather than purely what they made, to whom they sold products and so forth), noted that McNee (1958) was one of the first geographers to broaden the scope of location analysis to consider corporate decision-making in the petroleum industry. The limitations of previous approaches were apparent in that the location decisions were almost invariably associated with new firms entering business. Danielsson (1964) correctly pointed out that every investment, whether related to a new operation, expansion, relocation, the introduction of a new product line or even reinvestment, involves a *location* decision. Krumme (1969b) was able to broaden previous decision-making structures by drawing on a wide range of empirical work on location decisions: of particular interest was the notion of a 'locational range of tolerance'—first proposed by Thomas (1964)—which suggested that there existed, for most actions, a range of decisions within which success could be expected. These ideas are closely associated with Smith's (1966) concept of the 'space-cost curve' and Pred's (1977) attempt to relate decision-making from a matrix of information on to a 2-dimensional space. Krumme (1969b) suggested location decision-making required information on

(a) the external environment;
(b) decisions made by all other competitors;
(c) personal and external considerations; and
(d) the push and pull of spatial forces.

In some of these studies, the ideas of Alchian (1950) which were incorporated into Tiebout's (1957) articles on location theory, began to assume an importance that provided many inputs into the later work of Steed (1968, 1971a,b,c,d,e). Locational 'adaptation' and 'adoption' present 2 contrasting views by firms of a location decision: in the former case recognizing, while in the latter apparently 'oblivious' to, spatial concerns. However, successful firms would only survive if they could adapt to their 'incorrectly' chosen environment. In a broader sense, if the firm were either large enough and/or maintained a monopolistic or monopsonistic position in the industry, it could adapt the external environment to its eccentric location decision.

Steed (1968) applied some of these ideas in a study of the shipbuilding industry in Belfast, Northern Ireland, and traced the way firms adjusted and responded to internal and external factors. The period since the Second World War well illustrated the extent to which adaptation, or in this case, re-adaptation, could take place without the help of government intervention. Later, Steed (1971b,c,d,e) examined the impact of corporate structures on location decision-making. Of particular importance in this process was the influence of geographical inertia, in one sense an expression of adaptation by firms since relocation is usually far more expensive. However, the growth of multi-product corporations, which Pred (1974) calls 'major job providing organizations', has led to a different form of adaptation and adoption to changing geographic environments.

Dicken (1971) has argued that in large organizations, perception is less individually related: information tends to be collected by various departments with specific goals in mind (such as expansion of product lines or expansion of facilities). Törnqvist (1977) maintains that, given the multi-objective nature of decision-making within large multi-product firms, classical location theory would find little application in these contexts. The industrial environment comprises sets of activities, the most important being headquarters, R & D activities, sub-contracting plants and assembly plants. Törnqvist's theoretical model differs sharply from those of the early location analysts. In place of the usual restrictive assumptions are notions of bounded rationality, imperfect knowledge, little indication that decisions other than the physical location one *per se* have spatial consequences, and the fact that many decisions represent solutions to conflicts between incompatible objectives. Törnqvist also claims that the concept of transport cost, so prevalent in early location theory, needs to be broadened to embrace 3 levels of communication: (a) the transport of goods, (b) the transfer of information through personal contact, and (c) the transmission of information through telecommunications.

Dicken (1977), however, is not yet convinced that least-cost location theory has served its useful time or is irrelevant to the new industrial milieu of the latter part of the twentieth century. He suggests that each stage of the product life cycle is characterized by specific technology-demand relationships which, in turn, have a geographical expression. Subsequent research by Rees (1979a) and Erickson and Leinbach (1979) has provided continuing support for these ideas, showing that it is during the maturity stage of the product cycle the corporation will be most interested in securing lowest cost production sites. This fact was substantiated by Erickson and Leinbach (1979) in a study of 200 firms which had moved into non-metropolitan areas. Rees (1979a) suggested a causal link between structural and regional shifts in the United States and the assumptions embodied in the product life cycle hypothesis.

Some of the best work at the micro-level on location and relocation decision-making of industrial firms has been by Townroe (1969) using empirical data. He discovered that, in many firms, the pressure for change comes from internal forces such as growth in output, adoption of innovation, new facilities for employees, or changes in financial circumstances. He later showed (Townroe, 1972) that the need to adapt following the move was usually caused by many factors:

(a) unforeseen changes in conditions at the new site;
(b) inadequate information at the decision time;
(c) inadequate use of information; or
(d) poor judgement and insufficient evaluation.

Some responses by firms, once the new conditions were revealed, included changes in processes, in the origin and destination of inputs and outputs, and in personnel. In another study, Moseley and Townroe (1973) examined the changes in linkages which may occur after a firm moves, an aspect of the decision-making process which has particularly strong policy implications (discussed later) and represents an undernourished field of research.

Townroe (1972) commented that the most complete adaptation behaviour is closure. Apart from some early work by Churchill (1955) and Ferguson (1960), very little research has been undertaken on the causes and conditions for firm failure and, more importantly, the impact of failure on the regional economy. Firm closure or failure is just one extreme of a spectrum of actions which may be regarded as adaptation to the environment: relocation, merger, reduction in operations or changes in product lines may all represent alternatives to closure. Hewings (1977) noted that in Canada and the US there is a pronounced negative binomial relationship between age of the firm and its demise in any given year. Yet O'Farrell (1976), in a study of Irish firms during the period from 1960 through 1973, found that survival of firms was a linear function of size independent of age. However, these firms were grant-aided and were essentially new concerns under non-Irish ownership. In many cases firm closure may reflect relocation: while the net impact on society may be very small, the impact on specific regions may be very important. Gripaios (1977a,b), found that in southeast London between 1970 and 1975 most closures involved firm death, claiming that this phenomenon may be a long-term multiplier effect of past decentralization of activity out of the London region.

The considerations of firm survival become critical when related to regional development policies and to regions with a fragile economic base. There has been, however, little work identifying the success of business ventures in less prosperous regions which have been supported by central government assistance grants of various kinds (except for the work of

O'Farrell, 1976). Part of the reason may be that many grants are provided for several years and hence the vulnerability of the firm to traditional market pressures may be delayed beyond the critical first few years in the new location. This is very closely tied to regional comparative advantage, which becomes more critical when the modern firm with its varied linkage systems is considered.

INDUSTRIAL LINKAGES AND THEIR IMPACTS ON REGIONAL ECONOMIES

Inter-sectoral linkages play an important role in regional growth and development theories. The Tiebout-North debate of the 1950s focused attention on the way in which regions grow and, in particular, on the differing responses of regional systems to varying degrees of external *vis-à-vis* internal stimuli (Tiebout, 1956; North, 1955, 1956). While this particular debate was never satisfactorily resolved, a more elegant statement of the role of linkages was provided by Thompson (1965, 1966, 1968) who signalled that the nature of these linkages should be expected to change as the economy developed. The Thompson model also suggested the possibility that regions might specialize in consumer trade and service activity to the extent that such goods and services might be exported, an increasingly familiar aspect of regional systems.

Most models of regional industrial systems are premised on an assumed cause and effect relationship between sets of exogenous and endogenous activities. In the simple economic base model, the economy is divided into only 2 components on the basis of the disposition of the output from the various sectors within that economy. Input-output and econometric models operate at a more disaggregated scale but the same division applies, although sectors can, and do, trade internally and externally. The understanding of industrial linkages is mostly limited to these very simple divisions: with few exceptions, little has been done to identify the complex structure of spatial linkage patterns in a multi-regional system. Such attempts as have been made have resorted to non-survey estimation techniques having quality control on the holistic accuracy of the models but very little control over the quality of the rich detail of inter-industrial and inter-regional transactions. The models, such as those of Leontief and Strout (1963), Polenske (1972), Harris (1974) and others, have provided useful inputs into broad policy-making issues. Except for some exploratory work by Beyers (1978), little has been done to document the complexity of the intra-national structure of the industrial system.

In this connection, a body of literature has developed in relation to the identification of industrial complexes and measures have been proposed to identify spatial clusterings of industries. Czamanski (1971, 1973, 1974),

Richter (1969) and Streit (1969) have developed many alternative techniques; on a more theoretical level, Ghosh and Sarkar (1970), Roy (1971) and Blin (1973) have provided algorithms to relate inter-sectoral and inter-industry linkages. These inquiries document the existence of spatial multiplier effects which complement the topological inter-sectoral multiplier effects of traditional inter-industry analysis. One major problem is that this sort of analysis is restricted to only one type of linkage, what Thomas (1972) refers to as the propulsive system linkage. As Beyers (1974) has shown for the State of Washington, the laterally induced system of linkages (the multiplier effects from the payment of wages and salaries by local firms to consumers and their expenditure on local goods and services) may be far more important in regional economies than the previously considered inter-industry linkage effects. Furthermore, the capital goods multiplier and accelerator effects provide yet another dimension not often considered in the examination of the industrial system in regional economies.

More recently, the study of linkages has been moved into other domains—Pred (1974) and Törnqvist (1977) in the field of organization linkage systems, and King et al. (1969), Casetti et al. (1971), King et al. (1972) and Bannister (1976) into spatial macro-economics long ignored in traditional industrial analysis. The latter work, on spatial macro-economics, attempts to examine inter-regional linkage systems, but aggregation is usually very high. None the less, this body of literature provides the basis for an examination of the impacts of macro-economic policy on regional systems (see Clark 1978; Hewings 1978). Research progress is likely to be hampered because the accounting frameworks which have been borrowed from national macro-economics are themselves undergoing critical examination and review. Hence, it becomes difficult to investigate wage changes in industrial systems within the context of an implied trade-off between such changes and unemployment when the existence of such a trade-off (the Phillips' curve) is disputed at the national level. Yet analysis does provide guidance for future enquiry—for example, in identifying the differential effects of business cycles on regional economies (Cho and McDougall, 1978), an issue long ago raised by Siegal (1966) and McKee (1967), and the ways in which leads and lags filter through the regional system (Bassett and Haggett, 1971; Thirlwall, 1973).

Pred (1974) has provided an entirely different perspective: noting the differences in corporate structure that have been evolving over the last half century, he has attempted to document the existence of ownership linkages. Most regional growth models postulate response of the local economy to external influences (usually a 'region' called 'rest of the nation'). Pred suggests that the responses may be conditioned by the increasing concentration of decision-making in a relatively small number of metropolitan-centred regions. The implications of his analysis are provocative, namely, that the way in which the regional system will evolve in the future will no longer be a 'random walk' but a rather carefully orchestrated process conducted by a relatively small number of major job-providing organizations (including, of course, the various levels of government). The viability of communities may no longer be considered a function of the degree of competitiveness of their industrial base alone but a combination of this factor and the future role planned for the constituent firms by the multi-product operations of which most are part.

Finally, some consideration should be given to the fact that linkages between the industrial system (in a broad sense) and other systems have not received sufficient attention. In particular, population changes have altered the spatial distribution of demand in the United States and require careful evaluation of their likely impacts on the continued viability of industrial enterprises in regions experiencing net out-migration. Linkages between energy and industrial systems are, once again, receiving attention and, as a concomitant to this exploration, changes in the transport system in combination with population and energy changes will serve to create a different contextual environment for industrial growth in the rest of this century.

MULTINATIONAL INDUSTRIES AND REGIONAL SYSTEMS

Research on organizational and behavioural approaches to industrial location has been extended to consider the impact of extra-national control of regional activity on various regional economies. Pred (1974) pointed to a concern with the increasing concentration of decision-making in a few major metropolitan areas: an extension of this to considerations of international control would appear to be a logical development.

Dicken (1976) identified 2 types of studies undertaken in this area: (a) the headquarters locations of multi-plant firms and (b) the impact of external control on the development of a single region. Dicken could point to several dimensions of the effect of external control on British regional economies, particularly that the in-migration of branch plants and subsidiaries of multi-national firms has tended to be faster than the growth of local firms; externally controlled firms tended to be faster growing and technologically based; and finally, the process of external control was considerably accelerated by mergers and acquisitions. The merits of external control are debatable. Dicken notes several points of contention—reduction in local control, removal of profits from the region, removal of higher-level management and, as a reflection of their high-technological base, a substitution of capital for labour. McDermott (1976, 1977a) argues that some of these problems may not be well grounded in fact, especially as regional development policy has encouraged foreign-owned firms to shift from the more prosperous southeast of England to more peripheral regions.

While this may confer short-run benefits on such regions, McDermott also raises the question posed by Dicken about the substitution of non-local for local entrepreneurial talent. This would seem to parallel the findings in the US about firm location decisions at the mature phase of the product life cycle. In these cases, the production process requires a much lower level of sophistication of entrepreneurial talent than in the early and critical development stages. Firn (1975) examined a small region, Clydeside in Scotland, an area with few new enterprises and little indigenous employment creation. He found that most firms were controlled from the southeast of England and North America and that the larger the plant the more likely it was to be externally controlled (especially from North America). Indeed, Firn attempted to 'regionalize' the economic dependency theory argument evolved to explain the extent of control some developed economies have over less developed countries through ownership of capital, transport systems, marketing agreements and mineral exploitation. He presented evidence showing that the Scottish economy was moving towards a branch plant/ subsidiary economy in which the growth sectors were externally owned, a factor in pressures from some quarters within Scotland for greater independence from the British economy. Only 41 per cent of all Scottish manufacturing is controlled internally, so that a local plant's ability to expand may not depend entirely on its competitive stature and, with very little R & D in branch plants, employment opportunities for skilled managerial talent are diminished. Finally, the Scottish study also claimed that as a result of non-local control, local linkages may be reduced making the plants concerned more sensitive to fluctuations elsewhere in the economy which directly influence the parent firm and, indirectly, the externally controlled firm.

The work of Firn (1975) and Yannopoulos and Dunning (1976) suggests that, too often, simple assertions about multinational behaviour become part of the 'received theory'. In reality, many different types of multinational enterprises exhibit varying degrees of responsibility to the regional economic structure in which they have branch plants. Since multinational operations are likely to increase in importance there is considerable incentive for further research.

GOVERNMENT POLICY INFLUENCES ON INDUSTRIAL FACTORS IN REGIONAL SYSTEMS

The role of government policy and its influence on industrial development and hence on regional systems has become so intertwined in Western Europe and North America as to lead one to believe that regional policies in most countries were, *de facto,* industrial development policies.

One assumption about the lack of growth in certain regions is the role of a diversified economic base. Regions with considerable dependence upon a narrow range of industrial activities were shown to exhibit greater propensities for more severe impacts from business cycle activity. As a result, regional policy was aimed at broadening this base to ameliorate the impacts. The policy is admirably stated but assumes that diversification would tend to bestow positive benefits on the region under consideration. In many cases, regions are not diversified because either they lack endogenous demand or cannot offer significant comparative advantages for the production of a wider range of goods and services. Many new firms would find it difficult to adapt to what may be regarded as an unfavourable environment without significant financial assistance. Even where this has been provided, through central government incentives, capital allowances, job-creation grants and state and local tax incentives, there has been no guarantee of survival for the firm once aid terminates. Evidence for this is sketchy, however, and requires more longitudinal studies of regional industrial development.

Canadian development policy presents an interesting study in apparent contradiction. The espoused policy is directed at diversifying the regional economies of the less prosperous Maritime Provinces: yet the Department of Regional Economic Expansion located almost all new activity in this region which tended to exacerbate an already heavy dependence upon primary and manufacturing activity (the latter being closely tied to primary activities). This points to another difficult dilemma in regional development policy: the long-run versus the short-run issue and the encouragement of capital-intensive versus labour-intensive industries to locate in less prosperous regions. Woodward (1974), for example, has been very critical of the Canadian policy which has been a heavy subsidizer of capital development in these regions even though the greatest underutilized resource is labour. The time issue becomes critical as to whether policy should encourage firms which may be highly labour-intensive yet with some uncertainty about their ability to compete in 5 or 10 years' time, or should be aimed at those activities which have the greater probability of continued existence even if their short-run employment impacts may not be very high. It could be surmised that, through the development of inter-industry linkages, the latter's total employment impact on the regions may be rather respectable from an employment perspective, although the Yeates and Lloyd (1970) study of the Georgian Bay (Ontario) region and Moseley and Townroe's (1973) study of linkage adjustment following movement would not provide much promise for anything more than minimal indirect industrial development.

These issues bear very strongly on one of the most contentious policies relating regional planning and industrial development—the growth centre policy. The idea of concentrating growth initiatives into a relatively constrained spatial setting undoubtedly provided an attractive alternative to previous policies. Moseley's (1974) excellent review of the application of growth centres in the spatial planning process highlighted many difficulties of translating a theoretical concept into a workable policy tool. Extensions of this issue include consideration of aspects of identification of the key or leading sectors (see Beyers 1973, 1976; Hewings 1974) and the suggestion of a relationship between the growth centre idea and central place theory (Parr, 1973).

The general evaluation of the role of unbalanced spatial development has been relatively unfavourable, reflecting an impatience with the time taken for any anticipated effects to be observed and the fact that few countries have the control necessary in central government operations to provide the type of investment strategy which would be required to ensure any degree of success. The United States Economic Development Administration (1972) evaluation provides some scepticism about the extent to which the agency was committed to the growth centre development programme—especially in light of the relatively short period which was provided for the policy to take effect.

The impact of government programmes on industrial location has received mixed reviews in Britain. Moore and Rhodes (1973) and Buck and Atkins (1976) indicate that the policies of decentralization away from southeast England have yielded positive benefits to the less prosperous regions in net job creation. In Canada this is less clear; in some years the effect of government-sponsored job creation has been completely undermined through firm closure and there has been some evidence that firms choosing to locate in the less prosperous regions have regarded the incentives offered as windfalls (see Springate, 1972; Hewings, 1977).

RESEARCH NEEDS: A PRELIMINARY PROSPECTUS

From the foregoing review several research needs become clearly identified. These mostly reflect continuity with past research efforts rather than strikingly new avenues of inquiry. This does not imply a certain lack of lustre in this field but rather reflects the fact that many directions demand deeper research effort to yield a better holistic view of the interaction between industry and regional systems.

The increasing internationalization of industry has created a very different environment for analysis: much work on the organization of these enterprises is not yet paralleled by sufficient understanding of their impact on and control of regional systems. Cross-sectional analysis of the nature of the linkage systems of externally controlled firms in comparison to locally owned firms is required. Are these firms, as some suspect, located in, but do not form part of, the regional economy? Do they foster greater local ties over time or does their dependence on external inputs and outputs remain relatively unchanged?

The frameworks used for analysis reflect very traditional approaches to the nature of regional systems. While the era of large-scale integrated models has arrived, the packaging of component models together has seldom yielded very many new insights. Much more attention needs to be focused on the linkages between various sub-systems within the regional economy. Here the work of Beyers (1978) is important in integrating the population and economic/industrial system in a more useful manner than just combining an input-output model with a population growth model. Pressures imposed by the energy crisis demand more empirical analysis of production functions of major users of energy and of the changing geography of energy supply and demand. Some preliminary work in connection with the Ohio River Basin Energy Study Region (Page *et al.,* 1979) suggests that the impacts of fuel substitution are likely to be rather dramatic, especially if there is a return to coal utilization for the generation and cogeneration of electricity. As energy supplies of petroleum become more critically limiting considerable change can be anticipated in the production of goods and services. The models of Hudson and Jorgenson (1976) allowing complete substitution between all energy and non-energy inputs have been developed only at the national level, yet non-energy for energy input substitution will have a pronounced spatial impact, although its nature, direction and extent are, at present, unknown and the subject of much speculation.

While it is generally recognized that government activity has a pronounced effect on regional systems, very few studies have treated government as an industry and examined the direct and indirect nature of its production and consumption systems. The early work of CONSAD (1967) and the United States Department of Commerce (1967) suggested that the major impact of government policy would not be confined to those expenditures and actions related solely to the 'regional' arm of central government. Since each branch of government is involved in substantial expenditure programmes which often have very specific spatial concentrations, their impacts should be assessed and evaluated. Another area of interest which is tangentially influenced by government policy is the role of R & D. With few exceptions, the locational aspects of R & D components of US firms have not been well documented. Malecki (1979a,b) has provided some important ideas on this problem: in a sense, it complements the work of Erickson and Leinbach (1979) which looked at the mass production stage of the product cycle and its influence on spatial decision-making, by exploring location behaviour during the critical, high-risk innovative stage.

With very few exceptions, time has not been an important component of research inquiry in industrial systems analysis. The state of the art has not developed much beyond variations on shift and share analysis: paucity of data would remain a major limiting consideration but there are very many attractive models which could be examined for their use in explaining space-time dimensions of industrial change. Economists (e.g. Arora and Brown, 1977) have begun to appreciate that the space dimension is not just another trivial extension for econometric analysis. Specification of leads and lags over time and space provides a unique challenge for the use of existing theory and the development of new theory. Some early attempts to use combined cross-section/time series econometric models have produced statistically significant results in the identification of cause and effect relationships in employment change in the Illinois economy (White and Hewings, 1979). While the form of the model is to some extent prepackaged, the application to a 2-dimensional space presents many unique problems.

Another area of concern (from invasion and colonization by economists) is the continued development of industrial location theory, and perhaps some modest beginnings of challenging behavioural location theory could emerge. The influences of multi-plant establishments, be they multi-regional or multinational, present a location decision-making milieu which existing theory cannot accommodate, yet the work of Isard and Liossatos (1979) on space-time dynamics, which explores the utility of concepts like hierarchy theory, provides one of many possible starting points for extensions to the current conceptual notions about firm behaviour.

Other apparently marginal fields have an important bearing on research on industrial systems. Many models and much theory assume incremental growth; during the 1970s growth for the industrial system has become uncertain. Changes have had catastrophic impacts on the industrial landscape, especially the worldwide oil crisis. Greater focus should be given to conceptualizing the regional system within a framework which embodies notions from catastrophe theory and not a monotonic progression from one state to another. The work of Gilmore (1976) on boom-town growth phenomena in the western United States (associated with mineral and energy developments) suggests that standard regional socio-economic models fail to capture the dramatic cyclical interactions which accompany rapid development. In particular, the differential effects of construction and production phases of new industrial establishments create 'non-basic' demands of a very different kind both from the perspective of their quality and their timing. Yet our understanding of the mechanisms of decline is woefully inadequate; multipliers do not necessarily work in reverse in the same way that they do in measuring the impacts of a positive change. Regional adjustment to decline—precipitous or incremental—in industrial activity has not been carefully studied. The impacts are often the subject of conjecture whereas, in reality, the dimensions of change are many-faceted (as evidenced by the movement of textile firms back into New England from the south).

The research record is impressive in its breadth and in the sophistication of some of the insights into the role of industry in regional economies.

However, the analysis often falls short of providing the answers to many important questions. One general theme that arises is the provision of research in the direction sought by Dziewonski (1973), namely, for regional analysis to move more forcefully into prognostications of the future patterns of regional development. Industrial analysis research is heavily focused on explanation of historical trends and patterns; moving in the opposite direction will require considerable reorientation.

Spatial Analysis, Industry and the Industrial Environment. Vol. 3 Regional Economies and Industrial Systems
Edited by F. E. I. Hamilton and G. J. R. Linge

Chapter 3

Theoretical Problems in the Analysis of Technological Change and Regional Development

ANDREW SAYER

In the wealth of literature in regional studies concerned with proposing and evaluating particular hypotheses about such objects as labour markets, manufacturing decentralization and regional policy, analyses are generally conducted against a largely implicit background of theoretical views about the nature of the economy, the state and government policy. In one new area of research—the role of technological change in regional development—these normally implicit assumptions are revealed rather more clearly than usual (e.g. in the issue of *Regional Studies,* 14(3), 1980, on 'industrial innovation and regional economic development', and the special feature in *The Professional Geographer,* 31(1), 1979, on 'the North-South issue' in the US).

This chapter criticizes some aspects of this background by reference to this recent literature. The arguments centre on 4 main issues: the de-emphasis of economic explanations produced by the continued use of a behavioural approach; the view of the economic role and impact of technological change and the associated calls for an 'innovation-oriented regional policy' (Oakey *et al.,* 1980, p. 251); the meaning of regional development; and the dominant methodology. The chapter concludes with a sketch of a suggested alternative approach to the relationship between technological change and regional development using a largely Marxist background theory.

THE ORGANIZATIONAL VERSUS THE ECONOMIC IN THE BEHAVIOURAL APPROACH

Where regional research is concerned with industrial activity, the behavioural approach is still widely used, and this is especially true of the technological change and regional development literature. One of the most striking characteristics of research in the behavioural tradition is its de-emphasis of economic relations and forces and its reduction of these to their organizational forms within firms. Concepts such as 'decision-maker', 'linkage', 'channel' or 'environment' often serve only to provide a scientific relabelling of economic phenomena in such a way as to jettison the available

59

insights of economic theory concerning them. For example, the actual economic characteristics which constitute the environment, in terms of such features as the strength of competition, management-labour relations, rates of interest, taxation and other state policies, and indeed the general condition of the economy, are not easily accommodated within a behavioural framework.

These 'scientific' behavioural concepts also encourage a peculiarly idealized and technocratic view of planning at all levels—corporate, urban or regional. This is perhaps most obvious in the case of urban planning where, as Scott and Roweis (1977) show, planning appears as a set of practices based purely upon analytical tools with the aim of allocating resources in some rational manner. This technocratic view, with its systematic sequencing of goal formation, planning, and implementation of strategy, creates the impression that urban planning actually takes the dominant initiative in creating the built environment, when in fact, in most advanced capitalist countries this positive power is the prerogative of private (property) capital. The reduction of the activity of planning to its organizational form and self-perceived aims almost leads one to forget that hardly any urban development occurs without money being spent and without much of the investment being controlled or mediated by capital (cf. Harvey, 1975b).

At the regional level it is perhaps harder to exclude economic considerations, but even here it is common to find 'regional development' being discussed without any reference to the general condition of the economy concerned, its rates of profit and investment, and other indicators relating to the enabling conditions of capital accumulation. In recent literature on technological change and regional development, a distinct impression is given that the state has only somehow to create the organizational forms necessary for, or conducive to, innovation and a 'seed-bed' of new industry will develop. The problem is that these are only necessary conditions for the latter, and little or nothing is said about the sufficient conditions such as profitability, availability of market openings and investment funds. This reduction of the economic to the organizational can be seen where it is assumed that investment funds are created simply by setting up the organizational channels through which they flow.

At the corporate level, the determinants of investment and location planning of firms are reduced to functions of organizational form and perception of the environment. Again, such things as profitability, vulnerability to competition and recession, and labour relations are largely ignored as epiphenomena, as exceptions or as 'noise'.

Yet, the alternative offered by regional economic models are little better, for despite their explicit 'economic' content, their use encourages historically specific determinants of industrial or regional change to be ignored or collapsed into the conceptual 'black holes' of their variables such as labour supply or demand. Using this approach to explain the rapidly deteriorating British textile industry, for example, all the interesting determining relations—such as the dependence on cheap sources of labour among Black populations and women workers, the backward technology, the shifts in overseas competitors' positions, and the effect of the strong pound—would presumably be blandly reduced to the dimensions of determined 'variables' in an 'economic' model.

It also seems probable that the standard range of organizational concepts used by the behavioural approach would 'define out' the specificities of such a situation. In either approach—economic modelling or behavioural—information about the causes of industrial change is excluded simply by an unacknowledged 'normalization' for history (Massey, 1979b). The preoccupation with organizational forms has even started to neutralize some of the important benefits to be gained from the growing realization that regional development is increasingly tied up with production organized at an international level. There is a depressing tendency simply to use the old concepts of behavioural industrial geography (reinforced by the ample business studies literature on corporate organization) for use at this larger scale. When this happens the multinational firm is reduced from its status as a *prime bearer of economic forces* (with all the insights into the reproduction of uneven development which this generates) to little more than a novel form of organization in which a different kind of decision-maker faces a different kind of decision-environment. However, exceptions to this tendency to de-emphasize the economic implications for regional development are to be found in, among others, Murray (1972) and Perrons (1979).

TECHNOLOGICAL CHANGE AND ECONOMIC THEORY

Behind all these particular limitations are some fundamental misconceptions about the nature of capitalist economies. These misconceptions have languished for a long time in regional studies but have been thrown into particularly sharp relief by recent work on technological change and regional development. They stem, it seems, from a failure to distinguish between use-value and exchange-value.

If something is to be sold (i.e. have *exchange*-value) it must also be useful (i.e. have *use*-value) otherwise no-one would buy it. But the contrary is not true for while there are many products and services which have use-value, not all of them can be sold, and not all of those that can, can be sold at a profit. Capitalist production is orientated to the production of those use-values on which profit can be made when sold. The necessary conditions for capitalist production obviously include the technical (and social) feasibility of making the product concerned, but it is the possibility of realizing profit which constitutes the sufficient condition. Developments on the material, use-value side, such as the introduction of improved technology, certainly have an effect on the exchange-value side in reducing costs. However it is a disastrous, but common enough, error to suppose that the new technology serves as an end in itself and a sufficient condition for development, rather than as a means of raising or defending profitability. Even where the new technology is embodied in a product rather than a process innovation, the point of doing so is to obtain a return on investment in exchange-value terms. While writers on technological change and regional development are aware of the distinction between an invention and an innovation, in which the former only becomes the latter when it is produced commercially, this same literature seems to encourage the technological determinist view that technological change can be taken as an end in itself.

More support to this claim is presented later, but there are still some other misconceptions surrounding technology and the use-value/exchange-value distinction which need attention. Even though technological change is only a means to achieving profit-orientated ends, it is nevertheless true that economic development under capitalism, as under any system, primarily depends on technological development in expanding output per worker or raising the level of the forces of production. There are benefits from this development in that more use-values can be produced for a given amount of labour. But it is then grossly misleading to infer that (a) because technological change is so rapid under capitalism, it is an unqualified good; and (b), worse, that the means of development and its secondary effects are its primary goal and guide, as if capital accumulation were consciously designed to expand the productivity of labour and make commodities more abundant and affordable. Even where it is acknowledged that capital accumulation is not directed towards these goals, it is often assumed that the pursuit of profit will achieve these so adequately that no harm is done in assuming that capitalist development proceeds as if the latter were true.

When pressed few would accept either assumption, yet the superficial persuasiveness of technological determinism perhaps rests not upon these but upon a confident reflex rejection of the imagined preposterous Luddite claim of its critics that technological development is a bad thing. If technological change has enabled such considerable economic development, it would seem obvious that it can help to redevelop backward regions. This simple proposition has a superficial appeal but closer analysis shows it to be subject to a number of major qualifications.

The immediate regulator of capitalist production and investment is profit and not use-value; consequently the prime reason for introducing process innovations is to defend or raise profits *vis-à-vis* competitors by increasing the output per worker per hour. Similarly, in the case of product innovations, the sufficient condition for their introduction is the expectation that their production will yield the average or above the average rate of profit.

Certainly, these will have beneficial effects, but the ways in which detrimental effects will occur should be considered.

(a) Particularly in the case of process innovations, technological change may reduce average skill-levels, increase the intensity of work and reduce the quality of its subjective experience (see Braverman, 1974; Conference of Socialist Economists Microelectronics Group, 1980).

(b) It may, under certain conditions (elasticities of demand for the final product of less than 1) induce redundancies; under capitalism, there are no economic planning mechanisms which will ensure that the redundant are redeployed.

(c) It may put workers in competing branches or firms where technological change is slower, and management control over work intensity is weaker, out of work.

(d) In some cases (e.g. weaponry) the use-value of the product to its buyers may derive from its disutility to others.

(e) Where a leading industry manages to raise profits by adopting the most advanced technology, there is no necessary reason why workers in the most profitable branches should get any share in these profits: by far the most likely possibility is that the accumulated profits will be reinvested wherever they are likely to yield the best future profits. (Incidentally, mobility of profits is not just a feature of multinational enterprises and their branch plants. Indigenous firms have the opportunity of portfolio investment in firms in other regions or countries. British capital had a history of export of capital long before multinationals became established.)

(f) The relation between technical sophistication and incomes is very complex. At a society-wide level it would seem that technological development *must* produce increasing real incomes. But an examination of the concrete forms in which the former takes place in capitalism shows the relation to be contingent. For example, the introduction of the new technology of the green revolution (and the agricultural revolution that preceded the industrial revolution in the now advanced countries) often lowered the real incomes of peasants by displacing them from the land, by removing their subsistence crops and replacing them with cash crops which they could neither afford nor use. This shows that technological change under capitalism is not orientated towards needs-satisfaction in any simple sense. *Ceteris paribus*, where firm A and firm B use the same (new) technologies, but A has a cheaper supply of labour, A will make higher profits. Certainly, wages tend to be highest in the countries which use the most advanced technology, but this association does not follow automatically. It depends upon pressure from labour in terms of relative supply and demand conditions in the labour market and in terms of labour organization, and upon a large number of firms having a sufficiently strong competitive lead to be able to accommodate these pressures. What matters to the firm is not absolute wages but wage costs per unit of output, and the latter are usually lower in high-wage countries. Nevertheless, as will be argued shortly, this is always a relative matter, so that, *ceteris paribus,* raising output per worker only yields above average profits as long as competitors have *not* done so; competitive struggles only have winners when they also have losers.

The objections to the rose-tinged view of capitalist development implicit in modern versions of technological determinism can be put very simply: technological development could, among other things, make work easier and reduce the working day, but to allow this to happen on anything but a universal scale, firms would have to risk the conditions of their survival as profit-making concerns in the face of competition from other firms which managed to resist these pressures from their workers.

To each of the above points counter-claims may be made; for example against (c), it might be objected that new jobs may be created in other sectors where cost-lowering innovations are compensated for by a highly elastic demand. The reply to this and similar objections can only be that it is a contingent matter (i.e. it concerns states of affairs which are neither necessary nor impossible) and answers to it can only be found by empirical investigations. Moreover, universal regularity in the answers should not be expected precisely because the relations involved are contingent. Generally, there is little reason to expect the negative effects listed under (a) to (f) to be compensated in the right places at the right times and in the right amounts except by accident, as is known only too well from actual empirical regional studies. This is not to imply that capitalist development is a zero-sum game, but nevertheless there are negative as well as positive results. Although competitive economic struggles only have winners when they have losers, this does not of course mean that the absolute level of development of most of the competitors, or at least the average competitor, cannot rise over a long historical period.

However on this very question of the nature of competition, there are some further reinforcing misconceptions in regional research. Despite all the historical examples to the contrary, it seems to be supposed that with appropriate 'initial' assistance through some form of regional aid (which some British regions have been receiving for 50 years) backward regions can be 'made competitive' again. In some cases this may be possible but what seems absurd is the apparent belief that all regions and their industries can simultaneously take the lead in competition without there being any losers. Uneven development is unacceptable at the regional level, but if it can be cured at this scale by externalizing its negative effects at a larger scale on to other countries, only idealistic and altruistic believers in internationalism will worry. Uneven economic development encourages the growth of chauvinistic ideologies in which each region or nation engages in special pleading and beggar-thy-neighbour policies. The aim of making particular regions or countries within the structure of uneven development 'more competitive' does not transcend these ideologies but merely rearranges the support for them. Recently, Oakey *et al.* (1980) have acknowledged that technological change is a threat to laggard regions. This is true enough: under capitalism, technologies become backward and economically obsolete not when they are worn out but when technological advances are adopted by competitors. Even so Oakey *et al.* (1980, p. 251) see no contradiction in advocating an 'innovation-oriented regional policy' that, apparently, will introduce a new kind of technological change in which there can be advance without backwardness, or winners without losers:

> Innovation-oriented regional policies are expected to be of a long-term nature aimed at assisting areas to restructure in the face of international and national competitive pressures and, thereby, achieve self-sustained economic growth.

A similarly optimistic view is taken by Ewers and Wettmann (1980, p. 162): 'it can hardly be disputed that new markets and the quick adoption of technological innovations is crucial for the survival and growth of many industries'. Le Heron (1980) suggests that one of several 'long-standing tenets of regional growth theory' claims that 'innovation creates opportunities and propels industrial and regional growth'. The following 'tenet' may be added to the last 2 quotations: 'under the control of capital, technological change substantially contributes to the very problems that regional theory aims to solve'.

As has been noted already, such policies could do little more than create the necessary organizational and material conditions for innovations, and in the absence of any obvious means of ensuring the sufficient conditions (largely macro-economic) of innovation on a large scale, it must be wondered where the hoped for proliferation of innovation 'seed-beds' will come from. The extent of the wishful thinking becomes especially clear when what is being suggested would, even for a modest number of regions, constitute an absolute mass of R & D activities hitherto unknown in the history of capitalism.

> The second implication of the product cycle is that as decentralization of production progresses, external economies . . . can build up in the periphery and regional demand can grow to a critical threshold. At this point an industrial seed-bed effect can take place, particularly through the spin-off of small firms from "lead firms" and the migration of entrepreneurs to the new areas. In other words, a region that becomes the location for industries in the standardization phases of their product cycles can evolve as a focus of innovations. This is possible because small firms tend to be relatively more productive than large firms in the generation of innovations (Rees, 1979a, p. 49).

This argument is true, *provided* that careful attention is paid to the qualifying tone indicated by 'can build', 'can take place', 'can evolve', 'tend' and 'possible'. All these things are possible in a limited number of cases. But so, too, are their opposites. Not every region (or even a majority of them) can simultaneously experience this happy sequence of contingently related events. And some, but not all, of the reasons why this does not happen are actually given in conventional regional economic theory, with its emphasis on agglomeration economies, circular and cumulative causation, and increasing returns to scale. Interpreted literally, the defensive, qualifying tone of the quotation from Rees shows just how little theoretical, explanatory weight can be put upon accidental associations and 'chaotic conceptions' (cf. Sayer, 1982).

A more realistic line of argument is pursued by Goddard (1980) in his discussion of probable effects of current technological change on the British space economy. Here the negative as well as the positive effects on employment are evaluated, and indeed the overall future picture is far from optimistic and offers little support for beliefs in the possibility of an effective innovation-orientated regional policy. The complexity of juggling policy design to direct this tangled mass of employment-generating and employment-shedding processes into a pattern more in accord with the goal of reducing inter-regional disparities is mind-boggling. This is yet another example of a regional policy proposal hoping to solve structural problems by purely quantitative geographical rearrangement of the positive and negative effects of those problems.

Even then, this leaves unanswered 2 questions which policy-evaluation studies characteristically avoid: first, whether the institution (the state) which is supposed to implement the recommended policy is structurally capable of doing so, given its determining relations and, second, whether the economic structure which is the object of the policy can be manipulated in this way. The answer in both instances must be in the negative, as explained in the last section of this chapter which argues why, using contemporary examples, the 'regional problem' under capitalism cannot be solved.

This is not just a simple objection to unrealistic or infeasible policies because, on occasion, it may be worthwhile to put forward such ideas precisely to question the acceptance of the social structures which make them infeasible. For example, there is no objection to asking that technological advances be used to shorten the working week, reduce the drudgery of subaltern work and extend and enrich the opportunities for 'caring' and 'creative' activity, provided an acknowledgement is made that their achievement on a major scale is structurally incompatible with the continued survival of a capitalist economy, which has to make increase of time economies in production its overriding preoccupation.

THE CONCEPT OF REGIONAL DEVELOPMENT

Regions are 'chaotic' or loosely structured aggregates of objects and processes, some of which are internally or necessarily related (as for example in the way in which capital presupposes wage-labour) and some externally or contingently related (as in the case of adjacent but separate industries having no interaction). In a purely descriptive role, as a way of referring to coterminous bundles of phenomena, the concept of 'region' may be quite innocuous. But problems arise in explanations in which regions appear as unitary phenomena with their own undifferentiated powers and liabilities: here the concept's 'chaotic' character becomes a source of misleading notions (Sayer, 1982). For example, the idea of regional development can be misleading if it fails to say exactly what it is about the region which is being developed: without any such clarification, it is impossible to distinguish between development *in* a region and development *of* a region.

Where industry depends on cheap labour, industrial development, it could be argued, underdevelops the region concerned or at least blocks its development by reproducing low incomes. Regional theorists often note how some activities (e.g. R & D) reproduce relatively high incomes and hope to expand these, but little systematic attention is paid to the way in which poorly paid workforces are also a condition for the survival of many other activities. This selective view helps to reinforce the idea that development *in* a region always constitutes development *of* that region in some simple undifferentiated sense.

This conflation is entirely compatible with the misconceptions already discussed concerning technological change, for if the latter is always in everyone's interest, the special interests of capital can easily be assumed to be the same as the general social interest, such that development in and of a region must be the same thing. This confusion also obscures some important aspects of state intervention in regional development. The state usually presents aid to industry in backward regions (e.g. investment grants) as a means of support for those regions and the people in them. Yet in the last decade in the UK, regional assistance has become more and more directly a disguised form of aid to capital—see Morgan (1979, 1980) and, for international comparisons, see Carney *et al.* (1980) for a range of European examples; Dunford (1979a,b) on Italy and France; and Perrons (1979) on Ireland. Many researchers have of course noted that this aid often encourages capital-intensive industry and sometimes even creates redundancies instead of making significant increases in employment and incomes. But this point has rarely been treated as anything more than an aberration, a 'misguided' policy, instead of an indication of the divergence between the general social interest and capital's special interest, and the state's dependence on serving the latter in order to protect the national interest in economic prosperity. Moreover, this divergence of interests and this difference between development in and of regions have widened considerably in the last 15 years of 'jobless growth' (i.e. output expansion accompanied by employment stagnation or decline) that has characterized manufacturing in Western Europe (cf. Rothwell and Zegveld, 1979; Freeman 1979a,b,c). This trend may change, but while it lasts it suggests that technological innovation will produce negative rather than positive effects on employment.

It is not unreasonable both to acknowledge that technological change does, in the long-run, enable economic development and to challenge the wisdom of 'innovation-oriented regional policies' or (remembering the point about the interdependence between winners and losers in inter-firm competition), any other policy which proposes to help 'us' or 'the regions' to become more competitive.

METHODOLOGICAL INHIBITIONS IN THE CAUSAL ANALYSIS OF THE SPACE ECONOMY

It can be argued that substantive errors and distortions of the sort discussed arise partly as a result of certain methodological malpractices. Although the latter do not logically entail these particular substantive misconceptions, they can easily encourage or license them (a point discussed more fully in Sayer, 1982).

In the work being criticized, initial conceptualization and theoretical discussion are given very low priority. Having quickly noted an empirical regularity or association between technological change and economic development, this research characteristically jumps to the conclusion that the former must be good for regional development (the latter as has been shown, is very much a 'chaotic conception'). In support of this conclusion it is easy to point to spatial co-variances between relatively prosperous populations and R & D activity. Further research is then started to document these localized associations presumably in the belief that they represent some universal empirical regularity. It is then hoped that if the state can encourage the development of some of the phenomena in these associations, technological development and hence regional development will follow, and do so without serious counter-productive effects. In this research considerable time and effort is devoted to ensuring that the sample sizes in the surveys are adequate and the discovered associations statistically significant, while relatively little attention is paid to the prior question of whether all this 'scientific labour' rests upon concepts which are 'chaotic', such as that of regional development. The impatience to get hold of data and analyse them in terms of their quantitative dimensions, encourages a disregard of the study of the qualitative nature of the objects referred to and of the theory implicit in the generation of the original information by the data-gathering individual or institution. Without this qualitative study, it becomes very difficult to distinguish between causal or necessary relations and contingent or accidental ones precisely because these depend on the qualitative nature of objects. Quantitative descriptions of associations, whether they are arrived at inductively or deductively, do not themselves provide any means of distinguishing these types of relation.

Then follows a stage of interpretation of the data in which it is often noted that the results are somewhat ambiguous with respect to theoretical explanatory propositions, or that there is a 'lack of theory' or that 'more studies are needed'. Such weak conclusions are hardly surprising given that the main source of theoretical insight—the careful conceptualization of objects and relations which reveals what it is about these that *produces* or *causes* change—is so often impatiently glossed over as if it were merely an unimportant preliminary to the 'real' business of science: the search for quantitative order.

It may be hoped that strong quantitative associations indicate causal relations but whether they do can only be known by going beyond quantitative analysis of data to causal analysis, and this requires not a *concluding* theoretical interpretation but a *prior* one. In the particular case of the literature on technological change and regional development it is argued that researchers have frequently ignored this and made over-simplified leaps of inference across very complex systems of causal relations whose understanding requires a great deal more economic theorizing than is normally found. Thus when Malecki (1980, p. 226) writes that 'the large-scale variation in technological concentration by region is a major component of varying regional prosperity in advanced economies . . .' this must be understood as simply a descriptive statement about a quantitative association which itself says nothing about possible causal connections.

TOWARDS MORE RATIONAL ABSTRACTIONS IN REGIONAL THEORY

This conclusion proposes some more rational abstractions as a way of explaining some aspects of the extraordinary persistence of uneven development and the role of technological change in contributing towards it. The 2 main concepts to be used—the technical division of labour and the social division of labour—have recently been introduced into regional development theory by Massey (1980).

In the case of a single product being made within a firm, the division of labour involved in its production can be rationally planned by that firm, subject to the degree of cooperation forthcoming from the workforce. This technical division of labour is planned in accordance with goals or expectations regarding output or sales levels in the market. For example, in the early 1970s the British Steel Corporation conducted market research into expected levels of demand for its products and restructured its technical divisions of labour for each of these items in accordance with those forecasts and the associated expected returns on investment. This restructuring involved introducing further process innovations. The proposals were outlined in the ill-fated Ten Year Plan, announced in 1973.

How the division of labour between various products, either within or between firms, and that between different firms making the same commodity are determined must be considered. In contrast to the technical division of labour, this social division of labour is essentially unplanned for there is no agency in a capitalist economy to plan it. (However, when separately owned firms—usually former competitors—enter into planning agreements to produce certain commodities jointly, as has happened in the case of Peugeot and Citröen, there is a shift of labour processes from being determined within the social division of labour to being planned within the technical division of labour.) The 'hidden hand' of the market may ensure some fairly regular control where production planning lead-times for reorganizing the technical division of labour are very short. But even with these exceptions, the regulation of the social division of labour occurs a posteriori whereas the technical division is controlled a priori. Large sums may be invested over several years—even decades—before the end product appears on the market, often only to find (as did British Steel) that market conditions (including the success of competitors) were very different.

Where optimal scales of production expand more rapidly than the size of the final market (as has happened in many sections of the car industry) each producer will be forced to risk planning the technical division of labour at the optimal level even though it is clear that not all the contending firms can simultaneously achieve the market sales necessary to realize the planned economies of scale. The alternative is to forgo those economies and make the loss of market share more certain. Inevitably some firms suffer losses in this situation and they often appeal for state aid. As has been demonstrated in Britain recently, even when a firm is foreign-owned (such as Chrysler) it is difficult to refuse assistance. Whether this is given on what are curiously called 'social grounds' (cushioning redundancies) or on 'economic grounds' (to save an important part of the economy), the state is obliged to intervene. However, in order to prevent the crisis recurring, the state is liable to make this aid conditional upon major restructuring, including the introduction of new technologies, which inevitably causes many redundancies. Where the firm is already state-owned and subsidized, the state can resort to a draconian form of intervention called 'non-intervention' by cutting back loans and trying to force the firm into profit, incurring (as in the case of

British Steel) massive closures and redundancies. Such policies may some-times succeed in restoring the firms concerned but this cannot be ensured, and indeed the British experience has been largely one of recurrence of the problem, often on a heightened scale. This should occasion no surprise, for state intervention of this sort does not alter the rules of the game but merely helps the injured firm re-enter it with the stakes—and hence the risks— raised.

Although such policies are not called regional, they nevertheless have a profound and usually damaging effect on the regions. Morgan (1979, 1980) develops this point in the context of British state intervention and the regional development of Wales, and Dunford (1979a,b) discusses other European examples. Increasingly, in this era of jobless growth, many workers are being offered the choice of losing their job through the introduction of new technologies or losing it through a failure to introduce them. Since profitability is the sufficient condition for economic activity, the state can only support the latter by defending the former, even where this produces serious (and foreseeable) counter-effects. Suggestions such as that of Ewers and Wettmann (1980, p. 162) that we can 'operate from the assumption that national and regional economic policies are integrated with one another i.e. coordinated with regard to foreseeable counter-effects' must be refused. Even if this were qualified (against their apparent inten-tion) to mean economic policies with respect to capital within the regions and the nation, it is unacceptable because the state cannot hope to coerce individual capitals into adopting policies favourable to other capitals in particular regions without running the risk of making the former uncompeti-tive within the national economy. Such arbitrary attempts to impose a nationalistic order upon the anarchic development of the social division of labour only create as many problems as they solve. Recently, for example, in response to the attempt to force British Steel into profit this nationalized enterprise has had to cut back its purchases from another state-owned industry—The National Coal Board—to turn to cheaper imported coking coal so that it can reduce its costs. (It should be noted that in this instance only British, and especially Welsh, coal interests are being affected because the National Coal Board is itself involved in a consortium which extracts the Australian coal that British Steel imports—pers. comm. from K. Morgan.) This may help British Steel to develop more successfully *in* the regions in which it is located, but will hardly help the development *of* the South Wales region. The opposite policy of enforcing the purchase of Welsh coking coal would presumably save the state considerable outlays in terms of unemploy-ment and related benefits but it would not save British Steel's position in what is now an international market. It has already been stressed that the associated technological developments will not guarantee net benefits to particular regions either.

Those living in backward regions will obviously welcome regional policies which increase employment, but this purely quantitative, and often temporary, change does not end the problems of uneven development but merely aids their reproduction, perhaps in a new 'spatial division of labour' (Massey, 1979b). Recently in Britain, plants that were established in these areas and received regional aid have been as vulnerable to low pay, lay-offs, redundancies and closures as the establishments that existed there previously and sometimes in the case of British-owned branch plants, especially so (cf. Townsend, 1980a). What was proffered as a solution has turned out to be a reproduction of the problem.

This should occasion no surprise among students of the history of 'the regional problem', especially among those interested in what Schumpeter called the process of 'creative destruction' of technological change under capitalism. Mere relocation or quantitative change of capitals within the national space is unlikely to affect the inherent mechanisms of capital accumulation in such a way that they will now stop reproducing uneven development. Nor should it be expected that the state can fulfil its obligation to promote industry, whether private or nationalized capital, through regional policy or by other means, without contradicting any political 'welfarist' obligations that it may have. The goals or, more correctly, the conditions of survival, of capital accumulation and the manner of the regulation of the social division of labour are not directly related to general social needs in any simple way. Capital's immediate problem is to reproduce itself and in doing so it can only reproduce society on its own terms. The announcement in 1979 by the British Conservative government of plans to introduce 'enterprise zones' in which 'welfarist' controls on capital are relaxed is an extreme example of this situation: the only way the state can support capital at the present time is at the expense of the welfarist gains made by the working class in these areas. Once they are overridden within the zones it will be very hard to uphold them outside.

The difference between these conclusions and those of conventional regional theory partly result from a difference in methodology. The conventional approach seeks regular associations among empirical phenomena as a possible basis for generalization. The literature on technological change and regional development usually studies spatially regular associations of phenomena, held to be favourable, at certain conjunctures within the space economy. It is usually implicitly assumed that these are independent of less favourable associations elsewhere, such that the former can be reproduced without reproducing the latter. Since there is no attempt to show how causal mechanisms operate necessarily in virtue of the nature of phenomena, there is no way to distinguish between causation and accidental correlation and hence no way, other than by intuition, to distinguish necessary from accidental effects of particular forms of development. This lack of a methodological approach for differentiating relations encourages purely quantitative prescriptive suggestions which call for a change in the number and location of the regularities. Structural, qualitative changes are not suggested because the methodology does not aid the discovery of structures and their inherent mechanisms.

It would be unfair to say that conventional regional theory does not, at least implicitly, distinguish between the necessary and the contingent; but its empiricist methodology with its low priority of conceptualization and its preoccupation with purely quantitative (including statistical) relations between simple undifferentiated data nullifies what limited powers of theoretical differentiation it has. Agglomeration economies, increasing returns to scale and 'circular and cumulative causation' are important concepts in conventional regional theory: all refer to processes which contribute towards regional uneven development but either merely to the quantitative aspects of the latter or else reduce the causal processes to 'regularities' and then, especially in formal models, to 'functions'. Mathematical functions and empirical regularities, whether static or dynamic, do not of themselves indicate what it is about objects which makes them operate in the way they are described. To understand this one has to turn to structural analysis.

The structural approach seeks out mechanisms which operate necessarily because of the nature of the relations constituting the phenomena in question. These mechanisms do not relate to their empirical effects in a simple, fixed fashion but are mediated by contingently related phenomena in concrete situations. Despite this de-emphasis of the significance of empirical regularities in themselves, it is none the less possible to explain different empirical outcomes as a contingent combination (whose form has to be discovered empirically) of necessary relations, mechanisms and externally related conditions. This appears to be the method adopted, for example, by Massey and Meegan (1979) to show how the mechanisms of the economic crisis affected various types of firms in different ways. In the case of uneven development, many of the negative effects of capital accumulation are necessary in the sense that they could not be eliminated without eliminating capital. Hence, to intervene in the determination of the social division of labour so as to plan it according to the social needs of people, both as workers and consumers, would require the withdrawal of capital's power to dispose of its money-capital wherever in the world it sees the profit prospects to be best. To do this would be to dispossess and abolish capital.

Spatial Analysis, Industry and the Industrial Environment. Vol. 3 Regional Economies and Industrial Systems
Edited by F. E. I. Hamilton and G. J. R. Linge
© 1983 John Wiley & Sons Ltd.

Chapter 4

Capital Accumulation and Regional Problems: A Study of North East England, 1945 to 1980

RAY HUDSON

This chapter describes and accounts for the post-war restructuring of the economy of North East England (Figure 4.1; see also Carney *et al.*, 1976, 1977). Its central explanatory thesis is that the observed pattern of changes must be understood both as the outcome of, and to some extent a pre-condition for, the process of capital accumulation, i.e. not merely the expansion of value but also the extended reproduction of capitalist social relations. This entails a consideration of politics and policies (e.g. those of capitals—individual companies—labour and the state), of economic change in the narrow sense and of the crucial question of securing the legitimacy of those social changes that form an integral part of the accumulation process. (The thesis poses epistemological and methodological problems which are no less troublesome as a result of being well known—for instance, see Massey, 1978.)

Such a process is uneven, with an inherent tendency to crisis which, on occasion, actually occurs. As Mandel (1975, p. 438) suggests, accumulation, the central driving force of the capitalist mode of production, follows a course of 'successive phases of recession, upswing, boom, overheating, crash and depression' which is, as it were, genetically endowed. This arises because accumulation depends upon an increase both in the mass and in the rate of profit and because the capitalist mode of production is characterized by a tendency for the rate of profit to fall which then sets in motion counter-tendencies either to avoid crises or (temporarily) overcome them and restore profitability (hence the expanded reproduction of capital) by a process of restructuring, reducing the value of the component parts of capital. The onset of crisis and this restructuring at the level of 'capital in general' are brought about through, and made possible by, competition between individual capitals. These deploy strategies to try to guarantee or boost their profits, to attain surplus profits (that is, profits that are above average for a branch of production). Several strategies are open to individual capitals striving to raise profitability (Mandel, 1975, pp. 77–8). They can switch investments between branches or sectors of the economy or alter the spatial allocation of investment which, increasingly, are made possible

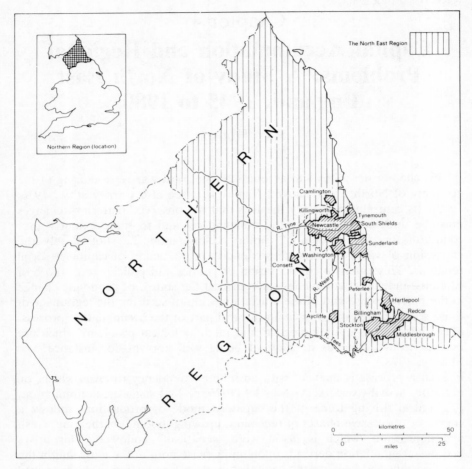

FIGURE 4.1 The Northern Region and the North East of England

because of the interrelated combination of the centralization of capital and an increased size of individual capitals (itself a product of competition); the larger scale of production associated with the concentration of capital; and concomitant changes in the labour process and division of labour as a result of technical progress which centralization and concentration both permit and require. Moreover, the pattern of spatial differentiation resulting from earlier periods of uneven capitalist development is an important pre-condition for such changes, with the state frequently and increasingly intimately involved through policies designed generally to reduce the cost of elements of the component parts of capital or selectively to lower the price of some of them to some units of capital, while legitimizing these actions as socially progressive.

Thus capitals' restructuring to avoid or overcome crises and maintain, increase or restore profitability requires a redefinition of capital:labour relations in favour of the former and this frequently, if not inevitably, implies the creation of crises (such as increased unemployment or cuts in living standards) when seen from the viewpoint of labour and the working class. At the same time, these changes must be justified, if not as legitimate, then at least as the outcome of natural economic processes, to guarantee the reproduction of capitalist social relations; in this the state is inextricably involved. The post-war history of the North East is considered against this brief background.

RECOVERY AND RECESSION: 1951 TO 1962

In sharp contrast to the inter-war years and the latter part of the 1940s, the 1951–58 period can be characterized as a 'Golden Age' for the region. The working class, a high proportion of which had experienced prolonged unemployment in the inter-war years, perceived this to be a time of full employment (although this was only maintained by the out-migration of a considerable surplus population to meet the expanding demand for labour in the South East and the West Midlands) and rising real wages (Figure 4.2 and Table 4.1). It was also a period favourable to the interests of capital. In manufacturing, for example, the 1948–51 profitability crisis was overcome: the mass and rate of profit both rose markedly (Table 4.1). For a time, then, it appeared that the objectives of capital and labour were complementary: how this apparent reconciliation of fundamentally incompatible interests could temporarily be maintained is not without significance.

Of considerable importance was the way that working class and trades union demands were formulated and pursued, these being greatly influenced by the region's inter-war experience. Even during a time of full employment, and no doubt reinforced by rising average real wages, memories of the 1930s served to shape these demands. As a result, the attainment and maintenance of full employment became an end in itself rather than being used as a platform from which to advance further and more radical demands. A recovery of profitability, therefore, was eminently feasible and, given a rising level of effective demand for labour both within this and other regions in the UK, was compatible with the maintenance of full employment within the North East. Several aspects of this process can be identified.

First, effective demand for many commodities 'traditionally' produced in the region recovered strongly. The British economy during this period remained essentially based on one fuel: the nationalization of coal-mining in 1948 reflected the need to guarantee production of a key element of

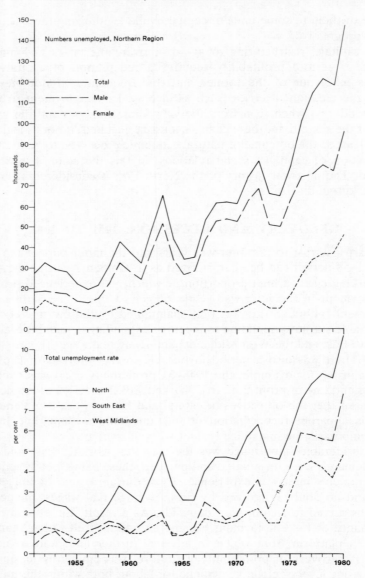

FIGURE 4.2 Regional unemployment changes in 3 regions of Great Britain, annual averages 1950 to 1980. From 1951 to 1964 the data for the South East include those for East Anglia. [Sources: United Kingdom, Department of Employment and Productivity, 1971; United Kingdom, Central Statistical Office, 1975, 1980]

circulating constant capital, the provision of which had ceased to be sufficiently profitable from the viewpoint of individual capitals. Since national economic recovery and expansion depended upon coal as an energy source, there were compelling pressures to maximize national coal output. Consequently, coal-mining employment in the North East was relatively stable (Table 4.2). Simultaneously and, to some extent relatedly, effective demand for some of the products of the region's 'traditional' industries—shipbuilding, marine engineering, mechanical and electrical engineering, metal manufacture, armaments—also recovered strongly.

This revival partly reflected the impact of the Second World War, the destruction wrought necessitating a period of reconstruction and leading to a relative lack of international competition facing North East producers. In addition, the upturn also reflected the demand for armaments during the Korean War of the 1950s. Output was boosted by increasing the size of the workforce (especially in shipbuilding) and by some increase in labour productivity (Table 4.1). In general, however, the restoration of profitability in these 'traditional' activities was based on expanded output resulting from fuller use of existing capacity. Productivity also improved, mainly from 'normal' incremental growth, as a result (essentially) of long overdue replacement investment in existing technology rather than with major outlays of fixed capital in new and qualitatively different modern technology and production methods. The recovery in profits largely resulted from an expansion in the mass of surplus value via increased outlays of variable capital at a time when, internationally, there was a tendency towards a sharp rise in the organic composition of capital (that is, the ratio of constant to variable capital advanced in production) and in the rate of surplus value. This pattern of accumulation was to assume considerable significance for the development of these branches in the North East, although in the conjuncture of their contemporary favourable position in the international division of labour and of the regional balance of class forces, and in particular in view of the way in which working class demands were formulated, it provided a short-term strategy that was extremely rational when observed from the viewpoint of the units of capital involved.

Second, effective demand for some products 'new' to the region also grew strongly, although from a low base level. These products were associated with activities (for example, in instrument engineering and parts of electrical engineering; clothing; and paper, printing and publishing) that had located there in response to the opportunities the North East offered for profitable production, allied to the newly emergent regional policies of the 1930s, the decentralization of war-time production, and the strengthened regional policies of the 1945–48 period. From 1948 the Labour government effectively sacrificed regional policy as part of the state's response to the balance of payments and sterling crises of the late 1940s while, during the 1950s. the

TABLE 4.1 Changes in total manufacturing and selected industry groups, Northern Region of England, 1951 to 1970

Industry group	1951	1958	1963	1968	1970
(a) *Employment (000)*					
Chemicals	40.6	59.2	57.3	49.1	55.0
Metals	58.9	58.3	52.2	50.3	57.5
Shipbuilding, marine engineering	51.7	60.0	39.9	36.2	34.4
Textiles	14.1	15.5	19.2	21.6	23.7
Paper, printing, publishing	12.7	13.0	14.4	18.4	19.7
Total manufacturing	374.7	410.1	393.2	413.7	448.6
(b) *Capital stock (£ million, 1970 constant prices)*					
Chemicals	242	455	660	957	1,072
Metals	197	311	441	580	612
Shipbuilding, marine engineering	149	162	171	166	165
Textiles	33	38	40	89	112
Paper, printing, publishing	33	39	46	63	72
Total manufacturing	1,085	1,554	2,008	2,647	2,910
(c) *Output (£ million, 1970 constant prices)*					
Chemicals	53.1	123.0	158.6	170.8	233.5
Metals	93.4	96.3	89.4	95.6	137.1
Shipbuilding, marine engineering	57.6	81.3	54.0	58.9	55.3
Textiles	8.5	14.5	41.3	56.8	40.6
Paper, printing, publishing	10.5	16.3	23.3	27.8	45.0
Total manufacturing	408.4	588.0	680.3	903.7	1,057.8
(d) *Profits (£ million, 1970 constant prices)*					
Chemicals	13.5	57.9	88.0	98.2	n.a.
Metals	38.8	34.8	34.7	35.6	n.a.
Shipbuilding, marine engineering	14.3	21.5	12.4	15.4	n.a.
Textiles	0.2	4.3	24.8	33.3	n.a.
Paper, printing, publishing	1.9	5.9	10.0	17.7	n.a.
Total manufacturing	115.2	209.2	281.1	431.9	n.a.
(e) *Wages (£ million, 1970 constant prices)*					
Chemicals	39.6	65.1	70.6	72.6	n.a.
Metals	54.6	61.5	54.7	60.0	n.a.
Shipbuilding, marine engineering	43.3	59.8	41.6	43.5	n.a.
Textiles	8.3	10.2	16.5	23.5	n.a.
Paper, printing, publishing	8.6	10.4	13.3	20.1	n.a.
Total manufacturing	293.2	378.8	389.2	464.4	n.a.
(f) *Capital per employee (£, 1970 constant prices)*					
Chemicals	5,975	7,689	11,511	19,497	19,491
Metals	3,350	5,338	8,446	11,523	10,636
Shipbuilding, marine engineering	2,880	2,695	4,278	4,575	4,796

TABLE 4.1—*continued*

Industry group	1951	1958	1963	1968	1970
Textiles	2,375	2,458	2,109	4,101	4,738
Paper, printing, publishing	2,583	2,985	3,187	3,408	3,640
Total manufacturing	2,896	3,789	5,110	6,398	6,486
(g) Output per employee (£, 1970 constant prices)					
Chemicals	1,308	2,078	2,768	3,479	4,245
Metals	1,586	1,652	1,713	1,901	2,384
Shipbuilding, marine engineering	1,114	1,355	1,353	1,627	1,608
Textiles	603	935	2,151	2,630	1,713
Paper, printing, publishing	827	1,254	1,618	2,054	2,284
Total manufacturing	1,090	1,434	1,730	2,184	2,358
(h) Profits per employee (£, 1970 constant prices)					
Chemicals	332	978	1,536	2,000	n.a.
Metals	659	597	665	708	n.a.
Shipbuilding, marine engineering	277	358	311	425	n.a.
Textiles	142	277	1,292	1,542	n.a.
Paper, printing, publishing	150	454	694	962	n.a.
Total manufacturing	307	510	715	1,044	n.a.
(i) Wages per employee (£, 1970 constant prices)					
Chemicals	975	1,100	1,232	1,479	n.a.
Metals	927	1,055	1,048	1,193	n.a.
Shipbuilding, marine engineering	837	997	1,043	1,202	n.a.
Textiles	589	658	859	1,088	n.a.
Paper, printing, publishing	677	800	924	1,092	n.a.
Total manufacturing	782	924	990	1,122	n.a.
(j) Profits as percentage of output					
Chemicals	25.4	47.1	55.5	57.5	n.a.
Metals	41.5	35.3	38.8	37.2	n.a.
Shipbuilding, marine engineering	24.8	26.4	31.1	42.5	n.a.
Textiles	2.4	29.7	60.0	58.6	n.a.
Paper, printing, publishing	18.1	36.2	42.9	46.8	n.a.
Total manufacturing	28.2	35.6	42.8	48.6	n.a.

Sources: Northern Region Strategy Team, 1975; Hudson, 1976b.

TABLE 4.2 Employees in employment, Northern Region of England, 1952 to 1975 (000)[a]

Composite industrial classification order groups	1952	1956	1960	1966	1971	1973	1975
A. Agriculture, forestry, fishing	39.0	36.5	34.0	24.8	19.1	19.2	17.6
B. Mining, quarrying	179.9	175.6	156.2	104.9	63.7	55.2	49.3
C. Food, beverages, tobacco	33.5	34.8	34.3	34.5	38.4	36.7	36.9
D. Chemicals, allied industries	44.1	50.1	59.8	57.3	58.7	52.9	51.1
E. Metal manufacture	58.7	59.8	62.1	57.9	47.6	44.6	45.0
F. Mechanical engineering	54.0	56.0	58.5	66.6	72.2	71.0	75.1
G. Instrument engineering	1.1	1.1	1.3	1.9	3.4	3.8	3.9
H. Electrical engineering	30.3	36.3	39.6	53.5	56.0	61.5	55.0
I. Shipbuilding, marine engineering	61.4	64.1	60.2	42.3	36.0	34.7	32.3
J. Vehicles	14.5	17.5	15.5	11.6	13.6	14.7	13.6
K. Other metal goods	12.7	13.7	12.1	14.4	13.8	15.0	15.3
L. Textiles	13.6	15.9	18.8	20.6	22.9	24.3	27.9
M. Leather, leather goods, fur	2.9	3.1	2.3	1.7	2.4	2.2	2.9
N. Clothing, footwear	28.1	30.0	31.7	34.7	35.5	36.4	35.5
O. Bricks, pottery, glass, cement	19.1	18.8	18.6	19.3	18.8	17.9	16.9
P. Timber, furniture, etc.	14.9	14.0	12.7	14.6	13.0	15.2	14.0
Q. Paper, printing, publishing	12.7	13.3	14.4	17.2	19.6	21.8	24.5
R. Other manufacturing	7.2	8.7	12.0	15.2	13.5	17.1	14.9
S. Construction	74.9	85.1	87.0	108.6	87.5	102.0	101.1
T. Gas, electricity, water	18.9	19.5	19.4	22.7	20.0	18.1	19.4
U. Transport, communications	101.2	98.0	92.1	86.6	70.5	67.2	68.6
V. Distributive trades	131.6	145.2	158.6	166.3	145.6	155.0	157.3
W. Insurance, banking, finance	12.2	15.3	16.9	20.5	23.6	25.1	25.8
X. Professional services	83.2	91.4	104.6	133.2	153.6	165.9	182.5
Y. Miscellaneous services	83.0	85.0	87.0	103.4	109.1	123.7	126.5
Z. Public administration, defence	71.7	68.2	69.3	74.1	80.0	84.4	95.7
Sub-total manufacturing industries (C to R)	408.8	437.2	453.9	463.3	465.4	469.8	465.2
Sub-total production industries (A to T)	721.5	753.9	750.5	724.3	655.7	664.3	652.6
Sub-total service industries (U to Z)	482.9	503.1	528.5	584.1	582.4	621.3	556.4
Total	1204.4	1257.0	1279.0	1308.0	1238.1	1285.6	1309.0

[a] These data are not strictly comparable with those in Figures 4.2 and 4.3 although the general tendencies are broadly similar.

Source: Fothergill and Gudgin, 1978, pp. 43–8.

Conservative government effectively suspended the implementation of formal regional policy and dispensed with programmes designed to steer new industries to the North East (Regional Policy Research Unit, 1979, Part 2). Displacement of surplus labour via migration to the South East and the West Midlands helped to meet the labour power requirements of capitals located there (so supporting national growth) while established employers in the North East had no interest in further tightening pressures on the labour market; in fact, they continued to vigorously oppose proposals for the introduction of 'new' (especially male-employing) industries into this region, as they had successfully done in the immediate post-war years (hence the spatial and sectoral concentration of such new industries as did invest there). In this, they were supported by the state. As the Northern Regional Controller of the Board of Trade informed the House of Commons Select Committee on Estimates, the 'last thing' his department would want to do would be to encourage firms to go to places with 'no unemployment' (cited by Bowden, 1965, p. 29).

Increased output in the new industries was for the most part achieved not by expanding labour forces or fixed capital stock but by gains in labour productivity. An important factor was that much of the workforce in these activities was female, often married and non-unionized, and being introduced to the regime of factory work for the first time (for example, see North Tyneside Community Development Project, 1978b).

However, the major focus of dynamism in the regional economy in this period was undoubtedly chemicals, associated not only with the continuing development of existing branches of production but also with the switch to, and development of, petrochemicals (notably at the Wilton complex of Imperial Chemical Industries Ltd) and the introduction of new technologies leading to great increases in productivity and profits per employee (House and Fullerton, 1960; Semmens, 1970; Taylor 1979; Hudson, 1981a). This and subsequent developments there were closely linked to general accumulation imperatives to produce new, synthetic raw materials as a means of reducing the value of elements of circulating constant capital. Thus, the development and expansion of the chemicals sector became a central component of the post-war 'long wave with an undertone of expansion' (Mandel, 1975), which had important repercussions on the overall pattern and pace of accumulation (Hudson, 1981b). Within the North East, much of the expansion of the manufacturing sector was associated with the development of chemicals—over 50 per cent of that in employment and over 45 per cent of that in capital stock, output and profits.

Third, in addition to net growth in the factory workforce there was also an expansion in service sector employment (Table 4.2), especially for women. In part, this reflected greater purchasing power from increased employment and wages in other sectors, enabling the further extension of capitalist social relations into the spheres of services and distribution. It also reflected the expansion of job opportunities in educational and medical services, which followed the establishment of the Welfare State in the immediate post-war years.

Thus for a time in the 1950s a generally profitable restructuring of capital co-existed with conditions of full employment within the region. It appeared that harmony prevailed between the interests of capital and labour. But 1958 saw a rupturing of this harmonious relationship and a turning-point in the region's social history, for it marked the beginning of the end of the brief period of full employment in the North East (and in other peripheral British regions) which led to pressures for increased state intervention to encourage the transformation of the region's economy, in the belief that this would provide the route back to full employment.

Employment loss in this period was, however, concentrated in 2 branches—coal-mining and shipbuilding. This reflected processes of restructuring set in motion in response to crises which had different origins. The crisis in shipbuilding and related activities (including steel production) reflected the changed status of North East producers as their world market share was sharply eroded by increasing competition from other producers using more modern production techniques (Cousins and Brown, 1970). Consequently, output and total profits fell sharply. In an attempt to maintain the rate of profit, outlays on wages were reduced equally sharply so that by 1963 profit as a proportion of the value of output had risen slightly but employment had fallen (Table 4.1). In coal-mining (and related activities, notably rail and water transport), employment began to fall quickly, although for different reasons. The regional decline in coal-mining employment reflected a decision—made possible by the availability on the international market of large amounts of cheap oil—at national level by the British state to switch to a multi-fuel economy in an attempt to cut energy costs, for these had implications to a greater or lesser extent for the international competitive position of all British manufacturing capitals. In the 1950s the drive to maximize coal output had resulted in increased unit production costs; among the implications of a switch to a multi-fuel economy were that, in general, total coal output be reduced and, in particular, high-cost collieries be closed (Regional Policy Research Unit, 1979, Part 4).

A corollary of this sectoral concentration of job loss was a spatial impact, especially in Tyneside and Wearside: the male unemployment rate in South Shields, for instance, rose to over 10 per cent in December 1958, reviving the spectre of the 1930s. In turn, this led to increased political pressure within the labour movement for stronger measures to combat unemployment. In response, the Board of Trade took a rather more active role in steering new industry to the region. It was able to do this because labour forces associated with coal-mining and shipbuilding began to disband and the labour market in the South East and the West Midlands remained inflexible, as full employment conditions continued there (Figure 4.2).

Moreover, these specific sectoral crises and male employment losses in the North East were overlain by broader, national 'stop-go' cycles of increasing amplitude, largely induced by state macro-economic demand management policies. The combination of these general and specific factors led to a particularly sharp unemployment increase in the region in December 1962 which continued into 1963 (Figure 4.2). In turn, heightened political pressure to combat this from the Labour Party and trade unions within the region, together with the desire of the Conservative government for re-election, led to the appointment of Lord Hailsham as Minister for the North East and the adoption of the 'Hailsham programme' (United Kingdom, Board of Trade, 1963; Carney and Hudson, 1974; Regional Policy Research Unit, 1979, Part 3). This represented a major switch both in Conservative ideology and practice, consisting of a combination of short-term measures to alleviate unemployment together with longer-term more fundamental measures. The latter amounted to an expanded programme of public sector infrastructure investment which, taking over elements of the prevailing planning ideology in the region (Pepler and MacFarlane, 1949; Durham County Council, 1951), was to be concentrated in certain key locations possessing 'growth potential' (growth points—such as new towns— and a growth zone, lying between the rivers Tyne and Tees and to the east of the A1(M) motorway). It was asserted that a once-and-for-all sharp increase in public sector infrastructure investment would set in motion processes of regional industrial 'modernization' and 'diversification' which, in turn, would provide a route back to 'full employment'.

While at national level the switch to intervention represented a marked change in the stance of the Conservative government, within the North East the regional modernization programme was seen as a consensus measure. The roots of such policies as a solution to the region's problems can be traced back to the response to crisis evolved in the 1930s by the region's bourgeoisie in an attempt to protect their own interests (Carney and Hudson, 1978). Crucially, they subsequently came to be accepted as a legitimate, even inevitable, solution by the Labour Party and working class organizations. Thus it was possible in the early 1960s for modernization policies to become the basis of a consensus, or a class alliance, as to how best to solve the region's problems. Given the Labour Party's political hegemony in the North East, this has meant its advocating and implementing policies which objectively meet the requirements either of 'capital in general' or of some individual capitals while legitimating these as being directed towards the attainment of declared social democratic goals (e.g. reducing unemployment and improving working class living standards).

Parallel with this renewed emphasis on modernization policies, important

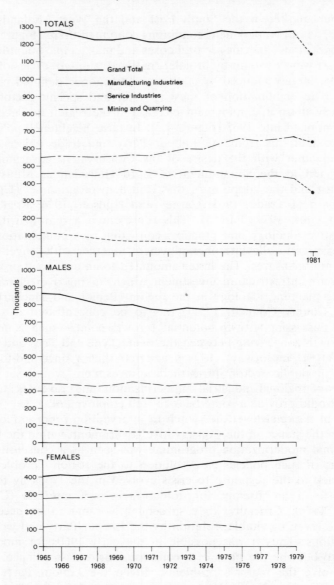

FIGURE 4.3 Employment change in the Northern Region, 1965 to 1981. [Source: United Kingdom, Department of Employment, 1976–81]

alterations were occurring in the remainder of the regional economy in response to declining employment, especially in coal-mining and shipbuilding. In manufacturing, apart from shipbuilding, the pattern of change between 1958 and 1963 exhibited little evidence of crisis from the point of view of capital; on the contrary, gross output, fixed capital stock, labour productivity and profitability all rose sharply. Thus, while there may have been a crisis in terms of falling employment in shipbuilding and coal-mining (which became generalized at a political level), the manufacturing sector continued to be restructured in a way that was favourable to the interests of capital. While the recorded increases on these indicators tended to be smaller than those in the 1951–58 period (although in some branches, notably textiles, the reverse was true), of particular interest are the more rapid rises in fixed capital stock and in the capital : employee ratio. While the increase in the latter to some extent reflects employment loss, of greater significance was the accelerated pace of fixed capital investment in the early 1960s (especially in chemicals and metals). In chemicals, the growth of fixed capital investment was related both to capacity expansion, as better capacity utilization was achieved, and the adoption of more sophisticated technologies. In metals, it reflected the recovery in demand that had come about by 1960 because, in response to this, several modernization and expansion schemes were initiated. Even so, this investment was, by international standards, in outmoded technology: for example, the South Durham Iron and Steel Company's integrated South Works at Hartlepool opened in 1962 based on open-hearth steel production.

Moreover, while manufacturing employment (with the exception of shipbuilding) continued to expand slowly during this period, employment in the service sector, in aggregate, grew more rapidly. This was particularly so in distribution and professional services, as in earlier years, and also in miscellaneous services: these gains offset losses in transport associated mainly with the run-down of coal-mining. Despite the slight upward trend in numbers of jobs (Table 4.2 and Figure 4.3), unemployment, particularly for men, continued to grow (Figure 4.2), not least because many of the new jobs in services, the major source of employment expansion, were for women. Thus from the viewpoint of labour, if not of capital, this was a period of continuing employment problems which culminated in the sharp unemployment increases of December 1962 and 1963.

MODERNIZATION, 1963 TO 1970

The 1963–70 period in many ways saw the reinforcement of previously established restructuring tendencies in the region's economy and the refinement and implementation of the modernization policies which emerged during the early 1960s. In manufacturing there were substantial increases in output, fixed capital investment, labour productivity and profitability while employment and wages also increased, although at a much more subdued pace. However, the rate and character of restructuring varied among different branches of manufacturing. These variations and their relationship to the overall pattern of change in the regional economy require a consideration of the specific conjunction of circumstances that made particular locations within the North East especially attractive to capitals involved in certain types of production. It is necessary to examine why, for a time, the region provided an attractive destination for a part of some capitals contemporary 'round of investment' (Massey, 1979b). Several elements may be identified.

First, enhanced central government financial incentives were made available to capitals investing in the region. This was particularly so after 1966 (Moore *et al.*, 1977), following the election of a Labour government in 1964. This was initially committed to strengthening regional policy in response to social-democratic aims of narrowing spatial inequalities but, increasingly over time, became committed to pursuing policies intended to restructure the national manufacturing base as an end in itself, or as a means to attaining macro-economic policy objectives, rather than as a way of narrowing regional inequalities. One symptom of this, which was carried over into the 1970s, was the concentration of state aid for R & D in the South East while subsidies for production were channelled to regions such as the North East (Table 4.3). Such policies thus encouraged the emergence of a new spatial division of labour within Great Britain (a point amplified later). State subsidies served to cut production costs by reducing the price of elements of fixed capital although without necessarily reducing their value: rather, the state assumed financial responsibility for an increased proportion of the costs of production. Consequently, in general this made the region an attractive location for investment in activities characterized by a high and rising investment in fixed capital (notably chemicals and steel); in particular, the availability of large, flat, stable sites and the possibility of deep-water port facilities led to such investment within the region being concentrated at Teesside (for a comparison with the West Netherlands see Läpple and van Hoogstraten, 1980).

Thus fixed capital investment in new productive capacity, output and labour productivity rose sharply in both chemicals and metals production. Although profitability continued to increase in the former, this was not so in the latter (Table 4.1): indeed, this was a crisis period for iron and steel production. From 1961 through 1966, effective demand for steel produced in the Northern Region slumped and profitability fell sharply. This collapse in profitability was not restricted to the Region and served as the immediate trigger for the re-nationalization of parts of the industry in 1967. The combination of a recovery in demand for steel and a programme of

TABLE 4.3 Expenditure under the Public Expenditure Survey Committee programme: trade, industry and employment

Programme	Northern Region (£ million current prices)					Northern Region as per cent Great Britain total				
	1969–70	1970–71	1971–72	1972–73	1973–74	1969–70	1970–71	1971–72	1972–73	1973–74
Regional support and regeneration	*65*	*56*	*53*	*49*	*85*	*33.3*	*30.8*	*30.4*	*25.3*	*26.7*
Selective assistance	—	—	—	2	12	—	—	—	18.8	18.8
Regional development grants	—	—	—	3	36	—	—	—	42.7	33.3
Regional employment premium	31	31	31	29	31	28.7	28.6	29.2	29.0	29.2
Expenditure under the Local Employment Acts	34	25	22	14	7	40.1	34.8	33.9	20.4	17.4
Industrial innovation	*5*	*3*	*4*	*4*	*4*	*3.7*	*1.7*	*1.4*	*2.0*	*1.9*
General support for industry	*81*	*88*	*82*	*60*	*53*	*13.5*	*14.5*	*14.7*	*16.1*	*18.5*
Assistance to shipbuilding industry	4	3	1	4	8	25.2	35.8	11.4	41.4	29.9
Investment grants	77	85	80	56	43	13.2	14.4	14.3	15.0	17.2
Functioning of the labour market	*7*	*9*	*11*	*13*	*12*	*8.6*	*8.7*	*8.6*	*7.8*	*8.8*
Industrial training	3	4	3	5	6	10.8	10.8	10.8	11.0	10.8
Total expenditure	171	168	160	153	208	15.5	14.3	13.1	12.1	12.8

Source: Northern Region Strategy Team, 1976b, pp. 108–21.

rationalization and fresh investment by the British Steel Corporation (following a period of relatively little investment), although mainly in obsolete production technology by international standards (Cockerill and Silbertson, 1974), led to a sharp rise in output and a continued increase in fixed capital investment in metals production between 1968 and 1970 (Table 4.1).

None the less, net employment in chemicals and metals tended to stagnate or decline. Employment growth associated with capacity expansion both by existing companies and those new to the region (e.g. US multinationals involved in various types of chemicals production such as Monsanto) was balanced by the closure or restructuring of existing capacity (Robinson and Storey, 1979). Thus, the 1960s saw an extensive programme of modernization of ICI's inorganic chemicals and fertilizer production at Billingham; labour-intensive ammonia-producing plants (dating from the 1930s), which used coal as a source of process gas, were replaced by new plant using first naphtha and then natural gas as a raw material (Hudson, 1981a). ICI pioneered this development in a search for technological rents (Mandel, 1975, pp. 192–4). The resulting loss of several thousand jobs (Taylor, 1979) was offset to some extent by employment growth accompanying a considerable expansion and modernization of organic chemical production at Wilton.

These state financial incentives also helped bring about some restructuring in other 'traditional' sectors, such as shipbuilding and related marine, heavy mechanical and electrical engineering. Moreover, on occasion, the state was directly involved by promoting mergers and amalgamations. But a consequence of this increased centralization of control was a restructuring of production and employment decline (North East Trades Union Studies Information Unit, 1976).

Second, the Hailsham programme was implemented and public sector infrastructure investment (on industrial estates, houses and roads) sharply increased. These outlays were designed to provide some of the pre-conditions necessary to attract fresh manufacturing investment in new (especially consumer goods) industries by reducing or taking over elements of their costs of production. This investment was selectively channelled to a few key locations, such as the various new towns with Washington (5 miles [8 km] south of Gateshead) perhaps being the supreme example (Hudson, 1976a; 1980a,b). Hence the state became increasingly involved in the coordination and programming as well as the financing of investment, especially on Teesside, in response to the expansion of chemicals production there (North East Area Study, 1975). Associated with this spatially selective modernization programme was a substantial involvement of private capital in speculative house building and central area commercial redevelopment schemes, which found their fullest expression in the redevelopment of central Newcastle as the regional capital (Burns, 1967; Regional Policy Research Unit, 1979, Part 9). Public sector infrastructure investment was not limited to the areas specified in the Hailsham proposals. In particular, the growing demand for water from the continuing industrial development at Teesside led to the controversial decision in 1967 to construct a reservoir at Cow Green in Upper Teesdale thereby flooding a unique assemblage of flora (Gregory, 1975).

Such public expenditure policies reflected the formation and maintenance of a consensus around the politics of modernization as being the only solution to the problems of unemployment in the North East. Briefly, following the publication of the National Plan in 1965, which represented an attempt to increase the national economic growth rate through indicative planning and reducing differences in regional growth rates, this specific programme for the North East became linked to these broader planning policies and the Keynesian notion of balanced regional and national growth (Shanks, 1977), which attempted to modify the inherently uneven nature of capital accumulation.

Third, the 1960s saw the reconstitution of an abundant reserve of labour within the region, which provided an important attraction to some capitals in manufacturing. This had 2 aspects. One was that female workforce participation rates in the region, especially for married women, (Table 4.4) had historically been relatively low so that female labour could be drawn on to the labour market, often for the first time (Hudson, 1980a,b,c). This was, in part, related to the second aspect, the accelerated and chaotic run-down of coal-mining and the break-up of the workforce in this and associated activities which released many men on to the labour market. This was particularly evident after 1967 when the run-down of coal-mining was hastened as part of the measures to combat pressure on the exchange rate and balance of payments (Crossman, 1976, pp. 451–2; Krieger, 1979; Regional Policy Research Unit, 1979, Part 4). Significantly, rather than

TABLE 4.4 Workforce participation rates, Great Britain and Northern Region of England, 1961 to 1975

	1961	1966	1971	1975
Northern Region				
Male	86.0	83.1	81.1	80.6
Female	31.4	38.3	40.4	43.6
Great Britain				
Male	85.1	83.8	81.2	79.6
Female	37.1	42.2	43.0	45.8

Source: United Kingdom, Central Statistical Office, 1975–80.

opposing closures the regional branches of the National Union of Mineworkers and the Labour Party negotiated only about the pace of closure: from within the relevant working class organizations, mining decline was seen as 'inevitable', an indication of the extent to which they had absorbed the dominant ideology as to the nature of regional change. These various changes provided flexibility for employers on the labour market and offered opportunities to recruit a variety of types of labour power. In particular, there were opportunities to employ many people who were both pliant (because they were non-unionized or recruited into unions which promised trouble-free production in return for the right to negotiate closed shop arrangements and thus increase their own membership) and cheap (particularly during the 1967–76 period when the state directly met part of the price of labour through the Regional Employment Premium, a subsidy paid to employers depending upon the size and composition of their workforces).

These second and third elements and—to some extent—the first, provided a combination of circumstances that capitals in some branches of production found particularly attractive. The growing tendency to centralization and concentration, allied to technical progress and changes in labour processes associated with Taylorist and Fordist techniques of scientific management (Braverman, 1974; Aglietta, 1979, pp. 111–22) enabled some capitals advantageously to locate those parts of their production activities requiring relatively large amounts of poorly skilled labour in branch plants in the North East. This was part of the process of corporate restructuring which, increasingly, was and remains globally rather than nationally based. Mandel (1975, p. 324) identified the internationalization of production as a distinguishing feature of late capitalism. Changes in the North East are clearly related to this changed international division of labour. Thus, in 1971 40 per cent of all manufacturing establishments in the Northern Region were branch or subsidiary operations, many of which resulted from investment decisions made in the 1960s by multinationals (North East Trades Union Studies Information Unit, 1977). One result was an increase from 8500 in 1963 to 24,400 in 1971 in the numbers employed in foreign-owned factories in the Region (Northern Region Strategy Team, 1976a).

These changes in the North East were part of much wider processes whereby the 'traditional' regional specialization of industry in the UK was changing to a new spatial division of labour. For a time, regions characteristically fulfil a particular role in the overall production process in which a widening range of activities are becoming organized on an international basis. Typically, assembly and semi-skilled component manufacturing operations are assigned to regions like the North East of England (Massey, 1978; Perrons, 1979; Lipietz, 1980b). Thus the characterization of the region as a 'global outpost' (Austrin and Beynon, 1979) is particularly apposite.

Within the North East, these changes were manifested in 2 main ways. First, because public sector investment in physical infrastructure was spatially selective this led to a geographical concentration of 'new' industry which was also associated with a spatial restructuring of intra-regional labour markets and changes in commuting patterns (Hudson, 1980a). During the 1961–73 period, 46 per cent of all new manufacturing firms moving into the Northern Region located in only 8 of the 77 Employment Exchange Areas there. These 8 were all in the North East and were associated with new towns (Aycliffe, Cramlington, Peterlee and Washington) or developments by the English Industrial Estates Corporation (Gateshead, Hartlepool, Stockton and Thornaby) as noted by Hudson (1976a, Vol. 1, pp. 139–40). Second, relatively strong rates of growth of employment, output and profits were recorded in industries like food, beverages and tobacco; engineering; clothing; textiles; paper; and other manufacturing; in others (notably textiles) capital stock also grew sharply. Greater output tended to be associated with gains in labour productivity as well as larger workforces but there is little evidence of sharp increases in fixed capital : employee ratios (except in textiles and other manufacturing where there was considerable fixed capital investment partly financed through state subsidies). This suggests an expansion of capacity using much the same technology but with a more flexible labour market enabling greater productivity by changing working conditions at the point of production.

Thus, the alterations brought about in the region's manufacturing sector in general constituted a successful, profitable restructuring from the viewpoint of some of the capitals involved—even in the shipbuilding sector profitability recovered, if only weakly and temporarily. Conversely, for the working class, these changes, together with those experienced in the remaining sectors of the regional economy, were not successful, particularly in increasing employment opportunities: some growth in net manufacturing employment has to be seen against employment loss in other sectors, notably coal-mining. The qualitative aspects of jobs lost and created also require consideration. Women accounted for almost half the net increase in the factory workforce between 1965 and 1970 (Figure 4.3), a symptom of the drive for supposedly non-militant, unskilled labour power: Lipietz (1980a) suggests that feminization can be taken as an index of de-skilling although this is not to suggest that women's work is necessarily unskilled but rather that unskilled jobs are frequently occupied by women. At the same time some capitals established new factories because of the availability of ex-miners, but the labour thus absorbed did not equal the supply released by the restructuring of coal-mining. In the services sector, too, net male employment fell (largely because of the decline in activities dependent upon coal-mining) while net female employment increased. Those reductions in female job opportunities which did occur (for example, in distribution, in part associated with commercial restructuring and central area redevelopment schemes) were more than offset by expansion in activities like education and medical services and public administration because of increased public expenditure by the Labour government in response to social reformist pressures. Moreover, this growth reflected a general expansion of these sectors as well as a restructuring within the state apparatus and changes in the spatial division of labour in the tertiary sector within the territory of the British state, in response to the possibilities offered by technological change and its impacts on labour processes. This was manifested by a decentralization of routine operations to the North East.

These various changes resulted in a steep rise in male unemployment, declining male workforce participation rates, a fall in males in employment and continuing net out-migration at the same time as the number of females in employment and female workforce participation rates grew. While to some extent policy objectives were realized (the employment structure for example being 'diversified'), state intervention failed to achieve its principal aim of lowering (male) unemployment and was associated with a pattern of changes which exacerbated the problems it was supposed to solve. (For an analysis of why intentions and outcomes *must* differ, see Offe, 1975a; Habermas, 1976.) This disjunction between intention and outcome *could* have served to call into question the legitimacy of the state and the progressive or, at worst, class-neutral, character of its interventions. But, given the general acceptance by working class organizations and the Labour movement within the region of an ideology which perceived economic change and employment decline as inevitable and modernization as the only alternative, that possibility was not realized and the consensus on the politics of modernization as the route to social reform remained intact, though not unaffected.

PERMANENT DEPRESSION: THE 1970s ONWARDS?

With the exception of a brief period of weak recovery in 1972–73, the 1970s were marked by a deepening depression in the North East, as unemployment mounted to levels last seen in the 1930s. This was a reflection of strategies adopted both by capitals and the British state to meet various crises. Moreover, the impacts of recession—initially the specifically British recession of 1971–72 triggered by the macro-economic policies of the newly elected Conservative government and then the post-1973 international recession (Mandel's, 1978, 'Second Slump')—were intimately related to the way in which capital, encouraged and supported by the British state, had utilized the opportunities offered by the region in previous years.

Some kinds of production, notably steel and petrochemicals (the latter

TABLE 4.5 Fixed capital formation by manufacturing industry, Northern Region of England and United Kingdom, 1971 to 1978 (£ million current prices)

Year	Gross		Net	
	Northern Region	Per cent UK total	Northern Region	Per cent UK total
1971	206	9.4	—	—
1972	178	8.7	—	—
1973	191	8.1	186.4	8.2
1974	305	9.9	309.5	10.1
1975	452	12.8	461.6	13.1
1976	491	12.4	478.8	11.8
1977	588	12.2	594.8	11.9
1978	630	11.0	—	—

Sources: United Kingdom, Central Statistical Office, 1975–80; United Kingdom, Central Statistical Office, 1981, p. 157.

increasingly related to the North Sea oil developments on Teesside) maintained substantial fixed capital investment and this was reflected in the Region's rising share of national fixed capital formation in manufacturing (Table 4.5). It was linked both to the continued international tendency for fixed capital investment to assume increasing importance and to the accelerated turnover time of fixed capital (Mandel, 1975, pp. 223–47). Such investment was part of a continued drive to increase competitiveness and retain or raise world market shares for existing products through greater labour productivity, largely allied with the introduction of automated production techniques (Aglietta, 1979, pp. 122–30) and the development of new products. Generally, however, restructuring has meant a decline in jobs as demand either fell or increased only slowly, leading to development without employment. This fixed capital investment has been substantially underwritten by the state, not only directly by reducing the cost of elements of fixed capital through industrial and regional policies (Tables 4.5 and 4.6) but also through transforming parts of the Region's rural periphery, particularly by constructing major reservoirs at Kielder and Cow Green to ensure water for expanded chemicals and steel production on Teesside.

Investment in metals was mainly associated with aluminium and iron and steel production. The former reflected Alcan's decision to build a smelter at Lynemouth (on the coast, about 25 km northeast of Newcastle) using state subsidies to cut the price of key elements of both circulating and fixed constant capital to encourage the production of aluminium within the UK. Investment in iron and steel was associated with the rationalization that followed the renationalization of parts of the industry, in an effort to cut

TABLE 4.6 Regional development grants to Northern Region of England, 1972 to 1980 (March) (£ million)

	Plant and machinery			Building and works			Total
	Special development areas	Development areas	Total	Special development areas	Development areas	Total	
Northern Region	237	394	631	56	64	120	751
Per cent of Great Britain total	33.2	42.7	38.5	33.1	34.8	21.3	34.1

Source: United Kingdom, Central Statistical Office, 1981, p. 116.

unit production costs of basic steel by belatedly erecting modern plant. (This was an attempt by the state to reduce the price of a central element of constant capital for many other manufacturing activities which had important implications for their international competitive position as well as that of the British Steel Corporation itself.) From 1973 the rationalization programme was particularly linked with the British Steel Corporation's 'Ten Year Development Plan' which entailed scrapping capacity and replacing it with modern plant. This necessitated spatial changes in production nationally and regionally, and the development of integrated, coastal works including that at Teesside.

In the early 1970s steel output fell sharply in the UK and in the Northern Region at a time when global demand for steel was growing, a reflection of the weakening international competitive position of British Steel. The subsequent simultaneous fall in global demand for iron and steel products and the expansion of modern capacity in some countries (Linge and Hamilton, 1981) called into question the intention of the Development Plan to increase output. This was reinforced by financial constraints imposed on the British Steel Corporation by the Labour government because of deepening fiscal problems in the mid-1970s, and then by the strict cash limits prescribed in 1979 by a Conservative government committed to monetarist policies, as well as the EEC's effort to cut capacity. The Development Plan was severely modified: plant closure was speeded up and schemes to expand new capacity abandoned. In the North East this resulted in the closure of works at Consett and Hartlepool, while at Teesside the second blast furnace at Redcar is not to be erected and employment is to be reduced. These steps will have consequences for the mining industry because of the decreased demand for coking coal. Employment in coal-mining continued to decline during the 1970s—though at a much slower rate than in the 1960s—as a result, in part, of the introduction of improved mechanized deep-mining techniques and the development of opencast methods in an attempt to reduce further the unit production costs of coal. Furthermore, financial constraints on the British Steel Corporation have led to policies of importing coking coal for the Teesside works (for example, from Australia), threatening employment in collieries on the County Durham coast.

Other manufacturing activities have also reduced capacity with companies writing-off fixed capital to maintain or boost the rate of profit. This process has occurred in both traditional sectors and in the new growth industries of the 1960s. The limited restructuring of the former was increasingly found inadequate as the recession deepened globally and weaker capitals were eliminated. The nationalization of the shipbuilding industry in 1977 followed a period of increased direct state intervention in response to a chronic profitability crisis and the impacts of accelerating inflation which were felt by capitals that had committed themselves to fixed price contracts in an attempt to finance belated and inadequate restructuring programmes from the late 1960s. But this was simply a prelude to the state's assuming responsibility for a severe rationalization in the face of serious overcapacity and the weak international position of British shipbuilders, particularly following the election of a Conservative government in 1979 which imposed tight cash limits on the industry as part of its wider monetary policy. Employment in shipbuilding in the North East between nationalization in 1977 and the election in 1979 declined by almost 20 per cent from 36,000 (North Tyneside Trades Council, 1979) and has since continued to fall.

Moreover, the 'new' industries were also affected by the recession; the earlier generation of plants from the 1940s were affected first, but as the recession deepened, the 'growth industries' of the 1960s also suffered, thus vividly demonstrating that the modern, diversified sector of the regional economy was extremely fragile in the changed world market conditions of the 1970s. Product diversity did not mean diversity of production processes and it was the latter that were most readily changed. Capitals which, in the favourable environment offered by the region in earlier times, had established branch plants to produce specific commodities, either reduced levels of capacity utilization in response to falling levels of demand or truncated the 'natural' life cycle of plants by closing capacity and writing-off the fixed capital investment in an attempt to restore the rate of profit. In other cases branch plants had been established to make commodities that were already technically obsolete and at the end of their life cycle but for which a specific, temporary demand then existed; once this disappeared they were closed.

Damette (1980) has introduced the concept of 'hypermobility' to embrace the accelerated switching of investment between locations as the turnover time of fixed capital is reduced (not least because of the state's taking over parts of the costs for individual capitals). Related to this is the possibility that part of the next 'round of investment' by these capitals will not be in the North East. Given the internationalization of production, there will be an increasing tendency for investment to be switched to other locations offering better opportunities for profitable manufacturing: for example, cheaper labour areas in Mediterranean Europe, especially when the EEC is enlarged, and the Third World (Fröbel *et al.*, 1980; Damette, 1980). This tendency is being reinforced by the policies of states in such areas to enhance the possibilities for profitable production. Such switches in investment strategy, from the viewpoint of the capitals concerned, represent part of a rational response to crisis. The net result of these changes in the North East was a sudden decline in factory employment after 1975, especially in jobs for women (Figure 4.3). Total declared redundancies (which understate job losses) in the Northern Region have increased and so also has the proportion of the UK total there. Between 1971 and 1975, some 77,300 redundancies were declared in the Northern Region (Table 4.7), 8.1 per cent of the UK total but between 1976 and 1980 this rose to 127,863, 10.9 per cent of the UK total (calculated from data in Benwell Community Development Project, 1978; Manpower Services Commission, 1981). Paralleling the growing tendency towards the internationalization of production is an equally strong tendency towards the regionalization of the associated consequences (Damette, 1980).

At the same time the capacity of the British state to intervene effectively to counter these consequences was severely limited. Macro-economic policies became increasingly monetarist—a response to the threatening fiscal crisis of the British state—and political goals have switched from those of

TABLE 4.7 Notified redundancies in the Northern
Region of England, 1970 to 1980

Year	Total	As per cent of UK total
1970	14,000	—
1971	24,506	7.8
1972	12,878	7.8
1973	8,252	10.0
1974	10,672	8.3
1975	20,999	7.9
1976	21,022	12.7
1977	21,931	15.1
1978	18,217	10.7
1979	20,493	—
1980[a]	20,000	—

[a] January to June *only*.
Sources: Benwell Community Development Project,
1978; Manpower Services Commission, 1981.

'full employment' to the containment of inflation and reduction of trade union power. While, for a time, net loss of manufacturing employment was to some extent offset by service sector growth, 'although the resulting jobs were typically part-time and associated with rising activity rates for married women' (Hudson, 1980c), this expansion was curtailed as a consequence of public expenditure cuts after 1975. Similarly, expenditure on regions was cut and the emphasis in regional policy swung even more strongly to restructuring Britain's manufacturing base as an end in itself (Geddes, 1978; Cameron, 1979). This met with scant success as 'deindustrialization' (Blackaby, 1979) accelerated, especially with the advent of the petro-pound and the increasing emphasis on controlling the money supply which was intended to 'shake out' weaker capitals but which further weakened the international competitive position of British manufacturing. Furthermore, restructuring within the British state and the creation of new Development Agencies for Scotland and Wales, partly to meet the perceived threat of a resurgent neo-nationalism precipitating the 'break-up of Britain' (Nairn, 1977), made these more attractive destinations for capitals seeking to invest in the United Kingdom. This had 3 consequences within the North East. First, it led to sporadic calls for a comparable Northern Development Agency, particularly from within the Labour Party. Second, in its absence, greater emphasis was placed on encouraging the formation and growth of indigenous small firms as a source of employment growth (Northern Region Strategy Team, 1977); this had a marginal impact in creating new jobs, not least because of the conflict between this goal and macro-economic policies. Third, the awareness of declining manufacturing employment and of service sector expansion meant that there was more emphasis on the latter as a source of future employment growth (Northern Region Strategy Team, 1977), ignoring both the type of service sector jobs provided in the past, the short-term impacts of public expenditure cuts on such activities and the probable longer-term effects of technological progress (Hines and Searle, 1979).

The combination of falling labour demand, both in the North East and in the South East and the West Midlands, and growth in labour supply (United Kingdom, Department of Employment, 1978) has resulted in further sharp increases in both male and female registered unemployment (Figure 4.2), the latter being a specific feature of the later 1970s, although a generalized effect of the world recession rather than one confined to the North East (Organisation for Economic Co-operation and Development, 1976; Mandel, 1978, p. 16). Even so, the increases in registered unemployment understate the magnitude of the problem because considerable numbers, especially of young people, have been kept off the unemployment register by various state temporary job-creation or preservation schemes (North Tyneside Community Development Project, 1978a, p. 94; Manpower Services Commission, 1979). Furthermore, given the sectoral distribution of employment

decline, some areas within the North East have experienced disproportionate shares of the overall regional unemployment increase; in some the
registered male unemployment rate is already in excess of 20 per cent (for
example, Hartlepool, Sunderland and Consett where it exceeds 30 per cent)
and will almost certainly increase further (for example, the male unemployment rate in Consett is forecast to rise to over 50 per cent).

An important issue is the trade union, Labour Party and, more generally,
working class responses to job loss. There have been a few well-publicized
campaigns to prevent particular plants closing, such as the British Steel
Corporation at Consett and Vickers-Armstrongs Ltd at Scotswood (Save
Scotswood Campaign Committee, 1979), which have mainly centred on the
arguments that such plants were, or could be made, commercially viable or
that the social costs of closure were unacceptable. While there may have
initially been opposition to closure, this has often dissipated in the face of
redundancy payments which, however, are rarely generous (North Tyneside
Trades Council, 1979). Perhaps the most significant challenge came early in
1981 when the threat of a strike by the traditionally moderate Durham
miners' union led to the abandonment of plans to close 5 collieries in the
region by the National Coal Board, although within a few weeks of this
plan's being abandoned the closure of one of these collieries had been
agreed. In general job losses have been seen, in some sense, as natural and
rising unemployment as inevitable. The boundaries to what is regarded as
the legitimate scope of state intervention have been reached but, within
these, the state is unable to effectively offset the impacts of the law of value.
The situation could be described as one of the politics of despair: to borrow
Offe's (1975b) evocative phrase, 'the necessary had become impossible, the
impossible necessary', in terms of state policy intervention.

CAPITAL, THE STATE AND REGIONAL CRISES

The central thesis of this chapter is that the pattern of changes observable
in the North East during the post-war period can only be understood in
relation to the process of capital accumulation, being simultaneously a result
of, and pre-condition for, this. Of decisive importance in this phase of late
capitalism has been the growing tendency towards the internationalization of
production and the emergence of a new international division of labour in
manufacturing. In turn, this has resulted in a reduction in the capacity of the
British state to manage and steer the national economy and cope with the
problems of the North East and similar regions. Rather than solving
problems at the economic level, the crisis tendency inherent within the
capitalist mode of production is internalized into the state apparatus to
appear in fresh forms—notably a fiscal crisis (which itself further restricts the

state's capacity to manage the economy) and a rationality crisis (a perceived disjunction between the intentions and outcomes of state actions). These could spill over into a socio-political crisis, challenging the legitimacy of the state and, indeed, of the capitalist mode of production (Habermas, 1976; 1979).

Carney (1980) has argued that the failure of state intervention in regional problems can give rise to opportunities for the growth of new nationalist and regionalist movements which may, temporarily, precipitate acute disruption of 'normal' political activity. He cites several examples: Belgium (Mandel, 1963); Lorraine and Nord Pas de Calais; and Scotland (Nairn, 1977). However, in North East England, where increased state intervention both directly and indirectly, has been a proximate cause of the deterioration in the region's economy, particularly in the declining job opportunities and rising unemployment, this has not been so. Rather, in general there has been a largely passive acceptance by the working class that economic decline, shrinking job opportunities and mounting unemployment are an inevitable part of the natural order, an acceptance made easier by memories of the 1930s and the cushion to consumption levels currently provided by the Welfare State. To account for this particular reaction, it is necessary to consider the character and role of the Labour Party and Labourism in the region. Historically, the Labour Party has been the prime representative of working class aims and aspirations and for some decades has effectively enjoyed a political hegemony within the region. But it has tended to adhere to a view that, in the final analysis, the interests of capital and labour are complementary; hence the emergence of a consensus around the politics of modernization in the early 1960s as the only route to full employment and social progress. The Labour movement held a key role in both establishing the legitimacy of the resultant regional modernization programme and implementing it. However, when this was at first accompanied and then followed by sharply rising regional unemployment, the limits of the consensus politics of modernization as the route to social reform were clearly revealed. Yet to transcend these limits would require extending both the scope and qualitative forms of state action and, ultimately, challenging the legitimacy of capitalist social relations.

Spatial Analysis, Industry and the Industrial Environment. Vol. 3 Regional Economies and Industrial Systems
Edited by F. E. I. Hamilton and G. J. R. Linge
© 1983 John Wiley & Sons Ltd.

Chapter 5

Organization of Production and the New Spatial Division of Labour in France

SUZANE SAVEY

During the last 15 years, the organizational framework of industrial production in the Western world has rested on finance capital and ever more advanced technology. Finance capital, a structural combination of industrial and banking capital, is both the product and the constituting element of the major conglomerates that arose in France in the 1960s through a series of mergers and take-overs leading to marked ownership concentration. Since only the major industrial and banking groups possess this type of capital they have a 2-way dynamic with which smaller firms cannot compete: (a) a worldwide mobility, in accordance with the relative reliability of natural and human resources and of political organization; and (b) advanced technological research, carried out in laboratories and experimental plants which test the industrial application of new processes that may yield no short-term profit. The widening sphere of activity of these firms and their constant search for the development and implementation of ever more elaborate technology have demanded a different organization of productive forces. New forms of production, controlling both capital and technology, have appeared with highly skilled and specialized jobs, while simultaneously new types of unskilled productive forces have extensively developed with tasks limited to mere execution.

The resulting spatial distribution shows a growing coincidence between the hierarchy of wages and that of the standards of living inherited from the primitive accumulation achieved during the competitive phase. Thus zones in which primitive accumulation had then been important, already strengthened by a concentration of decision centres, now exhibit an extensive concentration of new productive forces. Whereas these are becoming foci of increasingly privileged planning and management, at the other extreme the zones of limited accumulation coincide with areas where unskilled productive forces develop with low-paid workers merely undertaking actual manufacturing.

If the spatial distribution of the industrial system were simply organized into these 2 types of zones, corresponding to the 2-fold hierarchy of local standards of living and wage levels, the new organization of production which tends to establish a deep division between the zones of decision-making and of decision-implementation would not entail much reshuffling of existing social relationships. But in fact there is a third type of zone which was privileged by the organization of work during the competitive phase, thanks to the extensive use of highly skilled labour which the new organization now seeks to disband: this poses the problem of relocating these productive forces between the other 2 types of zones.

Such relocation is a 2-fold process: a new integration of the skilled productive forces in the production framework, either in higher-level managerial jobs or lower-level factory work, and a new spatial integration of these forces. This relocation process has been occurring very quickly during the last 15 years and is the driving force of the new spatial division of labour structurally linked to the transformation of social relationships within firms; simultaneously, it depends on state machinery to contain the collapse of the social consensus that it might entail.

THE CONCEPTUAL FRAMEWORK

Since the early 1970s, Castells (1972), Palloix (1973), Castells and Godard (1974), Lipietz (1977) and others have suggested a conceptual framework likely to bring about a radical revision of theory accounting for the upheavals currently affecting the world. This new approach makes it possible to explain the relationships between production and society on the one hand and space on the other; it is of outstanding interest for geographers who deal with industrial systems. Poche (1975) shows that the current phase of the capitalist mode of production involves the development of new productive forces. The first, scientific and technical, controls the innovation process and determines the products; the second is concerned with marketing and sales and endeavours to control the markets; and the third, responsible for the management of capital, controls the technical use of capital as money. The tendency for these new higher-level productive forces to develop and the growth, both relatively and absolutely, of new unskilled direct productive forces (both at the expense of the skilled direct productive forces) seem to be one of the hallmarks of production reorganization in the current phase of capitalism.

Lipietz (1977) argues that several types of space may be defined according to the extent of their integration in the different phases of capitalism: some are mere relics of the mercantile mode or of the competitive phase. Lipietz (1977, p. 59) put forward—as one of the possible explanations for the international division of labour—the tendency to have 'the value of manpower [for the different productive forces] determined with reference to the average standard of living in the zones from which the people concerned originate'. Thus, unskilled direct productive forces, the growth of which is one aspect of the struggle of finance capital against the falling rate of profit, seem to be forced towards the peripheral zones of all types; so, too, are the skilled direct ones, which used to be the engine of production during the competitive phase, as a result of dismissals and loss of specialization. The new productive forces, however, seem to cling to their central location.

This conceptual framework is relevant to the current changes in France concerning the distribution of industrial activities, the spatial division of labour and the specialization of space. It must be asked whether these can be consistently explained by the new demands put on large firms following their essential reorganization of production to counter the falling rate of profit. The main hypothesis of this chapter is that the new spatial division brought about by such reorganization must be accompanied by a radical alteration of social relationships, both within firms themselves and throughout society. This mutation, which gives rise to new types of conflicts, must be controlled and channelled by the state to forestall any disruption of the social consensus that might otherwise occur.

RESHUFFLING INDUSTRIAL PRODUCTION IN FRANCE

A turning-point in the evolution of the spatial distribution of French industry occurred in the late 1960s, for since then the relative attractiveness of the various industrialized regions to businessmen and investors has been changing considerably.

Inter-regional Population Mobility

Whereas the leading industrial regions (Paris, Nord, Lorraine and Lyon) attracted population throughout the first half of the twentieth century to the detriment of the extensive rural areas in west and central France, the opposite has been the case since the mid-1960s. Regions attracting more than their relative share of population are mostly in southeast France and to the southwest of Paris, while the Ile de France has been stagnating since 1975 and the Nord and Lorraine regions have collapsed (Figure 5.1). The differences between the regions are largely explained by internal migration (Figure 5.2). From 1954 to 1968 the 2 large industrial conurbations of Paris and Lyon gained population, whereas the Nord and Lorraine, with concentrations of activities like coal-mining and steelmaking now in decline, were already losing population. From 1968 to 1975 these trends accelerated although the population of the Paris region stabilized. At the same time the south of France and Brittany, which had not previously been industrialized, attracted people. Migrants from Lorraine and Nord mainly went to the south (Provence-Côte d'Azur and Languedoc-Roussillon) and, to a lesser extent, the Rhône-Alpes region.

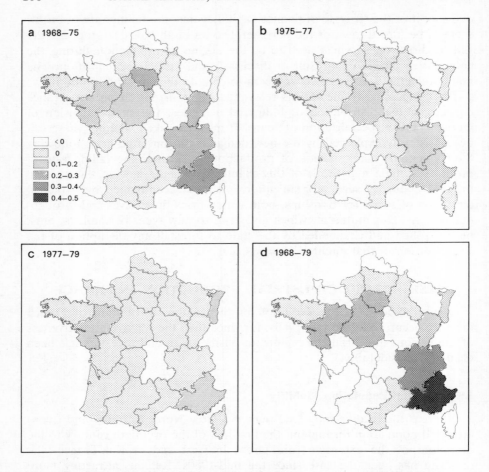

FIGURE 5.1 Changes in the percentage distribution of the national population in each administrative region of France between the years indicated. [Source: compiled from Institut de la Statistique et des Etudes Economiques, 1979]

Figure 5.3, showing the annual average migration rate of the working population, clearly reveals the seriousness of the situation throughout France but especially in Nord and Lorraine. This is further underlined by Figure 5.4: in Lorraine, in particular, the index of dismissals for economic reasons rose from 100 in 1975 to 183 in 1977. At the same time Provence-Côte d'Azur, although it had previously been a region of in-migration, was also badly affected because numerous workers were laid off, possibly because of the general restructuring of French industry.

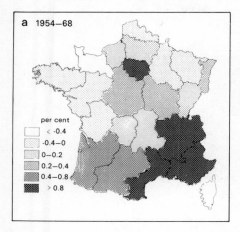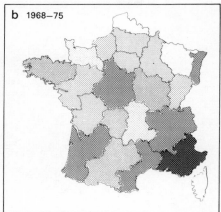

FIGURE 5.2 Total population—annual net migration rates (per cent) by regions in France, (a) 1954 to 1968, (b) 1968 to 1975. [Sources: compiled from Institut National d'Etudes Démographiques, 1972; Institut National de la Statistique et des Etudes Economiques, 1979]

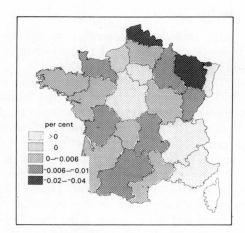

FIGURE 5.3 Total workforce—annual net migration rates as percentage of total population by regions in France, 1968 to 1975. [Source: Institut National d'Etudes Démographiques, 1975]

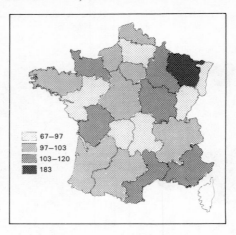

FIGURE 5.4 Total workforce—index of retrenchments for economic reasons by regions in France, 1975 to 1977 (1975 = 100). [Source: compiled from Institut National de la Statistique et des Etudes Economiques, 1979]

The New Deal in Industrial Sectors

These indicators bring to light a crisis affecting, for the most part, the traditional industrial regions. It must now be asked whether this results from the current recession or from fundamental changes in the organization of production. Consideration must be given to the way in which the spatial reorganization of the French workforce has affected industrial production. In 1968 and 1979 there were 4 main industrial regions: Ile de France (which includes the Paris region), Rhône-Alpes, Nord and Lorraine. But whereas Ile de France had 26 per cent of the French factory workforce in 1968 it had only 20.9 per cent in 1979; Nord dropped from 9.1 to 8.6 per cent; and Lorraine from 5.5 to 5.1 per cent. Only Rhône-Alpes consolidated its development, growing from 12 to 12.5 per cent (Figure 5.5).

Job opportunities in some other regions also increased relatively (Figure 5.6). Those in west France and to the south of the Paris Basin had their peak growth from 1968 to 1973; in Provence-Côte d'Azur, the peak was from 1971 to 1973. After recovering between 1971 and 1973 (Figure 5.6b), Nord and Lorraine continued to decline and eventually collapsed at the end of the period, whereas Rhône-Alpes, which declined for 4 years, made a spectacular recovery at the end of the 1970s (Figure 5.6e). The annual changes in the industrial workforce in each region from 1973 to 1976 (Figure 5.7) show

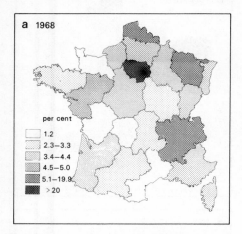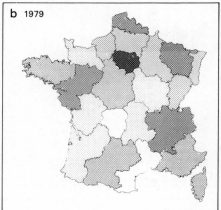

FIGURE 5.5 Percentage of total factory workforce in each region of France, (a) 1968, (b) 1979. [Source: compiled from Institut National de la Statistique et des Etudes Economiques, 1979]

clearly that the crisis of capitalism is affecting industrial production as a whole. The decline was general throughout France, except for 3 regions (Limousin, Poitou-Charente, Pays de la Loire) that had an insignificant amount of industrial activity at the beginning of this period.

A spatial reorganization is none the less taking shape. Apart from the redistribution of the workforce already described, this has manifested itself in the consumption of electricity for industrial purposes (Figure 5.8): between 1960 and 1976 there was a spectacular increase in usage in western France and a moderate one around the Paris region; in contrast in the older industrial regions (Nord, Lorraine and Rhône-Alpes) and in Massif Central the increase was much smaller and in Paris and Midi-Pyrénées it was negligible. Taken together, the upsurge in industrial employment and electricity consumption underline the trend for new enterprises to be located in the western, and relatively little industrialized, part of France.

These observations, along with the data in Figure 5.9a showing the annual average industrial wage in each region in 1974, might lead to the simplistic conclusion that a search for cheap labour was the main motive in selecting new locations, the traditional constraints in relation to raw materials and energy supplies having become less significant. This 'wage factor' might also account for the industrialists' reluctance to settle in Lorraine where from 1969 to 1974 the greatest increase in wage rates occurred (Figure 5.9b). But this explanation would fail to account for the take-off of Provence-Côte d'Azur, the recovery of Rhône-Alpes or the growth of Picardie, Alsace and

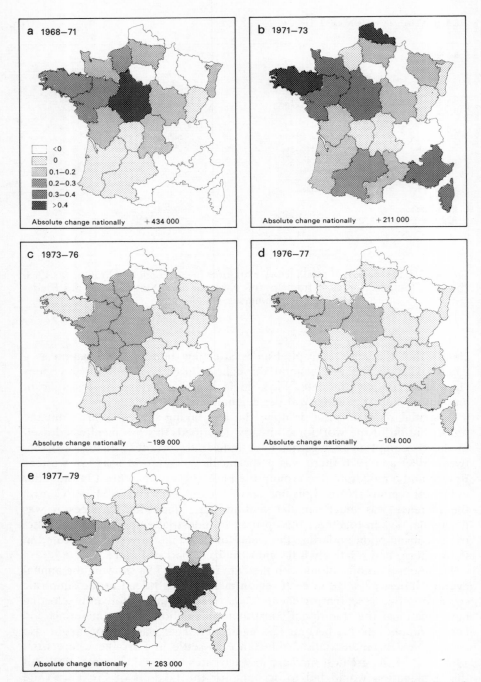

a 1968—71

Absolute change nationally   +434 000

<0
0
0.1—0.2
0.2—0.3
0.3—0.4
>0.4

b 1971—73

Absolute change nationally   +211 000

c 1973—76

Absolute change nationally   −199 000

d 1976—77

Absolute change nationally   −104 000

e 1977—79

Absolute change nationally   +263 000

FIGURE 5.6 Regional factory employment change as percentage of total French factory employment during periods indicated between 1968 and 1979. [Source: compiled from Institut National de la Statistique et des Etudes Economiques, 1979]

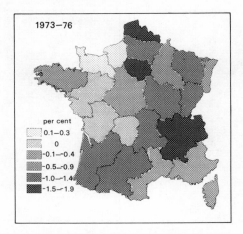

FIGURE 5.7 Annual percentage change in factory employment in the regions of France, 1973 to 1976. [Source: compiled from Institut National de la Statistique et des Etudes Economiques, 1979]

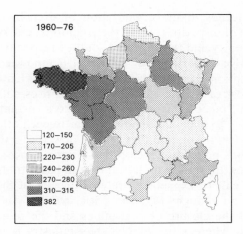

FIGURE 5.8 Index of changes in electricity consumption for all industrial purposes by regions of France, 1960 to 1976 (1960 = 100). [Source: compiled from Institut National de la Statistique et des Etudes Economiques, 1979]

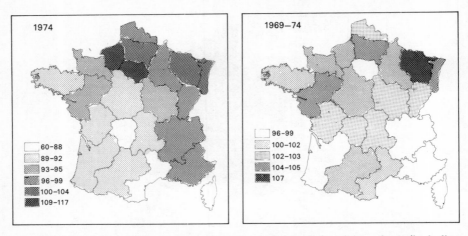

FIGURE 5.9 (a) Index of average gross wages paid to industrial workers (including those in building and construction) in each region of France, 1974 (France = 100), (b) change in annual average gross wages paid to all employed persons by regions of France, 1969 through 1974 (1969 = 100). [Source: compiled from Institut National de la Statistique et des Etudes Economiques, 1979]

Champagne-Ardennes, where average wages were already very high and rising sharply.

Thus the new trends in the organization of French national industrial space reveal 2 sets of disparities. First, the traditional one between the north and east of the country and the west and south, which still manifests itself in terms of the relative importance of industrial manpower, wage levels and electricity consumption. Second, recent changes have led to a fundamental reshuffle, with most of the new industrial enterprises still operating being located in western France. This seems to point to a current reshaping of the national space likely to make all regions similar to each other because of the scattering of industry, a situation that can be viewed as a direct result of the central government's policy to develop the national space.

Some exceptions to this overall trend still have to be accounted for although it is difficult to explain the rate of decline of the older industrial regions. It might be thought that the crisis in Nord and the collapse of Lorraine followed the closure of coal mines and the reorganization of the steel industry. But whereas the French steel industry is relatively healthy, Lorraine is having problems. Moreover, Rhône-Alpes (another traditional industrial region, with textile industries in Lyon, coal around Saint-Etienne and settlements in Alpine valleys with plants based on hydroelectricity) is still a focus of industrial innovation. It may be argued that insufficient diversification of activities—important in Lorraine and to a lesser extent in

Nord—is a major cause of decline, in contrast to Rhône-Alpes where new kinds of industry have been developing for a long time. But this is not a convincing explanation for the rise of manufacturing activities in rural areas in western France. Granted that it is more difficult to set up new activities than to modernize older ones, the spectacular successes achieved in Lyon still seem surprising. The prior existence of an important industrial framework—which used to be considered a prerequisite for establishing new enterprises and plants—now appears to be either totally irrelevant in some cases (as witness the success of the west and collapse of Lorraine) or very important in others (Rhône-Alpes and the decentralization of the Paris region's being confined mainly within the immediate neighbourhood of the Ile de France).

Thus, apart from technical necessity, now greatly reduced by so-called technological progress with the many contradictions that its current implementation involves, it must be asked whether there are other factors determining the reorganization of industrial space.

THE PROCESS OF THE NEW SPATIAL DIVISION OF LABOUR

The current economic and social crisis in France results from a process of reorganization of productive forces in which the new spatial division of labour is tending to divide French space into 2 major types of zones, thus progressively erasing the legacy of the phase of competitive capitalism. The central (or A-type) zone (Figure 5.10) has its main centre in Paris and a secondary one in Lyon, while the periphery is tending to become more or less homogeneous. The organization of the latter entails the decline of C-type zones (with highly skilled labour and an average standard of living), such as Lorraine, the Nord or the coal basins in the Massif Central, and the establishment of new industries in B-type (mainly rural) zones where labour is unskilled, the standard of living is low and income from agriculture can supplement the low industrial wages through various channels (such as vegetable gardens or help from relatives on the land, cheap rents or use of the family house). This is particularly the case in the west and southwest.

The decline of the C-type zones follows 2 main processes: (a) through technological sophistication, with a consequent move from skilled to unskilled workers; and (b) through geographical transfer, either by sending skilled personnel to other parts of the world (exemplified by firms that export technology), or by using local unskilled labour thought to be easily trainable in a few days or weeks and low-paid compared with the average standard of living prevalent in the zone from which the organization of production originates.

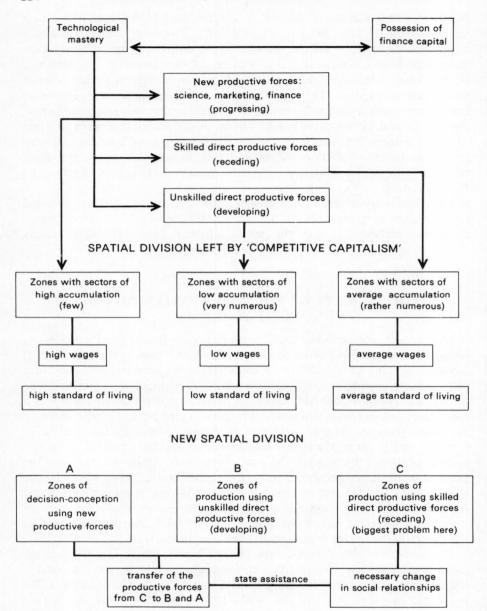

FIGURE 5.10 The new organization of production by the multinational corporations and the spatial division of labour

The B-type zones are the recipients of 2 major sorts of industrial capital.

(a) National investments as part of the 'decentralization' fostered and financed by the government's development agency or of the movement of large enterprises from old industrial regions. For instance, the steelmaking firms Union Sidérurgique du Nord et de l'Est de la France (Usinor) and Union Sidérurgique Lorraine SA (Sidelor) are shifting from the Nord and Lorraine to the south where the jobs thus created are unspecialized and low-paid.

(b) Foreign investments involving relatively generous wages so that they tend to dominate the local labour market. Moreover, the possibility of integrating, through sub-contracting, various small local firms sometimes enables foreign investors to control a large part of the local workforce (as does IBM France Cie in Languedoc).

Despite the relatively high wages paid by foreign firms and sometimes even by the 'decentralized' companies, the general trend is towards a coincidence between the hierarchy of wages and that of local standards of living. The new productive forces in charge of policy-making concentrate in the A-type zones of Paris and Lyon (nearly 3 million out of 5.9 million workers being managed from Paris alone in 1973) and the direct productive forces employed in the new settlements are scattered around the periphery of the Paris region, in the west and, to a lesser extent, in the south of the country.

This relocation of French industry would have created few difficulties had it not been accompanied by the collapse of the C-type zones. The workforce transfers necessitated by the exploitation of pools of labour with low living standards—shown by the growing number of dismissals for economic reasons, as in Lorraine—led to changes in social relationships both inside the firms and all over the country.

RESHAPING SOCIAL RELATIONSHIPS: A MUST FOR MONOPOLIES

Until the early 1960s French industrial space was characterized by the concentration of production in a few dynamic zones which had inherited traditional technology and national or, more often, regional capitalism. This type of industrialization had successfully changed the pre-existing social forms by concentrating the working population. However, there was no homogeneity in social relationships: in some regions the French style of paternalism prevailed; elsewhere some form of autonomous working class life had been established, on the basis of trade union action and socialist ideas. When conflicts appeared between the workers and employers, the state would intervene, either with police repression or through more gentle legislative action to protect the workers. This well-balanced situation was disrupted in the late 1960s.

The change in social relationships in the wider sense is in fact a manifestation of the tendency for the capitalist firm to circumvent legal constraints brought about by social reform. To achieve this, the firm has 3 possible strategies: (a) moving abroad (particularly to developing countries where labour is hardly, if at all, protected); (b) reorganizing its own productive forces; or (c) relying on the benevolent sympathy of the state. Major French firms have used all these devices although concern here is only with the latter 2.

Internal Reorganization

The French paternalistic tradition has given way to a new mode of management founded on bargaining and anonymity. The rules governing recruitment have changed: the specialized worker, highly skilled, who has learned his trade through long service to the firm (and who often has been 'brought up' in the company because his father worked there) has been succeeded by the unskilled worker hired for a 2-month probationary period after which he may be dismissed or hired on the basis of a contract that may or may not be renewable. De-skilling, the natural ingredient of the new bargaining policy, is fostered by 2 more characteristics: delocation and denationalization. Workers' delocation, advocated for a long time by industrial employers and politicians under the guise of workforce mobility, developed extensively over the last 10 years thanks to what was known as industrial redeployment. Guglielmo (1981) has shown that plant modernization makes it possible to replace the system of workers' grading based on their professional qualifications with a system based on their actual positions in production and that financial reorganization entails the geographical transfer of production from one plant to another of the same group. The resultant moving about of workers always has the same consequences: dismissals, dequalification (rather easily accepted by those who can thus remain employed), and social and geographical uprooting. Employing foreigners (denationalization) makes these aims easier to reach, at a lesser cost. Migrants, in most cases hired on short-term contracts without any professional qualification, were the first instances of temporary employment, which frees employers from the constraints entailed by dismissals for economic reasons or the payment of allowances to workers leaving the firm of their own accord. Job instability inside the firm and the systematic use of foreign labour may facilitate the dismantling of workers' organizations, the decline of unions and of labour protection generally. The growth of temporary employment agencies—with their relatively slack regulations—also facili tates this process: direct integration of labour in firms can be avoided and the selection of the best elements can thus proceed unchecked. Another destabilizing factor is the replacement of the policy of providing housing estates by long-term, low-rate building loans. Workers thus enter the general residential market and are left to their own devices when they have to move. Such changes amount to a destabilization scheme in which the transfer of labour from C-type to B-type zones plays the most important role. Similarly, the executives and, more generally, the new productive forces have also had to accept destabilization as a means to ensure employment and relative job security. Here again, recruitment conditions have changed: the traditional French high schools are no longer adequate and prospective executives are often required to supplement their training in the United States (e.g. at the Harvard Business School, or the MIT Sloane School). Moreover they, too, are kept mobile, both within a particular company and between firms located all over the world. For them, in fact, transfers over the national space inside a particular firm are the exact opposite of what they are for the workers: a kind of near stability, which they readily accept.

State Intervention

Planning Behind this relocation of industry and spatial reorganization seem to lurk new groups of interests which are more difficult to assess than the traditional industrial employers actually endangered. The new locations seem to be governed by an organization of space determined at the highest level of decision-making.

State intervention is necessary to ensure the social consensus on which the system depends by mitigating the consequences of harmful decisions that have to be made to compensate for falling rates of profit. These new conditions brought about some fundamental revisions both from the social and spatial viewpoints. Consequently, confronted by the discrepancy between a rich France (the north and east) and a poor France (the south and west)—the legacy of traditional industrialization and growing social tensions stemming from the changes brought about by the neo-capitalist outlook— the state had to accept a new role. This was to work out, usually in an *ad hoc* way but sometimes after deliberate consideration, a new regional distribution of manpower and economic activities. Thus, there is now more planning aimed at facilitating the 'redeployment' of free enterprise activity. Steps taken during the last few years correspond to some well-defined objectives.

(a) Facilitating the concentration of basic industries, particularly steelmaking, by establishing privileged zones and large concerns (e.g. at Dunkirk and

Fos-sur-Mer). This was achieved by restructuring the steel industry, which left only 2 firms in this field, and also by creating special facilities in some ports for large enterprises, which put massive amounts of public money at the disposal of the private sector.

(b) Redistributing manpower both by production location and residence through a reorganization of the older industrial regions. Their decline was managed by the state through a series of plans. Those for the liquidation of coal-mining and the restructuring of the steel industry determined the workforce transfers needed to create the new centres. Simultaneously some preservation steps were taken to ensure social consensus under 'Conversion Plans'. Then, the loosening of the major urban conglomerations of Paris and Lyon made it possible to reorganize and redistribute manpower. The policies of industrial decentralization on the one hand and urban planning on the other are tending to scatter the working population either into regions that are not industrialized or into suburbs that were formerly rural areas. Thus the revised social relationships needed by the new strategy of the large industrial firms can and must be established.

(c) Scattering industry into rural zones which has the 2-fold purpose of achieving some form of spatial homogeneity and facilitating industrial redeployment.

(d) Developing tourist resorts thus enabling the state to take care of underprivileged regions (such as Languedoc-Roussillon and Aquitaine). Infrastructure was planned both to create jobs and also to provide working people with inexpensive leisure facilities.

Legislation The destabilization of labour facilitated by geographical shifts can hardly be achieved without the state's support or at least benevolent neutrality. Thus, since the early 1970s, a wide spectrum of the workforce— traditionally highly protected and radically hostile to mobility—has been severely affected. The main nationalized services (electricity, gas, railways, education, post and telecommunications) have been partially dismantled by the transfer to the private sector of some of their traditional activities. The consequent redistribution of tasks has entailed both a reduction in the number of protected jobs and an easier development of facilities in B-type zones, at the expense of those in C-type zones.

The very slack regulations governing the operation of temporary employment agencies reflect the reluctance of the state to enforce the legislation appropriate to these enterprises, which appeared almost clandestinely in the 1960s and developed rapidly in the 1970s. By condoning their proliferation, the state has played a role in this 'grand' scheme aimed at the social and geographical destabilization of labour.

Conversely, there has been a reliance on the state to preserve social stability by taking steps to maintain the national consensus while fostering the policy of moving firms from C to B-type zones. Instances include subsidies to facilitate job opportunities; unemployment benefits; the 'national pact for the employment of young workers'; financial help for old people or workers willing to leave their home region; and subsidies paid to mountain zones or coal-mining regions to establish new activities. All these were aimed at alleviating the brutal consequences of the revised policy of the firms founded on the new division of labour.

NEW SOCIAL CONFLICTS AND THE DISRUPTION OF CONSENSUS

These precautionary measures taken by the state were not enough to prevent the emergence of new types of social conflicts. The progressive dwindling of the national policy of development since 1971 in favour of more freedom of initiative by the major firms and the growing control of the state over regions and local institutions (the increased powers of the *Préfets* meant that the representatives of the state became mere vectors to transmit decisions made in Paris) have resulted in resistance by labour or by whole regions striving for their survival or rejecting the new role imposed upon them.

It seems that, through the new organization of space brought about by the refashioning of the industrial system in its present monopolistic phase, political power is a kind of smoke-screen shrouding economic power (at least, until the 1981 presidential election). It reflects all the various kinds of political conflicts since it is responsible for the introduction of legislation through Parliament and for the implementation of the necessary executive measures; it finds itself at the very core of the conflicting situations it creates, while trying to redirect them towards other responsibilities or other centres of interest. In the name of the general public interest and collective welfare it will, for example, beg for a national effort to save the economy and stimulate expansion. Simultaneously, however, the state must take into account the conflicting interests of the different employer factions. The decline of regional bosses and local middle-class groups in favour of a ruling class at the national level (which also has international connections) lead to antipathies manifest in the conflicts opposing the large local institutions and the central government.

The state has to confront the resistance of the peasant class (its traditional support) which sees the dwindling of its production space in favour of new forms of activity (like tourism) that it does not control. Alliances may appear between the peasant class and local middle-class groups more or less deprived of their land capital by these new forms of activity. The state also has to face the resistance of the workers who refuse to accept instability of employment, mobility and de-skilling. Slogans such as 'we shall live and work at home' build up unanimous support in whole regions where all the social categories together contest the new organization that brushes them aside (Lorraine) or imposes upon them a specialization they do not want (Languedoc) by demanding regional power or even autonomy (Corsica).

The recent political changes that have occurred in France were in part a consequence of this simultaneous reshuffling of labour and space. It is worth noting that the emergency measures taken in 1981 by the new government were mainly in the fields traditionally aimed at alleviating the tension created by the previous economic and social reorganization: the minimum wage, the family and rent allowances, the raising of old age pensions and the release of people in prison for 'politically motivated crimes' (mostly regionalists). Another measure, instituting a special tax on temporary employment agencies, appears to signal an intention to enforce social laws inside the firms. The *Decentralization Act,* the first 2 sections of which cover the rights and liberties of local communities, has just been passed: this endows the chairman of the elected department council with powers previously retained by the *Préfet* appointed by the central government. This discontinuation of the tradition instituted by Napoleon enables local institutions (department and town councils) to deal with firms direct without having to submit to the control of the *Préfet* (i.e. the central power). Moreover, the Ministry of National Planning, rather dormant under President Giscard d'Estaing, was given a more important role. In addition, the nationalization of some of the most important French companies—including, for instance, Pechiney Ugine Kuhlmann (see Savey, 1981), Rhône-Poulenc SA, Saint Gobain SA, and Matra SA—has been foreshadowed by the Mitterrand Government.

France now stands at one of the great crossroads of its history, a point at which it is reconsidering the new organization of labour and the new spatial division brought about by the evolution of firms during the last 15 years. Whether or not the change in the nature of the state's action and in its relations with the large industrial and financial enterprises will reverse the current trend of plant and labour transfers is unclear. But what is now required is some system to monitor and assess the results achieved through the new legislation.

Spatial Analysis, Industry and the Industrial Environment. Vol. 3 Regional Economies and Industrial Systems
Edited by F. E. I. Hamilton and G. J. R. Linge
© 1983 John Wiley & Sons Ltd.

Chapter 6

An Economic Potential Model for the European Economic Community: A Tool for Understanding Industrial Systems

G. A. van der Knaap

In the study of regional economic development the 'centre-periphery' concept is often used as a framework for understanding spatial processes and spatial inequalities (cf. Myrdal, 1957; Friedmann, 1973; Gottmann, 1980). The mechanisms of these spatial processes are to some extent explained by the theory of polarized development (Perroux, 1955), but also by geographical diffusion theory (Hudson, 1972). Thus, a central element of the 'centre-periphery' concept is the spatial diffusion of economic development—from a developed core to an underdeveloped periphery—which is usually based upon industrial growth. When viewed from the core the key questions in this context relate, first, to the structure of the process of filtering down and its consequences for the location of industry and, second, to the definition of the core. Consideration has to be given as to whether the core is a geometric concept relating to the centre of gravity, a geographical concept relating to the centre of activities, or a combination of both. The way in which the concept of distance is operationalized becomes crucially important when trying to define the core. The essential contrasts between the centre and the periphery are expressed by the different levels of economic development and, usually, are summarized by the variations in regional income. Within a regional policy context the location or relocation of industry in backward peripheral regions is conceived as an instrument to diminish the observed differences in the standard of living between the centre and periphery (Thoss, 1977).

Here only the second question is examined by using both economic potential analysis to define the core and a multi-dimensional approach to regional income to describe spatial variations in demand within the EEC. Against this background, changes in the industrial pattern of the EEC are discussed in this chapter.

ECONOMIC POTENTIAL ANALYSIS

It can be asked why economic potential analysis—developed by Stewart (1947) and Warntz (1956)—should be reintroduced in modern industrial geographical analysis. Several arguments can be presented to support this choice. First, until very recently economic theory has cast industrial location into a predominantly Weberian context (cf. Hamilton, 1978) which has even shaped the way behaviour and uncertainty in decision-making are incorporated (Smith, 1971). Second, considering that nowadays most industry is footloose, demand orientation has become a key factor in studying location patterns (Lindberg and McCarty, 1966). Thus, the market and its location still play an important role in locational analysis. To this extent modern and traditional analysis converge and thus, when studying the industrial pattern in the EEC, the work of pioneers in industrial location analysis like Harris (1954) and Dunn (1956) who used potential models as a macro-geographic tool to study the location of manufacturing industries, gains even more significance.

In the late 1960s Clark *et al.* (1969) extended and applied this approach to Western Europe to study the locational consequences of the enlargement of the EEC to include the UK, Denmark and other countries. They defined economic potential as the sum of the regional incomes around any point, divided by the distance cost of reaching it from all points. Thus,

$$P_i = \frac{I_i}{M} + \sum_{j=i}^{n} \frac{I_j}{M + T_{ij} + F} \qquad \text{for all } i \text{ except } j \neq i, \qquad (6.1)$$

where

P_i = economic potential of region i;
I_j = regional income of region j;
T_{ij} = transport cost from i to j;
M = minimum cost;
F = tariff.

Three points are now of interest: (a) the theoretical assumptions or hypotheses which have been 'assigned' to the model; (b) the operational definition of the variables in the model and their relation to the centre-periphery concept; and (c) the limitations of the model caused by the first 2 points.

The Model and Its Hypotheses

According to Clark *et al.* (1969, pp. 197–8) the economic potential model can be used to measure the attraction of a region for industry. They apply the model to demonstrate the relative shift in locational advantage in the core region(s). The 2 fundamental (Weberian) variables that affect location decisions and which are incorporated in the potential model are (a) the location of the main sources of inputs and the location of the main markets for the products, and (b) the estimation of the distance cost of reaching these locations from any particular point in space. Following the hypothesis that the majority of industries can now be described as footloose in relation to markets and/or materials, 3 related assumptions were made by Clark *et al.*:

(a) 'to an increasing extent it is the areas of dense population which will provide some of the most vital inputs as well as being the main markets';

(b) 'the capacity of a region to act as a market and as a supplier of inputs can be measured by the regional income';

(c) 'the area of greatest attraction to industry will be the region where the distance costs are least to all possible markets'.

A first complication arises when considering locational problems across national borders, because other factors like international competition and different levels of technology may be important. When discussing the link between international trade theory and industrial location, Peschel (1975, pp. 31–2) concludes that the validity of potential models in this context is dependent upon the assumption that 'the relative importance of comparative advantage does not differ greatly among nations so that the foreign trade ratio is not significantly affected by the extent of a nation's comparative advantage'. If there are spatial differences in the impact of competition, technological progress, and the effects of specialization, these will affect the spatial equilibrium situation hypothesized by international trade theory.

A study into the various levels of technology in 4 EEC countries (West Germany, France, Belgium and the Netherlands) was carried out by Van Driel *et al.* (1975). The technology matrices presented were based on the 56×56 input-output matrix of 1965 for the 4 countries. They concluded that the main differences observed between these countries can be attributed to differences in definitions of sectors and sub-sectors in the input-output table and not in technology. When studying locational changes this conclusion puts more emphasis on the problem of 'limited factor mobility' and the importance of the size of the market as measured by population and regional income. Thus, in the case of footloose industry the comparative advantage of a region becomes one of the most decisive factors.

Differences in distance cost, which is the second key variable in the potential model, can be considered as only one aspect of a comparative advantage. These advantages are usually compounded in urban-industrial agglomerations (Isard, 1956; Pred, 1966) so that it is the agglomeration economies that strongly influence production costs by lowering the price per unit output, thus engendering considerable spatial inertia. From this perspective use of the economic potential model can reveal some of the forces behind the observed spatial inertia by comparing the theoretical and the observed locational patterns. the differences reflect *inter alia* the comparative advantage of the actual location and emphasize the functional structure of the regions concerned.

An Operational Definition of the Variables in the Model

Two key variables emerge from this discussion, namely, the concept of the market and the accessibility to the market. The total regional income can express a region's capacity to act as a market and as a supplier of inputs. However, when Clark *et al.* (1969, p. 199) discuss the use of exchange rates in comparison with purchasing parity, to standardize across the EEC countries, they conclude that 'exporters would be more interested in the money incomes of their markets and not in their purchasing power over local goods'. This justifies the use of exchange rates in standardization. It remains unclear whether 'the market' should be conceived as one for consumer goods, or as one for intermediate products or as a combination of both. In the first instance total regional income seems a more relevant approximation than the gross value of the total regional product. Both reflect a different type of demand and thus relate to different aspects of the industrial structure of a region. Here regional income is accepted as the approximation of the market.

Accessibility to the market can be expressed by the distance cost, a high degree of accessibility being reflected by a low distance cost. If it is assumed that total mobility within and between the EEC countries has the same modal split for every country, calculation of accessibility becomes straightforward. Observed differences in the types of infrastructure provided in various countries will be ignored, as the market considered—given the choice for total regional income—is for finished products. These issues regain importance when markets for raw materials and intermediate goods are introduced as they may give rise to variations in input prices based upon differences in transport cost.

Thus, when measured in this way the core region is defined as the region which offers the largest market with the least costs from an accessibility point of view.

Limitations of the Model

As has been shown, the concept was narrowed down to the location factors relevant to footloose industries. A general discussion of alternative centre-periphery models is provided by Keeble (1976, pp. 46–87). However, 2 questions specific to the measurement of centrality within an economic potential approach must be discussed here.

The first is the definition of an industry in which the organizational structure of the firm is a key variable. When using employment data to study changes in industrial location it is tacitly assumed that the structure of the firm remains the same and that no mergers, no internationalization and no branch-plant developments occur during the study period. Substantial research into the relationship between the organizational structure of the firm and the associated pattern of location has been carried out in Sweden (cf. Törnqvist, 1968; Pred, 1973). Its fundamental thesis is that each organizational unit of a multi-plant firm has its own locational requirements. This ranges from the head office with its emphasis on personal contacts to the primary production unit which has a Weberian emphasis on the supply of labour and raw materials. The concept of footloose industry becomes very difficult to apply in this context as it is relevant to some but not necessarily all units within an industry. A redefinition of the economic potential for different groups of industrial activity, each with the same locational requirements, may seem theoretically appealing but it is seldom possible to apply because of lack of data.

The second question is the definition of regional income related to industrial activity. According to the assumption previously stated, the regional income can be used as a proxy variable to measure the capacity of a region to act as a market for finished products or for intermediate products as a supplier of inputs to other industries. Regional income, when measured as the gross regional product (GRP), can be considered as an index of the absolute volume of the utilized production possibilities, but is not representative of the total production capacity of a region (cf. Peschel, 1975, p. 33). In this sense the GRP stresses the regional capacity to act as a supplier of inputs and not as a market for consumer goods. When considering the capacity of a region to act as a market it is income per capita which can be used to indicate the expected consumption in the region, so making standards of living and regional purchasing power important. When GRP is used, foreign exchange rates play a key role in the standardization of the income variables across the EEC sub-national regional units.

REGIONAL VARIATIONS IN INCOME IN THE EEC

Supply Variations

The distribution of the GRP over the 112 regions of the EEC can now be examined more closely. In Figure 6.1 the GRP is shown as an index figure relative to the EEC average, set at 100. The original data were given in European Units of Account so that a weighted conversion of the currencies of the member countries on the basis of exchange rates has already been

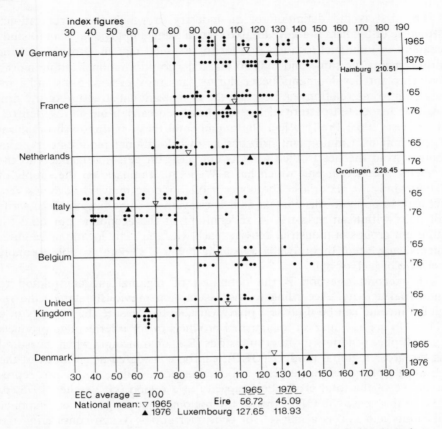

FIGURE 6.1 Regional concentration and change in the gross regional product
1965 to 1976

carried out. Besides the EEC average, the national mean has also been given special attention to demonstrate the shift in income during the 1965–76 period. The differences between the regional distributions for each country are striking, with West Germany showing the largest range followed closely by Italy and France (excluding the extreme position occupied by Paris). Two other exceptional cases should be mentioned: one is the 'city-state' of Hamburg as the smallest but most important producing region in West Germany; the other is the province of Groningen (which has been marketing its enormous reserves of natural gas since 1968) in the Netherlands in 1976.

Comparisons of the shifts in the national averages from 1965 through 1976 show the relatively stable position of France in contrast to positive shifts between 10 and 20 points for most other countries, though trends in the Netherlands and the UK were exceptional, with shifts above 35 points (although in opposite directions). Concomitant with these changing national positions 2 types of regional change can be observed. The first is a proportional shift in intra-regional income distributions. This pattern occurs, for example, in France, the Netherlands, Belgium and Denmark. The second type of change is a convergence of intra-regional income differences as in West Germany, Italy and, very strikingly, the UK.

More detailed consideration of the regional structure can be helpful not only in understanding the nature of the above differences but also in the composition of the GRP. The relationship between the 3 main sectors of economic activity has already been estimated for the EEC regions by Biehl *et al.* (1972, pp. 76–7) using a semi-logarithmic, a full logarithmic and a logarithmic second order polynomial specification, respectively (Table 6.1). Interestingly, in all 3 approaches, the agricultural sector responded indifferently whereas the industrial sector showed a better performance. Although the service sector showed only in 1 case a weak relationship with the third function this latter form was selected for further analysis because the relationships in the 2 other functions were not significant. The results are

TABLE 6.1 Estimates of the percentage contribution to the gross regional product of 3 sectors in 61 EEC regions, 1968[a]

Sector	Equations of regression	R^2	F
Agriculture (s_1)	$\ln s_1 = -0.56236 - 0.00102\,y$ (± 0.00009)	0.680	125
	$\ln s_1 = +11.33368 - 1.85124 \ln y$ (± 0.19390)	0.607	91
	$\ln s_1 = -2.75133 - 0.00119\,y +$ $0.33569 \ln y$	0.681	62
Industry (s_2)	$\ln s_2 = -1.05976 + 0.000145\,y$ (± 0.00005)	0.144	10
	$\ln s_2 = -3.83904 + 0.4095 \ln y$ (± 0.07957)	0.309	26
	$\ln s_2 = -12.54301 - 0.00073\,y +$ $1.76099 \ln y$	0.606	45
Services (s_3)	$\ln s_3 = -0.98531 + 0.0001\,y$ (± 0.005)	0.006	—
	$\ln s_3 = -0.48769 - 0.05991 \ln y$ (± 0.09838)	0.006	—
	$\ln s_3 = +8.42852 + 0.00075\,y -$ $1.44429 \ln y$	0.298	12

[a] For the purposes of these calculations the EEC has been defined as consisting of 61 regions because of the need to amalgamate some regions for which separate data are not available.

Source: Biehl *et al.*, 1972.

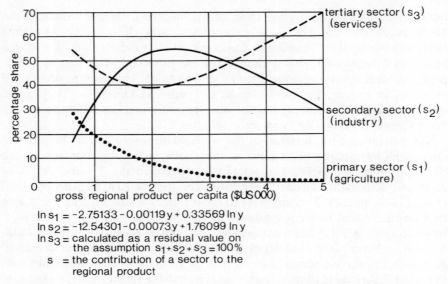

$\ln s_1 = -2.75133 - 0.00119\,y + 0.33569\ln y$
$\ln s_2 = -12.54301 - 0.00073\,y + 1.76099\ln y$
$\ln s_3$ = calculated as a residual value on
       the assumption $s_1 + s_2 + s_3 = 100\%$
s = the contribution of a sector to the
       regional product

FIGURE 6.2 The composition of the gross regional product by sector in 1968.
[Source: after Biehl *et al.*, 1972, p. 76]

shown in Figure 6.2 where the curve for the service sector is in fact the residual value of the other 2 sectors.

The difference in the percentage contributions of the 3 sectors for each GRP per capita value demonstrates that for a regional comparison the sector composition is of extreme importance in the explanation of GRP per capita. When evaluating the economic potential from the point of view of an industrial location in different regions, controlling for these influences may throw light on both the potential in principle as well as the regional differences created by the comparative advantages in other regions. These latter differences will probably reflect the magnitude of the development problem for the region concerned.

Whereas this part of the chapter has concentrated on the GRP per capita as an estimate of the magnitude of the supply side of the market, the discussion now focuses on income per capita or, more generally, on standards of living representing the capacity of a region to act as a consumer market for the finished product.

The Standard of Living and the Consumer Market

There is a gap between the measurable aspects of standards of living and the appreciation of those standards by people in different regions—a problem akin to the measurement of individual (implicit) preference functions in economics. Here explicit observable phenomena require analysis so that EEC regions can be compared on a common basis. This can be achieved by classifying many variables into a limited number of structural indicators describing the standard of living which should at least refer to:

(a) the *demographic structure* (variables 1–9);
(b) the *employment structure* (variables 9–14);
(c) the *level of urbanization* (variables 14, 15, 24 and 25);
(d) the provision of *social infrastructure* (variables 16–19 and 21);
(e) the *level of household expenditures* (variables 20, 22 and 23).

The 25 variables (Table 6.2) which can be associated with those indicators have been subjected to a principal axis factor analysis. When using Kaiser's criterion ($\lambda = 1$) 6 factors remained and these were subjected to a varimax

TABLE 6.2 List of variables

Number	Name
1	Population index figure, 31 December 1968, EEC = 100
2	Natural increase per 1000 inhabitants, computed from variables 3 and 4
3	Number of births per 1000 inhabitants, 1968
4	Number of deaths per 1000 inhabitants, 1968
5	Child deaths in 1968, computed as the ratio between the number of children aged less than 1 year and the total number of live births
6	Percentage of persons over 65 years in 1968
7	Number of marriages per 1000 inhabitants in 1968
8	Number of inhabitants per km^2 in 1968
9	Percentage employed in agriculture in 1968
10	Percentage employed in the secondary sector in 1968
11	Percentage employed in the tertiary sector in 1968
12	Number of unemployed per 1000 in 1968
13	The GRP per inhabitant as an index in 1969, where EEC = 100
14	Number of dwelling construction permits per 1000 in 1969
15	Number of finished dwellings per 1000 in 1969
16	Number of doctors per 100,000 inhabitants in 1969
17	Number of pharmacists per 100,000 inhabitants in 1969
18	Number of hospital beds per 1000 inhabitants in 1969
19	Number of hotel beds in 1969
20	Number of private cars per 1000 inhabitants in 1969
21	Number of buses per 1000 inhabitants in 1969
22	Electricity use by household as KWh per inhabitant in 1969
23	Number of television sets per 1000 inhabitants in 1968
24	Number of municipalities above 20,000 inhabitants, 1968
25	Percentage of the population living in municipalities with more than 20,000 inhabitants in 1968

Source: calculated from Commission of the European Communities, 1971.

TABLE 6.3 The factor matrix after rotation

Variable[a]	Factor					
	1	2	3	4	5	6
1 Population index		0.82987			0.45847	
2 Natural increase	0.94526					
3 Births	0.84401					
4 Deaths	−0.89655					
5 Child deaths					0.77157	
6 Aged over 65	−0.71201				−0.35628	0.34320
7 Marriages	0.52228		−0.60302		−0.31547	
8 Inhabitants per km²			−0.52531			
9 Per cent primary			0.43954	−0.77018		
10 Per cent secondary				0.93046		
11 Per cent tertiary			−0.77492			
12 Unemployment		0.35453			0.82098	
13 GRP per capita	−0.37868	0.31403	−0.30498	0.54334	−0.41521	
14 Construction permits		0.93371				
15 Finished dwellings		0.92650				
16 Doctors	−0.48599		−0.48406	0.38495		
17 Pharmacists	−0.82240					−0.38396
18 Hospital beds						0.86751
19 Hotel beds		0.40322			0.29961	0.50583
20 Private cars	−0.63940	0.32072	0.26788		−0.29456	0.31769
21 Buses		0.58093				
22 Electricity use			−0.56095	0.56946	−0.29254	
23 Television sets	−0.34379		−0.46940	0.48574		0.42576
24 Municipalities		0.52827			0.65678	
25 Population in muni-cipalities with more than 20,000 inhabitants		0.33641	−0.76512		0.26590	
Values	4.97	3.89	3.07	2.90	2.82	1.81
Per cent variation explained	19.88	15.56	12.28	11.60	11.28	7.24

[a] See Table 6.2 for more detailed description of variables.

rotation to improve the interpretation of the factors individually (Table 6.3). Without such a procedure the first factor emerges as a general factor, which is not the purpose of this exercise. The rotated factors can be identified as follows:

(a) general demographic structure index (Figure 6.3);
(b) general urbanization index (Figure 6.4);
(c) rural-urban index (Figure 6.5);
(d) industrialization index (Figure 6.6);
(e) socio-economic stagnation index (Figure 6.7);
(f) welfare index (Figure 6.8).

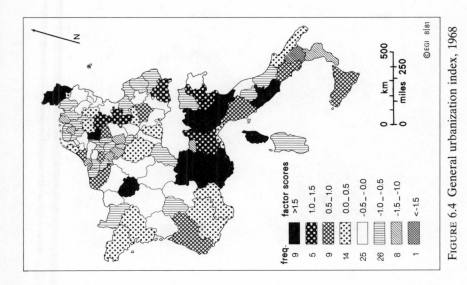

FIGURE 6.4 General urbanization index, 1968

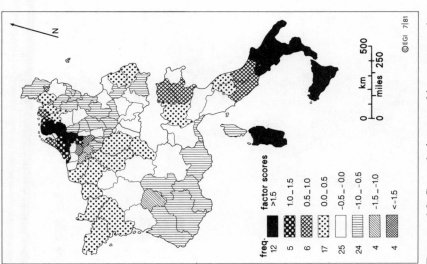

FIGURE 6.3 General demographic structure index, 1968

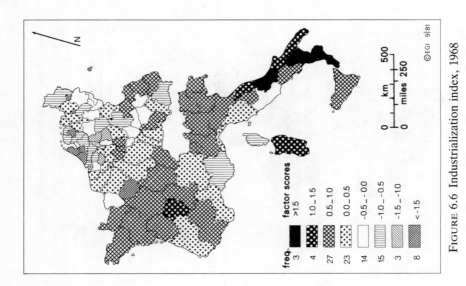

FIGURE 6.6 Industrialization index, 1968

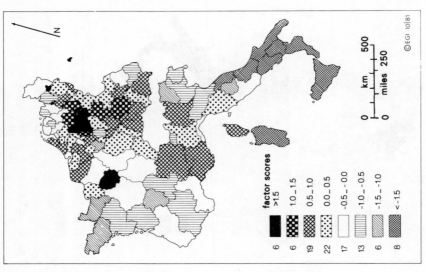

FIGURE 6.5 Rural-urban index, 1968

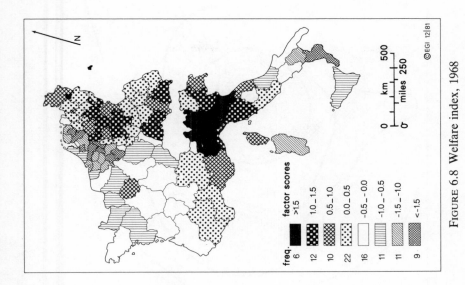

FIGURE 6.8 Welfare index, 1968

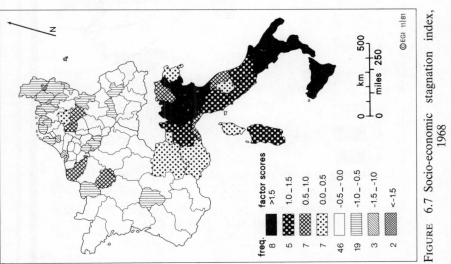

FIGURE 6.7 Socio-economic stagnation index, 1968

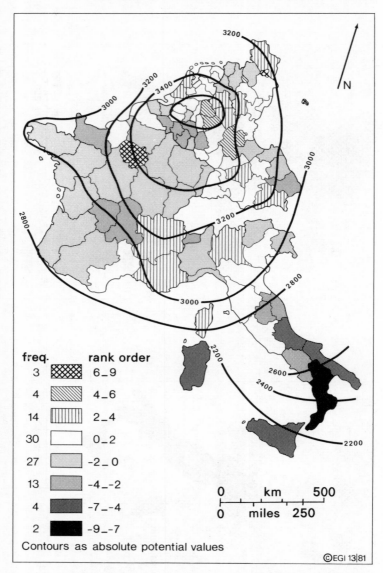

FIGURE 6.9 Distribution of regional welfare in the EEC. [Source: after Clark *et al.*, 1969, p. 204]

When comparing these results with the objectives already stated it can be noted that the level of employment and the degree of urbanization both appear twice in the interpretation of the factors. The second factor represents a general urban expansion and consumption pattern, while in the third factor the lack of services and service activities and low overall densities emphasize the contrast between rural and urban areas.

The level of employment is of general importance in the fourth factor in which spatial similarity is evident between employment in the secondary sector, higher GRP per capita and higher levels of consumption. Contrasting with this pattern is the fifth factor where not only the level of unemployment is associated with lower GRP per capita but also with unfavourable demographic conditions. It appears that household expenditures and consumption patterns do not create an independent dimension but are related in various ways with the other factors. Some type of welfare structure remains, however, and is weakly present in the sixth factor.

The combination of these results may yield an index representing the standard of living in each of the 98 sub-regions of the EEC. The question of how to combine them is, however, a difficult one. A first approximation could be obtained by putting the factor scores relating to 1 factor into rank order. Thus, instead of 6 factor scores a region has 6 rank numbers. As the mathematical results of the factor analysis are not directly related to the regional reality, the negative scores for some factors are considered to be positively related to a high standard of living. This is the case, for example, with the scores associated with the third factor, where the largest negative value has been assigned rank number 1.

The results of this procedure are shown in Figure 6.9 in which also the potential map of Clark *et al.* (1969, p. 204) is shown. The spatial pattern of the standard of living index is a structural phenomenon representing geographical variations in demand. The incongruence of this pattern with the supply surface is not predominantly caused by the difference between an isopleth and a choropleth map but by the difference between the actual and the hypothesized location of industrial production.

DEMAND AND SUPPLY PATTERNS

The comparison between the maps showing the economic potential surface and the average standard of living indicates not only the difference between theoretical regional analysis and observed structural realities but also the differences between the locational pattern of demand and supply. In this context the concurrence of regions which have a relatively low standard of living in the same areas with the highest potential values can be noted. The mismatch between the patterns is less when the standard of living is compared with the spatial distribution of industrialization (Figure 6.6);

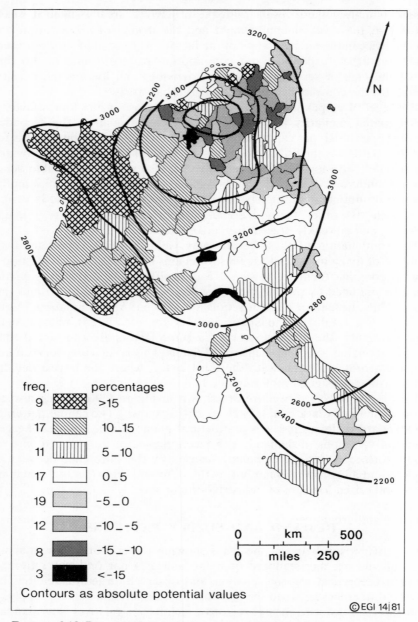

FIGURE 6.10 Percentage change in employment in the secondary sector,
1960 to 1968 (1960 = 100). [Source: after Clark *et al.*, 1969, p. 204]

indeed, this should provide the closest coincidence as it is nearest to the theoretical bases of the economic potential concept. As the 2 main variables in the industrialization index are employment in the secondary sector and the GRP per capita (see Table 6.3), this suggests that distance is not a key variable in the location of manufacturing industries for the EEC.

Alternative explanations become apparent when the industrial location question is not confined to the spatial organization of manufacturing but is broadened to incorporate the service sector as part of the new industrial structure. Then it may be hypothesized that manufacturing would increasingly decentralize away from the core region(s) and consequently employment in these activities in the periphery would grow. At the same time the jobs in the core regions may be displaced by new office technologies which interact with corporate organizations and patterns of control. It must be asked whether these possible patterns reflect a new spatial division of labour in which contact potentials coincide with the nodes of the European urban spatial system where second order cities gain in importance, or whether these patterns merely reflect statistical artefacts.

In Figures 6.10 and 6.11 the relative shifts in employment in the secondary sector are given for the 1960–68 and 1968–76 periods. The relative growth of secondary employment in the periphery is very noticeable on both maps while, at the same time, a decline continues in the core. This process proceeds, however, at a different rate. In the 1960–68 period peripheral growth was below 5 per cent, except in the regions in northern Italy. After 1968 a very rapid growth of 10 to 15 per cent occurred in many peripheral regions, indicating accelerated decentralization.

Comparison of this growth pattern with that in service sector employment in the 1968–76 period (Figure 6.12) is very interesting because it took place in both the core and the periphery, the highest rates being observed more in the periphery than in the core itself. Moreover, employment growth in the tertiary sector occurred everywhere in the EEC except for 2 regions.

Several explanations can be suggested. The growth of tertiary employment in the less central areas supports the hypothesis of the expansion of second order towns. The increased supply of low-skilled service jobs in the industrial and urban scenes coincides with the employment structure of these less central areas which were still predominantly agricultural in the late 1950s. At the same time growth of tertiary employment in the core region is possibly caused by a replacement of both low and high-skilled manufacturing jobs by employment opportunities in the service industries.

Although evidence is not available at the EEC level, there is some support for the speculative comments in a study of the Netherlands by Jansen et al. (1979) who found a 3-stage industrial decentralization process in operation during the past 25 years from the urban-industrial core to the rest of the country. The first stage comprised the decentralization of labour-

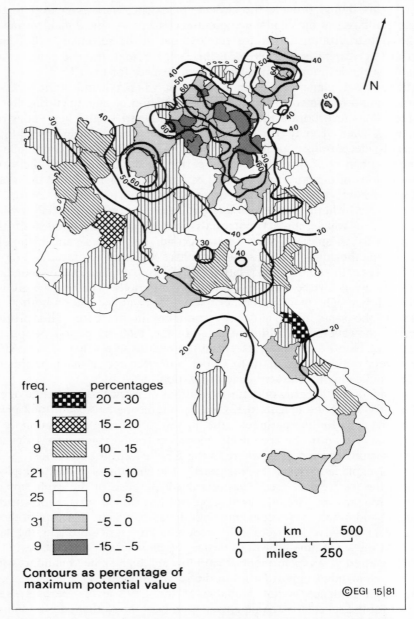

FIGURE 6.11 Percentage change in employment in the secondary sector, 1968 to 1976 (1968 = 100). [Source: after Keeble and Owens, 1980, Figure 2]

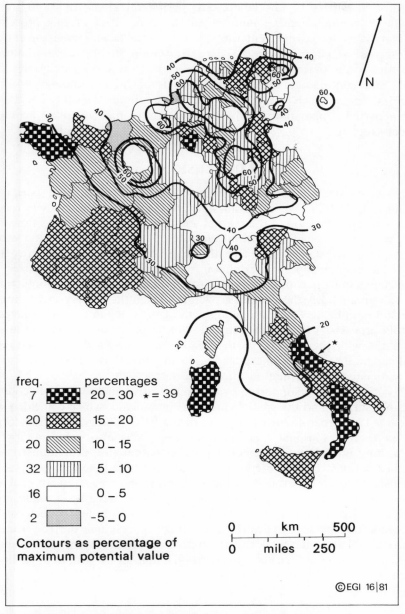

FIGURE 6.12 Percentage change in employment in the tertiary sector, 1968 to 1976 (1968 = 100). [Source: after Keeble and Owens, 1980, Figure 2]

intensive industries to low labour-cost peripheral areas, followed by the growth of capital-intensive industry in the core. Part of this process is stimulated by the government through rural area development incentives. The second stage involved the decentralization of the capital-intensive industries to the periphery and their replacement by service industries. The third, and continuing, stage is the growth of high-technology R & D activities, but conclusive evidence is not easy to obtain. This process gives at least a partial explanation for the continuation of high regional income in the core regions.

CONCLUSIONS

This economic potential analysis has identified central and peripheral regions in the EEC. Two important questions emerged. The first was related to the conceptualization of the market and focused on the nature of the core area, while the second focused on the role of transport costs or the way in which physical distance influenced the shape of the market. The growth of industrial employment in peripheral regions since 1960 emphasizes the diminishing influence of transport costs in the location of manufacturing jobs. Simultaneously there was a growth in jobs in the tertiary sector in both core and periphery. The sustained growth of the GRP in the core suggested a 2-fold process—a further concentration of 'information capital' in the core associated with the location of the head offices, and a decentralization of fixed capital into the periphery leading to the growth of second order cities and associated employment in the service sector.

This explanation is supported by the comparative analysis of the economic potential surface and the spatial variations in demand, which coincided with the early 1960 urban-industrial pattern of the EEC. The gradual transformation in these traditional manufacturing regions is also suggested by the diminishing differences in regional product within the most industrialized member nations. It can be concluded that economic potential analysis is a very useful tool in exposing both the conceptual and measurement problems in industrial location analysis. Various suggestions have been made about ways in which its application could be extended including a sectoral disaggregation of the potential surface or a focus on residuals derived from the comparison between actual and theoretical locations. Comparative advantages may thus be revealed for locational questions within a particular sector.

Spatial Analysis, Industry and the Industrial Environment. Vol. 3 Regional Economies and Industrial Systems
Edited by F. E. I. Hamilton and G. J. R. Linge
© 1983 John Wiley & Sons Ltd.

Chapter 7

Location of Manufacturing and Operational Urban Models

M. J. WEBBER

This chapter examines the nature of, and prospects for, operational models of the location of manufacturing activity in urban areas. At present, such operational urban models as the Lowry model avoid analysing the amount and spatial distribution of manufacturing in cities by implicitly treating the manufacturing sector as exogenous. Some previous attempts have been made to model the spatial distribution of manufacturing activity (e.g. Goldberg, 1967; Putman, 1972), but they ignore much recent evidence about its location. Within this context, the chapter has 2 aims: to introduce industrial geographers to the aims and methods of operational urban modelling; and to show how evidence about the location of manufacturing may be used to construct operational models of the manufacturing sector.

The geography of manufacturing examines 2 distinct issues. The first concerns the distribution of manufacturing among cities (inter-urban location patterns), and analyses the links between national economic performance and the relative success of the cities of that economy as manufacturing centres. The second issue focuses on the distribution of manufacturing activity within cities (intra-urban location patterns) and examines the link between the aggregate urban economy and the performance of individual zones within that city. Because both are large topics, the former is ignored here (though the methods of Gordon and Ledent, 1980, can be used to integrate several models of separate cities). It is assumed, therefore, that there exist known aggregate levels of manufacturing activity in a city and that these levels change exogenously; given a known, initial spatial distribution of manufacturing within the city, the modelling task is to specify the changes in that distribution which will occur over time. (This assumption and method imply that the directions of causality are nation→city and city→zone, and that the spatial distribution of activity in a city does not significantly affect the quantity of activity in that city. The assumption is not strictly correct, but is widely adopted because of its simplifying properties and because the zone→city influences are believed to be secondary when compared to city→zone influences.)

This task is approached by bringing together the 2 separate geographical traditions of operational modelling (the first 4 sections) and intra-urban location theory (the next 2 sections) within operational models of manufacturing location (the last section). The first section provides general background by discussing the distinctions and choices which must be made when constructing operational models, while the second describes the tasks that such models perform in geography and planning: the ideas discussed in these sections underlie the entire modelling enterprise. In the third, operational models—the Lowry model and EMPIRIC—are described and an effort is made to identify and to criticize the hypotheses of those models about the location of manufacturing activity. This introductory material is concluded in the fourth section by a discussion of the information minimizing method and a research strategy based on it, which are the frameworks within which the analysis is conducted. The next 2 sections examine the location of manufacturing within cities: the fifth briefly describes the history of intra-urban manufacturing location and the sixth reviews recent evidence about the factors that determine the spatial distribution of manufacturing. The last section then illustrates how this evidence may be used to construct operational models of manufacturing location and identifies additional research which is needed to expand and evaluate them.

OPERATIONAL MODELS AND THEORY

Operational models are widely used in geography (Wilson *et al.,* 1977) and in planning (Pack, 1978; Barras and Broadbent, 1979). One of the main traditions of mathematical modelling in geography is derived from the Lowry model (Wilson, 1977): it integrates ideas about the form of urban areas in a way that has been found scientifically fruitful as well as operationally useful. At the same time, spatial interaction and Lowry models are the most commonly used models in English structure plans (Barras and Broadbent, 1979, pp. 8–12) and are widely used in the US too (Pack, 1978, pp. 55–89).

Recipes can be written by which state-of-the-art urban models should be produced (Wilson, 1974; Wilson *et al.,* 1977) but, valuable though such summaries are, they miss the point that success in operational modelling for planning is not measured by the same criteria as success in scientific modelling. (This comment could also be made about Sayer, 1976.) Scientific urban models are designed to increase our understanding of the urban world and to integrate theoretical research: state-of-the-art modelling is vital in this undertaking. By contrast, operational planning models are designed to produce reliable forecasts in a believable manner, and their construction raises strategic and tactical issues which are not relevant to scientific models. (Batty, 1976, pp. 11–19, discusses some of these issues.) This section describes some of the consequences of this distinction.

Some Distinctions

The distinctions between applied and academic research are those of purpose rather than form and of degree not kind. Applied urban models are a tool, just as (say) an accounting procedure is a tool, designed to promote the aims of the capitalist enterprise: they provide development plans, and so are an integral part of the way in which capitalist societies now operate. Academic research is also a part of the society: it is not an exogenous force, but is produced by society in response to its needs and problems, and provides a general understanding of how societies operate and evolve. This is not to say that applied models are designed for action whereas academic theories are not of practical use, for understanding itself implies a particular way of acting and influences the evolution of the system. Planning models regard the form of society as given and are produced to make that society operate more profitably; scientific research examines the conditions under which the society operates and the manner in which it is changing, but need not regard the form of society as constant.

Theories and models must also be distinguished. A theory is a logically coherent set of statements about the way in which society is constructed and evolves: statements about the principles which govern social relations. For example, one view of the world is neo-classical, in which all societies are visualized as aggregations of private firms, public institutions and households, each making decisions in order to maximize profits, social welfare or utility (respectively), in a manner governed by externally fixed technological and preference relations and subject to payments to factors of production that are proportional to their marginal products. This core of beliefs is elaborated in neo-classical theory: the elaboration deduces details about decision rules, about outputs, prices and locations in the theoretical society (and their correspondence with actual societies) and about the consistency of the world view. Models are constructed by applying these principles to particular environments (and, in this sense, a theory is a rule about how to construct models). A well known model is that of perfect competition, in which the neo-classical principles are applied to an environment characterized by many small firms and households, none of which can control prices, by perfect mobility of factors between firms and products, and by complete information. A familiar geographical (central place) model is that in which all places are equally endowed with resources, households all earn the same income and are regularly distributed over space, and industries can be entered freely. By applying the theoretical principles to a particular environment, the model can be solved (the nature of the theoretical society can be deduced); to the extent that the theory and the assumed environment correspond to a real circumstance, so the model describes tendencies inherent in the actual society.

Two general types of scientific models can be identified. The first type is analytic, based upon a simple and idealized environment; such models produce general principles about the operation of abstract societies. Both the perfect competition and central place models belong to this class. The second type of model is realistic or operational, and describes a particular society at a particular place; for example, the Lowry (1964) model uses information about travel costs, the distribution of basic employment and other parameters which are specific to particular cities. In this way the predictions of the theory can be compared to the actual state of the city. Some models may be used for both purposes: an analytical version of the Lowry model could be constructed by assuming that travel costs are proportional to euclidean distance, the basic population is evenly distributed over space (or, perhaps, concentrated at a single point), and zones are indefinitely small (Webber, 1980a, pp. 283–351).

The degree of difference between an analytic and an operational model depends upon the style of their prior theory. In neo-classical economics, the analytical tradition diverges widely from the operational tradition of model building because the theory contains many unobservables, such as utilities, long-run profits (in an uncertain environment) and marginal productivities. The contrast between the Alonso–Mills–Muth analytical models of urban economics and the Herbert–Stevens operational version of the theory is particularly acute; analytical and operational models of neo-classical location theory differ similarly. By contrast, theories which rely on directly observable categories produce operational and analytical models which are more similar in form, and the use of the Lowry model for both analytical and operational purposes illustrates the attractiveness of this possibility.

Two classes of research have thus been identified—applied research and academic (or scientific) research. The first gives rise to applied models for planning; the second to 2 types of model, operational and analytic. This distinction is important because the criteria by which models are judged depend on the uses to which they are put. Confusion arises in evaluating the Lowry model because it is used both as an applied model in planning and as an operational model in urban geography; the 2 roles must be kept distinct, even though the general adjective 'operational' is applied to both categories of the model.

Operational models themselves can be constructed in several styles. Normative models define the way the world ought to be, at least from a particular point of view. A linear programming model of a city (e.g. Herbert and Stevens, 1960) describes what a city should be like if certain criteria of efficiency are to be satisfied. Postitive models, on the other hand, try to describe the way the world is. Lowry (1964) does not claim that cities ought to be constructed according to the conditions derived from his model, but rather that the model is a description (admittedly simplified) of actual North

American cities. (Of course, if one believes that cities are organized according to given criteria of efficiency, then the Herbert–Stevens model would have a positive as well as a normative role.)

But it is also important to distinguish descriptive and predictive power in positive models. The descriptive power of a model refers to its ability to reproduce the data on which it was calibrated. For example, suppose that a city is divided into I zones, labelled $i = 1, 2, \ldots, I$, such that the working population of zone i is O_i (O for origins), the number of jobs in the zone is D_i (D for destinations) and the cost of travel between zones i and j is c_{ij}; then a very simple model claims that the journey-to-work trips in the city from zone i to j (t_{ij}) will be

$$t_{ij} = O_i^\alpha D_j^\gamma \exp\left(-\beta c_{ij}\right) \qquad \text{for all pairs } i \text{ and } j. \qquad (7.1)$$

Now suppose that the values of the parameters, α, β and γ of equation (7.1) are estimated from 1966 data about the working population, jobs and journey-to-work trips in Hamilton, Ontario. The descriptive power of the equation is measured by the goodness of fit between the equation and the 1966 pattern of journeys to work. Next, suppose that predictions about the 1976 distribution of working people (O_i), jobs (D_j) and travel costs (c_{ij}) are used together with the 1966 values of α, β and γ to predict the 1976 journeys to work: the goodness of fit between the actual and predicted journeys measures the predictive power of equation (7.1). The example offers 2 reasons why good descriptive models may not be good predictive models. First, the estimated parameters may not remain constant over time. Second, the exogenous data (population and job distributions and travel costs) may be difficult to forecast accurately, so the model inputs may be inaccurate. A good predictive model requires parameters that are relatively constant and exogeneous data that are easy to forecast accurately; a good descriptive model needs neither of these attributes.

Styles of Theory

The nature of theories must also be examined briefly. Theories simplify: they attempt to make sense out of the world by ignoring inessential relations. Thus theories differ by virtue of what they choose to regard as inessential as well as by the nature of their claims about the way the world works. Theories can abstract relations about the world in 2 different ways (Dobb, 1937, pp. 127–36). The essential features can be chosen to be those that are common to all societies in the domain of the theory; for example, neo-classical economics interprets all social relations as exchange relations and all societies as markets—thus, wages become a universal category (the marginal productivity of labour) rather than a specific category (payment of a labourer by an employer); and macro-geographers examine distributions of populations and spatial interaction. If this theorizing is successful, the abstracted relations do indeed characterize different societies (for instance, the negative exponential population density equation and the spatial interaction equation apply in several different societies: see Berry and Horton, 1970; Ayeni, 1979), yet the danger is that the relations are merely contingent—that is, are the outcome rather than the cause of social forms. This is quite clear in the case of macro-geography and the Lowry model: the spatial interaction relations are produced by, rather than determinants of, city structure (Sayer, 1979). Such a theory can describe some aspects of future social forms, if the underlying causal relations and the environment do not change, but cannot identify what causes the present to evolve into the future society (nor yet the parameter values of the relations in the theory). In such theories, the Lowry model could be used both as a planning tool and as an operational model. The second mode of theorizing is grounded in actual situations (though does not attempt to generalize to all societies) but excludes some features of society which are less important or more variable than those which are included. The purpose of this abstraction is to isolate certain aspects of the real world for intensive investigation (Sweezy, 1942, pp. 11–22). Insofar as the forces that produce societies differ at different places and times, this type of theory is less likely than the first to identify contingent rather than determining relations; the corresponding danger is that of discarding important relations. A predictive model based on contingent relations and designed for planning cannot be also an analytical model in such a causal theory.

The dominant, neo-classical theory in economics and economic geography is of the first, generalizing kind. Yet several crucial disabilities arise from its focus on contingent rather than determining relations: the presumed exogenous variables (technology, preferences and income distribution) are themselves produced by society; a model of nineteenth century Papua which has the same form as a model of twentieth century America (apart from different technical coefficients) seems to miss many of the significant differences between the 2 societies; the required negative relationship between the price of capital (in relation to wages) and the capital intensity of production is not produced by the theory (Garegnani, 1970; Dobb, 1970); and the theory does not provide a means of interpreting the evolution of social systems from one form of production to another. These comments are amplified by Hunt and Schwartz (1972), Green and Nore (1977) and, in the context of urban models, by Sayer (1976).

An alternative, causal theory is Marxist and described in, for example, Sweezy (1942), Mandel (1968) and Howard and King (1975). The basic postulates of this theory are that the social, political and economic character of a society is generally determined by its mode of production (the manner in which the production of goods is organized), and that as an existing mode of production encounters problems or crises due to conflicts of interest between the classes in society, so a new mode of production evolves. This chapter is concerned with advanced capitalist economies, by which is implied that there exists a class of individualistic capitalists who own the means of production and a class of workers who sell labour power to the capitalists, and that most production is commodity production, in which goods are produced in order to be exchanged at a profit (Medio, 1972). It will later become necessary to distinguish between 2 kinds of advanced capitalist economy: an age of industrial capitalism, in which most sectors are competitive, and an age of monopoly capitalism, in which many of the sectors of the economy are subject to monopoly power (see also Mahdel, 1968, pp. 132–81, 393–547). This characterization generates 3 propositions which govern the manner in which the geography of urban areas may be investigated.

In simple terms, capitalist production is the following process. A capitalist holds money (capital), uses the capital in order to buy machinery and plant, raw materials and labour power, uses these capital items to produce new commodities, and sells the new commodities for money. The aim is to hold more money at the end than at the beginning of the process. Now, all production of commodities involves the use of plant and machinery that is long-lasting and immobile (both between uses and between locations) and capitalist decision-making is decentralized; since the profitability of a decision depends upon later decisions made by other capitalists, investors are uncertain about the outcome of their investment decisions. The first proposition is therefore that capitalist society operates so as to maximize the amount of profit made per unit of time and thus the rate of an accumulation of capital—over the long run and as perceived *ex ante*. Four kinds of action arise from this intent:

(a) those designed to increase the amount of profit made in any one production cycle, for example by using more efficient techniques than do rival capitalists;

(b) those designed to reduce the amount of time required in the production process (to increase the rate of circulation of money), for instance by speeding up the distribution of commodities to consumers;

(c) those designed to reduce the risk of production, by locational strategies, by diversification and increased size, and by state planning;

(d) those designed to preserve the social system, without which no profits could be made.

The second proposition qualifies the first: the decisions made by individual capitalists in a particular city do not necessarily appear to maximize profits *ex post* (Massey, 1973). *Ex post* and *ex ante* optima may differ if the expected state of affairs does not eventuate. Long-run profit maximization requires that the capitalist stays in business rather than merely maximizes the profit associated with each individual decision. The costs of small additions to a factory and of plant relocation imply that a factory may remain at the size and location chosen when it was built, at least until a major reorganization is necessary. The location, scale and type of production of a single factory are not chosen solely with respect to the operation of that factory but rather in the context of the profit-maximizing behaviour of the entire business enterprise of the capitalist owner. The concern in the system as a whole that the rate of profit be maximized may lead to state intervention designed to induce individual capitalists to locate factories at places that are not profit maximizing when viewed in isolation: regional planning, as practised in the UK and Canada, exemplifies such effects (Bourne, 1975). Although the capitalist enterprise as a whole is designed to maximize long-run *ex ante* profits, such a perception does not apply to the scale, type of production and location of any individual part of that enterprise considered by itself.

The third proposition directly challenges the central neo-classical tenet of consumer sovereignty. This notion is the postulate that all economic activity is directed to consumption and that consumers have exogenously determined and insatiable wants. The contrasting view asserts that the economic system is dominated by the supply side, by producers. The conditions deduced in utility theory from the assumption that consumers choose commodities so as to maximize their welfare, subject to a budget constraint, are replaced by a model in which prices, including wages, are determined by technological conditions (as expressed in input-output coefficients) and by the welfare level of workers' wages as a share of the surplus, while the marginal utility conditions determine the quantities produced (Sraffa, 1960; Johansen, 1963; Medio, 1972). In addition, preferences are not independent, for monopolistic or oligopolistic firms can set output levels and advertise rather than accept the production levels determined by existing tastes. The notion that production is directed to consumption illustrates how contingent relations come to be regarded as determining relations: production, as a matter of fact, does generally imply consumption, but that does not imply that production is undertaken in order to satisfy wants (for why, then, expend effort in expanding wants?). The purpose of production is to expand wealth: the capitalist economic system is supply dominated.

Principles for Models

Several principles about the methods of modelling the location of manufacturing follow from these propositions. In the first place, a particular model must be historically specific. On the one hand, models of the location of manufacturing differ according to whether they are to be used to describe early capitalist, advanced capitalist or state capitalist societies. On the other hand, at a smaller scale, much of the evidence about the factors that determine the location of manufacturing in cities was collected during the long post-war period of economic expansion and there is no guarantee that similar factors will be identified during periods of contraction of the manufacturing labour force in cities. (The scale of this contraction is described by Massey and Meegan, 1978; Linge, 1979; and Lloyd, 1979.) Such is the penalty for research which relies on contingent rather than causal relations. Similarly, such operational models as Lowry's reveal their date of birth by their assumption that the labour force is fully employed, an assumption that must obviously be relaxed now. Second, the modelling effort must identify and measure the linkages between national and aggregate urban performance (which are the statements about the nature of the economy) and the location of manufacturing activity in cities. Studies of the methods by which decisions are made and theories which emphasize the choices of individual capitalists, whether economic or behavioural, are not of primary significance; rather the location and growth of capitalist enterprise is regarded as a response to structural economic and social conditions. Therefore structures and constraints are emphasized, not individual decisions. The third principle concerns methods of analysing government interventions in the urban economy. Traditionally, economic geographers who study the location of manufacturing have regarded the state and its interventions as exogenous, with aims which are independent of those of the manufacturing section; thus, such textbooks as Lloyd and Dicken (1977) analyse the location of economic activity as a private process and then append material about the state's role in influencing location patterns. By contrast, the Marxist tradition regards the state as endogenous to the economic system, having institutions and policies which can be deduced from the needs of the capital enterprise; accordingly, the succeeding section examines the nature and role of the local state.

The principles govern the style of modelling adopted in the following sections. The first task, though, is to examine the role of the state in planning the urban economy and to determine the part played by operational models in that planning.

OPERATIONAL MODELS AND URBAN PLANNING

The standard notion of planning involves the ideas of forethought and objectives. In general, planning is a procedure for arranging beforehand (Bruton, 1974a,b), by deliberately sequencing actions so as to achieve an objective (Hall, 1975, pp. 3–18): to channel growth and to change and control its effects on society (Hall et al., 1973, p. 363). Urban planning (also called physical or spatial planning) refers to the spatial component of planning, which provides for the spatial structure of activities and the spatial coordination of policies (Rose, 1974; Hall, 1975, pp. 3–18).

Urban Planning Theory

In neo-classical economic theory, planning interventions are called forth by market failures. Such failures, whether caused by monopoly, external effects or uncertainty, reduce social welfare below the level attainable by a perfectly competitive market; and in neo-classical economics, the job of planning is to remedy the effects of these failures. The job can be accomplished in 2 distinct ways (Foley, 1964). Adaptive planning implements controls which prevent market failures: examples include anti-trust legislation or taxes on polluting firms (which internalize the external diseconomies), but the local state does not have the power to initiate and enforce such controls. In predetermined planning, a set of goals is deduced from a social welfare function, physical plans are developed which reflect these goals, and that plan which most nearly achieves the goals is chosen. But in the US during the 1960s, metropolitan plans were produced and policies deduced from them (Boyce et al., 1970, pp. 29–30) while in England and Wales, objectives and structural plans remain largely unrelated (Barras and Broadbent, 1979, p. 13), and although planning is supposed to be a goal-directed process (Harris, 1965), most of the models used are positive or forecasting rather then optimizing models (see the review of planning models in Pack, 1978). More fundamentally, the value of policies which maximize a social welfare function is not at all clear if preferences are endogenous.

Thus, theoretical and empirical objections can be raised against a theory of planning deduced from neo-classical economics. Planning agencies are an arm of local government and so an element of the state: their purpose is therefore part of the purpose of the state. The specific form of the state and the particular actions which it takes depend on the mode of production and the social relations within the society, and evolve historically in response to the particular circumstances of that country. In advanced capitalist economies several failures are evident. The purely capitalist processes of production and exchange do not automatically guarantee that the labour force is reproduced (that there is provided a supply of labour for commodity production), that the internally generated crises of over-production and unbalanced accumulation are controlled, nor that conflict over the division of the surplus does not destroy the system of social relations (Dear and Scott, 1981). The role of the state is to provide these guarantees in order to maintain a social system in which private enterprise can make profits and reinvest those profits in new or expanded spheres of activity (Sweezy, 1942, pp. 240–4; Mandel, 1975, pp. 474–5). This role generates 2 broad classes of activity: accumulation—assuring the conditions of production and reproduction which cannot be assured privately—and legitimation—ensuring that people continue to support the existing social system (Mandel, 1975, p. 475; see also O'Connor, 1973, pp. 1–10).

Popular allegiance to the institutions of the advanced capitalist economies is ensured by several activities, such as fostering nationalism, parliamentary elections, citizen participation and rising standards of living (Cockburn, 1977, pp. 51–7), but for present purposes the more important activity of the state is its assurance of the conditions of production and reproduction. Not all goods and services are commodities: the state directly produces some goods which at a particular time cannot be produced profitably by the private sector (for example, roads since the nineteenth century and, more recently, low-income housing) and owns or regulates producers (especially the utilities) which have become monopolies as economies of scale have increased (Roweis and Scott, 1978). The state guarantees the supply of factors of production, by stabilizing the supply of raw materials and providing education, medical and social services to ensure a continuing supply of labour, and safeguards national capital in the world market. As research and fixed capital costs have become larger, the state has begun to cover many R & D costs, to subsidize large industrial projects and to provide such markets as armaments, space research and overseas aid (Mandel, 1975, pp. 484–5). The state intervenes to overcome crises of over-production, unbalanced growth, market failure and monopolization that a system of private and decentralized decision-makers inevitably produces but cannot control (Scott and Roweis, 1977, p. 1103)—as, for example, the centralized economic management since the Second World War. Urban physical planning in the advanced capitalist economies has comprised 2 broad classes of activity— choosing the location and quantity of the physical infrastructure of a city, and guiding the location and quantity of land development (Barras and Broadbent, 1979, p. 2)—which correct particular urban problems.

The physical problems that arise in cities originate in the private land market (Scott and Roweis, 1977, p. 1104). A central institution of advanced capitalist economies is the private ownership of land: individual firms and households own land and have, within loose limits, the right to exchange and develop land in a system of decentralized decision-making. Yet developed urban land is not a commodity, for its value in use arises in 2 stages: the actual use to which a plot of land is put is determined privately but the profitability of that use is determined socially, by the decisions of all other land-owners about the development of their land (Roweis and Scott, 1978). Furthermore, the investment decision, once made, is immobile and long-lasting. It follows that the success of a development decision is essentially uncertain and uncontrollable by the private developer (Webber, 1972) and that exogenous changes must cause the urban built environment to deviate from efficient forms (Roweis and Scott, 1978). (A more detailed review of the conflicts which surround the uses of land and the rent paid for it is provided by Harvey, 1978.) Thus individual developers (whose investments are uncertain) and capital as a whole (the efficiency of whose fixed capital is threatened by the effects of myopic decisions and exogenous change on immobile investments) require that urban physical planning be instituted in order to stabilize the uncontrolled outcomes of private investment decisions.

This stabilization has 2 elements. The first is an *ad hoc* reactive element, in which the state corrects evolving imbalances in patterns of investment which threaten the stability of society and the profitability of private production. One imbalance in particular is relevant to American land-use planning—the use of automobiles for long-distance commuting before investment in freeways; a longer-lasting imbalance is the failure of private producers to build sufficient houses to accommodate low-income families in dwellings of good quality (Headey, 1978). The second element of the planning task is a continuing intervention to reduce the risks of development decisions. Private investment decisions have 2 components: fact (the existing state of the market) and judgement (about the continuity of social and economic trends), but even the factual component is weak because of ignorance about the decisions of others. The risks of development decisions can be reduced by a planning system which collects and makes usable the facts required for decisions; establishes common assumptions about social and economic trends and about the meaning of facts; provides a common expectation about government investment in infrastructure and social welfare projects; and sets standards to govern land development and building, so that the parties to a development decision can more easily agree on designs (Wheaton, 1964). These activities comprise the socialization of risk.

Urban Planning Practice

These ideas are borne out by the history of urban planning in the UK and US since the Second World War. There was little planning of American cities during the early post-war years. American cities continued the aggressive, peripheral expansion that had begun a century earlier (Walker, 1978) by constructing low-density suburbs based on commuting by car. Given ample space and sufficiently rapid rises in productivity to expand housing supply and pay for infrastructure, this policy maintained cheap land·and provided at least some houses for the poor (by filtering). The major planning task was to socialize risk by zoning which, after its introduction in New York City in 1916, proved very popular with private households, firms and local government. The system of zoning segregates land uses and social classes in order to protect investments in land development (Hall, 1975, pp. 263–4).

By contrast, the UK in the 1950s was much more highly planned, using machinery set up in the 1945–52 period. Urban planning was regulated by the 1947 *Town and Country Planning Act*, which required that counties and county boroughs produce 20-year physical plans for the use of land (to be revised every 5 years). A plan was a map of projected land uses together with a supporting policy statement. The development (that is, change in use) of a parcel of land required planning permission, which could be denied if the proposal did not accord with the plans. In addition, the 1946 *New Towns Act* and 1952 *New Development Act* provided some machinery whereby some of the growth of the population of London was diverted to smaller nearby communities and to new towns. (See also Hall *et al.*, 1973; Hall, 1975, pp. 99–124, 155–68.)

It is easy to over-emphasize the differences between American and British land-use planning during the 1940s and 1950s. The British machinery was comprehensive (for a few years, it even included expropriation of the profits from land development) and involved creating new towns. Yet the similarities between the 2 systems are fundamental: their inability to initiate land development and reliance on private development proposals; their exclusion from the production of goods and services for profit; their lack of explicit social goals; and the central role of the land-use plan or zoning ordinance which guided and protected urban development decisions. (Broadbent, 1977, pp. 128–65 discusses these characteristics of British planning.) In both countries, land-use control was executed by local governments which administered areas unrelated to the functioning of metropolitan regions.

However, conditions were changing. In the late 1950s, several states in the US had established metropolitan planning agencies and in the 1960–68 period over a dozen mathematical models were constructed during metropolitan plan-making. Lowry (1968), Boyce *et al.* (1970) and Brown *et al.* (1972) all describe some of these models, while Batty (1976, pp. 8–10) summarizes the history of the modelling projects. In the UK, too, wide-area transport and population studies were conducted in the early 1960s followed by some *ad hoc* cooperative studies of small regions and, in 1968 and 1972, by planning and constitutional acts which required that the newly reformed counties draw up long-range development plans (Hall, 1975, pp. 155–99; Barras and Broadbent, 1979). In both countries, the 1960s and 1970s were a period of strategic plan-making at the level of the functioning economic entity—the metropolitan area; increasingly, first in the US and later in the UK, this plan-making was accompanied by operational urban modelling.

Several factors came together in the late 1950s to prompt this new kind of American urban planning. The central structural need was that of maintaining suburbanization, based on the private car, while in some way alleviating the disbenefits of using cars (Boyce *et al.*, 1970, p. 11, and Batty, 1978 both emphasize that existing American cities were poorly adapted to the use of cars). Yet the mass-transit and freeway systems which were to accommodate this need had to be planned at the level of the metropolitan area rather than the individual city and had to reflect (and guide) suburban development of the entire metropolis. The interventionist mood was justified by social and aesthetic criticisms of American cities (Keats, 1957; Mumford, 1961; Blake, 1964) and the success of science in space, while the need brought forth the technology used to begin the planning task. As manufacturers and retailers joined the flight to the suburbs, they required to know the expected location of workers and markets: the new urban plans provided developers with the information needed to plan work and market places—where and at what pace the metropolitan area was going to develop. Operational urban models were the essential tool permitting plans to be produced which reflected, if only imperfectly, the integration of an entire metropolitan economic system.

Character of Applied Models

Although the operational models produced in the 1960s differed widely, they did share some common features, dictated by the task they were to perform. Operational models must be quantitative: while not all aspects of urban development can be reduced to numbers, nevertheless planners need numerical forecasts of, say, population growth and traffic flows in order to coordinate the provision of roads, services and residentially zoned land, while developers need numerical forecasts of the housing market. The models must be spatially disaggregated, for the demands for roads, services and housing must be satisfied at particular places in a metropolitan area. Operational models must predict the effect of change and development plans on various sectors of the urban economy, for households, retailers, manufacturers, office employers and transport firms all react in different ways to growth and development. Since the models were required for physical planning, they had to measure the effect of investment in infrastructure on the physical form of the city. Operational models had to use real data for real cities and be adapted to the particular geographies of those cities.

One other feature of operational models is more controversial. It is sometimes the complaint that the application of 'scientific' models to planning makes the existing city structure seem inevitable and so the future merely an extension of the present (Wurster, 1964). In fact, operational models must be *status quo* models in Wurster's sense, for planners, not having the power to initiate development, cannot control the future but only try to foresee it and by foreseeing it make the development process smoother and more profitable. If the housing market operates so that the poor are allocated the housing not wanted by rich households, then in the future the private development process will ensure that this allocation rule continues; therefore a model which purports to describe the future development of a metropolitan area to guide public and private investment must also assume that the poor are allocated residual housing. If planners do not have power over policies, models must be descriptive and predictive, not prescriptive.

In the 1940s and the early 1950s, urban planning had comprised the relatively simple operation of controlling land use and was performed by the lowest tier of the state. Increasingly, it has become a more complex operation, organized hierarchically, employing sophisticated mathematical models and embracing a wide range of planning tasks. The physical planning begun in the 1960s has continued (Barras and Broadbent, 1979; Pack, 1978, discusses the use of operational models in American urban planning) and the use of operational models has spread to many other countries (see the examples in Baxter *et al.*, 1975). The new urban planning tasks of citizen participation and welfare planning seem designed to maintain community support for the social system and to reproduce the labour force, whereas physical planning socializes development risks and guides infrastructure and public facilities (and is therefore more about production than about reproduction). The new tasks are additions to, rather than replacements for, the physical planning process.

OPERATIONAL MODELS

The publication of Lowry's (1964) monograph constituted a breakthrough in attempts to model urban systems. Many of the urban modelling efforts of the early 1960s had floundered or were floundering in a mass of detailed analyses which lacked a clear, comprehensive view of the way a city operates and which were ambitious far beyond the available computational capacities. By contrast, Lowry offered an extremely simple and elegant insight into the way an urban economy works, yet a view which integrated several employment and household sectors. The model was computable. Academics and planners have continued to be fascinated by the Lowry model because it can be operationalized, has a simple yet comprehensive structure, and offers opportunities for future development (Goldner, 1971).

This section of the chapter describes the original version of the Lowry model (see also Wilson, 1974, pp. 221–7). Since the concern here is to examine the central hypotheses of the model, only cursory attention is paid to more recent developments of it. Then the role of the manufacturing sector in the model is analysed and an attempt made to illustrate the contributions which industrial geography can make to the refinement of the model. Finally, a much simpler operational model, EMPIRIC (Hill *et al.*,

1966), is described and some evidence presented to show how well it forecasts.

Lowry Model

Although Lowry's model was originally built to represent a large American metropolitan area (Pittsburgh), it has been applied to smaller cities such as Reading in England (Echenique *et al.*, 1969a, 1969b) and to larger regions which contain several cities, such as Nottingham-Derby (Batty, 1976, pp. 111–37) and West Yorkshire (Mackett and Mountcastle, 1977). The area being studied is here called a region which is divided into small areas called tracts or zones. The Lowry model is intended to predict the spatial distribution of activities among the zones which comprise the study region.

The activities of the region are classified into 3 groups. One group is basic employment, i.e. employment in export industries, at a level which is determined by external demand rather than by events within the regional economy. Correspondingly, employment in basic industries is site-orientated rather than constrained by access to the regional market. Both the level and the zonal distribution of basic employment are given, exogenous to the model. A second group comprises the service employment sector or residence-orientated activities (which include schools as well as retail facilities and local government services). These activities require access to the residents of the region: the level and the location of employment in the retail sector is to be predicted by the model. The third group is the household sector—the size of which depends on the number of jobs—which in turn determines the size of the retail sector. The location of households is assumed to depend on the location of jobs. Given the level and the geographic distribution of basic employment in the region, the model calculates the level and geographical distribution of retail employment and the number and geographical distribution of households.

There exists a known distribution of basic employment over the zones of the region. The model first calculates the number of households needed to supply that employment and the accessibility of each zone to these basic jobs. Households are then distributed in proportion to the accessibility of each zone to jobs, subject to the proviso that the density of households on residential land in each zone cannot exceed a given maximum. Next, the number of retail jobs needed to serve these households is computed, and the level of retail employment is distributed over zones in proportion to their accessibility to households, subject to a constraint on the minimum number of retail employees per zone. But these retail jobs themselves require labour from additional households: thus the accessibility of each zone to jobs is calculated anew and the additional households distributed accordingly. The newly located households need retail services, which are again distributed in proportion to the accessibilities of zones to households. This iterative procedure of adding retail jobs and households continues until the pattern stabilizes.

These procedures are represented by a set of simultaneous equations, the solution of which describes the predicted spatial pattern of employment and residences. This solution cannot be interpreted as an equilibrium, because no processes are modelled, nor does it have a normative interpretation, for nothing is optimized. Lowry intended his model to simulate the actual behaviour of employers and households.

The model is expressed in 9 equations and 3 inequalities. In these equations the following notational conventions are used: upper case italic letters refer to variables (e.g. A = area of land, E = employment, N = number of households and T = number of trips), lower case italic subscripts (notably i and j) refer to individual zones (of which there are I in the region), while italic superscripts (e.g. k) refer to classes of retailing activity (of which there are K), and upper case superscripts denote sectors (B = basic sector, R = retail sector and H = household sector; also U = unusable).

The following identity describes the possible uses of land in each zone of the region:

$$A_i = A_i^U + A_i^B + A_i^R + A_i^H, \qquad i = 1, 2, \dots, I. \tag{7.2}$$

Both the total and unusable land area in each zone are known exogenously, so the land available for development in zone i is $A_i - A_i^U$. In competing for this land, the basic sector has first claim, while the retail sector can outbid households. At any stage in solving the model, then, the land available for basic employment in zone i is $A_i^B = A_i - A_i^U$; the land available for retail employment is $A_i^R = A_i - A_i^U - A_i^B$; and the land available for residences is $A_i^H = A_i - A_i^U - A_i^B - A_i^R$.

For each tract i, the amount of land used in basic employment (A_i^B) and the level of basic employment (E_i^B) are known exogenously.

For each of the K types of retail activity, let δ^k denote the number of retail employees required to serve one household. The values $\delta^1, \delta^2, \dots, \delta^K$ are given exogenously. Therefore the total employment in retail activity k is

$$E^k = \delta^k N, \qquad k = 1, 2, \dots, K, \tag{7.3}$$

The demand for the services of retail activity k derives from trips which originate at home and from trips which originate at work-places: let α^k denote the proportion of all trips to retail activity k which originate at home. The attractiveness of the retail activity k in zone i as a destination for home-based trips depends on zone i's accessibility to the population of the region,

$$\sum_{j=1}^{I} \frac{N_j}{T_{ji}^k},$$

where N_j is the number of households in zone j and T_{ji}^k is an empirically estimated function which measures the deterrent effect of distance upon trips to activity k. The work-based trips to retail activity k in zone i are assumed to be made on foot and to be short, so that the only employees who patronize retail activity k in zone i are those who work in zone i (and there are E_i of these employees). The level of retail activity in zone i is therefore proportional to

$$\alpha^k \sum_{j=1}^{I} \frac{N_j}{T_{ji}^k} + (1 - \alpha^k) E_i$$

with a coefficient of proportionality, η^k, chosen so that the zonal total of activity k sums to E^k, given by equation (7.3). Thus

$$E_i^k = \eta^k \left\{ \alpha^k \sum_{j=1}^{I} \frac{N_j}{T_{ji}^k} + (1 - \alpha^k) E_i \right\} \tag{7.4}$$

for $i = 1, 2, \ldots, I$ and $k = 1, 2, \ldots, K$. The parameter η^k is set so that

$$\sum_{i=1}^{I} E_i^k = E^k \quad (= \delta^k N), \qquad k = 1, 2, \ldots, K, \tag{7.5}$$

whence

$$\eta^k = \delta^k N \left\{ \sum_{i=1}^{I} \left[\alpha^k \sum_{j=1}^{I} \frac{N_j}{T_{ji}^k} + (1 - \alpha^k) E_i \right] \right\}^{-1}, \qquad k = 1, 2, \ldots, K.$$

The next identity describes how the 2 employment components are combined:

$$E_i = E_i^B + \sum_{k=1}^{K} E_i^k, \qquad i = 1, 2, \ldots, I. \tag{7.6}$$

The amount of land used in each zone by retail activity depends on the exogenously determined employment density coefficients $\psi^1, \psi^2, \ldots, \psi^K$:

$$A_i^R = \sum_{k=1}^{K} \psi^k E_i^k, \qquad i = 1, 2, \ldots, I. \tag{7.7}$$

Let γ be the exogenously given number of households per employee. (That is, γ^{-1} is the labour force participation rate, expressed per household.) Therefore the number of households in the region is:

$$N = \gamma \sum_{i=1}^{I} E_i. \tag{7.8}$$

The accessibility of zone i to the jobs in the region is measured as

$$\sum_{j=1}^{I} \frac{E_j}{T_{ij}}.$$

It is assumed that the population in a tract is proportional to its accessibility to jobs:

$$N_i = \rho \sum_{j=1}^{I} \frac{E_j}{T_{ij}}, \qquad i = 1, 2, \ldots, I. \tag{7.9}$$

The coefficient of proportionality, ρ, is chosen so that the sum of the tract populations equals N:

$$\sum_{i=1}^{I} N_i = N \tag{7.10}$$

whence, by equation (7.8),

$$\rho = \gamma \sum_{i=1}^{I} E_i \left\{ \sum_{i=1}^{I} \sum_{j=1}^{I} \frac{E_j}{T_{ij}} \right\}^{-1}.$$

These 9 equations are solved subject to 3 constraints. Economies of scale in retailing demand that the minimum number of employees in retail activity k in each zone must exceed Z^k, or else the retail centre is not viable:

$$E_i^k \geq Z^k \quad \text{or} \quad E_i^k = 0, \qquad i = 1, 2, \ldots, I, \quad k = 1, 2, \ldots, K. \tag{7.11}$$

Similarly, for each tract there is a maximum density of population per unit of residential land (Z_i^H), defined by building technology and zoning ordinances:

$$N_i \leq Z_i^H A_i^H, \qquad i = 1, 2, \ldots, I. \tag{7.12}$$

Finally, the amount of land used in retailing must not exceed the supply:

$$A_i^R \leq A_i - A_i^U - A_i^B, \qquad i = 1, 2, \ldots, I. \tag{7.13}$$

Together with equation (7.2), this constraint ensures that non-negative areas of land are available for residential uses.

These variables and parameters are summarized in Table 7.1; Figure 7.1 illustrates an iterative method for finding the solution of the model.

Commentary

Substantial improvements have been made to the Lowry model since it was first published. Batty (1976) has examined alternative methods of calibrating the model and calculating its solution. Garin (1966) has written the model in matrix notation and so examines the existence of its solution. Wilson (1970b) has improved on the spatial interaction models used by Lowry. Macgill (1977) superimposed an input-output model on Lowry's coarse classification of sectors, while Gordon and Ledent (1980) have

TABLE 7.1 Variables and parameters of the Lowry model

Variable/parameter		Symbol	Number	Source
Variable				
Land:	total area per zone	A_i	I	Exogenous
	usable area per zone	A_i^U	I	Exogenous
	basic sector area per zone	A_i^B	I	Exogenous
	retail sector area per zone	A_i^R	I	Equation (7)
	residential area	A_i^H	I	Equation (2)
Employment:	total per zone	E_i	I	Equation (6)
	basic per zone	E_i^B	I	Exogenous
	regional retail k	E^k	K	Equation (3)
	retail k per zone	E_i^k	IK	Equation (4)
Households:	number per zone	N_i	I	Equation (9)
	number in region	N	1	Equation (8)
Distance-deterrents:	work trips	T_{ij}	I^2	Exogenous
	retail k	T_{ij}^k	I^2K	Exogenous
Parameter				
Retail k:	employment per household	δ^k	K	Exogenous
	proportionality coefficient	η^k	K	Equation (5)
	proportion of home-based trips	α^k	K	Exogenous
	land use per employee	ψ^k	K	Exogenous
Households per employee		γ	1	Exogenous
Household proportionality coefficient		ρ	1	Equation (10)

Source: Lowry, 1964, pp. 9–13.

enriched the demographic structure of the model. Yet the role played by the manufacturing sector within the model has been ignored.

The model categorizes manufacturing and service employment into sectors. In Lowry's version, these are the export sector (which sells goods and services to people and firms outside the region) and the local sector (which sells goods and services to firms and households within the city), but in Macgill's version they are the sectors of an input-output model. It is then assumed that the size and location of the export sector are exogenous, independent of other aspects of the structure of the region; by contrast, the size and quantity of the local sector depend on the population of the region and access to markets. These ideas can be summarized as 3 hypotheses about the location of manufacturing employment:

(a) that the location of export-orientated manufacturing employment is independent of the region's spatial structure;
(b) that the households locate within the region with respect to access to jobs;
(c) that the location of locally orientated manufacturing employment depends on access to the markets (households within the region).

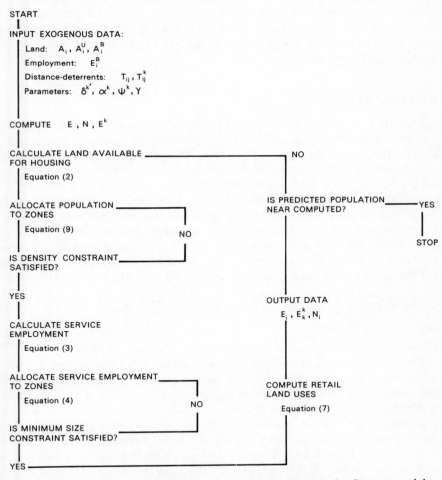

START
│
INPUT EXOGENOUS DATA:
   Land: A_i, A_i^U, A_i^B
   Employment: E_i^B
   Distance-deterrents: T_{ij}, T_{ij}^k
   Parameters: $\delta^{k'}$, α^k, ψ^k, γ
│
COMPUTE   E , N , E^k
│
CALCULATE LAND AVAILABLE ─────────────────────── NO
FOR HOUSING
   Equation (2)
│   IS PREDICTED POPULATION ──── YES
ALLOCATE POPULATION ──────────┐   NEAR COMPUTED?
TO ZONES   │   │
   Equation (9)   │ NO   STOP
│   │
IS DENSITY CONSTRAINT ────────┘
SATISFIED?
│
YES   OUTPUT DATA
│ E_i , E_k^k , N_i
CALCULATE SERVICE
EMPLOYMENT
   Equation (3)
│
ALLOCATE SERVICE EMPLOYMENT ──┐   COMPUTE RETAIL
TO ZONES   │   LAND USES
   Equation (4)   │ NO
│   │   Equation (7)
IS MINIMUM SIZE ──────────────┘
CONSTRAINT SATISFIED?
│
YES ──────────────────────────────────────┘

FIGURE 7.1 Flow chart of iterative procedure for solving the Lowry model.
[Source: Batty, 1976, p. 61]

There are good location-theoretic reasons for doubting the validity of each of these 3 hypotheses. For example, export-orientated manufacturers require access to a labour force and their ability to attract labour may vary according to the location they choose; also, modern manufacturing processes are extensive users of land and so may seek locations where land is cheap. Similarly, urban economic theory suggests that access to jobs is only one of the factors which influences the desirability of places as residences (Richardson *et al.*, 1975). And, third, the fact that an industry serves the local market does not imply that its location is market-orientated (Massey, 1971): for example, brickworks are site-orientated (raw material) although they typically serve only local markets. Thus one task of industrial geography is to assess evidence about the factors that affect the location of manufacturing in cities so as to improve the hypotheses contained in such operational techniques as the Lowry model.

EMPIRIC Model

EMPIRIC is a simpler model, for it comprises merely a set of simultaneous regression equations. Let R_{il}^t denote the proportion of the city's quantity of R_i^t which is located in zone l at time t (for example, R_1^t may be the city's population, R_2^t the number of manufacturing employees, and so on); and $\Delta R_{il}^t = R_{il}^t - R_{il}^{t-1}$; it is the ΔR variables that are to be predicted by the equations. Let Z_{kl}^t denote the proportion of the city's quantity of Z_k^t which is located in zone l at time t (Z_1^t may denote total highway access; Z_2^t length of sewers; Z_3^t area zoned for industry, and so on); and $\Delta Z_{kl}^t = Z_{kl}^t - Z_{kl}^{t-1}$; the ΔZs are explanatory variables. Then for each sub-region $l = 1, 2, \ldots, L$, and variable $i = 1, 2, \ldots, I$, the following regression equation system is estimated from data for times t and $t-1$ (Hill *et al.*, 1966):

$$\Delta R_{il}^t = \sum_{\substack{j=1 \\ j \neq i}}^{I} a_{ij} \, \Delta R_{jl}^t + \sum_{k=1}^{M-m} b_{ik} \, \Delta Z_{kl}^t + \sum_{k=M-m+1}^{M} b_{ik} \left(\frac{1}{L} - Z_{kl}^{t-1} \right). \quad (7.14)$$

Here, the a_{ij} and b_{ik} terms are estimated regression coefficients.

This model has been applied to over a dozen US cities (Putman, 1976). While many of the variables were similar from one application to the next, the specific variables used differed in each application, for they were chosen partly because of their performance as predictors in equation (7.14). The regression fits (to the data on which the model was calibrated) are good for the population variables, often having R^2 values between 0.7 and 0.9, with the numbers of zones lying between 100 and 400. But the model serves less well as a predictor of the location of change in the share of manufacturing employment: for the Twin Cities (of Minneapolis and St Paul), Putman used change in share of service employment, base-period service employment, base-period share of manufacturing employees, base-period net commercial area, base-period land availability and 2 measures (change in and base-period level) of highway accessibility to predict change in zonal shares of manufacturing employment with $R^2 \sim 0.7$; at the same time Masser *et al.* (1971) could only poorly predict change in the share of manufacturing employment in North West England ($R^2 < 0.5$). Although EMPIRIC has proved simple to use and apparently makes reasonable short-term forecasts, its theoretical structure is simplistic and it cannot be used to provide information about the causes of locational change.

The ideas in these models about the location of manufacturing in cities are rudimentary, even though they (and their descendants) have dominated the field of operational (planning) models. The task of this chapter then is to interpret the evidence about manufacturing change in cities in order to enrich the structure of operational models. This requires a model which is less applied than existing models, less directed to forecasting and more directed to understanding.

A FRAMEWORK FOR ANALYSIS

The operational model of the location of manufacturing foreshadowed at the end of the previous section must be consistent with models of other sectors of the urban economy. A method of analysing the spatial structure of urban areas which reflects the structuralist viewpoint of the first section and which integrates models of urban areas is now presented: it uses the principle of minimum information, which is therefore described and justified in the first part of the section.

A Measure of Information

Suppose that an event is about to occur: say, that a firm is about to choose to locate in one of the I zones of a region. A land developer has studied the firm and its needs, and concludes that the probability of the firm locating in zone 1 is q_1, in zone 2 is $q_2, \ldots$, and, more generally, of locating in zone i is q_i. The number q_i is the developer's guess about the likelihood of the firm locating in zone i; alternatively expressed, the ratio $q_i/(1 - q_i)$ is the odds of the firm choosing zone i. Clearly all probabilities and odds must not be negative (so: $q_i \geqslant 0$) and the firm must locate somewhere (so: $\sum_i q_i = 1$). The developer then receives an inside message that one member of the board favours a particular zone, say j. The developer is now forced to revise the estimates so that for each i, the probability of the firm locating in zone i is p_i (in an extreme case, the developer may conclude that $p_j = 1$, and $p_i = 0$ for all $i \neq j$). The message has evidently caused the developer to change his or her mind about the likely outcome of the event and has therefore imparted information. The question is: how much information?

The developer starts with the probability distribution $\mathbf{Q} = (q_1, q_2, \ldots, q_I)$ and changes the opinion to $\mathbf{P} = (p_1, p_2, \ldots, p_I)$. Let the information contained in the message that causes the change from $\mathbf{Q}$ to $\mathbf{P}$ be a number denoted $I[\mathbf{P}; \mathbf{Q}]$. Five desirable requirements are imposed on the measure $I[\mathbf{P}; \mathbf{Q}]$.

In the first place, it may in fact be that the 2 probability distributions are the same ($\mathbf{P} = \mathbf{Q}$): the message was ineffectual in changing the developer's mind. Since information is measured by its effect on beliefs, an ineffectual message is one that provides no information: that is, $I[\mathbf{P}; \mathbf{Q}] = 0$ if $\mathbf{P} = \mathbf{Q}$.

Second, suppose that there are 2 ways of listing zones in the city. One might be by alphabetical order; the other by order of increasing size. The order in which zones are listed does not affect the developer's beliefs about the likely location choice of the firm: evidently, it is reasonable to require that the information conveyed by the message does not depend on the order in which zones are listed.

Third, it is required that $I[\mathbf{P}; \mathbf{Q}]$ be continuous. Thus, if the message has only a small effect ($\mathbf{P}$ is very similar to $\mathbf{Q}$), only a little information is gained (and $I[\mathbf{P}; \mathbf{Q}]$ is nearly zero). Or, if there are 2 developers who have beliefs $\mathbf{P}$ and $\mathbf{P}^1$, and if $\mathbf{P}^1$ is only slightly different from $\mathbf{P}$, then $I[\mathbf{P}^1; \mathbf{Q}]$ is only slightly different from $I[\mathbf{P}; \mathbf{Q}]$. Or, if the 2 developers have different initial beliefs $\mathbf{Q}$ and $\mathbf{Q}^1$ but both change their mind to $\mathbf{P}$ after the message, then if $\mathbf{Q}^1$ is very similar to $\mathbf{Q}$, so $I[\mathbf{P}; \mathbf{Q}^1]$ is very similar to $I[\mathbf{P}; \mathbf{Q}]$. Quite reasonably, slight differences in probability distributions have only slight effects on information.

Next, suppose that the developer knows only the zones in which the firm will not locate. Lacking other information, the developer must believe that each of the possible zones is equally likely: if there are I such zones, then

$$\mathbf{Q} = \left(\frac{1}{I}, \frac{1}{I}, \ldots, \frac{1}{I}\right).$$

The message which the developer receives eliminates some more zones from contention, so that only $J+1$ ($0 < J < I$) are left:

$$\mathbf{P}^A = \left(\frac{1}{J+1}, \frac{1}{J+1}, \ldots, \frac{1}{J+1}\right).$$

On the other hand, another developer receives a message after which only J zones are thought to be possible sites:

$$\mathbf{P}^B = \left(\frac{1}{J}, \frac{1}{J}, \ldots, \frac{1}{J}\right).$$

A third developer begins by believing that $I+1$ zones are possible, but this number is reduced to J by the message. Each of the 3 developers believes that some zones are possible sites for the firms, but does not know how likely the zones are and so believes that each possible zone is equally likely. The 3 developers are:

A who initially believed that I zones were feasible, but reduced this to $J+1$ when given a message:

$$\mathbf{Q}^{\mathrm{A}} = \left(\frac{1}{I}, \frac{1}{I}, \ldots, \frac{1}{I}\right), \qquad \mathbf{P}^{\mathrm{A}} = \left(\frac{1}{J+1}, \frac{1}{J+1}, \ldots, \frac{1}{J+1}\right);$$

B who also believed that I zones were feasible, but reduced that to J when given a message:

$$\mathbf{Q}^{\mathrm{B}} = \left(\frac{1}{I}, \frac{1}{I}, \ldots, \frac{1}{I}\right), \qquad \mathbf{P}^{\mathrm{B}} = \left(\frac{1}{J}, \frac{1}{J}, \ldots, \frac{1}{J}\right);$$

C who initially believed that $I+1$ zones were feasible, but reduced that number to J when given a message:

$$\mathbf{Q}^{\mathrm{C}} = \left(\frac{1}{I+1}, \frac{1}{I+1}, \ldots, \frac{1}{I+1}\right), \qquad \mathbf{P}^{\mathrm{C}} = \left(\frac{1}{J}, \frac{1}{J}, \ldots, \frac{1}{J}\right).$$

In the sense of the number of zones taken out of contention by the message, A has received the least information and C the most; and $I[\mathbf{P}; \mathbf{Q}]$ is required to satisfy this ordering.

Lastly, the developer's beliefs about the firm's location decision can be described in several different ways. The obvious and simplest way is to list all the zones of the region and the probability ascribed to their being chosen as a site; this is the method used so far. Alternatively, the zones may be classified into 2 groups—say, those north of the harbour and those south of it, or those in the inner city and those further out, or those developed before and those after 1945. Suppose that the first group contains zones $1, 2, \ldots, J$, while the second group contains zones $J+1, J+2, \ldots, I$ $(0 < J < I)$. Now, the developer's beliefs can be expressed in the following way: first, what is the probability that the firm will locate in group 1 as compared to group 2, and second, if a given group of zones is chosen, what is the probability that the firm will choose a particular zone in that group? Let (q_1^*, q_2^*) and (p_1^*, p_2^*) be the prior and posterior probabilities assigned to the groups and let the probabilities of choosing a zone within each group be $\mathbf{Q}_1$, $\mathbf{P}_1$ for group 1 and $\mathbf{Q}_2$, $\mathbf{P}_2$ for group 2. Then, a message provides information about group membership (changes $\mathbf{Q}^*$ to $\mathbf{P}^*$) and about zone location, given the group (changes $\mathbf{Q}_1$ and $\mathbf{Q}_2$ to $\mathbf{P}_1$ to $\mathbf{P}_2$, respectively), and the expected total amount of information is:

$$I[p_1^*, p_2^*; q_1^*, q_2^*] + p_1^* I[\mathbf{P}_1; \mathbf{Q}_1] + p_2^* I[\mathbf{P}_2; \mathbf{Q}_2].$$

It is required that this quantity be equal to the quantity of info mation given by the message when beliefs are described in the simple and obvious way, $I[\mathbf{P}; \mathbf{Q}]$. (In the language of gamblers, the information provided about which card is drawn from a pack equals the information about the suit to which the card belongs plus the expected information about its face value, given its suit.)

The 5 desiderata are imposed on the measure of information. The first 4 are apparently necessary—it is hard to think of a numerical measure of information which would not satisfy these properties. It is the fifth desideratum which is most debatable, and it is possible to think of alternative properties which an information measure should satisfy. Together the 5 uniquely specify a measure of the information provided by a message that changes probabilities from $\mathbf{Q}$ to $\mathbf{P}$; it is

$$I[\mathbf{P}; \mathbf{Q}] = \sum_{i=1}^{I} p_i \log \frac{p_i}{q_i}. \tag{7.15}$$

(The base of logarithms is not determined by the desiderata; it is assumed here that logarithms are natural.) Equation (7.15) is Kullback's (1959) measure of information gain, which has been studied by Hobson (1969) and Webber (1980a, pp. 62–90); Snickars and Weibull (1977) obtain this measure by a combinatorial argument.

Another commonly used measure in information theory is Shannon's (1948) entropy. In equation (7.15), if $\mathbf{Q}$ is uniform (that is, if $q_i = 1/I$ for every $i = 1, 2, \ldots, I$), then

$$I[\mathbf{P}; \mathbf{Q}] = \sum_i p_i \log p_i/(1/I) = \sum_i p_i \log (p_i I)$$

$$= \sum_i p_i \log p_i + \sum_i p_i \log I$$

$$= \log I + \sum_i p_i \log p_i$$

$$= \log I - H[\mathbf{P}]$$

where $H[P] = -\sum_i p_i \log p_i$ is known as Shannon's entropy. Thus Kullback's information gain is linearly related to Shannon's entropy when prior probabilities are uniform. Shannon's entropy was introduced into the geographical literature by Wilson (1967) and has since been widely used (e.g. Wilson 1970a; Webber, 1980a).

Social Systems

Consider a social system, contained in a region. The system contains a population of individuals, say firms, each of which belongs to one and only one type. (A type may refer to a simple static class, such as a location; or may denote a more complex class, such as a classification of factories by location, size, type of product, number of employees, origin and quantity of raw materials of various kinds, size and location of markets; or may be dynamic and refer to, say, a classification of firms according to changes in their location.) It is believed a priori that the probability of a firm being of type i is q_i, for each $i = 1, 2, \ldots, I$. (In the absence of definite information, $\mathbf{Q}$ may be uniform.) Some structural or aggregate data are obtained which describe some properties of the firms in the region; call these data D. The problem is to predict the distribution of firms among the types: the problem arises because the data D are insufficient to specify uniquely the distribution of firms.

The method of solving this problem is called the minimum information principle. The data provide information, changing beliefs from $\mathbf{Q}$ to $\mathbf{P}$, where $\mathbf{P}$ is to be chosen to minimize $I[\mathbf{P}; \mathbf{Q}]$ (subject to the requirement that $\mathbf{P}$ be consistent with the data D). Thus the prediction is made which deviates least from the original beliefs, apart from the deviations demanded by D. This principle was first stated, in slightly different form, by Jaynes (1957) and used by Wilson (1970a); this form of the principle has been stated and used by Hobson and Cheng (1973), March and Batty (1975), Sheppard (1976), Snickars and Weibull (1977) and Webber (1980a). The principle is an inferential tool, for drawing conclusions from data, and forms the basis for the style of operational modelling conducted in this chapter.

The context in which this method is applied is an urban system. This context (or theory) emphasizes spatial structure and pays less attention to calculating aggregates: for example, the spatial allocation of employment is examined in more detail than the size of that employment, because of the orientation of this chapter to the intra-urban location of manufacturing. The theory is dynamic, because cities are evolving phenomena.

The rate of change of the spatial structure of a city depends on 2 opposing forces: the demand for change and the supply of investment to pay for that change. Lags occur and only some households and facilities relocate because there is insufficient surplus to invest in change or because the cost of moving is greater than the return on the move. Investment in urban change is limited by the surplus generated by the city and by the city's ability to attract the surplus of other cities, and so proposals for change must compete for these restricted funds. The demand for change is, however, a function of 3 processes.

One source of change is the city's response to external shocks. These shocks include variations in the demand for the city's goods and services, the migration of unemployed or retired people to and from the city, and changes in tastes and technology, all of which are independent of the spatial structure of an urban area. (In the longer run, they also include changes in the social structure.) The rate at which a city responds to external stimuli depends on the magnitude of the response which is required, on the size of the surplus available to pay for the response, and on the demand for other changes in the city. These external stimuli are equivalent to the forcing functions of dynamic systems theory; in urban theory they are supplemented by 2 internal sources of change.

Pressure for change is also created as the supply of, and demand for, urban facilities mutually adjust over time. In urban geography this adjustment is typically analysed by static models which belong to 2 distinct schools. The spatial response of households to the provision of jobs and services belongs to the province of land-use theory, which analyses residential location patterns, whereas the adjustment of jobs and facilities to a distribution of population is studied in location theory. The separate schools provide 2 independent and partial views of spatial structure, but theory must be comprehensive, for facilities locate and relocate (partly) in response to the spatial distribution of households and, in turn, people adjust their locations to the spatial pattern of facilities and jobs.

The third source of change is also internal—an aging process. A household evolves over time as its income changes, children are born and leave, and individuals grow older; consequently, the consumption, the location and housing demands of a household depend on its stage in this evolution. The nature of a housing unit changes over time as the character of a neighbourhood changes and as the unit deteriorates physically, so that the services which can be provided by a housing unit depend on its age, physical condition and setting. The value of the physical plant (fixed capital) of factories and shopping areas declines over time and the locational characteristics of sites change as a metropolitan area grows. The deterioration of physical structures can be arrested by investment, but other aspects of the aging process are halted only by the death of the person, household or factory.

Suppose, then, that there exists an urban region which contains a given quantity and spatial distribution of jobs, houses, services and households. Aggregate consumption levels are known. These quantities and their spatial distribution evolve over time in response to (exogenous) changes in export performance, household tastes, income, technology and population; to the aging of the population and the fixed capital stock; and to an endogenous force which tends to equilibrate the supply of and demand for services, at a rate which depends on the magnitude of the stimuli, on the deviation of the urban region from equilibrium and on the availability of a surplus to pay for changes. Since knowledge about urban areas is incomplete, the change in urban structure over time must be estimated by the principle of minimum information, which provides a minimally biased prediction of that structure subject to the known information and the present state of the urban region.

The principle is applied in 2 steps. Assume first the existence of distributions of employment, service facilities and housing (classified by types).

Then the principle of minimum information allows a population distribution to be inferred from the previous (known) state of the system, the assumed distributions and the given aggregate data. This theory therefore explicitly rejects the principles of urban structure derived from Alonso's (1964) work, in which spatial structure is the outcome of household-optimizing decisions; equally, in the second stage of the analysis, the theory rejects the principles of neo-classical location theory, in which the pricing and locational decisions of firms are modelled as profit-maximizing decisions. In this second stage, the distributions of employment service facilities and housing are chosen to minimize the information in the population distribution of the city, subject to the constraints that the costs of the new patterns do not exceed the surplus available for investment and that the patterns satisfy a minimum profitability constraint (for example, profits of each enterprise must exceed some given minimum level).

This framework is quite sparse. It is discussed in more detail in Webber (1980a, pp. 143–72). Static models derived from the theory are described in Webber (1980a, pp. 173–351) and a model of household mobility as a function of the aging process is examined in Webber (forthcoming). The following section of the chapter begins to describe the empirical information which is available to flesh out the aspects of the method that relate to the location of manufacturing employment in urban areas: it provides a social context.

HISTORY OF MANUFACTURING IN CITIES

There exist a great many studies of the location of manufacturing in cities, but few have managed to relate empirical evidence to a theory about the evolution of the capitalist enterprise. At one level, the question of manufacturing location may be approached by examining the effects of production processes, economic expansion and technical change on the factors which influence location, but more deeply the issue is one of the relations between urban form and the imperatives of capitalist accumulation. The history of the location of manufacturing in cities is now described and interpreted in the light of the Marxist theory briefly outlined in the first section, as a prelude to a study of recent trends in location pattern (which is continued in the next section). Scott (1980) has attempted to interpret the history of the location of manufacturing in cities, and much of this discussion overlaps with his book.

Cities of Industrial Capitalism

The implications of the capitalist manufacturing system for city structure began to become apparent in British cities early in the nineteenth century (e.g. Martin, 1966, pp. 1–22) and somewhat later elsewhere (Walker, 1978). The early locational patterns generally lasted throughout the nineteenth century until changes in transport technology began to cheapen significantly the movement of commodities within cities (Fales and Moses, 1972). The structure of manufacturing evolved throughout the nineteenth century as average firm size grew, the amount of material used per worker was reduced and some industry dispersed to the suburbs (Martin, 1966, pp. 20–2; Walker, 1978); nevertheless, the broad homogeneity of the period, particularly in comparison with later changes, justifies simplification of this history in the phase 'early manufacturing cities', that is, the cities of industrial capitalism.

Throughout the nineteenth century plants were typically small and operated in competitive markets. As late as 1909, 94.7 per cent of all American manufacturing plants employed fewer than 100 people (and 99.6 per cent employed fewer than 500 people—over three-quarters of the manufacturing labour force); in France in 1896, of all non-agricultural enterprises, 99.6 per cent employed fewer than 50 people and together they employed 74.4 per cent of the non-agricultural workforce (Mandel, 1968, pp. 396–7). Typically, nineteenth century factories operated in markets in which prices and output levels were determined by supply and demand and so they were forced to take, rather than to set, prices. In such conditions firms can protect profits only by reducing costs of production, and in particular, choose locations to minimize costs of production. Therefore, as Fales and Moses (1972) recognize, the location of manufacturing in the cities of industrial capitalism can be most readily understood in the terms of Weber's (1909) theory of industrial location.

In Weber's theory, the location of a plant is chosen with reference to access to material inputs, markets, labour and agglomeration economies. The implications of this principle in early manufacturing cities were determined by the fact that:

(a) such cities contain a core (dominated by financial and trading functions), several inter-city transport terminals (ocean, river, canal or rail) and a surrounding labour force, living at high density;

(b) the inter-city movement of commodities was cheaper than the movement of commodities within cities (Fales and Moses, 1972, cite data that indicate that intra-urban commodity movement cost between 10 and 30 times as much per ton-mile as inter-urban rail freight in the 1880s);

(c) the movement of people within cities was more efficient than the movement of commodities (Fales and Moses, 1972); and

(d) in most industries which processed raw materials, the weight loss during manufacture was great. Thus, input materials were either local (i.e. were generally bought from other plants, for most cities contain only limited local raw material sites) or imported (and so effectively located at inter-urban transport terminals); markets were non-local (again effectively located at inter-urban transport terminals) or local (and the easiest access to them was from the city core); labour, though spatially dispersed, was most readily available at the urban core; and agglomeration economies were available wherever linked firms were located.

These ideas allow 4 classes of manufacturing industry to be recognized (of course, in reality, the industrial geography of early manufacturing cities was more complicated than this).

The first class consists of industries which located with reference to local site factors. Although cities generally do not contain significant raw material sites, nevertheless some local raw materials are significant—brickworks (using local clay) and breweries (using local water) are notable examples. But this class also contains the noxious industries: in nineteenth century London as in twentieth century Boston and Cleveland, such industries are concentrated in the isolated or poorer parts of town (Martin, 1966, pp. 17–20; Struyk and James, 1975, pp. 115–22). Such industries, though locally significant, are not the major determinants of the geography of early manufacturing cities.

The second and third groups of industries are those which use large amounts of input commodities per operative and which therefore are dominated by attempts to minimize transport costs. The groups are distinguished according to the degree of weight loss suffered by the input commodities.

The second industry group was characterized by only slight loss (or even gain) of commodity weight during processing. Given the state of nineteenth century technology, this criterion implies that these industries predominantly used input commodities which had already been processed by other plants. Such industries seek market locations, either at terminals (if markets are non-local, e.g. shipbuilding) or at the city core (if markets are local: newspapers, furniture building, baking). (The core is also the point of maximum access to labour.)

The third group was characterized by a high degree of weight loss of commodities during processing and consists of what Scott (1980, pp. 96–9) calls the large-scale materials-intensive industries. These industries included slaughtering (in Chicago), steel manufacturing (in Pittsburgh) and heavy engineering (in London: Martin, 1966, pp. 15–20); they exhibited high capital to labour ratios and, especially, high ratios of commodity inputs per worker. Therefore, in an economic system in which the inter-city movement of goods by rail or water was cheap compared to the intra-city movement of goods, such industries had to minimize the costs of assembling input commodities and established themselves near the transport terminals, which were the effective location of imported materials. Such industries became concentrated near transport nodes and formed the early manufacturing heart of nineteenth century cities.

The fourth industry group used only small amounts of input material per worker. It is Scott's (1980, pp. 96–9) small-scale, labour-intensive group, and includes the clothing, jewellery, printing and precision manufacturing industries. In such activities, fashion and variable demand made production lines short; inputs were hard to standardize (even with respect to size or quality, for example); and manufacturing processes were often intricate (Scott, 1980, p. 96), so that organizational economy required small, vertically disintegrated factories, each closely tied to others by frequent, small-scale (and therefore expensive) commodity movements. Such industries had to concentrate together (to agglomerate) in order to obtain transport cost savings and external economies (Hall, 1959; Lichtenberg, 1960; Webber, 1972, pp. 204–9); and they centralized near the Central Business District (CBD) to be accessible to labour (Scott, 1980, p. 26; see also Martin, 1966, pp. 2–15).

Some of these distinctions are revealed in Fales and Moses' (1972) study of the location of manufacturing industry in Chicago after the fire of 1871. Table 7.2 summarizes some of their results. Consider, first, their class of large firms, which presumably contains our third group together with

TABLE 7.2 Density of employment, Chicago, 1870s[a]

Independent variable		Size of firm		
		Small	Medium	Large
	N:	42	46	28
River	Coefficient	−0.23	0.58	0.95
	Significance	—	0.01	0.01
Terminal	Coefficient	0.46	0.05	0.41
	Significance	0.01	0.01	0.01
Horse-car	Coefficient	−0.01	−0.21	0.24
	Significance	—	—	—
Core zone	Coefficient	11.61	7.29	3.52
	Significance	0.01	0.01	0.01
Log distance from core	Coefficient	−1.27	−1.21	0.12
	Significance	0.10	0.10	—
	$\bar{R}^2$	0.81	0.82	0.39

[a] N is the number of grid squares which contained firms.
Source: Fales and Moses, 1972, p. 163.

shipbuilding and some noxious industries. Such firms are attracted to river, terminal and core locations, but their density does not decrease with distance from the CBD. The class of small firms contains our fourth group and most of the second group of industries; though these firms are also attracted to terminal locations, they are highly attracted to the core and their density declines with increasing distance from the CBD.

Although this classification of industries is doubtless over-simplified, nevertheless it does permit a clear understanding of the geography of early manufacturing cities. One type of industry was located with reference to local site advantages, particularly local raw materials. A second group of industries sought access to markets and a third sought access to commodity inputs derived from inter-city transport terminals; in both cases to minimize transport costs. None of these industry groups was concerned with access to labour; rather the working class was forced to live at high densities near the favoured locations because of the slowness and relative expense of intra-urban passenger transport. The fourth group of industries agglomerated in order to save on inter-firm linkages, and locate near the city core, which was the point of maximum accessibility to labour (and, especially, to cheap labour provided by recent immigrants). This classification of industries bears some resemblance to Lowry's classification of activities as exogenous (classes 1 and 3) or as requiring access to markets or labour (classes 2 and 4). Furthermore, as Moses (1962) realized and Hoover and Vernon (1962, pp. 40–2) discovered for New York, this pattern of location implies that wages should be higher at the city centre than at the fringe, for locally employed fringe workers should be willing to accept lower wages than they could earn in the CBD in return for not having to pay commuting costs to the CBD.

Evolution of Monopoly Capitalism

But conditions were changing and, particularly during the twentieth century, the concentrated, high-density early manufacturing city exploded over the surrounding countryside. In part, this phenomenon has been associated with the increase of urban populations due to natural increase and the replacement of labour by capital in agriculture. But also cities have expanded because the density of activity in city centres has fallen. For example, Mills (1972, p. 45) shows that in 6 US metropolitan areas, the gradient of the density of manufacturing employment fell from an average of 0.94 in 1920 to 0.48 in 1963, while the average central density fell from 12,250 employees per square mile to 6210 employees per square mile. (Mills relates density, $D(s)$, to distance from the CBD, s, and central density, $D(0)$, through the equation $D(s) = D(0) \exp(-bs)$, where b is the gradient.)

Underlying this dispersal of urban activity lie 2 (related) phenomena. The first is the central process of capitalist economies—the drive to accumulate.

Capitalist commodity production is defined as the process of advancing capital to buy labour and material commodities which are transformed into other commodities having a greater exchange value than the original capital outlay. The difference in values between the capital outlayed and the commodities sold is surplus value or profit, which is used to expand the production of commodities in the next cycle of production. Both capital as a whole and individual capitalists need to accumulate, though their needs take somewhat different forms. This process has occurred in the context of the second phenomenon: the introduction of new techniques that have revolutionized production methods in manufacturing industry. New production techniques include the use of new sources of power (especially oil and electricity), new ways of making such basic materials as steel and aluminium and new industrial processes in the chemical and, more lately, electronics industries. In addition, new techniques of transport have been based on the internal combustion engine; the automobile and the truck have combined to produce a long-run trend which until recently at least, has significantly cheapened both inter and intra-urban transport (especially the latter). These changes in the techniques of production and transport are the crucial elements which have permitted the demands to accumulate to express themselves in the particular locational effects which have occurred during this century.

Among individual capitalists the drive to accumulate is based on an attempt to enhance profits by gaining an advantage over competing capitalists. Since markets are free and competitive in industrial capitalism, each capitalist can only try to gain as large a share of the market as possible by reducing selling prices, which in turn implies that, if profit rates are to be maintained, costs of production must be reduced, by means of new equipment, more rational production methods and a greater division of labour within the factory. The competition for market shares via new techniques thus implies that products are standardized, economies of scale are achieved by increasing plant size and labour is replaced by fixed capital (plant and machinery), all of which can reduce costs of production at the expense of long runs of a standard product. As production becomes more standardized, it can become more capital-intensive and, because the amount of control needed per unit of output falls, larger in scale (the new production techniques are both a cause and an effect of such standardization and scale changes). In many industries, this attempt has been successful, as the data in Table 7.3 illustrate, and as is indicated by the fact that the average size of manufacturing establishments in the US increased from 8 employees in 1850 to 10.5 in 1880 and 55.4 in 1954 (Mandel, 1968, p. 397). Some industries have been unable to standardize their product, particularly clothing, jewellery, publishing (if not printing) and some precision manufacturing; such industries remain labour-intensive and, because they buy and sell in small

TABLE 7.3 Characteristics of manufacturing production, United States, 1874 to 1964[a]

Year	Labour input index	Capital input index	Capital labour ratio	Output per unit of	
				Labour	Capital
1874	22.7	10.2	0.45	21.7	48.6
1884	32.7	15.2	0.46	28.4	60.9
1894	40.9	23.1	0.56	29.6	52.4
1904	59.7	32.4	0.54	34.6	63.7
1914	74.4	43.6	0.59	37.7	64.4
1924	80.5	54.0	0.67	48.5	72.4
1934	66.4	57.3	0.86	56.2	65.6
1944	97.3	61.6	0.63	69.2	109.3
1954	103.4	88.0	0.85	89.5	105.2
1964	111.3	118.7	1.078	119.1	111.7

[a] The capital and labour input indexes (1958 = 100) are measures of physical input, weighted by price. The output data are indexes (1958 = 100), weighted by price, and divided by the input indexes. For 1904 and later years, the data are averages of a 5-year period centred on the date given.

Source: Labour and capital input and output data are from Kendrick, 1961.

lots, their transport costs are high (Scott, 1980, pp. 97–9)—they still cluster and centralize.

This trend to increasing plant size has been accompanied by a concentration of capital and output in a few firms in each industry. The production of many industries is dominated by 1, 2 or 3 firms (Mandel, 1968, pp. 407–11 gives examples) and conglomerates are able to control output in several industries. Several factors have been conducive to this increasing concentration of market power in a few firms. The new technologies are generally capital-intensive and operate efficiently at large scales, which create barriers to the entry of new firms. New techniques of communication and computer control have permitted managerial control of ever larger numbers of employees and processes. Falling transport costs have allowed firms to sell over markets which are spatially more extensive (and so more populous) than previously. The risk and uncertainty of competitive markets can to some extent be controlled if monopolistic firms can set prices and outputs and use size as a defence against fluctuations (Rothschild, 1947). Finally, monopolistic firms are able to set monopolistic prices, higher than competitive prices, and so to secure monopolistic (or super) profits.

Thus the first major structural change which has affected the location of manufacturing within cities during the twentieth century has been the evolution from an industrial capitalist mode of production to a monopoly capitalist one. The latter is one in which the dominant industries in an economy are (implicitly or explicitly) organized by a small number of firms. This change has particularly been associated with the replacement of labour by machinery, the enlarged scale of operation of individual plants and the increasing extent of monopoly power within individual industries (though there do remain some industries which are dominated by small firms and competitive markets).

Some general implications of this evolution can now be noted. The trend to monopolistic control of most industries has freed the firms in those industries from the need to seek out maximum profit locations. In a competitive industry, where profit rates are low and firms can freely enter or leave, plants must be located at or near to profit-maximizing locations, for otherwise they are driven out of business (by negative profits). On the other hand, if prices are set at monopoly levels (so that the average firm in an industry makes the average level of monopoly profit) and there exist barriers to entry, then, while firms still generally aim at maximizing profits, there does exist some freedom of locational choice which is not available to competitive firms: a non-optimum location does not imply bankruptcy but only less-than-average monopoly profits. Furthermore, the spatial expansion of the markets served by plants, which follows from their increasing scale and from falling transport costs, has reduced the extent to which plants serve consumers only in a particular city: plants increasingly sell to many cities rather than to one. This trend implies that the proportion of plants which seek locations from which to serve an urban market cheaply is decreasing, so that the locational significance of the CBD as a point of easy access to the market within a city is diminished. Third, the falling cost of intra-urban transport has freed industry and labour from their earlier need to locate close to each other and has also freed the high commodity-using industries from their close dependence on market or terminal locations. (The rising technical efficiency with which input commodities are processed also helped to reduce the tie of industry to input sites.)

The firms within any one industrial sector are faced with a contradiction. On the one hand, they use monopoly power to keep prices high so that monopoly profits can be made and capital accumulated. On the other, the accumulation of capital in that sector increases the output capacity of those firms and so tends to drive prices down. To some extent monopolists are able to restrict output, but there still exists overcapacity in many sectors of American and British manufacturing (Mandel, 1968, p. 52; Massey and Meegan, 1978). The problem, then, is for monopoly capital to find new ways to invest its accumulated capital profitably and to defend its level of profits. The 2 solutions to this problem which have developed in this century are the search for new markets and the intervention of the state.

The search for new markets takes 2 forms. The first is trade, as the spatial extent of the market is expanded beyond the national boundaries, but this form is of little significance to this chapter. More important is the case in which capital's drive to accumulate takes the form of expanding the sphere of commodity production by the continuous introduction of new commodities, particularly at the expense of the domestic economy (food processing, appliances, radio and television, travel goods). These new commodities give rise to new industries. This expansion of the sphere of commodity production is the second major structural change to affect the location of manufacturing in cities during the era of monopoly capitalism.

A characteristic history of new product development has been identified. When a new product first appears its market is small and firms are uncertain about its market, design and production. Such firms are typically small—or small parts of large firms—and use labour-intensive techniques. If the product is accepted in the market, or well-advertised, 2 developments occur. The market for the commodity begins to grow rapidly as the proportion of households which buy it increases: this is the rapid growth phase of the diffusion of a new product (Beal and Rogers, 1960). At the same time, firms become more skilled at the process of manufacture and, since the market is growing rapidly, profit levels in the new industry rise: individual capitalists can seek to enlarge their share of the market by using the profits to standardize and to increase capital:labour ratios. (Often at this stage, the innovating firms are taken over by a monopolistic conglomerate.) The change from small, labour-intensive plants to larger, capital-intensive factories is confirmed in the history of the radio and clothing industries in New York (Lichtenberg, 1960) and of cheap clothing in London (Luttrell, 1962). The last stage of the production cycle occurs when the market is saturated and growth only occurs as population and wages grow; by now, plants are large and make standardized outputs under capital-intensive conditions at average monopoly rates of profit.

This idea about the product cycle has been associated with a particular hypothesis about the location of new industries within cities—the incubator (or seed-bed) hypothesis. Small-scale and labour-intensive plants in long-established industries are concentrated and centralized within cities to obtain external economies. Since plants in new industries are also small, labour-intensive and may need external economies, Hoover and Vernon (1962) hypothesized that such plants should also concentrate and centralize. In fact, there is no evidence that firms in new industries locate in central areas to any greater extent than elsewhere (Struyk and James, 1975, pp. 109–14). Actually, there exist some differences between the plants in new and in external-economy industries which may account for the failure of the incubator hypothesis. First, new industries must contain a high proportion of novice entrepreneurs, who simply make locational mistakes or (perhaps more commonly) choose the wrong product for their location and talents.

Second, a capitalist who sets up a new clothing plant is guided by existing locational choices whereas no such guidance can be offered to capitalists in new industries. Finally, new industries must contain a high proportion of new capitalists for whom a location near existing business and financial acquaintances may be optimal (Webber, 1972, pp. 106–7). In any event, the product cycle does not begin with factories more centralized than industry as a whole; nor does the central core offer such plants longer life expectancies than prevail in other parts of the city (Leone and Struyk, 1976).

Monopoly capital has also increasingly involved the state in the task of defending its profits and of finding new avenues for investment. Several particular areas of state intervention are significant. The state intervenes in the economy to guarantee monopoly profits by taking over unprofitable basic sectors; refloating enterprises which are in difficulty; transferring public property to private trusts; and providing subsidies (accelerated depreciation, postal rebates, oil depletion allowance) (see Mandel, 1968, pp. 501–7). The state sector expands to absorb the labour that is made redundant by technical change in the monopoly sectors of industry (O'Connor, 1973, pp. 25–9). The state has, particularly since 1945, begun to manage the economy so as to smooth out the fluctuations caused by private production for a public market, though the inflationary price of this management has only recently become clear (Mandel, 1968, pp. 529–34). But for present purposes, the most important role of the state has been in providing new markets for monopoly capital to exploit: 2 markets are particularly significant.

The armaments (and space) market is the one which, over the last 30 years, has provided the guarantee of capitalist expansion (Mandel, 1968, pp. 521–9). As long as there are unused resources in the society, this market tends to stimulate full employment of them (though, again, there is an inflationary price as purchasing power is raised without a corresponding increase of goods on the market). The state has consequently encouraged the expansion of a high-technology monopolistic sector which relies on cost-plus (rather than competitive) pricing. To this extent, the state has increased the number of plants which are highly capitalized and set monopoly prices and thus has enhanced the effects of the first structural change.

The state has also attempted to increase (and to stabilize) demand by establishing high, state-directed levels of investment in housing, urban freeways and transit systems, and automobiles. Beginning in the nineteenth century (Walker, 1978), but particularly since the Second World War, the housing industry has represented a crucial component in the state's attempt to manage the economy (Harvey, 1975b), in both North America and Western Europe (Headey, 1978)—and perhaps also to maintain the level of public support for the existing social and economic system. The provision of large quantities of urban housing at relatively low densities implies high levels of investment in transport infrastructure and automobiles. Therefore, just as the manufacturing sector has expanded over the physical space of cities, so the urban labour force has been required to buy larger amounts of housing and to live at lower densities than formerly: the urban population density gradient flattens as the workforce suburbanizes. According to Mills (1972, p. 49), the average population density gradient in 4 US metropolitan areas fell from 1.22 in 1880 to 0.31 in 1963 (while their populations grew 5-fold on average). Similarly, Schnore and Klaff (1972) show that in American Standard Metropolitan Statistical Areas (SMSAs) central city populations grew by 10.7 per cent in the 1950s and 4.7 per cent in the 1960s whereas the population of non-central city areas grew by 48.6 per cent and 25.5 per cent respectively. This is the third of the major structural changes which have affected the evolution of intra-urban patterns of manufacturing location.

The essential argument is that the evolution of the location of manufacturing activity within cities must be set within the context of the economic history of twentieth century North America and Western Europe. This era of monopoly capitalism was dominated by the effects of the drive of capitalists to accumulate and of the technical conditions of production and transport. These effects are 3:

(a) increasing size of plants and monopolization of many industrial sectors as labour is replaced by capital (and this includes the growth of the arms and space sectors);

(b) the continual introduction of new products as capital seeks new spheres of commodity production; and

(c) high, state-directed levels of investment in housing and transport systems, which have caused the suburbanization of urban workforces.

Locational Implications

These 3 manifestations of the drive to accumulate have, in the context of falling costs of transport within cities, combined to dramatically alter the pattern of location of manufacturing activity in cities by changing the relative attractiveness of different locations. The reduction in intra-urban commodity transport costs, the use of trucks for inter-urban transport and the rising efficiency of materials processing have freed the large-scale materials-intensive industries from their reliance upon inter-urban transport terminals near the central city (though some industries, such as oil refining, are still tied to terminal facilities). At the same time, the standardization of production processes has led to the replacement of labour by capital; part of this process is the use of greater amounts of land per worker to raise the efficiency of materials flows within factories; and the suburbanization of the workforce at low densities has resulted in the use of additional space for parking. Furthermore, as cities have grown in size and people travel more within them, so downtown congestion has been exacerbated and the cost of transporting people and commodities near the CBD has risen sharply in comparison to transport costs elsewhere in the city (Hoover and Vernon, 1962, pp. 34–6). Thus, as the materials-intensive industries were freed from their tie to central terminals and as the labour force and market dispersed to the suburbs, so space needs and congestion operated to push them from central locations. Meanwhile, the urban fringes exhibited 2 attractive features: initially, at least, they were areas of relatively low wages (Hoover and Vernon, 1962, pp. 40–3; Martin, 1966, pp. 44–8) and easily accessible to labour; and they were (and remain) areas of relatively cheap land (Scott, 1980, pp. 90–5). The consequence of this changing balance of locational advantages was that the second and third classes of manufacturing industry (the transport-orientated industries) dispersed towards the edge of the city. (Bluestone and Harrison, 1980, pp. 132–4, also point out that several provisions of the US tax code encourage business to change locations.)

Although the pattern of location of manufacturing as a whole has changed during this century, the first and fourth classes of industry have been less affected. Thus, for example, the noxious industries remain predominantly tied to poorer parts of the city. Similarly, the small-scale labour-intensive industries continue to be highly concentrated and centralized near the core of the city (Scott, 1980, pp. 97–9). In Minneapolis-St Paul in 1965, the central industrial districts contained half the SMSA employment in printing and publishing, but only a fifth of all manufacturing employment (Struyk and James, 1975, pp. 51 and 55); in Boston, the central industrial district contained only 4.6 per cent of the SMSA manufacturing employment in 1965, but 11 per cent of the employment in apparel industries and in printing and publishing (Struyk and James, 1975, pp. 68–73). Steed (1976) produces similar evidence of the concentration of clothing and publishing industries in downtown Toronto and Montreal, while Martin (1966, pp. 160–76) describes the location of the clothing industry in London.

The net effect of these changes seems to have been to make the industrial structures of many areas of the city quite similar. Data from the 1966 journey-to-work census in Sydney report the workforce distribution by 19 industrial groups and 171 districts. The districts were classified (MULT-CLAS) on the basis of the proportion of their workforce in each of the 19 industries. Although 7 groups were formed, 4 were small, including 2 inner city groups (dominated by clothing, and paper and paper products industries), a group of heavy chemicals and textiles districts (Botany) and a specialized petrochemical region (Silverwater). The other 3 groups of districts were poorly differentiated, though 1 identified areas of engineering and vehicles (construction and accessories) employment.

The causes of the evolution of the pattern of location of manufacturing industry must be distinguished from the correlates of that evolution. The drive to accumulate causes: (a) standardized production methods in large plants and a dispersal of the labour force within the context of falling transport costs and these in turn cause (b) the dispersal of manufacturing. On the other hand, several correlates of the dispersal of manufacturing production in cities can be anticipated: expansion of space usage per worker; relative labour shortages in the central city as households suburbanize; land prices in the central city which are too high relative to the benefits of central locations to manufacturers; and the existence of relatively old and congested plants which have not been relocated. The pattern of correlations can be deduced from the pattern of causality; but the correlates are not themselves the cause of dispersal. Two additional correlates of locational change are of particular significance.

This interpretation of the history of manufacturing asserts that relocation of industry is part of the process whereby production methods are standardized. As Table 7.3 illustrates, labour is being replaced by capital in manufacturing as a whole, and relocation is part of this process; but in some industries, production cannot be standardized and remains labour-intensive—such industries continue to locate near the central city. Therefore, there should exist a positive association between the degree of change in the capital:labour ratio in an industry and the reduction in the proportion of that industry's output which is produced in the central city. Scott (1980, pp. 102–6) does indeed find that such an association generally held in Montreal, Toronto and Vancouver during the 1956–74 period.

Although the long-run benefits to a capitalist from standardization and relocation can clearly be identified, nevertheless the short-run costs of the move are also large. Apart from the actual costs of acquiring land, building a new factory and transporting plant and equipment, production costs are also generally higher in a new factory than in an old one, at least for a while. Townroe (1976) estimated components of the cost of relocation by surveying a sample of about 180 factories in England in 1972. Of the managers surveyed, three-fifths agreed that costs of production were initially higher in the new plant than in the old, and over 10 per cent felt that the level of efficiency in the new plant did not reach that in the old until the plant had operated for 2 years. The high initial production costs were ascribed to a high labour turnover ratio (and so high recruitment and training costs and low productivity because of lack of experience), difficulties in finding local suppliers and services, and the start-up costs of running-in new equipment. This fact implies that plants are typically not relocated until they are forced to by lack of space, eviction or operating losses (Cameron and Clark, 1966; Keeble, 1968; Townroe, 1971): of manufacturing plants that relocated from London, expansion of output was cited as a major factor prompting movement of 72 per cent of firms, while site congestion was cited by 55 per cent (Dennis, 1978, p. 71). Although the cause of dispersal is the desire to standardize, the degree of dispersal is correlated with the rates of growth of plants and their managers' complaints about lack of space.

It is now possible to examine the evidence about recent manufacturing changes in cities in the light of this interpretation.

ANALYSIS OF RECENT RELOCATION OF MANUFACTURING

Evidence about the nature, components and correlates of the recent relocation of manufacturing activity in cities has been accumulated in a variety of studies. Most of these studies have examined the superficial correlates rather than the structural causes of locational change (Scott, 1980), but they do indicate the nature of the changes that have occurred recently in the cities of advanced capitalist societies. This evidence is now reviewed in order to provide the context for the operational models presented in the next section. The review has 4 parts: it is introduced by data which describe the magnitude of the recent dispersal of manufacturing activity and which analyse the components of this change (whether due to the closure and opening of plants, relocation, or *in situ* expansion); the correlates of manufacturing change are identified; the results of more sophisticated multiple-equation regression models are presented; and the section concludes with some comments on the implications of the results for operational models.

Components of Change

Manufacturing activity has been decentralizing rapidly in many cities. In 10 large US metropolitan areas, 79 per cent of the SMSA employment growth in manufacturing over the 1959–69 period occurred outside the central cities, compared to only 54 per cent of all employment growth (Hughes, 1974, p. 7). Whereas in 1947 the city of Cleveland contained 83 per cent of its SMSA manufacturing employment, this proportion had fallen to 59 per cent in 1968 (Struyk and James, 1975, p. 35); the corresponding proportions for Minneapolis-St Paul were 86 and 61 per cent, and for Boston, 34 and 29 per cent (Struyk and James, 1975, pp. 53 and 70). In Amsterdam over the 1966–74 period, the number of employees fell by 12 per cent but the number of manufacturing employees fell by 30 per cent (Kruijt, 1979). In Sydney, the inner core lost 31 per cent of its manufacturing employment over the 1968–76 period, while the rest of the metropolitan area lost only 1.7 per cent of its manufacturing jobs; in Melbourne, the core lost 27.5 per cent and the rest gained 3.2 per cent of its jobs in manufacturing (Linge, 1979, pp. 1419–20).

TABLE 7.4 Components of change in manufacturing employment, 4 Standard Metropolitan Statistical Areas, United States, 1965 through 1968

SMSA		1965 employment	Out-moving plants	In-moving plants	Plant openings	Plant closures	*In situ* change	Net change 1965–68
Cleveland	City	187,190	−13,424	8,983	5,084	−16,228	−3,061	−18,646
	Rest	110,802	−3,775	8,259	2,624	−6,864	4,383	4,627
	Total	297,992	−17,199	17,242	7,708	−23,092	1,322	−14,019
Minneapolis-	City	102,335	−9,385	6,621	6,722	−12,922	−6,635	−14,599
St Paul	Rest	49,256	−3,077	5,946	2,575	−4,021	5,218	6,000
	Total	151,591	−12,462	12,567	9,297	−16,943	−1,417	−8,592
Boston	City	92,601	−6,053	3,691	835	−11,570	10,132	−2,965
	Rest	205,517	−7,945	8,609	3,049	−12,324	22,748	14,182
	Total	298,118	−13,998	12,300	3,884	−23,894	32,880	11,217
Phoenix	City	41,063	−1,754	1,659	2,666	−2,292	9,216	9,495
	Rest	11,753	−711	747	3,726	−509	1,573	4,813
	Total	52,816	−2,465	2,406	6,380	−2,801	10,789	14,308

Source: computed from Struyk and James, 1975, pp. 41, 58, 75, 90.

These changes can be analysed into several components. Table 7.4 represents some evidence for US metropolitan areas for the 1965–68 period. In each SMSA, the central cities grew more slowly than the surrounding counties (and, apart from Phoenix, the central cities actually lost jobs). Most central city jobs were lost because of an excess of plant closures over openings (a net loss of 27,700 jobs); the relocation of firms contributed a net loss of 9600 jobs, while *in situ* expansion of plants led to a gain of 9600 jobs. By contrast, the remaining areas of the SMSAs gained jobs by means of *in situ* plant expansion and the balance of immigrant over out-migrant plants, though jobs were lost through an excess of closures over openings. Similar data for Amsterdam are contained in Table 7.5: the old city lost jobs primarily because of the mobility of plants and *in situ* change in employment, whereas the loss due to closures and openings was small. Lloyd (1979) found that job losses in the Merseyside Inner Area from 1966 through 1975 were almost equally due to plant closures/openings and *in situ* labour force

TABLE 7.5 Components of change in manufacturing employment, Amsterdam, 1966 to 1974

Area	1966 Employment	Loss due to out-moves (per cent)	Gain from in-moves (per cent)	Gain from births (per cent)	Loss due to deaths (per cent)	*In situ* change (per cent)	Net change 1966–74 (per cent)
Old city	150,882	−35.9	+14.3	+19.6	−25.6	−17.8	−37
Total	348,515	−26.4	+21.0	+22.7	−22.5	−7.2	−12

Source: Kruijt, 1979, p. 146.

TABLE 7.6 Changes of manufacturing labour force, Sydney and Melbourne, 1969 to 1976

Industry	Sydney					Melbourne				
		1969		1976			1969		1976	
	Jobs	Core as per cent whole	Core per cent change	Rest per cent change	Core as per cent whole	Jobs	Core as per cent whole	Core per cent change	Rest per cent change	Core as per cent whole
Food, beverages	42,509	41	−23	+8	33	40,739	21	−18	+9	17
Textiles	15,422	39	−53	−26	29	21,093	24	−41	+12	16
Clothing, footwear	38,438	54	−42	−32	50	58,788	46	−45	−13	35
Wood products, furniture	18,049	31	−45	+19	17	14,568	15	−25	+4	11
Paper, paper products	36,632	66	−22	+16	56	29,873	43	−9	+4	40
Chemicals, petroleum products	28,726	24	−27	+7	18	20,144	20	−4	−7	20
Non-metallic mineral products	15,961	39	−47	−1	25	11,100	6	−11	−2	5
Basic metal products	12,699	39	−26	+9	30	7,817	21	−1	+21	18
Fabricated metal products	36,493	26	−32	−6	20	32,835	15	−16	+5	13
Transport equipment	41,147	40	−42	0	28	46,888	8	−12	+12	6
Other machinery	80,897	25	−18	−10	23	57,354	14	−32	+2	10
Miscellaneous	27,015	28	−21	+4	23	27,831	20	−34	+8	13
Total	393,988	37	−31	−3	29	369,030	23	−28	+3	17

Source: Linge, 1979, pp. 1419-20.

reductions. In London, plant closures/openings dominated *in situ* changes in plant size (Dennis, 1978, pp. 68–9), which is the opposite of the New Jersey experience (James and Hughes, 1973). Metropolitan areas apparently experience different kinds of manufacturing employment change. Bluestone and Harrison (1980, pp. 24–8) also warn that the data used in these analyses are biased measures of locational change.

An additional way of viewing these changes is presented in Table 7.6, which illustrates the change in location patterns of industries in Sydney and Melbourne. The employment histories of the 2 cities are not very similar: cities' manufacturing location patterns are affected by idiosyncratic as well as common factors. The industries which dispersed least (measured by the ratio of their proportions in the core in 1969 and 1976) were, in Sydney, food and beverages, clothing and footwear, paper and paper products, other machinery, and miscellaneous products; in Melbourne, the less rapidly dispersing group did not include the other machinery and miscellaneous sectors but did include chemicals and petroleum products, non-metallic mineral products, basic metal products, fabricated metal products, and transport equipment. In fact the correlation between the dispersal ratios in the 2 cities is $r < 0.02$. It is necessary to be careful in generalizing from the evidence of a few cities.

Correlates of Change

The pattern of plant relocation does exhibit some regularities. In particular, the relocation of plants is constrained by distance; two-thirds of relocating New Jersey firms chose locations within their county of origin (James and Hughes, 1973), while the proportion of Chicago relocating plants which move a specified distance declines as the logarithm of that distance (Moses and Williamson, 1967). Furthermore, both studies find that distance is a more severe constraint upon the behaviour of small plants than large.

More generally, studies have investigated the characteristics of areas with different employment histories, many by estimating regression equations which purport to predict manufacturing employment change. (Yet the results of such regression analyses are not secure because of multicollinearity: any variable that varies with distance from the city centre will contribute to the explanation of employment change.) Essentially, these analyses imply 2 main propositions (see also Scott, 1980, pp. 89–90). Manufacturing industry leaves central areas because of lack of space (Logan, 1966); traffic congestion (Hoover and Vernon, 1962, pp. 34–5); high wages and labour shortages (Dennis, 1978, p. 71); planning restrictions on industry or lack of permission to develop (Dennis, 1978, p. 71); or high central land prices and taxes (Keeble, 1968). By contrast, manufacturing industry is attracted to

TABLE 7.7 Factors associated with plant relocation or expansion, Chicago, 1950 to 1964

Variable	Density of destinations per unit area for			
	Plants expanding at new locations		Relocating plants	
	Regression coefficient	Standard error	Regression coefficient	Standard error
Distance from Loop	−0.096	0.017	−0.083	0.015
Population density	0.018	0.012	0.015	0.010
Per cent of land in transport	0.767	0.931	0.341	0.819
Presence of highway	0.226	0.161	0.261	0.141
Per cent of land vacant	−0.614	0.862	0.479	0.758
Per cent of land in manufacturing use	−6.801	1.215	4.558	1.068
City of Chicago dummy	0.149	0.246	0.110	0.261
R^2	.247		.215	

Source: Moses and Williamson, 1967, p. 218.

areas accessible to transport and, especially, freeways (Hoover and Vernon, 1962, pp. 34–5; Moses and Williamson, 1967), accessible to labour and having developable land (Moses and Williamson, 1967; Webber and Daly, 1971a). The results of 2 different kinds of study are presented in Tables 7.7 and 7.8.

TABLE 7.8 Survey of firms relocating out of London, 1964 to 1967

Factor	Proportion of firms which claimed that the factor was		
	Major	Minor	Insignificant
Expansion of output	72	11	17
Reorganization of production space	41	18	42
Site congestion	55	8	38
Traffic congestion	8	14	77
Planning permissions	17	5	78
Labour shortages: males	25	13	62
females	35	7	58
skilled	16	10	74

Source: Dennis, 1978, p. 71.

Simultaneous Equation Models

More sophisticated analyses of manufacturing location change recognize that the relocation of manufacturing jobs and of the labour force may be related and investigate these relations in a system of simultaneous equations.

The earliest such model is that of Steinnes and Fisher (1974), for which more complete results were published in Fisher and Fisher (1975). They obtained 1970 data for a sample of 100 corporate suburbs or city neighbour-hoods in the Chicago SMSA. Their results are listed in Table 7.9. In addition to the variables listed, the regression equations included as explanatory variables: median income potential, park employees potential, rapid transit potential and property tax potential of zones, but none of them was significantly associated with employment level. The manufacturing employment equation shows that the amount of manufacturing employment in a zone depends on the number of residents and potential of residents in that zone, on the amount of industrial land and potential of residents in that zone, on the amount of industrial land and (positively) on the corporation tax rate. The residential population equations reveal wide discrepancies between the White and Black populations, with Blacks being relatively excluded from zones which have many jobs whereas Whites are attracted to such zones: residential land, median income, number of park employees, the lake, the elevated subway system and the tax rates all attract residents. The most significant result in Table 7.9 is the effect of manufacturing employment and residential location upon each other.

Steinnes (1977) offers another approach to the same idea (Cooke, 1978, corrects Steinnes' method, but does not affect his conclusion). Using data for 15 US SMSAs and 7 censuses of manufacturing between 1938 and 1972, Steinnes defines

R_T: percentage of SMSA population resident in central city at Tth census;

M_T: percentage of SMSA manufacturing employment located in central city at Tth census;

W: percentage of SMSA population which is White;

T: number of census (1938 census is 1, . . . , 1972 census is 7).

Steinnes estimates that

$$R_T = -0.74 + 0.00036T + 0.00082W + 0.9R_{T-1} - 0.068M_{T-1}$$

with $R^2 = 0.92$ and $|t| > 1.5$ for the coefficients of W, R_{T-1} and M_{T-1};

$$M_T = -2.34 + 0.0012T + 0.0008W + 0.30R_{T-1} + 0.67M_{T-1}$$

with $R^2 = 0.183$ and $|t| > 1.5$ for the coefficients of W, R_{T-1} and M_{T-1}.

TABLE 7.9 Relocation of population and employment, Chicago Standard Metropolitan Statistical Area[a]

Explanatory variable[b]	Dependent variable[b]					
	MFG	NMFG	WWC	WBC	BWC	BBC
WWC	+0.57	+1.62				
WBC		−2.60				
BWC	−6.11	−19.86				
BBC	+3.18	+9.00				
WWC POT		+17.39				
WBC POT		−26.39				
BWC POT	−62.75	−169.47				
BBC POT	+42.55	+91.00				
IND LAND	+0.92					
CORP TAX	+49.18					
HOSPITAL		+1.91				
GHETTO POT		+96.35				
MFG			+0.15	+0.38		−0.08
NMFG			+0.10		−0.01	
NMFG POT			+0.50		−0.33	−0.55
GHETTO			−29.62	−21.61	+15.24	+24.26
COLLEGE				−11.53		
RESID LAND			+0.34	+0.20		+0.06
MEDIAN INC				+0.32		
PARK			+102.63	+69.37		
LAKE					+21.03	+12.51
EL			+39.34		+13.76	+38.01
TAX			+29.33	+17.36		
CORP TAX POT				+108.64		
OLS R^2	0.62	0.64	0.68	0.79	0.72	0.76

[a] Coefficients only included if $|t| > 1.5$; estimates are 3SLS.
[b] Variables: WWC: number of White, white-collar residents
   WBC: number of White, blue-collar residents
   BWC: number of Black, white-collar residents
   BBC: number of Black, blue-collar residents
   IND LAND: thousands of sq ft zoned industrial land
   CORP TAX: corporation tax rate per $US10,000 value
   HOSPITAL: number of people employed in hospitals
   GHETTO: 1 if ghetto in zone, 0 otherwise
   MFG: number of employees in manufacturing
   NMFG: number of employees in non-manufacturing jobs
   COLLEGE: number of college faculty residents
   RESID LAND: thousands of sq ft zoned residential land
   MEDIAN INC.: median income
   PARK: number of park employees
   LAKE: 1 if Lake Michigan in zone, 0 otherwise
   EL: 1 if elevated subway passes through zone, 0 otherwise
   TAX: property tax rate per $US10,000 value
   POT: suffix indicating that the variable is computed as a potential.
Source: Fisher and Fisher, 1975, pp. 266–7.

(Mills, 1972, pp. 53–7, also concludes that 'time' is not strongly associated with locational change.) These results are evidence that manufacturing jobs have followed people to the suburbs but that people have tended to avoid locations with existing manufacturing jobs.

Clearly, little credence should be placed upon the precise size of the regression coefficients computed by Fisher and Fisher (1975) or Steinnes (1977). Both use extremely aggregate measures of location (counties or incorporated suburbs), which imply that regression estimates are unreliable (Webber, 1980b). Fisher and Fisher employ exogenous variables that may be collinear (e.g. median income and the property tax rate); use absolute numbers rather than densities, so that the different sizes of zones influence the regression results; calculate employment and population potentials exogenously rather than within the model and employ numbers of people or employees rather than change in numbers as endogenous variables, so that the significance of such exogenous variables as area of zoned industrial land is unsurprising. Furthermore, Webber and Daly (1971a) indicate that regression estimates are not stable over time.

Commentary

The simultaneous equation regression models do imply that Lowry made a specific error when constructing his model. Whereas Lowry assumed that the location of manufacturing was exogenous and that population follows jobs (via a spatial interaction model), in fact the dependence is mutual: as the structural analysis of the preceding section suggested, the location patterns of populations and of jobs are each dependent on the other. Furthermore, Fisher and Fisher's results imply that the relationship between the locations of people and jobs depends on both race and class—a sophistication that did not enter Lowry's model. Operational land-use models of the Lowry tradition must be adjusted to incorporate these facts.

Evidently, empirical studies of manufacturing location in cities have been conducted at the level of appearances (correlations) rather than at the level of economic structure. No reports have examined the evolution of an industry through the processes of standardization, replacement of labour by capital and increasing use of land per worker, as they are related to locational change within cities. Instead, the factors associated with relation and dispersal have been emphasized, factors that (like locational change itself) are products of the need to accumulate. Therefore, modellers need to observe that the economic environment of manufacturing industry has changed, from the rapid growth era up to the 1960s to the slow growth or declining cities era of the 1970s (Dennis, 1978; Massey and Meegan, 1978; Linge, 1979) and that there is no guarantee that the correlates of locational adjustment will remain stable over this change of environments.

This point is illustrated by a study of job losses in several British industries since the mid-1960s. Massey and Meegan (1978) conclude that jobs were lost primarily because of (a) standardization and scale increases of the kind discussed in the fifth section of this chapter and (b) rationalization and closure of labour-intensive plants in the face of overcapacity. Within any one industry, the locational effect of both processes is dispersal, but their aggregate effect on the location of manufacturing employment as a whole depends on the rate of loss of jobs in the various industries: if the clothing industry in Canada disappears, the central cities will appear to decline industrially, whereas if the electronic or automobile industries disintegrate, the suburbs will appear to decline. The particular factors which are apparently related to the movement of manufacturing thus differ according to the state of the economy and, more fundamentally, the evolution of capitalism; a structural theory (and one, moreover, that is more fully articulated than the version presented in the fifth section) is needed to understand these differences.

Furthermore, there exists little evidence about investment in the locational change of manufacturing activity over business cycles. True, the available data are sparse and difficult to obtain; nevertheless, the success of operational models depends in part on the continuation of the economic conditions under which they were built and calibrated, and the short-run performance of models is affected by cyclical phenomena. Webber and Daly (1971b) claimed that Sydney's industrial growth between 1954 and 1968 consisted of periods of rapid but localized growth, poorly predicted by regression models, which alternated with periods of slow, dispersed growth, well predicted by a regression model; in addition, they identified phases of rapid outward expansion of the zone of maximum employment growth, interspersed by periods during which this zone contracted towards the city centre. Harrison (1974) has also shown that rates of suburbanization of population and manufacturing employment in US SMSAs appear to behave cyclically. This claim is speculative because the period was short; but the understanding of such dynamics would enlarge the scope of operational models to short-term industrial change in cities, and offers the possibility of integrating the dynamics of industrial change with analysis of speculative booms in the urban environment (a task which Walker, 1978, has begun).

This review has provided several comments on the relation between studies of the location of manufacturing in cities and operational urban modelling. A specific error of Lowry's has been identified (that the location of manufacturing activity is independent of the distribution of the workforce). Several of the correlates of manufacturing change have been identified, and these may be used to construct an operational model of manufacturing location which is within the Lowry tradition, though the results of Webber and Daly (1971a) and Massey and Meegan (1978) warn that such models are unlikely to be stable over changes in the economic environment. The structural analysis of the preceding section suggests ways in which urban modelling may be adapted to reflect long-run causal forces rather than mere correlates of change. There also arises the intriguing possibility of investigating the short-term dynamics of manufacturing change by means of operational models, but this remains speculation at this point.

OPERATIONAL MODELS OF MANUFACTURING LOCATION

There already exist several operational models which purport to predict the location of manufacturing in cities. Perhaps the most famous of these is EMPIRIC, a simultaneous equation regression model (Hill, 1965); other models include LINTA (Seidman, n.d.; Goldberg, 1967). Putman (1972) has reviewed a large number of these models and Pack (1978) comments on their use. However, such models are not situated within the context of an explicit theory of commodity production and do not reflect the historical perspective on the geography of manufacturing which was developed in the fifth section; accordingly, these existing models are not reviewed here. Instead, this section first summarizes the argument so far as a set of principles to govern the construction of an operational model; next, it presents an input-output model of a (non-spatial) economy and briefly describes some of its properties; then a method of disaggregating the model by zones and of incorporating other effects of space is introduced; and finally an operational model form is built on to the spatially disaggregated input-output model. The development is informal: proofs are not offered nor are explicit solutions discussed, because the general nature of the model is more important than its specific form. It is also emphasized that the final model presented is large and unwieldy, and is operational in form only; its purpose, however, is to coordinate the ideas which were developed in the previous sections of this chapter, to direct research into the dynamics of manufacturing change and to offer a basis for theoretical analysis of the location of industry in cities.

Three distinctions which have been drawn in this chapter are fundamental to the model developed now. The first section distinguished applied models (used in planning) and scientific models; applied models must be *status quo* ones, in the sense that they assume that existing trends continue. At several points, the neo-classical tradition of social theory, which emphasizes the role of individual decision-makers, is distinguished from structural theories, in which individual businesses and households are regarded as subordinate to the social and economic structure. In the fifth section, a distinction is maintained between studies which analyse the correlates of locational change and those which investigate the causes of that change. Generally, existing models fall into the categories of applied, neo-classical and correlation models but, as the previous section warns, they cannot guarantee that the relations upon which they were calibrated will continue if the environmental conditions change. The model presented in this section is therefore a causal one in which urban structure is determined by the social and economic conditions of society and in which the role of individuals (and in particular of individuals' tastes) is secondary to the role of the production sector. Furthermore, as the first section requires, the model is specific to commodity capitalist economies and assumes as a guiding principle that the rate of accumulation is maximized; however, the role of the state is ignored. The particular details of the manner in which the model is constructed follow the guidelines outlined in the fourth section: a 2-step information minimizing location model which links the aggregate urban economy to the locational characteristics of industries.

Aspatial Input-output Model

Consider, first, a static, non-spatial economic system which is at equilibrium. There are I commodities, labelled $1, 2, \ldots, I$, produced by means of production which use other commodities and labour. Production methods in each industry are technologically fixed and independent of scale. Since the system is at equilibrium, the rate of profit π on advanced capital is the same for all industries; similarly, only one class of labour power is presumed to exist, paid a money wage w. Let a_{ij} denote the amount of commodity i that is used up in the production of one unit of commodity j (this term measures the amount of materials purchased for use in current production); γ_i denote the amount of labour power used to produce one unit of commodity i; P_i denote the price of commodity i.

The price of a commodity i includes several elements. The first element is the expense of material inputs per unit of commodity i, which is

$$\sum_{j=1}^{I} P_j a_{ji}.$$

Second, the price of commodity i must include a payment for the labour power used to produce a unit of the commodity, namely $w\gamma_i$. Finally, it is assumed that both labourers and input suppliers are paid before the returns from production are realized, so that wages and input payments are a capital cost which earn a profit equal to π times the expenditure. (The assumption that a profit is earned on wages advanced distinguishes this model from Sraffa, 1960, and from the model employed by A. J. Scott, 1976, 1979.) Observe that the model assumes that production uses no fixed capital which lasts more than one production period. Thus:

$$P_i = \left(\sum_{j=1}^{I} P_j a_{ji} + w\gamma_i \right)(1 + \pi) \qquad \text{for } i = 1, 2, \ldots, I. \tag{7.16}$$

The composition of the wage can also be expressed in terms of the commodities produced in the system. Let λ_j denote the physical quantity of commodity j consumed by a unit of labour power per unit of time. Then the wage rate must satisfy:

$$w = \sum_{j=1}^{I} P_j \lambda_j. \tag{7.17}$$

Equations (7.16) and (7.17) comprise a set of $I+1$ linear equations. There exist $I+2$ unknown quantities, namely $P_1, P_2, \ldots, P_I, \pi$, and w, whereas the coefficients (a_{ij}, γ_i and λ_i) are presumed to be known. The system is solved in the following manner. Substitute (7.17) into (7.16):

$$\begin{aligned} P_i &= (1 + \pi)\left(\sum_{j=1}^{I} P_j a_{ji} + \gamma_i \sum_{j=1}^{I} P_j \lambda_j \right) \\ &= (1 + \pi) \sum_{j=1}^{I} P_j (a_{ji} + \gamma_i \lambda_j) \qquad \text{for } i = 1, 2, \ldots, I. \end{aligned} \tag{7.18}$$

For brevity, equation (7.18) is rewritten as

$$P_i = \sum_{j=1}^{I} z_{ji} P_j, \qquad z_{ji} = (1 + \pi)(a_{ji} + \gamma_i \lambda_j),$$

the solution of which may be expressed in matrix notation as

$$(\mathbf{Z} - \mathbf{I})\mathbf{P} = \mathbf{0}, \tag{7.19}$$

$$\mathbf{P} = \begin{pmatrix} P_1 \\ P_2 \\ \vdots \\ P_I \end{pmatrix}, \qquad \mathbf{0} = \begin{pmatrix} 0 \\ 0 \\ \vdots \\ 0 \end{pmatrix}, \qquad \mathbf{Z} - \mathbf{I} = \begin{pmatrix} z_{11} - 1 & z_{21} & \cdots & z_{I1} \\ z_{12} & z_{22} - 1 & \cdots & z_{I2} \\ \vdots & \vdots & & \vdots \\ z_{1I} & z_{2I} & \cdots & z_{II} - 1 \end{pmatrix}.$$

The system of equations (7.19) has a solution $\mathbf{P}$ (not all equal to zero) if and only if $|\mathbf{Z} - \mathbf{I}| = 0$. Two points should be noted in this regard: (a) if $\mathbf{P}$ solves equation (7.19), so does $k\mathbf{P}$, for any constant k—that is the system is determinate only up to proportional prices; (b) there may be several linearly independent sets of prices which solve the system.

The economic system is meaningful only if it yields prices which are positive, and can exist in the long run only if $\pi > 0$. If $\mathbf{P} > \mathbf{0}$, then it must be for each i that

$$z_{ii} < 1,$$

which implies that

$$\pi < \frac{1 - a_{ii} - \gamma_i \lambda_i}{\gamma_i \lambda_i} \qquad \text{for all } i. \tag{7.20}$$

This condition sets an upper limit on the rate of profit. (There may, however, be several $\pi > 0$ for which equation (7.19) has a solution with $\mathbf{P} \geq \mathbf{0}$.)

Additional macro-economic relationships can now be specified for this model. If X_i denotes the physical quantity of output of commodity i, then total wages paid in the system are

$$W = w \sum_{i=1}^{I} \gamma_i X_i \tag{7.21}$$

and profits are

$$\pi = \sum_{i=1}^{I} \left(P_i - w\gamma_i - \sum_{j=1}^{I} P_j a_{ji} \right) X_i, \tag{7.22}$$

whence total urban income is

$$I = W + \pi. \tag{7.23}$$

If I is set at some given level (say, $I = I^*$), then this fact serves to determine prices uniquely (see also Scott, 1976, p. 339); other postulates of invariance include the selection of one commodity (usually a 'luxury good') as numéraire (Sweezy, 1942, p. 109), the equality of total value of output and total price of output (Winternitz, 1948) and the equality of total value of surplus and total (money) profit (Meek, 1956).

To determine levels of output, additional relations must be specified. Equation (7.17) defines the wage rate in terms of consumption per unit of labour power, with λ_j the consumption of commodity j per unit of labour power. But the total quantity of labour power used is

$$\sum_{i=1}^{I} \gamma_i X_i$$

as in equation (7.21); therefore the total consumption of commodity j by the workers is

$$C_j = \lambda_j \sum_{i=1}^{I} \gamma_i X_i, \qquad j = 1, 2, \ldots, I. \tag{7.24}$$

Finally, it must be that the total quantity of each commodity used equals the total quantity produced:

$$X_j = C_j + \sum_{i=1}^{I} a_{ji}X_i, \qquad j = 1, 2, \ldots, I. \tag{7.25}$$

In this equation, C_j is final demand and

$$\sum_{i=1}^{I} a_{ji}X_i$$

denotes the use of commodity j to produce the other commodities $i = 1, 2, \ldots, I$.

This simple model, equations (7.16), (7.17), (7.21)–(7.25), is modified from a model used by Johansen (1963) who shows that the system satisfies some Marxist propositions about the organic composition of capital. It is also evident that in this model, the consumption characteristics of workers (or, for that matter, of capitalists, if the model distinguished them) do not affect the prices of commodities, for the equations (7.16) and (7.17) are a determinate (up to a proportionality constant) subset of the whole system.

Spatial Input-output Model

As it stands, this first system is far too simple to be used in operational modelling. The first step in adapting it is to introduce the dimension of space, which requires that several changes be made to the model.

First, there must exist a commodity called transport, which is the $i = 1$ commodity. The price of this commodity, per unit of commodity i shifted from location m to location n is P_{1imn}. The price of transport satisfies the same relation as the price of any other commodity, equation (7.16).

Second, it must be explicitly recognized that land is used in the production process and that part of the surplus is paid to landlords as rent. Let r_m denote the price of land per unit area at location m in the city, and L_i the quantity of land used per unit of output of commodity i. It is presumed that the payment to landlords is, like other payments, made before the commodity is sold, whence the cost of the land component of the price of commodity i produced at location m is $(1 + \pi)r_m L_i$.

Third, prices and wages vary over space. Prices vary because transport costs must be added to the mill price of the commodity: the price of commodity i at location m delivered from location n is

$$P_{inm} = P_{in*} + P_{1inm},$$

where P_{in*} is the mill price of commodity i at location n. The price of labour varies over the city because some job locations are on average more accessible than others and hence cost less in commuting; w_m is the price of labour power at location m. It is also true that the wage must include payments not only for the commodities consumed, but also for commuting (P_{1wmn}) and for the land used in housing ($r_n L_w$).

And, finally, we must recognize that the urban economy is not closed: there are imports and exports. The rest of the world is denoted as zone number $n = 0$, and the cost of transport to the rest of the world from zone m is regarded as equal to the cost of transport from zone m to the edge of the city: P_{1im0}. The edge of the city is also the point at which the prices in the rest of the world are computed.

As a result of these changes, equation (7.16) must be revised to

$$P_{im*} = (1 + \pi) \left(\sum_{j=1}^{I} \sum_{n=0}^{M} p_{jnm} a_{jim} + w_m \gamma_i + r_m L_i \right) \tag{7.26}$$

for $i = 1, 2, \ldots, I$ and $m = 1, 2, \ldots, M$, with

$$P_{jnm} = P_{jn*} + P_{1jnm}. \tag{7.27}$$

For the transport commodity, the price does not include a payment for land since land is usually provided free to private transport companies in a city—

$$P_{1inm} = (1 + \pi) \left(\sum_{j=1}^{I} \sum_{l=0}^{M} P_{jln} a_{j1ln} + w_n \gamma_i \right). \tag{7.28}$$

Corresponding to equation (7.17) is the wage rate for labour power which works in zone m:

$$w_m = \sum_{j=1}^{I} P_{j**} \lambda_j + P_{1w*m} + r_* L_w, \tag{7.29}$$

where $*$ indicates that the corresponding variable is given a value which is averaged over the city: P_{j**} is the average price of commodity j in the city, P_{1w*m} is the average cost of commuting to zone m and r_* is the average price of land.

The system of equations (7.26)–(7.29) must also satisfy a land constraint, that the allocation of workers, transport and production to zones does not exceed the land available. This constraint may be written:

$$A_m \geq N_m L_w + \sum_{i=1}^{I} L_i \sum_{n=0}^{M} X_{imn}, \tag{7.30}$$

where N_m is the quantity of labour power which resides in zone m and X_{imn} is the amount of commodity i produced in zone m and shipped to zone n.

The system (7.26)–(7.30) consists of many equations and variables. The M equations in (7.20) serve to determine the wage rate (money price of labour power) at each location and the IM^2 equations in (7.28) determine the transport rates. Equation (7.26) contains IM equations and the following variables: the materials input coefficients (a_{ijmn}, which are known), the labour power input coefficients (γ_i, also known), and the land input coefficients (known); the prices of imports (P_{j0m}, which are assumed to be known); and $IM + M + 1$ unknown variables—the prices (P_{im*}), profit rate (π) and land prices (r_m). (The prices of transport and the wage rate can be substituted from equations (7.28) and (7.27).) Although there are $M + 1$ more variables than equations, the system must satisfy the constraints that:

$$P_{im*} \geq 0 \qquad i = 1, 2, \ldots, I; \quad m = 1, 2, \ldots, M$$

$$w_m \geq 0 \qquad m = 1, 2, \ldots M$$

$$\pi \geq 0$$

$$r_m \geq 0 \qquad m = 1, 2, \ldots, M.$$

(a total of $(I+2)M + 1$ constraints).

The division of the urban income into its components can be determined. The total wage is (if $X_{im*} = \sum_{n=0}^{M} X_{inm}$)

$$W = \sum_{i=1}^{I} \sum_{m=1}^{M} X_{im*} \gamma_i w_n; \tag{7.31}$$

rent from production is

$$R = \sum_{i=1}^{I} \sum_{m=1}^{M} X_{im*} r_n L_i; \tag{7.32}$$

and total profit is

$$\pi = \sum_{i=1}^{I} \sum_{m=1}^{M} X_{im*} \left(P_{im*} - w_m \gamma_i - r_m L_i - \sum_{j=1}^{I} \sum_{n=0}^{M} P_{jnm} a_{jinm} \right); \tag{7.33}$$

whence

$$I = W + R + \pi,$$

a condition that can, as before, be used to scale prices, profit and rent. The total consumption of commodity j by the labour force is

$$C_j = \lambda_j \sum_{i=1}^{I} \sum_{m=1}^{M} X_{im*} \gamma_i. \tag{7.34}$$

The equality of production and consumption must now recognize the existence of imports and exports, whence

$$X_j = C_j + \sum_{i=1}^{I} \sum_{m=1}^{M} X_{im*} \sum_{n=1}^{M} a_{jinm} + \sum_{m=1}^{M} X_{jm0} - \sum_{m=1}^{M} X_{j0m}, \tag{7.35}$$

for $j = 1, 2, \ldots, I$. In equation (7.35), the first term represents the final demand within the city, the second measures the use of the commodity in production, the third denotes exports and the fourth imports. (This equation applies also to the transport sector.)

The system of equations (7.26)–(7.35) represents a formal spatial disaggregation of the initial equilibrium model, equations (7.16)–(7.25). Although the system now approaches a form in which it can be used for operational urban modelling, nevertheless several deficiencies remain. In the first place, the I equations of (7.35) do not serve to choose production levels within the city (for there are IM values of X_{im*}): some means must be found whereby the aggregate production levels can be spatially disaggregated. Similarly, it has been assumed that the technical coefficients a_{ijmn} are known; in fact, it may reasonably be supposed that the aspatial coefficients a_{ij} can be found, but the inter-zonal trading disaggregation of the coefficients should be determined in the model. Third, some means must be found of determining the spatial distribution of labour power, which has so far been assumed to be given. Finally in this static form, the model is incapable of expressing some of the inter-temporal relations in production: for example, the profit on this year's production is used to expand the sphere of commodity production and to change the techniques of production. (Other necessary features of an urban model, such as spatial and inter-industry differences in profit rates and fluctuations in profit rates over time, are too complex and too poorly understood to be included in this first attempt at an operational, spatially disaggregated model of production.)

Operational Model of Manufacturing

We begin by assuming that at each point in time, the system satisfies equations like (7.26)–(7.35) and that at some initial time t the system is given and known. Over the period t to $t+1$ the exogenous parameters (i.e. those outside the direct control of the city system) change in some known way and the previous period's surplus is invested. At the end of the period, the city again satisfies equations like (7.26)–(7.35), but with new prices, production levels, profits, wages, rents and spatial distributions of output and labour power. The changes are predicted using information minimizing methods.

Let X_{****} denote the total output of all commodities in the city. Since outputs of different industries are being summed, they must be expressed in similar units; one possibility is to measure output in market prices, but this presumes that prices are known rather than determined in the model; more satisfactory, therefore, is to measure the value of a commodity as the (socially necessary) labour-time expended on its production. (The nature of this definition is explored by Sweezy, 1942, pp. 28–34.) Then for each $i = 1, 2, \ldots, I$, X_{i***} is the value of commodity i produced in the city (or imported), X_{i*mn} is the value of commodity i produced at location m and shipped to place n, and X_{ijmn} is the value of commodity i produced at m and shipped to place n for use in producing commodity j. Evidently,

$$X_{****} = \sum_{i=1}^{I} X_{i***} \qquad X_{i***} = \sum_{m=0}^{M} X_{i*m*}$$

$$X_{i*m*} = \sum_{n=0}^{M} X_{i*mn} \qquad X_{i*mn} = \sum_{j=0}^{I} X_{ijmn}.$$

The system can be built up in the following manner. The prices of commodities, the wage rate, rents and profit are all determined in equations (7.26)–(7.29), depending on the technical coefficients at time t. In fact, the inter-industry technical coefficients $a_{ij}(t)$ are regarded as known, but the inter-zonal component of the coefficients $a_{ijmn}(t)$ depends on trading relations within the city, for

$$a_{ijmn}(t) = X_{ijmn}(t)/X_{j***}(t) \tag{7.36}$$

$$a_{ij}(t) = \sum_{m=0}^{M} \sum_{n=0}^{M} a_{ijmn}(t),$$

whence the inter-zonal flows must satisfy

$$\sum_{m=0}^{M} \sum_{n=0}^{M} X_{ijmn}(t) = a_{ij}(t) X_{j***}(t), \tag{7.37}$$

and the full set of technical coefficients (a_{ijmn}) can only be determined when the X_{ijmn} are known. They, in turn, must satisfy

$$\sum_{j=1}^{I} \sum_{m=1}^{M} \sum_{n=0}^{M} X_{ijmn}(t) = X_{i***}(t) \qquad i = 1, 2, \dots, I. \tag{7.38}$$

The total quantities $X_{i***}(t)$ of each commodity produced at time t can be obtained from the input-output equations (7.35) and the consumption equation (7.34), again as a function of the variables which measure the location of production and the inter-zonal inter-industry technical coefficients. There remain, then, 2 sets of variables which must be explicitly modelled, namely the locations and inter-zonal flows of commodities and of labour. In addition, since this is a dynamic model, the uses of $\pi(t)$ must be accounted for.

First denote by $N_{mn}(t)$ the quantity of labour power that resides in place m and works in place n at time t. This quantity must satisfy the following relations: the amount of labour power used at place m is determined as

$$N_{m*} = \sum_{n=1}^{M} N_{nm} \tag{7.39}$$

where

$$N_{m*} = \sum_{i=1}^{I} X_{i*m*}\gamma_i;$$

the expenditure on commuting is given as

$$\bar{c}_w = \sum_{m=1}^{M} \sum_{n=1}^{N} N_{mn}P_{1wmn}, \tag{7.40}$$

and the wage rate at zone m must compensate for the aggregate commuting costs of the workers there—

$$w_m = w + P_{1w*m}, \tag{7.41}$$

where w is the spatially invariant wage rate net of commuting costs. These 3 equations (7.39)–(7.41) must remain true at all times t, though the quantities $N_{m*}(t)$, $X_{i*m*}(t)$, $\gamma_i(t)$, $c_w(t)$, $P_{1wmn}(t)$ and $w_m(t)$ may all evolve over time. Not only must $N_{mn}(t)$ satisfy these conditions, but also the investment in changing the pattern of residences must not exceed the part of the profit devoted to changing the urban form:

$$\sum_{m=1}^{M} P_{1m}^m |N_{m*}(t) - N_{m*}(t+1)| \leqslant \pi^1, \tag{7.42}$$

where P_{1m}^m is the cost of investing or disinvesting per unit of labour power entering or leaving zone m. The constraint on land uses, equation (7.30) must also be satisfied.

The particular values of $N_{mn}(t)$ are chosen to be minimally biased compared to a prior probability which reflects additional special information about the system (such as the lack of residentially zoned land in some parts of the city), while satisfying the constraints (7.30) and (7.39)–(7.42). The choice is information minimizing subject to the given data, and the prediction $N_{mn}(t+1)$ depends on the presumed spatial distribution of commodity production and demands for labour $(N_{m*}(t+1))$ and on the investment in residential change (π^1); thus denote the prediction by $N_{mn}[t+1; N_{m*}(t+1), \pi^1(t)]$.

The values of the spatially distributed production levels are chosen similarly. Equation (7.37) requires that the inter-zonal and inter-regional production levels satisfy the technical demands of production, and equation (7.38) that the location and quantity of trade flows must satisfy total production levels. Constraint (7.30) must also be satisfied. Finally, the degree of change in production levels from one period to the next must be paid for out of last period's profits:

$$\sum_{j=1}^{I} \sum_{m=1}^{M} P_{1jm}^m |X_{j*m*}(t) - X_{j*m*}(t+1)| \leqslant \pi^2. \tag{7.43}$$

Given these conditions $X_{ijmn}(t+1)$ is chosen to be information minimizing compared to a prior distribution which reflects particular details about the urban area (such as the legal exclusion of industry from particular areas). The model then predicts values of

$$X_{ijmn}[t+1; \pi^2(t)].$$

The model must also account for the distribution of the last period's profit. Two uses of this profit have been noted—to change the residential pattern and to change the spatial pattern (and quantity) of production in the system:

$$\pi(t+1) = \pi^1(t+1) + \pi^2(t+1).$$

These expenditures must be explicitly accounted for in the input-output equations (7.35) as demands for the output of the construction and capital goods industries, in order that those equations reflect the central dynamic of capitalism—change by distribution of the surplus. The remaining free variables are $\pi^1(t)$ and $\pi^2(t)$, which are chosen by embedding the model in a mathematical programme: choose $\pi^1(t)$ to maximize $\pi(t+1)$, an objective which reflects the orientation of the capitalist system.

The model is now mathematically closed.

CONCLUSION

This chapter has examined a theme which is fundamental to Marxist thought—the relation between analysis at the level of appearances and analysis at the level of structural causes. The theme is discussed by juxtaposing 2 geographic research traditions, of operational modelling and of intra-urban manufacturing location. It has been argued that operational urban models work at the level of appearances of phenomena and that even at that level they ignore much evidence which has accumulated about industrial locational change. Although such operational models may be used in applied planning work to predict the evolution of urban areas in the short run, nevertheless they are incapable of analysing changes which occur in the long run (when the economic structure changes) and they cannot be used to inform us about the 'deeper' structure of cities. Therefore, a particular operational model has been proposed which is consistent with a structural view of the way cities work and which incorporates the ideas that production is for profit and profit is for expanded reproduction. In this sense, the chapter provides an example of the argument of Sayer (1976).

The operational model of the location of manufacturing in urban areas enables the dynamics of a spatially distributed commodity production system to be examined in a way consistent with existing aggregate models of an economy and with ideas about the distribution of activities in urban areas.

The model is at once cumbersome, for it has many variables and has lost the independence of prices and quantities which characterized the first equilibrium model, yet at the same time simplistic in its representation of the urban economy. Nevertheless the model does recognize the central issues raised in the previous review of the literature—that the locations of labour and of production are interdependent and that the evolution of their locations arises directly from the central force of the capitalist system (the drive to accumulate). The model also provides a framework within which some important questions can be analysed: about the relationship between technical progress (as measured by changes in a_{ij} and γ_i), profits and the spatial organization of the city; and about the patterns of investment over economic cycles (as profit rates change in different industries). To investigate these questions, this model must first be analysed formally to determine its solution properties, and extended to accommodate spatial and temporal fluctuations in profit rates. A capital goods industry must also be explicitly included if the problem of the urban built environment is to be investigated. Although the model clearly cannot be operationalized in this form, it does potentially enable important urban issues to be treated formally.

The model satisfies several principles. It is historically specific—to an advanced capitalist economy, in which production of commodities dominates the system, and in which the system as a whole is driven by the need for private profit. It emphasizes structures and constraints rather than individual decisions. Although profits are maximized globally, it is not necessarily true that each individual location and production decision is profit maximizing *ex post*, because of uncertainty and because of the fact that decisions are interdependent (outcomes are social). The model also emphasizes production requirements rather than consumer demands: for example, prices are independent of consumption characteristics. Of course, the model remains rudimentary, particularly in its relation to prior theory, but it does indicate that dynamic, causal models of the urban economy can be constructed.

Spatial Analysis, Industry and the Industrial Environment. Vol. 3 Regional Economies and Industrial Systems
Edited by F. E. I. Hamilton and G. J. R. Linge

Chapter 8

An Input-output Framework for Measuring Economic Impacts: A Case Study of the Aluminium Industry at Gladstone, Australia

T. D. MANDEVILLE

The past decade has witnessed an increasing desire on the part of government and industry to assess the impact of new developments on host regions. Most new projects in Australia now require an Environmental Impact Assessment and recently governments have shown more interest in possessing information on the potential economic effects of new developments. Ideally this information should present a blueprint of the expected structure of the regional economy following the establishment of a new industry. This information is important for planning and decision-making at all levels, enabling business and government to perceive the magnitude of eventual effects, including likely gaps in both industry requirements and the provision of associated services.

At the local and regional level, information relating to the economic impact of major projects has generally not been available and this has made it difficult to develop a consistent approach to regional economic planning. Where the size or the importance of the impacting agent warrants serious attention, regional Keynesian multipliers, economic base multipliers or input-output multipliers can be developed. Of these 3 models, input-output is by far the most powerful technique. Input-output economics involves dividing the economy of an area into industrial groupings (sectors) and tracing the transaction flows in dollars between the sectors for a given year. Once the flows or transactions table has been compiled, simple mathematical transformations can be made to derive output, income and employment multipliers for each sector in the economy. The multipliers allow the analyst to determine the economic impact (in terms of industry output, income to households, and employment) resulting from a given economic stimulus in a particular year. The model can also be adapted to examine the impact on an area of a new firm or industry.

Input-output analysis is potentially a useful descriptive device and a flexible analytical technique. In practice, the time and expense required to construct survey-based tables have restricted the use of this methodology to 'research' rather than operational applications. Certainly input-output techniques appear to have played a relatively insignificant part in most regional planning decisions made by government, largely because of the inability of analysts to produce input-output tables in the time-span within which most decisions must be made. Recent work at the University of Queensland has altered this situation, thereby laying the groundwork for the case study presented here. This prior work (Jensen et al., 1979) involved the development of a methodology termed the Generation of Regional Input-Output Tables (GRIT) system, which provides the facility for users to develop holistically accurate regional input-output tables at relatively low cost. Although GRIT was originally formulated for the Queensland state government, it is now being utilized by planning authorities in South Australia, the Northern Territory and Victoria (West et al., 1979, 1980).

This chapter has 3 objectives. First, it provides some background to why the aluminium industry is becoming increasingly attracted to Australia in general and to the Gladstone region in particular. Second, a methodological framework for the analysis of the economic impact of new industry by means of input-output models is presented. Third, the methodology is applied to the case of an aluminium smelter presently under construction at Gladstone. Much of this material is fully documented in Mandeville and Jensen (1978a,b).

ALUMINIUM IN AUSTRALIA

The production of aluminium has 3 distinct phases: mining of bauxite, industrial refining of bauxite to produce alumina, and industrial smelting of alumina to produce the metal aluminium. The world aluminium industry exhibits a high degree of vertical integration and concentration of ownership, a pattern which is reflected in the Australian context. (Technological and informational reasons for this are discussed in Stuckey, 1979, while a full description of the Australian aluminium industry occurs in Australia, Department of Industry and Commerce, 1979a.)

Australia has the world's largest bauxite mining industry, accounting for about 30 per cent of total world production. The 4 alumina refineries currently operating in Australia supply about half the world trade in alumina. Historically, the major international aluminium companies have regarded Australia as an important supplier of raw materials for smelter operations located close to the major markets in North America and Western Europe. Thus Australia's current smelting capacity is small by world standards: 3 smelters with a combined annual capacity of 280,000 tonnes account for about 2 per cent of existing world primary aluminium capacity.

TABLE 8.1 Australia's aluminium production capacity and projected expansion, 1979

Smelter	Capacity (000 tonnes)	Start-up date
Existing		
Comalco—Bell Bay	112	
Alcoa—Point Henry	100	
Alcan—Kurri Kurri	68	
	Total 280	
Expansions of existing capacity		
Alcoa—Point Henry	57	1981
Alcan—Kurri Kurri	22	1981
	Total 359	
Committed/final feasibility		
Comalco—Gladstone	412	1982
Alcoa—Portland	120	1983
Alumax—Newcastle	236	mid-1980s
Pechiney—Newcastle	220	1983
Alcan—Gladstone	100	1983
Nabalco	150	
Total capacity	1597	

Sources: Australia, Department of Industry and Commerce, 1979b, p. 15; pers. comm., Comalco Ltd.

Recently, however, Australia has come to be seen as an increasingly attractive location for aluminium smelting plants. Table 8.1 indicates that the proposed expansion of existing smelters plus no fewer than 6 new smelters planned or under construction, an extraordinarily large addition in worldwide terms, will bring annual capacity to 1.6 million tonnes, or over 10 per cent of present world capacity by the mid to late 1980s. Most of this output will be available for export as domestic consumption of alumina should account for only 259,000 tonnes by 1985 (Australia, Department of Industry and Commerce, 1979a, p. 33). Reasons for this massive influx of industrial capacity to Australia need to be considered, albeit briefly.

Electricity costs are the prime factor affecting the location of energy-intensive aluminium smelting plants. Thus the rise in global energy prices beginning in 1973 has shifted the comparative advantage of aluminium smelter location to countries which have competitively priced and abundant energy resources for power generation. The main contenders for new smelter plants became Australia, Malaysia, Indonesia, Brazil, Venezuela, and some Middle East nations (*Australian Financial Review,* 7 June 1979). Australia's massive and readily accessible steaming coal reserves enable thermally generated power to be supplied at competitive rates for the production of aluminium. Elementary principles of location theory would suggest that the influence of rising energy prices on transport costs also makes Australia, with large bauxite reserves and an established alumina industry, more attractive for the location of further aluminium smelters. Location of smelting plants near the raw material source reduces the bulk of the product which has to be transported to the markets.

Information economics literature (e.g. Lamberton, 1971) provides a clue to a further closely related factor encouraging smelter location in Australia. International organizations responsible for further aluminium smelting investment decisions are already present domestically via their existing bauxite, alumina and smelting operations. Australia is thus a known and reliable location for the aluminium industry, lacking the costs of the uncertainties in many alternative countries with cheap energy resources. Once a few new smelter decisions are made, the bandwagon effect of locational interdependence helps attract others. During the brief period 1978 to 1980 decisions were made by international consortia concerning the 6 new smelters referred to in Table 8.1.

Political and economic stability plus government policy which actively encourages foreign investment and export-orientated manufacturing industry are further related factors encouraging the location of new aluminium smelting capacity in Australia (Study Group on Structural Adjustment [the Crawford Report], 1979; Australia, Department of Industry and Commerce, 1979a). The state governments, which have responsibility for the provision of infrastructure, are also keen to attract large-scale industrial developments, and the Australian press abounds with rumours that some very generous terms for electricity provision have been offered to aluminium producers (e.g. *The National Times* [Sydney], 16 December 1978; *Australian Financial Review*, 7 August 1979).

Environmental pressures are another factor discouraging the location of further smelting facilities in densely populated Western Europe, US and Japan. Countries with space available for industrial development away from population centres and those with less stringent environmental regulations obtain a locational advantage for new heavy industry. Environmentalists in Australia are now questioning, however, whether the proposed massive expansion of aluminium smelting capacity is in the nation's best interest (*Courier Mail* [Brisbane], 2 June 1980; *Sydney Morning Herald,* 9 October 1979).

Those factors helped to determine the location of new smelters, but the market outlook for aluminium in the 1980s triggered the rush to build them. Aluminium producers are forecasting a global production shortfall of 3 to 6 million tonnes by the late 1980s (*Australian Financial Review*, 7 June 1979; *The Australian*, 5–6 May 1979). Paradoxically, energy prices are helping to stimulate demand for the product of this energy-intensive industry. Energy conservation measures are resulting in the increasing substitution of light-weight aluminium for steel by such users as the automotive and aircraft industries. Solar collectors also incorporate aluminium in their design.

While the above remarks reflect the situation up to mid-1980, the subsequent decline in the world economy has depressed the outlook for aluminium. Concomitantly the recent fall in oil prices, as well as management problems within major electricity generating authorities, have eroded Australia's comparative advantage for the location of new aluminium smelting plants. These factors have meant that most of the plans for new aluminium smelters in Australia have been shelved.

Gladstone as a Site for Smelting

Two of Australia's 6 proposed smelters (the Comalco and Alcan projects) were planned to be located at Gladstone (see Figure 17.1), an industrial centre with a population of around 20,000 about 450 km north of Brisbane in Queensland. (However, the Alcan project has been deferred.) Gladstone's attractions as a site for aluminium smelting are discussed in Mandeville and Jensen (1978a) but may be briefly summarized:

(a) low-cost electric power available in bulk from the 1650 MW thermal power station located at Gladstone;
(b) supplies of alumina available from the 2 million-tonne capacity Gladstone alumina refinery—in which both Comalco and Alcan have part owner-ship—which will minimize alumina handling costs;
(c) Gladstone has a natural, deep-water port;
(d) the Gladstone sub-region could ultimately provide housing, infrastructure and community support facilities for further major industry;
(e) state government policy;
(f) the availability of prime industrial land adjacent to the sea.

METHODOLOGY

Regional economic 'impact' may be defined as the measured effects on the economy of a region of any difference or change attributable to an impacting agent. The regional economy is the network of individuals and organizations involved in the production, distribution and consumption of goods and services in a particular geographic area. The impacting agent can be any economic stimulus the analyst wishes to examine, and has traditionally been either the introduction of a new industry to the region or a change in the region's exports.

Impact studies have tended to concentrate on the effects of particular industries, for example defence industries and the space programme, educational institutions, the agricultural or mining sectors, and the steel or aluminium industries. The size of the area included in impact analysis varies from local studies which consider impacts on individual towns or cities and their surrounding areas, to state or regional studies. Finally, nation-region studies are generally concerned with analysing the effects of national policy on all the constituent states or regions of a nation. (The literature on regional economic impact is reviewed in Richardson, 1972; Stone, 1973; Mandeville and Jensen, 1978a.)

By defining impact in this way the concept is narrowed considerably to focus on only part of a potentially multi-dimensional concept. Only economic effects are considered, to the exclusion of social, political, psychological, quality of life, and environmental impacts (Stone, 1973). The emphasis on measurement implies a focusing on the quantitative as distinct from the qualitative aspects of impact. The impact of technological change is another factor difficult to incorporate into traditional quantitative impact analysis (Mandeville et al., 1980).

With the GRIT facility to produce regional input-output tables at relatively low cost, resources are freed to perform more detailed analytical applications of input-output for use in impact analysis studies. To further the objective of using input-output in the regional planning process, the various approaches have been combined into a framework which allows the analyst to measure the effects of both the construction and operating phases of new industries, plus the spatial incidence of impacts as they affect the local, regional, state, and national economies.

The impact analysis system is outlined below.

STEP I   Impact analysis in Economy 1 (the sub-region)

For each new industry or combination of new industries:

1. measure the impact of construction phase during a typical construction year;
2. measure the impact of the operational phase during a typical operating year;
3. measure the impact of possible satellite industries and/or infrastructure associated with each new industry;
4. consider the net result of any compensated change if appropriate.

STEP II   Repeat Step I for Economies 2–4 (region, state and nation).

STEP III   Presentation of results and discussion.

From the national input-output table and state, regional and sub-regional tables produced by GRIT, the incidence of economic impact can be detailed at 4 levels. This follows Stone's (1973) suggestion of micro-studies to complement the macro-picture. From the viewpoint of planning and policy, both perspectives are required. The relative importance of the impacts will be less the greater the size of the economy; a major effect in a sub-region could be a relatively minor one in Australia as a whole. However, since leakages via imports decline as the size of the economy increases, the multiplier effects will progressively increase along the continuum from sub-region to nation.

Step I involves completion of impact analysis in the sub-region economy. For each development the construction and operating phases are examined separately (Sadler *et al.*, 1973). The construction phase impact may be measured for a 'typical construction year', or the peak year, depending on the objectives of the analyst. Operationally its measurement will require information on construction costs incurred in the study region. If the data are sufficiently detailed, the input-output matrix for the area may be augmented with a new row and column representing the building and construction sector associated with the new industry plant. But if data are sparse, the construction impact can be measured via the existing building and construction industry multipliers.

Measurement of the impact of the operating phase will involve augmenting the input-output matrix with a new row and column representing the new industry (Tiebout, 1967), for which appropriate data will be required. The impact of possible satellite industries and infrastructure can also be measured. Several estimates could be made with alternative assumptions about the level of satellite industries in a continuum from minimum to maximum attraction of these industries. If more than one industry is expected to locate in an area at the same time, the developments can be measured in combination (Miernyk *et al.*, 1970) by augmenting the matrix with *n* rows and columns simultaneously (*n* being the number of new industries). Economic impacts can be measured in both aggregate and relative terms. In aggregate terms, total increases in output, income and employment resulting from the given economic stimulus can be calculated: in relative terms, the increases in output, income and employment can be related to a unit increase in the original stimulus, i.e. the sector multipliers are compared in some detail.

Step II involves repeating the procedures in *Step I* for each of the subsequent economies to be analysed, in this case the region, state and nation. In each instance, data requirements will vary, referring to expenditures in the appropriate area. The GRIT tables were designed to be produced at the 11, 19 and 36 sector levels, depending on the complexity of the economy under consideration. The decision of the analyst to (a) measure all impacts at the 11 sector level, or (b) measure impacts at the 19 and 36 sector levels respectively, for the sub-area/region and state/nation, or (c) do both (a) and (b) will depend on study resources and objectives. The decision made will have implications for overall data requirements for the impact analysis.

The detail and content of *Step III* (presentation of results and discussion) will again depend on the analyst's objectives and the resources available. The presentation of results can range from economy-wide effects to detailed effects on specific industries. It is possible to consider the net effects of any compensated change, or the results could be integrated into a larger cost/benefit analysis framework. In each economy the relative effects of the construction and operating stage can be illustrated and discussed, and the relative impacts of different new industries (if more than one is being considered) can be analysed. Between economies a comparison and contrast of the relative effects of the developments can be presented. Often the various input-output tables, or the data for the impact analysis, will relate to different years. Thus when measuring aggregate impacts, standard dollars for a particular year (ideally the year that the study is being published) should be utilized. Finally, a qualitative assessment of the quantitative results should be made. This will include comments on the timing of the impacts, the various assumptions made, non-economic factors and other aspects that will aid user interpretation of the results.

Although this system was designed to assess the impact of new industries, the overall framework can be easily adapted to measure other types of impacts. For example, if the analyst is simply concerned with measuring expansion or decline in an existing industry, the standard procedures for measuring impacts with input-output models (Richardson, 1972) may be applied in the context of the above framework as desired. Alternatively, some analysis may not require the augmentation of matrices with new rows and columns, but simply involve changing some of the existing coefficients; again this simpler analysis may be applied in the above framework. Finally, a major feature of this system is that it is based on GRIT. Thus not only can input-output tables be derived quickly and cheaply, but the multipliers for each are directly comparable, both conceptually and by sector definition.

IMPACT OF AN ALUMINIUM SMELTER AT GLADSTONE

The original empirical application of the impact methodology involved the analysis of the economic impact of a number of major industrial developments under construction or proposed for Gladstone (Mandeville and Jensen, 1978a,b). Part of this exercise involved the generation of appropriate GRIT-based sub-regional and state input-output tables. This section will discuss impacts in connection with an aluminium smelter only. The sub-region was defined as the city of Gladstone (128 km^2) plus the surrounding shire of Calliope (5875 km^2).

The Comalco-sponsored smelter presently under construction at Gladstone was the first of the 6 proposed Australian smelters. This project had its origin in the 1957 Agreement between the State of Queensland and Comalco, which provided for the development of Weipa bauxite deposits located on the Cape York Peninsula, and required the company to investigate the possibility of siting an aluminium smelter within Queensland or Australia. In April 1978, Comalco announced plans to establish a 2-potline smelter at Gladstone, producing about 206,000 tonnes of aluminium product per annum. By August 1979, the planned capacity of the plant had been increased to 4 potlines producing about 412,000 tonnes of output per annum (*Australian Financial Review*, 28 August 1979). The original studies referred to above examined the construction and operating phases of the smelter's development at both 2 and 4-potline capacity levels. Here only the operating phase of 412,000 tonne-capacity will be examined for the purpose of illustration.

Multiplier Effects

Aluminium smelting output, income and employment multipliers (Tables 8.2 and 8.3) were specially calculated by augmenting the local, state, and national input-output matrices with new columns representing the aluminium smelting industry. Comalco provided the required data on the smelter's cost structure.

Two types of multipliers were derived. Type I measures employment and income resulting from the operation of the smelter. It includes the smelter workforce and their income (wages and salaries) plus those additional jobs and incomes created in the various industries which service the smelting operation. Type II takes the Type I multiplier effects into account and also

TABLE 8.2 Aluminium smelter multipliers, Gladstone, Australia

Multipliers	Gladstone	Queensland	Australia
Output[a]			
Simple multiplier	1.512	1.759	1.805
Total multiplier	1.643	2.162	2.249
Income[b]			
Type I	2.170	2.934	3.347
Type II	2.739	4.308	4.748
Employment[c]			
Type I	2.676	7.138	12.268
Type II	4.249	12.319	19.903

[a] Indicates the economy-wide multiplicative effects of a $1 change in output of the aluminium smelting sector.

[b] Indicates the economy-wide multiplicative effects on household income of a $1 change in household payments of the aluminium smelting sector.

[c] Indicates the economy-wide multiplicative effects on employment of 1 employee change in the aluminium smelting sector.

Source: Mandeville and Jensen, 1978a.

TABLE 8.3 Adjusted aluminium smelter multipliers, Gladstone, Australia

Multipliers	Gladstone	Queensland	Australia
Output[a]			
Simple multiplier	1.013	1.015	1.018
Total multiplier	1.077	1.161	1.159
Income[b]			
Type I	1.063	1.067	1.067
Type II	1.342	1.567	1.514
Employment[c]			
Type I	1.148	1.331	1.344
Type II	1.919	3.133	3.778

[a] Indicates the economy-wide multiplicative effects on output of a $1 change in output of the aluminium smelting sector.
[b] Indicates the economy-wide multiplicative effects on household income of a $1 change in household payments of the aluminium smelting sector.
[c] Indicates the economy-wide multiplicative effects on employment of 1 employee change in the aluminium smelting sector.
Source: Mandeville and Jensen, 1978a.

includes the impact these jobs and incomes have on creating further employment and incomes in household consumer-related industries throughout the 3 economies. Output multipliers are classified as direct and indirect (which is similar to the Type I multiplier described above) and total (similar to the Type II multiplier).

The aluminium smelting sector multipliers, indicated in Table 8.2, are quite high and require careful interpretation and adjustment when they come to be applied to estimate the numerical aggregate effects of the smelter on the 3 economies. The historical pattern of development of the smelter support industries at Gladstone has been such that a large proportion of the output, income and employment impacts that will be attributable to the smelter already exists in the sub-region. Thus the Gladstone power station was located at Gladstone with the aluminium industry in mind. However, it is desirable here to be able to estimate the additional aggregate impacts in dollars resulting from the smelter. One way of doing this is to recalculate the smelter multipliers, leaving out the direct inputs provided by electricity and alumina. This has been done in Table 8.3.

Normally the impact agent, the industry represented by the multiplier, is viewed as creating additional economic activity through its demand for industrial support requirements and the further round-by-round effects subsequently generated. However, in this instance the major local industries producing inputs to the smelter, the electricity and alumina industries, existed prior to the smelter and sold their products to established markets—the state grid and overseas smelters respectively. Thus in the context of this study, the smelter will not directly stimulate increased local production of electricity or alumina, but will simply divert part of the output of these industries from other markets to smelter inputs and thus help maintain support activity that already exists. The multipliers in Table 8.3 can be interpreted as the additional effects on the 3 economies generated by the smelter. The multipliers appearing in Table 8.2, however, provide an estimate of the total effects attributable to the smelter. The difference obtained by subtracting figures in Table 8.3 from those in Table 8.2 is a measure of the smelter impacts already accounted for in each area's output, income and employment.

The direct and indirect output multiplier gives the most reliable indication of the flow-on effects attributable to an industry or project. The magnitude of an output multiplier indicates the extent of that industry's direct and indirect purchases of goods and services within an economy. The higher an industry's output multiplier, the greater the extent of local purchases.

Aggregate Effects

The estimated direct stimulus to the Gladstone sub-region, the Queensland and the Australian economies in terms of industry output, household income and employment resulting from a year's operation of the 4-potline smelter is:

Output	$A595,000,000
Household income	$A28,500,000
Employment	1900 jobs

Aggregate impacts on the 3 economies (Table 8.4) were estimated by applying respective multipliers to the direct stimulus associated with the smelter. Impacts on output, household income and employment are shown in the form of a range. This reflects direct, indirect and total output multipliers and Type I and Type II income and employment multipliers, respectively. In addition, the percentage changes to existing local, state and national economic levels as a result of the impacts are also shown. Discussion here of the impacts shown in Table 8.4 focuses on local and state effects. In the Gladstone area, the 4-potline smelter will increase employment in the range of 2181 to 3646 jobs or 23 to 39 per cent, household income by $A30 million to $A38 million or 37 to 46 per cent, and industry output by $A603 million to $A641 million or 175 to 186 per cent. Clearly this is a very significant impact. Queensland employment will increase in the range of 2529 to 5953 jobs or 0.4 to 0.9 per cent, household income by $A30 million to $A45 million or 0.7 to 1.0 per cent, and industry output by $A604 million to $A691 million or 3.7 to 4.3 per cent.

TABLE 8.4 Impact of operating phase of the 4-potline aluminium smelter, Gladstone, Australia

Economy	Industry output ($A million)	Household income ($A million)	Employment (persons)
Gladstone/Calliope			
Smelter (increases)	603–641	30–38	2,181–3,646
Per cent	175–186	37–46	23–39
Smelter (total)	900–978	62–78	5,084–8,073
Per cent	262–284	74–94	55–87
Queensland			
Smelter (increases)	604–691	30–45	2,529–5,953
Per cent	3.7–4.3	0.7–1.0	0.4–0.9
Smelter (total)	1,047–1,286	84–123	13,562–23,406
Per cent	6.5–8.0	1.9–2.7	2.0–3.5
Australian			
Smelter (increases)	606–690	30–43	2,554–7,178
Per cent	0.5–0.6	0.1–0.13	0.05–0.14
Smelter (total)	1,074–1,338	95–135	23,309–37,816
Per cent	0.9–1.2	0.30–0.42	0.46–0.75

Source: Mandeville and Jensen, 1978b.

The total effect of the 4-potline smelter on employment in the sub-region is estimated to be in the range of 5085 to 8073 jobs or 55 to 87 per cent of the local labour force, $A62 million to $A78 million or 74 to 94 per cent on household income and $A900 million to $A978 million or 262 to 284 per cent of industry output. The 4-potline smelter's total effect on the state labour force is estimated to range from 13,562 to 23,406 jobs or 2.0 to 3.5 per cent, $A84 million to $A123 million or 1.9 to 2.7 per cent on household income and $A1047 million to $A1286 million or 6.5 to 8.0 per cent of industry output.

Discussion of Results

Earlier the distinction was drawn between the smelter's impacts in terms of *increased* economic activity, and its *total* influence in terms of increases plus its contribution towards maintaining activity that already exists in the economy. It was argued that, in the context of this study, the smelter will not directly stimulate increased local production of electricity or alumina, but will divert part of the output of these industries from other markets to itself and thus help maintain support activity that already exists. However, further smelters attracted to the state would require increased investment in alumina refining and an expansion of coal production and electrical generating capacity. This has already happened; after the announcement of the Alcan smelter to be located at Gladstone (*Australian Financial Review*, 3 August 1979), the alumina refinery at Gladstone and the State Electricity Authority announced planned increases in capacity (*Australian Financial Review*, 4 September 1979, 7 August 1979).

In terms of the range of impact presented, the estimates found at the lower end of the range are likely to be more realistic. Reasons for this relate to the assumptions underlying the input-output model and the years on which the input-output tables are based. The period for the multiplier effects to be fully realized in the 3 economies is not precisely known. Multiplier effects are not instantaneous but may require some years to work their way through an economy.

Several impacts that will be associated with the smelter are not explicitly considered in the analysis. 'Non-economic' effects, such as environmental, social and political impacts are not considered; and some economic effects, such as tax payments to government and export earnings contributed to Australia's net balance of payments, are also not included in the analysis.

It may be queried whether economic impact case studies are simply academic exercises or have some efficacy for government, industry and other sections of the community. A catalogue of the diffusion of the results of the impact work at Gladstone since original publication provides some evidence for the latter view. The study has been reported at conferences (Mandeville, 1978, 1979), in the local press (*Gladstone Observer*, 1 August 1979), in the Queensland press (*Courier Mail* [Brisbane], 7 February 1979), and in the national press (*Australian Financial Review*, 7 February 1979; *The Australian*, 8 February 1979). The results have been used by local and state planning authorities to estimate future infrastructure requirements (e.g. Co-ordinator General's Department, pers. comm.); by businessmen seeking information on support requirements of the smelter (e.g. Vinidec Tubemakers, Email Ltd, pers. comm.); by academics in their research (e.g. Hughes, 1979; Auty, Brown, Tucker, pers. comm.); by the federal government (Australia, Department of Industry and Commerce, 1979a); politicians; and industry (Comalco Limited, 1980) to justify the expansion of the aluminium industry; by the Committee of Inquiry into Technological Change in Australia (pers. comm.); by environmentalists to oppose the expansion of the aluminium industry (Newcastle Ecology Centre, pers. comm.); by unionists (Builders Workers Industrial Union, pers. comm.) in connection with working conditions; and in a court case (Goodwin, pers. comm.) over the government procurement of land for the proposed Alcan smelter at Gladstone. Of course, the results have also been misused to calculate the 'cost' of each job in the aluminium industry (*Australian Financial Review*, 3 January 1980) and misapplied in order to estimate the impact of proposed aluminium smelters to be located in New South Wales and Victoria. Overall, however, it seems that information derived from regional economic impact studies has the potential to aid understanding, planning and decision-making at all levels of the economy. Whether sufficient effort will always be made to realize this potential is another matter.

Spatial Analysis, Industry and the Industrial Environment. Vol. 3 Regional Economies and Industrial Systems
Edited by F. E. I. Hamilton and G. J. R. Linge
© 1983 John Wiley & Sons Ltd.

Chapter 9

Innovative and Cooperative Entrepreneurship: Towards a New Thrust in Industrial Development Policy

DIANA HOOPER AND DAVID WALKER

An economic development commissioner faced with the problem of stimulating employment must be concerned with just what it is that creates growth. Every place has particular qualities that, in conjunction with the general economic environment, provide greater or lesser opportunities, but ultimately it is the human response which decides whether or not this potential is turned into reality. It depends on whether local people see the opportunity for creating new business, whether other entrepreneurs come in to capitalize on the situation, or whether decision-makers in large companies recognize that a place offers them something. Such questions of response have largely been neglected in location theory or, perhaps, have been covered simply as stochastic elements. Yet to the community or region whose future depends on them they are vital.

Increasing attention has been given lately to the dangers of relying too heavily on outside companies so that small, indigenous ones have been given new prominence in development strategies (Schumacher, 1973; Peterson, 1977; *Financial Times of Canada,* 26 March 1979, pp. 20–1). In turn, this has led to a renewed interest in the role of entrepreneurs and a recognition that innovation and risk-taking are important functions in the development process.

This chapter goes a step further and suggests that a *grouping* of lively minds focused on business problems, combined with a sense of action and a desire to overcome difficulties, is probably a necessary element in helping a 'backward' place to break into a more successful long-run development path. While this chapter does not prove the case, it does have a compelling logic relevant to development strategy.

ENTREPRENEURSHIP

Controversy exists about the definition of entrepreneurs and their role. Certainly they form a class which does not conform to the present but rather

217

encourages change. Traditional functions associated with entrepreneurs include the roles of organizer, capital accumulator, employer and risk-taker. Most importantly, an entrepreneur is the agent who introduces change by reorganizing the elements of production, resulting in a forward movement of the economic system (Thwaites, 1977, p. 17). This innovative function suggests that entrepreneurs are a central and important causal factor in promoting economic growth, a point emphasized in Friedmann's (1972, p. 87) view of true development in which the 'cumulative effect of successive innovations is to transform the established structure of society by attracting creative or innovative personalities into the enclaves of accelerated change', thus creating an environment and set of attitudes favourable to further development.

Certainly an entrepreneur must also be sufficiently skilled in management to maintain a profitable industry. Although innovation is his most important activity, it is an isolated event, occurring only at certain moments. On a day-to-day basis, an entrepreneur needs to ensure his business will run smoothly so as to capitalize on the potential of the innovations. But such management functions are readily acquired by non-innovative individuals lacking the entrepreneurial flair.

Despite this, however, every entrepreneur cannot be expected to make advances on a world scale. Kilby (1971, p. 6) argues that 'perceiving truly *new* economic opportunities and the carrying out of fundamental, pioneering innovations of the type envisaged by Schumpeter are largely irrelevant' in the underdeveloped world. He believes there is such a mass of known technology, which has neither been fully exploited nor adapted to particular situations, that 'the critical entrepreneurial function in the modernizing economy of the twentieth century' will be

> To obtain adequate financing, to adapt techniques and organization, to maximize factor productivities and minimize unit cost, to improve substitutes for non-available skills and materials.

A strong case can be made that Kilby's stance is also true of less advanced areas in developed countries. Nevertheless, more fundamental innovation cannot be ignored, especially if there is to be reduced dependence on areas from which the new techniques are imported.

Successful innovation requires a company to be sound both managerially and technically. Freeman's (1974) work in attempting to identify patterns of success and failure in innovation showed that firms must:

(a) recognize the needs of users of the new product;
(b) be prepared to deal with after-sales problems;
(c) have a fairly large project team working intensively;

(d) have a good communication with the related scientific community;

(e) place the project under a senior executive.

Freeman concludes (p. 190):

> The fact that the measures which discriminated between success and failure included some which reflected mainly on the competence of R and D, others which reflected mainly on efficient marketing, and some which measured characteristics of the business innovator with good communications, confirms that view of industrial innovation as essentially a coupling process.

Coupling in this context is between a potential market and a new product or process: hence government policies to encourage innovation must address both the technical and the managerial aspects of company requirements.

INNOVATIVE COMMUNITIES

Two of the factors that Freeman identified suggest the importance of team-work and of interrelationships with other innovators and researchers. Within large companies having a strong research focus these occur almost automatically, but the lack of them can inhibit the individual inventor or entrepreneur, especially when operating outside the main business regions. In contrast, a handful of like-minded individuals can choose to share and cooperate instead of continuing to function in strict isolation. History offers examples of such cooperation and there is no reason why such groups should not be even more important today: it must be asked why Boards of Trade and Chambers of Commerce so rarely focus attention in this direction (Ironside, 1977, p. 178).

The Lunar Society of Birmingham

Perhaps the best example of an association that helped businessmen to discuss all the latest ideas was the Lunar Society, based in Birmingham in the late eighteenth century during the formative years of the Industrial Revolution in England. At that time Birmingham was a relatively small and isolated place which had both skilled craftsmen and a tradition of non-conformity and freedom, but lacked major factors for industrial growth such as transport connections, materials, water power and large markets. A group of enterprising men began to meet there informally as early as the 1760s: by 1780 their meetings were regular (Schofield, 1963, p. 17). The name Lunar Society derives from the fact that it met on the Monday or Tuesday closest to a new moon.

The participants naturally changed somewhat from the time of the earliest contacts to the gradual fading of the Society in the 1790s. Key people initially were Matthew Boulton (son of a buckle manufacturer) and Erasmus Darwin (grandfather of Charles Darwin) who was a doctor at Lichfield, both of whom had strong interests in a wide range of scientific problems. In 1765, William Small, who arrived in Birmingham and became Boulton's doctor as well as scientific adviser, seems to have played a major role in linking people together (Schofield, 1963, p. 35). A very important connection was forged by Darwin in the mid-1760s with Josiah Wedgwood, the famous potter, who was drawn into the circle. Slightly later, 2 other key people joined—James Watt (who moved from Scotland to work with Boulton) and James Keir (another Scot mainly interested in chemistry). The last renowned addition was the chemist, Joseph Priestley, who came to Birmingham as pastor of the New Meeting House: his arrival in 1781 led the Society into its most productive decade but, as a result of riots related to his anti-conservative views, he was forced to leave the city in 1791. During the 1790s deaths, business pressures and further departures undermined the Society and it gradually faded away.

The interesting feature of this group is that some members were primarily businessmen and others doctors or scientists, but all concerned themselves with a wide range of investigations: they had a thirst for knowledge and a desire to solve problems, both theoretical and practical. Boulton and Watt were primarily involved in developing and exploiting Watt's ideas on the steam engine, and their factory at Soho attracted visitors from all over the world: they complemented each other because Watt was a technician and experimenter while Boulton had a flair for promotion and project planning (Schofield, 1963, pp. 149–50). Wedgwood's main investigations concerned clays and enamels, while Keir—a partner in a chemical works at nearby Tipton (Staffordshire)—experimented with and developed various processes to produce industrial chemicals. His best money-maker was a cheaper process for producing mineral alkali, but he also patented a metallic alloy. Keir's plant, started in 1780, became one of the largest in the country and, like Soho, a tourist attraction (Schofield, 1963, pp. 157–9).

However, other important members who were not entrepreneurs were interested in problems not directly connected with the business world: similarly those in business also discussed issues unrelated to their work. The range of topics reviewed was, therefore, very extensive. Schofield (1963, p. 89) notes:

> The introduction of a new topic, whether for profit motives or not, by one member was the signal for the rest to add their contributions, sometimes learned, more often not, but always with enthusiasm.

Discussions embraced, among other subjects, the chemistry of ceramics;

geology; botany; properties of metals; properties of chemicals and various chemical reactions; instrument design; various types of machinery; steam engines; electricity; astronomy; balloons; standards of weights and measures; and numerous elements of theoretical chemistry. Theoretical discussions were usually linked to scientific experiment and sometimes also to commercial exploitation; many learned papers were presented and several books written. The entrepreneurs involved in this group must have been greatly stimulated and challenged, with new ideas constantly being raised and discussed and their own problems and solutions subjected to critical comment. Schofield (1963, pp. 147–90) refers to a number of cases in which Boulton, Watt, Keir and Wedgwood were helped to overcome technical difficulties in their businesses.

Hamilton (Ontario) in 1900

The Lunar Society, while unique, was perhaps a model of entrepreneurial attitudes and of a willingness to search out and discuss new ideas. A possible example of more typical interrelationships among entrepreneurs in a community is that of Hamilton (Ontario) in the late nineteenth and early twentieth centuries.

Hamilton, on the western edge of Lake Ontario, has been one of Canada's most successful industrial cities. Undoubtedly its excellent location for industrial development in terms of transport facilities and large nearby markets has been vital to its growth, but these have not been the sole reason for the city's success: local businessmen played crucial roles.

Business achievements during the second half of the nineteenth century were numerous. Many individuals who initiated small, locally based companies prior to 1900 saw them develop into major industrial concerns in the twentieth century. For example, George Tuckett and John Billings started a small tobacco firm in 1860; when Billings retired in 1880 Tuckett's sons bought his shares to form the G. E. Tuckett and Sons Company. The following years saw numerous innovations, including the development of unique tobacco brands, 'T & B Plug Tobacco' and 'T & B Myrtle Navy Cut', as well as the company's own cigars, the 'Marguerite' and the 'Corona'. According to the Industry Clipping File in the Hamilton Public Library, the firm was the first local tobacco company to attempt to market its products overseas. Treatment of employees was also innovative: for example, working hours were adjusted to suit seasonal variations and bonuses were offered for hard work. At a time when exploitation of industrial workers was the norm, this was indeed unique (Bliss, 1974, p. 67). Eventually 3 separate companies were formed: George E. Tuckett and Sons Limited, the Tuckett Cigar Company, and Tuckett's Limited. In 1912 the firm was finally reorganized into a single joint stock company, Tucketts Limited, with a capital of

$C2 million (*Monetary Times,* 13 July 1912, p. 164) and branches across Canada as well as several in the US.

Tuckett's was only one of many successful firms in early Hamilton. Many were not making world-scale advances, but were important in identifying and adapting technology to local needs. Several firms developed brand-name products that came to be well known in the region or, in some cases, country-wide. These included the Wanzer Company with its popular 'Wanzer' and 'Little Wanzer' sewing machines, and D. Moore and Company's lines of 'Superior' and 'Treasure' cooking stoves, the only electric models produced in Canada in the early twentieth century. Other firms, including the Eagle Knitting Company and the B. Greening Wire Company, kept close ties with England and their owners travelled there periodically to familiarize themselves with the latest techniques and equipment. While few of these activities were important much beyond Hamilton, they contributed to the overall inventive atmosphere in the city.

There were, however, several major innovations that emerged from the city during this period as well. In many cases the innovative idea was not brought to commercial fruition in Hamilton itself, but it is significant that such large-scale innovations began there. For example, Thomas L. Willson was an early entrepreneur who developed and patented several important ideas in Hamilton: most notably the discovery of acetylene gas and the use of the dynamo to power electric arc lights. Although he left Hamilton before commercially establishing these ideas, he was later to invent calcium carbide which he sold to a group of individuals who later began the Union Carbide Company in Sault Ste Marie (Union Carbide Canada Ltd, n.d., pp. 4–10). Similarly, Harry Semple, an employee of the Hamilton Glass Works, invented a steam-operated machine to manufacture bottles, and it had the potential to reduce costs by 30 per cent. It proved successful after testing in Ohio (*The Canadian Manufacturer,* 16 March 1888, p. 201).

Many of the city's businessmen did not confine themselves to their own company; in fact, one of the earliest and most important business achievements involved the support and cooperation of many local entrepreneurs. A group of Americans had established a blast furnace at Hamilton in 1894 in response to federal and provincial bounties on iron-smelting, and additional inducements offered by the city (Kilbourn, 1960, pp. 48–50). Difficulties beset it even during the initial year. Recognizing the magnitude of the problems and not wishing to lose such an important development, local businessmen stepped in and bought out the American interests in 1895. Included were John Patterson, who brought Hamilton its first electric power; Cyrus Birge, important in the metal-working industry; and William Southam, a powerful businessman best known as publisher of the *Hamilton Spectator.* This move is almost unequalled in importance since The Hamilton

Blast Furnace Company survived to become the keystone to post-1900 iron and steel development in the city (Acheson, 1971, p. 230).

Another significant venture occurred in 1898 when Cyrus Birge, as the head of a syndicate of Canadians, bought out the Rhode Island interests that controlled Hamilton's Canada Screw Company. Henceforth the firm developed to become part of the 1910 merger which formed The Steel Company of Canada (STELCO). These 2 actions were important, not only because they provided the area with the foundation for its locally owned iron and steel industry (still dominant in Canada) but because they both exhibited a reversal of the traditional trend of Americans buying out Canadian interests.

Hamilton's entrepreneurs also fostered progress through their participation in local institutions and support of infrastructural developments. A Board of Trade had existed in the city since 1845 and was always active in issues affecting the business community. Businessmen were strongly represented on the city council (Middleton and Walker, 1980) which, despite being dominated by a merchant group, offered ready support in catering for manufacturers' needs.

Attracting railway facilities was of primary importance to Hamilton's business growth and was supported by businessmen generally, and specifically those on council. As early as the 1830s, lawyer, land-owner and (later) politician, Alan MacNab, recognized the need for rail transport. His efforts, along with those of Isaac Buchanan (a wholesale merchant and member of parliament), were fundamental in bringing the Great Western Railway through Hamilton despite an earlier proposal which would have bypassed the settlement (Campbell, 1966, pp. 95–6). Later, in the 1890s, substantial financial aid was given to the Toronto, Hamilton and Buffalo Railway. Despite a focus on that railway, the city was not remiss in trying to attract the Canadian Pacific Railway. Plans never came to fruition even though financial aid and valuable land grants were offered to Canadian Pacific on several occasions.

The offering of bonuses, another phenomenon of the later nineteenth and early twentieth centuries, also received unified support from local entrepreneurs, especially those on council. It was customary for companies to parade across Ontario seeking the municipality that would offer the best deal in terms of a free land site, tax exemptions or outright financial grants (Naylor, 1975, pp. 147–56). Since almost every municipality in the province engaged in this practice, firms had strong bargaining power and Hamilton's businessmen were shrewd enough to realize that they, too, had to participate or lose much of their competitive advantage. Support was offered, therefore, even when it meant hardship to existing enterprises such as by increasing competition and raising the cost of services. An excellent example of this attitude was the comment by Alderman Tilden (of the E. and C. Gurney Company) when referring to a bonus offer to the Canada Screw Company:

> while his company had to pay large taxes and were consequently not generally in favour of exemptions to factories, this was an extraordinary case and he thought the city should not let the opportunity go past without taking advantage of it (*Hamilton Spectator*, 29 April 1887).

Another issue on which businessmen cooperated was the controversial subject of hydroelectric power. This was a provincially owned facility in much of southern Ontario by about 1910 and as such was trying to make inroads into Hamilton. The city, however, had its own private enterprise—the Cataract Power Company—that had been operating successfully since the mid-1890s when John Patterson harnessed the water at DeCew Falls. This innovation gave Hamilton hydroelectric power before other cities in the region and was widely believed to have been crucial in giving it a competitive advantage and thus promoting new industrial development. Although the Cataract Power Company had always served local industry efficiently and at a reasonable cost, it gave the average citizen less favourable treatment. Thus even though manufacturers and merchants remained unified and launched a good fight on behalf of the enterprise, they eventually lost a close battle and in 1914 public hydroelectric power was incorporated in Hamilton (Lucas, 1976, p. 245).

The formation in 1872 of The Bank of Hamilton is a further indication that local businessmen worked together for the betterment of the city. Trigge (1934, p. 65) notes that the list of those present at the bank's first organizational meeting 'is thoroughly representative of the principal businessmen of Hamilton of that day'. Individuals present included Edward Gurney, founder of a local stove-making firm and foundry that grew to be one of the largest in Canada; James M. Williams, member of parliament, oil refiner, foundryman and railway promoter; and John Winer, proprietor of a large and prosperous drug business and an original founder of the local Board of Trade. Interest in Hamilton's primary financial institution did not wane: in fact, several Hamilton businessmen remained as directors even after the 1924 take-over by the Canadian Bank of Commerce.

Cooperation is also evident in the complex mix of directorships held by many individuals. They concentrated not only on improving their own companies but also actively directed or managed other similar or complementary firms. Undoubtedly much of the city's business spirit developed out of this direct business interaction among individuals of common interests. The example of an entrepreneur already mentioned illustrates this. Cyrus Birge, head of the Canada Screw Company and an original Vice-President of STELCO, was also a Director of Sawyer-Massey Company,

Vice-President of the Dominion Power and Transmission Company and President of the Bank of Hamilton at various times during his career. He was, in fact, included in Acheson's list of Canadian industrial élite in both 1885 (Acheson, 1972, p. 171) and the early twentieth century (Acheson, 1971, p. 465).

In Hamilton's early development many of its foremost entrepreneurs were immigrants from the United States and Great Britain. The fact that a majority of these men did not remain as outsiders but became strong forces at the forefront of business expansion goes a long way to indicate the positive atmosphere that pervaded the area. Entrepreneurs of foreign birth took up the causes of service development and business representation as readily as did local individuals. A case in point is the formation of STELCO. Many of its initial officers—including its first President, Charles Wilcox— had been of a different heritage but by the time of the 1910 merger had settled to become local citizens.

While the rapid influx of branch plants after 1900 (38 by 1914) cannot be accepted as entirely positive, there is no doubt that they played a crucial role in Hamilton's development. It is unlikely they would have settled in such numbers had Hamilton not been the successful, well-serviced business area that it was. Hamilton's ability to absorb this rapid infiltration without completely selling out to the Americans can be at least partially attributed to the strength of its close-knit entrepreneurial group. Thus, the area's identity was preserved and local control was maintained, for example, of the 2 major steel companies, STELCO and DOFASCO (Dominion Foundries and Steel Company).

Certainly Hamilton has been a successful industrial city, and the interest and cooperation of local businessmen played definite roles in this success. Local entrepreneurs were inventive in their own right; were prepared to buy into the foreign-controlled blast furnace company to maintain its operation; took interest in and supported a wide variety of the community's infrastructural and other business developments; played active roles in large numbers of related firms and were receptive to new industry, both local and foreign. Had this early spirit not existed, Hamilton might be a far different city today.

POLICY IMPLICATIONS

Traditional development policies have tended to focus on land, labour and capital. They have provided serviced lots at low rental, ready-made buildings, manpower and management training, and capital grants for new or expanding plants. Recently there has been more emphasis on encouraging innovation and entrepreneurship and it is helpful to review some of the current approaches. However national technological policy is not discussed here even though it provides a framework for what can happen in smaller spatial units. Rather, the concern is with policy approaches that can link more explicitly into regional or local development efforts, recognizing with Feller (1975, p. 100) that a region 'can achieve sustained economic development only if it continually adjusts to changes in market demand, resource availability and technology'. Having considered some existing policy initiatives, the extent to which they foster the cooperative entrepreneurial spirit described already can be questioned. A final issue is whether in fact public initiative does much to encourage such a situation to develop where it does not arise spontaneously.

Innovation Centres

Innovation centres are a recent thrust 'aimed at promotion of innovation and entrepreneurship' (Research Triangle Institute, 1977, p. 1). They are directly tied to the process of establishing successful companies based on new ideas. Three of them were set up in the United States with National Science Foundation funds in the early 1970s at the Massachusetts Institute of Technology, Carnegie-Mellon University and the University of Oregon. In Canada, the University of Waterloo, after operating such a centre under a temporary arrangement for one year, now has full federal approval. These centres aim to solve problems associated with the gap between researching an innovative idea and reaching the stage of commercial production, and hence 'provide innovation processing assistance in a centre of entrepreneurial excellence combined with training to upgrade innovative and entrepreneurial skills of future innovators' (University of Waterloo, 1978, p. 3). They also 'allow for innovation development in an atmosphere which allows failure without negative consequences' (Research Triangle Institute, 1977, p. 7) and therefore eliminate the financial and other difficulties apparent in the period between the transfer from ideas to full commercial production. Location at or near a university is preferable to permit utilization and commercialization of university-held technology. Potential entrepreneurs are brought together in this setting to experience university education, clinical exposure, policy guidance and assistance from the business world.

Studies illustrate the great scope for this approach. In the US '27 new products have been developed by three centres and 29 new venture businesses have been staffed with 33 centre-trained entrepreneurs, having total gross sales of $30,000,000 in 1976' (University of Waterloo, 1978, p. 7). Results suggest that classroom training combined with direct clinical experience in the innovation process increases the probability of future successful entrepreneurs.

The range of activities that could be covered by such a centre is illustrated by the proposal for a centre at the University of Waterloo. The implementa-

TABLE 9.1 Users of the Ontario Industrial Innovation Centre

Client	Client needed
Faculty	Assistance to commercialize research results by any means that will succeed
Students	Guidance in invention and new enterprise development beyond that encountered in regular course work
Independent inventors	Response to perceived needs which commonly include protection of the idea and assessment of patentability
Entrepreneurs in action	Fast, direct response to the current question, frequently a short cut to finding money without surrendering equity
Prospective entrepreneurs	Assistance to understand the mysteries of business start-ups including incorporation, business structures, financing, and the like
Innovators and innovation managers	Guidance to improve in-house management of R & D programmes
Manufacturers	Leads to new products and processes
Venture capitalists	Large payback investment opportunities well developed by a competent manager
Bankers	Well developed and well secured investment opportunities
Colleges and universities	Educational materials for courses and projects

Source: Ontario Industrial Innovation Centre, 1980, p. 7.

tion plan (Ontario Industrial Innovation Centre, 1980) sees the centre as serving many clients (Table 9.1). Five objectives have been set:

(a) invention development and utilization—concerning the actual inventions themselves;
(b) enterprise and entrepreneur development—to help entrepreneurs relate their technology to business opportunities;
(c) student inventors and entrepreneurs—to guide students to a stage at which they can put inventions and business proposals to profitable use;
(d) education for innovation—special courses to encourage inventors, innovators and entrepreneurs;
(e) research into innovative processes.

The University has already been working for several years in some of these areas such as evaluating inventions from all over the country, helping student inventors and teaching courses on innovation.

Enterprise Workshops

A relatively recent development idea, the enterprise workshop, has emerged in Britain. Unlike the innovation centres already described, these encourage innovation that uses well known technology in new ways: they consist of workshop space equipped with machinery and supervised by experienced businessmen, where individuals can develop their ideas into a prototype. Low-rent nursery units of approximately 500 to 600 square feet (46 to 56 m^2) are associated with the workshops for entrepreneurs ready to begin commercial production. Strathclyde Regional Council, which has the longest experience in their operation, covers much of western Scotland—a region relying heavily on coal-mining, shipbuilding and engineering which have long had problems of industrial decline and unemployment. As part of a development strategy, enterprise workshops are the newest programme to help alleviate these difficulties. By the end of 1976 2 workshops were approved: one at Hamilton (23 km southeast of Glasgow) and the other at Paisley (12 km west of Glasgow). These were commissioned, respectively, in April and July 1977 and are located in converted buildings owned by the Strathclyde Regional Council. Workshops are about 2500 square feet (232 m^2) and include a small office, kitchen and storage area. Space is common to accepted users with supervisors performing an important advisory function as well as allocating and maintaining the machinery available. Workshop managers, with many years of industrial senior management experience, control the organizational and financial aspects of these enterprises. Strathclyde has been fortunate in obtaining men with pensions from early retirement who do not demand salaries commensurate with their experience.

Vetting of applicants is difficult and is handled in Strathclyde by a team with diverse experience. Criteria considered include market and job-creation potential and financial and technical feasibility. Only about a quarter of the applicants have so far been accepted. Entry is normally approved for a 3-month occupancy but, in practice, additional periods are always permitted. By June 1978, 30 projects had been accepted for the Hamilton Workshop and 12 for that in Paisley: at Hamilton, however, there were only about a dozen active users, most of whom came from within 12 miles (19 km). Promising projects included a collision-proof traffic bollard, a semi-automatic filling machine, an up-and-over door, a reclining invalid chair, and electronic bagpipes; other ideas had already progressed to the production stage.

Three nursery units, each of 500 square feet (46 m^2), are also available at Hamilton for inventors ready to attempt commercial production. Rents are attractive compared to commercial rates but these units are designed only for short-term use with a maximum of 12 months.

Communication is maintained between Strathclyde's team and specialists at local colleges of technology as well as the nearby National Engineering Laboratory. Such contact is important especially for technical advice and testing. Years of business experience also provides valuable contacts with local firms and personal knowledge of technical, financial and patent specialists in the private sector.

Judging from the number of marketable new products emerging from these British workshops the idea could be very successful. The low-cost approach appears ideal for fostering growth and development utilizing well known technology and local inventors. Its small scale and low cost makes it feasible in a much greater variety of locations than the innovation centre.

Venture Founders

Venture Founders Corporation, a private company with head offices in Waltham (Massachusetts), specializes in developing and providing capital for enterprises with substantial growth potential. The company operates mainly in economically depressed areas and uses investment capital from local development groups. A key element in its approach is the techniques used for finding entrepreneurs with the potential for success: entrepreneurs are seen as central to development and the corporation's operations are geared towards this belief.

Aggressive, active searching for potential entrepreneurs and the provision of a far broader range of services than is normal for a venture capital firm makes Venture Founders' approach unique. In addition to finding potential innovators through media coverage, meetings and mailings to prospective candidates, Venture Founders conducts New Business Development Workshops at which evaluation of entrepreneurial ability and selection of the most capable candidates takes place. They are conducted by a behavioural scientist and a venture capitalist who assess such factors as attitude towards risk-taking, drive and energy level, ability to persist, and specific management skills. Responses to simulated business situations are observed and those most likely to succeed are then selected from the large workshop group. Venture Founders assist the chosen individuals to make business plans, to organize and launch their business ventures, to secure a competent management team and to arrange the necessary initial capital.

Based on this company's successes in relatively undeveloped parts of the United States, the province of Nova Scotia hired Venture Founders to search out entrepreneurial talent as part of its development strategy. This eastern part of Canada is generally considered to be lacking in this sphere (George, 1970) but Nova Scotia officials are extremely pleased with their experience so far. Venture Founders are now into their third contract each of which embraces 3 weekend workshops designed to identify potential entrepreneurs and then follow-up sessions with those who show promise. The first contract resulted in 3 new facilities and the second produced 4.

Enterprise Zones

Many writers concerned with small business have argued that a major factor inhibiting the entrepreneurial spirit is the burden of taxation and bureaucratic red tape. After visiting Asian cities, Peter Hall in 1977 recommended 'enterprise zones' which allowed a great deal of freedom from such restrictions (*The Observer,* 30 March 1980, p. 21). The British government accepted the idea in its 1980 budget as a way of renewing areas with severe economic and physical decay—essentially old, run-down industrial districts. The zones will be up to 500 acres (202 ha) and businesses there will be exempt from development land taxes, property taxes and certain restrictions: in addition they will receive 100 per cent capital allowances on buildings and be subject to special help in simplifying planning procedures and reducing government requests for statistics (*Economic Progress Report,* May 1980). Although this scheme does not relate directly to innovation, it is hoped that the proffered freedom will stimulate entrepreneurship; moreover, by concentrating businesses together in a small area, discussions and sharing of ideas could be encouraged.

The specific proposals have been criticized on a number of grounds, not least of which is that it would be advantageous to remove restrictive burdens from firms wherever they are located in the country. The Association of Independent Businesses (1980) is concerned that larger companies will in fact benefit most because they have the time and the expertise to use the proposals to best advantage. The Association, further, sees a danger in commercial and warehousing uses squeezing out manufacturing. In its view also, these zones should be reserved for new business development. Nevertheless such difficulties could certainly be dealt with.

COOPERATION AND COMMUNITY IN ECONOMIC DEVELOPMENT

Policies to encourage small business, entrepreneurship, research and innovation have clearly come more to the fore in recent years. Various combinations of the policies discussed in this chapter could be powerful agents in influencing long-run economic change. Moreover, they could, with little modification, encourage the kind of cooperative relationships which spark community development. Workshops of the kind operated by Venture Founders, as well as management training programmes, bring entrepreneurs together and may lead to long-term contacts, but they are generally short-term and geared to individual advancement. In the case of enterprise zones, enterprise workshops and innovation centres, however, the scope for long-term interrelationships is much greater.

Workshops and innovation centres could both be used to stimulate discussion of ideas by inventors and entrepreneurs. They already encourage joint use of buildings and laboratories, interaction with specialists and supervisors whose function is to help, and systematic links with the scientific community and continuing research in other companies. Linked with advertising which encourages people with ideas to try them out, and programmes such as Venture Founders' that identify potential entrepreneurs, the basis for long-run supply of innovators is laid. Educational courses to encourage independence and open the vista of self-employment, such as are available at the University of Waterloo, can also play a part.

In most communities, other important elements of a long-run cooperative development strategy usually exist already. Thus businessmen's associations look after the requirements of the commercial community as a whole, and there are many courses in management skills. These should be drawn together with the innovative thrust into a carefully thought-through development strategy.

Development plans are designed to benefit the community as a whole. The question arises as to whether businessmen in the industrialized West are really interested in anything other than their own situation, or whether they are prepared to encourage new entrepreneurs or discuss their latest ideas with potential competitors. Excessive secrecy and individualism have perhaps kept the level of development below what it could be, but given patent laws and the demands of the market-place, perhaps successful companies will always opt out of effective cooperation.

A further consideration is what this means for underdeveloped areas. In the past, a successful entrepreneur may have built up a strong company only to sell out (often to one based far away) and invest most of the returns elsewhere; or, perhaps, a wealthy dynasty has arisen to control the whole economy in paternalistic fashion. Somehow a community or region must build up a breed of entrepreneurs who are good but can think socially as well as individualistically and who are not motivated by the desire to control others. The only alternative in a democracy is public or cooperative ownership.

Established businessmen's associations do not appear to have been very successful in pioneering new ideas or creating innovative developments in less developed areas. Perhaps the success of a Quebec association, the *Caisses d'Entraide Economique,* suggests a way forward. Essentially this is a credit union, receiving funds from a variety of individuals and firms in a place which invests in local enterprises, encourages local economic development, and brings businessmen together to discuss a wide variety of issues.

Started in the small town of Alma, the movement is sensitive to the needs of rural and peripheral areas and judging from the increase in the number of branches and of invested capital, has proved very successful. It suggests a way around the financial problems of small business and a mechanism for preventing take-overs by outside interests.

The new British enterprise zones might also help to foster greater co-operation simply by concentrating many small businesses close together. Business discussions and social ties could well be created in such an environment, although they cannot be automatically expected. Many modern industrial parks, for example, show quite restricted interrelationships between firms (see Barr's chapter in this volume).

Government policies, at least those directly related to economic development, can probably do little more than promote necessary changes in this direction. Attitudes in the business sector must adapt correspondingly, and human progress must be seen as a product not just of competition but also of cooperation. In the long-run, only education can facilitate these changes, but it may not be easy. Specific development policies can help find entrepreneurs, encourage innovation, improve management, and aid in financing, but they cannot force businessmen to work together for their own and the common good.

Spatial Analysis, Industry and the Industrial Environment. Vol. 3 Regional Economies and Industrial Systems
Edited by F. E. I. Hamilton and G. J. R. Linge
© 1983 John Wiley & Sons Ltd.

Chapter 10

The Effect of International and National Developments on the Clothing Industry of the Manchester Conurbation

DAVID C. GIBBS

The rapidly growing integration of the global economy has raised a number of major tensions between and within nations, arising especially from problems inherent in existing mechanisms of adjustment to the quickening pace of change (Steed, 1978a, p. 35).

The decline of the clothing industries in many Western developed nations has been greeted in these countries with considerable distress and consternation:

> Their fast changing international specialization and competitiveness have probably created more anguish and led to greater contention between, as well as controversy within nations, than almost any other manufacturing industries over recent years (Steed, 1978a, p. 35).

Much has been made of the apparent importance of imports, especially those from developing countries, as a direct cause of declining employment and production capacity. It is thought that by undercutting prices and paying low wages the developing countries (especially Taiwan, Hong Kong and South Korea) have somehow 'undermined' the strong position of developed country clothing industries (e.g. National Union of Tailors and Garment Workers, 1978). This chapter examines changes in the employment fortunes of a major clothing manufacturing centre—the Manchester conurbation—and evaluates the impact of import penetration and other factors on employment. A major problem, however, is to attribute cause and effect. Although imports of clothing from developing countries increased during the 1966–75 period as employment simultaneously declined, it is difficult to directly attribute the latter as an effect of the former. Moreover, it is virtually impossible to divorce the influence of import penetration from other industry changes such as restructuring, demand and new technology. None the less, the call for selective import controls—even total protection—is growing and is often reflected in government policy. 'Trade Unions and employees in those industries wanting import restrictions often find a ready response in Whitehall' (Cable, 1977b, p. 1). Similarly, the problems of the clothing industry cannot be separated from overall economic management of the economy (inflation, interest and exchange rates, unemployment and the balance of payments). The serious slump in the fortunes of the developed world since 1973 has markedly increased the attraction of 'beggar-my-neighbour' trade restrictions largely designed to export unemployment. Protection, though, represents a short-term Keynesian approach to unemployment and is largely irrelevant to a major long-term industrial problem—the deep-rooted structural inadequacies of the UK economy (Cable, 1977b).

The chapter first establishes the importance of Manchester as a leading centre of clothing manufacture in the most recent year for which data are available, 1975, and compares its structure to that at the national level. It outlines aggregate change in employment within the conurbation between 1966 and 1975, decomposing its constituent components, which is then evaluated in terms of developments 'external' and 'internal' to the conurbation. It becomes clear that the rise in protectionism around the world in response to the perceived 'threat' from developing countries is based upon over-simplified assumptions. In Manchester, while imports have played a role in employment loss, local changes inherent to the conurbation remained important. The most significant of these was the structure of its clothing industry and, especially, its relationship with fashion change.

BACKGROUND DEFINITIONS

'The clothing industry . . . really comprises a collection of industries producing a wide variety of products' (Davies and Kelly, 1972, p. 36). Here, the clothing industry is defined at the Minimum List Heading (MLH) level to include the 5 sectors listed in Table 10.1. While this definition is valid at the local and national scales in Great Britain, it cannot be used internationally; neither OECD nor UN data define the clothing industry in comparable terms and import data published by the Joint Textile Committee (1976) are not organized in this way.

The 'Manchester conurbation' used here corresponds with the old SEL-NEC (South East Lancashire, North East Cheshire) area, and was defined by data availability, being covered by Factory Inspectorate information collated at the University of Manchester by the North West Industry Research Unit for the years 1966 to 1975 (Figure 10.1). Among other advantages, this enabled the research to be free of administrative boundaries and to look beyond the aggregate to the individual components of change (Lloyd and Mason, 1976, 1978; Dicken and Lloyd, 1978; Lloyd, 1979).

At the national scale, data on employment at the MLH level are published in the *Department of Employment Gazette,* while trade figures and supplementary employment information are published by the Joint Textile

TABLE 10.1 The structure of Manchester's clothing industry compared with that of the British clothing industry, 1966 and 1975

Minimum List Heading	Manchester						Great Britain			
	Employment (000)		Per cent		Employment as per cent of Great Britain total		Employment (000)		Per cent	
	1966	1975	1966	1975	1966	1975	1966	1975	1966	1975
441 Weatherproof outerwear	14.5	8.8	36.9	29.2	48.5	47.1	29.9	18.7	8.1	6.9
442 Men's and boys' tailored outerwear	3.4	3.4	8.7	11.2	2.9	4.2	118.8	81.7	32.3	30.0
443 Women's and girls' tailored outerwear	4.5	3.2	11.5	10.6	7.1	7.4	63.6	43.1	17.3	15.8
444 Overalls, men's shirts and underwear	7.2	5.5	18.4	18.1	16.3	15.4	44.1	35.6	12.0	13.1
445 Dresses, lingerie and infants' wear	9.6	9.4	24.5	30.9	8.6	10.1	111.4	93.0	30.3	34.2
Total	39.2	30.3	100.0	100.0	10.7	11.2	367.8	272.1	100.0	100.0

Sources: North West Industry Research Unit, unpublished data; United Kingdom, Ministry of Labour, 1967, p. 167; United Kingdom, Department of Employment, 1976, p. 484.

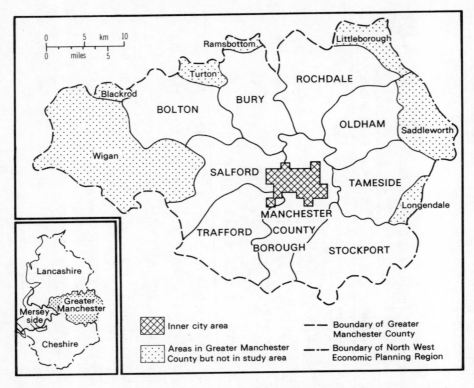

FIGURE 10.1 The study area in the context of the Greater Manchester conurbation

Committee and by the National Economic Development Office. The Manchester and national data are not strictly comparable; the former refer to manual workers in employment, the latter include all workers in manufacturing. Because clothing industries have a 'flat' management structure and paucity of office staff (National Economic Development Office, 1971) this may not be too great a problem, but should be borne in mind when studying the tables. International data on production and employment have been culled from UN and OECD reports on the industry and tabulations relating to trade.

MANCHESTER'S MANTLE

In 1975 781 clothing firms (13.5 per cent of all enterprises) in the Manchester conurbation had 30,347 manual employees, 9.0 per cent of all manual workers in the area and 11.2 per cent of the labour force in this industry in Great Britain. Characteristically, the industry is very labour-intensive (Helfgott, 1959), has a low technological content and relies on women for 70 to 80 per cent of its workforce (Hague and Newman, 1952; National Economic Development Office, 1971). Table 10.1 reveals, however, that structurally Manchester's industry differs considerably from that in Great Britain as a whole, being dominated by weatherproof outerwear and containing much less than the national share of employment in men's and boys' tailored outerwear. Similarly, Table 10.1 also shows the importance of overalls, men's shirts and underwear (MLH 444) and dresses, lingerie and infants' wear (MLH 445).

Decline

During the 1966–75 period, the Manchester conurbation lost 8904 manual jobs in clothing. Despite this absolute decline, the clothing industry has increased its relative share of the job market in the area from 8.7 per cent of manual employees in 1966 to 9 per cent in 1975; this was a relatively good employment performance. The conurbation as a whole lost 111,314 manual jobs in manufacturing during the same period, a 25 per cent decline as compared with 22.7 per cent in the clothing industry. At MLH level, contraction in Manchester differs from that at the national level (see Table 10.2), the percentage change in men's and boys' tailored outerwear and in dresses, lingerie and infants' wear being less than in the nation as a whole. In the case of the former, however, Manchester is under-represented and this may be an anomalous figure.

Table 10.2 suggests also that on the whole the conurbation performed

TABLE 10.2 Percentage change in the clothing industry employment in Manchester, the North West and Great Britain, 1966 to 1975

Minimum List Heading	Manchester	North West	Great Britain
441 Weatherproof outerwear	−38.9	−11.8	−3.0
442 Men's and boys' tailored outerwear	+0.3	−4.0	−10.0
443 Women's and girls' tailored outerwear	−29.0	−5.5	−5.5
444 Overalls, men's shirts and underwear	−18.2	−5.1	−2.3
445 Dresses, lingerie and infants' wear	−2.4	−2.2	−5.0
All clothing	−22.7	−28.6	−26.0

Sources: as for Table 10.1.

slightly better relatively than the North West and Great Britain. If the massive decline in weatherproof outerwear manufacturing, which was the most important single change within the conurbation, is excluded sectors 442–5 contracted by 13.1 per cent in Manchester compared with declines of 22.7 and 27 per cent, respectively, for the North West and Great Britain.

Components of Change

These aggregate changes are the net results of various components of change during the 1966–75 period. As Leone (1972, p. 172) states, 'aggregated data sources reveal the results, but obscure the processes of change'. Use of establishment-based data can focus research on micro-level explanations of aggregate employment shifts, such that 'the components of change approach can be described as working backwards from the effects to the causes' (Gudgin, 1978, p. 49). Such an approach has recently gained considerable currency (for example, Swales, 1976; Firn and Swales, 1978; Gudgin, 1978; Lloyd and Mason, 1978; Lloyd, 1979). Table 10.3 differentiates the components of change at the MLH level.

Closures Of the total 15,032 jobs lost through closures, about 40 per cent were concentrated within the weatherproof outerwear sector; only 8954 jobs were lost by the other 4 sectors combined. Closures were concentrated among the smaller and predominantly single-plant firms that went out of business altogether. Rates were high in all sectors, although weatherproof outerwear, and women's and girls' tailored outerwear were most prone to closure (Table 10.4). Moreover, these rates were high compared with other industries in Manchester. During the 1966–75 period 225 clothing establishments closed (13.5 per cent of all industrial establishments in 1966 and 1975, and 24 per cent of the 1966 stock of clothing establishments).

New entrants Entries are significant since they represent those sectors of the industry for which the Manchester conurbation still offers some locational attraction, and hence represent an element of employment creation. Altogether, 5967 jobs were created in new plants, offsetting closures by only a third. As Table 10.5 shows, weatherproof outerwear in job terms played an important role in entry activity, although it performed less well than expected from the sector's share of 1966 employment. Entry rates vary between sectors: Table 10.5 reveals that the highest entry rates were in dresses, lingerie and infants' wear, although most entry rates were above the average for the conurbation as a whole. A comparison of Tables 10.4 and 10.5 underscores the fact that in no single case did entry rates approach closure rates, and that the largest sector—weatherproof outerwear—had a particularly low opening rate.

TABLE 10.3 The components of change, Manchester's clothing industry, 1966 to 1975

Minimum List Heading	Net change in employment	= Openings	− Closures	+ Transfer destinations	− Transfer origins	+ Net change in survivors
441 Weatherproof outerwear	−5,650	1,420	6,078	1,126	1,462	(−656)
442 Men's and boys' tailored outerwear	10	695	879	1,520	1,401	(+75)
443 Women's and girls' tailored outerwear	−1,315	835	2,331	603	522	(+100)
444 Overalls, men's shirts and underwear	−1,721	418	2,345	1,057	960	(+109)
445 Dresses, lingerie and infants' wear	−228	2,599	3,399	1,800	1,512	(+284)
Total	−8,904	5,967	15,032	6,106	5,857	(−88)

Source: North West Industry Research Unit, unpublished data.

TABLE 10.4 Closure rates for the clothing industry in Manchester and comparative rates for conurbation and selected industries, 1966 to 1975

Minimum List Heading	Closure rate[a]
441 Weatherproof outerwear	41.92
442 Men's and boys' tailored outerwear	26.07
443 Women's and girls' tailored outerwear	51.49
444 Overalls, men's shirts and underwear	32.48
445 Dresses, lingerie and infants' wear	35.03
412 Spinning and doubling of cotton and flax	39.70
339 Other machinery	18.61
361 Electrical machinery	26.34
399 Metal industries n.e.s.	26.59
All clothing industry	38.22
Manchester conurbation	27.53

[a] Calculated as a percentage of 1966 base employment figures. In 1975 MLHs 412, 339, 361 and 399 were the leading industries in the conurbation.
Sources: North West Industry Research Unit, unpublished data; Mason, 1978.

Survivors The 349 firms surviving in their existing locations throughout the study period performed relatively well, maintaining about 18,500 manual jobs. By comparison, the conurbation overall incurred a total *in situ* loss of 19,433 manual jobs. The MLH level picture was more variable. Excluding weatherproof outerwear, the other 4 sectors added 568 manual jobs, but these have to be set against a decline of 656 in weatherproof outerwear. Even so, this latter sector still provided nearly 36 per cent of employment within the survivors sub-group, a total of 6736 jobs in 1975.

TABLE 10.5 Plant entries, Manchester's clothing industry, 1966 to 1975

Minimum List Heading	Employment in plant openings		
	Employment	Per cent of total	Opening rate[a]
441 Weatherproof outerwear	1,420	23.8	9.78
442 Men's and boys' tailored outerwear	695	11.6	20.55
443 Women's and girls' tailored outerwear	835	14.0	18.44
444 Overalls, men's shirts and underwear	418	7.0	5.79
445 Dresses, lingerie and infants' wear	2,599	43.6	27.01
Total	5,967	100.0	14.60
Manchester conurbation	28,861	—	6.44

[a] Calculated as a percentage of 1966 base total.
Source: North West Industry Research Unit, unpublished data.

Transfers Transfers can be subdivided between those plants closing in the study area to re-open elsewhere within the conurbation, and those moving outside its boundaries. In the former intra-urban category 166 plants involving 5857 jobs transferred into 159 plants creating 6106 jobs (i.e. in some cases 2 or more plants relocated into only one establishment). Intra-urban transfer dynamics differed at the product sector level. Whereas employment in weatherproof outerwear manufacturing declined by 336, the workforce in the other 4 sectors grew by 585. Employment in about 70 per cent of the plants that made intra-urban transfers declined, in about 28 per cent it expanded after the move, and in the rest it remained static.

Some closures can be reclassified as transfers out of the study area. Some 14 plants (involving 13 firms) moved out of the conurbation to other destinations within the North West area: these represented barely 3 per cent of total employment lost through closures. But these relocated firms created 740 new jobs, a 69.3 per cent increase over 1966, and hence represent the loss to Manchester of an important growth element. The figures exclude the movement of 'closures' to other regions, or to the North West under a different company name.

INTERNATIONAL TRENDS

Given that Manchester's clothing industry has an unusual structure, it could be postulated that the causes of such changes differ from those operating nationally in that the conurbation performed better than the nation as a whole (Table 10.2). While a more traditional approach would emphasize factors operating at the local scale as of prime importance to any interpretation, a more useful analytical framework is in terms of broader scale national and international developments. More importantly, it must be questioned as to how much of the employment change in Manchester has resulted from imports from developing countries. In a relative sense, the global distribution of the clothing industry has altered markedly in recent years having become increasingly important in some of the developing countries (Table 10.6). The growth of exports from Third World countries (Table 10.7) has led to concern by employers and unions in the developed world who, perceiving this trade to be a threat to their livelihood, have provoked government action, mainly in the form of non-tariff barriers.

The increased comparative advantage of the developing countries has largely been a function of labour costs and the clothing industry's low technological content. The differential between wage rates in developed and developing countries is a major reason for the changing location of production (Steed, 1981). Hence, 'lines of production that previously made cost sense in a national setting lose their justification in a global setting, being followed by the international shifting of production' (Ádám, 1975, p. 90).

TABLE 10.6 Growth in employment in clothing industries, selected developing countries, 1967 to 1976 (index 1970 = 100)

Country	1967	1969	1971	1972	1973	1974	1975	1976
Hong Kong	69.7	98.5	117.9	130.7	137.7	134.2	153.4	185.3
South Korea[a]	—	98.7	120.6	100.0	131.8	132.6	136.7	153.3
Singapore[b]	—	—	128.0	176.9	200.6	169.5	159.5	—

[a] From 1973, base 1972 = 100.
[b] Includes textiles.
Source: United Nations Economic and Social Commission for Asia and the Pacific, 1977, pp. 158, 247, 406.

Productivity rates in developing countries may equal or be slightly less than those in the developed world, but the differential in labour costs makes such comparisons meaningless. The high labour intensity of the industry is closely related to its low technological content:

Clothing as it exists at present is a low technology product that can be manufactured by any country from internationally available raw materials. It can therefore be sold only on a basis of price and quality (including design) unless fashion provides a temporary market advantage (National Economic Development Office, 1971, p. 79).

In the absence of any generally accepted alternative to sewing seams, the possibilities of reducing direct labour content in the industry are severely limited (National Economic Development Office, 1971). Clothing therefore belongs to a group of industries which 'for one reason or another have resisted the whole trend of technology in developed countries, which has been to mechanize production wherever possible' (Sharpston, 1975, p. 107). Consequently, the price of a garment prior to the retail stage depends largely

TABLE 10.7 Exports of clothing from selected developing countries, 1966 and 1975[a] ($US million)

Country	World		United States		Western Europe		United Kingdom	
	1966	1975	1966	1975	1966	1975	1966	1975
Hong Kong	354	1965	117	609	176	977	71	308
Taiwan	26	n.a.	15	n.a.	3	n.a.	—	n.a.
South Korea	32	1132	16	444	12	371	1	74
Singapore	16	117	5	45	1	440	1	5

[a] Clothing defined as SIC 841 (clothing not of fur).
Sources: United Nations Economic and Social Commission for Asia and the Far East, 1969, p. 114; United Nations Economic and Social Commission for Asia and the Pacific, 1978, p. 181.

on labour costs. The industry in developed countries therefore faces a situation in which units with comparable technology can be quickly established anywhere in the world (Clothing Economic Development Council, 1979). Because of the very few technological changes that have been made in the industry since its inception—which in any case have been diffused and adopted very rapidly (Sharpston, 1975)—no one country has a particular competitive edge (Steed, 1978b).

The major clothing exporting countries in the Third World, Taiwan, Hong Kong and South Korea, 'have to a great extent built their economies on the manufacture and export of low-cost textile and clothing products, aided by investment from the industrialised world' (National Union of Tailors and Garment Workers, 1978, p. 9). International sub-contracting, defined by Sharpston (1975, p. 94) as 'all export sales of articles which are ordered in advance, and where the giver of the order arranges the marketing', has grown in response to the difference in labour costs between developed and developing countries. For the latter it allows access to developed countries without the risks and problems of marketing, a circumstance that has been encouraged by the buying practices of large retail organizations which may either sub-contract out the manufacture of certain garments or operate their own factories in Third World countries (Helleiner, 1973; Sharpston, 1975; Richards, 1981; Steed, 1981).

NATIONAL DEVELOPMENTS IN THE CLOTHING INDUSTRY

Essentially, the comparative advantage of developing countries is expressed through the cost advantage of Third World producers, the demand for clothing, and the role of imports in meeting part of this demand.

The UK trade balance in clothing products deteriorated during the 1966–75 period (Table 10.8). The developing countries accounted for over half of all such imports, nearly a third of which (worth £165 million) came from Hong Kong (Richards, 1981). The trade deficit rose from £16 million to £240 million (1976 prices) during the decade, with the value of imports being about twice the value of exports by 1975. Because the developing countries have concentrated on the cheaper end of the market, value data underestimate the volume of imports into the UK.

Although Third World countries were important sources in 1975, high-cost areas—especially the EEC and the European Free Trade Area—supplied no less than 39.6 per cent of all clothing imports into the UK. The British industry does not seem to have been competitive even with other West European producers: Cable (1979, p. 52) has noted that 'the role of developing countries has been small . . . and imports from other industrial countries have been more important in import penetration terms'.

In addition to the growth of imports, the 1966–75 period saw a relative fall

TABLE 10.8 United Kingdom trade balance in clothing products, 1966 and 1975 (£ million)

Source/destination	1966			1975		
	Imports	Exports	Trade balance	Imports	Exports	Trade balance
EEC	21	16	−5	123	110	−13
European Free Trade Area	5	8	+3	77	64	−13
Other Western Europe	—	2	+2	15	5	−10
CMEA	1	1	—	17	4	−13
Other developed countries	5	15	+10	18	43	+25
Developing countries	32	6	−26	255	39	−216
World total	64	48	−16	505	265	−240

Source: Joint Textile Committee, 1976, p. 12.

in consumer expenditure on clothing (from 7.4 to 6.9 per cent), although there were considerable differences between product sectors (Table 10.9). A declining domestic market may have meant both declining job opportunities in a labour-intensive industry and also diminishing capacity unable to meet short-term upsurges in demand: hence, 'the industry did not have the capacity to meet demand and retailers, particularly in 1973, turned to imports to satisfy their needs' (National Union of Tailors and Garment Workers, 1978, p. 10). Even more important has been the failure of the

TABLE 10.9 Expenditure on clothing by product sector, United Kingdom, 1966 and 1975

Product sector[a]	As per cent of total annual expenditure	
	1966	1975
Men's outerwear	19.9	21.0
Men's underclothing, hosiery	9.0	8.3
Women's outerwear	30.1	33.8
Women's underclothing, hosiery	12.6	10.3
Boys' clothing	4.8	5.9
Girls' clothing	5.4	5.9
Infants' clothing	4.8	4.8
Other	13.4	10.0

[a] Not Minimum List Heading.
Source: Joint Textile Committee, 1976, p. 5.

industry to anticipate and respond to trends in fashion, particularly in menswear (an industry-specific problem), the increasing popularity of less formal clothing and the boom in leisurewear as distinct from made-to-measure garments. As the National Union of Tailors and Garment Workers (1978, p. 11) reported,

> These changes in fashion have had a profound effect on the men's outerwear sector of the clothing industry—an impact that, at times, still does not appear to have been fully understood by manufacturers. Adjustments to take account of modern trends have been slow and painful. Too often the failure to respond has resulted in rundown and redundancy.

IMPACTS ON MANCHESTER'S CLOTHING INDUSTRY

The question arises as to how international developments have affected the British clothing industry in general and whether factors peculiar to the Manchester conurbation are important in explaining employment changes within this region. On the one hand, Manchester's small share of men's outerwear manufacturing (11.2 per cent in 1975) may have meant that its response has been atypical; on the other, the declining demand for weather-proof outerwear, and hence employment in this sector, may best be explained by fashion change (a move to less-formal wear) plus social environmental change (including better heating facilities and increased car ownership).

Figure 10.2 shows that in 1976 import penetration levels for raincoats were less than 30 per cent of UK total consumption (by volume), some 15 to 20 per cent of the total being from developing countries. For Manchester's other major product sector—dresses, lingerie and infants' wear—import penetration levels for dresses and skirts are about 23 per cent, with some 14 to 15 per cent coming from Third World sources.

These 2 product groups, MLH 441 and MLH 445, provided 60 per cent of the jobs in the Manchester clothing industry in 1975. If imports of clothing were a significant causal factor leading to the industry's decline in Manchester, it could reasonably be assumed that the major effect has been upon the other 3 sectors. In the case of MLH 442, MLH 443 and MLH 444, import penetration levels were, respectively, about 50 to 55 per cent, 54 per cent and 60 per cent. It can be supposed, in view of these import levels, that manufacturers in Manchester were constrained by lack of demand even though these 3 sectors provided less than 40 per cent of manual employment within the industry.

Several attempts have been made to quantify the impact of imports on employment in the clothing industry, notably Cable (1977a,b), United Kingdom, Foreign and Commonwealth Office (1979) and Fröbel et al.

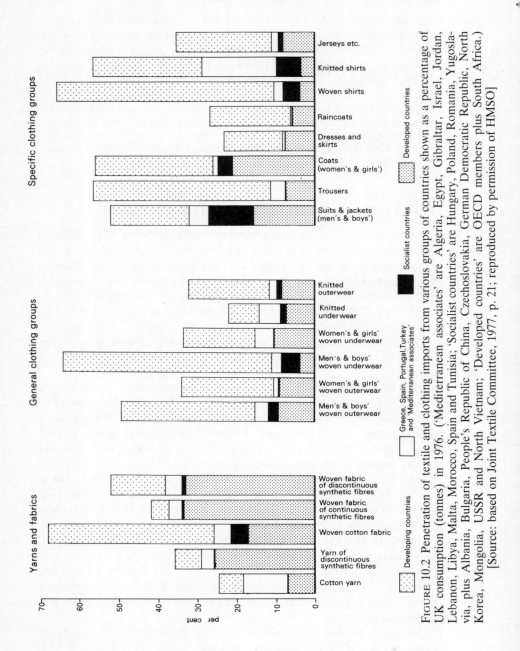

FIGURE 10.2 Penetration of textile and clothing imports from various groups of countries shown as a percentage of UK consumption (tonnes) in 1976. ('Mediterranean associates' are Algeria, Egypt, Gibraltar, Israel, Jordan, Lebanon, Libya, Malta, Morocco, Spain and Tunisia; 'Socialist countries' are Hungary, Poland, Romania, Yugoslavia, plus Albania, Bulgaria, People's Republic of China, Czechoslovakia, German Democratic Republic, North Korea, Mongolia, USSR and North Vietnam; 'Developed countries' are OECD members plus South Africa.) [Source: based on Joint Textile Committee, 1977, p. 21; reproduced by permission of HMSO]

(1980). Table 10.10, derived by using the method applied by the Government Economic Service, assesses the absolute impact on the Manchester conurbation of trade in clothing with the developing countries to try to assign responsibility for clothing employment changes between 1966 and 1975.

Clearly, losses of employment have largely ensued from increased productivity which led to the shedding of 13,035 jobs, while imports from all sources accounted for the loss of a further 8510. More specifically, imports from developing countries accounted for gross losses of 4223 jobs (nearly half the employment loss attributable to imports). To arrive at the net job losses of 8904 by this method, it is postulated that the workforce increased by 12,641 as a result of home demand and expanded exports.

The method, however, does have shortcomings. In particular, it assumes that the sources of employment change operated independently of one another whereas, in reality, interdependence is the more likely. Of greater importance, domestic productivity increases may have been stimulated by Third World competition: in the absence of any rises in productivity, domestic demand and exports would probably have increased less and imports might have increased more. This view is shared by the National Union of Tailors and Garment Workers (1978) and the Clothing Economic Development Council (1980, p. 27):

> The EDC rejects completely any supposition that greater productivity rather than the incursion of imports has been responsible for the loss of employment in the UK. Without improvements in productivity employment losses would have been even greater, as a result of companies becoming uncompetitive and going out of business.

Table 10.10 shows that in all sectors imports from developing countries were a less important source of employment decline than either gains in productivity or losses attributable to imports from high-cost sources. Work by Cable (1977b) and the National Union of Tailors and Garment Workers (1978) also suggest that productivity increases were the major source of employment loss. Only about 17 per cent of gross employment losses can be attributed to net import penetration from the developing countries and those belonging to the Council for Mutual Economic Assistance (CMEA) (Cable, 1977b).

Both studies propose that imports from developing countries accounted for 1 per cent out of a loss of 2.4 per cent each year in UK clothing employment as a whole. On this basis, the decline in Manchester during the 1966–75 period averaged 2.3 per cent annually (a crude rate derived by dividing the total decline by the number of years concerned). A loss of 1 per cent annually (of an annual total of 2.3 per cent) would be equivalent to a

TABLE 10.10 Sources of employment change in the Manchester clothing industry, 1966 to 1975

Minimum List Heading	Overall change in employment	Increase in employment attributable to		Decrease in employment attributable to		
		Home demand	Exports	Productivity	Total imports	Imports from developing countries
441 Weatherproof outerwear	−5,650	2,301	245	4,959	3,237	(1,606)
442 Men's and boys' tailored outerwear	10	2,070	220	1,379	901	(447)
443 Women's and girls' tailored outerwear	−1,315	1,390	148	1,726	1,127	(559)
444 Overalls, men's shirts and underwear	−1,721	1,431	153	2,000	1,305	(648)
445 Dresses, lingerie and infants' wear	−228	4,233	450	2,971	1,940	(963)
All clothing	−8,904	11,425	1,216	13,035	8,510	(4,223)

Source: North West Industry Research Unit, unpublished data.

total decline of about 890 jobs over the entire study period. If the data are further disaggregated into the 2 periods for which they are available, the main employment decline (17 per cent, or 3 per cent annually) occurred between 1966 and 1972 as against an overall decline of 5.8 per cent, or 1.9 per cent annually, from 1973 to 1975.

Given that the greatest contraction in employment occurred during the first period, it would seem likely that events in the Manchester industry were caused mainly by fashion changes, productivity rises and imports from high-cost sources rather than from increased competition from Third World products. This is especially so when it is considered that import penetration rates rose after 1972, 'a crucial period before MFA [Multi-Fibre Arrangement] restraint was effective' (Cable, 1977b, p. 26). But both these analytical methods ignore more parochial causes of employment decline. In Manchester, the local changes now to be discussed have led to a reduction in the number of clothing firms and employment.

THE MANCHESTER SCENE

Characteristically, clothing firms tend to be concentrated in the inner parts of large metropolitan areas to which they are attracted by agglomeration economies (Martin, 1966; Dicken, 1968). Consequently, forces operating within such areas have had an important effect on the job opportunities available in the clothing industry (Falk and Martinos, 1975).

At the local level a major influence on decline has been local government redevelopment activity (Gripaios, 1977a).

In the 1960s and early 1970s inner Manchester underwent massive urban renewal. The city cleared large tracts of housing and areas of mixed land use. Inevitably industry has been affected and given the nature of planning philosophy and the locational distributions involved, it has been the small plants and lighter industries which have suffered the most (Lloyd and Mason, 1978, p. 86).

Much local redevelopment has occurred through application of Compulsory Purchase Orders (CPOs) by local authorities. Under the *Town and Country Planning Act* of 1971 local authorities can be authorized by the Secretary of State to compulsorily acquire land in their area for purposes of redevelopment or improvement. Compensation is paid to the occupants of the land under the principle of market value compensation, i.e. the amount which the land if sold in the open market by a willing seller might be expected to realize (Heap, 1978). While large-scale industry has been left undisturbed, clothing, with many small plants, has been most affected by redevelopment activity (Stedman and Wood, 1965; Manchester City Planning Department, 1970). However, CPOs have not necessarily exacerbated closure rates. Lloyd and Mason (1978) found that only 12 per cent of plants that closed during the 1966–75 period in Manchester County Borough, which contained 20 per cent of the population and 9 per cent of the Greater Manchester County area in 1971 (United Kingdom, Office of Population Censuses and Surveys, 1975), were directly affected by CPOs, although they suggest that CPOs more strongly influenced the transfer of plants. This concurs with Chalkley's (1978) thesis that several small firms in Leeds turned CPOs into opportunities to move to better premises. No data are available about clothing firms as such but the total number of inner city plants affected by CPOs in Manchester County Borough is indicated in Table 10.11. Clothing firms were also dominant in the absolute numbers of transfers (24 per cent) and number of inner city plants (32 per cent). If this surrogate measure of the impact of redevelopment be accepted, the many clothing factories involved in transfers (24 per cent of all those in the Manchester conurbation during the 1966–75 period) can be partly explained by external factors. However, for the 20 per cent of intra-urban transfers which expanded after movement this may not be true since these may be more successful enterprises, at least in employment terms.

Mason (1978) argues that factors producing high potential mobility include small plant size, undemanding requirements about site and premises and low capital investment, all of which apply to small clothing factories. Moreover, it is impossible to quantify the effect of CPOs on closure rates as a result of loss of either business confidence or cheap premises through demolition (Warnes, 1977). The latter may also have exacerbated the low level of entry rates shown in Table 10.5 and high closure rates in Table 10.4. In many cases the simultaneous redevelopment of residential areas may have deprived firms of their previous labour supply (Foreman-Peck and Gripaios, 1977). Many workers have been displaced from the central labour market to peripheral housing estates, and family and home commitments often prevent women from undertaking long journeys to work; the centrally

TABLE 10.11 Plants affected by CPOs in Manchester County Borough, 1966 to 1975

Impact	Total number of plants		Per cent of plants affected by CPOs
	in Manchester County Borough	affected by CPOs	
Closure	866	82	9.5
Transfers within inner city	174	37	21.3
Transfers outside inner city	89	27	30.3
Total	1129	146	12.9

Source: Lloyd and Mason, 1978.

located clothing industry, employing a high proportion of females, has been particularly hard hit (McKean, 1975). A survey by Manchester City Planning Department (1970) concluded that many factories, especially in the clothing industry, faced labour shortages and this was confirmed during fieldwork by the author in mid-1979.

Redevelopment may also have affected the birth of new firms to replace those lost by CPO activity. The 'seed-bed' hypothesis proposes that the inner parts of large cities function as nurseries for small plants and the first-time entrepreneurs who occupy them (Fagg, 1978). The cheap, although often poor quality, premises available there present relatively easy entry to aspiring manufacturers (Cameron and Johnson, 1969) aided by the range of external economies offered, in terms of services and labour (Struyk and James, 1975). High labour intensity and low technological content, characteristic of the clothing industry, fit in with the seed-bed concept since such firms have low initial factor thresholds and can commence operations in a small way.

By destroying low-cost premises in Manchester's inner areas, redevelopment may have reduced the applicability of the seed-bed concept (Mason, 1978). Empirical studies suggest that the birth of new firms is most typical in industries (like clothing) possessing ease of entry in terms of technological and premises requirements, needing minimal capital investment, and demanding skill and innovative capacity in product design (Townroe, 1970; Keeble, 1976). While Taylor (1969) has suggested that a high closure rate may provide an impetus for a high birth rate (because of the ready availability of second-hand premises and equipment), Mason (1978, p. 287) claims that 'Greater Manchester's employment problem is . . . one of a very high closure rate and a low opening rate' a view borne out by Tables 10.4 and 10.5. Redevelopment may have destroyed the conditions necessary for seed-bed growth and led to high closure rates and low opening rates, not only in Manchester but in the other major UK conurbations (Cameron, 1973; Dennis, 1978; Firn and Swales, 1978).

The seed-bed concept suggests that the migration of industrial establishments is a progression whereby successful small firms, established in cheap premises, expand *in situ* until the existing site becomes too restrictive. At this stage there is a search for new premises, perhaps in the middle urban ring if such sites are available, but more likely on a suburban estate (Lloyd, 1979). Only the successful shift out, and these are likely to have more employees than those remaining in the inner areas unless they substitute capital for labour (Lloyd, 1979). Firms that made inter-regional moves also tended to increase their workforces (Keeble, 1971).

Because the clothing industry is labour-intensive little capital substitution is, in fact, likely, and it seems safe to assume that 'success' will result in increased employment (Firn and Hughes, 1973). But since some 75 per cent of the clothing workforce are women (National Economic Development Office, 1974) who are generally unwilling or unable to travel long distances to work (Andrews, 1978), the choice of location may be related to the availability of new labour markets or continued accessibility for the existing workforce.

Much relocation has occurred within the central area of Manchester which is readily accessible by public transport. Since 27 per cent of the 1966 clothing workforce was located in the inner city and that the mean distance moved by relocating firms was 2.5 km, shifts to fringe areas of the conurbation have been insignificant. Intra-urban transfers are important, however, in determining the long-term viability of the source areas. If mobile firms tend to be the more successful and expanding ones, their loss removes an important long-term growth component from the area of origin, especially where the industry has important local linkages. Movement may therefore lead to a long-run cascade effect of closure (Lloyd and Mason, 1978).

MANCHESTER AND THE NORTH-SOUTH DEBATE

Manchester's decline as a clothing centre seems to have been related more to changes in fashion and local redevelopment activity than to import competition from developing countries. Links with retailers, fashion trends, the weather, labour supply and local redevelopment are all factors that have affected Manchester's clothing industry and, in particular, that section of it producing weatherproof outerwear. Changes in this sector have resulted from an absolute decline in demand rather than from an increased share of the market being taken by imported items. Market decline has been mainly due to changing fashion and social trends away from the purchase of weatherproof outerwear; this sector is likely to decline further.

Manchester's most important sector for employment, dresses, lingerie and infants' wear, will probably see increased import penetration from high and low-cost sources, especially given the increasingly overseas-orientated purchasing practices of retailing chains which accounted for 45 per cent of all women's clothing sold in 1971 (Joint Textile Committee, 1976). In other sectors, too, there is no cause for complacency. For example, the post-1975 rationalization of the Burton Group Ltd meant the closure of the 2 largest clothing plants in Manchester producing men's and boys' tailored outerwear. (The Burton Group Ltd is based in Leeds and is the parent of a group of subsidiaries engaged as retailers and manufacturers of clothing; in 1981 the company employed 13,250 people in the UK (Dun and Bradstreet, 1981).) This sector has high import penetration levels (especially from CMEA countries), although these particular closures were blamed by management on fashion changes.

Absolute decline caused by such import penetration from developing countries may have been about 10 per cent of the total job losses during the 1966–75 period. More important were structural factors stemming from fashion change and local redevelopment, relationships that policy-makers should consider before seeking to control clothing imports from Third World countries. As Cecil Parkinson, then Minister at the Department of Trade, has reportedly said (*Financial Times,* 1 February 1980):

> What the Government cannot do is to regulate fashion changes, protect firms that do not up-date their designs, protect workers who will not operate modern machines effectively or generally stop or control imports . . . from other developed countries, many of whom have wage costs far in excess of our own.

Despite such findings unions and producers will probably press for continued, if not increased, import controls through the Multi-Fibre Arrangement. The rationale for protection has been largely based upon a 'conservative social-welfare function' (Corden, 1975, p. 80).

> The fact that the protected industries are not usually dominated by large international firms and tend to be located in depressed areas and to employ the least affluent workers of the rich countries produce wide political backing for the joint pleas of labour and capital in these industries for defence against low-wage products (Helleiner, 1973, p. 28).

Short-term political considerations, set against a background of depression, inflation and unemployment, have largely governed policy. Whereas losses of employment from whatever cause are immediately obvious (especially if they emerge in electorally sensitive areas), any gains from expanded exports to developing countries are more diffuse and less visible since, in part, they accrue outside the manufacturing sector and in very different locations.

Advocates of trade restrictions seem to rule out the concept of specialization and international trade. Obviously trade-induced change does have costs (as do changes due to fashion, technical innovation and industrial reorganization), but it can also lead to substantial gains in real income, despite the devastating impacts of structural unemployment. The basic problems are how 'industrial change can be made less traumatic such that specific groups of workers do not pay the price for general economic advance' (Cable, 1977b, p. 5), and how adequate adjustment assistance can be provided; anything less denies the low-paid workers in advanced countries the chance of anything better (Mukherjee, 1974).

Yet it is unreasonable to penalize people in developing countries fortunate enough to have job opportunities. Clothing exports are an important source of foreign exchange, and 'the issues presented by trade in these items have an important bearing on North-South relations as a whole' (Cable, 1979, p. 40). Developing countries cannot be expected to remain dependent within the world economy; therefore, instead of preventing trade, developed nations should take the opportunity to redeploy their capital in more productive occupations (Cutajar and Franks, 1967). Although this may involve short-term costs and human hardship the long-term gains both to North and South could be considerable.

Spatial Analysis, Industry and the Industrial Environment. Vol. 3 Regional Economies and Industrial Systems
Edited by F. E. I. Hamilton and G. J. R. Linge
© 1983 John Wiley & Sons Ltd.

Chapter 11

Industrial Innovation and Regional Economic Development in Great Britain

J. B. GODDARD

THE REGIONAL POLICY CONTEXT

Policy Performance: Past and Present

This chapter examines industrial development in lagging regions of a mature economy (Great Britain) and public policy responses to this problem. However, studies undertaken for the Commission for the European Communities reveal similar problems throughout most of Western Europe (Ewers and Wettmann, 1980). Economic adjustment problems in older industrial areas have long been recognized, especially those in the peripheral regions of national space-economies, although exceptions are the Ruhr in West Germany and of many cities in the US manufacturing belt. In various countries the response has been to attempt to stimulate economic development in lagging regions by industrial investment incentives and (less commonly) by controls on industrial development in more prosperous areas (Allen and Yuill, 1979). Such policies have successfully plugged the employment gap created by the rundown of traditional industries like shipbuilding and heavy engineering. Much new investment has occurred in assisted areas but this has chiefly been diverted from more prosperous regions and has taken the form of new branch plants of national or international companies (cf. Keeble, 1976).

There is, however, mounting evidence that policies successful in the 1960s were less so in the 1970s and will have very limited effect in the 1980s. Moreover, while they achieved the short-run objective of providing immediate employment, past regional policies have probably been insufficient to create the basis for internally generated self-sustained economic growth in lagging regions (Segal, 1979).

Two broad groups of reasons explain why the 1980s will be different.

'Cyclical' factors Many OECD economies are well into the most prolonged recession since the 1930s, restricting mobile industrial investment available for lagging regions. This mobile investment is strongly correlated with the business cycle (Moore *et al.*, 1977; and Figure 11.1). Labour

255

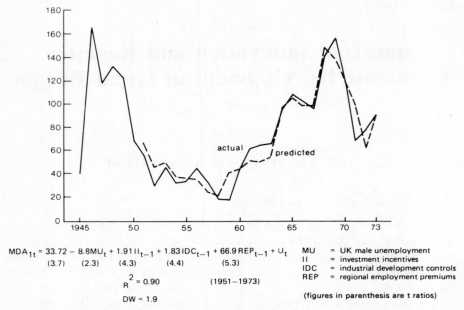

$$MDA_{1t} = 33.72 - 8.8MU_t + 1.91II_{t-1} + 1.83IDC_{t-1} + 66.9REP_{t-1} + U_t$$
$$\quad\quad (3.7) \quad\; (2.3) \quad\;\; (4.3) \quad\quad (4.4) \quad\quad\;\; (5.3)$$

$$R^2 = 0.90 \quad\quad\quad (1951-1973)$$

$$DW = 1.9$$

MU = UK male unemployment
II = investment incentives
IDC = industrial development controls
REP = regional employment premiums

(figures in parenthesis are t ratios)

FIGURE 11.1 Actual and expected movement of firms to Development Areas in Great Britain, 1951 to 1973. [Source: Moore *et al.*, 1977]

shortage, one of the chief push factors in diverting industrial investment from more prosperous regions, is less important when unemployment is rising generally; in this situation industrial development controls are more difficult to apply. The net result has been less job creation in assisted areas as a result of regional policy in the 1970s (11,000 jobs per annum cumulative in UK assisted areas during the 1971–77 period as against 20,000 in the more prosperous 1960s) (Marquand, 1980). The general state of the economy also limits public funds available for regional industrial subsidies. For example, during the period from 1971–72 to 1977–78 the gross direct exchequer costs of UK regional policy were £4930 million. While the net exchequer costs are less, because of increased tax revenues and reduced unemployment benefits, the response of the Thatcher Government—concerned to lower public expenditure—has been to drastically reduce the areas eligible for automatic regional investment assistance to those with the worst unemployment problems but possibly the lowest growth potential (Townsend, 1980b). These responses reflect both the current economic situation and a general climate of opinion about national fiscal policy.

'*Structural*' *factors* The increased ineffectiveness of traditional regional policy instruments is explained also by possibly more fundamental structural changes in the nature and location of industrial investment. Lagging regions have sought to attract totally new industrial or green-field developments. However, with reduced investment a larger proportion is going into replacement rather than new investment. In West Germany, for example, data on gross and net investment, capital stock and capital coefficients reveal that rationalization as a proportion of total investment has increased in the 1970s (quoted in Ewers and Wettmann, 1980).

Part of the explanation for this trend is changing international investment patterns. West European companies are increasingly turning to newly industrializing countries (NICs) where operating costs are lower than in the peripheral regions of their own countries even after taking account of industrial subsidies. Lagging regions of industrialized nations have lost their competitive advantage of low-cost industrialized labour. At the same time, inward investment to countries like the UK from the US is slowing down or increasingly taking the form of the acquisition of indigenous companies rather than green-field development. Moreover, whereas the latter tended to favour assisted areas, acquisition is generally concentrated in more prosperous areas because that is where more successful firms are to be found (Smith, 1980).

In the long run the dichotomy between structural and cyclical factors may be false. Perhaps the present recession represents a major trough in a Kontratiev long wave and is associated with current technological progress (Freeman, 1977a,b; Ray, 1980). From an analysis of patent data Mensch (1979) suggests that there is currently an innovation trough and the benefits of technologically introduced growth resulting from the widespread diffusion of micro-electronic based goods and services are yet to come. Thus, very many electro-mechanical products are at the end of their life cycle but as yet few new products have entered the production system to take up the slack.

Whatever the causes, the current economic and technological situation has revealed some longer-term weaknesses in traditional regional policy, namely that sectoral diversification of industrial structures in lagging regions has not been accompanied by diversification of occupations so that manual (as opposed to professional) jobs prevail (Northern Region Strategy Team, 1977). Regional policy tended to foster new employment in branch plants with truncated management hierarchies. Lagging regions have not participated as much as more prosperous areas in the general shift towards the white-collar employment both within manufacturing industry and producer services (Goddard, 1979).

This trend may be related to another apparent failure of past policy in that many of the jobs created have not been permanent: evidence indicates an increasing closure rate of mobile manufacturing plants recently established in UK assisted areas, and plants set up since 1966 have consistently had lower survival rates than those established in non-assisted areas, irrespective of their origin (Henderson, 1979). The reasons are several. For example, mobile plants may be particularly vulnerable to overseas competition especially from NICs and also from technological displacement because of a tendency to manufacture goods at the end of their product life cycle. But even more serious is employment loss through *in situ* contraction of indigenous establishments; in Scotland this has not been compensated either by totally new openings or by in-movement from other areas (Marquand, 1980) and has led to the demise of older industry in the larger conurbations. Despite the limitation of employment data as an indicator of economic performance at the establishment level, there is clearly a general failure of competitiveness amongst both indigenous and mobile industry in Britain's lagging regions.

Towards a New Local Economic Development Strategy

The manufacture of new products and the rapid diffusion of new production techniques appears to be central to the international competitiveness of national economies (Denison, 1962; Freeman, 1979d). Hence governments have become actively involved in innovation at a national level, frequently adopting an aggressive stance towards technological development (Freeman, 1978). In the face of intensified competition between advanced economies and also between them and NICs, many governments have sought to increase the human capital input into production, for example through public R & D effort, thereby creating totally new markets or moving 'up market' within existing product ranges (Science Council of Canada, 1979; Britton, 1980). However, such strategies will not achieve the much desired goal of self-sustained regional economic growth because presumably the ability of a firm to participate in technological progress is in part *spatially determined* by its particular locational environment. Many of the constraints on the innovation process are locational, including shortages of required skills, problems of access to specialist information and the lack of subcontractors. There are thus systematic spatial variations in the *potential* for innovation, and lagging regions generally have the poorest environment. A spatial dimension to national innovation policies is thus necessary to achieve national objectives and an innovation dimension to regional policies is necessary to attain regional objectives. Both types of policy will be concerned with raising the technological capacity of economic activity in *all* parts of national territories. While such a strategy may not be directly job-creating in every case, it is preferable to wholesale industrial collapse arising from a loss of competitive advantage by industries in backward regions.

Unfortunately, governments frequently fail to link regional and national policy adequately (Cameron, 1979). This is clearly demonstrated in Figure 11.2 where there is a heavy concentration in South East England, the most

FIGURE 11.2 Location of micro-electronics applications consultants licensed by the UK Department of Industry

innovative region, of consultancies licensed by the UK Department of Industry to provide advice on micro-electronics applications. More and not less effort should be devoted to the stimulation of technological change in lagging regions. This is supported by empirical evidence in the remainder of this chapter, the regional aspects of the innovation process having been adequately reviewed elsewhere (e.g. Thomas and Le Heron, 1975; Thwaites, 1978b).

REGIONAL VARIATIONS IN INNOVATION POTENTIAL

Research and Development

The important contribution of systematic research work to industrial innovation is widely acknowledged, as is the fact that R & D inputs vary systematically between industries and between small and large enterprises (Freeman, 1974). Yet significant regional disparities exist in the location of R & D laboratories, with a marked concentration in South East England outside London. The pattern of public-sector laboratories is very similar. In the US there is a considerable concentration of R & D laboratories in major metropolitan centres (Malecki, 1980). Industrial structure partly explains this, particularly as the more successful regions tend to specialize in industries with a high R & D component. However, Crum and Gudgin (1978) and Thwaites (1978b) indicate that regions like South East England have significantly more R & D workers and the Northern Region significantly less than would be expected, given each Region's industrial structure.

Other factors are clearly at work. Multi-site organizations in all industries tend to centralize R & D functions in core regions because of the advantage of access to technical information which may not be *specific* to individual industries. Possibilities are thus opened up for the transfer of knowledge from one product or process field to a totally new product or process field and may be facilitated not only by personal contact but also by the actual job mobility of R & D personnel between laboratories—and this can be more readily achieved in areas of concentrated R & D employment opportunities where individuals can change jobs without necessarily changing residence.

Other Management Functions

Successful innovation comes about with the linking of scientific research and development to actual or perceived market needs (Langrish *et al.*, 1972; Sappho, 1972) which have been identified by a number of management functions. Such functions as market research may be provided 'in house' in headquarters or purchased by headquarters as business services on a consultancy or contract basis. Evidence again points to a concentration of company headquarters and specialist services in more prosperous regions. For example, Crum and Gudgin (1978) in a study of 415 manufacturing sites in the UK for 80 of the largest multi-regional manufacturing companies, found much lower proportions of non-production workers to total employment in branch plants as compared with those sites with an associated headquarters (usually a divisional office). Moreover, branches in a lagging region like the Northern have proportionately fewer non-production workers than branches elsewhere (Table 11.1). This is especially conspicuous in marketing and distribution. Smith (1979) reveals that 77 per cent of manufacturing establishments employing more than 100 workers in the Northern Region were not locally owned in 1973, an increase from 42 per cent in 1963 partly resulting from the in-migration of branch plants, but primarily from the acquisition of indigenous companies by firms based outside the Region (Table 11.2). Other research has suggested that acquisition is associated with centralization of many management functions of the acquiring company (Leigh and North, 1978).

There is also evidence that single region companies may have fewer non-production workers in lagging regions as compared with those elsewhere. In a survey of 96 indigenous and non-locally owned *establishments* in Northern England, Marshall (1979a) discovered that management functions accounted for 28 per cent of total employment in indigenous companies

TABLE 11.1 Non-production function proportions[a] by status of establishment, Northern Region of England and United Kingdom, 1976

Department/function	Branch		Non-detached head office[b]	
	Northern Region	UK	Northern Region	UK
General management	1.2	4.5	3.3	5.2
Specialist services	2.4	3.7	4.1	5.8
Personnel and maintenance	6.2	6.2	5.2	6.9
Production-related	10.7	7.6	10.6	8.4
Research and development	0.3	0.7	2.8	1.7
Marketing and distribution	2.5	7.2	4.8	13.3
Other	0.0	0.6	0.0	0.4
Total non-production functions	23.5	30.4	30.7	41.7
Number of observations	15	352	7	64

[a] Per cent of all employment (production and non-production).
[b] Containing both non-detached head offices of multi-site firms and single-site firms.
Source: Crum and Gudgin, 1978.

TABLE 11.2 Ownership status, Northern Region manufacturing establishments, 1963 and 1973

Ownership status	Per cent of regional manufacturing employment (establishments with over 100 employees)	
	1963	1973
Independent plant	10.6	4.4
Branch controlled within region	13.3	7.9
Regional parent plant	23.9	9.9
Plant acquired by company with headquarters outside region 1963–73	17.2	31.4
Externally controlled branch never locally owned	35.0	46.3
Total	100.0	99.9

Source: Smith, 1979.

compared with 37 per cent and 36 per cent, respectively, in subsidiary and large establishments (Table 11.3). As with Crum and Gudgin's (1978) national study of multi-site *organizations*, production management was the predominant function in the non-locally owned sector while indigenous companies contained a broader range of functions. Unfortunately no data are available for independent companies in other regions; nevertheless the low absolute numbers of workers in management functions in independent companies in the Northern Region in comparison to the externally owned

TABLE 11.3 Proportion of non-production employees in Northern Region manufacturing firms by ownership status

Non-production functions	Independent[a]	Subsidiary[b]	Branch[c]
General management services	7.0	6.9	4.5
Legal and financial services	3.8	4.2	3.7
Personnel	3.6	8.8	8.2
Production	4.6	8.3	11.7
Research and development	0.5	0.4	0.4
Marketing and distribution	8.0	7.6	7.1
Other	0.3	0.9	0.3
Total non-production employees	27.8	37.1	35.9
Sampled establishments	28	13	42

[a] Independent establishments: share capital completely controlled by the establishment.

[b] Subsidiary establishments: those whose share capital is at least partially controlled from outside the establishment.

[c] Branch establishments: completely owned by another establishment elsewhere.

Source: Marshall, 1979a.

group of establishments indicates a limited commitment to those types of activities related to innovation and diversification.

In theory the absence of management functions 'in-house' can be compensated for by the purchase of specialist business services but these, too, are highly localized (James, 1978). For example, only 1.4 per cent of UK employment in market research and advertising is in the Northern Region compared with its 5 per cent share of total employment. Despite this, another study has shown that indigenous companies purchased 72 per cent of their business service requirements within the area, while externally owned firms meet 77 per cent of such requirements from outside it (Marshall, 1979b). Whether the *absolute* level of business service inputs varied between the 2 groups of establishments cannot be determined because of lack of information.

Information Inputs

While much technical information is widely available through specialist trade journals, this does not necessarily lead to innovation decisions. The extensive literature on intra and inter-organizational communications suggests the hypothesis that decisions to adopt new production processes in manufacturing like computer-controlled machine tools are greatly influenced by personal contacts especially with existing adopters (Rogers and Agawala-Rogers, 1976; Grønhaug and Fredrikesen, 1978). In theory the more geographically widespread the contact network of management in a company the greater the probability of connection with sources of information relevant to its own innovative performance. If the contact network is highly localized, the value of the information input would depend very much on the diversity of the immediate environment.

McDermott's (1977b) investigation of information linkages of marketing managers of electronics firms in 3 contrasting regions of the UK—Greater London, the Outer Metropolitan Area and Scotland—confirms the findings of others as to the dominance of the local environment in information flows, especially those external to the organization. He (p. 233) considered that this placed

> Scottish firms at a disadvantage as their local region does not coincide with or adjoin the current centre of market-related information for the electronics industry as it does for London and Outer Metropolitan Area respondents.

Contact fields of marketing managers in the Outer Metropolitan Area were less localized than those of their counterparts elsewhere, a finding which gains significance when considering the quality of information flows, with the more routine contacts tending to take place over longer distances. Thus, although the local environment is relatively more important to the Scottish-based firms, the quality of non-routine information obtained from that environment is likely to be poorer than for those firms based elsewhere. McDermott (1977b, p. 247) concludes:

> in day-to-day external communications the marketing sub-system maintains relatively wide spatial horizons with respect to those functions for which it holds primary responsibility, the maintenance and monitoring of customer relations. However, in less routine functions, functions which may well be more critical in terms of general firm management and alignment, respondents were, on average, considerably more constrained in their spatial interaction, suggesting a greater degree of dependence upon local information.

While the information fields of Scottish firms were more locally peaked, their spatial extent was greater, reflecting a peripheral location *vis-à-vis* the rest of the UK; as far as information via personal contacts is concerned, marketing managers in Scottish-based firms are inevitably involved in extensive business travel. An information theory of regional development would suggest that firms based solely in peripheral areas would also be peripheral to the dominant information flows in the space-economy. Because of the travel time involved, fewer business contacts will be maintained than by equivalent firms in core regions, possibly resulting in less innovative activity especially in industries for which managers perceive a relatively stable market and technological environment. In contrast, contacts in multi-site organizations with regional establishments would be predominantly internalized and confined to lower levels of the managerial hierarchy.

Marshall's (1979b) study of the contacts of key communicators in 96 manufacturing units in the Northern Region reinforces McDermott's findings, revealing that independent companies (and small units using jobbing technology) there have a predominantly locally orientated contact network, even though they sell their products in national and international markets. In contrast, non-locally owned and larger establishments using more continuous production technology have a non-local contact orientation. These results are confirmed at a more aggregate scale by business travel by air and rail from the Northern Region to the South East Region of England (James, 1978). After allowing for the relative importance of each sector of the Northern Regional economy, the analysis revealed that the *less* travel-intensive sectors included more representatives of top management from small headquarters workplaces while the *more* travel-intensive sectors included more representatives of technical staff from large subsidiary or branch establishments, journeying principally to other company sites (Figure 11.3). Although no ownership breakdown is available, all diary studies emphasize the dominant importance of the local environment in business contacts (Thorngren, 1970; Connell, 1974; Goddard, 1975), results totally

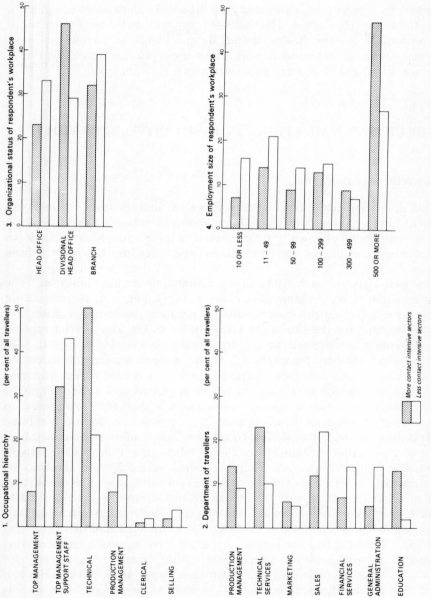

FIGURE 11.3 Inter-regional business travel by rail and air between the Northern and South East Regions of England

consistent with basic principles of space-time geography. However, the *range* of information relevant to technological change within a given time distance in a lagging area, particularly for the small independent company, is likely to be severely limited. The multi-site company with a larger number of non-production workers has more staff time available for contact via inter-personal communication and can also draw upon information derived from company sites located in more information-rich environments.

REGIONAL VARIATIONS IN INNOVATIVE BEHAVIOUR

Measurement of Innovation

This discussion has drawn upon a range of findings from research not explicitly concerned with technical innovation. The case that regional variation in some factors known to be inputs to the innovation process also leads to differences in innovative behaviour between localities has not yet been proven.

One major reason is the difficulty of actually measuring innovation. The most common proxy is patent data (Taylor, 1977), but many patents do not become products and the data recorded are usually for company headquarters rather than for the site of the invention or its first commercial application. Patents thus represent the invention rather than the innovation stage in technological advance. Furthermore, many products are manufactured but have no real economic or technological impact. A way round these problems is to seek the opinion of a range of technical experts in a variety of fields, asking them to name *significant* innovations within their own area of competence. Freeman (1974) adopted this approach in his study of the contribution of small British firms to technological innovation undertaken for the Committee of Inquiry on Small Firms (the Bolton Committee). Experts in industry, government and academic research were asked to list the principal post-war innovations and, where possible, to name the innovating firms. If several experts mentioned an innovation the companies concerned were asked to confirm the information. This strategy produced 1200 major innovations attributable to about 800 firms in 55 industries covering half the UK manufacturing output. An alternative approach to identifying innovative activity is by the annual competition, operating since 1966, for the Queen's Award to Industry for Innovation. Up to 1975, 3585 entries had been received by this scheme and 241 awards made and the data set has been extensively used in a non-regional context by Langrish *et al.* (1972).

Regional Distribution of Innovative Manufacturing Establishments in Great Britain

Neither the coverage nor the representativeness of both sources of information is known to have a spatial bias in its mode of collection. Yet in the belief that firms in more dynamic regions are more likely to enter a competition than equally innovative firms in a lagging area, Oakey *et al.* (1980) undertook a postal survey of firms identified in the 2 data sets, aimed at finding the location of the first commercial production of each innovation. The survey covered 323 innovations, 288 of them being product innovations, introduced during the 1965–76 period. The survey concentrated on the most recent innovation in those firms attributed with several and, by removing the non-respondents untraceable because of movement, acquisition or closure, the final response rate was 86 per cent.

In absolute terms the South East and Midlands Regions contain the most establishments accredited with the first commercial production (or utilization) of an innovation (Figure 11.4 and Table 11.4). Relative to the number of workers in manufacturing industry in each Region, however, the West Midlands appears to have fewer innovations and East Anglia and the South West more, while the South East maintains its leading position. These rankings concur with regional employment performance and thus highlight the success of the East Anglia and South West Regions and the relatively poor performance of the West Midlands (Keeble, 1976). Levels of R & D effort and innovative activity generally vary significantly between industrial sectors and Oakey *et al.* (1980) show that 5 sectors—mechanical engineering, electrical engineering, chemical engineering, instrument engineering, and vehicles (which includes aerospace)—account for 75 per cent of all innovations, with instrument engineering being the most innovative sector relative to its labour force. A reasonable hypothesis is that regional variations in industrial structure largely account for the distribution of innovative establishments described in Table 11.4. For example, the high-ranking position of the Northern Region may be explained partly by innovations in shipbuilding there. But the results achieved by Oakey *et al.* suggest that the paucity of innovations in the development areas could not be attributed solely to their industrial structure; in contrast the industrial structure of the South East favoured innovation while remaining areas have industries with a poor innovation record. In general, the development areas were less innovative than might have been expected by their industrial structure whereas the reverse was the case in the South East.

Arguably the key personnel involved in innovation are non-production workers, and therefore it is incorrect to include all workers in each sector as the basis for the standardizations for industrial structure. Oakey *et al.*

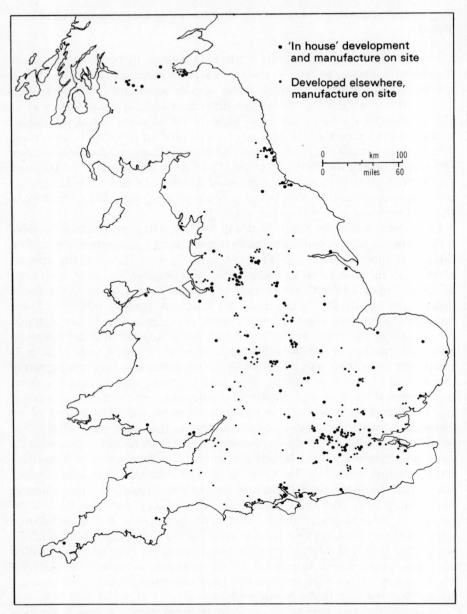

• 'In house' development
and manufacture on site

• Developed elsewhere,
manufacture on site

0 _____ km _____ 100
0 _____ miles _____ 60

FIGURE 11.4 The first commercial manufacture locations of innovating plants in
Great Britain

TABLE 11.4 Number of workers per survey innovation in the planning regions, Great Britain

Region	Number of innovations per region	Number of manufacturing workers per innovation (000)	Index GB=100
1 East Anglia	12	17.1	154
2 South West	22	19.4	136
3 South East	98	20.3	130
4 Northern	21	22.5	117
5 East Midlands	19	31.5	84
6 Yorkshire and Humberside	24	31.8	84
7 West Midlands	33	32.1	82
8 North West	33	33.0	80
9 Scotland	19	34.6	76
10 Wales	6	55.5	48
Great Britain	287	26.4	100

Source: Oakey et al., 1980, p. 243.

(1980), using only non-production workers in each sector, show that regional innovative performance can largely be 'explained' by the distribution of non-production workers; the level of non-production employment has a particularly adverse effect on innovation in the development areas and other regions in contrast to the positive influence in the South East.

One explanation of regional variations in the distribution of non-productive workers outlined earlier related to the absence of many such functions in branch plants in the spatial structure of multi-site organizations. Assisted areas are often 'branch plant economies'. Oakey et al. (1980) attributed 192 innovations to multi-site companies, of which 126 were first introduced in branches and not headquarters factories (i.e. a ratio of 2:1). They note (p. 242):

The significance of this ratio depends on the population of branches to head-quarters factories in the population at large. Crum and Gudgin's (1978) sample of admittedly large corporations suggests a ratio of branch plants to manufacturing head offices of approximately 6:1. Smith (1979) in his work on ownership and control in manufacturing industry in the Northern Region of England suggests a ratio of 4.5 branch plants to 1 headquarters plant. But perhaps the most reliable data which covers all establishment size bands for Scotland by headquarters and branch plant activity suggests for indigenous industry a ratio of 3.5:1. Based upon the limited evidence offered in this study it is tentatively suggested that the branch plant population has not produced its expected share of innovations.

This may be explained in that 42 per cent of innovations manufactured in branch plants were developed in another company location, compared with only 18 per cent in plants attached to headquarters' factories. The study also revealed that the bulk of technology transferred between one company site and another occurred *within* regions. Thus it was in the South East Region, the major source of specification of innovation in multi-site companies, that the majority of these innovations were first commercially manufactured. Very few were transferred to the assisted areas at this very early stage in their life cycle.

An important policy inference is that, even in large multi-site companies, local inventive activity tends to generate local results. Measures designed to stimulate the diversion of investment from more to less dynamic regions will not necessarily result in the transfer of the newest products because products need close monitoring early in their life cycle. Controls on industrial development in more prosperous regions in the pursuit of regional objectives could also seriously constrain innovative activity altogether without benefiting the lagging areas. This confirms the need for policies designed to raise directly the level of innovative activity in lagging regions. Yet the analysis indicates little about the relative importance of establishment, organizational and regional factors as critical determinants of technological change at the establishment level. Moreover, because emphasis has been placed on major innovations, Oakey *et al.* (1980) ignore the many minor improvements to existing products and processes which can be of considerable economic, if not technological, significance and the diffusion of process innovations which might significantly lower production costs and improve the quality of existing goods.

Scientific Instruments, Electronic Components and Metal-working Machine Tool Industries

To overcome these limitations a study has been undertaken in the Centre for Urban and Regional Development Studies, University of Newcastle upon Tyne, which examined technical change at the establishment level in 3 innovative and regionally dispersed sectors of manufacturing—scientific and industrial instruments, metal-working machine tools, and electronic components. This has involved either interview or postal questionnaire to all 1600 establishments which could be identified in these sectors throughout the UK. Interviews have been concentrated in 3 regions with different levels of government assistance: the Northern Region (a development area), the North East (an intermediate area) and the South East (no assistance). All plants in the Northern and a random sample in the other 2 Regions were covered by interviews; those in the North West and South East Regions and the rest of the UK were sent a postal questionnaire.

In both surveys innovation was defined as the most technically advanced and most economically significant new product or process introduced into the plant during the 1973–77 period. Of the 807 plants in the sample, 84 per cent had introduced a new product innovation and 63 per cent a new process. It was possible to distinguish between diversification product innovation, existing product innovation and innovations leading the establishment into high as opposed to low-growth product groups. Product and process innovations were also classified along a scale of technical sophistication by industry experts to provide indicators of the technical innovativeness of the plant which can be related to several establishment, enterprise and regional characteristics.

A preliminary cluster analysis of the 807 plants used a subset of 31 attributes relating to location, innovative activity, size and organizational status. Each attribute was represented as present or absent and a cluster analysis undertaken using a hierarchical divisive technique with relocation. The most efficient partitioning of the data in the percentage change in the error sums of squares occurred with 7 clusters (Table 11.5). The chief limitation of this analysis is the crude measure of innovative activity (introduction or non-introduction of a product or process innovation), particularly

TABLE 11.5 Grouping of establishments in relation to their organizational characteristics and innovative activity

Group 1: 13 per cent of cases
Small single-site enterprises in development areas
   Product innovation: 16.2 per cent of group
   Process innovation: 41.9 per cent of group
Group 2: 19 per cent of cases
Small single-site enterprises in the South East
   Product innovation: 100 per cent of cases
   Process innovation: 54.9 per cent of cases
Group 3: 17.7 per cent of cases
Small branch establishments with low autonomy and located in
   Development areas
   Product innovation: 79.7 per cent of cases
   Process innovation: 60.1 per cent of cases
Group 4: 10.3 per cent of cases
Small headquarters establishments of small company groups in
   Intermediate areas
   Product innovation: 88 per cent of cases
   Process innovation: 69.9 per cent of cases
Group 5: 10.6 per cent of cases
Large branch plants of large company groups located in
   Development areas
   Product innovation: 99.8 per cent of cases
   Process innovation: 89.8 per cent of cases

Source: Thwaites *et al.*, 1981.

given the frequency of innovation overall. Yet it is possible to identify groups of plants with different levels of innovative activity and fairly distinctive corporate and locational features. Cluster 1 contains most non-innovative establishments, only 16 per cent of them introducing a product innovation compared with 84 per cent in population overall. Plants in this cluster are typically small independent firms in the electronic components industry in development areas, often remotely located in the outer metropolitan ring of urban areas. Independent status is not, however, the only explanation of low innovative activity: every plant in cluster 2 recorded a production innovation and, while single-site companies, they are located in inner urban rings in the South East and manufacturing in the highly innovative scientific instruments industry.

Similar, although less marked, distinctions can be drawn between more and less innovative plants which are parts of multi-site companies. The least innovative are in cluster 3 and typified by branches in development area locations and with headquarters in the South East; they are less innovative than the headquarters sites of small multi-plant companies which are concentrated in cluster 4, where 88 per cent have introduced a product innovation. The most innovative multi-site company plants are in cluster 5 where 99 per cent have introduced a product innovation as compared with 80 per cent in cluster 3. What really separates these 3 clusters is not so much location as the size of company group, the most innovative plants being large ones that are part of a firm with more than 10 manufacturing sites. (Cluster 6 is similar to cluster 5 but with less commitment to innovative activity and more plants with fewer than 500 employees.)

Only cluster 7 does not fit this pattern and contains highly innovative independent companies in the machine tool and electronic component industries located in intermediate areas. Apart from sector and location this group is distinguished from cluster 2 by the high level of process innovation (70 per cent of cases as compared with 55 per cent in clusters 2 and 5 respectively). This partly results from sectoral differences in production technology, the scope for process innovations being restricted in the scientific instruments industry because of its largely unstandardized products (Oakey, 1978). That independent firms in a semi-peripheral region do not seem constrained in introducing process innovations may seem surprising but one possible explanation is that such innovations frequently take the form of 'off the shelf' machinery of a type widely advertised in trade journals. Also the intermediate areas consist basically of regions centred on Manchester and Leeds, both of which contain a wide range of manufacturing service firms able to sell and to maintain such equipment.

Notwithstanding the impressive performance of this group, process innovations are most likely to be introduced in the large plants of organizations; thus 90 per cent of the plants in cluster 5 have introduced process innovations compared with 63 per cent of the entire sample. Evidence from the interview survey suggests that this is because such plants tend to use forms of mass production technology where the scope, and indeed requirement, for process innovation to increase productivity is greatest.

The Inter-regional Diffusion of Production Innovations

Many product innovations being generated by the 3 sectors are also process innovations in others; for example, numerically controlled machine tools are a potential process innovation in many industries. Given the very serious obstacles to product innovation in lagging regions, a more realistic policy option could be to stimulate the rapid diffusion of such new production processes. The constraints on diffusion are very different from those on innovations and may be more amenable to local policy influence.

While the selection of plants for the manufacture of new products may be a matter of group strategy, the initiative for the adoption of new processes may emanate from lower down the corporate hierarchy. Such decisions are often the preserve of production management, a function which is widely dispersed in British manufacturing industry. If production management is unaware of the availability of new techniques they may fail to press higher levels in the organization for resources to purchase the equipment. Conversely, making top management aware of new processes may not lead to their actual implementation at the production level.

If these suggestions are correct then policy designed to stimulate rapid diffusion of new production techniques should be targeted at plants as much as firms. Before such a policy can be promulgated, however, more needs to be known about the mechanisms underlying the inter-regional diffusion of production innovations. Unfortunately the design of the research here described does not allow a clear distinction to be drawn between the determinants of regional variations in the speed of take-up of established processes and determinants of regional variations in innovation *per se*. In future research, therefore, a range will be selected of the products of varying degrees of technical sophistication that have been identified in the current investigation and which are potential process innovations in a number of 'target' sectors. The research will cover all plants within the target sectors to distinguish the plant, organizational and regional influences on adoption and non-adoption and will be modelled on studies by Mansfield *et al.* (1971) with an explicitly spatial dimension.

POLICY IMPLICATIONS

Telecommunications and Improved Information Access in Lagging Regions

The previous section examined product and process innovation; of equal importance are managerial innovations that influence the ways in which

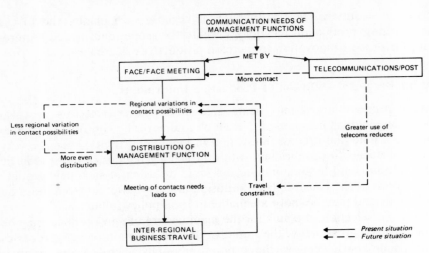

FIGURE 11.5 Contact possibilities, the location of management functions and
the impact of telecommunications

companies use managerial resources (particularly time) in coming to important decisions. Recent developments in information processing and exchange
technology herald a managerial revolution with important spatial consequences (Goddard, 1977, 1980). Of particular regional importance are developments in telecommunications technology which should enable companies in peripheral regions to gain much easier access to information with
less need for time-consuming business travel. Figure 11.5 suggests that
multi-site companies might be able to devolve more non-production functions to manufacturing sites in peripheral regions, while single-site companies would not need to recruit more managerial personnel to create time
to maintain contact with customers, suppliers and innovation centres. The
net impact would be to improve substantially the milieu for industrial
innovation in lagging regions. Thus policies designed to improve the telecommunications infrastructure of such areas could provide an important part
of an innovation-orientated regional policy.

The study of inter-regional business travel between the Northern and
South East Regions of England (James *et al.*, 1979) assessed the possibility
of using telecommunications instead of face-to-face contact for the meeting
that prompted the trip. This assessment was based on the principal feature
of the meeting recorded by travellers and the known performance capability
of different telecommunications systems (see Pye and Williams, 1977, for an
evaluation of the methodology for assessing telecommunications substitution
potential). Respondents were asked to score a list of 8 functions of the
meeting (such as delegation of work, information seeking, negotiation) and

4 descriptors of the meeting (such as problem-solving or inspection of fixed objects), and these scores, together with information on the number of participants involved and work-places represented, were used to determine the probability of the meeting being suitable for video communications, multi-point and audio-conferencing or a straightforward telephone call. The methodology was broadly similar to that adopted in other surveys of business meetings, the results of which are compared in Table 11.6. While there is much scope for the use of telecommunications as an alternative to inter-regional business travel this is considerably less than is recorded for those studies covering *all* meetings recorded by individuals over a period of time. This is not surprising given that the time and cost involved in long-distance travel would have already acted as a filter on the decision to meet as opposed to using telecommunication.

Thus, more widespread use of telecommunications is unlikely to have the same impact on interactions between peripheral and core regions as on more localized contact patterns. However, comparisons of studies of the total contact network of individuals in different locational situations produce another interesting feature, namely that there is greater potential for using telecommunications in Northern Region manufacturing firms than in other instances. The only situation with comparable levels of substitution potential are offices which have decentralized from London, the majority of which consist of routine functions with a low contact intensity (Goddard and Morris, 1976). The implication is that industry in this particular peripheral region sample also has relatively routine communication requirements.

TABLE 11.6 Telecommunications substitution potential: comparison of business meetings recorded in different surveys[a]

Survey	Per cent				Sample size
	Telephone and post	Audio	Video	Face to face	
1 Inter-regional	6	21	1	71	1759
2 Northern Region manufacturing establishments	25	54	0	21	615
3 Decentralized offices	13	38	27	22	344
4 Random sample 4 regions	45		8	47	1377
5 Central London Civil Service	3	40	23	34	6379

[a] Each of these surveys used different procedures for sampling establishments, individuals and meetings and for allocating these meetings to communications channels. In terms of allocation procedures surveys 1, 2 and 4 and 3 and 5 used similar methodologies (see Pye and Williams, 1977; Goddard, 1980).

Sources: Surveys 1 and 2: James *et al.*, 1979; Survey 3: Goddard and Morris, 1976; Survey 4: Tyler, 1973; Survey 5: Connell and Sokoloff, 1972.

This is confirmed when the substitution potential of meetings recorded from the 2 Northern Region surveys (of inter-regional business travel and of manufacturing plants) is compared with the characteristics of the participants. Meetings to which respondents journeyed from the North East but which are held in the South East are less substitutable than in the reverse situation. Similarly, meetings attended by individuals from single-site companies are less substitutable than those by individuals from multi-site companies, while meetings by individuals from the service sector are more substitutable than those recorded by individuals from manufacturing industry. The survey of Northern Region manufacturing firms reveals that contact with suppliers is more substitutable than that with customers or in situations when no commercial relationship is involved. Hence intra-company contacts are also more substitutable than those between companies.

Clearly there is greater scope for telecommunications in the control of routine production activities in peripheral areas from headquarters in core regions. Large organizations have the greatest scope for installing compatible equipment in all their sites. Small independent firms, which tend to be less communication-intensive, have proportionately more higher-level contacts with other organizations. Yet because of greater constraints on managerial time for business travel, the need to use telecommunications is greater in the small independent firms in peripheral regions. Research on the availability and use of various telecommunications hardware in Northern Region manufacturing and service units reveals less availability and use on the part of this group as compared with units which are part of multi-site companies. A survey asked 456 key communicators in 132 Northern Region manufacturing and service industry units whether each item of equipment was (a) present in their establishment; (b) available to them; (c) used by them. Individual responses to these questions were summed scoring 1 for a 'yes' response and 0 for a 'no' for each type of hardware. A mean score for managers in particular types of units (independent, subsidiary or branch) was obtained. The higher the mean for each group of managers the more important hardware was in the unit. Although there are problems of combining information on utilization and availability, the results clearly suggest that, as with product and process innovations in manufacturing, small independent firms in this peripheral region do lag behind large non-locally controlled companies in the adoption of new communications technology.

Thus, until new telecommunications devices such as facsimile transmission are very widely diffused, developments in this form of technology will not benefit lagging regions. Without some policy initiative further disadvantages in access to specialist information are likely to emerge in such regions. Policy initiatives might include campaigns to increase awareness of the potential for telecommunications among small and medium-size firms in lagging regions and subsidies to cover initial installation costs. The opening of public audio-conferencing studios in several strategic locations in these regions is another policy option. Yet availability of facilities does not necessarily imply greater use. The need for contact has first to be appreciated. Telecommunications becomes most relevant in maintaining established business relationships and not in making new contacts. Additional policies are therefore required to channel the information relevant to innovation and diversification to firms in lagging regions.

Regional Technology Transfer Agencies

The important role of professional change agents in the innovation process is widely acknowledged in the literature (Rogers and Shoemaker, 1971) but is not yet fully recognized by those concerned with regional aspects of national industrial policy. (A comparison of Figures 11.2 and 11.4 should suffice to demonstrate the point that technology transfer agencies are currently located where the need is least.) The inadequacy of existing regional policy instruments which emphasize general investments incentives is also beginning to be appreciated. For example, the quota-free element of the European Regional Development Fund contains several provisions to stimulate innovation in small and medium-size enterprises in lagging regions of the EEC (such as subsidies for technical feasibility studies). The existence of the instruments themselves will not ensure that the incentives are taken up. Existing policies often fail to reach small and medium-size enterprises in lagging regions because of inadequacies in the implementation system (Sørlie, 1978; Hjern and Hull, 1980). Much effort is needed to ensure the delivery of policies designed to influence the decisions of firms on technological innovation. This implies not merely advertising but detailed appreciation by the agencies concerned of the internal (production) and external (market) conditions prevailing in local enterprises. As is widely recognized in agriculture, this requires the setting-up of specialized services which bring together managerial and technological expertise with sufficient resources not only to advise but also to assist practically with such tasks as prototype developments or with de-bugging problems arising from the introduction of new machinery.

Spatial Analysis, Industry and the Industrial Environment. Vol. 3 Regional Economies and Industrial Systems
Edited by F. E. I. Hamilton and G. J. R. Linge

Chapter 12

High-technology Industry, Industrial Location and Regional Development: The British Case

RAY OAKEY

Manufacturing in advanced economies is becoming increasingly dominated by new high-technology forms of production. Forecasts about the impact on national and regional job markets in the United Kingdom have ranged from euphoric when considering totally new industries based on new products (e.g. home computers and micro-chip toys), to doomladen when assessing the employment impact of other spin-offs of the new technology (e.g. computer-controlled lathes, robots and word processors) (Barron and Curnow, 1979; Hines and Searle, 1979). Much of this confusion, which has stemmed from generalizing about high-technology industry, can largely be dispelled by returning to basic manufacturing principles.

Technologically, manufacturing activity in a particular plant can be dichotomized into product and process developments. These are linked in that a product innovation in one plant can become a process innovation in a purchasing plant (e.g. machinery). But at the *individual plant* level they can be separated to good effect enabling a 2-fold categorization of manufacturing as it applies to both products and processes. Hence a conceptual matrix can be constructed into which any production plant can be inserted. This fundamental categorization allows for the 'real world' phenomenon of plants which have high-technology processes but low-technology products (e.g. food processing), and those which make high-technology products using low-technology process methods (e.g. scientific instruments) (Oakey, 1978). This failure to distinguish between product and process innovations when considering the impact of new technologies on specific industries has caused muddled thinking about their employment effects. For instance, many innovations have greater potential impact on manufacturing employment as subsequent processes than as original products (e.g. robots and word processors). Confusion is avoided by adopting a plant-level approach in which innovations can be seen as either product or process improvements implying widely different employment impacts.

The encouragement of new and existing high-technology activities has been proposed as a means of correcting imbalances in British regional development by diversifying the manufacturing base of economies traditionally dominated by heavy industries now in decline (Northern Region Strategy Team, 1977; Ewers and Wettmann, 1980). Here again, the thinking is muddled if job creation is the main objective. Unless massive increases in output and subsequent sales ensue, the technological upgrading of existing industry through high-technology process improvements will at best leave employment levels static, and at worst create large-scale redundancies. These process improvements may be essential to the survival of some traditional industries (e.g. iron and steel production) but they cannot be viewed as job generators if their employment effects are taken in aggregate.

Initially, the stimulation of new product technologies in the indigenous industries of development regions seems a brighter prospect. But the major industrial sectors of development areas in Great Britain are dominated by mature or senile activities where the scope for incremental improvement in product specifications is, in the main, restricted (e.g. textiles and shipbuilding), and where the substitution of related new process innovations tends to occur in newer, more prosperous regions or abroad (Schon, 1964). Moreover, the potential to acquire new product technologies by attracting new technology industries from outside the development regions is poor for several reasons.

While process innovations may diffuse easily through normal sales networks between companies from region to region, affording cost saving advantages for the plants which adopt them, the technology associated with product innovations tends to be spatially less mobile. Since product development is a highly competitive process between firms in similar types of manufacturing, it tends to be internalized and confidential (Oakey, 1979a). Of course, once in the market place a product of one industry sold as a process to another loses its confidentiality. However, a robot-welder manufacturer, for instance, would not sell his machine to a competitor although he would to a car-maker. A competitor could, of course, surreptitiously purchase the welder and 'reverse engineer' it by taking it apart and making a slightly altered copy, but the lead time involved would frequently render the imitation obsolete before it could be marketed. Even a capacity to make copies implies a high level of technical and engineering competence (Bundgaard-Nielsen and Fiehn, 1974). Internalized product development, innovative or imitative, demands skilled workers to transform innovative ideas into saleable items. It is here that this discussion is relevant to regional development problems. Unlike high-technology process innovations which can be purchased from specialist makers, the creation of high-technology products in a region requires on-site skilled and semi-skilled workers. Indeed, if Vernon's (1966, 1971) cogent arguments on the need for new technologies to be produced at or near the development location are accepted, then skilled development workers would also need to be present in, or available to, the development region production plant. But since most development regions have senile industrial structures, low levels of R & D activity, and generally lack skilled production and development workers of the type needed by high-technology activities, they are not an obvious location for such new forms of production (Buswell and Lewis, 1970; Thwaites, 1978a).

Given the dubious employment effect of the diffusion of new process innovations to the development regions and notwithstanding the labour skill difficulties already discussed, an inflow of new high-technology activities based on product innovations remains a possible vehicle for technological improvement and structural employment change in British development regions (Thwaites, 1978b). Yet a vicious circle seems to have formed in which, because there is a shortage of skilled development and production workers in British development regions, high-technology industry remains in southern England: the problem of the development regions attracting high-technology industry is thus being compounded. Government could begin to break this circle by encouraging high-technology industry to locate in development regions. However, it is not without significance that in 1979–80 it failed to direct the *state-owned* Inmos Ltd's micro-chip headquarters and R & D centre to a development area despite considerable political pressure from development regions in favour of an assisted area location. Inmos executives argued, however, that skilled R & D labour recruitment problems ruled out a development area as against an environmentally attractive site at Bristol (*Newcastle Journal*, 27 February 1980). Although, as acknowledged, these labour difficulties are very real, there appears little resolve by the British government to enforce change by influencing the location of enterprises it controls: such behaviour does not augur well for possible policies aimed at promoting development areas for high-technology production in the private sector (Oakey, 1979b).

In manufacturing, 'high technology' must ultimately be defined in terms of new products and processes introduced at plant level. Except in the case of purchased process innovations, high-technology production requires a skilled labour input at least once in the manufacturing process during development. However, some forms of production need skilled or semi-skilled workers from conception to construction of the product. The latter are frequently associated with 'tailor-made' or small batch production runs and high value added in an environment where performance is often more important than price, the tasks undertaken intricate, and their assembly complex (Pred, 1965). Hence the scope for the substitution of capital production equipment for skilled labour is low and restricts the spatial mobility of such production to concentrations of the required labour skills (Segal, 1960). The high value added in production allows high labour costs and subsequent economic viability.

The Case Study

As an example of a high-technology form of production, this chapter discusses the British scientific instruments industry (Minimum List Heading

354), and seeks to relate its locational requirements and growth characteristics to the problems of regional development and the potential for future high-technology expansion in assisted areas. Although many of the foregoing comments on high value added forms of production are relevant to this analysis, MLH 354 should not be taken as a surrogate for high technology in general since particular industries will vary in the extent to which any given production resource will affect performance and spatial requirements. Thus MLH 354 needs highly skilled labour for both the R & D and production phases. Other high-technology industries may depend on skilled workers only in the development phase with production being entrusted to semi-skilled operatives or machines (as in some sections of the electronics industry). None the less, this analysis contributes to the widening debate on the impacts of high-technology manufacturing on industrial growth by providing direct evidence about a particular sector that has production characteristics contrasting with many of the generalizations made about high-technology industry.

The data have been derived from 2 separate studies of British MLH 354. (In both instances, constraints on resources precluded a UK study which would have included Northern Ireland production.) The first was a wide-ranging survey of the location of the instruments industry (Oakey, 1978) from which information has been selected here to give a broad impression of the nature of MLH 354 production and to highlight important aspects of organization and labour utilization which influence manufacturing techniques and subsequent ties to particular locations. The second study examined regional variations in industrial innovation levels in Great Britain (Thwaites *et al.*, 1981) and included a comparison of MLH 354 with other industries. These analyses are compared and examined in the context of high-technology industry's regional employment potential in the concluding section of this chapter.

THE BRITISH SCIENTIFIC AND INDUSTRIAL INSTRUMENTS INDUSTRY

The first data set was obtained from a survey of 102 establishments in the North West and South East British Standard Planning Regions during 1976 (Oakey, 1978). This analysis is preceded by a brief description of MLH 354 and its constituent product sub-sectors and an indication of the distribution of the industry throughout the planning regions of Great Britain.

Data Availability

The scientific and industrial instruments and systems industry—created in 1968 from the 1963 'Scientific, surgical and photographic instruments'

MLH—excluded some peripheral products (e.g. photographic instruments and spectacles) but included other new or rapidly growing innovative ones (e.g. instruments for measuring and testing electronic magnitudes, ultrasonic instruments). Table 12.1 lists the main product groups within MLH 354 and their percentage contribution to total sales in 1975. During the last 20 years the relative significance of traditional optically based instruments (e.g. surveyors' instruments, microscopes) has declined while control instrumentation for other manufacturing sectors has increased. This is reflected in the share of sales recorded in 1975 for process measuring and control instruments (42.9 per cent). Although there has been a shift in the types of

TABLE 12.1 MLH 354, per cent of sales by major product headings, Great Britain, 1975

Optical instruments and appliances	7.01
Surveying, hydrographic navigational, meteorological and geophysical instruments (non-optical except magnetic compasses and gyroscopes)	2.35
Instruments for engineering meterology	1.63
Instruments, apparatus or models for educational or exhibition purposes	0.67
Instruments, apparatus for testing physical and mechanical properties of materials (inc. hardness, strength, compressibility, elasticity) and for non-destructive testing of homogeneity (excluding ultrasonic equipment)	1.82
Process measuring and control instruments and equipment (including systems)	42.94
Analytical instruments	6.96
Liquid, gas and electricity supply meters and pre-paid meters	6.79
Counting and velocity measuring instruments	4.08
Electrical measuring, testing and controlling instruments and apparatus	12.18
Ultrasonic instruments and equipment	0.42
Scientific laboratory instruments and apparatus not elsewhere specified	1.46
Other scientific and industrial instruments not elsewhere specified	3.91
Total	92.22[a]

[a] Does not sum to 100 per cent due to the exclusion of parts and accessories and unclassified work done.
Source: United Kingdom, Department of Industry, 1975a.

TABLE 12.2 MLH 354 size, employment, net output and output per head, by firm size categories, Great Britain, 1972

Size group	Establish-ments	Enter-prises	Employ-ment	Net out-put (£000)	Net output per head (£)
1–10	470	455 ⎫			
11–24	255	249 ⎪	16,514	42,272	2,559
25–49	77	76 ⎬			
50–99	108	104 ⎭			
100–199	68	64	10,552	26,638	2,524
200–499	68	67	20,762	52,053	2,507
500–749	19	14	11,621	32,280	2,777
750–999	9	9	7,872	16,905	2,147
>1000	22	19	43,671	96,316	2,205
Total	1,096	970[a]	110,992	266,464	2,401

[a] The sum of the figures in the size groups exceeds the total for the industry because certain enterprises made returns for establishments in more than one size group.
Source: United Kingdom, Department of Industry, 1975b.

skills required by the industry this does not imply a reduction in their quality or quantity.

MLH 354 had only 1096 establishments in 1972, 91.2 per cent of which employed fewer than 100 people. However, these 884 companies made sales worth only about £42 million whereas those of the 19 firms with over 1000 employees totalled £96 million. The most interesting evidence in Table 12.2 is the data on output per head. In most industries larger plants tend to have greater scale economies that yield savings which increase output per head despite the inevitable growth in administrative staffing. Industry groups as diverse as soap and detergents; rubber; tractors; radio and electrical components; and jewellery and precious metals all displayed a general increase in output per head with size (Oakey, 1978, pp. 196–7). However, in MLH 354, while plants in the 100–749 range produced the best results, those with fewer than 100 workers had an average output per head greater than those with 750 or more employees.

The evidence to be presented here suggests that, although increases in bureaucracy are encountered by MLH 354 firms in the same way as by other manufacturing organizations, the complexities of instrument production inhibit the use of mass purchase or production methods that normally accompany increases in size of plant (Oakey, 1978). Large MLH 354 firms may well experience the disadvantages of size without the benefits; thus their output per head is less than that of very small firms which maintain a much healthier direct to indirect labour ratio.

Distribution of MLH 354 Production in Great Britain

MLH 354 is concentrated in a few British planning regions, with the South East alone containing 53 per cent of the jobs in this industry (Table 12.3). The 16 per cent share in the North West Region is, however, more surprising, especially in view of the poor representation of the West Midlands. However, the West Midlands has never had a tradition of instrument manufacture and this partly explains its poor current performance, particularly in a view of the following comments on the industry's inertia.

TABLE 12.3 Regional distribution of MLH 354 employment, Great Britain, 1971

Region	Number (000)	Per cent
Northern	2.3	2
Yorkshire and Humberside	3.2	3
East Midlands	3.4	3
East Anglia	4.2	3
South East	62.9	52
South West	7.7	6
West Midlands	5.0	4
North West	18.8	16
Wales	1.9	2
Scotland	10.3	9
Total	119.7	100

Source: United Kingdom, Department of Industry, 1974.

ORGANIZATION OF THE BRITISH INSTRUMENTS INDUSTRY

The expanding literature on the organization of the multi-plant firm has contributed greatly to an understanding of the location process (Parsons, 1972; Rees, 1972, 1974; Leigh and North, 1978; Goddard and Smith, 1978; Smith, 1979). However, when individual plants in multi-site organizations are compared with single plant independent firms at the plant level, the latter frequently display the more complex organizational structure. Single plant firms are not, by definition, externally complex because all the functions of the company are contained under one roof. But the extent to which MLH 354 multi-plant establishments are externally controlled by headquarters may be affected by the unique high-technology nature of this particular industry: the complex technology embodied in products may make considerable control at the plant level essential since the on-site expertise of key personnel forms the most competent rationale for decision-making.

Branch plant autonomy in MLH 354 The strength of autonomy in the MLH 354 sample was measured by asking the 41 branch plants to indicate their freedom to purchase or sub-contract: 36 had total freedom, 4 had freedom for some items, and 1 had to obtain permission from headquarters for all such actions. A comparison was also made between single plants and branch plants that purchased more than half their materials locally. Of the 12 plants in the first group, 8 purchased 50 to 75 per cent locally and the others bought more than 75 per cent; for the 14 in the second group, the comparable figures are 12 and 2. In effect the purchasing behaviours are not markedly different and the extent of the autonomy is surprisingly great when compared with the results obtained by Luttrell (1962) and Townroe (1971).

Corporate control and MLH 354 The extent to which the general move towards industrial concentration in recent years (Prais, 1976; Meeks, 1977; Goddard and Smith, 1978) has affected the instruments industry was also examined. Although none of the 44 multi-plant firms had acquired other businesses during the previous 10 years, 25 had themselves been taken over. Since only 4 of these acquiring firms had more than half their manufacturing establishments in MLH 354, the instruments industry does not appear to be subject to large-scale horizontal acquisition such as has occurred for example in the textile industry. Take-overs in MLH 354 are mainly initiated by large and powerful companies in other industrial sectors such as electronics (e.g. GEC; Thorn; Philips; and Rank). The instruments industry is a relatively secure form of business because its highly technical products often promote captive markets. The very complexity of these high-value outputs and the small fragmented markets means, however, that rapid growth and large size through acquisition are rare among MLH 354 companies. While MLH 354 firms appear attractive to large firms outside this industry, there is no evidence that such take-overs are a means of internalizing externalities. Exhaustive examination of multi-plant input and output linkages between MLH 354 multi-plant establishments show the flow of materials to be very low (Oakey, 1978).

Much of the substantial acquisition activity in MLH 354 during the past decade has been initiated from outside the industry. Branch plants, both new and acquired, have a strong propensity for on-site control—the summary data presented here being supported by the more detailed findings in Oakey (1978). McNee (1974) may have pointed up a reason for MLH 354 branch plant autonomy by suggesting that companies which expand into other industrial sectors often purchase 'going concerns' because their knowledge of the acquired firm's technology is poor and management expertise can be purchased with the firm. This motive is clearly relevant both to MLH 354 acquisition within Great Britain and to foreign plants purchasing British companies. The complex nature of MLH 354 production demands that decisions about purchasing, product design and manufacturing methods be made 'in house' where the best information is available: this ensures great autonomy at the individual MLH 354 branch plant level.

Technical Information and MLH 354 Production

Evidence exists that information availability varies over space and that this affects the performance of both manufacturing and tertiary organizations (Thorngren, 1970; Pred and Törnqvist, 1973; Goddard, 1978). Buswell and Lewis (1970) show that in Great Britain R & D activity, which is often related to innovation in industry, has a strong South Eastern bias. While there appears to be agreement that most information acquisition largely depends on search effort invested (Cyert and March, 1963; Webber, 1968; Pred and Törnqvist, 1973), this present analysis (based upon Oakey, 1979a) questions this view insofar as it applies to technical information in manufacturing plants.

Information on product technology in a given plant can be divided into (a) high-level and (b) low-level categories. Examples of the latter would be supportive information—extracted from technical libraries on the performance of components—which is generally available in proportion to the search effort invested. In contrast, high-level technical information—for example specifying the design of new and improved products—is confidential to the developing firms since, in a high-technology industry, improved performance can be more important than low price in a competitive market. This argument appears to hold for MLH 354 since 94 of the 102 firms in this survey maintained internal R & D departments.

US evidence suggests that external sources of high-level R & D information might stimulate MLH 354 production in certain concentrated locations. Deutermann (1966) and Gibson (1970) argue that technically orientated universities in the US were strong foci for instrument firms (e.g. Massachusetts Institute of Technology, Stanford University). Thus, the 102 survey firms were asked whether they maintained information links with any research establishments within a 30-mile (48 km) radius. Surprisingly, 37 had no local research establishment contacts at all (Table 12.4). Moreover, of the 65 firms that acknowledged local contacts 55 indicated that such links had no locational significance. The survey suggests a marked difference in the importance of universities to instrument industry production in Great Britain and the US. Collaboration between MLH 354 firms and British universities would undoubtedly be beneficial but the paucity and weakness of such links is probably mainly due to the lack of confidential contract research facilities. Unlike those in the US, British universities are for the most part publicly funded and academics have reservations about financial links with industry and the constraints of confidentiality that might ensue.

TABLE 12.4 Technical contacts with local research establishments, MLH 354 firms in Great Britain,[a] 1976

Contact	North West Region		South East Region		Total	
	Number	Per cent	Number	Per cent	Number	Per cent
Academic	19	53	30	45	49	48
Government	13	36	31	30	44	43
Private	7	19	21	32	28	27
None	13	36	24	36	37	36
Total establishments	36	35	66	65	102	100

[a] Responses in this table, when totalled, exceed the regional and survey totals due to certain individual firms acknowledging more than one type of contact.
Source: fieldwork.

The survey results may reflect a reluctance by industrialists to seek university assistance and a lack of motivation by academics to disseminate their expertise into the wider social and economic environment.

However, in an industry such as MLH 354 where technological change is rapid much product development work must be based within the manufacturing plant itself. While university collaboration could help eliminate particular design and construction problems, much of the effort to transform concepts through design and into production would, in any case, need to be located under one roof; in most cases all these phases of evolution involve specialists who interact to iron out development snags. In an industry with generally small and fragmented markets, where improved specifications and special variations to suit individual customers are common, design and production can never be far apart. British MLH 354 firms survive and prosper through the market advantage afforded them by skilled researchers who generate high-level internalized confidential information on the design and construction of new and improved products.

Labour and Locational Inertia

The broader study of MLH 354 location pointed up the role of labour—especially the powerful constraints imposed by the existing workforce—as the most important determinant of instrument industry location. The locational significance of existing labour supplies to MLH 354 firms is borne out by the fact that only 15 of the 99 established plants surveyed had relocated during the previous 5 years (3 new firms being excluded). Of the other 84 only 7 (all in the South East) had plans to progress towards relocation; 11 (all but 1 in the South East) had considered but rejected a move, while 66 indicated that action had been taken or planned. None of the 15 mobile firms had shifted more than 30 miles (5 in the North West and 10 in the South East). Moreover, 13 of them (including all those in the South East) acknowledged that existing local labour skills had greatly influenced the shortness of their move: existing workers had been retained without any of them having to shift house. This factor was considered particularly important for skilled shop-floor workers.

In short, the general impression is of immobility. Most firms had neither relocated nor considered a move, while those that had shifted had remained within their local area. That there are pitfalls in moving MLH 354 workers far appear to be borne out by the absence of long-distance relocation in this survey. In the broader study from which these data are extracted (Oakey, 1978, pp. 270–81), 3 case studies of firms which had recently undergone long-distance relocations revealed that all had experienced severe problems in attracting existing skilled personnel to the new location and in employing or training fresh workers there.

INNOVATION IN THE SCIENTIFIC AND INDUSTRIAL INSTRUMENTS INDUSTRY

The following data were derived from a major study of regional innovation levels in Great Britain (Thwaites *et al.*, 1981) which involved a national questionnaire survey of 807 establishments in the scientific instruments (MLH 354), metal-working machine tools (MLH 332) and electronic components (MLH 364) industries. These were chosen because in recent years they have achieved high levels of industrial innovation (Thwaites, 1978a; Oakey *et al.*, 1980).

If the comments at the outset of this chapter about the differences between product and process innovation are correct the results that follow might be expected to confirm significant differences in the case of MLH 354. Indeed the data already presented have indirectly supported claims about the minor importance of process innovation in MLH 354 because of the lack of economies of scale in large instrument firms and the continued employment of skilled shop-floor labour. Since a central theme of this chapter is that constantly changing high technology and the complexity of MLH 354 products inhibit mass production methods, considerable product innovation but a lower level of new process innovation might be expected. Initial results of this survey confirm the earlier research in that 90 per cent of the 373 MLH 354 establishments carried out on-site R & D (compared with 92 per cent recorded in the earlier study).

The following data on innovation propensity during the 1973–77 period stem from questions about whether any product or process innovations *new to the plant* had been introduced during those 5 years. While these data do not indicate the volume of innovations (since plants may have innovated several times during the period concerned), they do distinguish between innovators and non-innovators.

Sectoral Comparisons of MLH 354 Innovation Levels

Table 12.5(a), summarizing product innovation across the 3 industry groups, shows that MLH 354 has a 10 percentile point higher incidence than the others, a result which is enhanced when it is recalled that all 3 sectors are very innovative. Conversely, but as anticipated, Table 12.5(b) indicates that MLH 354 establishments displayed the lowest level of process innovation.

These results generally support the argument that MLH 354 has a high level of product innovation but a lower level of new process introduction. That process innovation is lower in MLH 354 because of the difficulty of applying new process techniques in manufacture is given further credence by the data in Table 12.6 which show that although MLH 354 records the lowest absolute level of process innovation it has, marginally, the highest level of 'in-house' developed processes using tailor-made rather than on-the-shelf equipment.

TABLE 12.5 Level of (a) product innovation and (b) process innovation in the British scientific and industrial instruments industry, 1973 to 1977

Industrial sector		Yes	No	Total
(a) *Product innovation* (N = 795)				
MLH 332 (Metal-working	Number	143	36	179
machine tools)	Per cent	79.9	20.1	100.0
MLH 354 (Scientific	Number	334	39	373
instruments)	Per cent	89.5	10.5	100.0
MLH 364 (Electronic	Number	192	51	243
components)	Per cent	79.0	21.0	100.0
(b) *Process innovation* (N = 790)				
MLH 332 (Metal-working	Number	112	69	181
machine tools)	Per cent	61.9	28.1	100.0
MLH 354 (Scientific	Number	217	153	370
instruments)	Per cent	58.6	41.4	100.0
MLH 364 (Electronic	Number	182	57	239
components)	Per cent	76.2	23.8	100.0

Source: fieldwork.

TABLE 12.6 Level of in-house process developments in the British scientific and industrial instruments industry, 1973 to 1977

Industrial sector		Processes developed on site ($N = 503$)		
		Yes	No	Total
MLH 332 (Metal-working	Number	51	61	112
machine tools)	Per cent	45.5	54.5	100.0
MLH 354 (Scientific	Number	117	91	208
instruments)	Per cent	56.3	43.7	100.0
MLH 364 (Electronic	Number	94	89	183
components)	Per cent	51.4	48.6	100.0

Source: fieldwork.

Innovation and Plant Size

It might be supposed that, because of their scale of operation, large plants would be more product innovative and be more able to use new process machinery. Table 12.7(a) indicates that there is a steady increase in product innovation with establishment size, although the difference between the smallest and largest size groups is less than 15 percentile points. However, when process innovation levels are measured against plant size, as in Table 12.7(b), they show a 37.2 percentile point difference between the smallest and largest size groups. Taken in the broader context of earlier results, the relatively high level of product innovation in small, mainly independent, establishments must in part reflect the significant in-house R & D undertaken in most MLH 354 plants. Although, as might be expected, larger MLH 354 plants produced a higher incidence of process innovation performance, this result is tempered by a lower aggregate MLH process innovation performance when compared with other sectors (Table 12.5b).

Regional Variations in MLH 354 Innovation Levels

Given earlier comments about MLH 354 labour requirements, the possibility of relocating such establishments to create employment in, and diversify the industrial base of, development areas is a hazardous prospect. There is, of course, the possibility that the minority of high-technology firms indigenous to development regions may grow. But the South East Region's monopoly of R & D activity (Buswell and Lewis, 1970), high productivity levels (Cameron, 1979) and corporate control (Goddard and Smith, 1978) suggest that indigenous innovation and growth within high-technology firms

TABLE 12.7 Size of plant by (a) product innovation and (b) process innovation in the British scientific and industrial instruments industry, 1973 to 1977

Size of plant (number of employees)		Yes	No	Total
(a) Product innovation (N = 371)				
1–99	Number	182	31	213
	Per cent	85.4	14.6	100.0
100–499	Number	104	7	111
	Per cent	93.7	6.3	100.0
500–999	Number	31	1	32
	Per cent	96.9	3.1	100.0
>999	Number	15	0	15
	Per cent	100.0	0	100.0
(b) Process innovation (N = 368)				
1–99	Number	105	107	212
	Per cent	49.5	50.5	100.0
100–499	Number	70	39	109
	Per cent	64.2	35.8	100.0
500–499	Number	29	3	32
	Per cent	90.6	9.4	100.0
>999	Number	13	2	15
	Per cent	86.7	13.3	100.0

Source: fieldwork.

in development areas would be less vital than technological change in South East England.

The following analysis of regional differences in MLH 354 product and process innovation levels aggregates national results on a generalized 'core-periphery' basis into 3 groups: the South East of England; the development areas of Scotland, the North of England and Wales; and the remaining areas termed 'intermediate'. The level of product innovation in South East England was higher by 25 percentile points than that in the development regions (Table 12.8(a)), whereas process innovation levels between the 2 regional groupings differed by only 8.6 percentile points (Table 12.8(b)). More detailed research strongly suggests that process innovation levels over selected industries are bolstered in development regions by capital grants for purchasing new process machinery (Thwaites *et al.*, 1981). If the incidence of product innovation is viewed in terms of a dichotomy between indigenous internally controlled single plant firms and plants belonging to a larger company group, the trend of Table 12.8(a) is considerably sharpened for indigenously owned firms. Table 12.9 shows that single plant independent

TABLE 12.8 Regional variations in (a) product innovation and (b) process innovation in the British scientific and industrial instruments industry, 1973 to 1977

Region		Yes	No	Total
(a) Product innovation (N = 371)				
Development regions	Number	31	14	45
	Per cent	68.9	31.1	100.0
'Intermediate areas'	Number	102	12	114
	Per cent	89.5	10.5	100.0
South East England	Number	199	13	212
	Per cent	93.9	6.1	100.0
(b) Process innovation (N = 368)				
Development regions	Number	23	22	45
	Per cent	51.1	48.9	100.0
'Intermediate areas'	Number	68	44	112
	Per cent	60.7	39.3	100.0
South East England	Number	126	85	211
	Per cent	59.7	40.3	100.0

Source: fieldwork.

firms in South East England were more than twice as innovative as those in development regions. These results are supported by other research on regional differences in significant British product innovations (Oakey *et al.*, 1980). Since new products are the life-blood of any industrial firm, these results do not augur well for the growth of development area MLH 354 plants in general, and indigenous single plant independent firms in particular.

TABLE 12.9 Plant status by regional variations in product innovation in the British scientific and industrial instruments industry, 1973 to 1977

Region		Single plant (N = 183)			Group plant (N = 189)		
		Yes	No	Total	Yes	No	Total
Development regions	Number	9	13	22	22	1	23
	Per cent	40.9	59.1	100.0	95.7	4.3	100.0
'Intermediate areas'	Number	44	7	51	58	5	63
	Per cent	86.3	13.7	100.0	92.1	7.9	100.0
South East England	Number	101	9	110	96	4	100
	Per cent	91.8	8.2	100.0	96.0	4.0	100.0

Source: fieldwork.

Earlier analysis of its labour requirements indicated that MLH 354 is an unsuitable industry for long-distance relocation: it is unlikely, therefore, that development regions could be seeded with instrument industry production. Moreover, MLH 354 establishments indigenous to the development regions are less innovative in terms of new product introduction so that *in situ* growth does not appear to be a likely means of changing the industrial mix in such areas.

MLH 354: HEALTHY BUT NOT A REGIONAL SAVIOUR

The instruments industry is a healthy and growing part of British manufacturing with a strong small-firm sector which seems to thrive on short production runs. Not surprisingly, activity in MLH 354 is becoming dominated by various types of control instrumentation which reflects the general drive to introduce new process technologies. The considerable autonomy enjoyed by MLH 354 branch plants is facilitated by the production complexity of the industry which demands that decisions on purchases, R & D, manufacturing methods and customer contact can only be handled by the on-site skilled personnel who construct the wares. These people need to be readily available in any case for control tasks. This is in sharp contrast to other externally controlled plants in lower-technology industries where production can be undertaken with one factory manager and a staff of semi-skilled and unskilled workers while control functions (e.g. purchasing and sales) remain at headquarters (Townroe, 1971).

The complexity of MLH 354 products creates the need for an on-site team of highly skilled development production workers to perfect their exclusive and confidential products. Since many firms specialize in 'one off' products or very small batch production, modifications to specification or construction can be introduced without great trauma; there is no great pressure for perfection before commitment to a mass production run. But the high proportion of skilled workers required brings problems of locational inflexibility to instruments production. Indeed, the powerful influence of existing skilled workers was the most striking location factor to emerge from the wider study of MLH 354 production (Oakey, 1978). The immobility of most of the firms surveyed was pronounced and was largely due to fears about the consequences of relocation on the allegiances of existing skilled workers in general and skilled shop-floor workers in particular. The immobility of MLH 354 production may help to explain the spatial concentration of this industry in Great Britain to areas of previous specialization and its surprisingly poor representation in areas like the West Midlands. This evidence about MLH 354 has clear implications for the contribution that certain high-technology industries can make to the alleviation of industrial development problems in depressed areas.

The innovation survey supported many of the themes emerging from the earlier work. The introductory comments of this chapter about the differences between product and process technology and their impact on high-technology industry were substantiated by the data on product and process innovation. While the incidence of internal R & D was consistently high for MLH 354 (and product innovation levels were highest for instruments as against other sectors), process innovation was generally much less important. These results support the underlying theme that MLH 354 production methods do not lend themselves to mechanization and emphasize the continuing importance of shop-floor labour.

The analysis of regional MLH innovation levels emphasized that the small proportion of the instrument firms located in the development areas introduced fewer product innovations than their counterparts in South East England. Not only is the distribution of high-technology MLH 354 firms set against the development regions, but the innovation levels of those that do exist provide little hope for much indigenous self-sustained MLH 354 growth.

While it is reasonably safe to predict a continuing steady growth in MLH 354 output in real terms, it is difficult, given the labour constraints, to see how this growth will find its way to development regions in Great Britain. There will be a strong and understandable desire among MLH 354 executives to expand *in situ* or near their existing locations. Moreover, new high-technology industries may well be attracted to areas where MLH 354 and electronic industries are found together (e.g. London and the South East). There are valid arguments for such a location based on *in situ* skilled labour, good sub-contracting facilities and nearness to customers and suppliers.

Not only do the prospects for increased MLH 354 employment in the development regions look bleak, but the expected growth in MLH 354 output could lead to job losses in these regions as process control instrumentation accelerates the substitution of capital equipment for labour in traditional industries, like textiles, common in depressed areas. This points up 2 important conclusions. First, the instruments industry does not appear to be a suitable vehicle for sectoral diversification and employment growth in depressed areas. Second, it should not be assumed that the new high-technology industries will automatically take up the workforce now being shed by other previously labour-intensive industries like motor-vehicle building. While new high-technology industries may well produce wealth, they will not usually fill the social and economic need to employ large numbers of unskilled workers. The example discussed in this chapter suggests that the term 'high-technology industry' encompasses a wide range of heterogeneous activities with growth characteristics that will have markedly different productivity and employment impacts on industry in general.

Spatial Analysis, Industry and the Industrial Environment. Vol. 3 Regional Economies and Industrial Systems
Edited by F. E. I. Hamilton and G. J. R. Linge
© 1983 John Wiley & Sons Ltd.

Chapter 13

Structural Adaptability of Regions during Swedish Industrial Adjustment, 1965 to 1975

LENNART OHLSSON

A major ingredient in European regional policies has been financial incentives for industrial location and expansion in backward areas. This has also been the case in Sweden, where selective financial incentives to industry, apart from regionally motivated ones, were small and few before 1975. In most countries with such policies the root of regional employment problems appears to be related to an inability to quickly adapt the regional structure to altered patterns of external demand and competition. In Sweden the structural problem of the north was too much employment in the primary sectors and a settlement dating back to the time when exploitation of raw materials and land was still profitable.

When active regional policies began in Sweden in 1965, industrial development was still a dynamic force behind economic growth. Northern Sweden then had industries that were rapidly expanding and enjoying strong international competitiveness. Unfortunately, this growth was insufficient to absorb the unemployment increase resulting from the declining labour needs of the primary sectors and of the stagnating parts of manufacturing. The concept underlying regional policies was therefore to stimulate competitive regional producers to expand at a faster rate and to induce companies in southern Sweden to locate a greater share of their increased production in designated Aid Areas.

This concept was based on 2 important premises. One was the existence of a relatively large core of competitive production in the Aid Areas, since the time required for the migration or entry of new enterprises to create sufficient employment opportunities was known to be rather long. The other was that southern Sweden had a prosperous industrial sector that could withstand some drain of its competitive production. This, of course, required that the areas to be aided were small compared with the size of industry elsewhere in Sweden and especially that part which was competitive.

Since 1970 areas to be aided and the level of subsidization have kept increasing. Lately 2 of the 3 metropolitan regions have been allocated special industrial aid to alleviate severe industrial employment problems in the shipbuilding industry, a step that calls into question the bases of Swedish regional industrial policies. Moreover, the evolution of industrial problems in southern Sweden without a solution of those in the north may call for a revision of the basic premise of general economic policies, if the presumption of an industrial sector that is capable of providing a steady and prosperous growth and secure employment opportunities proves to be false.

After the 1978–80 oil price increases such a revision has gradually gained political momentum, although it is often perceived as a consequence of this and other events abroad such as sluggish global market growth and depressed world market prices, new international protectionism, and the appearance of Newly Industrializing Countries (NICs) as suppliers of cheap manufactures. While all these external causes have played a measurable role, they are not a priori the main causes of the poor Swedish performance. Other industrial countries have been able to adjust more successfully: Sweden's overall and industrial growth performance in the 1970s was substantially worse than that of the Organisation for Economic Co-operation and Development as a whole *and* also that of OECD's small countries. Another reason is that Sweden was earlier viewed as a flexible adjuster, at least partly because the economy was small and open.

Maintenance of a high degree of adaptability does not merely require an early recognition of changing external market signals. It also demands rapid shifts of productive resources to expanding sectors and regions. With a population density of 18 persons per km^2 Sweden is one of the most spatially extensive economies in Europe. Although population is concentrated in southern Sweden it is dispersed everywhere in small villages or towns and commuting distances are large or costly, owing to a comparatively small number of commuters. Unless the geographical mobility of capital and labour compensates for the 'over-extensiveness' in space this establishes a higher threshold for the inter-sectoral mobility for a given set of external impulses.

During the 1965–75 period, people voted for and obtained policy alterations that were meant to decrease the need to move because of unemployment. High and rapidly increasing labour force participation rates for married women and a shift towards settlement in private, single family dwellings also imply enhanced economic barriers to geographical mobility of labour. These changes appear to reinforce the greater structural adaptability of the densely populated metropolitan area compared with the sparsely inhabited region. In addition, the former has better access to a variety of the resources necessary, such as early information, fast accumulation of knowledge, labour skills and capital. A comparison of the structural flexibility of regions with different population densities, initial industrial structure and access to regionally endogenous or exogenous supplies of productive resources, can consequently be crucial to a better understanding of the adjustment of the economy as a whole.

This chapter considers the 'structural adaptability' of regions with potentially different adjustment capabilities during a period of transformation of Swedish industry. Such an investigation may indicate whether regional industrial aid is based upon a true understanding of the regional dimension of industrial adjustment. The approach is to compare changes in the composition of manufacturing in 11 regions, emphasizing (a) the so-called footloose industries and (b) the metropolitan and coastal regions of Stockholm, Göteborg and Malmö.

EXTERNAL STRUCTURAL IMPULSES AND COMPARATIVE REGIONAL ADAPTABILITY

During the study period Sweden's role in the international division of labour changed. Historically, the country was a major supplier of raw materials and manufactures thereof to European industry. Already at the turn of the century a successful engineering industry had been established; being based on domestic innovations, it meant a substantial diversification of Swedish industrial exports both as to products and foreign markets. However, even as late as 1960 neither this industry nor the 'footloose' industries taken together generated export surpluses. Table 13.1 demonstrates several influential changes in Sweden's net trade composition between 1960 and 1975. First, its historical net export position in raw materials exchange disappeared—a development that was not a consequence of increased oil prices after 1973 alone. Second, manufactures from raw materials grew substantially in net exports but not enough to compensate for the deterioration in the trade balance for raw materials. In part, the gradual switch towards highly manufactured raw materials was delayed by higher EEC protectionism in the markets for steel and paper. Free trade in such products will not be achieved, according to the European Free Trade Association

TABLE 13.1 Net exports from Sweden by type of sector, 1960, 1970 and 1975 (SKr 000 million)

Sector	1960	1970	1975
Foreign trade-sheltered industries	−0.4	−0.2	−0.0
Raw material-based industries	1.1	1.7	3.4
Footloose industries	−3.4	−2.8	−1.2
Raw materials (including miscellaneous goods)	1.0	0.1	−2.6
Commodity trade	−1.7	−1.1	−0.4
Commodity and service trade	−0.6	−1.4	−3.3

Source: special calculations of unpublished and published data provided by the National Central Bureau of Statistics.

(EFTA) settlement, until the mid-1980s. Later policy changes have introduced stronger protectionism, raising doubts as to whether this settlement will be realized. Third, there was a sharp decline in the net imports of the footloose sector. This clearly marked Sweden's secular evolution away from a typically resource-based economy. The decline was also necessitated by the balance of payments constraint induced by the shift from a net export towards a net import of services resulting mostly from the steep rise in tourist expenditures abroad after 1959. Other important factors were increased foreign aid, the inadequate expansion of shipping incomes and net exports of know-how and related services.

Within footloose industry several trade changes can be observed. If the 78 detailed sub-industries (see Ohlsson, 1977a) are classified according to their technical personnel/total employee ratio into 4 groups, each group had net imports in 1960. The 2 groups that made least use of technicians experienced successive increases in their net imports position, i.e. their international competitiveness seems to have diminished. The most technical personnel-intensive group switched into net exports during the 1960s, and the 1970–75 period saw a further strengthening of its competitiveness as measured by net trade. The net trade of the second most technical personnel-intensive group showed no clear trend over the 1960–75 period.

These results imply an adjustment towards a more human skill-intensive based pattern of specialization and in turn may result from a change in Sweden's comparative advantage *during or before* the period (Ohlsson, 1977b, 1980a). It obviously involves the spatial composition of the industrial production system in some sense because of the declining importance of geographically immobile (or low-mobile) resources and the growing weight of human capital—a very mobile production factor. The associated spatial adjustment problem can be of small or large magnitude depending on whether

(a) there is an historically determined *regional* division of labour drawing on regional, resource-based comparative advantages and/or on a regionally differentiated accumulation of human skills;

(b) existing specialization acts to restrict the subsequent specialization changes owing to established advantages and regional imbalance creating mobile factor movements;

(c) the changing specialization is strongly factor-biased also in terms of inputs other than raw materials and highly skilled labour.

Thus, the combined regional and industrial adjustment is best studied if regions and industries can be defined in a factor proportions framework that allows for more than 2 factors and differential mobility of both certain key factors and the output of certain industries.

REGIONS BY FACTOR ABUNDANCE AND INTERNAL ADJUSTMENT CAPACITY

The division of Sweden into 11 regions (Ohlsson, 1977c) uses the concept of areas that are homogeneous in factor endowments and relative factor costs. Broadly, they were defined on the basis of historical differences in regional factor abundance with the partial exception of Aid Areas for which policy-induced differences in relative factor prices during the study period served as an additional criterion. Secondary, but important, criteria were the size, the population density and the existence of a developed local labour market. These latter grounds were used to delineate the metropolitan regions where human skill is abundant. Equipped with air, land and sea transport facilities and with an internal capacity for, and control of, human and non-human capital formation, these regions can be treated as the closest approximations in Sweden to the assumptions underlying the notion of 'perfectly functioning' factor markets. Moreover, their better contact with external market signals might suggest earlier information about impulses from abroad to altered comparative costs. In a small, flexible, open economy, which is extended over a large surface, the metropolitan regions should on these a priori grounds be hypothetically regarded as early and rapid adjusters. Apart from the metropolitan regions of Malmö, Göteborg and Stockholm, the East Middle region is also skill-intensive (Figure 13.1). This is a highly urbanized region with several middle-size cities and 3 universities.

There are 2 regions with an initial heavy physical capital-intensive industrial composition: the so-called Outer Aid Area, which received investment and land transport cost subsidies as well as temporary subsidies for training new employees, and the Bergslagen region, most of which coincides with the 'Grey Zone' of the regional aid system so that its industries benefited from investment loans with a small interest subsidy and assistance for training programmes. In contrast to these physical capital-abundant aid areas, there are 2 others—the Inner Aid Area in the north of Sweden and the Borås region near the Göteborg metropolitan area—endowed with abundant raw labour, but they are otherwise very different. The Inner Aid Area has top priority in regional policies: it has been granted the highest and the most varied assistance including investment, training, land transport cost, and incremental and total wage cost subsidies. In contrast Borås received only investment loans for part of the study period and some support for training schemes. Moreover, the Borås region is largely a local labour market surrounding the medium-size city of Borås and there is daily commuting to Göteborg whereas the Inner Aid Area is the most remote and extensive of all the regions with, in 1975, only 25,000 factory workers. Although its total population is comparatively large because of its high share of employment in

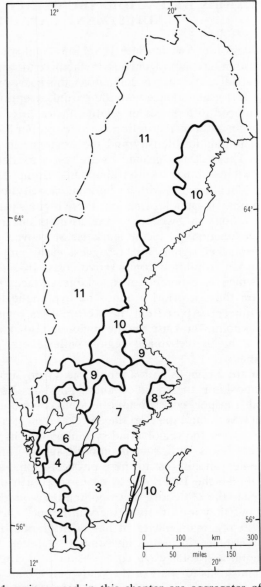

1 Malmö
2 Southwest
3 Southeast
4 Borås
5 Goteborg
6 South Lake Vänern
7 East Middle
8 Stockholm
9 Bergslagen
10 Outer Aid Area
11 Inner Aid Area

FIGURE 13.1 The 11 regions used in this chapter are aggregates of Sweden's 274 local communes (in 1975). Two are regional policy Aid Areas as at 1974. The others were defined so as to create regions with (a) internally homogeneous factor endowments; (b) differing factor endowments—including regions abundant in skilled labour (1, 5, 7 and 8), unskilled labour (4 and 11) and capital (9 and 11); and (c) large enough manufacturing sectors to allow inter-regional comparisons of industrial specialization

primary and tertiary sectors, it has a low labour force participation rate. Settlement is extremely scattered with only 3 local labour markets with populations of 40,000 to 50,000. The remaining 3 regions are all relatively urbanized. Compared with other countries in Europe, production units are more dispersed, being located in small urban places.

This summary of regional definitions and differences stresses that Sweden is a large country with a small population. The inter-regional differences are emphasized by the fact that Stockholm—a relatively small capital city by international standards—alone had 18 per cent of the population in 1975 and 20 per cent of the workforce. These percentages are equivalent to the sum of the 2 other metropolitan regions which, in turn, are roughly of equal size. Stockholm has an extremely specialized employment structure with a particular concentration in the banking and insurance sector and, to a lesser extent, in the public service sector. Despite its relatively small size, manufacturing industry in Stockholm is significantly larger than that of the other 2 metropolitan regions.

THE USE OF INDICATORS THROUGH THE CLASSIFICATION OF INDUSTRIES

The 110 manufacturing industries were classified into 3 basic groups: there are 15 trade-sheltered industries making, for instance, semi-processed foodstuffs (e.g. flour), forest-based and building materials, and 17 raw material industries, namely trade-exposed food (e.g. biscuits), beverages and forest-based activities (e.g. paper) and petroleum refineries. The other 78 industries (including steel) are 'footloose' in that backward and forward linkages to resources and local, regional and national markets are negligible. Trade exposure is high for their outputs and their intermediate inputs. Prices of both inputs and outputs can be assumed to be given internationally because of the smallness of the economy. Inter-industry differences in the technology of the value-added process can also be viewed as externally determined as far as best practice technology is concerned. Thus the variation in international competitiveness between industries is largely a function of inter-industry differences in (a) factor intensity-based comparative advantages, and (b) the efficiency with which production factors are used.

A comparative regional analysis of industrial adaptability should ideally be organized to reveal the response to the same impulses as those from the international market which lead to changes in Sweden's overall specialization. Therefore the development of the national pattern of specialization as an indicator of an inter-regionally homogeneous stimulus can be used, although only for the study of trade-exposed industries and, because of their competitive conditions, of footloose industries. The latter are classified by a revealed comparative advantage measure.

304 SPATIAL ANALYSIS, INDUSTRY AND THE INDUSTRIAL ENVIRONMENT

A second external source of differential regional industrial growth is the rate of expansion of domestic demand, a criterion best utilized in industries with products that are easily traded. Industrial development can then be investigated for footloose industry classes which differentiate industries according to their demand growth rate.

A third impulse is inter-sectoral differences in the development of input/ output and input/input coefficients: these can be studied for all manufacturing and be complemented by an examination of inter-regional variations which can then be seen as a direct study of intra-regional adaptability. Another direct approach is to compare the adaptability of regions by analysing changes in plant size or by the net formation of new establishments in expanding versus contracting sectors.

Finally, a fourth type of external impulse is regional policy. There are 2 possible direct impacts: (a) the relocation of industrial production to aid areas of new, affiliated and migrating plants or firms which would otherwise have been located elsewhere; and (b) the competition effect originating in a policy-induced faster expansion of existing establishments (or less contraction of existing ones) in the Aid Areas. Neither this latter impact nor the various kinds of indirect ones are considered in this chapter.

These 4 largely external impulses are now analysed: many of the comparisons are made in terms of employment rather than production to achieve greater comparability and because of the greater policy interest in employment. All comparisons are between years at the height of the business cycle, i.e. in years of full or nearly full capacity utilization.

REGIONAL SPECIALIZATION CHANGES IN SPATIALLY TIED SECTORS

Changes in the composition of Swedish manufacturing between 1965 and 1975 are summarized in Table 13.2. Total factory employment increased by only a few thousand or less than 1 per cent with the footloose sector gaining somewhat at the expense of the raw material-based sector. Table 13.2 also demonstrates that metropolitan areas seldom specialize in raw material-based industries. The Malmö region has the strongest concentration but this is simply a reflection of its large trade-exposed food sector, which in turn is closely associated historically with its high intra-national competitiveness in agriculture and basic food industries.

In contrast, Stockholm and Malmö have a comparatively large trade-sheltered sector, the scope of which is much influenced by population size and whether the individual industries have inter-regionally tradeable products. Ohlsson (1980b) shows that the 3 metropolitan regions have complementary specializations with a strong base at Malmö for that part of the food industry which is sheltered by policy-imposed trade barriers. Only this

TABLE 13.2 Employment share of 3 sectors in 3 Swedish metropolitan regions, 1965 and 1975 (per cent)

Sector	Stockholm region		Göteborg region		Malmö region		Total Sweden	
	1965	1975	1965	1975	1965	1975	1965	1975
Trade-sheltered	27.3	24.6	16.9	17.9	23.2	24.4	19.0	19.0
Raw material-based	6.0	5.9	6.9	5.8	10.5	11.3	13.1	12.2
Footloose	66.7	69.6	76.2	76.3	66.2	64.3	67.9	68.8
Total manufacturing	100.0	100.0	100.0	100.0	100.0	100.0	100.0	100.0
Employees (000)	118	105	80	81	83	78	896	902

Source: as for Table 13.1.

region has, according to Table 13.3, a higher share of national sectoral employment in the trade-sheltered sector than its total employment share (9.4 per cent in 1975). Only the Göteborg metropolitan region maintained its share of the factory workforce (see Table 13.3). Unlike the others it maintained its share of the footloose sector. Stockholm lost employment shares in each major sector. Manufacturing employment was thus either stable or contracting in the metropolitan areas as a whole and at the level of the major sectors. There is little evidence of a long-run shift of employment from a resource-based sector either in these areas or in Sweden as a whole.

Table 13.4 indicates that there is a slight tendency for manufacturing employment to become more equal in the 8 other regions, so that the standard deviation of their employment shares declines from 4.62 to 4.42. This decrease occurred in all 3 sectors, although it was less pronounced in the footloose one—the largest and regionally least specialized. Another feature is that the raw material-based sector has the strongest regional

TABLE 13.3 Regional shares of sectoral and national employment, in 3 Swedish metropolitan regions, 1965 and 1975 (per cent)

Sector	Stockholm region		Göteborg region		Malmö region	
	1965	1975	1965	1975	1965	1975
Trade-sheltered	19.0	15.0	8.0	8.5	11.4	11.1
Raw material-based	6.0	5.6	4.7	4.3	7.5	8.0
Footloose	13.0	11.8	10.1	10.0	9.1	8.1
Total manufacturing	13.2	11.6	9.0	9.0	9.3	8.6

Source: as for Table 13.1.

TABLE 13.4 Regional shares of sectoral and national employment in 8 Swedish regions, 1965 and 1975 (per cent)

Region	1965				1975			
	Trade-sheltered	Raw material-based	Foot-loose	Total manu-facturing	Trade-sheltered	Raw material-based	Foot-loose	Total manu-facturing
Southwest	5.6	5.6	5.0	5.2	7.2	7.3	4.9	5.7
Southeast	12.8	13.9	12.9	13.0	12.8	14.6	14.0	13.9
Borås	2.0	0.9	5.8	4.4	1.8	1.2	4.7	3.7
South Lake Vänern	5.3	4.1	5.8	5.5	5.7	4.4	6.6	6.1
East Middle	17.2	9.5	18.8	17.3	16.8	9.5	17.9	16.7
Bergslagen[a]	5.3	14.0	10.2	9.8	4.5	14.1	9.8	9.3
Outer Aid Area[b]	10.8	30.3	8.5	11.8	12.8	26.3	10.5	12.9
Inner Aid Area[b]	2.6	3.6	0.9	1.6	3.7	4.6	1.8	2.5
Sum of Stockholm, Göteborg and Malmö regions	38.4	18.2	32.2	31.5	34.6	17.9	29.9	29.2
Total Sweden	100.0	100.0	100.0	100.0	100.0	100.0	100.0	100.0

[a] This region approximates the so-called Grey Zone Area of regional policy.
[b] Appointed Aid Areas of regional policy.
Source: as for Table 13.1.

specialization (measured by the standard deviation of the regional employment shares) followed by the trade-sheltered sector. For obvious reasons, the latter seems to be relatively large in the remote, very sparsely populated Inner Aid Area. The raw material-based sector is, for equally obvious reasons, most important in sparsely populated and usually sparsely cultivated regions.

Attention must be drawn to 4 regions which have received special consideration in Swedish regional policy.

The Inner Aid Area, which contributed little to Sweden's manufacturing employment in 1965, increased its share by more than 50 per cent during the study period. Each of the 3 sectors contributed to this rise, but the footloose sector displayed the most pronounced relative growth. Since this sector also obtained a larger share of the total manufacturing employment in Sweden, the growth rate of that sector in the Inner Aid Area was clearly very high. Table 13.4 suggests, therefore, that the most resource-based regional economy is rapidly expanding in more highly manufactured industries.

The Outer Aid Area, The aid area next in priority, enhanced its role in Swedish manufacturing employment from 11.8 to 12.9 per cent. This was attributable to the trade-sheltered and footloose sectors in which the region was not specialized. Clearly, it has obtained a more diversified production structure and increased employment in a direction leading it away from a natural resource-based industrial sector.

The Bergslagen region, almost equal to the Grey Zone Area, has traditionally been strongly specialized in industries based on forest products and metal and therefore has a composition similar to that of the Outer Aid Area. In contrast to the latter, however, manufacturing employment in the Bergslagen region decreased and became more concentrated in the raw material-based sector. After 1975 this region experienced employment problems in this sector and in its iron and steel industry.

The Borås region was in 1965 the most specialized of them all, hardly surprising since it is small and compact. Despite its specialization in the footloose sector, this region decreased its manufacturing workforce and especially that in the footloose sector.

In short, the employment shares of the footloose sector did not vary as much across the regions as the share of the other 2 sectors. In principle this may be attributable to the spatial immobility of factors and products associated with these 2 sectors, but another possible explanation is the sheer size of the footloose sector, which had 4 times the number of workers than either of the others.

REGIONAL ADAPTABILITY TO DIFFERING MARKET GROWTH RATES BETWEEN FOOTLOOSE INDUSTRIES

Because of its weaker forward and backward linkages and product variety, footloose industry can be regarded as more flexible than the trade-sheltered or raw material-based sectors. One source of varying growth rates between parts of the footloose industry is the cross-industry differences in market growth. At the level of detail in the industrial classification used here it is not possible to measure the rate of expansion of external markets, but this may not greatly affect inter-regional comparisons because the domestic market is the largest or one of the largest for each industry.

If it is assumed that changes in trade specialization and labour/output coefficients of the 78 industries are not correlated with the development of the domestic market the evolving employment composition of the footloose sector would be closely associated with inter-industry differences in the rate of domestic market growth. If these 2 assumptions also hold for the 11 regions, the primary cause of regional employment share changes would presumably be the capability of the individual companies in an industry to adapt. This is rather a strong claim to make for each individual industry. However the interest here is not in the adaptability of individual industries but of individual regions, primarily with respect to features that might be

TABLE 13.5 Employment composition of footloose industries, Sweden, 1965 and 1975, aggregated by market growth rates 1960 to 1975[a]

Region	Year	Total footloose sector (per cent)	Per cent manufacturing employment of industries in footloose sector with			
			Rapid market growth	Good market growth	Slow market growth	Stagnating or contracting market
Malmö	1965	66	10	21	15	21
	1975	64	14	25	11	14
Göteborg	1965	76	6	47	8	15
	1975	76	10	55	5	6
Stockholm	1965	67	13	34	14	5
	1975	70	15	36	14	4
Total Sweden	1965	68	14	22	17	15
	1975	69	18	24	17	10

[a] The market growth rate underlying the classification $= \frac{(C_{1975} - C_{1960})}{C_{1960}}$, where $C =$ domestic apparent consumption.

Source: as for Table 13.1.

associated with changes in the regional division of labour. Thus, the 78 industries were aggregated into 4 groups of roughly 20 industries according to their rate of growth of domestic apparent consumption during the 1960–75 period. The initial specialization of each region in the 4 groups was investigated for the 1965–75 period to see how it affected the subsequent long-run trend. The results are presented in Table 13.5.

For Sweden as a whole, employment shares improved when the growth rate of the domestic market was higher, with a corresponding drastic reduction in the employment shares of industries facing a stagnating or contracting domestic market. In 1965 none of the metropolitan regions had a relatively high employment share in industries with a rapid market growth; their position was best in industries with a good market growth and especially so in Göteborg and Stockholm. The Malmö region had a high proportion of employment in industries with the worst market conditions, and this helps to explain why it experienced a decline in the employment share of the footloose sector as a whole. All 3 regions improved their employment balance in industries with good or rapid domestic market growth, but Table 13.6 indicates that it was only the Malmö and Göteborg regions that improved relative to Sweden as a whole. Stockholm, with the best initial industrial composition, obtained instead a larger than average employment increase in industries with poor market growth. Accordingly,

TABLE 13.6 Index of relative employment size by region and sector 1965 and 1975
(index = 100 for all Sweden each year)

Region	Year	Total foot-loose sector	Footloose industries with			
			Rapid market growth	Good market growth	Slow market growth	Stagnating or con-tracting market
Malmö	1965	98	72	94	85	140
	1975	93	80	104	67	135
Göteborg	1965	112	47	215	44	99
	1975	111	56	226	32	60
Stockholm	1965	98	93	157	83	36
	1975	101	87	149	84	40
Southwest	1965	96	126	67	72	140
	1975	87	118	63	59	138
Southeast	1965	99	170	88	91	62
	1975	101	142	89	98	65
Borås	1965	131	49	42	37	440
	1975	126	55	67	52	506
South Lake Vänern	1965	106	159	110	52	115
	1975	107	159	105	57	104
East Middle	1965	109	136	80	110	124
	1975	107	123	76	118	136
Bergslagen	1965	104	37	86	243	34
	1975	105	51	89	235	25
Outer Aid Area	1965	72	71	46	117	61
	1975	82	90	46	126	78
Inner Aid Area	1965	56	106	48	44	37
	1975	72	119	59	51	58
Total Sweden	1965 1975	100	100	100	100	100

Source: as for Table 13.1.

there is no clear evidence that the dense urban regions with, it is assumed, well-functioning (factor) markets have adjusted better to demand changes than Sweden as a whole. The initial specialization did not seem to make any difference.

The Borås region had the highest employment share in the footloose sector (Table 13.4). It lost employment in this sector and Table 13.6 suggests that one of the main reasons for this was its extremely bad initial composition with respect to market growth. This region had more than 4 times the national average employment share in industries with stagnating or contracting markets, largely as a result of the high concentration of textile and clothing industries in and around the city of Borås. During the 1965–75 period, when employment in those industries contracted rapidly, the Borås region was less severely affected than the nation as a whole. This gives some support to the hypothesis that a region performs better in industries in which it has a good competitive strength (Ohlsson, 1979b). The industrial composition of the Borås region between 1965 and 1975 improved more than that of Sweden, providing yet another explanation of why the total employment loss was relatively limited. The improvement may in part have been due to regional aid to firms establishing new plants in the region. All the other 3 regional Aid Areas also improved their industrial composition considerably. Moreover, 3 of the 4 Aid Areas had initially unfavourable compositions, the exception being the Inner Aid Area which had a relatively large employment in industries with a fast market growth. The South Lake Vänern region appears to have had the best industrial composition and it was the only area with a good initial composition which did not suffer a relative deterioration.

Thus, it is far from true that the 3 metropolitan regions adjusted more favourably to demand growth conditions. Nor can this be attributed to a lesser need to adapt because of a particularly good, initial industrial composition since several regions of southern Sweden had a more favourable specialization. Rather, the regions that improved the most were those that had the worst initial composition and that, due to employment problems within or outside the industrial sector, received regional aid during at least part of the period. Although the instruments and the degree of subsidization varied, they all obtained at least investment aid in the form of 'soft' loans. By and large, Tables 13.5 and 13.6 suggest that the market conditions of the footloose sector of the regions were more equal in 1975 than in 1965. The variations among industries in market growth rates also seem to be clearly reflected in the employment changes. As mentioned already, this is not at all self-evident since even at the national level there are 2 possible countervailing powers, namely the industry variations in international competitiveness and in labour/output ratios.

REGIONAL ADAPTABILITY TO DIFFERING COMPETITIVENESS CHANGES FOR FOOTLOOSE INDUSTRIES

Regional adjustment flexibility can be partially examined to see how the regional clusters of industries adapted to changes in Sweden's international competitiveness. For footloose industries with a high international tradeability of output, a measure of revealed comparative advantage changes can be chosen which is fairly insensitive to inter-industry differences in product tradeability. The measure of specialization changes chosen is the ratio:

$$\Delta\left[\frac{X-M}{C}\right] \tag{13.1}$$

where:

X = exports (f.o.b.);
M = imports (c.i.f.);
C = apparent domestic consumption.

This measure appears to complement the market growth rate of the preceding section and, in addition, maintains the idea of revealing a country's comparative advantage by its foreign trade specialization (cf. Balassa, 1965). The main difference from earlier studies is that comparative advantage is viewed here as a non-static concept, i.e. the specialization measure is chosen to reflect long-run trends in comparative advantage, trends which affect production and, indirectly, employment development.

The classification of footloose industries after revealed comparative advantage also has 4 groupings (Table 13.7). In 1965 almost 30 per cent of manufacturing employees in Sweden were engaged in footloose industries with declining or strongly declining international competitiveness, while another 40 per cent worked in those that strengthened their competitiveness. By 1975 the former share had decreased by 5 percentage points and the latter had expanded by 6 percentage points. The employment gains of industries with enhanced international competitiveness were not great since they merely compensated for workforce reductions in non-competitive footloose industries.

Of the 3 metropolitan regions, only Stockholm had a better than average industrial composition in 1965, about half its manufacturing employees being

TABLE 13.7 Employment composition of footloose industries, Sweden, 1965 and 1975, grouped by changing international competitiveness 1960 to 1975

Region	Year	Total footloose sector (per cent)	Per cent manufacturing employment in industries with competitiveness			
			Strongly increased	Increased	Slightly increased or decreased	Strongly decreased
Malmö	1965	66.2	18.6	17.3	7.5	22.9
	1975	64.3	21.0	17.9	6.0	19.5
Göteborg	1965	76.2	19.1	8.9	8.0	40.2
	1975	76.3	29.3	9.8	5.1	32.1
Stockholm	1965	66.7	33.1	17.5	7.4	8.7
	1975	69.6	42.0	15.1	6.3	6.3
Total	1965	67.9	18.1	20.8	12.0	17.0
Sweden	1975	68.9	24.8	20.1	10.5	13.5

Source: as for Table 13.1.

in industries with strengthening competitiveness. Only in industries with a much enhanced revealed comparative advantage did this region manage to enlarge its workforce (by about 5000). This absolute growth meant an even stronger upward trend in the employment *share* of these industries owing to the declining job opportunities in all other sub-sectors and sectors. The Göteborg region began with a poor competitiveness composition due to its dependence on large firms in industries like shipbuilding and the manufacture of ball bearings that were declining in competitiveness: this was not completely compensated for by the expansion of the Volvo truck and car assembly plant. The Malmö region also depended largely on industries with a poor international performance, and its industrial composition did not greatly improve between 1965 and 1975. Again, then, there is no evidence that the dense metropolitan regions adjusted better than the rest of Sweden to changes in international competitiveness. It seems that these areas, during this 10-year period, were relatively locked into the industrial composition they had at the outset. That the Stockholm region performed structurally better than the other 2 is consistent with this hypothesis since it had by far the most favourable composition. Its best characteristic was its ability to rapidly withdraw from less competitive industries.

Table 13.8 presents data on the relative employment size of all regions. Since the variations in performance across regions are similar to those discussed in respect to the market growth rate in the previous section, only brief comments are appropriate here. The Borås region had by far the worst industrial mix and the least favourable comparative advantage composition. The situation in the Inner Aid Area was not much better. None the less, both of them—but particularly the latter—improved their competitiveness composition more than Sweden as a whole. But up to 1975 they also increased their national employment share in industries that were quickly becoming less competitive internationally. This could create future employment problems unless regional and industrial subsidies maintain a protectionist shield. In 1965 the Bergslagen region and the Outer Aid Area each had a much more favourable industrial mix largely because of their specialization in the metal industries which successfully, but with decreasing profitability, adjusted to decreasing relative world market prices throughout the 1960s. During the last few years, the worldwide problems of this sector have also reached Sweden, and were reinforced by the sudden contraction of the domestic shipyards and the stagnation of domestic car production. It is generally believed that the problems of the metal industries are not only short-run. The lack of private risk capital led to the partial nationalization of the 3 largest basic steel producers in 1978: simultaneously they merged and a contraction plan, which implies a substantial loss of employment in the Bergslagen region and the Outer Aid Area, was agreed upon. The former region has also been struck by a rapid contraction of several high quality steel producers.

TABLE 13.8 Index of relative employment size by regions, footloose sector 1965 and 1975 (index = 100 for all Sweden each year)

Region	Year	Total footloose sector	Footloose industries with competitiveness			
			Strongly increased	Increased	Slightly increased or decreased	Strongly decreased
Malmö	1965	98	103	83	62	135
	1975	93	85	89	57	145
Göteborg	1965	112	106	43	66	236
	1975	111	118	48	49	239
Stockholm	1965	98	183	84	62	51
	1975	101	169	75	60	47
Southwest	1965	96	63	68	183	105
	1975	87	68	62	172	94
Southeast	1965	99	107	80	135	89
	1975	101	100	87	138	95
Borås	1965	131	26	47	244	266
	1975	126	35	71	242	286
South Lake	1965	106	148	74	128	83
Vänern	1975	107	156	47	166	61
East Middle	1965	109	106	111	110	108
	1975	107	107	116	104	97
Bergslagen	1965	104	20	252	86	27
	1975	105	24	252	82	53
Outer Aid	1965	72	79	109	57	31
Area	1975	82	93	109	70	30
Inner Aid	1965	56	50	34	70	79
Area	1975	72	74	51	67	106
Total	1965	100	100	100	100	100
Sweden	1975					

Source: as for Table 13.1.

Even if the metal industry is regarded as an exception, it can be concluded that, with respect to revealed comparative advantages, regions receiving investment aid appear to be relatively fast adjusters. It seems to be of small importance as to whether or not the initial industrial composition was poor. Consequently, an important key to a better understanding of regional industrial change may be Swedish regional policy and its inter-regional employment distribution effects, a theme developed in more detail elsewhere (Ohlsson, 1980c, Chapters 6 and 7). The fact that metropolitan regions were not found to be comparatively adaptable to altered competitive conditions is supported by a more detailed and alternative competitiveness classification of footloose industries (Ohlsson, 1980b). The dense metropolitan areas with their access to large and varied internal factor markets appear to be poor *structural* adjusters to both demand and competitiveness changes. This conclusion, when set against the opposite one for the regional Aid Areas, demands further elaboration of the nature of the adjustment process.

NET FORMATION OF PLANTS AND PLANT SIZE CHANGES AS SOURCES OF STRUCTURAL EMPLOYMENT CHANGE

An appropriate next step in this adaptability analysis would be to disaggregate the change in employment composition by more detailed subsectors or by categories of firms. The former was tried, with similar conclusions, in Ohlsson (1980b); the latter is only partially possible because of data limitations that prevent a full investigation of the evolution of entries, exits and permanent firms. However, it is possible to analyse employment data which may provide information about the net change of entries, exits and permanent firms if the concept of the 'firm' can be interpreted to mean establishment or plant. Swedish industrial statistics are based on plant data and include all those with 5 or more employees.

During the 1965–75 period the footloose sector gained employment, the trade-sheltered sector maintained constant employment (and employment share) and the raw material-based sector lost employees. It is evident from Table 13.9 that the comparatively good performance of the footloose sector

TABLE 13.9 Changes in the number of establishments and employees per establishment, Sweden, 1965 to 1975

Sector	Number of establishments			Employees per establishment		
	1965	1975	Change (per cent)	1965	1975	Change (per cent)
Trade-sheltered	4845	3968	−18	35	43	23
Raw material-based	1786	1311	−27	66	84	27
Footloose	6908	6383	−8	88	97	10
1. Competitiveness						
a. Strongly increased	1472	1803	22	110	124	13
b. Increased	1811	1712	−5	104	105	1
c. Slightly increased or decreased	1698	1551	−9	62	62	0
d. Strongly decreased	1927	1317	−32	79	92	16
2. Market change						
a. Rapid growth	1924	2158	12	63	74	17
b. Good growth	2106	2076	−1	97	110	13
c. Slow growth	1100	1046	−5	131	133	2
d. Stagnating or contracting	1778	1103	−38	78	87	12

Source: as for Table 13.1.

was associated with a smaller decrease in the number of establishments. Both the other sectors had a larger increase in employment per plant.

Increased plant size in manufacturing industry is commonly attributed to economies of scale or an optimal production scale inducing longer production runs. If this can be taken for granted the limited foreign competition in trade-sheltered industries did not seem to prevent the utilization of these scale economies. According to Table 13.9 relatively many small establishments appear to have ceased operations between 1965 and 1975; even so in 1975 this sector still had, on average, less than half the workforce per plant compared with the footloose sector. The raw material-based sector also experienced a relatively large contraction of small-size establishments, a development that would probably have been even more evident had not the 1973 energy crisis brought about a steep rise in the prices of raw materials and raw material-intensive products.

Inter-sectoral differences are even more striking within the footloose sector when disaggregated into groups with different changes in international competitiveness or demand growth rates. In industries with strongly improved competitiveness (and with a rapid market growth) the number of plants increased rapidly and the workforce per plant expanded more than on average. The lower the industries ranked according to these growth criteria, the more they lost establishments. Plant size in the group with the worst record increased probably because of a more rapid closure of small plants.

TABLE 13.10 Changes in the number and size of establishments by regions and sectors, Sweden, 1965 to 1975

Region	Number of establishments per cent change 1965–75			Employees per establishment					
				1965			Per cent change 1965–75		
	Trade-sheltered	Raw material-based	Foot-loose	Trade-sheltered	Raw material-based	Foot-loose	Trade-sheltered	Raw material-based	Foot-loose
Malmö	−18	−38	−13	43	85	91	19	62	3
Göteborg	−20	−22	−19	36	54	114	33	9	25
Stockholm	−18	−31	−14	50	91	82	−4	25	7
Southwest	−13	−30	−4	28	41	63	50	73	5
Southeast	−22	−25	−5	33	40	60	30	30	17
Borås	−10	−26	−17	24	17	59	0	76	0
South Lake Vänern	−27	−26	−13	31	66	82	45	35	33
East Middle	−18	−26	−8	41	56	118	20	27	6
Bergslagen	−22	−24	−4	32	142	202	9	24	1
Outer Aid Area	−15	−28	8	27	98	98	41	13	15
Inner Aid Area	−11	−15	42	18	36	31	61	42	48
Total Sweden	−18	−27	−8	35	66	88	23	27	10

Source: as for Table 13.1.

A rise in the number of establishments in a sector cannot be interpreted as an increase in the number of firms, yet the establishment data in Table 13.9 seem to reflect the very strong influence of the 2 criteria behind the comparative growth performance of industries and firms. The earlier finding that the metropolitan regions did not adjust as well as the Aid Areas can be reappraised by examining establishment data (Table 13.10). The number of plants decreased throughout Sweden in all 3 sectors with the exception of the footloose industries in the 2 Aid Areas. In general the decreases were smaller for the footloose sector. Only in the case of the raw material-based sector at Göteborg did the number of plants in a metropolitan region decline less than the rate for Sweden as a whole. Moreover, in only 2 instances in 1965 was the workforce per plant less in a metropolitan region than the Swedish average, and in only 3 instances was the 1965–75 percentage increase in plant size larger in these regions. Lack of employment growth in manufacturing in the 3 metropolitan regions thus appears to be associated with a less than average creation of new plants and growth of existing ones. In both respects the 2 regional Aid Areas had a better record, especially the most highly subsidized Inner Aid Area.

In Table 13.11 more details are given for the footloose industries grouped by changing international competitiveness: these underscore the results of Table 13.10. The metropolitan regions had less favourable changes in the number of plants than other Swedish areas, particularly those receiving regional aid. In addition the Malmö and Stockholm regions both had a smaller increase or decrease in the average workforce per plant. Göteborg was more favoured in this latter respect, and this may account for the fact that it was the only metropolitan region which managed to maintain its manufacturing employment from 1965 to 1975. Table 13.11 provides further striking evidence about the good performance of the Aid Areas and, particularly, the Inner Aid Area: there the number of plants, especially in industries with an improved competitiveness, and the average plant size both increased. Regional policy may at least partially account for this good record (Ohlsson, 1980c, Chapters 5 and 7). In principle, at least, regional policies may also explain the poorer performance of other parts of Sweden and, in particular, the metropolitan areas. If the analysis is restricted to direct effects alone, there are 2 possible mechanisms which may have worked in this direction.

First, direct competition from Aid Area producers—stimulated by subsidies—may have brought about reductions in the market shares held by other domestic producers. While this is possibly true, its importance is probably limited because the 2 northern Aid Areas only employ 15 per cent of the Swedish manufacturing workforce and because the employment effects of regional policy are fairly minimal. The decline in the employment share of the 3 metropolitan regions was roughly equivalent to the estimated

TABLE 13.11 Changes in number and size of establishments by regions and by footloose industries grouped by changing international competitiveness, Sweden, 1965 to 1975

Region	Number of establishments per cent change 1965–75				Employees per establishment							
					1965				Per cent change 1965–75			
	Strongly increased	Increased	Slightly increased or decreased	Strongly decreased	Strongly increased	Increased	Slightly increased or decreased	Strongly decreased	Strongly increased	Increased	Slightly increased or decreased	Strongly decreased
Malmö	19	−7	−18	−41	125	70	50	126	−11	0	4	32
Göteborg	−10	−9	−7	−47	108	47	63	232	71	17	−27	54
Stockholm	5	−20	−15	−36	129	57	67	64	6	−11	0	−2
Southwest	21	−5	1	−23	54	98	63	45	33	−5	−8	2
Southeast	35	−1	−18	−21	97	58	38	70	2	12	21	14
Borås	63	−9	−11	−30	49	51	81	53	−4	39	−19	2
South Lake Vänern	21	−1	−9	−41	171	106	47	53	35	−29	51	9
East Middle	22	−1	2	−42	141	148	99	93	10	−3	−16	17
Bergslagen	27	−7	−11	−27	46	379	155	66	22	1	−12	106
Outer Aid Area	44	7	8	−28	107	173	60	42	23	−2	12	19
Inner Aid Area	109	47	32	12	37	29	37	25	57	66	0	56

Source: as for Table 13.1.

total employment effect. Such localization of the negative impact of regional policies outside the Aid Areas would be more likely if they and metropolitan regions shared the same type of industrial specialization. The definition of regions demonstrates that this is probably not the case. Another possibility is that the pattern of change in market shares of the Aid Areas may be competitive with rather than complementary to that of the metropolitan regions. Results published elsewhere (Ohlsson 1979b) suggest that this was true for the footloose sector of the Malmö region but only when compared to the Outer Aid Area. The relationship does not appear sufficiently strong to account for other than a minor part of the poor structural adjustment performance of the Malmö region. Thus, negative regional policy effects on non-aided regions through commodity market competition appear to be so weak that they cannot explain the poorer performance of the metropolitan regions.

Second, non-aided regions may have suffered from an out-migration of plants. At the end of 1975 the stock of plants consisted of 2 distinct groups: (a) all plants in operation in 1965 minus those discontinued between 1965 and 1975; and (b) new plants established between 1965 and 1975, minus those discontinued before 1975. The former group can be labelled 'existing plants' and the latter 'plant entries'. It is clear from evidence given already that their combined production in non-aided regions was little hindered by direct competition with Aid Area plants but, even so, high mobility of factories may have produced a significant negative impact in particular industries. This is an issue already highlighted by Ohlsson (1979c) in an investigation of entries of affiliated and immigrant plants that began production in the Aid Areas with the help of regional aid. Roughly 0.5 per cent of all manufacturing establishments in 1975 belonged to each category and their average workforce was less than the Swedish average. Their total employment made up some 5 or 6 per cent of the factory workforce in the 2 northern Aid Areas. They were relatively most important in the footloose sector and especially the sub-groups having increasing competitiveness and rapid market growth. More than 40 per cent of the employment in these aided plants in 1975 'originated' in Stockholm. This represented only 4 per cent of the jobs remaining in the capital though this was more than twice the decrease in employment between 1965 and 1975. The distribution of the 'potential employment losses' via this out-migration of production had a clear bias towards a larger such 'loss' in those footloose industries with poor competitiveness and market growth situation.

This result reinforces the findings of other types of analyses: Stockholm deviates from the 2 other metropolitan regions primarily in its ability to diminish its non-competitive productive activities rapidly. Given that ambitious national employment goals meant a continuing labour shortage even in the depressed years of the 1965–75 period, it may be concluded that it was the competition for low and unskilled workers from the fast-expanding public and private service sectors that facilitated this result. Industrial firms that were not very competitive or had a low rate of market expansion could not afford to raise their wages enough to obtain adequate labour, a conclusion supported by the high turnover of the workforce throughout the business cycle. If this is correct a more severe consequence for metropolitan regions was that regional aid restricted the migration of labour from areas receiving it. As a result, workers from Finland and southern Europe tended to make up for the lower in-migration of Swedes from the northern parts of the country. While this may have affected the magnitude of manufacturing in Stockholm and other parts of southern Sweden, and its weak industries in particular, there is no evidence to suggest a negative impact on its ability to start and expand production with favourable competitive and growth conditions. The earlier conclusion of a comparatively bad structural adaptability of metropolitan regions still holds.

INTER-SECTORAL TECHNOLOGY AND TECHNOLOGY CHANGE DIFFERENCES AND THEIR ROLE FOR THE REGIONAL BALANCE OF FACTOR MARKETS

These inter-sectoral and inter-regional analyses have largely been based on employment. It has been demonstrated that differential development of domestic demand and international competitiveness of sectors and sub-sectors influence both national and regional industrial adjustment. Changes in demand and competitiveness directly affect the gross output of the sectors but only indirectly affect their use of labour. It is important, therefore, to investigate the impact of indirect links. The 2 sectoral classifications used already were again adopted since this permits a distinction to be made between various causes of structural employment change at the national and regional levels. It is possible to derive *ceteris paribus* (or partial) impulses to the inter-sectoral and inter-regional development of factor demand by combining initial conditions in 1965 with actual developments in sectoral demand and competitiveness between 1965 and 1975. Technological change can also give rise to similar impulses for the regional balance of factor markets by, for instance, encouraging a more intensive use of some inputs at the expense of others. (This will induce regionally different consequences only if the factor bias differs between sectors.) This presupposes technological change to be a given, whereas in fact regional technology at the sectoral level can alter differently as a result of the development of intra-sectoral and intra-regional specialization. At this level it is impossible to distinguish between shifts in this specialization and 'pure' technological change.

This section analyses interrelationships *between* the inter-sectoral differences in initial technology and in technology change *and* the corresponding ones in the demand and competitiveness changes. The results are interpreted in *ceteris paribus* terms, the possibility that regional variations in technology or in technology change occurring thus being disregarded.

A comparison of technology differences between sectors that have influenced the relative use of labour can easily be done with existing data, but a cross-sectoral comparison of how the corresponding change has affected the use of labour and therefore sectoral employment composition is far more intricate. Mainly this is because the 1965–75 period was an inflationary one which involved relative price changes and because input and output price data at the sectoral level are unavailable. None the less some information is available as evidenced by Table 13.12 which presents some aggregate technological characteristics by sector for Sweden as a whole. Recalling that alterations in international competitiveness and differences in market growth rates primarily affect the development of sales, Table 13.12 shows the levels in 1965 and relative changes during the 1965–75 period of the value added/sales and value added/employee ratios.

The value added/sales ratio in 1965 was substantially higher in the footloose sector than in the other 2; this, together with a lower labour productivity, explained its much larger labour use per unit of sales (in current prices). Despite some levelling of the ratios from 1965 to 1975, the differences remained considerable. Consequently, a given increase in the value of final demand had a larger direct impact on production and employment in footloose industry. But the inter-sectoral employment shifts between the 3 sectors were insignificant, primarily because of the small differences in the growth of sectoral demand and changes in competitiveness.

The lower value added/employee ratio in the footloose sector in 1965 compared with the trade-exposed raw material-based sector can also be contrasted with the much larger measured differences in capital intensities (and electricity consumption/employee). If international competition were working well (i.e. there were no severe market imperfections in external commodity and factor markets), the much smaller productivity difference should be attributable to a higher human capital intensity in the footloose sector. As demonstrated later, this is true, but may not be the whole story. Until 1975, the relative value added/employee ratio increased much faster in the raw material-based sector than might be accounted for by the simultaneous relative rise in capital (and electricity) intensities. The probable explanation is the drastic relative price rise of raw material-based products after the energy crisis in 1973, following a 20-year decline. Over the 1965–75 period the relative changes in labour use per sales value in the 2 trade-exposed sectors were about the same.

Within the footloose sector in 1965 both the value added/sales and the

TABLE 13.12 Some characteristics of sectoral technology variations and technical change in Swedish manufacturing industry, 1965 to 1975

Sector	Index (1965 = 100) for 1975				1965 values of			
	Value added/ sales	Value added/ employee	Motive capacity/ employee	Electricity consumption/ employee	Value added/ sales[a]	Value added/ employee[b]	Motive capacity/ employee[c]	Electricity consumption/ employee[d]
Trade-sheltered	123	266	133	151	39	37	6	11
Raw material-based	103	320	142	142	35	40	31	88
Footloose	89	251	105	139	52	35	8	21
1. Competitiveness								
a. Strongly increased	78	220	104	162	58	43	5	11
b. Increased	88	245	108	134	51	36	5	42
c. Slightly increased or decreased	100	267	101	127	52	33	6	8
d. Strongly decreased	107	283	127	169	45	28	6	14
2. Market change								
a. Rapid growth	104	263	104	116	46	34	6	21
b. Good growth	81	234	101	130	57	40	7	20
c. Slow growth	86	234	102	130	51	36	16	31
d. Stagnating or contracting	102	276	128	239	49	27	4	12

[a] per cent.
[b] SKr 000 per employee.
[c] kW per employee.
[d] kWh (000) per employee.
Source: as for Table 13.1.

value added/employee ratios were higher for the groups of industries having the better comparative advantage rankings. The labour productivity differences were not then positively correlated with the non-human capital intensity variations. In a well functioning world market this would imply a closer, positive association with the human capital intensity. Between 1965 and 1975 the 2 value-added ratios increased relatively more the poorer the competitive ranking of the industries. *Ceteris paribus* these results counteract each other in their effects on labour use per unit of sales value. But since the differences in the value added/sales ratio changes were the larger ones, the net result was that relative labour use declined more in industries that improved their international competitiveness. Since there were no systematic relationships between the shifts in competitiveness and in the capital/labour ratio, it can be concluded that, for a given magnitude of final demand, technological change induced somewhat lesser demand for labour in competitive than in non-competitive sectors. But this impact was limited. The large differences in the labour/sales ratio in 1965 were basically unaltered in 1975 and they were negatively related to the change in competitiveness criterion. Hence, the changes registered in international competitiveness between footloose sub-sectors tended to save labour in the value-added processes and, on average, they also decreased intermediate input demands of these processes. It is the former effect that kept the relative employment gain of the footloose sector small despite its increasing role in domestic demand and for net exports. The stronger labour-saving bias in competitive sectors underlined this but its influence was not very significant.

The net impact of all this on the inter-regional distribution of the labour market is rather limited. The consequences of a strong *initial* regional specialization in sectors with different demand and competitiveness changes were reduced not only by a *subsequent* levelling tendency in this specialization but also by the relative labour use differences between the footloose sector sub-groups. These 2 countervailing forces substantially reduced the inter-regional imbalances in the labour markets and possibly also net migration between the same regions. At least in part, capital appears to have migrated more in a compensatory way through regional policies.

The shifting sectoral composition and differences in technical change among the sectors also have implications for the kinds of labour required. As Table 13.13 suggests, the increased emphasis on products from the footloose sector has apparently stimulated the demand for non-manual labour. In particular it has strongly enhanced the need for technical personnel, such as engineers, rather than for management and sales personnel. In all 3 sectors between 1965 and 1975 there was an increase in the proportion of technical personnel. Within the footloose sector, international competitiveness improved with increased use of non-manual labour, especially technical personnel. Consequently, the growth of industries with an im-

TABLE 13.13 Shares of selected non-manual labour occupations in total employment by sector, Sweden, 1965 and 1975

Sector	1965 (per cent)			1975 (per cent)		
	Total non-manual labour	Technical personnel	Management and sales personnel	Total non-manual labour	Technical personnel	Management and sales personnel
Trade-sheltered	25	3	4	27	4	5
Raw material-based	18	3	2	21	5	3
Footloose	27	8	2	29	10	2
1. Competitiveness						
a. Strongly increased	31	12	2	31	13	2
b. Increased	29	9	2	31	10	3
c. Slightly increased or decreased	25	6	3	28	8	4
d. Strongly decreased	21	6	2	23	7	2
2. Market change						
a. Rapid growth	26	7	3	27	9	3
b. Good growth	30	11	2	31	12	2
c. Slow growth	27	8	2	29	10	2
d. Stagnating or contracting	23	6	3	28	10	3

Source: as for Table 13.1.

proved comparative advantage must have boosted the demand for technically educated, and also skilled, workers.

This discussion of the national and sectoral nature of technical change and structural development provides a background for the analysis of the possible regional differences in the demand for labour. It has already been mentioned that in 1970 the 3 metropolitan regions (but especially Stockholm) together with the East Middle region had the most abundant human capital. Since all 4 of these regions were also the best developed in respect of the formation of new both human and non-human capital, it could be presumed that they would have had the best capacity to transform their industrial composition into a more human skill-orientated specialization profile. According to the evidence in Table 13.13, this generates the already rejected hypothesis that the metropolitan regions would have displayed a particularly rapid expansion of the 2 footloose sectors that had improved their international competitiveness; instead, the Aid Areas demonstrated the best sectoral adjustment performance. Nevertheless, the metropolitan regions may still be deemed to have performed better in this respect if it can be shown that their intra-sectoral adjustment meant that the human skill-intensive industries and activities remained and flourished while elsewhere, and in the Aid Areas in particular, the least skill-intensive industries grew rapidly. This issue is considered in the next section especially in relation to

(a) technical personnel and (b) management and sales personnel. The latter group is not usually closely integrated into the physical transformation of inputs into finished products and hence it may or may not be a typical activity of urban and metropolitan regions. Technical personnel are, on the contrary, typically associated with activities at the plant level, including in certain industries, their R & D departments. To the extent that technical activity dominates over management and sales activity the metropolitan concentration of the former would be expected to be larger.

REGIONAL VARIATIONS IN THE USE OF SKILLED LABOUR

Variations between regions in the proportion of the factory workforce in selected non-manual occupations are set out in Table 13.14. The 3 metropolitan regions each have a higher proportion of non-manual workers than in Swedish manufacturing industry as a whole. This is especially so in the Stockholm region, mainly due to its substantially higher use of technical (highly skilled) and clerical (mainly low and unskilled) labour. The other highly skilled category—managerial and sales personnel—is not as concentrated in the metropolitan regions as technical personnel. But the latter group only accounts for 14.4 per cent of the factory workforce even in Stockholm. Thus, from the point of view of having a diversified local or regional labour market, a greater problem appears to be the concentration of clerical activities since this is related to the availability of low-skilled jobs for female labour.

During the 1965–75 period total employment remained almost stable but the proportion of non-manual labour increased by about 10 per cent and technical personnel by 27 per cent. The absolute expansion of the latter category did not, however, mean further regional concentration. The coefficient of variation dropped slightly, despite an above-average increase in the use of technical personnel in the 3 metropolitan regions. Rather, the levelling was attributable, in particular, to the Borås region and the Inner Aid Area, both of which displayed an increased use of technical personnel at more than double the rate of Sweden as a whole.

Along with earlier findings these results indicate that increased technical personnel usage in the metropolitan regions, and especially Stockholm, appears to be at least partially attributable to the rapid decline of employment in non-competitive sectors. In Stockholm, the absolute decline of employment in all but those industries in the footloose sector which had a strongly improved international competitiveness clearly worked in this direction, since the latter sector was by far the most technical personnel-intensive in Sweden as a whole. Regional Aid Areas in general, and the Inner Aid Area in particular, obtained the fastest improvement in their sectoral composition, implying either a higher than average increase in technical

TABLE 13.14 Per cent of workforce in manufacturing industry in selected non-manual occupations by regions, Sweden, 1965 and 1975

Region	1965					1975				
	Non-manual labour	Managerial and sales personnel	Technical personnel	Clerks	Foremen	Non-manual labour	Managerial and sales personnel	Technical personnel	Clerks	Foremen
Malmö	27.3	3.5	6.3	12.7	4.2	30.8	4.0	8.4	13.4	4.1
Göteborg	27.9	2.7	8.2	12.2	4.4	31.7	2.7	10.8	13.8	4.0
Stockholm	37.2	3.6	10.8	17.5	4.3	42.7	3.7	14.4	19.2	3.9
Southwest	20.4	3.0	3.7	9.3	4.0	22.3	3.5	4.8	9.6	4.1
Southeast	20.3	2.9	4.2	8.8	4.1	23.1	3.2	5.8	9.7	4.0
Borås	17.2	3.6	2.1	7.5	3.9	21.3	4.5	3.5	9.0	4.0
South Lake Vänern	21.5	2.2	5.7	9.2	4.2	22.2	2.1	6.8	9.0	4.0
East Middle	27.3	2.3	8.4	12.0	4.4	29.5	2.3	10.2	12.5	4.1
Bergslagen	24.0	1.3	7.6	10.5	4.4	26.4	1.7	8.9	11.0	4.6
Outer Aid Area	19.6	1.9	4.3	8.4	4.5	22.2	2.2	5.9	9.0	4.5
Inner Aid Area	17.6	4.0	1.9	6.9	4.2	18.5	3.5	3.4	6.9	4.3
Total Sweden	25.3	2.7	6.6	11.2	4.3	27.8	2.9	8.4	11.8	4.2
Mean value	23.66	2.82	5.75	10.45	4.20	26.43	3.04	7.54	11.19	4.15
Standard deviation	5.91	0.83	2.81	3.02	0.19	6.89	0.89	3.39	3.39	0.23
Coefficient of variation	0.25	0.30	0.49	0.29	0.04	0.26	0.29	0.45	0.30	0.05

Source: as for Table 13.1.

personnel usage or, if this is not correct, inter-regionally varying technical personnel intensity rankings.

Higher technical personnel intensity in metropolitan regions is not due to a higher usage in every sector (Table 13.15). Stockholm's very high share of technical personnel can be attributed to both an inter-sectoral specialization in sectors where this share is high and an intra-sectoral specialization in industries or activities with a high technical personnel intensity. A comparison between the coefficient of variation between regions (Table 13.15) with the corresponding coefficient estimated for each region over 6 sectors (trade-sheltered, raw material-based and the 4 footloose sub-groups) reveals that in 1965 the inter-sectoral variation in technical personnel intensities was often higher than the inter-regional variation. Between 1965 and 1975 the inter-regional relative differences declined in all sectors except those with the initially smallest differences, where they remained stable. Accordingly, the growth of the Swedish technical personnel intensity involves a tendency towards declining regional (relative) differences. Table 13.15 suggests that the inter-sectoral variations in technical personnel usage are similar across regions. The footloose sector always has a higher intensity than the others, followed as a rule by the raw material-based sector. The 2 footloose sub-groups which improved their international competitiveness have higher shares of technical personnel in 10 of the 11 regions than the other 2 sub-groups. This inter-sectoral stability is all the more surprising since:

(a) the principles of aggregation of the 110 industries do not take any account of the factor intensities of production;

(b) the varying size of the regions causes differences in the degree of their production diversification;

(c) one of the leading principles of spatial aggregation into regions was the differences in human skill intensity of spatial micro-units.

These results suggest that the inter-sectoral variations in technical personnel intensities remain stable between regions and may be one of the most important factors behind the changing international competitiveness in the footloose sector. The former conclusion compares well with an earlier finding (Ohlsson, 1980a, Chapter 6) for about half the footloose industries, namely that 33 engineering industries had remarkably stable relative differences in the technical personnel intensity between 1954 and 1968. The latter conclusion also conforms with an earlier report (Ohlsson, 1980a) that the Swedish engineering industries increased their international specialization in technical personnel-intensive production between 1960 and 1970. This chapter adds the spatial dimension of this adjustment process and demonstrates that all regions seemed to share common incentives to adapt their industrial composition in the same direction with respect to skill intensities. Moreover,

TABLE 13.15 Regional variations in technical personnel percentages of employees by sector, Sweden, 1965

Region	Trade-sheltered	Raw material-based	Footloose	Footloose industries with competitiveness			
				Strongly increased	Increased	Slightly increased or decreased	Strongly decreased
Malmö	2.4	5.2	7.8	7.9	7.8	6.1	8.4
Göteborg	2.5	3.4	9.9	13.4	9.3	4.3	9.5
Stockholm	3.6	6.6	14.1	18.5	10.5	10.2	8.0
Southwest	2.4	2.9	4.3	4.0	6.7	3.7	1.7
Southeast	3.2	2.7	4.8	7.0	4.8	2.7	4.3
Borås	1.1	0.5	2.3	3.9	4.4	2.7	1.4
South Lake Vänern	2.7	3.0	6.9	9.7	8.0	4.5	2.6
East Middle	2.6	2.8	10.4	16.1	11.7	7.7	4.8
Bergslagen	1.8	3.6	9.5	4.8	10.0	11.6	3.1
Outer Aid Area	2.1	2.7	6.1	7.0	7.3	3.8	1.6
Inner Aid Area	1.5	1.3	2.8	4.0	6.7	1.0	1.2
Total Sweden	2.7	3.3	8.4	12.2	8.9	5.7	5.6
Mean value 1965	2.35	3.15	7.17	8.75	7.93	5.30	4.24
Standard deviation 1965	0.72	1.66	3.60	5.13	2.30	3.29	3.07
Coefficient of variation 1965	0.30	0.53	0.50	0.59	0.29	0.62	0.72
Mean value 1975	3.56	4.42	9.07	10.26	9.17	7.92	5.86
Standard deviation 1975	1.02	2.18	4.39	5.27	2.69	4.43	3.33
Coefficient of variation 1975	0.29	0.49	0.48	0.51	0.29	0.56	0.57

Source: as for Table 13.1.

the most backward regions managed to improve the most while the seemingly good adaptability of the metropolitan regions did not in practice lead to rapid industrial adjustment. Finally, there are indications that differences in adaptability are partially associated with the regional variations in the creation of new establishments and the locational incentives of Swedish regional policy.

Relative changes in the technical personnel intensities by sector and region are shown in Table 13.16, where it can be seen that they tended to increase more the lower the initial value of the sector or region in 1965. This is also true for the Malmö and Göteborg regions in the case of footloose industries with strongly decreased competitiveness since this sub-group had unusually high initial values in these 2 regions. Thus, Table 13.16 suggests 2 different tendencies towards a levelling of technical personnel ratios. An earlier indication of a slight such tendency was found for the above mentioned 33 engineering industries between 1959 and 1968 (Ohlsson, 1977b, 1980a). Two different kinds of interpretation were offered. One was based on the assumption of an exogenously given, biased technological change; the other assumed the 'intensive factor saving bias' (Johnson, 1963) in Sweden's technical change to be endogenously determined. The former implies that the comparative advantage differences due to the factor abundance of the country and skill intensity differences between industries both declined during the period. But if the intensive factor saving bias was endogenously determined, one possibility would be that it was brought about by a change in Sweden's factor abundance and/or relative prices, meaning an increased comparative advantage in human capital-intensive production. Such a change creates incentives for the producers of non-human capital-intensive production to lower manufacturing costs and/or alter the product mix. In both cases technical personnel are the key category upon which the possible success of the adjustment depends. In this perspective the relatively large increases of technical personnel usage in the least intensive sectors may be viewed as an intra-industry and inter-activity change in specialization within sectors losing comparative advantage. For sectors gaining in comparative advantage there are no strong incentives for a similar intra-industry or inter-activity specialization change. Instead the production expansion due to this gain may involve a move towards products with less intense technical personnel requirements.

The tendency towards a regional levelling of the technical personnel intensities came during a period which initially experienced a balanced national market for engineers for the first time in at least 15 years. Later there were even excess supplies leading to a further increase of engineers in manufacturing employment over and above the increased technical personnel intensity. It is not surprising that such an alteration of market conditions is associated with a rapid increase in technical personnel intensities even in

TABLE 13.16 Percentage changes in the intensities of technical personnel by sector and region, Sweden, 1965 to 1975

Region	All sectors	Trade-sheltered	Raw material-based	Footloose	Footloose industries with competitiveness			
					Strongly increased	Increased	Slightly increased or decreased	Strongly decreased
Malmö	33	63	54	29	30	29	67	19
Göteborg	32	104	65	26	15	17	63	19
Stockholm	33	19	21	31	19	15	69	23
Southwest	30	29	69	26	38	13	32	47
Southeast	38	47	44	33	47	46	33	28
Borås	67	82	60	65	36	59	19	93
South Lake Vänern	19	67	10	13	−9	−18	78	73
East Middle	21	35	29	20	−8	19	47	33
Bergslagen	17	28	17	15	35	17	5	126
Outer aid Area	37	38	52	26	23	14	63	63
Inner Aid Area	79	93	69	50	33	85	230	83
Mean value	36.9	55.0	44.5	30.4	23.5	26.9	64.2	55.2
Standard deviation	19.7	28.7	21.8	15.2	18.2	27.5	59.6	35.4
Coefficient of variation	0.52	0.52	0.49	0.50	0.77	1.02	0.93	0.64

Source: as for Table 13.1.

TABLE 13.17 Regional variations in managerial and sales personnel, percentages of employees by sector, Sweden, 1965

Region	All sectors	Trade-sheltered	Raw material-based	Footloose	Footloose industries with competitiveness			
					Strongly increased	Increased	Slightly increased or decreased	Strongly decreased
Malmö	3.5	3.4	5.7	3.2	1.8	3.9	6.2	2.7
Göteborg	2.7	4.3	3.2	2.3	1.8	5.3	5.6	1.1
Stockholm	3.6	3.8	5.7	3.4	2.7	4.1	4.6	3.5
Southwest	3.0	4.4	3.2	2.6	2.8	2.1	2.8	3.0
Southeast	2.9	4.0	2.2	2.7	1.7	2.7	3.9	2.9
Borås	3.6	4.1	4.3	3.5	3.5	4.5	3.0	3.6
South Lake Vänern	2.2	3.6	1.7	1.9	0.8	1.8	2.7	3.3
East Middle	2.3	3.2	2.8	2.0	1.3	1.9	3.1	2.0
Bergslagen	1.3	4.0	1.1	1.0	2.1	0.8	1.3	1.8
Outer Aid Area	1.9	4.3	1.1	1.6	1.3	1.2	2.6	2.9
Inner Aid Area	4.0	5.4	2.1	4.4	2.9	3.1	5.4	5.5
Total Sweden	2.7	3.8	2.3	2.4	1.8	2.2	3.5	2.5
Mean value 1965	2.82	4.05	3.01	2.60	2.06	2.85	3.75	2.94
Standard deviation 1965	0.83	0.59	1.64	0.98	0.82	1.45	1.52	1.14
Coefficient of variation 1965	0.30	0.15	0.54	0.38	0.40	0.51	0.41	0.39
Mean value 1975	3.04	4.70	3.62	2.60	2.32	3.28	3.87	2.64
Standard deviation 1975	0.89	0.73	1.82	0.93	1.03	1.54	1.62	1.03
Coefficient of variation 1975	0.29	0.16	0.50	0.36	0.45	0.47	0.42	0.39

Source: as for Table 13.1.

TABLE 13.18 Percentage changes in the intensities of managerial and sales personnel by sector and region, Sweden, 1965 to 1975

Region	All sectors	Trade-sheltered	Raw material-based	Footloose	Footloose industries with competitiveness			
					Strongly increased	Increased	Slightly increased or decreased	Strongly decreased
Malmö	14	32	26	3	39	21	−5	−30
Göteborg	0	21	13	−9	−17	−2	11	−9
Stockholm	3	13	0	−3	−19	17	39	−6
Southwest	17	−9	19	19	25	14	14	23
Southeast	10	30	18	4	24	37	3	−14
Borås	25	46	23	23	20	16	33	17
South Lake Vänern	−5	6	35	−11	13	78	−22	−21
East Middle	0	16	32	−5	−8	0	6	0
Bergslagen	31	38	55	20	24	13	46	−33
Outer Aid Area	16	7	9	13	15	33	−4	14
Inner Aid Area	−13	−9	29	−30	14	−19	−43	−40
Total Sweden	7	18	26	0	0	18	6	−8
Mean value	8.91	17.36	23.55	2.18	11.82	18.91	7.09	−9.00
Standard deviation	13.25	18.11	14.69	16.02	18.61	25.15	26.28	21.13
Coefficient of variation	1.49	1.04	0.62	7.34	1.58	1.33	3.71	−2.35

Source: as for Table 13.1.

the most backward regions. However, there is enough evidence from the analysis here of a relatively successful adjustment of these regions in terms, for example, of their industrial mix and entries of new plants to suggest that this increase was not merely a lagged adjustment of initially low technical personnel intensities.

Tables 13.17 and 13.18 provide similar data for the managerial and sales personnel intensities and show that in manufacturing industry they were at least as high in the metropolitan regions, the Inner Aid Area and in some other non-urban regions as in Sweden as a whole. It is difficult in fact to find any systematic pattern. The managerial and sales personnel intensity is obviously not playing the same role for the changes in Sweden's international competitiveness nor for that matter in the regional division of labour. In fact, the variations in the employment shares of the low-skilled clerical category appear to be more important regionally.

THE DILEMMA OF SLOW STRUCTURAL ADJUSTMENT

One of the main findings of this chapter is that the 3 metropolitan regions did not switch their employment relatively quickly to sectors which either had a high market growth rate or had gained much in comparative advantage. The largest metropolitan region, Stockholm, already had at the outset of the study period a favourable employment mix especially with respect to the latter criterion but improved it largely as a consequence of a rapid contraction of employment in sectors which ranked low on both growth criteria. Analysis of the changes in the number and workforce of establishments suggests that the bad performance of the metropolitan regions was probably in part associated with the relatively few new firm entries and an out-migration of establishments in industries ranking high on the 2 growth criteria. In addition, 2 of these regions only had slight increases in the average workforce per plant. The study supports the conclusion that the best adjusters were not the metropolitan regions but rather those which received regional aid because of employment problems within or outside the industrial sector. Since these usually had an initially poor employment mix, this implies a tendency towards eliminating regional differences in the mix.

Technical change is seen to be another source of employment change. At the start of the 1965–75 period, footloose industry had a much larger labour requirement per unit of sales value than the foreign trade-sheltered and raw material-based industry but this difference diminished during the decade. Within the footloose sector, industries which gained in comparative advantage and therefore tended to expand sales and employment more, decreased their labour requirements per unit of sales value more rapidly and had a lower initial such requirement. Such industries were also using skilled, and especially technical, personnel more intensively. Therefore, the inter-industry and inter-regional adjustment to changing international conditions also implied, *ceteris paribus*, a smoothing out of the regional differences in the endowment of skilled labour.

The much higher technical personnel intensities in each sector of industry in the Stockholm region imply a pronounced inter-sectoral or even inter-activity specialization in production requiring a high proportion of technicians. But the other 2 metropolitan regions were not dissimilar in this respect to other regions in all sectors. In fact, regional differences in sectoral technical personnel intensities diminished during the study period. Although the inter-sectoral skill intensities remained stable, the inter-regional relocation of production and the inter-sectoral, inter-regional levelling tendencies for these intensities have brought about a higher relative growth of realized demand for skilled labour in regions where it was initially scarce. Since this occurred when there was no excess demand for engineers and technical personnel, it appears that educated labour has tended to move as a response to the out-migration of industrial production from the metropolises.

The comparatively good structural adaptability of the Aid Areas is a necessary but not a sufficient condition for the long-run success of the regional employment goal. Since this emphasizes the need to create alternative employment in internationally competitive production, the adaptability result appears to be a direct indication of a partial goal fulfilment. Ohlsson (1980c) shows that the good adjustment performance was achieved at least partially because of the investment aid system of regional policies. However there are still severe employment difficulties in the north of Sweden and the structure reached in 1975 was still substantially worse in several respects than that in the rest of Sweden. But the good adaptability of the Aid Areas may simply be a reflection of a bad adaptability elsewhere *if* Sweden as a whole was comparatively slow to adjust to its altered comparative advantages. Such a result was indicated in a study of the engineering industries in the 1960s in a comparison with other OECD countries. Moreover, the net export surplus in technical personnel-intensive footloose industries was reached only in the late 1960s and after. The development of Sweden's industry since 1975 has suggested a deteriorating adjustment performance. Throughout the 1970s the economic growth of Sweden has been one of the lowest among OECD countries; severe industrial problems have arisen in such major industries as iron and steel, mining, pulp, and shipbuilding alongside a continuation of the longer-term difficulties in the footwear, textile, clothing and other labour-intensive industries; the important car industries have also entered a period of sluggish demand and increased competition from Japanese vehicles.

Since 1975 the northern Aid Areas have shared the general industrial employment difficulties of Swedish industry as a whole, suggesting that regional policies were relatively successful as long as Swedish industrial growth was relatively rapid. As the external *and* internal conditions for industrial expansion gradually deteriorated during the 1970s the same policies seem to have become less successful. The lesson is similar to that of the UK: unless general economic policies provide good industrial prospects there is little scope of ambitious fulfilment for *any* regional policy. However, in contrast to the UK, Sweden has for a long time had a growth-orientated regional policy. Then in the 1970s more regional structure-preserving instruments were introduced, which meant a decline in the net employment effects per unit of aid. The need for increased industrial expansion and for more rapid adjustment to establish the future basis for such an expansion suggests that a more growth-orientated mix of instruments will become necessary.

The results for the Aid Areas and the 3 metropolitan regions suggests 3 possible reasons for the slow structural adjustment in Sweden. First, regional policies meant that the government took greater risks to lower costs for new firm entries and for expanding existing establishments than private shareholders and the capital market would do. Perhaps this can be taken as a sign of a risk-averse capital market which may or may not be associated with legal restrictions and taxation rules. A second possible explanation is related to the small size of the economy and the associated high degree of specialization. A small and open economy is generally more flexible in adjusting to changes in the world market because of the higher transparency throughout the economy of the role and importance of the international linkages. Hence, everything from the supply of educated manpower to economic policies is organized to meet industrial need. However, in at least 2 instances this advantage over the large economy may turn into a disadvantage. One case may be a period that has been preceded by many years of prosperity which may have led to less attention being paid to industry, especially if its share of the economy ceased increasing and a trade-sheltered public and private service sector created the net employment increases. This forgetfulness has lately been touched on in the economic debate of the possible role of the new labour market laws in the 1970s for the adjustment flexibility in industry as well as in the economy as a whole. Other related issues are the unfavourable taxation laws for shareholding as against other types of investment. The other case is when a fundamental shift occurs in the comparative advantage of the economy which calls for a rapid and equally fundamental change in industrial composition. The strong specialization not only of industry itself but also the production system as a whole may then develop to be a handicap. The world market signals to start up and expand companies in relatively small industries may not be noticed by the capital market institutions, the educational system, entrepreneurs and policy-makers. Hence, too many resources are continually devoted to the needs of traditionally competitive industries and firms at ever decreasing economic returns. This problem is evident in the Swedish iron and steel, iron-ore mining and shipbuilding industries.

The third possible reason for the slow adjustment of the Swedish economy is the combination of its small size, large spatial extension and historical spatial specialization. A high degree of flexibility has to be related to a high degree of geographical factor mobility. Structural adjustment becomes then for labour more painful for both economic and social reasons. Moreover, the economic reasons against such mobility have increased because of (a) increased household capital formation in partially immobile resources such as housing, and on the job training which is firm specific, and (b) increased female labour participation. The dispersed, small local labour markets in Sweden then become a barrier toward mobility.

One possible type of solution to these dilemmas is suggested by the results reported in this chapter. All Sweden shares increasingly the same kind of comparative advantages, and therefore its major regions are likely to develop a similar industrial mix based on an abundance in each region of human skills. Policies aiming at establishing a greater regional supply of such skills and also of industrial capital appear to be a likely ingredient. Other important policies are mobility-stimulating labour market policies that increase both inter-regional and inter-sectoral mobility. Finally, the capital market should be reorganized in such a way that risk-taking in the industrial sector is not reduced by taxation or other legislation.

Spatial Analysis, Industry and the Industrial Environment. Vol. 3 Regional Economies and In
Edited by F. E. I. Hamilton and G. J. R. Linge
© 1983 John Wiley & Sons Ltd.

Chapter 14

The International Location of Manufacturing Investments: Recent Behaviour of Foreign-owned Corporations in the United States

JAMES E. MCCONNELL

The multinational corporation is one of the most influential and highly diffused international institutions. The pervasiveness of multi-plant, multi-country enterprises during the last 20 years reflects managerial, technical and institutional changes that are the hallmark of the capitalist industrial system. Traditionally, these corporate giants have operated from bases in large developed countries and concentrated their foreign business activities in other developed economies (Jumper *et al.*, 1980, pp. 436–9). More recently, however, such enterprises are also emerging from developing nations (Wells, 1977), intensifying their investment activities in the Third World (Elsaid and Darling, 1978), and becoming heterogeneous in their size and geographical diversity (Aharoni, 1978).

Three phases of foreign investment activity can be identified since the Second World War (United States Department of Commerce, 1976, pp. 9–10). Between 1946 and 1957, worldwide investments were heavily concentrated in petroleum and other raw materials. The US was the leading exporter of foreign capital, concentrating its investments in Canada, Latin America and the Middle East; European overseas investments, although less than those from the US, were also evident in the Middle East, Africa and certain areas of South-East and East Asia.

From 1958 through the early 1970s, foreign investment began to concentrate on manufacturing and trade activities. With the establishment of regional trade blocs in Europe, and with the economic recovery of Western Europe and Japan, new direct foreign investments began to flow into Europe. The US, which accounted for almost half the total book value of foreign direct investments at the close of this period, continued to be the principal source of such activity, followed by the UK, West Germany, Switzerland, Canada and Japan (Sauvant, 1976, p. 45).

Throughout the 1970s, and particularly following the realignments of most key currencies and the depreciation of the US dollar during the 1971–73 period, a third phase of direct investment activity emerged. Although the

US remained the largest exporter of overseas direct investments, outward flows from Western Europe, Japan and Canada increased more rapidly (United Nations Economic and Social Council, 1978), especially to the US. From 1970 through 1979, for example, direct investments in the US from foreign-owned corporations grew from $US13,300 million to over $US50,000 million, or by an annual average of 31 per cent (United States, President, 1978, p. 372; United States, Bureau of Economic Analysis, 1980, pp. 32–3). Meanwhile, in contrast, overseas direct investment by US multinationals rose at an average annual rate of only 16 per cent. International *net* direct investment flows of the US and the other major industrial countries are rapidly converging (Christelow, 1979–80, p. 22).

The potential impacts of these trends on the US industrial system and on the international economic environment are quite significant. For example, foreign direct investments not only affect the global patterns of capital flows but also directly and indirectly the diffusion of technology, the extent of technological and organizational interdependence among companies and countries, the patterns of commodity trade, the competitive advantage of industrial corporations and countries, and the dynamics of political and social change. Equally important, foreign direct investments in the US influence industrial location patterns, regional growth dynamics, domestic business and employment conditions, and related public policy issues. Analysis of these activities of foreign corporations thus provides the basis for investigating the dynamics of national and international industrial systems.

This chapter examines the recent flow of foreign direct investments into the US with attention initially focusing on the conceptual frameworks associated with the international direct investment decision and on the empirical research on such investments in the US. The analysis then considers the direct investment patterns of European, Canadian and Japanese subsidiaries, with special emphasis on their national and sub-regional locational patterns. A foreign direct investment is defined by the US government as a foreign equity equal to, or greater than, 10 per cent.

This study extends from 1974 through September 1979, dates that coincide with the first comprehensive benchmark survey prepared by the US government on the status of foreign direct investment activity in the country (United States Department of Commerce, 1976, pp. A123–4) and the most recent data available from government and private sources (United States Department of Commerce, 1977–79; The Conference Board, 1977–79; Angel, 1978). Because data on the value of foreign direct investments in the US are incomplete, the number of foreign-owned subsidiaries is employed as the measure of the foreign presence. Ideally these should be used in combination with other indices of the actual significance of the investment because a single measure may distort the full impact of the project. The industry affiliation of each foreign direct investment project is reported here (because of lack of data) at the 2-digit level using the Standard Industrial Classification (SIC) system.

THE DECISION TO INVEST IN THE UNITED STATES

A Conceptual Framework

The decision by an industrial corporation to make direct investments outside its home country is a culmination of many complex, interrelated factors. The diverse motives include the desire to spread business risks through geographical diversification; the need to be closer to a foreign customer to provide better service; the eagerness to get behind tariff and non-tariff barriers to protect the company's market share; the wish to expand into new markets to improve profits or to extend sales cycles of specific product lines; the desire to capitalize upon cheaper labour and supply costs to maintain competitive production capabilities; and the need to gain access to foreign-controlled technological know-how and managerial expertise. The analysis of international flow patterns of direct investments, therefore, necessarily requires an understanding of the multinational corporation as an actor in the international space-economy (Root, 1978, p. 517).

One of the most crucial decisions associated with an international direct investment programme is the location strategy (Schollhammer, 1974, p. 1). A company must choose the country or countries in which to establish its foreign business activity, how many investment projects to develop and where to locate them. It must also determine whether to acquire established firms or to identify desirable sites to construct new production facilities; thus the decision to invest internationally is as much a location decision as an investment one (Daniels, 1971, p. 91; Thomas, 1980 p. 10).

Much remains to be accomplished in integrating foreign direct investment theory with location theory, neither of which fully accounts for international corporate behaviour. Foreign direct investment theory, unlike international trade theory, is a relatively new research field with the first empirical study appearing less than 25 years ago (Leroy, 1976, pp. 39–40). Prior to the early 1960s the international flow of direct investments was presumed to be explained by differentials in rates of return on portfolio investments (Leroy, 1976, p. 47), but subsequent empirical studies demonstrated that it involves much more than the movement of capital stock.

Similarly, economic theories that relate to the international location of economic activity have originated from 2 distinct traditions (Vernon, 1974, p. 89). One has been concerned with the geographical configuration of production points and markets, usually within a national spatial structure, in which an 'economic equilibrium in space' results from the structure of factor costs (Vernon, 1974, p. 89). However, the rise of the multinational corporation and the enhanced importance of oligopolistic market structure in certain industry sectors mean that comparative costs alone cannot explain the locational behaviour of foreign-owned subsidiaries (Vernon, 1974, p. 102). Moreover, because traditional location theory has focused on aggregate economic variables, it does not provide an operational guideline for arriving at locational decisions in an international business context (Schollhammer, 1974, p. 2; Thomas, 1980, p. 10). The other relevant tradition has been the theory of international trade, which specified how the global specialization of national economies is determined (Vernon, 1974, p. 89). The conceptual link between location and trade is based on the assumption that the determinants of the commodity patterns of international trade and of foreign direct investment activity are closely interrelated (Baldwin, 1979). Again, however, the rise of multinational enterprise and oligopolistic markets reduce the credibility of perceiving international trade theory as the theory of international industrial location (Dunning, 1973). For example, the former theory traditionally assumes that market structure precludes the dependence of one factor on the behaviour of others. Because multinationals in some product sectors are strongly influenced by the 'move-countermove' type of behaviour (Knickerbocker, 1973, p. 5), their locational decisions often directly depend on the behaviour of competitors.

Another factor retarding the integration of foreign direct investment and location theory is the complexity of the investment decision. The diversity of motives, opportunities, and strategies behind foreign investment has produced multiple theories (Leroy, 1976; Root, 1978; Dunning, 1980) which differ according to the principal objective of the investing corporation and its associated industry and market characteristics. For example, strong arguments are made to support the neo-classical model of profit maximization as the major determinant of foreign direct investment (Aliber, 1970; Horst, 1972, Stevens, 1974; Ray, 1977; Findlay, 1978), whereas others have favoured theories emphasizing behavioural constructs (Aharoni, 1966; Miller and Weigel, 1973; Eiteman and Stonehill, 1973) or growth maximization objectives (Stubenitsky, 1970; Shapiro, 1977; Håkanson, 1979). Others, again, argue that major determinants of foreign direct investment are based on many assets peculiar to the industrial organization (Kindleberger, 1969; Caves, 1971; Hymer, 1976), or on special characteristics of its product, market structure and industry (Knickerbocker, 1973; Flowers, 1976; Graham, 1976; Ozawa, 1979a): monopolistic scale or product differentiation advantages and market structure make foreign direct investment a way of maintaining market-share position within national and international industrial environments. Finally, a growing number of hypotheses attempt to link foreign direct investment and international industrial location through the theory of international trade (Vernon, 1966; Wells, 1972; Dunning, 1973; Baldwin, 1979). Proponents argue that factor endowments of countries have a direct impact on international trade structure and on propensities of home-based enterprises to engage in external direct investment activities. The latter involves the international movements of factor inputs as transfers of resources occur between one part of the multinational firm and another.

Thus, a unified, generally accepted explanatory theory of foreign direct investment is lacking and existing hypotheses must be viewed as partial explanations. The difficulty of formulating a broadly based conceptual framework arises partly because empirical studies designed to test hypotheses from these multiple theories have not had quality data available nor have they contained explicit derivations of foreign direct investment equations (Ray, 1977, p. 285); consequently, rival theories have not been rigorously tested and quite contrary explanations of investment behaviour are often afforded empirical support (Ray, 1977, p. 285).

Overview of Empirical Research

Most case studies of foreign direct investment in the US date from the early 1970s but the 1950s saw the first research on US multinational activities abroad (Barlow and Wender, 1955). Investigations have focused on the motives for foreign enterprises to invest in the US; many reveal that the conceptual frameworks developed to account for the overseas investment behaviour of US-based multinationals are incompatible with recent strategies of foreign firms locating plants in the US.

Two of the earliest studies of foreign direct investment in the US (Business International SA, 1971; Daniels, 1971) noted that some Canadian and West European companies sought to capitalize on a perceived monopolistic advantage while others identified profit maximization as their primary motive. Others, again, claimed that they were forced to locate in the US because of slower growth rates at home, US trade barriers, or a need to be near their customers. However, both authors identified the size and growth of the US market as the main attractions (Business International SA, 1971, p. 32; Daniels, 1971, p. 101), although the latter (p. 91) concluded that no single existing theory completely explains the inward movement of such investments.

Backman and Bloch (1974), in a revealing study of manufacturing, noted that the investment activities of European companies were motivated by different objectives from those stimulating overseas investment by US corporations; hence, a reverse application of the investment model followed by US multinationals is not helpful. Their hypothesis (p. 94) was that 'European companies want subsidiaries in the United States as an *offensive* measure; i.e. to strengthen their capacity to compete with the United States in the world and European (home) markets'. Once these corporations became financially strong enough they could gain access to technological and marketing skills by buying US subsidiaries: these take-overs were an expedient way to secure such assets and, given the gradual devaluation of the US dollar during this period, a relatively inexpensive one. As far as these findings typify the behaviour of foreign investors in the US, they are a setback for the product cycle model, which is based upon the export-substitution motivation that characterized much of the earlier overseas investment activities of US corporations.

Of all the empirical studies published in the early to mid-1970s (Faith, 1972; Leftwich, 1973; Webley, 1974; The Conference Board, 1974; Arpan and Ricks, 1974; Boarman and Schollhammer, 1975), the most comprehensive is that undertaken by a private consultancy for the US Department of Commerce (Little, 1976). This used interviews with 72 foreign parent companies in West Germany, the Netherlands, Switzerland, the United Kingdom, Canada and Japan, and discussions with international investment and banking institutions and government agencies to construct detailed country profiles of foreign direct investment activity between 1970 and 1974. Four important conclusions were reached.

(a) The surge of foreign direct investments in the US in the early 1970s was attributed to the extraordinary growth in sales and assets of foreign corporations, and to the trend towards mergers and consolidations (Little, 1976, pp. 10–11). These factors, combined with ambitious growth objectives, worldwide macro-economic and political developments, and depressed US stockmarket values made direct investments exceedingly attractive.

(b) While less than a third of all announced investment projects were acquisitions of US firms, these accounted for most of the investments in value terms (Little, 1976, p. 18). Moreover, the foreign companies that chose this mode of entry were generally in industries in which the country concerned was internationally competitive or had a strong investment position in the US. This preference for take-overs, which also characterized the domestic expansion of US corporations throughout the 1970s, reflected the undervalued market price for many US firms and the relatively strong cash position of many foreign enterprises (Rappaport, 1979, p. 99). Most of these growth industries were quite high-technology ones such as chemicals and pharmaceuticals, electrical machinery and electronics, transport equipment, and non-electrical machinery.

(c) This research also showed that investment decisions are seldom solely based on a desire to maximize profits or to grow; rather, corporate executives frequently *assume* that increased profits and corporate growth are underlying goals of *all* investment activity and, hence, discuss other objectives that are presumed to contribute to them. Little (1976, p. 46) concluded that the goal of profit maximization may be quite reconcilable with non-profit maximization objectives.

(d) Because of the diversity of objectives and motives underlying the direct investment activity of foreign subsidiaries in the US, both offensive and defensive strategies were evident (Little, 1976, p. 49), depending on whether firms were attempting to maintain market position by matching the actions of competitors or by keeping abreast of changing technological and marketing innovations. Apart from trade barriers and transportation costs, production-cost criteria were not considered to be decisive considerations (Little, 1976, p. 54).

Flowers (1976) also offered strong support for the oligopolistic reaction hypothesis of foreign direct investment with the hypothesis that the fewer the number of firms in an industry the more intensely firms would respond to each other's moves and countermoves. He demonstrated (1976, p. 47) that about half the European and Canadian subsidiaries entering the US since the Second World War were associated with firms in concentrated industries following the behaviour of their leading corporations. These counter-investments are not only especially typical of firms from the same country but also tend to follow a preceding surge of US direct investment into that country (Flowers, 1976, p. 47). This provides further support for Graham's theory (1978, p. 89) of cross-investment which argues that price-cutting competition in Europe by US subsidiaries, whose parent corporations are maintaining prices and profits at home, causes European firms to invest in the US as a defensive measure.

Several writers have recently assessed the impact of foreign direct investment on the spatial and economic systems of the United States (Little, 1978; United States, Office of Community Planning and Development, 1979; McConnell, 1980; Papa, 1980). Their findings are of 4 kinds.

(a) While the traditional US northeast manufacturing region continues to attract the largest number of foreign direct investments, their relative growth, especially since 1976, has been faster in the southeast and southwest. The latent response of foreign investors to earlier moves by US firms is attributed to the lack of adequate information and experience and to the initial desire of many foreign parent enterprises to take over existing plants that are more likely to be located in the established industrial core (McConnell, 1980, p. 270).

(b) A comparison between the regional and state shares of all foreign-owned manufacturing plants and their shares of US-owned manufacturing establishments shows that foreign and domestic investors have locational preferences that differ between industry sectors (Little, 1978, pp. 52–5). Foreigners appear to place more weight than US firms on factors like state wage differentials and the availability of large port facilities but seem less sensitive to differences in power costs (Little, 1978, p. 56).

(c) States in older industrial areas, with low population growth and high unemployment, have been less successful since 1976 in attracting foreign direct investments which suggests that they are relatively worse off in gaining employment and income benefits than the more 'healthy' areas (United States, Office of Community Planning and Development, 1979). This disparity is further compounded because the bulk of foreign direct investments in lagging regions involves take-overs of 'healthy' companies; in contrast, most new foreign-owned subsidiaries are constructed in the south-east and southwest which are therefore benefiting disproportionately from employment and income effects.

(d) After classifying the per capita income of US metropolitan areas into high, medium, and low-income groups, Papa (1980) found that only 9 per cent of all foreign-owned subsidiaries established since 1978 were in low-income areas; that these areas were more likely to attract low-technology rather than technology-intensive projects; and that these areas were likely to involve the construction of new facilities rather than acquisitions of existing firms. Thus, while such areas were not attracting the higher wage projects, they were benefiting from additional capital expenditures associated with new plant construction.

Empirical research on foreign direct investments in the US is thus still at the formative stage. Much remains to be accomplished in identifying the locational strategies behind these investments, in comparing these strategies with those of US multinational investment overseas, and in determining the specific impacts of these projects on the US space-economy. So far, too, most research has been at the regional or state level, but the development of a more definitive spatial perspective of foreign direct investment activity requires investigation at a finer spatial scale.

INVESTMENT PATTERNS OF FOREIGN-OWNED SUBSIDIARIES IN THE UNITED STATES

A National Perspective

Foreign multinational corporations from 8 principal investing nations claimed at least 10 per cent of the equity of 2484 American manufacturing facilities by mid-1979. The UK, Japan, and Canada together accounted for 65 per cent of these investment projects, followed by West Germany, France, Switzerland and the Benelux group; other countries accounted for less than 8 per cent of all foreign direct investments. In value terms, Canada, the UK and the Netherlands led all other investing nations, as they did in 1974.

TABLE 14.1 Standard Industrial Classification categories ranked by per cent of total foreign direct investments, United States, 1979

SIC	Description	Per cent of total foreign direct investment
35	Non-electrical machinery	17.75
28	Chemicals and pharmaceuticals	12.16
36	Electrical machinery and electronics	10.36
38	Professional and scientific instruments	8.62
34	Fabricated metal products	8.53
20	Food and kindred products	7.88
33	Primary metal industries	5.52
26	Paper and allied products	4.47
27	Printing and publishing	3.74
22	Textile mill products	3.38
37	Transport equipment	2.86
32	Stone, clay, glass and concrete	2.74
39	Miscellaneous manufactured products	2.58
23	Apparel	2.42
29	Petroleum refining	2.13
24	Lumber and wood products	1.73
30	Rubber and miscellaneous plastics	1.53
31	Leather and leather products	0.93
25	Furniture and fixtures	0.40
21	Tobacco manufactures	0.27
Total US		100.00

A dissection of foreign direct investments using SIC reveals that 6 categories accounted for over 65 per cent of all such activity in US manufacturing in 1979 (Table 14.1). The leading 4 are also the major technology-intensive industries judged by the number of scientists and engineers engaged in R & D per 1000 employees and R & D expenditures as a percentage of net sales (United States National Science Foundation, 1977, pp. 36–7); they have not only exceeded the 23.8 per cent growth rate of all foreign direct investments during the 1974–79 period, but are also growing the most rapidly in value-added and employment terms as a result of the investment activities of US domestic firms (Rees, 1979a, pp. 46–7).

Most projects in the industry sectors that lead the country's foreign direct investments came from only a few of the 8 principal countries (see Table 14.2). Firms from the UK, West Germany, Canada and Japan, for example, are responsible for over 76 per cent of the projects in the non-electrical machinery sector; Japan stands out as the major foreign investor in the chemical and electrical machinery and electronics industries; Japan and the UK are leading investors in the professional and scientific instruments

TABLE 14.2 Per cent of foreign direct investment in industry sectors listed by principal investing country, United States, 1979

Country	Non-electrical machinery	Chemicals and pharmaceuticals	Electrical machinery and electronics	Professional and scientific instruments	Fabricated metal products	Food and kindred products
United Kingdom	21.08	16.56	19.84	25.70	24.06	22.96
Japan	17.01	24.17	40.86	26.17	26.89	22.45
Canada	18.59	10.26	14.01	5.14	22.64	23.98
West Germany	19.95	13.58	6.61	15.89	10.38	1.02
France	7.50	13.91	8.95	6.07	8.49	7.65
Switzerland	9.98	12.91	3.11	16.82	3.30	14.80
Netherlands	2.49	5.96	6.23	1.87	3.30	6.63
Belgium-Luxembourg	3.40	2.65	0.39	2.34	0.94	0.51
Total	100.00	100.00	100.00	100.00	100.00	100.00

Sources: tables in this chapter were compiled by author from United States Department of Commerce, 1977–79; The Conference Board, 1977–79; Angel, 1978.

sector; and Japan, the UK and Canada dominate the fabricated metal products and food and kindred products industries.

The extent to which firms from a particular foreign country concentrate their direct investments in specific US industry sectors is closely related to that country's exports to the US (McConnell, 1981); a high correlation thus exists between the commodity trade specialization of a country and the industrial sectors within which its firms concentrate their direct investments. In essence, given the monopolistic advantage theory and the product cycle model of direct investment many foreign firms have compelling reasons to protect their established export markets in the US through direct investment activities.

Another important national trend is the increase in the foreign direct investment preference for acquisitions *via-à-vis* newly constructed production facilities. While acquisition of existing US corporations accounted for most of the value of such investments in 1974, this form of entry was used in less than a third of the total number of projects (Little, 1976, p. 18); by the late 1970s, however, this entry method was preferred for over half the projects (The Conference Board, 1977–79). This shift is attributed to the depressed stockmarket and the impact of high inflation on new construction costs (Little, 1978, p. 48); to the investment strategies of increasing numbers of foreign firms seeking quick access to US technological and managerial know-how to compete more effectively in their home markets (McConnell, 1980, p. 263); and to the fact that until recently multinational enterprises from the UK and Canada, which have traditionally preferred the acquisition route, were among the largest investors in the country. Japanese enterprises greatly increased their number of direct investments in the US after 1974 but continue to favour newly constructed facilities.

Although the annual sales and employment of foreign-owned subsidiaries in the US vary greatly, most are not large by US standards: few have annual sales over $US100 million (United States Department of Commerce, 1976, p. 64). Moreover, in 1979 less than 5 per cent of the 1000 largest US corporations were foreign owned, and only 7 of them were in the 4 high-technology sectors identified above (Time Incorporated, 1978).

Foreign-owned subsidiaries in the US have consistently been concentrated in relatively few states. In both 1974 and 1979 the same 17 states accounted for approximately 75 per cent of all foreign-owned manufacturing subsidiaries, and no other state had more than 2 per cent. Of the 17, 10 are located in the traditional northeast and midwest manufacturing core, 1 is on the west coast and the others are in the south and southwest. Most new foreign direct investments during the 1974–79 period were located in the west and south, hence paralleling the strategies of US firms to go outside the traditional industrial core (McConnell, 1980, pp. 267–9).

To ascertain which states are relatively more attractive to foreign than to

US manufacturing investors, ratios of each state's share of foreign direct investments in 1979 versus its share of US firms in the mid-1970s were calculated for each of the 6 major industry categories. The only ones with ratios greater than 1 for all 6 industries, indicating that they are consistently more attractive to foreigners than to American investors, were New York and New Jersey in the northeast, and Georgia in the southeast. Foreign-owned, low-technology activities tended to be attracted to the west coast and the northeast while technology-intensive categories were attracted to the eastern seaboard. Moreover, more states have ratios greater than 1 within the low-technology industries than within the high-technology ones, indicating that foreign-owned subsidiaries in the former industries are more dispersed spatially than their US counterparts.

Metropolitan and Regional Dynamics

The spatial distribution of foreign direct investments in the US has usually been analysed at the state or broad regional level, largely reflecting the primary emphasis of the 1974 government-sponsored benchmark study of foreign-owned subsidiaries on states and their relative shares of investment projects (United States Department of Commerce, 1976). Moreover, it can be argued that the state, as a spatial unit, is an important component of the 'mental map' of a foreign-owned corporation in that, when such companies are determining where to locate or to purchase a subsidiary, their perceptions of locational opportunities often consist of several states. Interviews by the author with locational consultants at the government's Office of Foreign Investment in Washington suggest that states are indeed the most important spatial framework used by enterprises in the initial locational search process. Hence the state is a convenient focus for gathering information about locational alternatives and for developing investment strategies. Little (1978, p. 55) suggests that most foreign firms consider only one state. However, the same government consultants in Washington also indicated to the author that as foreign parent enterprises become more familiar with the US business and economic environment their awareness and perception of locational options are heightened and they begin to perceive alternatives based on specific labour markets, R & D axes, growth centres or resource regions. The spatial framework of the foreign investor then focuses on a particular urban area or economic region.

Few studies have examined the spatial distribution of foreign direct investments at the sub-state level; hence the recent work set out here. The Bureau of Economic Analysis (BEA) of the United States Department of Commerce has divided the country into 183 economic areas (United States, Bureau of Economic Analysis, 1977), each of which consists of an economic node—typically a Standard Metropolitan Statistical Area—and the surrounding counties economically related to it. Each BEA area embraces the place of work and place of residence of its labour force and is, in effect, an urban region. About 80 per cent of all foreign-owned subsidiaries are located in 19 (10 per cent) of the 183 BEA areas: no others have more than 1 per cent of the total (Table 14.3). New York, Los Angeles and Chicago together account for half the country's foreign-owned corporations. The 19 BEA areas are largely concentrated within the traditional manufacturing belt and along the southern and western peripheries of the US (Figure 14.1). Within the regional context of the country's 9 major geographical census divisions (see Figure 14.2 and Table 14.3) 11 of the 19 BEA areas are in the traditional manufacturing belt (consisting of New England, Middle Atlantic and East North Central divisions), 4 are in the 3 southern divisions, 1 (St Louis) is in the interior division, and 3 are in the Pacific division.

TABLE 14.3 Bureau of Economic Analysis economic areas with at least 1 per cent of all foreign direct investments, United States, 1979

BEA areas	Number of foreign direct investments	Per cent of total direct investments	Geographical division
New York (New York)	891	35.87	Middle Atlantic
Los Angeles (California)	210	8.45	Pacific
Chicago (Illinois)	141	5.68	East North Central
San Francisco-Oakland-San Jose (California)	81	3.26	Pacific
Philadelphia (Pennsylvania)	76	3.06	Middle Atlantic
Boston (Massachusetts)	75	3.02	New England
Buffalo (New York)	66	2.66	Middle Atlantic
Atlanta (Georgia)	54	2.17	South Atlantic
Seattle (Washington)	45	1.81	Pacific
Detroit (Michigan)	43	1.73	East North Central
Houston (Texas)	42	1.69	West South Central
Cleveland (Ohio)	37	1.49	East North Central
Pittsburgh (Pennsylvania)	33	1.33	Middle Atlantic
Greenville-Spartanburg (South Carolina)	30	1.21	South Atlantic
Hartford-New Haven (Connecticut)-Springfield (Massachusetts)	28	1.13	New England
Charlotte (North Carolina)	28	1.13	South Atlantic
Syracuse (New York)	25	1.01	Middle Atlantic
Albany-Schenectady-Troy (New York)	24	1.00	Middle Atlantic
St Louis (Missouri)	24	1.00	West North Central
Total US	1953	78.70	

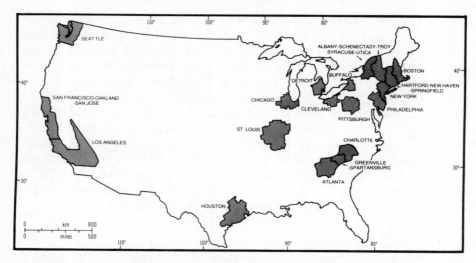

FIGURE 14.1 United States Bureau of Economic Analysis areas with 1 per cent or more of all foreign direct investments in 1979

The geographical dispersion of foreign direct investments is closely correlated with the population of the BEA area and the number of R & D facilities of US private corporations. A ranking of the number of foreign direct investments in the 19 BEA areas and their 1977 population gives a Spearman rank correlation coefficient of +0.7404: in short, as the population of a BEA area increased so did the number of foreign direct invest-

FIGURE 14.2 Major geographical divisions of the United States

ments. Moreover, 13 of the 19 areas are among the 20 urban places that had the greatest concentration of corporate-owned R & D laboratories in 1977 (Malecki, 1979b, p. 312). The 19 BEA areas are also specialized by principal investing countries and leading industry sectors: this becomes clear from Table 14.4, which includes only the countries and industry sectors with at least 20 per cent of the total number of foreign direct investment projects in each BEA area.

TABLE 14.4 Principal investing countries and leading industry sectors in the 19 Bureau of Economic Analysis areas, United States, 1979

BEA areas	Principal investing country	Number of foreign direct investments in leading industry sector of principal investing country	
New York	UK	135	Non-electrical machinery
	Japan	129	Chemicals and pharmaceuticals
Los Angeles	Japan	118	Electrical machinery and electronics
Chicago	Japan	57	Non-electrical machinery, electrical machinery and electronics, and professional and scientific instruments
San Francisco-Oakland-San Jose	Japan	30	Professional and scientific instruments
Philadelphia	UK	21	Professional and scientific instruments
Boston	UK	18	Fabricated metal products
	Canada	11	Non-electrical machinery
Buffalo	Canada	28	Non-electrical machinery
	UK	15	Professional and scientific instruments
Atlanta	Canada	16	Non-electrical machinery
	Switzerland	7	Chemicals and pharmaceuticals
Seattle	Japan	19	Food and kindred products
	Canada	6	Food and kindred products
Detroit	Canada	8	Non-electrical machinery
	West Germany	7	Fabricated metal products
Houston	UK	12	Chemicals and pharmaceuticals, and fabricated metal products
Cleveland	UK	11	Non-electrical machinery
	Canada	7	Non-electrical machinery
Pittsburgh	West Germany	13	Non-electrical machinery
	UK	10	Non-electrical machinery
Greenville-Spartanburg	Switzerland	10	Non-electrical machinery
	West Germany	5	Non-electrical machinery
Hartford-New Haven-Springfield	UK	7	Fabricated metal products, non-electrical machinery, and electrical machinery and electronics
	Switzerland	5	Non-electrical machinery
	West Germany	4	Non-electrical machinery
Charlotte	West Germany	7	Non-electrical machinery
Syracuse	Canada	6	Electrical machinery and electronics
Albany-Schenectady-Troy	Canada	13	Fabricated metal products
St Louis	Switzerland	6	Food and kindred products
	Canada	2	Food and kindred products

TABLE 14.5 Major spheres of influence of principal investing countries, United States, 1979

Country	BEA area	Number of direct investments in BEA area	Per cent of investing country's total direct projects	Leading sector of investing country in BEA area
Canada	Detroit	44	9.64	Non-electrical machinery
	Buffalo	43	8.84	Non-electrical machinery
	Atlanta	28	5.62	Non-electrical machinery
	Boston	23	4.62	Non-electrical machinery
	Albany	20	4.02	Fabricated metal products
	Syracuse	19	3.82	Electrical machinery and electronics
	Chicago	15	3.01	Food and kindred products, fabricated metal products
United Kingdom	New York	241	45.13	Non-electrical machinery
	Philadelphia	34	6.37	Professional and scientific instruments
	Boston	31	5.81	Fabricated metal products
	Buffalo	19	3.56	Professional and scientific instruments
	Chicago	19	3.56	Non-electrical machinery
	San Francisco	17	3.18	Food and kindred products
Japan	New York	205	35.04	Chemicals and pharmaceuticals
	Los Angeles	159	27.18	Electrical machinery and electronics
	Chicago	60	10.26	Non-electrical machinery, electrical machinery and electronics
	San Francisco	39	6.67	Professional and scientific instruments
	Seattle	30	5.13	Chemicals and pharmaceuticals, non-electrical machinery
Switzerland	New York	81	39.32	Non-electrical machinery
	Greenville	11	5.34	Non-electrical machinery
	Chicago	9	4.37	Food and kindred products, professional and scientific instruments

Country	City			Industry
	St Louis	9	4.37	Food and kindred products, fabricated metal products
	Atlanta	8	3.88	Chemicals and pharmaceuticals
West Germany	New York	119	45.77	Non-electrical machinery
	Chicago	16	6.15	Non-electrical machinery
	Pittsburgh	15	5.77	Non-electrical machinery
	Detroit	9	3.46	Fabricated metal products
France	New York	147	58.80	Chemicals and pharmaceuticals
	Los Angeles	13	5.20	Fabricated metal products
	Chicago	10	4.00	Fabricated metal products, non-electrical machinery, electrical machinery and electronics
Netherlands	New York	39	40.21	Electrical machinery and electronics
	Chicago	9	9.28	Chemicals and pharmaceuticals, non-electrical machinery
	Hartford	5	5.16	Non-electrical machinery, electrical machinery and electronics, professional and scientific instruments
	Houston	4	4.12	Chemicals and pharmaceuticals
	San Francisco	4	4.12	Food and kindred products, electrical machinery and electronics
	Boston	3	3.92	Food and kindred products
	Buffalo	3	3.92	Chemicals and pharmaceuticals
Belgium-Luxembourg	New York	15	27.78	Professional and scientific instruments
	Chicago	3	5.56	Chemicals and pharmaceuticals
	Houston	3	5.56	Chemicals and pharmaceuticals
	Atlanta	2	3.70	Non-electrical machinery
	Detroit	2	3.70	Non-electrical machinery
	San Francisco	2	3.70	Professional and scientific instruments

The UK and Canada are the leading investment sources in most BEA areas followed by Japan, West Germany and Switzerland. Canadian-owned subsidiaries operate in 114 of the 183 BEA areas, or almost twice as many as any other principal source: the Canadian presence in the US is thus the most dispersed whereas that of foreign direct investment activity by country and industry sector within the 19 areas further reveals the extent of its spatial concentration and industry specialization. Certain spheres of influence are particularly associated with some source countries (Table 14.5).

Canadian projects tend to be concentrated in 3 Canadian-US border regions—the East North Central, Middle Atlantic and New England—and South Atlantic divisions (Figure 14.2). Along the eastern seaboard, Canadian investments are mainly in non-electrical machinery whereas in the interior they are in food, fabricated metal products, and non-electrical and electrical machinery. Such spatial and industrial specialization reflects the proximity of Canada's industrial core to the major US urban and industrial centres. The desire by many Canadian firms to grow, escape from increasing governmental regulation, avoid economic and political risks, and penetrate tariff barriers have motivated their heavy investment in the US. Several of the principal objectives identified by Little (1976, pp. 232–3) include the penetration of new growth markets through geographical diversification, the maintenance of control over production costs through vertical integration, the acquisition of technological know-how and marketing expertise, and the stabilization of long-term earnings and profits through product diversification. The recent preference of Canadian investors for the South Atlantic division reflects a desire to take advantage of comparatively inexpensive skilled labour, low corporate taxes, good transport, and industrial-revenue-bond financing with low interest rates (United States Department of Commerce, 1980, p. 16).

United Kingdom direct investments are, in contrast, largely concentrated in the northeast reflecting the fact that many British parent enterprises have been developed as exporters and as direct investors in this industrial heartland for the past 3 decades or more. Recently British enterprises have stepped up their investment activities in the US because of increased government regulation, high taxes and the deteriorating economic environment in the UK and to meet worldwide competition from US and European multinationals (Little 1976, pp. 188 and 193). Access to technological and marketing know-how through the acquisition of US firms is also particularly important in explaining the locational behaviour of British direct investors, thus confirming the initial empirical work by Backman and Bloch (1974) who claimed that this is an expedient way for European firms to compete internationally.

Japanese subsidiaries are mainly on the Pacific coast and in the East North Central and Middle Atlantic divisions. The greatest range of manufacturing activities is on the west coast where it has subsidiaries in all 4 high-technology sectors: this reflects the relative nearness of this part of the US to Japan and early Japanese business influence there. The concentration of Japanese direct investments in the New York, Los Angeles, Chicago and San Francisco areas is also expected because until recently most of that country's total investments were in commercial outlets, finance, insurance and banking (Little, 1976, p. 264). When the Japanese began in the early 1970s to shift their investments from the service sectors into manufacturing they tended to remain in areas with which they were familiar. Moreover, the emphasis of the Japanese on technology-intensive projects in the US reflects their worldwide investment preference for capital-intensive industries (Little, 1976, p. 263).

The other 5 foreign source countries have strongly concentrated their foreign direct investments in the traditional manufacturing belt and eastern seaboard areas, although France has electrical machinery projects on the west coast, the Benelux firms have chemical investments in Houston and machinery and instruments projects in San Francisco, and the Swiss are most active in the South Atlantic division. The latter reflects the typical investment strategy of Swiss companies to take over small and medium-size companies with growth potential (Little, 1976, p. 163): such firms are common in the southeastern region of the country.

IMPLICATIONS

Decisions by manufacturing enterprises to establish subsidiaries outside their home countries are typically complex, multi-faceted processes, the motives for which vary from factors internal to the business organization to others associated with national and international events and trends. Only partial explanations of foreign direct investment thus exist. Most empirical research examines the behaviour of US-based multinationals but studies of foreign enterprises *in* the US became more numerous during the 1970s. This research has mainly focused on the investment decision and, in particular, on whether the foreign firms buy existing US companies or construct new plants. However, there is more concern with the location of such projects and the impact that these have on the US space-economy. The research has usually been based on data from interviews with only a few foreign companies or from the government's 1974 benchmark study; these have seldom been analysed at a finer spatial level than the states or, on occasion, broad census regions. Foreign parent corporations are tending to concentrate on technology-intensive industries, investing in only 1 or 2 leading sectors, entering through acquisitions rather than new construction, remaining relatively small by US standards, and skewing their locational choices towards a few states.

Analysis at the level of BEA economic areas further demonstrates the concentration and specialization that typify the locational and sectoral preferences of European, Canadian and Japanese firms. Four-fifths of all foreign direct investments in the country are located in 19 BEA areas which are mainly metropolitan ones with large populations and high concentrations of corporate-owned research laboratories. Locational preferences and industrial structures lead firms from the same country to cluster in various areas of the US thus reflecting historical patterns of business activity and proximity to the home countries of the foreign investors.

This chapter, along with other recent empirical work on foreign direct investment in the US, raises questions about its policy implications and about its significance for foreign direct investment theory. Two policy viewpoints are noteworthy.

First is the belief that foreign direct investments in the US should be more carefully monitored and stringently controlled because foreigners are 'taking over the country'; American technology and managerial know-how are being expropriated by foreign parent corporations and weakening the international competitive posture of American firms; foreign-controlled subsidiaries are less responsive and less subject to US national and regional policy objectives; and large-scale foreign presence could negatively affect domestic and regional growth and development.

A second position is that foreign direct investments should be actively encouraged and promoted through policy directives from national and state agencies because they strengthen the US dollar exchange rate, increase local employment, instil new working capital into declining firms, bring new tax revenues into distressed regions and enhance managerial and technological capabilities.

Many argue that the lack of information on the full impact of such activity prevents a reasoned policy stance (Backman and Bloch, 1974, p. 103). The paucity of data has caused one government agency to support stronger regulatory policy for a more comprehensive registry of foreign involvement in the US (United States, Office of Community Planning and Development, 1979, p. 9.1), arguing that more urban and regional data should specify impacts of foreign direct investments on employment, inter-regional growth, income and output, distressed regions, defence-related industries, high-technology outflows and the international competitiveness of American companies. Moreover, the agency notes that, while states and localities have done much to attract foreign firms, they have done very little to assess the net impacts of their actions (United States, Office of Community Planning and Development, 1979, p. 9.4); a national-level policy should thus be adopted to measure, assess and, if necessary, control direct investment by foreign-based corporations.

While the need for more data is clear, the US government should not conclude prematurely that the foreign presence is a negative influence. Foreign-owned subsidiaries still only account for a fraction of all US manufacturing and pose little threat: the number of foreign-owned industrial plants is about 1 per cent of all such plants in the country, while foreign subsidiaries produce no more than 6 per cent of the total output of any 2-digit SIC industry sector, although as much as 30 per cent of the output at the 4-digit level may be from externally controlled firms (United States Department of Commerce, 1976, p. 46). Moreover, the government believes that the US is gaining more technology from foreign direct investments than it is losing (United States Department of Commerce, 1976, p. 216). Also, investors are constructing new production facilities in low-income areas, creating new jobs and tax revenues. Because many foreign parent corporations continue to prefer locations in the older industrialized areas, the foreign presence is actually helping to offset high unemployment caused by the recent exodus of many American domestic firms. The US must not erect barriers to inflows of direct investments from major industrial countries; instead it must work with these nations to harmonize national policies if free trade and mobility of direct investment are to prevail.

Equally important are the implications of research for the further development of direct investment theory. Root (1978, p. 518) suggests that a theory of foreign direct investment should answer several fundamental questions, such as why firms go abroad as direct investors; how they compete successfully with local firms in the host country; why firms prefer direct investment to other forms of international business; and why reverse investment occurs at both the country and industry levels. He claims that such a comprehensive theory demands a synthesis of international trade theory, international business enterprise theory, and foreign direct investment theory (Root, 1978, p. 531).

Although an integrated model of international business enterprise has not yet emerged, there is a consensus that the propensity for foreign direct investment depends upon how far an enterprise possesses assets which its competitors do not, is willing to internalize these assets, and can profit from exploiting these assets in foreign countries *vis-à-vis* the home country (Dunning, 1980, p. 9). Moreover, Frank and Freeman (1978, pp. 85–110) and Johanson and Vahlne (1978, pp. 9–27) try to integrate international capital flows and technology and managerial transfers into a long-run dynamic model. Thus while the research outlined here adds to an understanding of the investment and locational behaviour of European, Canadian and Japanese multinationals in the US, it has yet to generate explicit derivations of foreign direct investment theories. And differences in behaviour between foreign direct investors in the US and American multinationals overseas create further gaps in efforts to integrate foreign direct investment theories. Yet, despite the difficulties of acquiring sufficient data, further research must analyse reverse investment within specific industries over time as space and time cannot be separated analytically (Sack, 1974). This will require detailed information at the firm and industry levels on the relationships between the firm's temporal horizons and the various alternative forms of international behaviour open to it. Following Massey (1979a), such an approach will also require analysis of the firm's direct investment decision within the context of national and international environments.

Spatial Analysis, Industry and the Industrial Environment. Vol. 3 Regional Economies and Industrial Systems
Edited by F. E. I. Hamilton and G. J. R. Linge
© 1983 John Wiley & Sons Ltd.

Chapter 15

The Role of Finance in the Evolution and Functioning of Industrial Systems

MICHAEL TAYLOR AND NIGEL THRIFT

Explanations of spatial patterns of economic activity in industrial geography are at worst inadequate and at best no more than partial, largely because of the subject's preoccupation with only the *use of funds* and hence with investment decision-making and allocation processes in enterprises and organizations (Townroe, 1969; Dicken, 1971). Little attention has been paid to the *sources of funds* (retained earnings, equity and borrowings) which must be equally important. Thus the functioning of industrial systems has focused on the input of materials, their transformation by one technological process or another, and the distribution of products to a consumer population arranged in some particular geographical configuration. Nowhere is this view better expressed than in studies using input-output tables and analyses (Czamanski, 1971, 1974, 1976; Roepke *et al.*, 1974; Hoare, 1975; Todd, 1978).

Unfortunately, few geographers have taken into account the sources and types of funds available to different types of enterprise even though the availability of these funds obviously constrains all aspects—not only the locational ones—of investment decision-making. Indeed, although industrial geography has spawned simple descriptive models of corporate growth (McNee, 1974; Taylor, 1975; Håkanson, 1979; Rees, 1979a; Watts, 1980) it has never developed models akin to Marris's (1964) formal economic model which postulated that the rate of growth of a firm depended upon the funds it could garner through borrowing (constrained by gearing ratios), new share issues (constrained by the need to avoid 'dilution') and retained earnings (constrained by the need to issue dividends) (Devine *et al.*, 1979). Reasons for this major and fundamental omission in industrial geography perhaps lie in the persistence of classical partial equilibrium models of location which have, by and large, assumed capital to be both freely available and perfectly mobile (Weber, 1909; Lösch, 1954; Greenhut, 1956). Thus, Smith's (1981) *Industrial Location...*, an explicitly neo-classical text, devotes only a handful of its 492 pages to any consideration of a firm's capital requirements.

For industrial geographers to continue to ignore the role of sources of funds in investment decision-making is both increasingly unreal and potentially dangerous for 2 important reasons. First, the capitalist world has seen the progressive intermeshing of the circuits of industrial, commercial and banking capital, especially during the past 20 years (Gershuny, 1978; Gregory, 1978). As large manufacturing corporations have taken on financial functions, so too have financial institutions acquired more non-financial functions to understand their clients' needs, vet their proposals and be able to participate in project financing (Taylor and Thrift, 1980). Second, since the Second World War the capitalist economic system has become increasingly segmented as various types of enterprise and organization have become more strongly differentiated through technological change, corporate growth and increased concentration (Averitt, 1968; Taylor and Thrift, 1981). Such segmentation reflects the unequal power relationships that have developed among different sets of enterprises and their very different abilities to both attract and command resources, especially the finance they need (Pfeffer and Salancik, 1974, 1978; Salancik and Pfeffer, 1974; Benson, 1975). A proper appreciation of the nature and availability of various forms of finance is, therefore, central to an understanding of the functioning of modern capitalist production.

This chapter seeks, at least partially, to redress this major imbalance in industrial geography by examining, in general terms, the evolution since the beginning of the nineteenth century of both financial institutions and external sources of finance for industrial development, principally in the UK and USA. Throughout this period of industrialization financial institutions have both led and been led by their industrial and commercial counterparts, an increasingly symbiotic relationship having developed between these 3 types of enterprise.

The traditional role of financial institutions has been to mobilize capital resources to satisfy the credit hunger of industrialists. However, as Walker (quoted in Cameron, 1967a, p. 53) wrote of banks in 1857, they 'never originate with those who have money to lend, but with those who wish to borrow'. But the relationship of finance and industry has not always been equal because financial institutions and systems have tended to labour under legislative restriction; e.g. the Jacksonian ethic in the US (Trescott, 1963), the Bank of England's near monopoly in England (Cameron, 1967a), paralysing legal restriction and centralization in France (Cameron, 1967b), or near free enterprise in Scotland. Each of these environments has developed different instruments to supply capital needs and these have combined to form the armoury of the currently internationalizing financial world. Since the advent of the Industrial Revolution the financial requirements of business organizations have progressively changed and this has necessitated constant evolution in the functioning of financial institutions.

Moreover, these evolutionary trends have had specific geographical implications both for the location of financial institutions and for industrialization and the evolution of space-economies in general. Reserve requirements, correspondent relations, note issue, government restriction, access to commercial bills markets, lending criteria, centralization, concentration and control all have spatial dimensions and repercussions. The literature on finance and financial institutions is rich in tantalizing hints on the spatial aspects of the supply of funds for industrialization and the growth of industrial enterprises, but they remain only hints, severely limiting analyses such as those attempted here.

This study is divided into 3 broad periods:

(a) industrialization and competitive capitalism which ended during the first 2 decades of the twentieth century;

(b) monopoly capitalism which can be traced from the early twentieth century to the 1940s and 1950s;

(c) global capitalism, the era of the multinational corporation in both production and finance, from the 1950s and 1960s to the present.

In each period, the relationship between finance and industry has been very different, becoming not only more complex and comprehensive but, in some important respects, also more conservative and constrained. It is these characteristics which the chapter seeks to explore, indicating wherever possible their geographical ramifications.

THE INDUSTRIAL REVOLUTION AND COMPETITIVE CAPITALISM

The United Kingdom Experience

From 1760 through the 1850s industry's financial needs were very restricted and were mainly for short-term credit to be used as working capital rather than for long-term credit to finance fixed capital investment. In part, this reflected the nature of early industrial organization. In British industrial centres, for example, a 'factor/outworker' system persisted until as late as the 1870s and 1880s. Under this arrangement, which was more strongly related to commercial capitalism than to production, a warehouse owner or 'factor' put materials out to 'outworkers' but without relinquishing ownership. Outworkers most frequently made products at home, their principal input being labour and, where necessary, fuel (Allen, 1929; Court, 1953). An individual was financially committed to a trade such as making nails, chains or guns in the English Midlands for no more than one week at a time—a flexibility which really only favoured the factor. Plainly, this system of production was incompatible with some forms of mechanization and the introduction and development of new technologies. It is all too easy to overestimate the significance of the steam engine in the Industrial Revolution in England: until the 1870s and 1880s there was little mechanization in most British industries, muscle power being the principal prime mover (Samuel, 1977; Joyce, 1980; Pollard, 1981). Iron making, coal-mining, chemicals manufacture, cotton and the railways were the obvious mechanized exceptions. Similarly in the West Midlands, for example, large factories employing up to 500 or even 1000 workers had existed in the japanning trade, jewellery manufacture, brass founding, gun making, lock making and other engineering activities from 1780s onward, but they were uncommon and even in the 1860s most of the region's labour operated under factor/outworker arrangements (Allen, 1929; Timmins, 1967).

There was also a legal restraint in England to company formation and, therefore, size, mechanization and the demand for capital. Cameron (1967a) contends that this limited demand arose from the influence of the *South Sea Company Act* (the 'Bubble Act'), 1720 (7 Geo. I, c.c.1,2), which remained in force until 1825 and continued to be a significant influence on company law until 1875. The Act severely restricted incorporation and hence the flow of capital into industry (John, 1950), probably impeding the rate of industrialization in England in comparison with its later starting rivals, Germany, France and the United States.

In this period in England fixed assets rarely exceeded half the total assets. The ratio of fixed to total assets for the Lancashire firm of Black Dyke Mills, for example, was only 41 per cent in 1841 after the construction of a new factory and had been reduced to 5 per cent by 1860. It was less than 42 per cent in Thomas Attwood's ironworks in 1812, less than 10 per cent in the firm of Boulton and Watt in 1822 and no more than 17 per cent in the brass and copper trades before 1830. More important were liquid assets and access to the short-term credit needed to purchase materials, pay wages and extend trade credit to buyers (Cameron, 1967a).

The scale of these requirements, too, was limited. To start in business the early nineteenth century English woollen industry needed only £100 to £150, an amount usually borrowable although certainly not beyond the savings capacity of many individuals. Furthermore, through the trade credit offered by suppliers, one week's wool could be obtained on credit allowing firms to operate on a hand-to-mouth basis (Cameron, 1967a).

Short-term working capital was supplied by a rapidly expanding but vigorously controlled banking sector (Cottrell, 1980). Privileges of the Bank of England severely restrained English banking: until 1826 country banks were limited to partnerships of not more than 6 persons, making the financial system unstable (Pressnell, 1956). The need grew for money-broking and remittance facilities, especially in London, and for issuing tokens and paper currency for local circulation to overcome coinage deficiencies. These needs brought people engaged in retailing, wholesaling, manufacturing, mining and tax collecting into banking. Private banks frequently became adjuncts of other enterprises facilitating the raising of capital at virtually no cost. The *Banking Act,* 1826 (7 Geo. IV, c. 46), removed the size restriction in country banking by permitting joint stock banks, but only outside London. However, developments which culminated in the *Bank Act,* 1844 (7 and 8 Vic., c. 32), imposed new restrictions on note issue and freedom of entry into the financial system. As a direct consequence demand deposits drawn on by cheque and short-dated bills of exchange were developed to offset the inadequacies of an inelastic currency. By 1840 as many as two-thirds of payments into banks were by cheque; by 1865 this proportion exceeded 97 per cent. Bills of exchange have a long history of usage in England and they, too, played an important monetary role especially in Lancashire where, after several bad experiences with private banks, bills for as little as £5 would circulate between merchants with scores of endorsements (Cameron, 1967a).

In other countries different short-term credit instruments were created to overcome official restrictions. The virtually unfettered Scottish banking system fostered branch banking, the acceptance of small deposits and the cash credit as a lending instrument, all of which tended to popularize the banking habit. In the more constrained German system (Tilly, 1967), private banks assumed an investment as well as a commercial function and developed giro banking, a variety of bills of exchange and acceptance business as money substitutes. By contrast, however, state control of the French financial system stifled financial innovation and retarded industrial development in that country (Cameron, 1967b). US banking also became increasingly controlled during the nineteenth century, in the first instance to finance government debt during the 1861–65 Civil War (Trescott, 1963; Cameron, 1967c, 1972; Sylla, 1972).

These financial measures were eventually assembled into the armoury of short-term instruments employed in twentieth century banking. However, important though short-term credit was for the operation of industry in the early nineteenth century, capital loans were also significant. Technological developments; increasing firm size; the breakdown of local, regional and national monopolies through advances in transport; and the legal sanctioning of limited liability joint stock operations in the UK all helped to stimulate the growth of large corporate enterprises. In turn, these developments necessitated the creation of new forms of company financing: these were largely pioneered by the mid-nineteenth century railway companies of the US and the UK.

Railway capital was raised in 2 forms as shares and as loans in the 1820s, 1830s and 1840s in England. Although share capital was quantitatively the more important source, with a part being played by London investors and the Stock Exchange, it generated insufficient capital so that more traditional loans—usually as fixed term debentures at 5 per cent interest—were of disproportionate significance for railway financing. In the early 1800s the securities market had been largely used to finance the National Debt. The mechanism was, in part, redirected to raising railway capital after 1820 following the reduction of the National Debt, marking a significant stage in the development of the English capital market. More significantly, railway companies began to draw on new classes of investor, particularly traders (Reed, 1975), ranging from small shopkeepers to wealthy merchants; manu-facturers were relatively small railway shareholders, so diluting claims that their investment patterns indicated local patriotism. Through the 1830s and 1840s increasingly large investments were made by 'gentlemen' and women testifying to a significant *rentier* component to investment.

Not surprisingly, a provincial investment mechanism emerged in the regional stock exchanges, usually formed when the railways boomed. Invest-ment in railways was particularly forthcoming from Lancashire, stimulating the formation of the Liverpool and Manchester Stock Exchanges in 1836; the remaining provincial stock exchanges were established in 1844–45, so encouraging wider diffusion of the investment habit in England and making the business community more familiar with the advantages of limited liability.

Institutions also invested in English railway companies: as government securities became less attractive, banks (including the Bank of England), insurance companies, friendly societies, religious bodies and their trustees, and statutory bodies (such as gas companies and even the railway com-panies) made loans to transport operators.

There is great danger, however, in overemphasizing the significance of large corporations in the UK economy in this period. Large joint stock ventures existed in very few sectors: banking, transport, insurance and mining (see Table 15.1). Yet their significance extended beyond their numbers, mobilizing new sources of finance and, to some extent, reorientating existing sources of investment. By commanding such funds they set them-selves apart from the vast majority of industrial firms which were usually small and had minimal capital requirements either brought to the businesses by their partners or raised by private contract. Quite simply, a segmented 'dualistic' economy had begun to emerge (Averitt, 1968; Taylor and Thrift, 1980), and this dichotomous pattern of financing continued virtually un-changed in Great Britain through to the 1920s (Lavington, 1921). Although the securities market supplied funds for coal-mining, shipping and shipbuild-ing, iron and steel, cotton spinning factories and picture palaces [cinemas], this stream of investment was 'of quite secondary importance in relation to the flow of resources by way of private contract and the reinvestment of profits' (Lavington, 1921, p. 277). Small private companies were the rule and not the exception until the 1920s in cotton weaving, the linen industry,

TABLE 15.1 Public companies known on the London market *c*. 1843

Activity	£1 shares (000s)
Railways (70)	57,448
English, Scottish and Irish joint stock banks	46,500
Companies in shipping, land, asphalt, cemeteries, loans, salt, bridges and miscellaneous activities	*c*. 28,000
Assurance companies (102)	26,000
Canals (59)	17,862
Docks (8)	12,077
Turnpike trusts	8,775
Gas and water companies (38)	6,863
East India Company	6,000
British mining companies (81)	4,500
South Sea Company	3,663

Source: after Reed, 1975, p. 46.

the Northampton boot trade, the woollen and worsted industries and the Yorkshire engineering industry.

It was not the lack of an adequate financial system dealing in securities that restrained the emergence of the corporate economy on a larger scale in Great Britain. From the 1850s until the First World War the numbers and types of financial intermediary operating in London increased greatly to include joint stock banks, overseas banks and agencies, companies via their bankers, investment trusts, finance, land and property companies, issuing houses with stock exchange connections and special purpose syndicates (Cottrell, 1975, 1980). But this system was firmly wedded to foreign business: of the £199,715 new share capital raised on the London Market between 1911 and 1913 for instance less than 18 per cent (£35,811) was destined for use in the UK, the remainder going to British possessions and foreign countries.

The spatial implications of this first stage in the evolution of the British financial system are plain. Regional banking systems had been established, operating initially as private banks, which were either strongly tied or legally controlled by London-based organizations and institutions (especially by the Bank of England). These systems had also been bolstered by the formation of regional stock exchanges before 1850. Yet centralized London-based financial institutions were more involved in financing first the National Debt and then later, overseas development and investors. They were little concerned with funding industrialization in the UK itself and should perhaps bear partial responsibility for the tardiness of mechanization and technological change in British industry, leaving it ill-equipped to deal with growing foreign competition after 1870.

The United States Experience

A very different situation pertained from 1850 to 1914 in the US: large corporations on a scale unknown in the UK emerged mainly because the American banking and financial system had long been recognized as a prime mover in the creation of a corporate economy (Nelson, 1959; Sylla, 1969, 1972). Financial institutions, especially a small number of investment banks like the successful one founded by J. P. Morgan, were important in promoting American railway expansion, much as they had in the UK. They began by channelling British and European investment into the developing American economy, but later extended their control over the companies they had originally floated, fostering merger and conservative management to ameliorate the excesses of over-zealous competition (Kotz, 1978). However, individuals (such as the Rockefellers) were more ready to shift money to other types of investments but when the rate of railway expansion began to decline even the investment companies began to float and trade in other securities.

Development of a national banking system in the years 1863–65—to enable the American government to meet the exigencies of the Civil War and to raise money when inflation was high—had a major, though unintentional, effect on the form and location of industrialization in the US. Note issue became a federal government monopoly, replacing the paper mania which had characterized the free enterprise banking of the ante-bellum years. The collapse of Southern banking after the Civil War and the restriction of note issue initially to $US300 million led to a concentration of banking in the northeast. Furthermore, the capital stock required by a national bank depended on the size of the centre in which it was located: $US50,000 in cities of fewer than 6000 population; $US100,000 in cities of 6000 to 50,000 population; and $US200,000 in cities with more than 50,000 population. The biggest cities got the biggest banks. But national banks were denied the mortgage lending instrument, virtually excluding them from operation in rural areas where that type of finance was in greatest demand. Country banks filled this gap, gaining, in effect, monopolies of rural business and hence high profits from high interest rates.

The *National Currency Act*, 1864, also created a reserves pyramid, 3 classes of national bank being distinguished with designated reserves. New York was chosen as the central reserve city and its national banks had to maintain reserves equal to 25 per cent of their deposits and note circulation. Next in the pyramid were 18 cities whose banks were given reserve city status; these also had to maintain 25 per cent reserves but only half this had to be in legal tender and the rest could be held as deposits in New York banks. The remaining national banks had to maintain 15 per cent reserves,

60 per cent of which could be held as deposits in reserve city banks. Interest was paid on these deposits and this is where the country banks were tied into the system. Rather than hold idle funds generated by their monopolistic activities, excess funds could be sent off to the cities where they earned interest and acted as deposits for the whole banking system as a result of the overlapping reserve provisions.

This system channelled funds from the countryside to the cities, particularly as the principal agricultural areas moved progressively away from the northeast after 1850. Funds were available for lending in the cities— principally located in the northeast—and loans were inevitably directed towards manufacturing industry. The location of the principal investment banks in New York reinforced this spatial effect of the banking system.

The investment banks that directed capital into the developing American economy until 1914 gradually turned the US from a borrower into a lender. The distinction between investment banks and commercial banks became blurred during the decade preceding the First World War as the commercial banks moved into the securities market (Kotz, 1978) assuming the investment function long undertaken by their German counterparts. Why this combination movement did not occur as early or as vigorously as in the UK has been a subject of great debate, but the capital market was certainly no constraint on finance.

The foregoing suggests that the Industrial Revolution and its nineteenth century progress brought about parallel development in any country of both an industrial (or manufacturing) system and a financial system which were largely independent of each other. This was particularly so in the UK in the early decades, and in the US in the third quarter of the century. Nevertheless, the American (and indeed also the German) financial system from the 1860s onwards could channel significant volumes of money from both domestic and foreign sources into industrial undertakings, so generating an early form of corporate economy (Hilferding, 1981). While Chandler (1959) explains why mergers were instrumental in creating the corporate economy in the US in this period, Nelson's (1959) quantitative analysis supports the hypothesis that this largely resulted from the prior existence of a highly organized capital market capable of absorbing the massive securities issues generated by this process. Indeed, Grosvenor (quoted in Sylla, 1972, p. 256) wrote in 1885 that 'in ordinary times, securities were offered to the end that railroads may be built. But in 1881, railroads were built to the end that securities might be offered'. By contrast the linking of the financial and industrial systems in the UK was mostly fortuitous and almost certainly unintentional. The small firm still predominated in virtually all industrial sectors and partnership principles predominated in both the UK and the US. Thus, the Committee on Finance and Industry (the Macmillan Committee)

(1931, para 307) was able to say of the pre-1914 era in Britain that:

> Industry in those days was, so far as each unit was concerned, on a comparative-
> ly small scale; its basis was in the main a family basis . . . its capital was provided
> privately and it was built up and extended out of profits; insofar as it required
> banking facilities, it found them from the independent banks, often family
> banks, which in general had their headquarters in the provinces . . . where the
> new industries flourished. Moreover, there had existed for many years in this
> country a large class of investors with means to invest, who exercised an
> independent judgement as to what to invest in, and did not rely . . . entirely on
> their bankers.

In essence, then, the ingredients of a dualistic economy, comprising the
large combine and the small family firm, had been created. It remained for
the 1920s and 1930s to witness the nurturing and deepening of this division
with the creation of finance 'gaps'.

MONOPOLY CAPITALISM AND THE FINANCING OF INDUSTRY

After the First World War the sources of funds for industrialization and
the growth of industrial organizations changed substantially, especially in the
UK. Gone was Victorian confidence in the permanence of things and
investors sought investments of which they could easily dispose, diverting
them away from local enterprise (Balogh, 1950; Frost, 1954). Purchases of
War Loans in the UK and Liberty Bonds in the US, for example, stimulated
investor interest in securities such that after 1918 new opportunities were
sought for private investment (Grant, 1937). Coupled with these changes
was a post-war growth in conspicuous consumption amongst the better-off.
Changes in taxation also affected the flow of funds from private investors:
imposition of heavier death duties made it desirable to keep investments in a
realizable form, which purchased stocks and shares allowed but which
purchases of private loans and investments did not. New taxation levels also
began to redistribute wealth from rich savers, reducing this long standing
source of finance for the industrial sector (Thomas, 1978). Indeed, surtax
rose from a maximum rate of 6 pence in the pound in 1913 (2.5 per cent) to
6 shillings in 1920 (30 per cent) (Frost, 1954), but Grant (1937) has warned
against exaggerating the impact of this factor.

At the same time, however, British banks—unlike their American and
mainland European counterparts—had all but abdicated their role as suppliers of capital to industry. Their guiding principle was that their funds
should not be 'locked-up' for long periods (Weston, 1931): advances should
be liquid and easily recalled (Steele, 1926). Banks, therefore, were most
attracted to self-liquidating investments of 6 to 12 months duration to

finance stocks, raw materials, work in progress or finished work. To quote Weston (1931, p. 35), 'The British banker embarks his funds upon these constantly maturing loans, not upon plant and equipment, not upon mortgages, not upon hire purchases'. It was thought appropriate for insurance companies to lend 'long' since their money was not repayable on demand. For banks to do so was unthinkable and, in support of this stance, Steele (1926) quoted the 1895 financial crisis of the Australian banks which apparently resulted from their over-commitment to locking up funds in mortgages. For Ellinger (1933), however, the refusal of British banks to lend long was their saving grace because recession in Germany in 1931 had necessitated government support of the banks just as recession in the US had seen 10 per cent of the banks there fail in the same year. A statement made by Barclays Bank in 1936 (quoted in Grant, 1937, p. 185) clearly corroborates this:

> as our deposits are repayable on demand or at short notice, our advances must be arranged on the same conditions. This does not mean that in practice the repayment of advances is arbitrarily demanded but that, in making an advance, we must be reasonably confident that the transaction will be self-liquidating in a comparatively short period, or alternatively, that the amount advanced will be forthcoming with reasonable promptitude in the event of a demand for repayment being made.

The conservatism of British bankers was in no way altered by bank amalgamations which continued after 1918. Take-overs and mergers had begun in the early 1800s initially to overcome the problems of private country banks which were progressively absorbed by joint stock ventures whose establishment had been sanctioned by Act of Parliament in 1833. Sykes (1926) identified 4 reasons for amalgamation:

(a) the administrative difficulties of small banks;
(b) the high agency costs incurred by small banks in meeting increased demands for customer services;
(c) some small banks had surplus funds which they could not invest to advantage in their regions of operation, especially rural areas;
(d) some banks needed London representation.

The aggressive management of some London banks and their geographical expansion by absorbing strong provincial banks accelerated concentration and centralization. By the early 1930s, apart from 28 commercial banks in London, British banking was dominated by the 'Big Five': Barclays, the Midland, Lloyds, the National Provincial and the Westminster (Weston, 1931). Bankers argued that amalgamation had been necessary to keep pace with the growth of large businesses generally, but it resulted in lending policies becoming more uniform and evenly applied (Thomas, 1978). Bank managers lost their local discretion and 'local elasticity' but, equally, it was said that their powers to finance industry had been increased and that there was no lack of loan capital for the use of British industry (Committee on Industry and Trade [the Balfour Committee], 1927). Together, these facts could only mean that bank amalgamation made funds freely available to large organizations which could provide the 'reasonable security' that was demanded, while small firms and newly established enterprises were denied access to anything other than short-term bank finance (Grant, 1937).

The consolidated savings of small savers were becoming a major source of external funds for industrial development in the 1920s and 1930s. They were being garnered by a range of both new and established financial institutions such as insurance companies, pension funds, investment trusts and, from the 1930s onwards, unit trusts which linked the investing public and business. Not only did they mobilize small savings, they also gave the smaller investor the chance to spread his risks.

In inter-war Great Britain insurance companies were the largest institutional investors with over £1500 million in invested funds, the relative disposition of which is shown in Table 15.2. Clearly they shifted from investments in government and overseas ventures to industrial and commercial securities, especially after 1932 when the yield became low (3 per cent) on long-term government securities (Clayton and Osborn, 1965). In 1920, for example, debentures, preference shares and ordinary shares made up only 13 per cent of the total assets of the 4 largest insurance companies in the UK (Prudential, Pearl, Alliance, and Sun Life of Canada), whereas in 1933 this had risen to 29 per cent. Insurance companies, especially those in life insurance, assumed a similar though somewhat less marked role in financing industry in the US after 1930.

Investment trusts in Great Britain commanded considerably smaller resources and, with paid-up capital of only £296 million and security holdings

TABLE 15.2 The disposition of the assets of British insurance offices, 1922 to 1935 (per cent of total assets)

Asset	1922	1927	1932	1935
Mortgages and loans	24.4	27.7	27.2	22.0
British government securities	35.0	23.4	20.4	19.5
Debentures	12.6	33.6	15.9	18.4
Preference stocks and shares	—	—	6.7	8.7
Ordinary stocks and shares	3.1	4.9	5.1	7.5
Land, houses, property, rents, offices, etc.	—	10.4	10.1	9.5

Source: after Clayton and Osborn, 1965, p. 254.

of only £332 million in 1934, were not much larger in aggregate than one insurance company, the Prudential. After having grown rapidly in numbers in the 1890s, investment trusts, being small, were mainly security holding organizations involved in overseas financing, and hence suffered heavily during the slump. This encouraged the formation of unit trusts (trusts with defined holdings) after 1932 and, although they were an innovation to which only £50 million had been subscribed by the end of 1935, they were important because their holdings were mainly in UK industrials. By contrast, investment trusts in the US grew to prominence only after 1920. Within 10 years over 60 per cent were sponsored by investment banks, brokers and dealers, and additional sponsorship came from commercial banks and their security affiliates so that highly pyramidal ownership structures had developed which were to prove disastrous in the 1930s (Galbraith, 1954).

Table 15.3 sets out the phenomenal growth of British financial institutions which mobilized the funds of small savers. This list is by no means complete and necessarily understates the true situation.

Finance companies were another type of intermediary which assumed some significance in inter-war Great Britain and some financed domestic industry through the provision of hire purchase (credit) facilities. But business organizations themselves were also becoming important suppliers of each others' capital requirements, and Grant (1937) has shown that railway companies and large and 'mature' industrial firms like Courtaulds, Shell, Imperial Tobacco, Pacific and Orient, and Imperial Chemical Industries, held millions and even tens of millions of pounds of securities by the late 1930s.

In these years, however, not only were private investors turning to the UK securities market, either directly by purchasing stocks and shares or

TABLE 15.3 The growth of some savings institutions in Great Britain, 1903 to 1938 (£ million)

Institution	1903	1913	1923	1938	Growth factor 1913–38
Building societies	66	66	125	759	11.5
Post Office Savings Bank	146	187	273	524	2.8
Trustee Savings Bank	52	69	103	243	3.5
Friendly societies	—	53	80	152	2.9
Provident societies	40	78	188	361	4.6
Collecting societies	—	11	31	85	7.7
Industrial asurance companies	26	56	123	359	6.4
Other life assurance companies	247	380	1	1322	3.5
Total	577	900	924	3805	3.9

Source: after Cleary, 1965, p. 275.

TABLE 15.4 New issues in Great Britain, averages for the period shown 1913 to 1935 (£ million)

Issues	1910–13	1927–30	1933–35
Home			
Production and trade	19.1	89.0	66.6
Other	25.1	81.5	54.6
Sub-total	*44.2*	*170.5*	*121.2*
Overseas	177.4	121.3	34.1
All new issues	221.6	291.8	155.3

Source: after Grant, 1937, p. 134.

indirectly by garnering small savings, but new issues in this market were also becoming more domestically orientated. Consequently, financial institutions and intermediaries (such as insurance companies, investment trusts and finance houses) were becoming more closely interdependent with domestic industrial fortunes, a trend demonstrated in Table 15.4. Clearly the fall in overseas investment was dramatic, particularly after 1931, and can be attributed to continuous restriction on foreign borrowing in London throughout the entire inter-war period; London's loss of attraction to foreign depositors; political instability in various overseas areas; and the entry into the world market of the US as a large-scale lender (Grant, 1937; Thomas, 1978). Moreover, investment in railways declined rapidly, ending a technological era which had been financed mainly by British capital.

Despite these very radical changes in the British financial system between the wars—the growth of financial intermediaries and reorientation of flows from overseas to the domestic market—the private investor was still by far the major supplier of equity capital to manufacturing industry. Grant (1937), for instance, estimated that individuals' holdings in home industry in the late 1930s were at least 10 times those of insurance companies and investment trusts. Yet private sources of industrial capital were also acknowledged then to be at full stretch; any future growth in this supply would have to come from financial intermediaries and would, therefore, be governed by their particular and inevitably conservative lending criteria.

Just as the supply of funds to industry changed radically so, too, did the demands for funds. Technological changes increased firm size and hence the demand for finance after 1918, a trend paralleled by a widespread desire to reorganize production (Thomas, 1978). Indeed, Frost (1954) has maintained that the owners of many small firms which had grown on lucrative wartime contracts wanted to realize their gains, but as capital gains to avoid taxation. A vogue for private company flotation was the inevitable result and 3 new issues booms occurred in 1919–22, in 1927–28, and in the mid-1930s. The target sectors for new issues also changed, beginning with heavy industries and extending to light, power and telegraphy companies and leisure activities in the early 1930s and then to engineering industries associated with rearmament in the late 1930s. Institutions in this market were very poorly organized and inefficient (Lavington, 1921) so that 'only one or two first-class houses in the city performed for certain first-class companies the same functions as the older issuing houses performed for foreign borrowers' (Piercy, 1955, p. 1). Frequently, flotations were made by *ad hoc* syndicates with little sense of responsibility. Underwriting issues became extremely expensive and issuing houses extracted commissions as high as 50 per cent before restrictions of 10 per cent were imposed in 1929. Public issues by prospectus, a common method of flotation in the 1920s, could incur a broker's fee of as much as 1000 guineas (£1050) simply for allowing his name to be printed on the prospectus.

There were, in fact, very definite economies of scale to be gained from making new issues: costs ranged from 15 per cent for those of less than £150,000 to only 7 per cent for those of more than £150,000 (1937 estimates by J. B. Selwyn, quoted by Thomas, 1978), while Henderson (1951) showed that in 1926 small-to-average placings (£198,000) incurred costs of 24 per cent as opposed to 9 per cent for average-to-large placings (£636,000). Drawing together some of the available evidence, Figure 15.1 demonstrates the approximate form of this scale-curve for new issues in the late 1930s. This scale-curve implies that small issues were almost prohibitively expensive. Indeed, the Macmillan Committee reported in 1931 (para 404) that 'great difficulty is experienced by the smaller and medium-sized businesses in raising the capital which they may from time to time require, even when

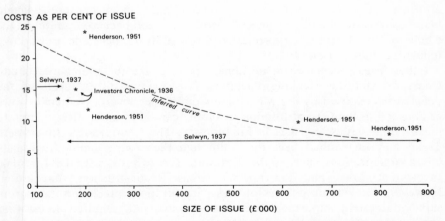

FIGURE 15.1 Inferred scale curves for new issues in the United Kingdom in the late 1930s. (The 1937 estimates by J. B. Selwyn are quoted by Thomas, 1978)

the security offered is perfectly sound'. This is the celebrated Macmillan 'gap' which points to a progressive dichotomization of UK industrial and commercial structure with (a) large firms and corporations having ready access to investment funds through a complex but integrated system of financial institutions and intermediaries and (b) small and medium-sized firms being thrown squarely on to their own resources. The latter, deprived of the private investment funds that had been available to them before 1914, faced dependency on banking sector lending criteria for external funds. Firms wishing to raise up to £200,000 on the London Stock Exchange in the early 1930s fell right into this finance gap although issues as small as £40,000 could still be floated on provincial stock exchanges (Frost, 1954). The principal problem of small issues was, and remains, that no ready market could be created in them and the trading of only small blocks of shares could cause severe price instability.

Capital supply to existing firms was not the only gap in the financial system that first emerged in the inter-war years. The venture capital gap became significant too, i.e. the scarcity of capital for investment in new and often experimental enterprises (Holborn and Edwards, 1971; Thomas, 1978). Rich private investors had provided funds for these ventures before the First World War but, being small in size and having no established borrowing record, supplying the needs of these organizations fell outside the realm of the rapidly expanding institutional finance sources. Attempts were made in the 1930s to overcome this problem. The Bankers Industrial Development Company was set up under the auspices of the Bank of England itself and so, too, was the Securities Management Trust, although its business was to salvage existing enterprises rather than to finance new industry proper. From the late 1920s the United Dominions Trust (UDT) also financed much industry, but was unique in 2 respects because it sought loan business (unlike other financial institutions) and because it searched the whole of the UK for opportunities through its branches in most large industrial cities (Grant, 1937).

Other firms specialized in instalment finance like the Mercantile Credit Company and the Banking Facilities Trust. As a direct result of the deficiencies exposed by the Macmillan Committee, several companies were established in the City of London to supply capital to enterprises unable to make public issues, e.g. Credit for Industry, The Charterhouse Investment Trust, and Leadenhall Securities, although there were similar regionally based organizations such as the Northern Territories Trust, the Lonsdale Investment Trust and the Special Areas Reconstruction Association. However, the lending policies of these organizations precluded them from supplying certain important sections of demand. All required access to a firm's accounts, most demanded a share in a firm's equity (usually as preference shares) and some expected direct participation in a firm's profits.

Such conditions were anathema to the small businessman who sought privacy and independence of action. Not surprisingly, therefore, despite the activities of these financial institutions, the venture capital gap and the new issues gap remained virtually unchanged.

Development of these gaps did, in fact, compound other serious problems which confronted small firms in the inter-war years. Accelerated technological change, for example, escalated R & D expenditure beyond the resources of many small firms and also favoured increased firm size. Transport improvements broke down local markets, reduced spatial monopoly and intensified competition, heightening the attraction of investment to gain economies of scale. Government, too, penalized small firms both through its purchasing and tendering policies, which favoured large enterprises, and nationalization schemes.

Most importantly, however, government taxation penalized the small firm by treating 'close' companies (50 or fewer shareholders before 1927; 5 or fewer shareholders after 1927) as potential tax shelters (Confederation of British Industry, 1970; Thomas, 1978), so reducing the potential savings of a sector which relies heavily on retained profits to finance its operations. In total, therefore, the financial difficulties of the small firms became monumental—their internal generation of funds being taxed, their access to the securities market being denied, their principal source of external funds being the banking sector to which, paradoxically, they became net lenders (Committee of Inquiry on Small Firms [the Bolton Committee], 1971): yet, on these limited means, they remained net givers of trade credit to large firms.

Thus sources of industrial finance changed substantially in the 1920s and 1930s: the rich private investor had been replaced by the institutional investor for whom the principal index of the worth of an investment was the stock exchange quotation. Formalization of the finance sectors in both the US and the UK denied funds to the small firm and substantially deepened a segmentation of these national economies which had emerged in the late nineteenth century.

Notwithstanding the more sharply differentiated access to funds experienced by the 2 segments of the dualistic economy in the inter-war years, significant regional variations existed in the availability of funds for new and growing enterprises (Grant, 1937). Generally, there was little or no shortage of capital for established and successful businesses although its price could be high. New enterprise faced most difficulties in securing external funds. The West Midlands apparently disposed of considerable funds for investment particularly in the many new small firms supplying parts to the large assembly trades, especially vehicles. Funds for small firms came mainly from private sources or through trade connections with solicitors and accountants. In general, though, industry in this region was self-financed. The same conditions existed in Manchester but solicitors and accountants there played a more active role in new small firm foundation. Although established Manchester businesses could approach the banks for funds, new share issues had almost invariably to be floated in London, so that the underwriting of northern enterprise was being creamed off in the City of London.

In Liverpool, before the First World War, prosperous local merchants and shipowners—operating essentially family businesses—were ready to place, or at least discuss placing, capital in new companies. But after 1918 business concentration saw the control of Liverpool's industry and commerce shifted to London where it became fashionable to establish head offices. Local financial independence was lost, so depressing capital supply for newly establishing industrial firms. Bristol experienced similar change.

The 4 common characteristics of this supply of funds in inter-war Great Britain have been summarized by Grant (1937):

(a) all public issues by companies from all regions of Great Britain were made in conjunction with the London capital market;

(b) there was no shortage of funds for established industry in all regions including the Special Areas (Central Scotland, West Cumberland, North East England, and South Wales);

(c) new enterprises had to seek *local* promoters, but innovation with the risks it entailed favoured established firms;

(d) no machinery existed in the 1920s and 1930s to move risk-bearing capital for new enterprises from one region to another.

Citing information on openings, extensions and closures of factories between 1932 and 1935 (Table 15.5), Grant (1937, p. 231) demonstrated the consequences of this regional bias in access to finance, arguing that the

TABLE 15.5 Factory development in Great Britain, 1932 to 1935

Region	Opened	Extended	Closed	Net change[a]
South and South West	118	43	54	+85.5
Greater London	927	174	549	+465.0
Wales and Monmouth	21	15	16	+12.5
Midlands	317	120	321	+56.0
Eastern Counties	90	30	40	+65.0
North West	420	131	519	−33.5
North East	165	85	219	−11.5
Scotland	75	28	104	−15.0
Total	2133	626	1822	+624.0

[a] Number of establishments opened minus those closed plus half those extended.
Source: Grant, 1937, p. 232.

'rapid growth of London ... must largely be explained by proximity to finance, or more exactly, proximity to financiers'. The pattern of disparity was to persist for at least 4 decades.

GLOBAL CAPITALISM AND THE FINANCING OF INDUSTRY

The concentration, centralization and institutionalization of capital supply for industry in both the UK and the US not only continued after the Second World War but even accelerated. The finance system was, in fact, becoming overcapitalized largely because of an explosion during the 1950s in contractual savings (insurance schemes, pension funds and unit trusts). This greatly intensified the institutional control of funds, heightening conservatism in lending and investment policies and heralding a significant redirection of funds away from manufacturing and productive sectors of the economy towards non-productive sectors, especially property and local authorities. Inflation in the 1960s and 1970s also increased the repayments burden of borrowing by firms or 'front end loading' (*The Economist Newspaper Ltd,* 1978), bringing about a decline in industrial demand for capital. Not surprisingly, three-quarters of British industry's capital needs were still met in the early 1970s through self-financing, mainly from retained earnings (Thomas, 1978).

The declining significance of the personal investor as a *direct* supplier of funds for UK industry has been examined extensively (e.g. King, 1977; Erritt and Alexander, 1977): from holding at least 90 per cent of UK equities in the 1930s these had declined to less than 40 per cent by 1975. By contrast the shareholdings of institutional investors, particularly the pension funds, insurance companies and investment trusts, rose from 27.7 per cent in 1963 to 46.8 per cent in 1975 (Table 15.6). In the US, however, the private investors maintained a major role in stocks and shares into the 1970s and only relatively recently have they been displaced by institutional investors (*The Economist Newspaper Ltd,* 1981).

Insurance companies became more important after the Second World War as their collection of savings increased from rising real incomes, inflation and high tax rates, and their involvement in house purchasing (Dunning, 1971). They have tended to switch their investments from government securities—partly because they were used by government to supply cheap money to finance the war itself—to tradeable securities and, with holdings amounting to almost 16 per cent of all issued ordinary shares in the mid 1970s, they had obviously acquired considerable power. But insurance companies, at least in the UK, have shied away from using that power by considering their investments as only trade interests. Unfortunately, this responsibility cannot always be abdicated as the Prudential found in the thalidomide settlements because of its holdings in Distillers Ltd.

TABLE 15.6 Beneficial holders of ordinary shares in the UK, 1963 to 1975

Holders	Per cent contribution			Change
	1963	1969	1975	1963–75
Persons	54.0	47.7	37.5	−16.5
Insurance companies	10.0	12.2	15.9	5.9
Pension funds	6.4	9.0	16.8	10.4
Unit trusts	1.3	2.9	4.1	2.8
Investment trusts	10.0	8.7	10.0	—
Banks	1.3	1.7	0.7	−0.6
Other	17.0	18.1	15.0	−2.0
Total	100.0	100.0	100.0	100.0
Market value of holdings (£ million)	27.5	37.9	44.6	17.1

Source: Erritt and Alexander, 1977, pp. 104–5.

UK pension funds have grown particularly rapidly through the 1950s and 1960s; some are now extremely large, especially in public sectors like those of the National Coal Board and the Post Office (over £1000 million in 1978) (*The Economist Newspaper Ltd,* 1978). Although heavily committed in the securities market, they have, in some instances, also invested much in their parent companies since their investment activities are relatively uncontrolled (Minns, 1980).

In the US a similar growth of institutional investment has occurred in the post-war years (Blumberg, 1975; Kotz, 1978) but with significant differences in emphasis. American financial institutions resumed their role in 1945 as suppliers of external finance to non-financial corporations. Yet whereas earlier this provision of capital had been the main avenue through which the financial institutions exercised power and control over the corporations, stockholding being only of secondary importance, after 1945 this stockholding function developed into the financial institutions' primary source of power (Kotz, 1978). In 1900 they owned only 6.7 per cent of all corporate stock, rising to 9.6 per cent in both 1922 and 1939, and from 16.5 per cent in 1945 to 33.3 per cent in 1974. This involved both the disproportionate purchase of new issues and the purchase of existing stock, presumably from individuals as in the UK. It is a moot point as to whether the financial institutions actually wield the power they possess. Blumberg (1975) argues that they do not at present but might in the future, citing evidence from the settlement of thalidomide claims in the UK. However, Pfeffer's (1972a,b) work on the composition of boards of directors in the US would suggest, indirectly, that financial institutions may already wield considerable power after the manner of the investment bankers in the late nineteenth century.

TABLE 15.7 Assets ($US000 million) and per cent holdings in common stock by US financial institutions, 1965 and 1972

Holding	1965		1972	
	Assets	Per cent	Assets	Per cent
Life insurance companies	158.9	4.0	239.4	8.9
Property and casualty insurance	41.8	21.6	75.9	23.7
Non-insured pension funds	59.2	42.4	117.5	63.5
State and local pension funds	33.1	4.2	72.1	19.0
Investment companies	47.0	85.1	79.6	80.4
Foundations	28.7	66.6	39.5	70.9
Educational endowments	11.7	59.0	15.0	66.7

Source: extracted from Blumberg, 1975, p. 95.

But some US financial institutions are more deeply involved than others in the securities market and in the provision of equity capital to the corporate sector (see Table 15.7). The largest collectors of funds are the insurance companies with assets of $US239,000 million in 1972. Yet only 9 per cent of these funds are held in common stock owing to regulations which were imposed in 1905 and which have been only slowly lifted. Other types of insurance company suffer far less regulation of their investments and hold more assets in common stocks. The massive growth of all types of pension funds is clearly displayed in Table 15.7 and results from increasing affluence, the decline of the extended family, and the rejection of social security coupled with a desire, essentially amongst the middle class, to minimize insecurity in old age (Kotz, 1978). Investment companies held approximately 25 per cent of all financial institutions' holdings in the US. They have always invested heavily in common stock, laying themselves open to periodic investor disenchantment, and in large but not the largest companies, concentrating on so-called 'special situations'.

No mention has yet been made of the role of the commercial banks in financing American industry. It is in this that a fundamental difference exists between the UK and the US. Banks in the US have long assumed an investment function which British banks have not, their power being much greater and emanating from a well-developed management function especially of personal trusts, investing the funds of the wealthy. Before 1914 these trusts held up to 6.5 per cent of corporate stock (three-quarters of that held by all financial institutions) (Kotz, 1978). Yet although the personal trust may have declined relatively, the business of trust departments of US commercial banks has continued to grow—by acquiring the management of a large proportion of non-insured pension funds. This function combines with legal restrictions imposed on insurance companies to make the commercial banks of overwhelming importance within the corporate sector of the US economy.

In the 1970s British commercial banks have also begun to broaden their activities and to take on an investment function, bringing them more closely into line with their US counterparts. Five factors have stimulated this quite radical change in British banking (Frazer, 1976):

(a) access after 1971 to medium term finance on the inter-bank market;
(b) the squeeze on company liquidity after 1974;
(c) the lengthening periods demanded for trade credit;
(d) the shortening life of industrial equipment;
(e) political pressure.

Moving into merchant banking and 'project financing' (Hall, 1976) has also necessitated this shift to medium and long-term financing. Moreover, to vet the proposals they receive, banks have had to acquire new skills in non-banking fields, so blurring further the distinction between industrial, commercial and financial institutions.

In no small way, these innovations in banking in both the UK and the US have been facilitated by the growth of international money markets, most notably that dealing in Eurocurrencies, which is in part an inter-bank market. Deposits of US dollars in Europe were acquired first under the Marshall Plan and later when the US went into balance of payments deficit. As restrictions on interest rates payable on deposits in the US combined with bank rate changes in the UK making sterling no longer available for its traditional uses, dollar holders began to deposit in Europe rather than in the US (Tew, 1977; *The Economist Newspaper Ltd,* 1979; Barclays Bank Ltd, 1979a). Other currencies have now entered the market which involves about $US475,000 million. Two instruments exist within this market, the short-dated, variable interest bank credit (70 per cent of Eurocurrency lending) and long-dated, fixed yield bond, often referred to as 'stateless' money. Development of this market from about 1960 was partly a response to the growth of multinational corporations; but it also encouraged the multinationalization of banking and finance, as exemplified by the movement of US and other foreign banks into London (Schoeppler, 1976), and the development of new forms of international financing, the most recent being the currency swap (Barclays Bank Ltd, 1979b) which represents a step towards the international integration of industrial and financial organizations.

The rapid institutionalization of the supply of finance for industry (Committee to Review the Functioning of Financial Institutions [the Wilson Committee], 1980) has had important ramifications for the segmentation of both the UK and the US economies. In the UK, economies of scale in the new issues market still persist as the Bolton Committee (1971) and Davis and Yeomans (1974) have demonstrated. While the Bolton Committee showed costs of issue for issues of £250,000 to be 6.7 per cent and of £1 million to be only 3.2 per cent in the early 1970s, Davis and Yeomans prove these estimates to be at least 50 per cent too low and to show the costs of the smallest issues to have risen from 10 per cent to 12 per cent in the 12 years to 1971. Clearly, access by smaller firms to institutional funds through the new equities market is becoming progressively more restricted. It is further restricted by the lending policies of the financial intermediaries: British pension funds and insurance companies have tended to invest in only the larger companies (Franklin and Woodhead, 1980; Minns, 1980). Of the insurance companies, Clayton and Osborn wrote in 1965 (p. 172) that their 'preference [is] for the more readily marketable shares of the larger industrial companies'. This sentiment was both endorsed and elaborated by Dunning (1971, p. 29) with the statement that 'their investments tend to be concentrated in the very large and rapidly growing companies'. Minns (1979) has demonstrated precisely the same trend in the investment policies of British pension funds. This tendency, however, has been exacerbated by the rapid growth of these organizations with investment strategies centred on a relatively restricted portfolio of holdings and a desire to take up no more than 5 per cent of a company's shares. Only the very largest companies receive the investment attention of both insurance companies and pension funds (*The Economist Newspaper Ltd,* 1978).

However, the equities of large manufacturing firms as a whole are barely adequate investment opportunities for the financial institutions, especially in comparison with property (Boddy, 1979). Ambrose and Colenutt (1975) commented that the 1974 value of the Commercial Union Building in the City of London was twice as great as the market capitalization of British Leyland at that time. Moreover, investments in property tend to be less 'visible' than investments in equities with a once-yearly valuer's certificate replacing daily quotations and fluctuations of equities. Under these circumstances property obviously becomes the most attractive investment from the fund manager's point of view.

There are 2 consequences of these investment strategies of pension funds and insurance companies in the UK. First, funds are redirected away from productive sectors (Minns, 1980) and, second, the investment that does go to productive organizations tends to be directed only to the very large ones. Predictably, therefore, the numbers of small firms (with fewer than 100 employees) in the UK declined from 136,000 in 1935 to only 60,000 in 1963.

The same penchant for financial institutions to invest in only the very largest corporations has also become evident in the US. For example, the 10 largest US banks in the early 1970s held around 30 per cent of Polaroid, of Xerox and of Avon Products and nearly 40 per cent of Walt Disney. As

Blumberg (1975, p. 107) summarizes, since the Second World War there has been a 'concentration of the vastly increased volume of institutional funds in a relatively limited number of companies, embracing many of the largest corporations in the nation'.

But as global capitalism progresses, financial institutions *per se* are becoming increasingly difficult to identify as the circuits of industrial and banking capital become increasingly intertwined (Thompson, 1977; Overbeek, 1980; Minns, 1981). As Taylor and Thrift (1981) have remarked, large business organizations in the UK are taking on more financial functions, especially in connection with currency shifts, as steadily increasing profits are harder to glean from purely industrial operations. This trend is also occurring in the US. Quoting the Chairman of Citicorp, *The Economist Newspaper Ltd* (1981) noted the burgeoning financial operations of firms such as General Electric, the National Steel Corporation, American Express, The Prudential Insurance Company of America, and Merrill Lynch.

Indeed, the intertwining of the industrial and banking circuits of capital has been dubbed by *The Economist Newspaper Ltd* (1981, p. 10) as 'converging into confusion'. It can only restrict further the supply of funds to firms other than the very largest and fits perfectly with what might be called the 'lemon-lime pie' syndrome in manufacturing organizations. The growing significance of the marketing function and the marketing ethic in large industrial enterprises is suggested by Hayes and Abernathy (1980) as reorientating firms towards only those products which can be shown through market research to have profit potential. Under these circumstances fundamental research on machine tools, for example, will never attract corporate investment when its merits must be judged in comparison to the market potential of a new flavour of pie filling.

The geographical ramifications of corporate and spatial concentration, international expansion and the blurring of the distinction between financial and industrial organizations during the period of global capitalism are also very clear. The concentration of power and resources which these have produced has further enhanced the significance of the main national financial centres such as London, New York, Tokyo or Paris. Liberalization of banking regulations in many of the states in the US has done nothing to counter this trend and the collapse of the property market in the UK in 1974 put paid to the establishment of regional offices by merchant banks, which briefly held out the prospect of funds for industry being made more readily available in the regions of the UK (*The Economist Newspaper Ltd,* 1978). Local funds still exist in some regions as, for example, through the investment strategy of the Midlands-based Britannic Assurance Company which has invested heavily in the equities of smaller quoted engineering enterprises of the West Midlands. But this is an exception, external capital sourcing of industry having become ever more concentrated organizationally and spatially.

REINFORCING REGIONAL DEPENDENCY

Research into the UK and US economies suggests that in developed capitalist countries the *sources of funds* available for industrialization and the development of industrial enterprises have changed substantially since the nineteenth century through the phases of competitive, monopoly and global capitalism. Several significant trends have been evident. First, the demise of the private individual, especially in the UK, as a direct supplier of funds for industrial investment; after the Second World War individuals there became net sellers of stocks and shares to institutional investors. There has, however, been a countervailing second trend, the rise of financial intermediaries to draw together the small savings of an ever-widening spectrum of society. Owing to the commitments these institutions enter into with their small savers, their investment strategies tend to be very conservative as the unwillingness, until recently, of British banks to invest or 'lend long' demonstrates. The US has suffered far less of this and risk capital has remained more readily available and may explain in part the continued significance there of small firms while their numbers have dwindled in the UK.

Institutionalization of money supply for industry resulted in more concentrated control of finance (J. Scott, 1979; Francis, 1980), though it was held back in the US to some extent by anti-trust legislation, and in the multinationalization of financial institutions and in functional diversification of some extremely large organizations to embrace financial and also commercial and industrial operations. In combination, these trends have redirected investment funds away from both small and also newly established industrial ventures which have been unable to meet the criteria of institutional investors seeking mainly low-risk opportunities for their funds. Large enterprises have been more favoured, although with time only the very largest have readily attracted funds. A dualistic or segmented economy has thus been created in which different sets of organizations and institutions hold very different amounts of power and control over available resources.

The spatial implications relate to the access individual enterprises have to funds and are expressed very simply in Figure 15.2. Until 1914, private sources of risk capital were available from individuals throughout the country, the capital and provincial cities offering slightly more access than other areas. Institutional sources were small and, in any case, the capital city's money markets were more strongly orientated to overseas investment (Figure 15.2a). Industrialization was possible at any location, but not so

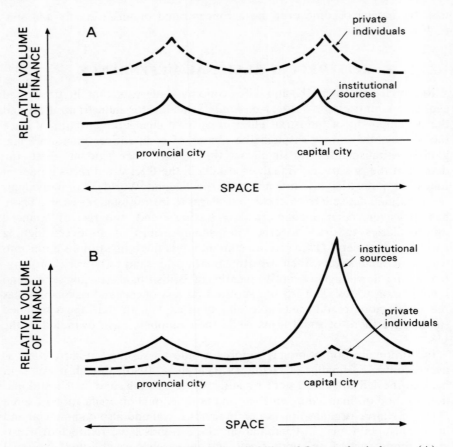

FIGURE 15.2 Spatial variations in the availability of finance for industry: (A) pre-1914 (competitive capitalism), (B) post-1960 (global capitalism)

after 1918 in the UK. Since the 1950s and 1960s the control of finance has been shifted to a country's capital city (Figure 15.2b). Local institutional sources have not dried up altogether, but have been reduced through corporate and institutional concentration. The private individual has ceased to fund industry significantly. A spatial version of institutional myopia has also developed which directs funds mainly to the very largest organizations. Now regions are also starved of funds from sources other than government.

Given this scenario of industrial development and financial institutionalization, regional economic problems in developed capitalist countries are a function both of the *use of funds* by industry (investment decision-making) and also the *supply of funds* to industry: a region's economic problems probably begin when it loses control of its local financial institutions and sources of investment funds. Such a hypothesis requires more research, yet it may explain the demise of the UK's periphery and the continued vitality of small businesses in the US; but it does suggest also that the current trends in the organization of financial institutions and their control in the US may leave this vitality little time to survive.

Spatial Analysis, Industry and the Industrial Environment. Vol. 3 Regional Economies and Industrial Systems
Edited by F. E. I. Hamilton and G. J. R. Linge

Chapter 16
The Regional Industrial System

GERALD J. KARASKA, CRAIG L. MOORE AND PAUL SUSMAN

The regional industrial system emphasizes the linkages between an industrial enterprise and all other components of society. The system perspective reflects a view of industrial geography whereby the firm is seen in its relationship to the total environment. This emphasis upon the total system suggests that the development of a region—its growth and decline—is a function or result of changes in certain 'lead' sectors to which other 'lag' sectors respond. The concern is for *both* the lead and lag sectors and the dynamics inherent in their interaction. Industry, then, is the sector which initiates growth responses, and it is a specific combination of linkages between the lead and lag sectors which distinguishes a particular regional system. Within this system for the advanced capitalist society the financial and governmental interactions are most profound in determining locational efficiency.

While a broader theoretical formulation has not been articulated, its foundations have been suggested as incorporating world, regional and local systems. Hamilton and Linge (1979) have described the dimensions of the world system and have also highlighted certain commonalities for all levels of industrial systems. Unfortunately, the world view does not touch upon certain relations and interactions that are more important in a *regional* context. The purpose here, therefore, is to establish the parameters of the regional industrial system, thereby emphasizing the uniqueness of the regional perspective.

A TOTAL SYSTEMS PERSPECTIVE

The regional system views the industrial firm in terms of its relationships with the total environment. The emphasis is on the linkages and their spatial manifestations, as well as the dynamics of the system with concern being placed on development, growth and change.

The following discussion is biased in that it focuses on an advanced economy—the United States. None the less, systems perspectives on Third World economies are approached in some of the development literature, particularly with reference to the roles of multinational corporations (Langdon, 1975; Wilbur, 1979). In centrally planned economies, collaboration with Soviet industrial geographers (notably Bandman) has revealed strong conformity of ideas on the regional industrial system in the context of the 'territorial production complex'.

Multiplier Models

Models commonly employed in economic impact studies are convenient descriptions of regional systems which highlight interactions and interdependence. Although they have only been used to measure inter-industry relationships, they can describe total system interactions once appropriate measures are defined.

Traditional multiplier models have suggested that the total impacts of change in the system can be evaluated since all elements within it are interconnected. Because these models have focused upon the calculation of simple coefficients or ratios, which purport to measure total interdependence, they have not found wide popularity. If attention is shifted to identifying the structure of the system as revealed by the linkages, the multiplier models have great utility. Following the logic inherent in the multiplier models, it is here suggested that the focus of attention in a regional industrial system should be upon the *total system,* of which the industrial firm or sector is the key element. Multiplier models have concentrated on the industrial sector, with the resulting coefficient measuring its impacts. Equally, industrial geography has been dominated by a myopia in which much attention has been centred on the *location* of the manufacturing firm. The paradigm of industrial geography for the 1980s should, it is argued here, shift concern to the complexity of the total system as the manifestation of the impacts of the industrial sector or firm.

This view proposes that the growth or decline of a region is a function or result of changes in certain 'lead' or growth sectors to which other 'lag' sectors respond. The total system's view is on *both* the lead and lag sectors and the dynamics inherent in their interaction. Industry, then, by definition, is that sector which initiates growth responses. Manufacturing and primary industries have commonly been considered as lead sectors, but tertiary and quaternary activities may also serve as leading sectors, generating growth and development. The critical issue is the interrelationships among *all* the sectors. Hence a regional industrial system perspective focuses on *both* 'lag' and 'lead' sectors. A particular combination of linkages between the lag and lead sectors characterizes each regional industrial system.

The Post-industrial Era

Advanced economies have a declining proportion of their workforces engaged in manufacturing and primary sectors, and even within these, 'white-collar' occupations have become more important. Clearly the tertiary and quaternary sectors are assuming greater significance in the economic structure of advanced economies but this does not mean that primary and secondary activities are becoming less important since they remain critical components of growth and change. The point again is that the advanced economic structure of a region is achieved through mechanisms that develop or enhance *all* sectors of the system.

Along with this contemporary trend, the spatial components of change have also been distinct. In the modern economy the spatial interactions of the primary and secondary sectors have expanded to cover national and international space, while the interactions of the tertiary sector which were once considered to be predominantly regional and local have now assumed international character.

Thus the advanced economy is no longer best understood in terms of physical or commodity flows but in terms of *monetary* flows and linkages. In the past input-output models have depicted interactions among sectors as commodity flows, albeit measured in monetary terms. But recently detailed studies have shown that commodity flows among manufacturing industries within the regional system constitute a relatively small proportion of all interactions. Shifting attention to the total set of monetary flows suggests that each sector—whether lag or lead—becomes more intimately involved in system interdependence. Put another way, previous research has focused on industrial capital, whereas the thesis advanced here is that flows of financial capital better highlight the interactions in a regional economy. The regional export base is very diversified because capital flows in from a multiplicity of sources; thus the monetary exchanges within the area concerned best reveal the total nature of the regional interdependence.

Concomitant with the heightened importance of financial capital in the regional industrial system, the contemporary industrial firm is characterized by a very complex organizational structure which includes financial, legal and fiscal relations that cover national space and often stretch across the globe. The production function comprises many components—headquarters, main plant, branch plants, sales offices, subsidiaries and sub-contractors—established in widely scattered locations. These firms not only make a great variety of products but also provide multi-faceted services. Thus, the previous research emphasis on technology in production now focuses on technology in management services, administration and control. Further, organizational decision-making now includes global coordination of such matters as the adoption of technological innovations, the relocation of investment concentrations and the maintenance of international markets.

The intricate organizational structure of the modern industrial firm imposes complicated linkages on the national and international system, and at the same time depends heavily upon the local regional system. It demands a multitude of services from the local system—of products, labour, housing, infrastructure, public services and financial capital—which usually can only be found in a large metropolitan region. The agglomeration effects of such a metropolis (region) thus provide the resources or 'externalities' that facilitate efficient management.

Pred (1974) has advanced a view of a national industrial structure in which the behaviour of organizations coincides with the location of industrial components, and the national hierarchical system of cities serves as the system structure. His logic is that this organizational structure depends on jobs concerned with the exchange and processing of specialized *information*. Similar views have also been expressed by Goddard (1971) and Törnqvist (1973) and are rooted in the growth and development process expounded in Hägerstrand's models of information diffusion. The inherent reasoning is identical to the 'financial flows' framework advanced here, since this simply reflects an economics perspective.

THE REGIONAL SYSTEM

The regional industrial system coincides spatially with a metropolitan region which encompasses an effective commuting zone around the central city, including suburban and exurban areas. Within this exists a set of linkages among all components which manifest the state of economic health of the region. The industrial component serves as the lead sector which acts as a stimulating mechanism for the total system. The initial phases of that interaction are described here as *economic* linkages, although these reverberate through the system as cultural, political and environmental impacts.

The industrial lead sector produces a good or service which is exported from the region and, in turn, generates an inflow of dollars representing the total value of all exported goods and services. These imported dollars then circulate within the local region as purchases of goods and services from local firms. The 'territorial production complex' model highlights certain efficiencies in this structural relationship (see Bandman, 1980).

At another level the industrial firm generates a set of responses by all households and businesses in the region through the wages and salaries paid by all the productive units concerned, creating local demand as described by the Keynesian multiplier models. However, these models are simplified and do not adequately account for the extreme complexity of linkages in the regional industrial system.

Other linkages occur within the system through the financial or banking sector. The mechanisms inherent in the banking system can be illustrated by a mathematical framework, beginning with a simple Keynesian model (Moore *et al.*, 1981):

$$Y = C + I + E - M \qquad (16.1)$$

where:
Y is regional income;
C is consumption by households in the region;
I is investment in the region;
E is regional exports;
M is regional imports.
Further, consumption is a function of regional income;

$$C = a + mpc(Y) \qquad (16.2)$$

where, $dC/dY = mpc$, the marginal propensity to consume. Finally, a new term, $mpcl$, is introduced here to embrace the marginal propensity to consume local goods, a simple relationship that can be extended (Tiebout, 1962) to generate the so-called regional trade or income multiplier:

$$dY/dE = \frac{1}{1 - mpcl} \qquad (16.3)$$

If, hypothetically, $mpcl$ equalled 0.5—indicating that, on average, half the value of goods and services consumed in the region was supplied by local factors of production—the multiplier would be 2.0. In such a case an initial change in regional income resulting from increased export sales would be doubled in the region's economy.

Earlier, emphasis was placed on regional flows of money payments and of goods and services. Whilst the latter are exchanged in a direct supplier-to-customer manner, payment is not. Most payments in the United States (and some other developed economies) are made through the banking system which does *not* have a neutral effect on the region's money supply and consumption. Banks create money. Money is not just cash or currency; over 90 per cent of the money supply is in demand deposits which are entries in account ledgers. As the volume of deposits increases in a commercial bank it is able to extend more credit and increase the level of spending in the economy based on changes in its deposit base.

When a regional household receives a weekly pay cheque, the first step is usually the commerical bank. The householder takes part of the money in cash to be used for pocket money and small purchases during the week (c). An additional portion (t) is often deposited in a savings or time deposit account, and the balance goes into a cheque account or *demand deposits* (r). The bank must place part of the demand deposits on reserve as required by the federal reserve system. A different reserve rate (r') is required on time deposits. The bank also keeps part of the money to run its business which can be thought of as till money or excess reserves (i). The balance of the money is then either invested in securities, which cause funds to flow outside the region (I_o), or loaned out as credit to local businesses (e.g., short-term payroll needs) and to households (Cr) (e.g. Mastercharge, Visa, car loans).

392   SPATIAL ANALYSIS, INDUSTRY AND THE INDUSTRIAL ENVIRONMENT

This relationship is illustrated by the following equation:

$$Cr = Y(1 - c - r - i - I_o - r't) \qquad (16.4)$$

By adding the banking system to the model of the region's economy, it incorporates flows of credit and interest between the banking system and each of the sectors described earlier. The addition of banking to the model of the local economy makes the impact on regional income from a change in export sales more complex. If more income is received by households they will be able to increase their expenditures to the same extent. But when they deposit this money the bank can extend credit to businesses and households in the region; in time this money will be spent on goods and services, which will generate still more income. Increased export sales result in a change in the flow of income which raises average demand deposits and therefore credit to a new level. The deposits are always spent and replaced by more income in the next period, which maintains the new increased level.

Equations (16.3) and (16.4) can be combined to generate a new multiplier describing the impact of a change in the industrial sector including the banking sector, whereby,

$$C = mpc(Y) + mpc(C_r) \qquad (16.5)$$

and more formally

$$dY/dE = \frac{1}{1 - mpcl - mpcl(1 - c - r - i - I_o - r't)} \qquad (16.6)$$

The potential significance of this change in the multiplier can be tested hypothetically by comparing it with the simple example given earlier where an *mpcl* of 0.5 gave a multiplier of 2.0. If it is now assumed that the *mpcl* has the same value of 0.5 and that the new term in the denominator, $(1 - c - r - I_o - r't)$, is equal to 0.4 (a reasonable level for a medium-sized banking system), the multiplier equals 3.33. This is a very significant increase.

THE INTER-REGIONAL INDUSTRIAL SYSTEM

The previous discussion has implied that the region is a 'closed' system having no linkages or interactions with the rest of the world (except for the initial import of dollars by the exporting industrial firm). That assumption is now relaxed. The internal linkages of a region are clearly responsive to events and conditions outside it. Put another way, the regional industrial system is a part of a larger one in which inter-regional interactions have a profound effect upon the regional relationships. Two major components of the inter-regional system—the role of financial transactions and government policies—have been singled out.

Dynamic Properties

The previous discussion noted several important characteristics regarding industry in a mature economic system. One was that each firm is linked to other firms and institutions via corporate controls—financial, legal and fiscal—and that these linkages covered national and international space. Corporations, being extremely decentralized both spatially and sectorally, produce a high degree of integration at the national level, and lately at the international level. The implications are that the economic health of each region is very responsive to events in the larger total system, and that changes in one region may have profound effects on the structure of another. One of the mechanisms for change in these inter-regional systems is the financial flows among industrial components.

First the cyclical character of the national and regional economies must be considered. At the macro-level, exogenous forces induce change in the national system; the national economy thus experiences periodic cycles of recession and growth. The net effect is an alteration in the structure of the inter-regional linkages. Also, each industry experiences shifts in output, reflecting changing demand and technology (Thomas, 1980). Thus the industrial structure and composition of each region alter as the economic health of one region wanes while the economy of another expands.

These inter-regional relationships become manifest through corporate structure and institutional arrangements. For example, there is great mobility of productive capital between regions as corporations and financial institutions seek to gain advantages by shifting the sites of investment. Through a process of disinvestment and reinvestment productive capital flows out of declining regions into growing ones. This can take the form of industrial corporations closing plants in one region and opening plants in another, or of large insurance and other financial institutions allocating investments to growing regions. Bluestone and Harrison (1979, p. 21) suggest that there are at least 4 ways in which industrial corporations may move their capital from one place to another. Companies may

(a) run down their older facilities (e.g. not replacing worn-out machinery) and use the savings to reinvest in other branches of their own firm, in other businesses or in other investment opportunities;

(b) close the older facility, reinvesting in other firms or portfolios, or by the owner taking pensions or other retirement benefits;

(c) gradually shift machinery, skilled labour, managers, or corporate responsibilities from older to newer facilities—the old facility remains in operation, but at a lower level of activity;

(d) not physically remove any of the older plant's capital stock in the short run, but profits earned from the plant's operations are reallocated to its newer facilities—the 'milking' of a profitable plant.

Bluestone and Harrison document the high mobility (hypermobility—see Hudson's chapter in this volume) of productive capital by US industry. They report (p. 11) that 'in 1974, an historic relationship was reversed, as manufacturing employment in the South passed that of the North for the first time', contending that the Sunbelt regions represent pools of investment capital siphoned from the older, declining Frostbelt regions:

> The average ratio of "closings" . . . for the four Frostbelt regions—the twenty-one states that make up the North—is 1.11 (weighted by each state's 1974 employment). That means that, for every one hundred jobs created by the private sector over this period through business openings one hundred and eleven jobs were destroyed through closings. The average for the three Southern regions, plus those Mountain states—is only 0.80. This means that, for every hundred jobs created by private investment in the form of openings or immigrations, eighty jobs were eliminated through closings or outmigrations . . . leaving a net growth of twenty new jobs (Bluestone and Harrison, 1979, p. 42).

DEVALORIZATION AND THE RESPONSE TO CRISES

Another body of theory exists which suggests explanation for the exchange of capital between regions (Sweezy, 1942; Harvey, 1975a). Its cornerstone is the influential role played by large corporations and especially the transnational corporations. These are depicted as being very responsive to changing factors of production in one region; pursuing a continued high rate of profit, they quickly shift productive resources elsewhere. The fluctuations in regional economies are labelled as responses to *crises* in the firm. One response may be to direct capital elsewhere; another may be to destroy the capital stock in the declining region by accelerating the depreciation of machinery. This reduction in capital value is called *devalorization* and it leads to conditions conducive to future capital accumulation in other regions and sectors (Susman, 1979; Gibson *et al.*, forthcoming). While devalorization is most apparent during crises, it is a continuous process as industries and associated capital are destroyed and renewed. Productive industries and larger firms are least affected while low productivity firms are hardest hit. Corporations may selectively devalorize certain plants which are operating at below average levels of profitability, thus establishing, for the affected region, new norms for prices and the social allocation of labour. Destruction of fixed capital by devalorization in the below-average firms and sectors reduces absolutely the capital extant in the society. Combined with lower real prices emerging from competition, this may result in less available capital, but more profitable conditions for future investment. This is true for several reasons.

First, as constant capital is devalorized any production that continues is contributing to a higher rate of profit. Second, higher unemployment leads to less bargaining power for labour, which may result in lower real wages. Third, a cheapening of commodities via competition preceding devalorization results in a reduction in the cost of labour subsistence and the wage. If the consumer commodity package that constitutes the wage is reduced in value, the amount of variable capital investment for labour power may be reduced. In effect, there has been a devalorization of labour power and a consequent increase in the rate of surplus-value and rate of profit.

Reducing the value of capital by devalorization is achieved in the price sphere by depreciating fixed capital holdings. Depreciation policies, often enforced by banks, respond to declining sectoral rates of profit. Thus, devalorization processes are independent of individual capitalists, and reductions in capital value are as involuntary as the need to develop the forces of production and to maintain at least the average rate of profit. In devalorization processes, the individual firm must have alternative sources of capital expansion available, and the reserves must be ample to maintain the firm's capital in a competitive position. As a result, the impact of devalorization will be least on giant enterprises with larger capital and with access to credit from the same financial institutions that deny capital to smaller firms.

Regions with high concentrations of industries undergoing devalorization are likely to experience significant changes in the local economic structure and in the welfare conditions of the affected population. Over time, a systematic shift in investment would be expected, from older industries using more skilled labour inputs to new industries employing members of the secondary labour force, including unorganized, minority, and newer entrants into the labour market. Easily hired and fired, easily trained and threatened, and receiving lower wages, the labour force in the new sectors is less likely to confront employers with demands for a greater share of surplus-value or for changes in the work process. The regional workforce is peripheralized in this way. Its role in the international division of labour is maintained as long as more profitable conditions elsewhere do not supplant it.

Thus, devalorization can bring about qualitative changes in the social relations of production and substantial alterations in the economic profile of affected regions. It can lead to new economic growth in one region and to stagnation in an older, deficit region. The impacts on the latter can be profound: it means 'secondarization' of the labour force in terms of greater employment of women, minorities and younger people—all of whom are unskilled and receive low wages—as well as substantial lay-offs, especially of the high-wage, skilled labour force.

The impact of this kind of capital restructuring can also be seen in a changing economic base in the deficit region. Subsidiaries of large corporations may be forced to make different products, hence the demands of these firms on the local region may be profoundly altered. Besides changing patterns of procurement, this can lead to population resettlement and new social relations as some neighbourhoods are destroyed and new towns developed. The extra costs to the households in the region can be immense.

THE ROLE OF GOVERNMENT

This process of capital mobility in an advanced economic system is aided and abetted by government and public institutions, which attempt to act as equalizing mechanisms compensating for the shifts in private capital investment.

The profit maximization motives of the private sector result in behavioural decisions which generate the highest rate of return. In the process, other factors of production become the responsibility of other segments of society. 'Indeed, in a purely competitive product market, the entrepreneur is under tremendous pressure not to worry about what happens to land, labor and social infrastructure' (Bluestone and Harrison, 1979, p. 26). Furthermore, productive capital moves with amazing speed while labour moves very slowly, if at all, leaving behind communities with severe economic and social problems.

Government in Western society has essentially been left with 2 functions: (a) promoting the accumulation of capital in the private sector; and (b) maintaining some minimal level of welfare service in order to establish and demonstrate its legitimate right to rule and to ensure the acceptance of rule by the population. The state has performed supportively to promote capital accumulation while maintaining order, protecting capital interests from invasion, and usurpation of productive facilities. Contemporary government has thus found it acceptable to:

(a) pay for the social services of the poor and destitute;
(b) provide the regional infrastructure;
(c) pay for the training and education of workers;
(c) finance industry, either through direct grants such as tax relief or low rents, or through indirect grants like loan guarantees or trade agreements.

Government has also aided the worker by supporting the social wage, in the form for instance of unemployment insurance benefits, pension rights, public assistance, disability insurance and a legal minimum wage.

SUMMARY AND SYNTHESIS

The regional industrial system as promoted by the International Geographical Union Commission on Industrial Systems is a synopsis of contemporary views in industrial geography. It emphasizes that the industrial plant is only one element of a larger system, and that a proper evaluation or analysis of that industry or firm can only be offered in terms of its linkages to the other elements in the system. The location of industry, its productivity or efficiency, and its changing character are all reflections of the linkage structure of the system.

Here this logic is carried a step further by suggesting that the emphasis for research should be upon the *total* system, in conjunction with investigations of the more direct industrial linkages. This chapter has attempted to outline the nature and character of the larger, broader systemic framework by noting 2 dimensions—the regional system and the inter-regional system. It is also argued that, in addition to the industrial sector, financial and government institutions are especially important components of the system relationships. Further, the organizational structures of industry, finance and government are dominant forces in the dynamics of the system.

The outline proposed begins with the regional system. The first level describes the direct linkages between the industrial exporting firm and other enterprises and industries in the region, as manifested in the flows of goods and services. These linkages are most commonly depicted by the input-output table, which explicitly measures the product-service flows in the regional system.

The second level focuses on the households in the region which are linked to industrial firms by wages and salaries. Interdependence follows as households purchase goods and services from the other businesses in the region, generating a series of rounds of consumer spending. The Keynesian multiplier articulates the final impacts of the consumption effect. Such things as housing demand and commercial growth are obvious direct effects of industrial wages and salaries, while land-use patterns and public capital programmes, for example, are long-range, indirect effects.

A third level of interaction is called into play as financial institutions intercede in the economic flows. In the process of handling the monetary transactions, these institutions actually enlarge the consumption effect by allowing more consumption, hence greater impacts from the industrial sector. At the same time, this role permits the institutions to generate those financial resources that are essential to industrial growth—such as loans and credits.

A fourth level of interaction is equally important to the economic health of the region and, thus, critical to the environment in which the industrial firm operates. Government and other public and private institutions and organizations make the policies and execute the plans, leading to effective administration, constructive investments and worthwhile societal goals. Indeed, the quality of life in the region is directly related to the structure of public organization and indirectly to industrial structure and organization.

At the inter-regional scale there are exogenous impacts which are also effective in shaping the industrial structure of the region. One level of linkages, macro in character, reflects business cycles in which the national economy and the region respond to fluctuations in the world market. Equally, each industry undergoes changes in demand which are related to the life cycle of the goods and services produced and the changing technology of the industry.

Another level of inter-regional interaction is the differential rate of investment in each region, as corporations and institutions move resources in the pursuit of profit. These flows of resources clearly reflect the linkages inherent in corporate structures. For example, the transnational corporation plays a central role in certain cyclical fluctuations associated with regional decline as a result of capital outflow. As overseas investments start to occupy a greater proportion of available capital, domestic crises and down-turns within the advanced capitalist countries occur with greater frequency.

Finally, as yet another level of influence is the role of government and other organizations. These act to promote development in certain regions while, at the same time, providing the stabilizing mechanisms to prevent disastrous impacts in others. Government policies may also lead to complete reorientation of the regional space economy via locational decisions for subsidies, industrial parks, public housing provision and construction, and other investment. Thus, the legitimation function is tied to the accumulation function and may result in fundamental changes in the mode of social reproduction such as the way communities are organized. The outcome of the capital restructuring process always includes a change in household consumption and organization in the affected area.

What is being suggested here is that the industrial structure of a region, and environment for any particular firm, is the result of a combination of factors:

(a) the direct-cost factors of production, related to location and delivery costs;
(b) the indirect linkages within the region;
(c) the macro-effects from national (and increasingly, international) forces;
(d) the organizational relationships within and between corporate entities;
(e) the stabilizing effects of governments and institutions.

The viability of an industry or firm is not strictly a function of competitiveness alone, but results from a combination of factors concerned with the way that each firm fits into the linkage structure of the region as well as the firm's fit into the structure of larger, decentralized, organizations (industrial, governmental and institutional).

Spatial Analysis, Industry and the Industrial Environment. Vol. 3 Regional Economies and Industrial Systems
Edited by F. E. I. Hamilton and G. J. R. Linge
© 1983 John Wiley & Sons Ltd.

Chapter 17

The Mobility of Manufacturing and Capital: Implications for Regional Development

M. T. DALY

GROWTH CENTRES

The first generation of regional planners depended on the mobility of capital and labour to balance spatial unevenness within nations. By the 1960s, however, it seemed clear that in the many countries which had chosen industrialization as the means of developing, spatial imbalances were great and increasing. Klaassen (1972, p. 1) summed it up thus:

> Urbanization and industrialization are so closely linked with each other that it is hardly possible to think of the one without implicitly thinking of the other ... Large cities become still larger, and even for the largest in the world there seems to be no limit to their further growth.

The idea, therefore, of using this 'natural' and seemingly irreversible process to boost lagging, depressed or frontier regions was both attractive and compelling. Perroux's ideas of growth poles provided theoretical respectability, albeit with some licence being given to the original concepts; as Petrella (1972, p. 190) observed:

> It cannot be denied that the simplicity of these ideas and their apparent connection with the facts described ... should have guaranteed their immediate acceptance and dissemination in the scientific community and among policy making circles.

It is now history that growth centres were not only accepted but became a talisman for regional planners; the panacea for spatial imbalances in every situation:

> Actively promoted ... through international agencies, including the United Nations and its agencies, the private foundations and consultants, the idea quickly spread from Western Europe and the United States and Latin America, first in Chile then Venezuela, Brazil and so on, and finally to Africa and Asia, particularly Japan, South Korea, India and to a lesser extent Southeast Asia (Lo and Salih, 1978, p. xii).

At the peak of the acceptance of growth centres by policy-makers there grew a deep sense of disillusionment about the effectiveness of those methods:

> At issue is not that what is conceived . . . by the planners is consistent with what has been written and advocated in the literature, but whether the proposed strategy will actually achieve the goals set for it. For the problems it is supposed to solve are wide ranging and certainly difficult . . . the efficacy and ability of growth centres to generate positive impact on their regional hinterlands, are in too many instances being questioned (Salih *et al.*, 1978, pp. 115–16).

There are many aspects to the debate about growth centre strategies. There have been numerous problems in translating the theory into practice, and strategists have found difficulty in answering such basic questions as where to locate growth centres and how to decide on the mix of activities which ensure that they do grow. The disappointments felt about growth centre strategies derive from such basic technical issues, and have affected almost every application of the idea. One of the most ambitious attempts to apply growth pole theory was undertaken by the Australian government during the 1970s and this is discussed in the next section of the chapter.

The relative failure of the Australian attempt was only partly a result of the inadequacies of the selection procedures and the nature of investment in the centres. More fundamental was a shift in the structure of the Australian economy brought about, in large measure, by the international changes in industrial systems and international finance described by Linge and Hamilton (1981). These changes have posed a new set of questions for theorists studying regional development processes, and in terms of the worldwide changes some commentators, such as Linn (1978), have drawn attention to situations of 'polarization reversal'. One interpretation of this is that in certain circumstances mobile factors of production have worked towards reducing spatial disparities, as the earlier theorists had predicted. A more plausible explanation of polarization reversal, however, lies in the spatial behaviour of multinational manufacturing firms and in the effect of development projects organized by governments but funded by international banks. In the final section of the chapter it is argued that there is likely to be a different locational pattern of multinational manufacturers in the 1980s and that the banks will favour large projects in resource-rich areas. These factors will prescribe the boundaries of regional planning approaches.

GROWTH CENTRES IN AUSTRALIA

Worldwide, the popularity of growth centres reflected an optimism, current in the 1960s, that growth was almost inevitable and that spatial imbalances could be solved simply by reallocating growth mechanisms,

TABLE 17.1 Capital city populations as a proportion of state populations, Australia, 1947 and 1971

City	State	1947	1971
Sydney	New South Wales	55.3	63.6
Melbourne	Victoria	63.0	71.5
Brisbane	Queensland	36.4	47.4
Adelaide	South Australia	59.4	71.8
Perth	Western Australia	54.6	68.2
Hobart	Tasmania	30.3	39.2
Darwin	Northern Territory	—	42.3

Source: Australia, Commonwealth Bureau of Census
and Statistics, 1947, pp. 1, 127, 209, 287, 361, 435; 1971.

particularly manufacturing. In Australia the regional problem was perceived
as one of imbalance between large and expanding cities and the rest of the
nation. Australia's colonial history and its federal system produced one
primate city within each state, and after the Second World War the
historical trend of increasing metropolitan dominance accelerated (Table
17.1). By the late 1960s governments in New South Wales, Victoria and
South Australia had developed policies aimed at attracting industry and
population to provincial centres. The focus of the debate shifted away from
the problems caused by the depopulation of rural areas to focus squarely on
the ills of the cities. This was because there were only small differences in per
capita incomes and levels of welfare between the various regions while in the
cities there were marked contrasts between rich and poor areas and the
cities in general were viewed as having more acute social problems, poorer
quality of life, unequal levels of access to services, and deteriorating
environments. By the late 1960s (Stilwell, 1974, pp. 104–35) social factors
were being stressed more than economic conditions.

Revealing the Pitfalls

The piecemeal efforts of the state governments had proved largely ineffectual in counterbalancing metropolitan growth and there was strong pressure
to make a spatially more concentrated attack on the problem of metropolitan
dominance; it was in this context that the growth centre ideas were
embraced in the early 1970s. Under the previous schemes the state governments had offered low interest loans for land and buildings; freight concessions; subsidization of training schemes; and the provision of housing for key
personnel for industrialists who wished to set up plants in provincial centres.
Political factors dictated that the grants and loans had to be available for any
town and this meant that the decentralized industries were thinly scattered
throughout a large number of towns, and the investment produced only

small multiplier and accelerator effects. Furthermore, the funds provided were too limited; in New South Wales in 1972–73 only $A9.9 million were allocated for decentralization programmes. The sense of directing the efforts into a few centres to be funded on a much larger scale by both federal and state authorities was accepted by most commentators. In 1972 the Australian government adopted a policy of growth centres.

Having pinned its faith in growth centres the government was confronted by 2 basic issues scarcely elucidated by the literature, one being the location of the centres and the other what activities to put into the centres to make them grow. There were 2 fundamental locational choices: undeveloped sites with particular advantages could be obtained and new centres established; or centres already established, but possessing potential, could be nominated. In Australia the latter procedure was followed so the identification problem was reduced to an examination of the relative merits of a few specified sites.

In many ways the set of methods used in other parts of the world to identify growth centres was inappropriate in the Australian case. Many investigators, such as Berry (1969) in Chile and Hodge (1978) in Ontario, had employed factor analysis in which town growth was measured by several variables and urban places were then classified according to their scores on the major factors. Semple et al. (1972) in a study of São Paulo factor analysed 9 variables in 96 cities during 2 decades. The growth rate of each centre was correlated with the reciprocal of distance to each of several evenly spaced reference points, and the primary growth centre in a region was identified on the basis of the largest correlation coefficient. More sophisticated was Kuehn and Bender's (1969) use of shift and share analysis in a study of 32 economic sectors in 125 counties in the Ozarks. Composition and component elements, and the sum of elements gave a 125×66 matrix from which the 66 scores for each county were correlated with those of each other county; the coefficients were summed to reveal those which had undergone unusually great structural change, and these were nominated as growth centres.

With factor analysis there was a substantial problem of interpretation to uncover which aspect of growth each factor was measuring and how, collectively or individually, the various aspects of growth might influence growth patterns. The theoretical shortcomings in the translation of Perroux's aspatial ideas into a spatial context meant that there was little theoretical illumination of the practical problem of interpretation. The sophistication of the techniques used to identify such centres was out of phase with the understanding which people had of the growth processes. In Australia the problems were complicated by a lack of suitable data. Censuses have been unable to publish certain kinds of information (such as the details of manufacturing in company towns) while other useful data (like retail sales) have been collected irregularly. Both the definition of particular items and the range of items have varied between censuses so that a lack of comparability has reduced the interpretation of growth trends.

The choice of growth centres was further complicated because some state governments acted independently of the Australian government in selecting centres. The latter adopted 8 general principles in selecting growth centres while the New South Wales government put forward 14 reasons to explain its choice of Bathurst-Orange as a growth centre (New South Wales, Department of Decentralisation and Development, 1973). Many points were common to both governments; these included a sound physical and economic base, satisfactory levels of services and recreation facilities, accessibility to metropolitan areas, and a positive environmental impact of development. The criteria outlined by the Australian government put more emphasis on welfare, and included 2 factors not considered in the New South Wales case: (a) the location of the prospective growth centres with respect to the national infrastructure of capital investments; and (b) the obtaining of a political consensus. The nature of federal-state relationships in Australia meant that the second factor predominated in some cases (including that of Bathurst-Orange).

Patchy Performance 1960 to 1980

To assess the location decisions made under the Australian growth centre policy an analysis was made by Daly *et al.* (1974) of the growth performance of the 52 non-metropolitan centres with populations exceeding 10,000 in the states of New South Wales, Victoria, Queensland and South Australia using data for the census years 1961, 1966 and 1971. The variables employed were: rates of population growth; changes in the major sectors of the workforce (manufacturing, retailing, government); changes in salaries and wages and per capita income; total investment in construction in each town; male and female workforce participation rates, unemployment, and level of qualifications of the workforce for 1971; migration rates; and the changes in the level of residential construction in each town.

Although several growth centres were designated, only Bathurst-Orange in New South Wales, Albury-Wodonga on the Victorian-New South Wales border and, to a lesser extent, Geelong in Victoria, were to receive substantial government aid. None of the towns chosen as growth centres ranked in the top 10 centres in terms of a composite growth index (based on z scores) for 1961–71. The top-ranking towns fell into 3 groups. First were the mining or mineral processing centres of Gladstone, Whyalla and Mount Isa: Gladstone, for instance, grew by a remarkable 73 per cent between 1961 and 1966, and by a further 25 per cent from 1966 to 1971. The second group comprised Campbelltown, Gosford, The Entrance, Budgewoi Lake and Werribee—all towns within commuting range of Sydney or Melbourne. The

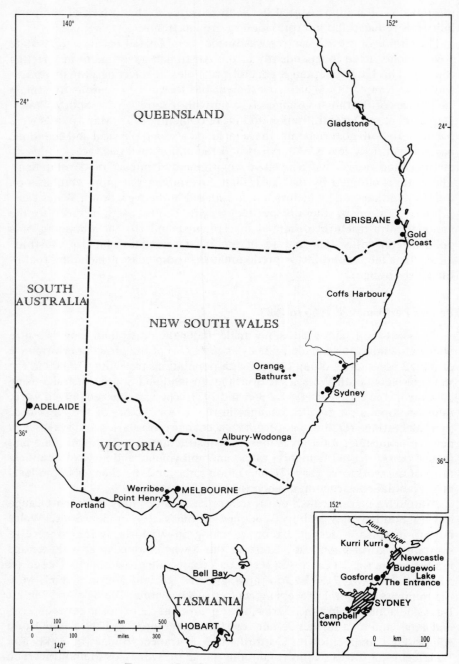

FIGURE 17.1 Southeastern Australia

third group were the coastal resorts of Gold Coast and Coffs Harbour. Of the major growth centres Albury ranked twelfth, Orange sixteenth and Bathurst fortieth of the 56 towns analysed.

Measured across several variables, the nominated centres did not perform well. Moreover, Albury-Wodonga and Bathurst-Orange were inland towns, and such places in general had unfavourable growth records throughout the 1960s, despite a high level of mobility in the population: 324,000 internal migrants moved into or out of Sydney between 1966 and 1971 with the metropolitan area suffering a net loss of 10,000 people. This decline, after decades of rural-urban drift, fortified the governments' confidence in their ability to create growth centres as alternatives. Daly *et al.* (1974) in a survey of 1000 householders in Sydney found that 52.7 per cent affirmed a desire to live outside the metropolitan area if the opportunity arose, the majority perceiving a better physical and social environment away from the city. Nearly two-thirds of persons aged less than 25 were favourably inclined towards non-metropolitan areas. But when asked the speculative question of where outside Sydney they would like to live, only 18 per cent nominated an inland centre while 52 per cent opted for coastal areas, the remainder suggesting interstate movement or a location close to Sydney. Specifically quizzed about the prospect of their moving to the Bathurst-Orange growth centre (if jobs were available) 23 per cent responded affirmatively. A similar survey in Melbourne about the same time (*The Age,* 4 August 1975) revealed that 20 per cent of respondents would consider moving to a new city such as Albury-Wodonga, but only 5 per cent said that they would 'seriously consider' moving.

Despite the relatively poor growth record of inland towns and the acknowledged preference of Australians to live near the coast the Australian government, in concert with the state governments, began a large investment programme centred on Albury-Wodonga and Bathurst-Orange designed to create centres which would provide viable alternatives to Sydney and Melbourne. The growth centres were to be big by world standards. Albury-Wodonga was designed to grow to 300,000 by the year 2000; Bathurst-Orange was initially planned to reach 250,000 by 2000 but in 1975 this target was scaled down to 186,000. Between 1973 and 1980 the governments invested at least $A167 million in the 2 growth centres (Table 17.2), mostly for housing and infrastructure. The governments produced only hazy indications of what was to provide their economic base. Three sources were suggested. First, the Australian government entered into negotiations with 2 Japanese car manufacturers and proposed that at least one of them establish a plant in Albury-Wodonga. These, and the accelerated rate of decentralization of city-based industries, would help stimulate an industrial base. Second, there was the expectation of government departments moving their headquarters to the growth centres. Finally, there was a strong faith in

TABLE 17.2 Commonwealth and state financial assistance for the Albury-Wodonga and Bathurst-Orange growth centres ($A000)

Year	Commonwealth finance		State loan funds	Private borrowings	Total
	Loan funds	Municipal works[a]			
(i) Albury-Wodonga					
1974–75	37,188	2,812	—	—	40,000
1975–76	36,937	2,926	—	—	39,863
1976–77	19,191	1,809	—	—	21,000
1977–78	5,000	—	—	2,000[b]	7,000
1978–79	5,000	—	—	2,000[b]	7,000
Total	103,316	7,547	—	4,000	114,863
(ii) Bathurst-Orange					
1974–75	4,407	593	3,797	—	8,797
1975–76	7,000	1,355	4,000	700	13,055
1976–77	3,222	768	4,000	3,000	10,990
1977–78	1,500	—	—	8,700	10,200
1978–79	—	—	—	9,000	9,000
Total	16,129	2,716	11,797	21,400	52,042

[a] Two-thirds loan, one-third grant.
[b] $A1 million from each state.
Source: unpublished data supplied by New South Wales Department of Industrial Development and Decentralisation.

the effect of the 'urban-size ratchet': that once a centre reached a certain minimum it would become self-sustaining in its growth as a result of circular and cumulative causation.

Factors in the Stagnation and Decline of Australian Manufacturing

Basically the Australian growth centre plans were founded on the belief that the boom of the 1960s would continue. That decade provided the climax of a long period of industrialization which had proceeded unhindered since the 1920s, and which had commenced when Prime Minister Deakin adopted the first substantial set of federal tariff measures in 1907. Accordingly the percentage of the Australian workforce engaged in manufacturing rose from 16 in 1901 to 19 in 1931 through 25 in 1947 to reach 27 per cent in 1966. The number of factories in Australia reached a peak of 57,782 in 1960–61 but the number of manufacturing employees continued to rise from 1,145,000 in 1960–61 to 1,301,639 in 1971–72 to decline briefly before reaching a peak of 1,338,379 in 1973–74. There was then a dramatic

TABLE 17.3 Employment in manufacturing industry, industrial classes, Australia, 1972–73 to 1977–78

ASIC	Industry group	1972–73	1977–78
21 + 22	Food, beverages, tobacco	206,101	194,118
23	Textiles	54,816	37,266
24	Clothing, footwear	112,032	80,998
25	Wood, wood products, furniture	83,366	75,460
26	Paper, paper products, printing	107,765	97,238
27	Chemicals, petroleum, coal products	65,416	61,444
28	Non-metallic mineral products	53,101	46,523
29	Basic metal products	95,923	91,671
31	Fabricated metal products	116,460	101,568
32	Transport equipment	153,901	135,092
33	Other machinery and equipment	186,436	160,784
34	Miscellaneous manufacturing	73,415	63,840
21–34	Total manufacturing	1,308,732	1,146,002

Source: Australian Bureau of Statistics, 1975, 1980a.

downturn in manufacturing. The number of factory workers fell by 193,821, or 12.15 per cent, between 1973–74 and 1976–77. The decline was quite severe in certain industrial groups (Table 17.3), most notably textiles (a 32 per cent fall from 1972–73 to 1977–78), clothing and footwear (28 per cent fall) and the category other machinery and equipment (15 per cent). In New South Wales and Victoria, the states with the largest cities and the most advanced plans for growth centres, the collapse of certain sectors of manufacturing was even more pronounced (Table 17.4) and because manufacturing was so concentrated in the major cities the effect of the changes there was quite drastic. In Sydney, for example, between 1973 and 1980 the textile and the clothing and footwear industries each lost 43 per cent of their workforce; non-metallic mineral products lost 29 per cent; fabricated metal products 19 per cent; and other machinery and equipment 24 per cent.

TABLE 17.4 Manufacturing employment, New South Wales, Victoria and Australia, percentage change in selected industrial groups, 1972–73 to 1977–78

ASIC	Industry group	New South Wales	Victoria	Australia
23	Textiles	−33.5	−33.5	−32.0
24	Clothing, footwear	−31.8	−26.0	−27.7
28	Non-metallic mineral products	−22.7	−13.1	−12.4
31	Fabricated metal products	−16.1	−9.5	−12.8
33	Other machinery and equipment	−15.2	−17.8	−14.8

Source: derived from data in Table 17.3.

Throughout the 1960s the hopes of boosting the non-metropolitan urban population of the Australian states had been based on the simple strategy of siphoning off a portion of the city-based manufacturing by enticing it to decentralize, and the same crude hopes underlay the thinking about the economic bases of the new growth centres. By the mid-1970s it was clear that Australian manufacturing as a whole was in a desperate fight for survival and there was little prospect of such plans, which had not worked in the prosperous 1960s, of succeeding in the recessionary years of the 1970s.

Shifts in Industrial Structure and Sources of Finance

Some signs of decline in manufacturing had begun to appear by the late 1960s although few people perceived them; manufacturing employment in 1972–73 was 11,435 less in Australia than in 1968–69. The fall of manufacturing was paralleled by a dramatic increase in the importance of minerals to the economy. Mineral exports in 1967–68 represented only 16 per cent of the total value of Australian exports but this moved to 24 per cent in 1969–70 and then levelled at about 29 per cent by the late 1970s. In relative terms the growth was staggering. The value of all Australian exports increased by 368 per cent between 1967–68 and 1978–79, but the value of mineral exports rose by 673 per cent over the same period. The development of Australia's huge mineral reserves attracted significant flows of

TABLE 17.5 Annual inflow of direct private overseas investment in companies in Australia ($A million)

Year	Primary industry[a]	Secondary industry	Other	Total
1965–66	128	186	179	493
1966–67	114	152	68	334
1967–68	176	214	154	544
1968–69	262	181	177	619
1969–70	265	187	287	740
1970–71	300	248	381	928
1971–72	356	190	329	874
1972–73	61	31	171	262
1973–74	58	269	223	550
1974–75	64	278	294	636
1975–76	33	223	304	560
1976–77	−53	485	641	1074
1977–78	57	360	591	1008

[a] Includes agriculture, forestry, fishing, mining, quarrying, and oil exploration and production.

Sources: Australia, Commonwealth Bureau of Census and Statistics, 1970, p. 355; Australian Bureau of Statistics, 1974, p. 317; 1980b, p. 684.

foreign capital. Direct private foreign investment in primary (mainly mineral) industry by companies grew from \$A114 million in 1966–67 to \$A356 million in 1971–72, and in the latter year it was almost double the level of investment of foreign capital directly in manufacturing companies (Table 17.5). There was then a decline during the 1970s, until 1979 when a new and much larger wave of foreign investment directed towards mining companies took place; capital inflow into Australia reached record levels setting off a spree on the stock markets which in October 1980 sent the All Ordinaries Index at Sydney above 1000 and the mining index above 6500. In the financial year 1980–81 over \$A6000 million of foreign capital entered compared to \$A1700 million in 1978–79; this enabled Australia to achieve a positive balance of payments for the first time in many years. In both the late 1960s and the late 1970s there was popular talk of a mineral boom despite substantial differences between the 2 periods.

THE INTERNATIONAL SETTING

The scale of the new mineral developments and their often remote locations implied enormous development costs, far beyond the limits of the rather unsophisticated capital markets which existed in Australia in the 1960s. Foreign investment was essential for the growth of the mining industry and this, combined with legislation in 1965 which prevented foreign firms from raising funds from Australian sources, attracted the attention of foreign banks and other financial intermediaries. The result was a broadening and deepening of Australian capital markets with overseas groups becoming particularly important. This produced a significant change in the role of the cities. In Sydney, for example, there were no merchant banks in 1965 but 80 by 1972, and there were only 3 foreign banks established in 1964 whereas 40 were there by 1971. Sydney became an important financial centre, and on a world scale. Davis (1976, p. 75) drew up a 'top league table of international investment centres' in which Sydney was ranked ninth in the world. Sydney, and to a lesser extent other Australian cities, received perceptible benefits from the structural changes in the economy which favoured mineral developments and reduced the importance of manufacturing. There was no way in which these changes could be made to assist the designated growth centres.

Import Penetration and Lost Competitiveness

The decline of Australian manufacturing was closely linked to international factors. Manufacturing had been developed behind solid tariff walls and has been assisted at various times by other incentives and subsidies. The result was a highly artificial structure in certain industries. In the whitegoods industry (the main component of the other machinery and equipment category of the census) Australian domestic demand stood around only 350,000 units per year whereas efficient manufacturers in other parts of the world were looking at 500,000 units per year as a minimum; Australia in 1972 had 9 manufacturers operating in 14 locations and producing 80 models. Between 1975 and 1979 there was a 39 per cent decline in employment in the manufacturing of appliances and electrical equipment. The motor vehicle industry was another in which Australia was at a decided disadvantage in terms of economies of scale. Thus instead of the car industry providing the basis of Albury's growth, the Australian vehicle industry entered a period of decline with falling levels of sales, rising imports and the virtual closure of one of the 4 major domestic manufacturers and the sale of another.

Despite small markets and high costs Australian manufacturing had flourished during the 1950s and 1960s partly because its stable political setting was attractive to foreign manufacturers. In contrast there were relatively low levels of investment by manufacturers in the Third World nations of the region just then emerging from colonial domination. By the 1970s, however, South-East and East Asian manufacturing had grown to such an extent that it offered Australian manufacturers severe competition. Japanese and East Asian (Taiwan, South Korea and Hong Kong) firms accounted for about 40 per cent of imports of textiles, clothing and footwear into Australia whilst ASEAN countries (the Association of South-East Asian Nations consisting of Indonesia, Malaysia, Philippines, Singapore and Thailand) began to make inroads in other sectors. ASEAN imports into Australia grew at 29.5 per cent (1975), 36 per cent (1976), 29.2 per cent (1977) and 15.3 per cent (1978) in comparison with increases in imports from all sources in each of those years of 2 per cent, 26.3 per cent, 7.3 per cent and 23.3 per cent. A 1977 government report by the Industries Assistance Commission estimated that the direct price effects of tariffs and quantitative restrictions on imports of textiles and clothing and footwear to Australia represented a total tax of about $A800 million on consumers and consuming industries. Rapid increases in the cost of labour in Australia (about 120 per cent between 1970 and 1975) and some lowering of tariffs helped to boost Asian imports and to cause the reductions in Australian industry noted in Tables 17.1 and 17.2.

Population Immigration and Revised Expectations

The pressures on Australian manufacturing caused by overseas competition and inflation coincided with a set of revised expectations about Australia's future growth rate. In 1975 the Australian government received a detailed report (Borrie, 1975) which forecast that far from reaching an

TABLE 17.6 Average annual rate of growth of population, Australia, 1951 to 1975 (per cent)

Year	Natural increase	Net migration	Total[a]
1951–55	1.38	0.95	2.31
1956–60	1.40	0.83	2.22
1961–65	1.27	0.74	1.98
1966–70	1.11	0.91	1.94
1971–75[b]	1.08	0.49	1.59

[a] Discrepancies between the sum of the rate of growth due to natural increase and net migration and the rate of total growth are due to intercensal adjustment.
[b] The rate of growth in this period incorporates revisions resulting from examination of evidence of under-enumeration in the 1971 census.
Source: Australian Bureau of Statistics, 1980b, p. 93.

anticipated population of between 22 and 28 million by the year 2000 Australia would be lucky to reach 18 million. In 1980 the projected population for the year 2000 was set at only 16.7 million. The average annual rate of growth of the Australian population had in fact declined continually from the 1950s (Table 17.6), with the significant factor between 1971 and 1975 being a reduced impact from immigration. Throughout the 1950s and 1960s immigration had been a parallel force with overseas capital in helping develop Australian manufacturing because it provided both workers and an expanding market. There was sudden fall in the number of immigrants from 121,000 in 1974 to 54,000 in 1975, and the level remained between 58,000 and 75,000 during each of the following 3 years. The decline of immigration affected the growth of the cities. Between 1966 and 1971 Sydney's population had grown by more than 10 per cent, and 56 per cent of that growth came from migration from overseas, intra-state or other parts of Australia. Between 1971 and 1976 Sydney's growth rate fell below 4 per cent. As well as the decline in overseas arrivals there was a reduction in the level of inter-state immigration, and New South Wales suffered losses in inter-state migration of 16.3 per cent in 1974, 11.1 per cent in 1976 and 13.5 per cent in 1977. Sydney's growth prospects were sharply reduced. As early as 1968, when the *Sydney Region Outline Plan* (New South Wales, State Planning Authority, 1968) was framed, the government had anticipated being able to direct as many as 500,000 of Sydney's projected population for the year 2000 to non-metropolitan centres. The growth centre plans of 1973 focused these hopes on Bathurst-Orange and Albury-Wodonga. By the mid-1970s there were doubts about Sydney's having any 'surplus' population to serve the needs of the growth centres.

The level of government and private investment in the growth centres allowed them to improve their rate of population increase through the 1970s from levels of 0 to 10 per cent in the latter part of the 1960s to as much as 18 per cent (Bathurst, 1976 to 1980) and 21 per cent (Albury-Wodonga, 1971 to 1976). The 12,930 people added to Albury-Wodonga's population between 1973 (start of the growth centre programme) and 1980 were supported by $A115 million of direct investment in infrastructure; the 12,350 additional population in Bathurst-Orange had been assisted by government investment of $A52 million (Table 17.2). Yet many centres which had received no special assistance in terms of government spending were able to grow much more rapidly during the 1970s.

The decade of the 1970s ended with official expectations of large-scale resource and resource processing developments in the 1980s costing anything from $A30,000 million to $A60,000 million. The resource-based developments have thrown up 'natural' growth centres such as the Hunter Valley (near Newcastle, New South Wales) and Gladstone (Queensland). These are being developed in response to overseas demand for minerals, such as coal, and through the investment of multinational aluminium corporations attracted by Australia's bauxite (of which it is the world's largest producer), and the promise of cheap electricity (see Mandeville's chapter in this volume).

The rise of these 'natural' growth centres prompted by international factors directs the discussion back to Perroux and his original contributions. Growth relates to the comparative economic advantage of each place and this rests on a blending of resource-base advantages and infrastructure. The realization of these advantages largely depends on demand and technology, and the major surges of growth have been associated with innovatory leaps. Perroux's great contribution was to focus on the unevenness of economic growth, noting how development impulses were directed by a few, innovative growth industries which propelled economies forward through their links with other sectors. Perroux, of course, was concerned with 'economic' space; the central role he gave to innovations has generally been neglected by geographers and regional planners who attempted to provide a spatial interpretation of his ideas. By their very nature innovations are unpredictable and, in a spatial sense, impossible to replicate. The Australian experiment ignored this.

It is not surprising to see the hopes of the Australian government shifting from the fabricated growth centres to new boom areas like the Hunter Valley and Gladstone. The total history of Australian development has reflected a reliance on the international economy. Again, Perroux (1964, p. 22) had made an eloquent plea for an international view of development:

We go on depicting to ourselves the relations between different nations as consisting exclusively in men and things in *one* space, conceiving them as *material* objects *contained* in a container ... This central conception of "container" and "contained" is contradicted on all sides by modern life, especially in its economic aspects. The concept remains tyrannical however ...

The developments of the 1960s and 1970s make such a plea most relevant to regional planning not just in Australia but in all parts of the world.

Multinational Corporations and Regional Development

The impact of multinational corporations has been immense. There are now at least 10,000 of them with 50,000 foreign affiliates, involving an international direct investment of $US287,000 million and accounting for 20 per cent of the GNP of the capitalist world (Wheelwright, 1980, p. 43). Curiously, the literature on regional planning says little about multinational corporations although they have directly affected the spatial distribution of economic activity in both Western and Third World nations. One reason for the failure of regional planners to account fully for the influence of multinational manufacturers is that the process of expansion occurred in 2 distinct phases and had quite different effects on different nations.

As already observed the great period of expansion of manufacturing in Australia occurred in the 1950s and 1960s and was significantly stimulated by the expansion of US firms. US manufacturers in the same period moved into Europe and some parts of the Third World, the expansion being directed by similar sets of forces. One factor was the need for US companies to extend the life of their products and to counter trading challenges. Through the first half of the twentieth century the United States grew to dominate world manufacturing, and that domination was based on, and represented the end of, a long evolution of machine tools. In the era of machine tools the American north and northeast became the geographical focus of manufacturing and provided the economic base for the most prosperous regions of the country. The capital-output ratios of machine-tool industries had begun a slow secular decline as early as 1919 (Watkins and Perry, 1977, p. 46) and between 1909 and 1947 the share held by the established 'manufacturing belt' of the total of US manufacturing output fell from 73 to 68 per cent (Norton and Rees, 1979, p. 142). The opportunities provided by industrial reconstruction or industrial development in Europe, Australia and elsewhere provided the opportunity for US manufacturers to extend the life of their products in the new locations.

In new settings, such as Australia, the locational patterns which had characterized the growth of US manufacturing during the first half of the twentieth century were repeated. Agglomeration economies were a decisive factor and manufacturing in Australia became concentrated in a few cities (Sydney, Melbourne and Adelaide). The prosperity which accompanied the first wave of post-war industrial growth bred the illusion that deconcentrating the engines of growth and centralization (the manufacturing industries) through the implantation of growth centres was both possible and necessary.

Associated with the expansion of US manufacturing abroad was a necessary evolution of the organizational structure of United States firms. The experience gained in the early part of the century in creating national corporations was extended into the development of multinational corporations (Hymer, 1979a, p. 42). This had a substantial effect on the spatial distribution of activities. Then as Hymer (1979b, p. 157) observed:

> A regime of multinational corporations would tend to produce a hierarchical division of labour within the firm. It would tend to centralize high-level decision-making occupations in a few key cities in the advanced countries, surrounded by a number of regional sub-capitals . . .

Mercantile cities turned industrial centres thus evolved into office centres containing the major corporate headquarters and, just as importantly, the banks and other financial institutions which served the system. As Schumpeter (1934, p. 126) noted, 'the money market is always the headquarters of the capitalist system from which orders go out to its individual divisions'. Corporate organization and international financing in the period of the greatest expansions of US multinational firms led to a more complex set of spatial interconnections. As well as the hierarchy of cities, towns and regions *within* nations there developed a most important, but complicated, international hierarchy of cities, towns and regions. Further, the nature of the changes meant that the associations between centres at the upper level of the hierarchies were more significant than the movement of ideas, goods, people and capital down the hierarchy. Horizontal relationships became as vital as vertical relationships in the system and at the highest level were the associations between the largest, most important centres such as New York, Chicago, London, Frankfurt, Paris and Tokyo. In nations with a small industrial base (and these included both Third World countries and semi-peripheral nations such as Australia, Brazil and Argentina) the path to development was seen in boosting import-substitution or export-valorization industries. Here the port-capitals, the largest cities, provided the external economies and linkages which attracted the often subsidized industries. The result was the well-publicized rural-urban migrations and the subsequent overgrowth of the major cities. Agricultural areas became marginalized while in the industrializing cities the 'abnormal became the stomping ground' of 'visions of progress and development. Fantasy was piled upon fantasy' (Naipaul, 1978, p. 44). Evidence of overgrowth was related to the wealth of each nation: from the squatter settlements of the Third World to the pollution, congestion and inflation of Australian cities. In the context of this broad malaise a broad solution, growth centres, was proposed.

The spread of United States manufacturing into other countries was partly stimulated by the stages reached in the product cycle by certain key industries. Tariff protection, subsidies and tax holidays made the transition easier. Another stimulus emerged out of the trade cycle. US firms had to meet competition in foreign markets by establishing manufacturing plants abroad, and the great spirit of nationalism in the decolonized nations and the formation of regional economic blocs in other places made this imperative. In Third World countries the rapid growth of the cities did not generally mean substantial, direct employment benefits from the expansion of the modern sector. In Kenya, for example, the increase in jobs in the modern sector between 1964, when the *Foreign Investment Protection Act* was introduced, and 1969 was only one-sixth that of the informal sector (Leys, 1975, p. 35). The economies of the Third World nations also failed to receive all the expected benefits of industrialization. Again using Kenya as the example, net private direct foreign investment between 1964 and 1969 was only £27 million whereas losses through expatriation of profits, transfer pricing, over-invoicing, and the sending out of money by Asian businessmen reached £103 million (Leys, 1975, p. 40).

A third factor explaining the spread of multinational manufacturing, which complements product and trade cycle effects and political considerations, has been the comparative advantages of different nations and different regions in terms of the cost of labour. In the UK, for example, during the 1960s and 1970s regional differences in levels of unemployment and the importance of manufacturing tended to decline, and Massey (1979b, p. 241) argued that these changes resulted from the changed relationship of the UK to the world economy. The separation and hierarchical arrangement of technical, control and management functions in manufacturing already discussed, and the effects of competition pushed the mass production and assembly stages of the process into areas where semi-skilled workers would accept low wages and had little history of industrial organization or militancy. Foreign firms in the UK have been largely instrumental in setting up such operations, a fact well demonstrated by the rise of foreign ownership of manufacturing in Scotland.

Export Platforms and Resource Development

The same kinds of factors lay behind the setting-up of free trade zones or export platforms in such countries as Taiwan, South Korea and Malaysia (see chapter by Salita and Juanico in this volume). The majority of firms in the free trade zones were foreign owned in the 1970s and it was their impetus that then caused the problems in Australian manufacturing.

Another element which emerged through the latter part of the 1960s and increased in importance in the 1970s was the development of resource-related projects. These ranged from the petrochemical plants in Saudi Arabia and Singapore through to power, coal and aluminium projects in Indonesia, Brazil and Australia. Not unrelated to such development was a tendency for multinational manufacturers to divide processing on a global scale according to the comparative advantage of places and the willingness of governments and workers to cooperate. Thus while multinational manufacturing in the 1950s and 1960s tended to produce repetitions of complete or partly integrated plants within nations or regional blocs, the emerging system of the 1970s restricted activities in one place to a narrow range, the world car being a perfect example of this.

Other significant changes occurred in the 1970s. The momentum of growth of the US multinational manufacturing corporations declined substantially. Ten per cent of all their overseas subsidiaries were sold off between 1971 and 1975; by the latter date only 1.4 new investments were being made for each disinvestment compared to 3.3 in 1971 (Rose, 1977, p. 112). Competition was much greater. The number of multinationals competing in the same manufacturing industry in 3 or more overseas markets increased 4-fold between 1950 and 1970, and 7-fold in some industries. Firms producing prosaic goods found themselves in particular trouble while the major growth sectors were in the technologically more advanced industries. Australian manufacturing was particularly hard hit by the competition offered by the developing nations as a result of the international division of labour. By the mid-1970s the largest cities were experiencing a drastic decline in their industrial bases, and were struggling to maintain their own growth rates let alone disperse part of that base to new growth centres.

The changes in the 1970s affected spatial distributions in both advanced and developing nations. In the United States the proportion of the nation's manufacturing located in the north and northeast had fallen to 56.3 per cent by 1969 and those areas lost 1.7 million manufacturing jobs between 1963 and 1976. In contrast the southern and western peripheral states gained 1.6 million jobs. It was not a simple transfer, however. The growth of the Sunbelt cities owed much to the stimulus which the government gave the military-industrial complex to develop electronics, calculators, semi-conductors, aeronautics, scientific instruments and other similar activities in the south.

The great cities of the north thus became less reliant on local manufacturing whilst their role as the focus of corporate headquarters and financial institutions was enhanced. As well many of the manufacturing enterprises which had spread around the world had a large share of their profits generated from abroad. By the mid-1970s, 41 per cent of the total foreign sales of 'Fortune 500' firms were generated by firms headquartered in New York and 39 per cent of the total sales of New York-based 'Fortune 500' firms were foreign sales (Cohen, 1977, p. 217). Places like New York and Chicago became important multinational corporate headquarters.

Another significant change which began in the 1960s and continued through the 1970s was the challenge thrown out by the spread of Japanese firms. In terms of direct investments funded through capital outflows between 1967 and 1974 Japan recorded an average annual growth rate of 31 per cent, peaking at over 50 per cent in 1972 and 1973; during the same period West Germany's rate was 26 per cent and the United States' 10 per cent (Ozawa, 1979b, p. 3). Overseas production became an integral part of Japan's economic growth strategy and foreign economic diplomacy. Japanese factories were set up abroad because of the declining competitive position of small manufacturers following rising labour costs; 70 per cent of the Japanese labour force in manufacturing work in factories employing fewer than 300 people and having an investment of less than ¥100 million ($US330,000). Because many factories were located in provincial areas the Japanese government, in conjunction with the great trading houses, found it politically expedient to assist the firms to set up in cheap labour areas especially in Asia. Other internal factors, such as the cost of pollution and ecological destruction, and external factors, such as the reaction to the growth of Japanese exports and the strength of the yen, contributed to the moves into other countries. Japan's interest in the resource-rich nations reflected its concern about the lack of indigenous resources; projects such as the $US693 million power and aluminium plant in the Amazon Basin in Brazil and Japanese involvement in aluminium plants in Australia demonstrate this. Japanese-headquartered multinational manufacturing has brought about important changes in the spatial distribution of some activities. There has been a tendency towards some decentralization related to the establishment of free trade zones and the exploitation of natural resources. The attempt of the Australian government to entice Japanese car manufacturers into establishing plants in one of the new growth centres was ill-timed in relation to the stage of growth of the Australian car industry (which lacked sufficient economies of scale to support new manufacturers) and in terms of the character of Japanese expansion abroad. At the same time Japanese demand and more recently Japanese direct investment have been responsible to an important degree for the development of the 'natural' growth centres in Australia.

The suggestions of 'polarization reversal' are closely related to the important changes in multinational development in the late 1960s and the 1970s. Tendencies towards more balanced regional development have been noted in places as different as the United Kingdom, and Taiwan and South Korea, and Colombia and Brazil. In each case they are explicable in terms of the factors already mentioned—the movement into cheaper labour areas associated with transferable technology and the de-skilling of the workforce, and the heightened awareness of the finite nature of some resources. Yet such tendencies have been countered by other factors. By the late 1960s cities as varied as Bogota, Nairobi, Bombay, Caracas and Djakarta gained half their growth from natural increase, and the percentage continued to rise through the 1970s. Such places have become self-sustaining in their growth and will continue to have a dominant effect on their national space-economies.

There is a new era of large-scale developments. The great power of the multinationals and the attendant oligopolistic nature of supply have created a need for huge volumes of resources whose development often necessitates enormous capital outlays both directly and for infrastructure. Thus there have been created 'natural' growth centres. In contrast, the increasing levels of vertical integration and the dominance of the major multinational producers will lead to a dispersal of particular aspects of manufacturing around the world. The complete and integrating factory complexes of the 1950s and 1960s, primarily concentrated in the major cities, will be replaced by a global sharing of manufacturing in the largest and in the most rapidly growing industries. This destroys much of the point of the 1960s spatial translations of Perroux's growth pole ideas.

The International Banks

Related to all these developments has been a dramatic restructuring of the banking sector of the international financial community. By 1980 there was reportedly $US3,000,000 million held by banks off-shore in Euro-dollar, Asia-dollar and other markets. Even before the massive input of petro-dollars the Euro-dollar market had grown at the compound annual rate of 31 per cent between 1969 and 1974, and by the latter date the total market held funds of about $US380,000 million. Branches of US banks abroad increased from 124 to 723 between 1960 and 1973. The 13 largest US multinational banks increased their international earnings from $US177 million to $US836 million between 1970 and 1975, at which date half the income of these banks came from overseas activities, and this earning rate had been growing annually at 36 per cent.

To some extent the expansion of the multinational banks was related to the growth of multinational industry and had the effect of reinforcing the hierarchical patterns created by the manufacturers. By the 1970s the diverse business of the banks, their worldwide modes of operation, and their freedom from government control had created a new set of relationships between cities. The international nature of this meant that some cities began to function somewhat independently of their national economies: for example London, which in 1976 had 449 banking establishments and dominated the world financial centres (Davis, 1976, p. 28). By 1979 the City of London employed 500,000 people and was earning almost $US3000 million in invisible exports from insurance, banking, commodity trading and shipping—a performance contrasting starkly with the wretched condition of the British economy in general. The relaxation of US foreign exchange regulations in the early 1970s led to the reassertion of New York as an international finance centre with the number of foreign banks growing by 136 per cent between 1972 and 1979, and their assets by 371 per cent to reach $US80,000 million. London, which in the early 1970s accounted for 40 per cent of the worldwide Eurocurrency business, had only 32 per cent of it by 1980. Further changes are forecast for the 1980s because of the United States Federal Reserve's approval for International Banking Facilities (operations free from domestic reserve requirements and interest rate controls) in New York. Regional centres such as Singapore, where the Asia-dollar market was set up through collaboration of the government with the Bank of America in 1968, service major regions of the world. At a lower level come national or sub-regional centres such as Sydney in Australia. Accompanying Sydney's rise to prominence in the international financial system there has been a boisterous rebuilding of the central business district and a transformation of its pattern of land uses which left financial and allied services as the principal consumers of office space. The very nature of the new international financial system required centres to be finely atuned to the nuances of interest differentials and flows of capital; nearness to competitors and linkages with other parts of the world gave banks the speed and flexibility of decision-making which were their major competitive strategies. Australia could have only one centre intimately linked into the world system and this was Sydney. Thus, the Australian government was attempting in the early 1970s to counter Sydney's expansion by the creation of growth centres just at a time when that city was developing a new role and stature in the international community. The development of the financial role was just one of those innovatory leaps which Perroux had seen to lie at the heart of major phases of growth. Curiously the misunderstood and stunted spatial version of Perroux's ideas formed the backbone of Australia's most ambitious programme of settlement reform just as the international forces were transforming Sydney's role.

These alterations to international financing have had other important effects. For example, by the 1980s many of the large corporations with US headquarters had begun to shift to foreign branches of US banks for their financing to reduce borrowing costs. In the first quarter of 1981 business borrowings from US domestic banks declined by $US5500 million while loans by foreign branches of US banks to local residents rose by $US2700 million. The Euro-dollar rate is established by the London Interbank Offered Rate (LIBOR) and most companies pay between half and one percentage point above this. In December 1980 and January 1981 the prime rate of the United States varied between 20 and 21.5 per cent whilst LIBOR was around 17 per cent.

While the major banks operating with Euro-dollar and Asia-dollar markets have become significant to firms throughout the Western industrialized world, they have become critical to developing nations. Faced by sluggish economic conditions in the industrialized nations in the second half of the 1970s, by the slow-down in the rate of expansion of the multinationals, and by the collapse of such favourite loan areas of the 1970s era as real estate, the banks looked to the Third World for investment. The banks provided only 20 per cent of the financing needs of the Third World during the 1971–73 period but 42 per cent during 1974–76: meanwhile the current account deficits of non-oil producing non-industrialized nations had multiplied 3-fold.

The movement into the Third World has posed many problems for the banks. The volume of funds to be invested has, at times, sent rates down to a level many consider dangerous. In 1975 major loans were made to Brazil at 1.75 points above LIBOR and to Guyana at 2.5 points above. In 1977 more than half the loans were at 1.5 or less points above LIBOR and one loan to finance a Malaysian electric power plant was less than 1 point above LIBOR.

The suspicions about the Third World loans became magnified by such events as the nationalization of all foreign banks in Nigeria in 1977 and by the crisis surrounding the $US6500 million loan to the Indonesian oil producer, Pertamina. The failure of many Third World nations to improve their economic performance casts doubts on their abilities to service their bank loans, and even the best performing nations are now very critically assessed by the bankers. South Korea (one nation to be spurred by the spread of Japanese-headquartered multinationals) had a growth rate of over 15 per cent in real terms each year during the 1970s (except 1974 and 1975) whereas Japan did not top 10 per cent during this period. By 1977 South Korea ranked seventeenth among the exporting nations of the world (Yamamura, 1979, p. 81). Yet when loans of $US500 million and $US200 million with 2 of Korea's largest organizations, Korean Air Lines and Honam Oil Refinery, were renegotiated in 1981, funds were frozen for a time. Banks have required covenants related to cash flows, the ratio of current assets to liabilities, and the ratio of debt to equity. Many companies, even with government guarantees, have had trouble in keeping up repayments on loans.

At every level, therefore, the commercial banks have had difficulty in assessing the soundness of loans to Third World governments and organizations. Banks have formed syndicates to provide some of the largest loans but while this has spread the risk it has not solved the basic problem. The future will mean ever stricter criteria governing loans: taken in conjunction with the trend towards large-scale, resource-orientated developments and the changing pattern of multinational developments the prospects for the poorer, stagnating or resource-depleted regions are grim. In the light of such changes the remedies so favoured in the 1960s, including the growth centre strategies, seem strangely out of place. In fortunate nations, such as Australia, the growth centres promulgated by the government will be replaced by others stimulated by resource developments. But for many other places there can be no such substitution, and regional development planners are faced with challenges greater than ever before.

Spatial Analysis, Industry and the Industrial Environment. Vol. 3 Regional Economies and Industrial Systems
Edited by F. E. I. Hamilton and G. J. R. Linge
© 1983 John Wiley & Sons Ltd.

Chapter 18

Industrial Parks as Locational Environments: A Research Challenge

BRENTON M. BARR

Industrial parks have become such an important component of the locational milieu of the Western industrialized world, especially since the Second World War (Bale, 1974b; Conway Publications Inc., 1977, p. 344; Stafford, 1979, p. 95), that their general absence from the geographical literature is remarkable. As a discipline priding itself in spatial analyses and possessing a rich heritage of investigation of location factors, geographers seem to have treated industrial parks as if they were a neutral force in that economic space within which a host of locational attributes exert their influence. Bale (1972, p. 12) has noted, however, that industrial parks are 'independent of the firms eventually to locate' in them and consequently play

> a vital role in the location decision of the firms. Indeed, it is tempting to suggest that existing studies on the location decision have been perhaps over occupied with analysing the point of view of the firm and paying insufficient attention to the role of the site-providing agency, which to some extent could be said to choose the firm's location for it.

In North America, for example, the number of industrial parks under development has increased from about 800 in 1957, 2000 in 1967, to between 4000 and 4500 in 1978 (when adjusted for incomplete survey returns) (Conway *et al.*, 1979, p. 14). About two-thirds of all new industrial facilities are reported to locate in industrial parks (Conway Publications Inc., 1977, p. 345). Although these figures do not reveal the total number of such parks in operation (as distinct from those being developed), and although comparable estimates are not available for all countries (earlier data are in Bredo, 1960), the relative importance of the industrial park in North America, the United Kingdom, and in developing countries (United Nations Industrial Development Organization, 1978) must not be excluded from future research.

Many non-geographical practitioners of the locational art, including land developers, real estate agents and community planners, have contributed to a literature replete with examples and evaluations which portray industrial parks as positive and purposeful locational environments. The insights contained in these discursive and expository analyses are too important for the future development of industrial systems and spatial analyses not to be scrutinized by geographers. The modest research findings about industrial parks also must be firmly incorporated into the mainstream conceptual development of industrial geography and be integrated into the diverse and fertile heritage of numerous other locational disciplines such as regional development and planning, regional science, and economics, environmental design and relevant fields of urban study. The methodological rigour, theoretical base, and conceptual coherence of industrial geography can probably enrich the literature on industrial parks and ensure that the trends observed in the evolution of these environments are organized to achieve taxonomic coherence and analytical insight.

This chapter considers whether industrial parks are still viable components of the industrial structure, whether they are being modified into innovative forms that are useful to developers and firms alike, and whether they are likely to comprise even more significant locational environments in the future.

THE STUDY OF INDUSTRIAL PARKS

Conceptual Disparity and Taxonomic Diversity

The literature on industrial parks contains much semantic confusion about their functions and the role of companies in their development and management. Such parks, notwithstanding diverse definitions, can contain numerous secondary, tertiary, quaternary (information manipulation and managerial control) and quinary (forecasting, orientation and long-range planning) economic functions. As industrial entities they need not be directly associated with changing the form of materials but often engage in facilitating the production or consumption of goods, or in conducting some function recognized as having utility to the local, regional, national or international economy. 'Industrial Park' is a generic term (outside North America the term 'Industrial Estate' is preferred) for a form of spatial concentration of economic activity. Many discussions on their role are biased towards advantaging at least one of 4 groups:

(a) the industrial land developer and merchandiser;
(b) the firm;
(c) the industrial park and its owners;
(d) members of local communities or governments concerned in some way with the associated benefits and/or costs.

Failure to distinguish between these groups frequently leads to confusion in analyses of industrial parks because they perform different roles for the members of each group.

Here, industrial parks are viewed as a type of land use with a diverse range of economic activity and specific economic, social or political objectives. They can probably best be conceptualized as a commercial form which is just as important to secondary, non-retail tertiary, quaternary or quinary industry as the shopping centre is to retailing and professional and personal services. Both occur in a range of sizes, serve a system of markets of different sizes, are a dominant function of urban space and urban expansion, and have become the spatial focus of economic activity created in many developed economies since the Second World War. The similarities in roles played in the urban environment by industrial parks and shopping centres appear to have gone unnoticed although Fisher (1966, p. 3) inappropriately described industrial parks as 'the industrial twin of the residential subdivision' which clearly they are not. Fisher did note, however, that today they are 'the best solution for most industries in search of an ideal industrial environment', an observation reminiscent of the need for tertiary services to locate in shopping centres.

Developed economic environments which escape total inclusion in either of these forms are the Central Business District, Central Manufacturing District, and sites dominated by the production facilities of a single large firm. Nevertheless, industrial parks with office functions are found in traditional business areas, and large firms may dominate industrial parks. In many regions of western North America, for example, development of new industrial facilities outside industrial parks is as rare as the establishment of retail services away from shopping centres or their immediate environs. The analogy between industrial parks and shopping centres appears especially apt where industrial parks having new commercial forms are locating near shopping centres to offer facilities requiring large amounts of floor space per dollar of sales and drawing on the higher density of patronage in the retail area. In other cases, new forms of the industrial park located on the urban periphery are becoming physically integrated with shopping centres (such as Marlborough Town Square and Franklin Industrial Park in Calgary) both to attract customers and to ensure adequate tertiary services for employees who would otherwise be reluctant to leave established commercial districts. Shopping centres have been given the lead in combining tertiary services and housing but industrial parks are about to follow suit by creating innovative aesthetic environments that will allow people to live near their work-places. Many industrial parks in Calgary, for example, now contain hotels with itinerant and special-purpose recreational, entertainment and business-service facilities. Diversification will 'carry the industrial park concept forward from its current emphasis on distribution to becoming more or less a self-contained community' (Society of Industrial Realtors of the National Association of Real Estate Boards, n.d., p. 7).

Concern about the definition and classification of industrial parks in business and academic literature should be no less important than that shown for shopping centres in the published work on retailing and central places. The analogy between industrial parks and shopping centres, however, does not always apply: for example, large industrial plants often locate away from other firms; large retail establishments, however, prefer locations in proximity to other firms.

Definitions

Increasing awareness by industrial developers and commercial firms of the benefits accruing through industrial compatibility, comprehensive infrastructure, and nourishing physical and psychological environments has led recently to the development of industrial parks that attempt to meet broad design and operational criteria. Definitions of industrial parks by geographers are keeping abreast of this more sophisticated approach. Hence, Matthews (1979, p. 31) has modified Bale's (1974a) earlier definition of industrial parks by stating that they are

> groupings of compatible industrial establishments provided with green spaces, and certain common services and utilities, laid down in advance of demand and established as a result of enterprise and planning by an independent organization.

Bale (1972) had rejected many existing definitions of industrial parks (estates) and had discussed the taxonomic gymnastics often pursued in earlier writers' attempts to produce a single definition covering the numerous subspecies of this phenomenon.

The definition of the industrial park used here stems directly from Matthews and Bale but emphasizes that the park of the 1980s can embrace varying amounts of secondary, retail and non-retail tertiary, quaternary and quinary industry; that external green spaces may be buffers between public roads and private facilities, be integrated with parking structures, or be internalized as arboreta or recreational space; and that multi-level structures are becoming more numerous as rising land costs limit the extent of development. Attempts to redefine industrial parks to incorporate each new activity have little merit because the essential components of the developed space remain the same. The key issue for geographers appears to be the changes in functions performed by firms in industrial parks, and hence in the expanding comprehensive utility of parks to the local, metropolitan/regional, national and international urban/economic milieux. If parks are accepted as possibly comprising economic activities not normally called 'industrial', then entities like office parks, research parks, university parks and airparks belong to a broadening continuum embracing the concepts already defined and freeing the researcher to focus on important variables, problems and issues related, for example, to industrialization, economic development and community planning. The changing appearance of the industrial park pales in significance compared to the host of operational, functional and organizational characteristics undergoing constant metamorphosis within them.

Operational characteristics figure prominently in the practical definitions of industrial parks which have evolved in the considerations of those associated with their development, management and utilization (reviewed in Urban Land Institute, 1975, pp. 3–8). Regardless of the particular function of the park envisaged, developers and tenants share a common concern for physical and operational standards comprising some degree of comprehensive planning, zoning, control, development strategy, design, architectural harmony, management, supervision, compatibility, protection of investment, effective community relations, avoidance of internal and external land-use conflicts, and the prospect of profitability (Baldwin, 1958, pp. 1–2; Urban Land Institute, 1975, pp. 3–8). Thus, 'whatever the name, the presumption is that the *industrial park* is a project which has been planned and developed as an optimal environment for industrial occupants' (Urban Land Institute, 1975, p. 3).

The American National Association of Industrial Parks (NAIP), while adopting definitions of industrial parks proposed by special-purpose organizations such as the American National Industrial Zoning Committee (the commercial need for definition and the problems faced by this Committee are described by Redman, 1967, pp. 22–4) and the Dartmouth Conference on Industrial Parks (Baldwin, 1958), has greatly facilitated the general definition of industrial parks by focusing on physical and operational standards and on behavioural criteria:

> An industrial park is the assembly of land, under one continuing control, to provide facilities for business and industry consistent with a master plan and restrictions, resulting in the creation of a physical environment achieving the following objectives: (1) consistency with community goals, (2) efficient business and industrial operations, (3) human scale and values, (4) compatibility with natural environments, (5) achieving and sustaining highest land values (Urban Land Institute, 1975, p. 7).

This comprehensive definition appears to supersede previous individual attempts, many of which have drawn on that derived at the Dartmouth Conference (Bredo, 1960; Boley, 1962; Malinowski and Kinnard, 1963; Griefen, 1970; Evans, 1972b; Hartshorn, 1973). The NAIP definition, in association with those of Matthews and Bale, facilitates transnational analysis of industrial parks and ensures that new forms of park can be accommodated without unnecessary semantic delay.

Industrial parks are, however, different from

(a) industrial 'quarters'—areas developed as a result of linkage in an unplanned environment, using utilities and sometimes buildings originally intended for other activities;

(b) industrial complexes—industrial development centred around one major industry;

(c) industrial areas/industrial districts—sites improved as an inducement to the establishment of industry of all types and sizes;

(d) industrial zones—unimproved or partially developed areas reserved for industrial use.

(These are discussed extensively in Anonymous, 1967, pp. 57–76; Bale, 1974a, pp. 31–3.) Although industrial park and industrial estate are basically synonymous, the former term is adopted here, in keeping with North American usage, to reflect the extensive areas of parking, external storage and green space relative to the land occupied by buildings (see Fogarty, 1959, p. 195; Bale, 1974a, p. 31; Pollina, 1975, p. 41), and to accommodate many of the new forms of 'park' increasingly associated with research, office management, and mixed industrial/commercial and retail services.

Sources

Although many fragmentary references to industrial parks appear in studies of other locational phenomena, most material about them has been published in academic, professional and trade sources. No study of industrial parks *per se* can be complete without reference to this literature: geographers concentrate on particular aspects, such as agglomeration economies and industrial incentives.

References to industrial parks are the subject of 4 special listings in the series produced by the Council of Planning Librarians (Vance, 1961; Karl, 1968; Bale, 1976; Starbuck, 1976); several specialist-applied catalogues (Karl, 1968, p. 3); entries in basic geographical bibliographies (Stevens and Brackett, 1967; Miller and Miller, 1978; Fisher *et al.*, 1979); parts of compilations for professional use (Boykin, 1969); and sections of Ahn's (1974) functionally organized bibliography. Although some are annotated, none classifies studies of industrial parks according to research method, source of information, extent of analysis and degree of universality. The need for critical evaluation remains despite important contributions and analyses by Bale (1972), Pollina (1974) and Matthews (1979). These demonstrate that the single greatest defect of existing studies is probably the lack of connection between the park as a taxonomic construct and as an integral part of spatial analysis.

Recently, professional and trade personnel have issued practitioners' guides to facilitate the development of industrial parks. The basic reference (Bredo, 1960) has been described by Bale (1976, p. 6) as 'the definitive overview on the subject'. Bredo's study, although dated, is a yardstick against which subsequent specific investigations can be measured because he reviewed the history, economic characteristics, sponsorship and organization, planning, location, layout, development, building types, facilities, services and financial management of industrial parks throughout the world. Many of the basic professional investigations since Bredo's study have elaborated how industrial parks can meet the locational needs of the firm, and how they can serve the multiple objectives of local and regional planning (Bredo, 1970).

The comprehensive literature of the last 2 decades demonstrates clearly that industrial parks themselves involve risk and must be planned, designed and managed as carefully as the individual firms comprising them. Professional organizations in the US and Canada have published extensive guides and site selection check-lists elaborating principles and practices to be followed in their creation and management (Boley, 1961, 1962, 1967; Urban Land Institute, 1975; Society of Industrial Realtors of the National Association of Realtors and the National Association of Industrial and Office Parks, 1979; Conway et al., 1979). Developers appear to know how to design and locate industrial parks (Society of Industrial Realtors of the National Association of Real Estate Boards, n.d.; Griefen, 1970), but the economic and industrial problems of the 1970s have now led them to focus on detailed analyses of financing, marketing, management, environment, energy, technological change, and inter-regional changes in the location of industry (Urban Land Institute, 1975).

Industrial parks, however, comprise only one—albeit a major one—of the locational environments of the developer and of the firm (see Kinnard and Messner, 1971, Chapters 15 and 16). As locations they must be placed clearly within the range of spatial alternatives available to the developer and the firm; they represent a particular kind of pre-planned, but semi-manufactured, locational environment with a real cost which is likely to be more expensive than raw sites (unless developed sites are subsidized or development on green-field sites is legally prohibited) because of the developer's need for a return on his investment and because of the costs he must incur between initial development and the sale or lease of the various portions. Where industrial sites are readily available outside industrial parks (which is not the case in Calgary), a firm may seek an alternative location to reduce land costs, maintain corporate identity, avoid undue operational and land-use regulation usually found in the parks, ensure greater flexibility in product mix and site expansion (Barrows and Bookbinder, 1975, p. 38), and participate in land development and speculation of its own by initially purchasing a site larger than its needs and causing the land to appreciate in value by its own presence (Evans, 1972a, p. 18). In the US annual growth in the number of industrial parks in the 1970s exceeded 14 per cent and this led

Barrows and Bookbinder (1975, p. 38) to remark that 'for many manufacturers, the advantages of selecting a site in an Industrial Park outweigh the disadvantages'.

Industrial parks are especially important when there is a need to reduce environmental conflicts or to locate near residential areas. As community groups become more vociferous, some industrial activities are having their locational choices circumscribed. Nevertheless,

> it appears that light, secondary manufacturing industry has the greatest flexibility in location, and will be least affected by these changing attitudes towards industry and development. Heavy industries appear to be faced with mounting difficulty in finding suitable areas for plant location. Site-selection managers in these industries should seriously consider locating in Industrial Parks which are zoned for heavy industry; locating in these Parks may help to eliminate environmental friction between industry and the community (Barrows and Bookbinder, 1975, p. 40).

Some communities arbitrate between potentially conflicting land users by providing industrial parks with different zoning characteristics (see Matthews, 1979), and by maintaining development areas for those firms which, on occasion, cannot be accommodated in any kind of park.

That such parks are only one of the locational choices available to the firm is often missed or conveniently overlooked by those who seem to assume that they are beneficial locations, that they generate externalities, and that they themselves are infallible. The private sector in developed economies like the US is clearly aware of the limitations, both economic and social, in the locational effectiveness of industrial parks; planning agencies, however, appear to have accepted the industrial park as a development tool without critical scrutiny (see United Nations Industrial Development Organization, 1968). Inclusion of such parks in discussions of world industrial growth is, however, so common (see examples for the 1960s in United Nations Industrial Development Organization, 1968, pp. 179–80) that the relevance of the term to the concepts, goals and successes of industrialization probably should become the focus of periodic re-evaluations in national and international development programmes.

Significance

Information sources about industrial parks contain a plethora of definitional, conceptual and empirical studies representing the interest shown in them by the academic, professional, trade and planning communities. But this diverse literature contains many equivocal concepts and statements which suggest that much rigorous investigation is required before the locational significance of industrial parks can be established. With notable exceptions, the existing professional and trade literature on the industrial park is exploratory, tentative, promotional, limited in scope, and often self-fulfilling. Moreover the problems and issues raised require cataloguing and codifying if they are to serve as precedents in specific future studies. Yet the legitimate diversity in the purpose and role of the industrial park suggests that this phenomenon cannot meet any single rigid criterion but must be examined for the support it offers to many notions, concepts and models (Matthews, 1979; Barr and Matthews, 1980) of interest to the systematic investigator.

CHANGING FORM AND FUNCTION OF THE INDUSTRIAL PARK

The industrial park is effectively a twentieth century phenomenon facilitated by the development of the motor vehicle and the widespread social reaction to the crowded mixed residential/industrial districts or quarters which preceded it in association with ports, waterways and railways. Such paths have radically transformed many districts of the urban and periurban environment and have accompanied residential suburbanization. In various guises they have followed the changing forms and functions of road transport although many still retain connections with rail and water transport and more recently have developed forms and functions suited to air services. As the transport revolution of the past century has dramatically altered accessibility, the industrial park has emerged as the locationally fixed counterpart to the increased flexibility of spatial movement. Industrial park development has also been facilitated by the electronic transfer of information, with the technological revolutions enabling the growth of light manufacturing, services and other non-manufacturing functions, and rising affluence.

If the friction of distance increases because of rising fossil fuel costs and reduced use of road transport the locational flexibility of the industrial park will probably change to accommodate new priorities; such parks will become more important antidotes to industrial obsolescence and many new ones will perform a renovative or infill function in decaying urban core or peripheral areas. Furthermore, as the technological and administrative sectors gain in importance, industrial parks related to activities like research and consulting will become more noticeable, especially in or near the multiple foci of the modern city, and they may contain more multi-storey rather than single-storey buildings. Whether urban environments retain their extensive present suburban and exurban forms, or whether they eventually become more compact with multiple centres, the industrial park with its many physical and operational standards will undoubtedly remain the basic means by which developers and planners try to ensure profitability of investment and realization of acceptable working and social environments.

Origins

Development of the world's first planned industrial park—or estate—commenced in 1896 in Manchester, orientated to navigable deep water; Trafford Park Estates Ltd remained the largest park of its kind in the world until after the Second World War when the concept gained acceptance in North America (Urban Land Institute, 1975, p. 10). The first parks in the US appeared in Chicago (the Original East District, the Pershing Road District, and the Clearing Industrial District) between 1902 and 1910 to facilitate the rail transport needs of manufacturers (Urban Land Institute, 1975, pp. 11–12), the capital being provided by railway interests and private real estate developers—sources of finance with goals inextricably concerned with the promotion of many similar developments throughout North America.

The 2 world wars left surplus military buildings in the UK and North America, many of which also had extensive all-weather surfaces for external commodity storage. In 1920, the Slough Trading Estate (west of London) became the first industrial district to occupy a former military complex (Urban Land Institute, 1975, pp. 13–14). The use of such facilities as replacement sites by industry became particularly important after the Second World War, particularly where the buildings and adjacent support areas were originally developed to service and store aircraft (McEwen and Barr, 1975, 1977). Redundant military infrastructure provided relatively inexpensive space and facilities for factories as well as an important seed-bed for communities otherwise devoid of industry and too peripheral to major urban centres to generate manufacturing employment.

The emergence of the industrial park as a major feature of the economic landscape accompanied the recovery of the UK and North America after the worldwide depression of the 1930s and the military priorities of the Second World War. The redevelopment of obsolete or damaged industrial areas in the UK along with suburbanization; conversion of intra-regional transport systems from rail to road; changing priorities in inter-regional transport (following the increasing quantities of manufactured goods moving on inter-state (US) or inter-provincial (Canada) highways and national motorways (UK), and the relative decline in industrial raw materials shifted by rail); the changing forms of industrial activity which eschewed multi-storied factories in crowded urban communities; and the advent of land-use zoning all assisted the industrial park to gain prominence during the 1950s. The growth of parks as a location for industrial activity 'was both encouraged and constrained by the parallel evolution of land use controls' (Urban Land Institute, 1975, p. 15). Growing social or community control over land uses also resulted in the widespread prohibition of residential development in industrial areas. Most commercial uses, too, were initially prohibited although more sophisticated land-use zoning later provided for judicious mixtures of commercial and industrial activities, especially in communities where heavy industry is uncommon, or in industrial parks where firms now accept that segregation of land uses is no longer in their best interest. As a result, residential, commercial and industrial activities have become segregated because of the growth of the industrial park as a major locational environment.

An important trend during the 1970s was the growing integration of commercial functions with the industrial ones traditionally found in these parks (Urban Land Institute, 1975, p. 206). A greater variety of activities is locating in parks which themselves are serving many more functions for the surrounding community. Without sacrificing parks' traditional basic role as industrial and business environments, new ones seek to create a diversified environment comprising offices, commercial convenience establishments, professional and business services, public and municipal services (such as police, fire fighting, health clinics and motor-vehicle licensing), food services, transient lodging, and recreational services (Urban Land Institute, 1975, p. 207).

One of the most important changes in the form and function of the industrial park during the 1980s and 1990s will be the emergence of hybrid entities (Urban Land Institute, 1975, p. 203) which judiciously combine commercial (including retail) and residential functions. Behind such new forms of industrial park are:

(a) the developer's need to reduce the burden of rising land and service costs of industrial development;
(b) the community's desire to reduce the rising friction of distance associated with the journey to work;
(c) society's growing ability to create and regulate industrial activities in the post-industrial age which are compatible with the noise and health standards protecting residential environments.

Some groups oppose the integration of industrial parks with residential and commercial land uses, or diversification from functionally compatible activities. They envisage:

(a) the ability of diverse industrial parks to accommodate functional and technological change;
(b) an overriding of the basic principles of planning security through zoning by non-industrial social and non-business considerations;
(c) vandalism during non-business hours arising from the proximity of loosely guarded industrial parks to adjacent residential communities (Urban Land Institute, 1975, pp. 211–12).

The increased prominence of industrial parks as industrial environments in the 1970s has also included the creation of very specialized and interrelated industrial parks with a narrow range of industrial and commercial functions emphasizing many economic advantages in clustering, concentration, proximity and flexible all-purpose buildings. Such areas are chiefly associated with warehousing, distribution, technology, research, combined wholesaling/retailing, food processing, and a variety of commercial and personal services located in offices. Others are emerging with forms and facilities related to specific purposes, including the 'Decoplex' (development-ecological complex) combining basic elements related to waste treatment, resource recovery, energy consumption and industrial processing (see diagrams in Conway et al., 1979, pp. A139–42) and the 'Pipe Park' attracting interrelated chemical processors using each other's products (see diagram in Conway et al., 1979, p. 67). Both are manifestations of the growing need to recover valuable waste materials and by-products, and the importance of advanced-technology chemical processing which accompanies manufacturing in developed economies.

The growth of corporate aircraft and all-freight airlines and the importance of speed in the distribution of high-value industrial commodities, have prompted 'Airport' and 'Fly-in' parks having special facilities located on airport land with access to taxiways (Conway et al., 1979, p. 61). These usually develop at an existing facility, often a former military airfield (see McEwen and Barr, 1975, 1977) but often land beside former air force establishments has become too valuable to leave in runways, or has been sub-divided for roads and non-industrial uses. Where buildings on such sites now comprise an industrial park, the architectural style is an indelible reminder of the area's original function.

INDUSTRIAL PARKS AND LOCATIONAL ENVIRONMENTS

Few studies have rigorously attempted to analyse the locational characteristics of industrial parks: investigators have not been able to establish whether such areas fulfil locational and spatial requirements that differ from other sites or districts. The suspicion is aroused and persists that industrial parks, while having community attributes that differ from other sites and particular design and architectural characteristics, may be indistinguishable from many other locational environments. The existing geographical literature, though small, is commendable, unlike much of the trade literature which contains glib generalizations that create more confusion than understanding. Bale (1972), Pollina (1974) and Matthews (1979) demonstrate that an effective understanding of the locational significance of industrial parks cannot be achieved without rigorous conceptual and theoretical analysis, that care must be exercised in choosing variables to measure attributes, and

that existing statistical techniques and mathematical models may be inadequate for the task or unable to overcome inherent data limitations. Yet as
Gottlieb (1972, pp. 600–1) has appropriately noted, purely statistical and
technological aspects of industrial parks and developments are now fully
understood:

> Industrial developments, however, are changing, as are shopping centres, apart-
> ment and office complexes and residential communities. The old formulas and
> check points cannot be ignored, but a *change in emphasis is imperative.* The old
> sociological cliché "a revolution of rising expectations" applies to the American
> businessman [i.e. the developer and occupant of industrial parks] as well as
> those for whom it was originally intended.

The functional diversity emerging in the types of industrial parks now
being built (discussed in Conway *et al.,* 1979, pp. 106–11) strongly suggests
that the associated locational requirements may be much greater than those
reputedly associated with early and less sophisticated developments. The
industrial park, synonymous with suburbanization of industry after the
Second World War (Evans, 1972b), is an important component of the shift
of manufacturing away from metropolitan areas generally, and in the US
particularly from the northeast and Great Lakes areas to the south and west.
Redevelopment of some inner city communities, however, has resulted in
their undergoing revitalization through specialized industrial parks, particularly in urban areas possessing skilled labour, a fully developed transport
network and developmental incentives. Many of these inter-regional trends
are too recent to evaluate fully and require extensive research before the
implications are fully understood. National relocation of manufacturing
industry such as that underway in the United States, and international shifts
in manufacturing from the developed, high-wage areas of North America,
Western Europe and Japan towards lower cost Third World environments
will be accompanied by changes in the location and functions of industrial
parks in both donor and recipient nations. The standards and functions of
such parks in developed nations are unlikely to be transferred immediately
to those in the Third World if the economic and social processes which led
to their initial creation are not demanded or supported by newly industrializing societies. Creation of 'free-trade zones' or 'export processing zones' in
developing countries, however, seems to serve as a rapid transfer of industrial park development expertise away from established industrial areas (see
the following chapter by Salita and Juanico).

Although the consequences of many locational shifts in the industrial
milieux of Western Europe and North America have still not been fully
comprehended, the influences that stimulated industrial park development
after the Second World War now seem less relevant. Forces related to the
deterioration of downtown industrial areas, limited availability of suitable

central land, growth in horizontal production-line methods, increased use of trucks, and the general antipathy by business and developers alike toward congested industrial environments—once the focus of eloquent research endeavours (Nunnally and Pollina, 1973, p. 356)—have been already accommodated in the advanced industrialized countries and are no longer novel research topics. Concern about the cost and availability of energy, environmental protection, humanization of the workspace, and numerous variables associated with cost of land and of production in addition to international competitiveness suggest that future research into the location of the industrial park will have different objectives (particularly from those pre-dating the energy crisis of 1973) and will need to incorporate issues of global concern relating to the purpose, function and even the very existence of Western industrial society.

The role of the industrial park in the industrializing world is unlikely to follow the precedents of the developed nations if social and political revolutions in the purpose of industrialization or in the unfettered investment of capital occur. Thus, in Portugal the development of industrial estates which commenced shortly before the political upheavals of 1974 has not proceeded according to initial expectations. Industrial parks were originally planned for the free market, to emphasize growth, to attract foreign investment and for channelling imported capital to peripheral regions. Since 1974, however, the role of industrial parks has been changed to facilitate a dominance of state planning, a policy of regional equalization and innovation, and permanent state investment in the economic transformation of the underdeveloped Portuguese hinterland (Von Weber, 1977, p. 135).

Although Portugal is not wholly representative of developing nations, this recent experience emphasizes that the role of industrial parks cannot normally be isolated from issues of national and regional economic development (as it has been in much of the North American literature). Furthermore the relatively untrammelled inter-regional flow of investment capital in North America whereby institutional leaders, development organizations and the corporate approach to land development provide capital for industrial parks, supported by investors' application of sophisticated tools of analysis and decision-making (discussed in Kinnard and Messner, 1971, pp. 549–50), should not be accepted uncritically as an appropriate model either of Third World spatial development or for understanding other developed nations. Various forms of state intervention in locational decision-making in most developed and developing nations alike suggest that future analyses of industrial parks will have to incorporate the role of government influence and the operation of planning policies on the form, function, and location of parks of all types.

While industrial parks are frequently viewed in the practical and professional literature as phenomena whose main purpose is to accommodate developers, firms, and community planning, some analysts see them as but one level within a land-use hierarchy (Urban Land Institute, 1975, pp. 19–22; Conway Publications Inc., 1976, p. 298). The extent to which parks form part of a functional hierarchy within industrial systems and their environments also requires further research.

The significance of the classification of planned developments in Table 18.1 lies not in its definitional rigour but in its demonstration of how the

TABLE 18.1 Locational levels of planned environments

Level	Attributes
Site	Limited size; specific and restricted land use; single firm
Complex site	Extensive size; specific and restricted land use; integrated processing; single firm with possible ancillary firm(s)
Industrial park	Comprehensive definition (see text); range of sizes; multiple firms in single or diverse land uses
	Includes: manufacturing (light, medium, heavy; specialized) commerce warehousing distribution office function research development waste management ('Decoplex') process sharing ('Pipe Park') transport orientated (water, rail, road, air) replacement (former military site; obsolete industrial site) renewal (obsolete and decayed urban sites, mining districts, etc.) planned unit development with mixed but compatible land uses; comprehensive planning
Micropolis, mini-city or micro-city	New city within a larger urban area; multiple land uses; associated with inner renewal, peripheral revitalization, metropolitan development
Satellite new town	On the periphery of established urban area; dependent on metropolitan and regional economic stimulus; likely occupational and economic-functional imbalance if viewed as separate entity
Frontier or free-standing new town	Functional, locational and economic autonomy; economic diversity, but likely sectoral imbalance; related to private and/or state resource and/or comprehensive regional development

Sources: derived and modified from Urban Land Institute, 1975, pp. 17–31; Conway Publications Inc., 1976, p. 298; Conway *et al.*, 1979, pp. 58–74.

industrial park is part of the continuum of community land-use planning which extends from initial sites to complete urban systems. Whatever its specific and increasingly varied form, the industrial park comprises a significant micro-locational environment which is inseparable from the function and performance of urban systems. It combines many specific sites and individual complexes; amalgamations of them may comprise almost the total industrial environment of new or replacement micro, meso, and macro-urban areas represented by districts or boroughs, new towns, or regional and national metropolitan areas. (These latter are not shown in Table 18.1 although the industrial environments of emerging metropolises in North America may be largely comprised of industrial parks—see Matthews, 1979.) If industrial location in developed and developing countries is virtually synonymous with some form of comprehensive state planning or state economic intervention, and if the industrial park is now recognized as the key form of planned locational environment, such parks should be a key element in future analyses by industrial geographers.

PARKS AND PRIORITIES

In his review of research priorities for industrial location analysts, Wood (1978, p. 5) noted that much of the existing research has focused on data collection and analysis of industrial structure and change in particular areas, but that the trend in research is

> towards the testing of hypotheses derived from models of *corporate behaviour in various regional and local environments.* The realities of the modern organization of industry, commonly into multi-plant firms, have encouraged this trend, together with the evident inability of "classical" location theory to provide positive guidance in an era when location has become a major consideration in many aspects of official planning.

Although based on British work, Wood's estimation of research priorities clearly transcends the national economic and regional planning needs of the UK. He recommends judicious balance of macro and micro-studies of changes in firms, overcoming the problems of inadequate and confidential data bases; longitudinal studies of regional and sub-regional variation in industrial activity and of industrial regeneration and corporate change; investigations into the significance of changing information flows; deeper analyses of decision-making by multi-plant firms; analyses of the importance of local conditions to small and medium-size firms; and renewed vigour in the derivation of theoretical solutions to the influence of economics, technology and labour on the location of industry (Wood, 1978, pp. 22–4).

Although he does not mention the industrial park as either a specific type of locational environment or corporate organization, Wood's analysis has as much portent for this phenomenon as it does for regional planning and the geography of the firm because of the bridge it forms between them. Parks reduce risk both for the industrial and regional planner and also for the private corporation—especially the multi-locational corporation unfamiliar with the vicissitudes of economic activity in particular regions; they reduce the initial costs of location and ensure rapid accommodation of product growth and the expansion of facilities. Industrial parks also fill the gap between macro and micro-environments because they form a meso-scale location which, depending on size, is akin to a small region or large district. As industrial parks become the dominant form of locational environment, many private and state data collection agencies are compiling economic and operational statistics about them, thus assisting locational analysts and obviating the need for expensive private surveys. Researchers can then concentrate on acquiring specific information still regarded as confidential by firms or government agencies.

Industrial parks seem to have a locational and terminological stability which can greatly facilitate studies of change through time. Although parks undergo modification in function and operational composition, the management concerned is likely to know the various reasons for the death or migration of particular firms, changes in product mix, and other details about the corporate policy and locational strategy of subsidiary, parent or single independent firms which the researcher cannot ascertain after an individual firm has gone out of business or has moved.

Parks may also be a much more nourishing and comprehensive local environment than raw or poorly planned industrial sites and districts as a seed-bed for new firms and nursery for the growth of firms from small to intermediate size (prior to a large corporation's decision to develop its own site). They also provide a focus for government regional development assistance and avoid the need to deal with a host of locational agencies or firms while offering security of numbers and a formal sense of community—something lacking in most other industrial locations.

The industrial park is a prime candidate for theoretical analyses because of the great expectations—many as yet totally unproven—which developers and analysts alike have placed on it in enhancing regional economic planning and accommodating many changing needs of the firm. Factors of locational behaviour which require more effective incorporation into the theory of the firm also require greater application to analyses of the industrial park. Most new investments are made by firms already located in industrial parks; because the number of these parks is limited nationally and internationally, such companies may be able to weigh the relative advantages of a finite number of sites. Firms are thus more likely to apply normative approaches to their spatial decision-making (in ways long refuted by location analysts) and behave systematically. Such rigorous decision-making will greatly enhance the researcher's subsequent ability to model the influence of economic and behavioural variables on the firm's location.

The industrial park appears to have direct relevance to the priorities outlined by Wood. Furthermore, it is an integral component of national locational environments and the national multi-locational structure of the firm; in an era of multinational, multi-locational enterprises, it also comprises part of the international locational environment and part of the corresponding spatial organizational structure of the firm. In the priorities established in Tokyo in 1980 by the International Geographical Union Commission on Industrial Systems for research between 1980 and 1984, industrial geographers were urged to focus on the ramifications of the new international division of labour emerging as a result of:

(a) governmental and institutional constraints and incentives;
(b) inter and intra-organizational relationships;
(c) diffusion and development of technologies; and
(d) demand and supply of material resources.

As the venue for industrial development and as a tool for regional economic expansion and intervention by government, the industrial park has a most appropriate role to play in the research objectives of the international industrial geographical community which correspond to those established by members of developing nations themselves (see Von Weber, 1977) and recognized by a major forum of scholars not aligned with the specific needs of any one country.

Spatial Analysis, Industry and the Industrial Environment. Vol. 3 Regional Economies and Industrial Systems
Edited by F. E. I. Hamilton and G. J. R. Linge
© 1983 John Wiley & Sons Ltd.

Chapter 19

Export Processing Zones: New Catalysts for Economic Development

DOMINGO C. SALITA AND MELITON B. JUANICO

During the last 2 decades, export processing zones (EPZs) have emerged as important agencies for economic development in developing countries, particularly in Asia where they have been most active and successful. They have become one of the major agents for earning foreign exchange, attracting foreign investments and creating employment as well as acting as an important vehicle for technology transfer and regional development in the Third World. Their sudden popularity stems from the benefits they provide to foreign investors which include low-cost labour; low rental costs on land and factory facilities; less strict anti-pollution measures; full remittance of profits; tax concessions; and duty-free import of raw materials. The proliferation of EPZs thus depends on the fact that they are mutually beneficial to both the host country and the investing firm. Despite this, however, controversy regarding the merits of EPZs continues.

This chapter examines the evolution, characteristics, aims, impacts, issues and prospects of this mid-twentieth century phenomenon, particularly in developing Asian countries.

EVOLUTION OF EXPORT PROCESSING ZONES

Precursors of the Export Processing Zone

The seminal idea behind the EPZ as a special form of free-trade zone goes back over 2 millenia when Romans transhipped, stored and re-exported goods from various ports in the Mediterranean. Traders continued to use free zones in the Middle Ages; it was, however, during the period of colonization, specifically from the eighteenth to the nineteenth century, when such zones conspicuously increased in number and gained importance in the international economic scene. Free ports in strategic places were set up to divert part of the trade that developed between the colonial powers and their colonies. Among those that still exist are Gibraltar (established in 1704), Singapore (1819) and Hong Kong (1842)—free ports that were chiefly involved in storing and re-exporting goods (Kelleher, 1976, p. 1). These

441

ports were just a convenience, designed to allow goods to be gathered together and subsequently shipped to distant parts of the world.

The idea of a free-trade zone as mainly a warehousing and re-exporting centre prevailed until after the Second World War when such zones were established at key points along international trade routes. In addition to the 3 already cited, other free ports like Aden, Colon, Port Said, Tangier and the Canary Islands vied with each other in attracting exports. Usually, in such free ports

> ships may enter . . . discharge, load and depart without customs formalities. The goods may be stored, repacked, manufactured, and re-exported without customs formalities. Only when the goods pass the barrier to reach the consuming public of the country do they undergo customs revision and pay the necessary duty (MacElweè, 1926, p. 381).

The Modern Export Processing Zone

EPZs started to become popular in the mid-1960s. The new ones were less concerned with trading activities than with expanding manufactured exports and providing employment for the surrounding area. The initiative came from those former colonies which wanted a share of international investment in manufacturing. In 1974 the Secretariat of the United Nations Industrial Development Organization (UNIDO) articulated the EPZ concept (in an unpublished document) as being

> the establishment of modern manufacturing plants inside an industrial estate, by offering a suitable package of investment incentives to both foreign and domestic entrepreneurs. To encourage this, legislation must be passed, giving investors such incentives as fixed term corporate tax exemption, duty exemption on production machinery imports, freedom to repatriate profits at a certain rate, and other facilities. Pre-built factory buildings with all services are usually made available at reasonable rates.

The EPZ must also be distinguished from the industrial estate, a more general term that refers to a 'tract of land which is subdivided and developed according to a comprehensive plan for the use of a community of industrial enterprises . . . with a view to protecting the investments of both the developer of the estate and tenants' (Bredo, 1960, p. 1). More specifically, such estates have an industry mix utilizing local manpower, raw materials and other resources, with products destined for both local and foreign markets. An EPZ, in contrast, utilizes imported raw materials (but not manpower) and has products mainly intended for sale abroad.

Generally, EPZs belong to a special category of customs-privileged facilities—along with others like free ports, transit zones and free perimeters—which aims to facilitate world trade and minimize encumbrances caused by

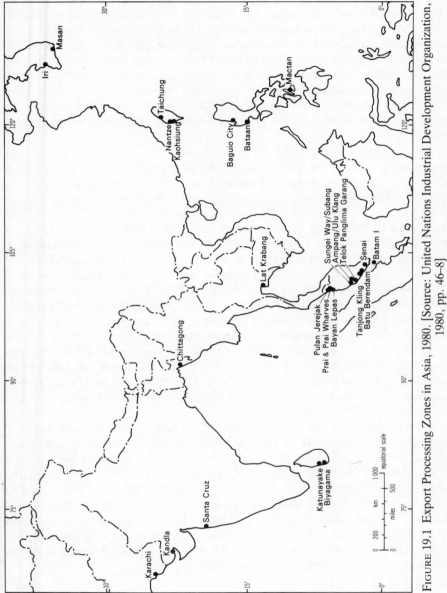

FIGURE 19.1 Export Processing Zones in Asia, 1980. [Source: United Nations Industrial Development Organization, 1980, pp. 46–8]

various import restrictions. EPZs are, however, the most popular primarily because of the flexibility they provide the marketer. At a free port, inward shipments of goods are stored or processed without the payment of duty until they are shipped or transferred into a duty area. Transit zones and free perimeters are similar to free-trade zones (like the free port and EPZ) except that they are smaller, have fewer facilities and hence undertake only storage. Other arrangements include 'special customs privileges' that range from duty exemptions to allowing companies to operate their own customs-free areas (*Business International*, 26 October 1973, p. 339). Altogether there were about 225 customs-privileged facilities around the world early in 1981.

The concept of the EPZ as a manufacturing area started with the establishment in Eire in 1959 of the Shannon export free zone, initially with the object of maintaining employment at nearby Shannon International Airport 'whose position as a refuelling centre was threatened by the development of longer range jet aircraft' (Currie, 1979, p. 2). Trade was promoted by attracting manufacturing activities which would generate air freight. This zone was established when Eire reorientated its industrialization policy from import substitution to export-led expansion, which had to be done amidst the diminishing supply of local raw materials and the small and already saturated Irish local market. Thus importing raw materials, manufacturing them at the free zone and exporting the finished products proved to be a successful venture (Kelleher, 1976, pp. 1–2).

Other countries, particularly the developing ones, which had been trying to develop their export sector followed suit and established EPZs. Notable examples are the zones at Kaohsiung in Taiwan and Kandla in India (both established in the 1960s), Sungai Way and Bayan Lepas in Malaysia, Port Louis in Mauritius, Bataan in the Philippines and Masan in South Korea (all set up in the 1970s) (Figure 19.1).

UNIDO played a significant role in stimulating the diffusion of the EPZ concept as demonstrated by the fact that it sponsored seminars and workshops for EPZ administrators. It also organized conferences at Barranquilla (Colombia) in 1974 and Alexandria (Egypt) in 1977 that touched on the need for an association of EPZs. Then, on 30 January 1978, UNIDO co-sponsored with the Philippine government a meeting at Manila and Baguio City at which the World Export Processing Zones Association (WEPZA) was formally organized: this Association aims to promote coordination and cooperation among EPZ managements and hence avoid an 'incentives war' developing between them.

SALIENT FEATURES

Site Based on a sampling of zones around the world, an EPZ may be as small as the 41 ha of Santa Cruz near Bombay in India or as big as the

Table 19.1 Selected Export Processing Zones classified by size and industry

Zone	Year established	Size (ha)	Type of industry
Port Klang (Malaysia)	?	850	Medium/heavy
Changwon (South Korea)	?	400	Medium/heavy
Bataan III (Philippines)	1969	207	Heavy/shipbuilding
Bayan Lepas (Malaysia)	1970	200	Light
Masan (South Korea)	1971	175	Light
Pulan Jerejak (Malaysia)	?	160	Heavy
Prai (Malaysia)	1973	110	Medium/heavy
La Romana (Dominican Republic)	1969	93	Light
Iri (South Korea)	1975	92	Light
Bataan II (Philippines)	1969	91	Medium/automotive
San Bartolo (El Salvador)	1974	86	Light
Shannon (Eire)	1959	80	Light
Bataan I (Philippines)	1969	67	Light
Sungai Way (Malaysia)	1971	52	Light
Santa Cruz (India)	1974	41	Light

Source: Kelleher, 1976, p. 16.

850 ha of Port Klang in Malaysia (Table 19.1). A zone is usually located near a dock or airport to facilitate the entry of imported equipment and raw materials. It is fenced in and usually patrolled, with the level of security dependent on the zone's location and the kind of merchandise passing through it (Kelleher, 1976, p. 2).

A considerable initial investment goes into the development of an EPZ to purchase land, erect factories and provide infrastructure. Most zones easily recoup such outlays through a brisk development brought about by accessibility to urban centres, a favourable location and liberal incentives. Bataan is one of the few which has not repaid the investment, a failing attributed to the large outlays needed for infrastructure development because Bataan is a hilly area previously inaccessible to metropolitan Manila. Meanwhile, it is attaining its other objectives that, in the authors' opinion, could compensate for the diminished foreign exchange earnings: it is providing employment, effecting transfer of technology and promoting regional development.

Imports The EPZ allows the import, free of duties and quota restrictions, of raw materials and capital equipment needed for manufacturing or processing products to be exported. This privilege, which greatly reduces the cost of production, excludes goods prohibited by law or by trade embargo such as arms and drugs. Some countries and trading groups, including the EEC, impose some restrictions on free importation for manufacturing purposes. Most commonly, these provide that in cases where goods made by the host country or by its trading partners are the same in price and quality as imported ones, those produced by the host country must be used (Kelleher, 1976, pp. 2–3; Fujimori, 1980a, p. 3). Since EPZs are primarily aimed at overcoming tariff barriers, they assume less importance for goods with low duties (Terpstra, 1972, p. 333).

Shipment of goods Products assembled and processed at EPZs are normally exported, this being a particular characteristic of those set up in the 1960s and 1970s with an emphasis on the export of goods to Western Europe, North America and Japan. In the older zones, in contrast, the stress is on trading; they function basically as assembly points for gathering and distributing products in local and regional markets. Normally, goods produced by the zone and used for personal consumption within it are subject to customs duties. Goods produced in the zone must be as competitive as foreign-made ones and, in this, foreign firms enjoy a comparative advantage over those not similarly situated (Kelleher, 1976, p. 3).

Legal status All laws of the host country (except those relating to customs) apply within the zone. Customs authorities have jurisdiction in the zone, with substantial powers to inspect and document goods, hold up deliveries, and search inside and around the zone. The extent of surveillance and control depends on the attitude of the customs authorities, on the type of merchandise passing through, and on the revenue risks involved. It is primarily with this authority, and secondarily with other authorities in the vicinity, that the zone management must establish a working relationship (Kelleher, 1976).

Operation Goods at a zone may be packed, unpacked, mixed, blended, assembled, stored, subjected to break of bulk, manufactured and transhipped, although not all these activities are allowed in every EPZ. Normally no limit is imposed on the length of time goods can be stored (Kelleher, 1976, p. 3).

Incentives A major incentive offered by EPZs is that 100 per cent foreign ownership is permitted as well as tax concessions, repatriation of all profits and capital dividends, and a guarantee of non-expropriation and non-requisition of foreign property except in the interest of national welfare and security (when just compensation will be made). Simplification of export-import rules and exclusion from cumbersome domestic laws and regulations, particularly those relating to labour and business practices, also act as considerable incentives.

Type of industry Most EPZs, particularly those in Asia, attract labour-

TABLE 19.2 Selected Export Processing Zones classified by type of firm

Industry group	Shannon	Bataan[a]	Masan	Other EPZs[b]	Total
Electronics	8	5	26	106	145
Engineering, machinery	19	3	45	33	100
Clothing, textiles, footwear	4	23	8	87	122
Other[c]	6	18	26	75	125
Total	37	49	105	301	492

[a] Based on data in Bataan Zone *Annual Report*, 1978.
[b] Includes Bataan Phase I (for light industries), Bataan Phase II (for medium and automated industries), and Bataan Phase III (for heavy industries).
[c] Includes those EPZs that were in operation by 1976.
Source: Kelleher, 1976.

intensive industries—such as clothing and electronics—that capitalize on the cheap wage structure of developing countries (Table 19.2).

OBJECTIVES AND IMPACTS

Objectives

The EPZs in developing countries came about as a result of a redirection from import substitution to export-orientated industrialization. Most Asian countries, in particular, were forced to change their development efforts towards export of light and heavy manufactures as a result of the partial failure of import-substituting industrialization during the 1960s and 1970s. This stemmed from the restricted demand on the home market for the limited range of light consumer goods being produced. Further industrialization necessarily calls for entry into export markets. The change-over, however, is not usually smooth because the developing countries have to face the challenge of trading efficiently in an international market and consequently may be forced to alter their domestic policies with regard to their export sector. Usually, moreover, an industrial sector, previously developed under protection, is deficient in managerial and technological skills and so is not in a sound position to export. The EPZs, as a special segment of the economy, present themselves as a training ground for the acquisition of skills (Kelleher, 1976, p. 5; Mok, 1980, p. 5).

The emergence of EPZs initially related to the policy of tariff-enclosed countries to liberalize import restrictions through minimizing duties, quotas, exchange controls and multiple exchange rates on shipments of foreign goods for export to a third country. Yet even the minimal controls have become administratively cumbersome and costly especially for foreign investors. The EPZ emerged, therefore, as a means of overcoming the difficulties or inconveniences presented by normal bureaucratic and administrative import-export procedures (Philippines Investment Coordination Committee, 1980, p. 3).

The oft-quoted basic objectives of establishing EPZs (Vittal, 1977a, p. 44) include:

(a) increasing foreign exchange earnings through export trade;
(b) creation of employment opportunities;
(c) attraction of foreign investment;
(d) transfer of technology and managerial skills;
(e) promotion of regional development.

Other minor objectives or benefits of EPZs include eliminating administrative or bureaucratic red tape, increasing the value of land and promoting international cooperation. But the important objectives are the generation

TABLE 19.3 National objectives pursued and/or resulting from Export Processing Zones[a]

Item	Very important	Important	Not important
1. Economic development	3	—	—
2. Regional development	1	3	—
3. Export expansion and diversification	4	—	—
4. Increased employment and incomes	4	1	—
5. Increased government earnings	5	—	—
6. Increased government revenues	1	1	2
7. Technological transfer (spillover)	3	2	—
8. Managerial technological transfer	1	3	—
9. Efficient utilization of domestic material resources including processed ones	1	3	—

[a] Based on a survey conducted by Van (1975) on behalf of the Asian Productivity Organization into national objectives related to EPZs. The countries surveyed were India, the Philippines, South Korea, Taiwan and the Republic of Vietnam.
Source: Van, 1975, pp. 2–3.

of foreign exchange, the provision of job opportunities and the attraction of foreign capital: these were perceived to be the major goals during a survey of countries in the Asian Productivity Organization (APO) region (Table 19.3).

Impacts

Foreign exchange earnings While direct government foreign exchange earnings from EPZ operations in terms of taxes and duties may not be as great as those in an industrial estate or in a tariff territory, the foreign exchange benefit (objective) derived from EPZs results mainly from indirect foreign currency earnings through salaries and wages of local employees and directly from receipts of rent, taxes, duties on domestic raw materials, and public service charges. These benefits are often considered in cost-benefit studies of EPZs to determine their viability. Thus the Masan Free Export Zone (MAFEZ) in South Korea obtained good returns from investments (Table 19.4) with foreign currency earnings increasing from 24.9 per cent of exports in 1971 to 36.9 per cent in 1975. Such earnings occur in 3 general forms: domestic raw material duties; salaries and wages; and lease charges, supporting firms' service charges processing outside the EPZ, and repairs and public service charges (Cha, 1977, pp. 87–9).

Another good example of an EPZ recouping investments after a relatively short period is the Kaohsiung Export Processing Zone (KEPZ) in Taiwan. In a cost-benefit study, the latter was measured by labour return (salary and

TABLE 19.4 Foreign currency earning effects in the Masan Free Export Zone, South Korea, 1971 to 1975

Year	Exports ($US000)	Earnings ($US000)	Earnings rate (per cent)	Percentage earning rate against MAFEZ investment[a] (per cent)
1971	956	238	24.9	1.4
1972	9,739	2,991	30.7	17.4
1973	70,376	25,881	36.8	150.5
1974	181,534	72,144	39.7	419.4
1975[b]	255,000	94,000	36.9	546.5
Total	517,605	195,254	37.7	1,135.1

[a] $US17,201,000.
[b] Estimates.
Source: Industrial Estates Administration (Republic of Korea), reported by Cha, 1977, p. 88.

insurance); government property return (rental and interest); net income of KEPZ Administration and its supporting agencies; and taxes collectable. The costs included investments by the government for infrastructure and other construction; investment by domestic entrepreneurs for setting up factories in the zone; maintenance costs; taxes exempted; and residual value of land and buildings. The study covered the 4-year construction period up to 1974 plus a 10-year generating time and an assumed 10 per cent annual depreciation rate (equivalent to the then current interest on government loans). As Wang (1977, p. 82) states:

> Up to December of 1974, the "added value" had accumulated to US$565,214,658 which was equivalent to more than 47 times of the total development cost. The "added value" is the difference of FOB value of exported products and the value of imported raw materials or components for making the products. Out of this amount US$31,593,500 had been remitted to foreign countries in the form of net profit, or dividends, travelling expenses, salaries of foreign employees etc. of the investors, while the remaining US$533,621,158 were the net foreign currencies the government actually earned in the forms of wages and salaries of local employees, taxes collectable, and other indirect costs etc. of the factories operated in EPZs, or an equivalence of 36% (well over the minimum required 25% added value) of the accumulated total amount of export value (US$1,526,773,900) from the three zones up to December 1974 had been attained. It also means that the government invested [sic] on developing EPZs had nearly 45 times been rewarded.

Employment Perhaps the most important benefit or impact of EPZs is the creation of employment for the local population in their immediate vicinities. In Asian developing countries, the EPZs with their small and medium-scale labour-intensive industries present a solution to the twin problems of urban unemployment and rural underemployment (International Labour Office, 1962, pp. 61–3). This has been shown, for instance, in the Masan EPZ in South Korea which has attracted rural workers from the surrounding hinterland following the urbanization process that has been termed 'population implosion' (Cha, 1977, pp. 91–2). No doubt, the zone has also provided employment to urban labourers in the fairly large city of Masan where it is located. The Mactan EPZ, on Cebu in the Philippines, is another example of a zone employing both urban and rural labour: it has been drawing urban workers from the nearby cities of Cebu, Mandaue and Lapu-Lapu as well as rural job-seekers from the islands surrounding it. This is also related to what has been termed 'production sharing' in which manufacturers in developed countries seeking unskilled labour turn to the developing world for help as their domestic supplies diminish. Employment creation is perhaps the foremost benefit of the EPZs as is illustrated in Table 19.5.

New jobs provided by industries in a developing country have a multiplier effect by creating new markets for consumer products. Bolin (1978, p. 79),

TABLE 19.5 Employment in Export Processing Zones,
selected Asian countries, 1979

Country	Number of zones	Area (ha)	Number employed (000)
South Korea	2	267	120.0[a]
Taiwan	3	181	77.4
Malaysia	10	663	56.0[b]
Philippines	1	345	17.3
Sri Lanka	1	202	5.2
India	2	325	3.2
Total	19	1983	279.1

[a] UNIDO estimate.
[b] In mid-1980 employment estimated to be 80,000 (Kobe, 1980, p. 1).
Source: Currie, 1979, p. 6.

an industrial estate expert, points out that

> As a rough rule of thumb, each new direct manufacturing job in a labor-intensive industry in the developing world, together with the two indirect jobs created at the same time, produces about $800 of GNP. If the three job-holders support themselves and five others, or eight persons in all, the per capita GNP of the group is $1000. If half of this is spent by the group as a whole (or $500/capita) for consumer goods, the purchases of the group amount to $4000 of consumer goods per year. Thus each new job in your industrial free zone may mean ₱40 million retail sales per year. Suddenly, you have created a new market for consumer goods which never existed before and which must now be satisfied with new supplies from your zone or some other zone.

Foreign investments With their cheap labour costs and other inducements such as exemptions from taxes and duties and full repatriation of profits, EPZs are attractive to entrepreneurs all over the world who are looking for possibilities of profitable overseas investment. Nearness to markets also attracts transnational corporations (TNCs) as this reduces production costs and freight charges, as has been demonstrated by the successful EPZs of Taiwan and South Korea. Since local industry plays a minor role in the EPZs, there is a need to attract foreign capital to boost the economic growth of the host country and, more specifically, to develop the related industries in the peripheral tariff territory (Vittal, 1977b, p. 5).

Certain countries have been instrumental in supporting the growth of Asian EPZs, with Japan accounting for the bulk of investments, particularly in those of South Korea and Taiwan, amidst the persistent fluctuations of production and employment in them in the 1970s. The increase in Japanese

EPZ investments is attributed to the rising labour costs in Japan, limited sites for expansion, and the restructuring of the Japanese economy towards liberalization of overseas investments (Fujimori, 1980a).

Second to Japan, investments by TNCs have also favourably influenced the growth of certain Asian EPZs. This was a manifestation of the strategy of US companies which, beginning in the mid-1970s, took advantage of value-added tariff arrangements that permitted products to be assembled and processed abroad for re-export back to the US duty-free (Sharpston, 1975; Linge and Hamilton, 1981, p. 78). The main motivating factor was the availability of an easily trained, cheap labour force. For instance, in 1980 the mean hourly wage costs for skilled and unskilled female labour in some developing Asian countries was less than $US0.50 as against $US9.00 in the US (Fujimori, 1980a). A survey by Business International Ltd in the Pacific Basin, as at 10 June 1980, showed that developing Asian countries have much cheaper labour markets than Australia and Japan (Table 19.6). The Philippines, Indonesia and Thailand have the lowest average monthly salaries, based on 6 major types of skilled employment (Anonymous, 1980, p. 1).

Chinese investment is specially significant in the development of EPZs in Taiwan. Overseas Chinese living in Hong Kong and Macao have steadily increased their investments since the mid-1960s, with the exception of certain years affected by international politics. Another factor partly responsible for the rapid growth of EPZs is the stimulating effect of the expansion of international trade at least until the mid-1970s. Thus during the

TABLE 19.6 Labour rates in selected Pacific Basin countries

Country	Average salary of skilled workers ($US per month)	Index[a] (Hong Kong = 100)
Philippines	156	40
Indonesia	156	46
Thailand	226	50
Taiwan	273	62
Malaysia	394	71
Singapore	427	79
Hong Kong	508	100
South Korea	669	108
Australia	1,232	185
Japan	1,331	236

[a] Includes 6 major types of occupation.

Source: Survey by Business International Ltd reported in Anonymous 1980, p. 1.

1965–75 period 'the rate of export growth recorded 25.8 per cent as compared with 17.8 per cent recorded in the developed countries as a whole' (Fujimori, 1980a).

Data about actual investment levels in EPZs are incomplete but Fujimori (1980c) has compiled information available from various sources for some of the zones in 5 countries (Table 19.7). According to the Central Bank of the Philippines, the Bataan, Mactan and Baguio City zones attracted $US21 million-worth of foreign direct investment in the 1970–80 period. As at the end of December 1979 the 75 investments in these 3 zones had the following ownership structure: Filipino, 29; European, 7; United States, 5; Filipino-European, 5; Filipino-Japanese, 5; Filipino-Other Asian, 4; Japanese, 3; Australian, 3; Overseas Chinese, 2; Other Asian, 1; Filipino-United States, 1; Filipino-Australian, 1; and other ownership combinations, 9.

Transfer of technology The transfer of technological as well as managerial skills appears to be a subsidiary but nevertheless significant benefit that it is hoped can be gained from TNCs in EPZs by technology-deficient developing countries. Local recruits can learn skills not available in cottage industries outside the EPZ. Some may be used to find better employment, others may be passed on to members of the family: together these skills can lead to greater productivity. In developing countries there are actually formal arrangements and policies ensuring that technology is transferred from one industry to another. For example, in the Philippines, Presidential Decree No. 1520 created the Technology Transfer Board with which all technology transfer arrangements are registered. As defined by the decree, technology transfer arrangements are contracts or agreements entered into directly or indirectly with TNCs which have as their major or accessory aim the transfer, assignment or licensing of technology or trade marks. TNCs usually provide special training for their recruits in addition to that provided by the zone management—an arrangement that constitutes outright transfer of the latest industrial skills. Usually, foreign companies do not bring in many administrative staff since most responsible managerial posts are filled with local recruits that are trained beforehand or on the job.

Regional development Another rationale for encouraging EPZs involves the promotion of regional development within their respective countries. Most of the successful zones today are in urban places located away from the capital city and close to rural areas. In India, for instance, the Kandla Free Trade Zone was located in a depressed area which was at the same time lacking in infrastructure. Iri, an industrially lagging area in South Korea is 255 km from Seoul, the capital, while Masan lies 60 km west of Pusan, South Korea's second largest city. In the Philippines, Bataan is 170 km away from

TABLE 19.7 Investment in Export Processing Zones of selected countries in South-East Asia ($US million)

Country	Export Processing Zone	Japan	Japanese joint ventures with local capital	US	US joint ventures with local capital	Overseas Chinese	Others	Local capital	Total
Malaysia	Bayan Lepas	1	2	10	1	2	11	1	28
	Prai ⎫ Prai Wharf ⎬	0	1	0	0	1	7	0	9
	Pulan Jerejak	0	0	0	0	0	1	0	1
Philippines	Bataan	3	7	4	2	2	26	28	72
	Mactan	0	0	0	0	0	2	1	3
	Baguio	0	0	1	0	0	0	0	1
Sri Lanka	Katunayake	0	2	0	5	12	18	6	43
South Korea	Masan	72	19	3	4	0	2	0	100
	Iri	6	0	0	0	0	2	0	8
Taiwan	Kaohsiung	30	24	6	12	17	0	34	123
	Nantze	18	24	5	6	12	0	32	97
	Taichung	23	4	4	2	1	0	6	40

Source: Fujimori, 1980c, p. 19.

Manila by road, Mactan is 1 hour away from Manila by commercial jet, and Baguio is 4 hours from Manila by road. The locations chosen for Taiwan's 3 EPZs are good because they are dispersed to accelerate regional development in lagging areas. The first zone in Malaysia located at Bayan Lepas on Penang Island is about 25 km from Georgetown, the district capital, while Port Klang, one of Malaysia's major ports, is 35 km from the national capital, Kuala Lumpur.

In developing Third World countries with parasitic primate cities that siphon off developmental impulses from the hinterland, EPZs are seen as counter magnets that would help hasten the 'spread/trickling down' process in regional development through industrial dispersal (Juanico, 1977, pp. 25–6). In the Philippines, EPZs are perceived to be significant instruments in the growth centre strategy which underlies the government's regional development programme. Considering EPZs as catalysts aiding regional dispersal, the Philippine government plans to add another 15 dispersed zones to the existing 3 in Bataan, Mactan and Baguio City, bringing the total number of EPZs operating by 1985 to 18 (*Business Day*, 1 December 1980, p. 8). In comparison, Malaysia, which claims (on the basis of a survey of 12 countries) that its industrial zones are very successful in contributing to the national economy, had 15 zones operating at the end of 1979, all located in West Malaysia.

Aside from other benefits, EPZs help in developing areas that are industrially backward, even though considerable outlays are needed initially to provide the necessary infrastructure. They can, in particular, stimulate ancillary industries in the host nation. As Wang (1977, pp. 32–3) has stated in relation to Taiwan:

> the supply of raw material, components, packaging material and services, the improving of infrastructure constructions and other types of activities by the existing domestic industries to the enterprises in EPZs could bring a favourable impulse of improvement and level-up of their technique towards international standards. Besides, the foreign entrepreneurs usually bring the export markets as well as marketing techniques, experience and knowledge of markets with them. This fact would save this country from going through the painful exercise of preparing deep market surveys and investigations during the pre-planning stage before the decision of establishing EPZs.

Developmental impulses from EPZs can also change the lifestyle of inhabitants in outlying rural areas. This presumes that, as their community becomes urbanized, they could become well-off, literate, well-nourished, leisure-seeking, high-consuming residents. In many instances, zone managements have gone out of their way to promote community development projects in the zone periphery, particularly with regard to education, nutrition, recreation and public health.

ISSUES AND PROSPECTS

Despite the many favourable aspects, major issues surround the establishment of EPZs in developing countries, particularly those in Asia.

Foreign Exchange Earnings and Investments

The claimed impact of EPZs as generating considerable foreign exchange earnings by attracting investments from abroad is questioned by detractors on the ground that inputs are imported free of tariff and duty payments that would otherwise accrue to the national government. In Bataan, for instance, significant direct earnings consist only of rentals for buildings, land, housing, telephone and other equipment; electricity and water bills; and escort and import-export fees, the latter being minimal. Any benefits from foreign exchange earnings enjoyed by the government are only indirect (most being through salaries and wages of local citizens): the social value of such benefits is, of course, considerable.

Despite this valid criticism, EPZs have performed the role of a catalyst in the industrialization efforts of developing countries in Asia. Simply by presenting a picture of dynamic industrial activity they may inspire other industrial and entrepreneurial ventures around the country. The maximization of land utilization can also be a strong justification for setting up EPZs, considering that the wealth derived from agricultural land is limited compared with that used for industry: the productivity of a given piece of agricultural land is not flexible whereas the productivity of a similar area used for manufacturing can be increased depending on entrepreneurial initiative. In the Kaohsiung, Nantze and Taichung EPZs in Taiwan, the utilization value of the land in these 3 zones was 4000 times more than the same area of agricultural land. As Vittal notes (1977b, p. 6), in the Kaohsiung Export Processing Zone

> each hectare of land . . . exported products worth US$5,170,000; however, every hectare of agricultural land could only turn out sugar worth about US$1,200 or produce rice worth about US$1,250 per annum.

More specifically, EPZs encourage export manufacturing nearby. Capital from Japan, North America and Western Europe as well as indigenous sources can stimulate the growth of local firms or the establishment of ancillary industries around the zone by providing a market for raw materials and components for assembly industries. This tendency to create backward linkages reflects the value of EPZs as catalysts of regional growth. The role is even more enhanced if industrially backward areas, like Bataan in the Philippines, are developed as EPZs. Such depressed areas will stimulate more investment in terms of increased expenditure for infrastructure development.

EPZs also encourage the establishment of support services within their perimeter like banking, communications, transport, recreation and sub-contract engineering. Thus, as Bredo (1960, pp. 43–9) suggests, such customs-privileged zones function as a way of mobilizing the investment of smaller blocks of capital into small- and medium-size concerns around them.

Transfer of Technology

Some observers note that the technologies being transferred to EPZs are the simple, less sophisticated and repetitive operations characteristic of assembly and production-line work. However, since most foreign companies still have to train their recruits, despite experience and the completion of vocational or technical courses offered by the host government, it appears that the skills are not that ordinary and in fact could constitute 'trade secrets'. These, in turn, can be used or imported in other ventures outside the zone.

While it is true that most workers may do only a couple of simple operations on the production line, there is still transfer of technology in that they are exposed to the essential principles of modern technology such as assembly-line production and the maintenance of quality control. Imbibing such ideas can redound to greater and high-quality production. Further, as Wang observes (cited by Vittal, 1977c, pp. 32–3), the greater impact of technology transfer occurs among those with responsible positions such as the foreman, shop supervisor, production engineer, quality control technician and employees with managerial functions. Foreign entrepreneurs also bring knowledge of export markets, marketing techniques and industrial management.

Manpower

The lack of trained and skilled manpower which appears to be the problem in Bataan, for instance, is sometimes cited as a disincentive to companies. However, the benefit of relatively low wages in the long run offsets the initial outlays on manpower training. Moreover, the experience of firms in EPZs is that rural recruits can be easily trained to become efficient industrial workers.

The tendency of zone enterprises to hire more women who are suited to light assembly work is also pointed out as a possible source of social problems. A former Filipino public official (Paterno, 1978, p. 35) has observed that in Bataan, for example, the ratio is 4 female to 1 male worker, a situation that can displace male bread-winners. One answer is to promote enterprises that employ more, or a significant proportion of, men. The present preponderance of women—especially if the EPZs are in rural areas—should actually be viewed as an opportunity for unemployed and underemployed rural women to contribute to the family income. The males in a family can always turn to farming as a primary occupation and perhaps to some zone activities as a secondary one.

EPZs in Relation to Local Industries

Export-orientated local industrialists have expressed fears about the adverse impact on their market potential of the preferential treatment given to EPZ industries making similar goods. The EPZs, however, do not always prejudice local industries outside the zone. When import restrictions have been imposed in developing countries, the limiting or banning of further entry of such industries into EPZs has overcome the disadvantage to local exporters. Such was the case in Taiwan and Sri Lanka for clothing and textiles after 1974 and 1978, respectively (Fujimori, 1980b, p. 3). In the Philippines, the proliferation of garment industries and the resulting over-production has led to recent imposition of quotas in foreign markets. The Bataan EPZ now discourages garment and footwear manufacturing and promotes semi-conductor electronic components and precision instruments.

In South Korea, no evidence of EPZ piracy of the foreign markets of local industries has been observed because foreign investors already have their overseas markets when they apply for entry into the zone. It is not their practice to invest first and look for markets afterwards (Vittal, 1977b, p. 8). The fact, too, that EPZ industries are not ordinarily allowed to sell locally while local export-orientated ones are allowed to sell both on domestic and overseas markets is an advantage that the latter enjoy. However, EPZ products that are still not available on the domestic market are usually allowed to be sold there upon compliance with appropriate taxes and duties for import substitution.

Proliferation of EPZs

A current major issue affecting both host countries and investors is the proliferation of EPZs in Asian countries that could lead to unhealthy competition and a diminution of benefits. This is likely to be a particular problem for those EPZs producing the same goods. Moreover, the situation may be exacerbated by the growth of exports of similar goods from the People's Republic of China. The unsettling possibility of destructive competition, however, is offset by such varied constraints as

limitation of wage bill payable to workers, changing political and industrial climate, negligible contribution of EPZ exporters in world trade etc. on the

part of host countries. The other set of factors that will prevent undue competition on the part of investors would be [the] approach of existing and prospective
investors with regard to the investment climate both political and social as well
as natural endowments available [within the] host country. The composition
aspect is, therefore, taken care of by the selectivity of investors as well as the
inherent constraints in the countries offering EPZ facilities. In the meantime,
healthy competition should be encouraged to fulfill the functional role of EPZ as
an instrument of economic development (Vittal, 1977a, p. 45).

More concretely, according to the United Nations Industrial Development
Organization (1977, p. 80), there are 3 reasons why the occurrence of an
'undesirable escalation of incentives' among EPZs is unlikely:

(a) such facilities are very much in demand as labour costs rise in
developed countries;
(b) most EPZs constitute only a minor industrial sector, with all their
exports put together not making up even 0.1 per cent of total world
manufactures;
(c) with the increase in EPZs, investment analysts will not only evaluate
the incentives offered by each but also other factors, such as the attitudes of
governments, standard of labour, sophistication of infrastructure, and the
availability of service facilities.

Following a recommendation by an Export Working Group on Industrial
Free Zones held at Barranquilla, Colombia, in October 1974, UNIDO was
asked 'to assist in the formulation of some form of association of all Free
Zone Authorities in the developed and developing countries' (United Nations Industrial Developmental Organization, 1977, p. 80).

There is also the potential problem that, as a result of competition, each
EPZ will try to attract some of the limited amount of 'footloose' industry
globally available and, in turn, that TNCs will frequently change the location
of their enterprises in an effort to maximize benefits. The constant
shifting of industries at short notice can adversely affect the benefits enjoyed
by host countries. One remedy is proper project evaluation. The zone
management should make sure that an industrial applicant is prepared to
invest in training local staff, construct its own factory or other facilities, raise
money from local sources, or comply with certain schemes to obtain its
loyalty to the zone. Once the plant starts operating, a tested way of
maintaining its loyalty and confidence is to provide efficient administration,
an aspect which many investors consider even more important than the
package of inducements and benefits offered. Such incentives should be
realized, not simply allowed to remain as 'offers' in print.

As Bolin (1978, p. 79) suggests, industrial free zones should think of
themselves as partners or 'friendly competitors'—the major aim behind the

organization of the World Export Processing Zone Association in Manila, Philippines, in 1978. This relationship can be achieved through production sharing, with foreign manufacturers looking for cheap labour in developing countries involving them in producing the world's commodities. Production sharing 'fits the manufacturing needs of the world and helps expand world markets'. Related to this is the 'network' concept by which 4 zones, for instance, may band together to respond to the needs of a particular manufacturing group and simultaneously set up a plant in each zone.

This type of cooperation has also been suggested as applicable and favourable to countries belonging to the Association of South-East Asian Nations (ASEAN), whose present techniques of promoting economic co-operation consist of regional industrialization projects, industrial comple-mentation schemes and preferential trading arrangements. The latter pre-sents a possible means of implementing the idea, recently mooted, of making the whole ASEAN region of Thailand, Malaysia, Singapore, Philip-pines and Indonesia a single vast EPZ. As Thai Deputy Minister Boonchu Pojanasthien has reportedly said (*Bulletin Today*, 18 February 1981, p. 14), the scheme of economic integration can enhance the development of ASEAN members by removing quantitative restrictions and tariffs, forming a customs union for standardizing tariffs against those of other regions, and establishing a common market that would allow unrestricted flows of com-modities within the region. At present, however, Indonesia is less enthusias-tic about such an idea, pending the mobilization of its economic potential and the attainment of a socio-economic level comparable with the other ASEAN members.

PANACEA OR PASSING PHASE

EPZs in developing Asian countries are most advanced because of the region's progressive entrepreneurial spirit, large numbers of unemployed, availability of managerial staff and high literacy rate. But EPZs should not be considered as a panacea for accelerating economic development as many of the proponents of this concept would claim. EPZs are actually provisional establishments that aim to speed up economic development in a developing country while the opportunity they provide lasts. Thus, as long as cheap surplus labour is available in developing countries and wage levels continue to rise in developed ones, EPZs will continue to remain viable ventures. EPZs are, of course, vulnerable to changing world conditions as well as those in local economies, resulting sometimes in mass lay-offs. In the mid-1970s, for instance, shrinking employment was observed in EPZs fol-lowing pervasive retrenchment moves brought about by global recession. This sensitivity to fluctuating global economic conditions is a fact with which zone planners and employees have to contend (Fujimori, 1980a). The EPZ can only hope to

> accomplish its role at the time when the economy of the host country develops to such an extent that the increased labour cost, as a result of decreasing unemployment, will make labour intensive industries no longer attractive to many profit-seeking investors. It is, therefore, essential to consider the establishment of EPZs as only useful measures (or instruments) for accelerating industrial development of the host country (Vittal, 1977b, p. 13).

Meanwhile, the Third World should take advantage of the demand by foreign investors for the benefits offered by EPZs. This should be done before the spectre of massive unemployment in the investors' home countries brought about by economic fluctuations becomes a reality and forces the investors to bring employment back home. But, as the United Nations Industrial Development Organization (1977, p. 75) points out,

> world production of manufactured goods increases annually, even during recessions . . . Businessmen know that unless they can increase their profits by higher productivity, they can only survive by passing on higher costs in their prices. To avoid increasing prices and losing a share of their market for a product, the obvious strategy is to produce more and sell more.

EPZs conveniently fit into this strategy and, for this and other reasons, it is difficult to see their role as catalysts for growth diminishing in the near future.

Spatial Analysis, Industry and the Industrial Environment. Vol. 3 Regional Economies and Industrial Systems
Edited by F. E. I. Hamilton and G. J. R. Linge

Chapter 20

The Kibbutz Industrial System: A Unique Rural-industrial Community in Israel

BARUCH A. KIPNIS AND AVINOAM MEIR

Kibbutz settlements in Israel, constituting a quarter of the nation's settlements and less than 3 per cent of its 3.7 million population (1979), evolved as a symbol of Israel's rural agricultural community. Contrary to this prevailing image, however, the internal physical, social and economic structure of the Kibbutz is rapidly changing to conform to the attributes of an urban entity (Kipnis and Salmon, 1972). A leading constituent of this change is the evolution of the Kibbutz industrial system which in 1979 accounted for 5 per cent of the nation's value of manufacturing production.

Unlike most industrial systems, which strive for efficient operations under expanding organizational circumstances, the Kibbutz system is moving towards small production entities, fully controlled by their owner-operators, aiming to balance revenues and personal welfare. This distinction stems from the fact that in most Western social structures group ideology plays little more than a latent and implicit role, beyond individual aspirations. However, in the Kibbutzim [Hebrew plural of Kibbutz] ideology—the group philosophy of a voluntary communal way of life in which there is no private property and in which each individual contributes socially and economically according to his ability and receives within the framework of acceptable norms all his needs—is explicit, recognized and shared by all its members. This ideology directs almost every facet of the Kibbutz social and economic activities, industry included. This chapter considers the unique pattern of this system, why and how it has evolved, the organizational structure that generates its operations, and the current issues and future prospects in the context of emerging sophisticated national industrial operations.

Kibbutz industrial activities do not fully conform to the system as defined by Hamilton and Linge (1979). For the most part the industrial units of the Kibbutzim do not operate locally or functionally together. The units maintain their linkages externally with the entire national system, and only limited inter-unit flows have emerged recently. However, 2 organizational elements cause the Kibbutz industry to operate as a system. One is the Kibbutz Industrial Association (KIA), an 'umbrella' body which acts as a 'voluntary' coordinating and advisory agency without controlling the individual operating units. The increasing role of the KIA in recent years makes the Kibbutz industry function as an industrial system from an organizational rather than an economic viewpoint. The other is the Kibbutz Federations' framework with which each Kibbutz is affiliated. These are political-ideological organizational entities that determine the patterns and operational principles of the socio-economic activities. These 2 organizational elements therefore create the 'task environment' (Fredriksson and Lindmark, 1979) of the Kibbutz industrial system, a unique national sub-system confined to industrial production operations within ideologically and organizationally confined principles.

THE NATURE OF THE KIBBUTZ

The industrialization of the Kibbutz and the issues associated with this process are generated by the nature and evolution of the Kibbutz as a collective system (Soshani, 1973; Peseh, 1979). The Kibbutz was intended to be a small agricultural democratic community of several dozen families, with mutual responsibilities among members excluding any kind of individualism, and all productive efforts and consumption patterns equalized and cooperative. The community, being a non-wage system, provides all the economic, social and cultural needs of its members on equal bases. Ideally, it was supposed to become an autarkic closed system, with self-employment in all economic activities. Since the Kibbutz owes—through the Kibbutz movement's criteria—social responsibility to other Kibbutzim, an extreme rise in the standard of living is not desired so that excessive revenues are reinvested within the Kibbutz in existing and new economic ventures. The decision of what, when and how to reinvest is the responsibility of the elected officials of the community pending, in major issues, the approval of the majority of the Kibbutz general assembly.

During the 70 years of the Kibbutz movement the basic ideology has been modified in response to internal processes and the influences of the external environment (Peseh, 1979). First, due to the acceptance of the principle of economies of scale, the Kibbutz has become a larger community, with a desired minimum size of 100 families. This increase provided for more flexible allocation of physical and human resources to innovative economic ventures. Second, the larger size permitted more liberal relationships to evolve among individuals of the community and the establishment of contacts between them and the external environment. These relationships and contacts increased individual aspirations for life-style, standard of living and job opportunities. Labour mobility is, up to a point, managed on the basis of individual choice rather than by communal necessity. With the continuous weakening of the group-ideology discipline, the Kibbutz has become a pluralistic society adjusting to a wider array of human needs and wants. It is more open than ever to absorb change from, and more ready to initiate change towards, the external environment, in terms of impacts from and on society at large, the national economy, and the regional socio-economic order.

CAUSES OF KIBBUTZ INDUSTRIALIZATION

Industrialization of the Kibbutz originated from internal as well as external factors. The internal causes were derivatives of Kibbutz organizational philosophy and of changes in the nature of the human resources, as well as their number (Meir, 1982). The main factor, however, relates to the size of the Kibbutz as an economic unit. During the 1920s and the 1930s there were various philosophies about the optimum size and economic orientation of the Kibbutz, according to the affiliation of the Kibbutzim into 'Federations' (political-ideological factions). Some Kibbutzim favoured a large unit, unrestricted in growth. Although agriculture was, and remains, the main focus, these large Kibbutzim were able to mobilize labour for other economic activities indicating the change towards an agro-industrial society. Another group of Kibbutzim advocated controlled growth, thus affecting the Kibbutz's flexibility to mobilize labour, resulting in a more balanced movement towards industry. A third group favoured a small, slowly growing unit, with agriculture as the sole economic activity: these Kibbutzim established industry relatively late. In time these philosophical differences as to size and economic base largely disappeared and, since the late 1950s, most Kibbutzim have recognized the need to become an agro-industrial society.

This reassessment was brought about, in part, by changes in the number and nature of human resources due to demographic processes. Natural growth and immigration caused high population growth rates. Although most early immigrants were orientated primarily to agricultural work, their short-term impact on industrialization was associated with the reassignment of old-timers from farm activities to manufacturing. In the long run they added, together with the veterans, to the natural increase of the population of the Kibbutz. The outcome was that while in 1936, 53 per cent of the Kibbutzim had fewer than 200 inhabitants, by the early 1960s—at the outset of the great leap towards industrialization—about 45 per cent had populations of over 400, and by 1979 the average number per Kibbutz was about 500 (Meir, 1982). With an annual growth of 2.7 per cent in the early 1950s (Barkai, 1977), it was anticipated that the total Kibbutz population would double in 25 years, thus creating an urgent need to diversify the economic base.

The nature of human resources has also changed, primarily due to the aging population. During the 1930s most people were under 45 years but by the early 1960s about 15 per cent of the population had reached this age, and the proportion is increasing (Barkai, 1977). The implication for the Kibbutz economy has been the growing need to shift the aging labour force from agriculture to less strenuous occupations.

An additional source of change is the technical and managerial experience accumulated from the long involvement in modern agriculture (Meir, 1977). This experience could no longer be absorbed within farming activities that were already very sophisticated. During the 1960s and especially the 1970s this trend was further intensified as more Kibbutz members acquired formal academic and technical qualifications. The high level of competent human capital has generated an internal pressure for involvement in new economic activities.

The internal causes have been accompanied by external constraints on the Kibbutz as an agricultural community. Starting in the early 1940s, a shortage of farm land and water affected the growth potential of the agricultural economy of the Kibbutzim. Moreover, directed by the political dictates of the Jewish settlement authorities, many Kibbutzim were established in peripheral arid, mountainous or swampy areas, and had to limit their farm production because of lack of fertile soil and water. With the growing pressure for agricultural land, many Kibbutzim developed small workshops and factories and this trend was intensified during the Second World War when some Kibbutzim established small plants to make basic military supplies such as clothing, shoes, packing material and ammunition. During the early 1950s the Kibbutzim were forced to decelerate agricultural development due to government intervention to maintain low food prices and to support the new *Moshavim* (semi-communal agricultural settlements), inhabited by new immigrants. With water and land quotas being further reduced, food prices strictly regulated, production costs raised due to new duties on imported inputs, and more people added to the Kibbutz, agricultural profitability and per capita income declined. For example, in 1945 the average per capita income of the Kibbutzim was 33 per cent higher than the national average while in 1965 it was 7 per cent below (Barkai, 1971; Don, 1976; Meir, 1982).

In the mid-1950s the Israeli government initiated an aggressive industrial development policy which strongly affected the Kibbutz economy. Supported by a generous *Capital Investment Encouragement Law* (1950), this encouraged manufacturing on the basis of industrial type, market orientation (preferably export) and location (Gradus and Krakover, 1977). The Law defined 'approved' and 'preferred' enterprises, stating the level of government aid, support and incentives available if located in 'priority regions'. Support included fully developed sites in industrial parks, loans, and grants, income tax reductions and export promotion incentives. In addition, the Law provided for the recruitment of new managerial employees and for the training of low-skilled labour. The Law was particularly favourable to Kibbutzim located near new Development Towns which had limited job opportunities. These could qualify for aid funds on the most favourable terms. From the late 1950s and during the 1960s the Kibbutzim moved quickly into agro-industrial and industrial activities: the seniority and status of the Kibbutz industrial system in the Israeli economy can largely be attributed to this Law. Yet it is the cooperative nature of the Kibbutzim and their ideology, their outstanding record in innovative agriculture, and their internal and external social responsibilities, that have made the benefits of the Law successful implements for industrial development.

THE PROCESS OF INDUSTRIALIZATION

The development of the Kibbutz industrial system has evolved through interrelated spatial and functional processes.

The Spatial Process

The process of the spatial diffusion of Kibbutz industry can be observed both regionally and locally. At the regional level, an adoption threshold is defined as the point at which 25 per cent of the Kibbutzim in a given subdistrict (an administrative subdivision) allocate at least 30 per cent of their labour force to industry. Figure 20.1 illustrates a general progression of industrial diffusion from core to periphery. With a few exceptions, the correlation between the year when this threshold was attained and the distance from the initiator subdistrict is relatively high (Meir, 1980), with the evolution of a smoother diffusion field over time (Meir, 1979a, 1979b). The initiators were Kibbutzim of the Rehovot subdistrict, located south of the Tel-Aviv metropolitan area, the nation's largest urban agglomeration. The diffusion process began there when the nearby Kibbutzim developed new plants or converted old workshops into factories in response to the growing demand for manufactured goods in Tel-Aviv. Neighbouring Kibbutzim learned about the 'successful venture': as each was an 'individual' decision-making entity, they absorbed the information gradually transmitted from the core towards the periphery until Kibbutzim in all subdistricts adopted industry. Kibbutzim, at various stages of development, with different physio-ecological constraints on agriculture, agricultural profitability, demographic pressure and ideological rigidity, demonstrated diverse sensitivities to diffusion factors, such as neighbouring and hierarchical affects (Meir, 1980). Blaut's (1977) notion that information flow cannot be taken as the sole determinant of innovation diffusion processes is also true with respect to the Kibbutz industrial system.

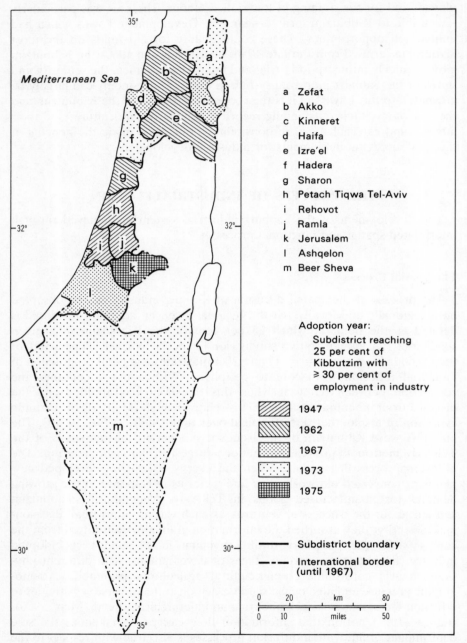

FIGURE 20.1 The spatial spread of Kibbutz industry. [Source: compiled from data supplied by the Kibbutz Industry Association]

The Functional Process

The functional evolution of the Kibbutz industrial system has followed 2 different trends. One involves the changing market orientation; the other, more recent, has emerged through the changing nature of industry towards capital-intensive specialization. Kibbutz industry dates back to the early 1930s, 20 years after the establishment of the first of these settlements. During that decade, the embryonic stage, industry was characterized by small workshops engaged in food processing and in the construction of agricultural implements for local use. The first move towards a commercial industrial system occurred during the 1940s when food, textile and metal industries supplied the Allied Forces and later the Israel Defence Forces. Large-scale penetration of the civilian market began during the second half of the 1950s, and was followed by rapid penetration of foreign markets in the late 1960s and early 1970s. The late 1950s to the early 1970s is considered to be the 'take-off' period of the Kibbutz industrial system (Barkai, 1977; Meir, 1982). In the late 1930s about 55 per cent of the Kibbutzim allocated 10 per cent of their income-earning labour days to industry. In the early 1950s some 35 per cent of the Kibbutzim allocated more than 20 per cent of their productive labour to manufacturing as against 60 and 30 per cent, respectively, 20 years later (Meir, 1980). During the Second World War 10 per cent of the Kibbutzim had 1 factory, whereas in the early 1970s 78 per cent had 1 industrial plant and over 20 per cent had at least 2.

The early 1970s saw Kibbutz industry consolidating previous trends and can be characterized as the 'drive for maturity' stage when it simultaneously strove for more output and higher productivity, searched for new external markets and crystallized an industry branch structure compatible with both the inherent communal characteristics of the Kibbutz and national development policy. In its drive for maturity the Kibbutz industrial system increased its output, employment, investments and exports (Figure 20.2). The rates of growth, influenced by world and local political and economic events, were uneven. Output and employment suffered as a result of the war between Israel and the Arab states in October 1973 and from the partial recession of the late-1970s, whereas exports have significantly increased, taking advantage of government incentives and favourable European markets. In 1977 Kibbutz industry sold 53 per cent of its exports to Europe, mainly to EEC countries. The leading exports have been foodstuffs, furniture, and metal, plastic, rubber and electronic products.

The most notable change was in the structure of industry (Table 20.1 and Figure 20.3). While the traditional labour-intensive industries declined, the more technologically advanced and capital-intensive industries, like plastics and electronics, expanded. (Chi-square [χ^2] values are sufficiently large to

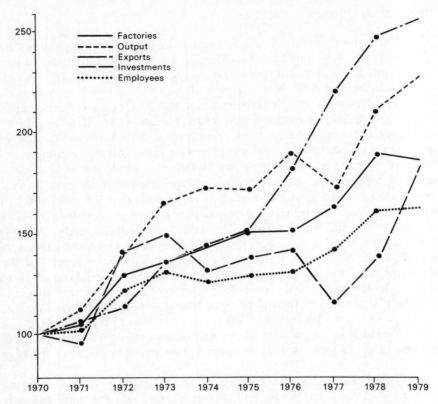

FIGURE 20.2 Index of changes in Kibbutz industry characteristics 1970 to 1979
(1970 = 100). [Source: Kibbutz Industry Association, *Annual Reports,* 1971 to
1980]

reject the hypothesis of similarity between the percentage distribution of the
variables of the attributes shown in Table 20.1 at the beginning and the end
of the decade.) Table 20.2 indicates the diversity of products, many of which
are technologically advanced, currently fabricated by the Kibbutz industrial
system.

Such moves into high-technology capital-intensive operations generated a
tendency towards smaller plants. In the late 1960s, 53 per cent of Kibbutz
factories employed more than 30 workers but by the mid-1970s such
establishments accounted for only 39 per cent of the labour force. Factories
with fewer than 10 workers rose from 14 to 24 per cent of total Kibbutz
industrial establishments during the same period (Meir, 1980), though
recently the growth of this group has halted in favour of factories employing
10 to 30 workers. This latter group, which accounts for 38 per cent of

TABLE 20.1 Changes in the percentage distribution of Kibbutz industrial activities, Israel, 1970 and 1979[a]

Branch of industry	Output			Exports			Employees			Establishments			Investments
	1970	1979	$\frac{1979}{1970}$	1970	1979	$\frac{1979}{1970}$	1970	1979	$\frac{1979}{1970}$	1970	1979	$\frac{1979}{1970}$	1970–79
Metal products	28.3	24.0	1.9	18.1	25.3	3.6	31.0	28.4	1.5	34.6	26.0	1.4	24.4
Plastics	15.4	30.1	4.5	9.7	24.6	6.5	12.4	17.6	2.3	15.6	19.6	2.3	29.4
Foodstuffs	16.3	13.2	1.8	39.4	26.6	1.7	17.7	8.8	0.8	10.1	5.7	1.1	13.4
Wood and furniture	22.2	10.9	1.1	29.0	9.8	0.9	22.8	16.3	1.2	7.8	5.4	1.3	8.7
Electronics	2.4	5.5	4.6	0.2	4.2	53.0	2.9	6.3	3.5	8.4	9.6	2.1	5.5
Others	15.4	16.3	2.4	3.6	9.5	6.8	13.2	22.6	2.8	23.5	33.7	2.7	18.6
Total	100.0	100.0	2.3	100.0	100.0	2.6	100.0	100.0	1.6	100.0	100.0	1.9	100.0
χ^2 values Ei = 1970[b]	23.09			124.39			20.41			11.7			

[a] Diamonds excluded.
[b] χ^2 of α at 0.05 = 11.1 and α at 0.01 = 15.1.
Source: Kibbutz Industry Association, *Annual Report*, 1971, 1980.

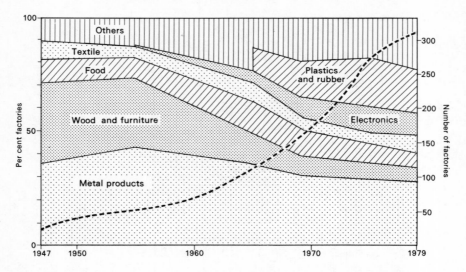

FIGURE 20.3 Change in composition of Kibbutz industry, 1947 to 1979. [Source: published and unpublished data from Kibbutz Industry Association]

Kibbutz factories, has been dominant both relatively and absolutely since the mid-1970s implying an emerging pattern of factory size. A notable reduction in the average workforce per plant occurred in the traditional labour-intensive industries; electronics—a growth industry—alone showed a significant increase (Table 20.3). These trends reflect the growing desire to comply with Kibbutz ideology by abolishing reliance on hired labour and reverting to self-employment on the one hand (Table 20.4), and the emerging shortage of blue-collar employment opportunities among Kibbutz members on the other. The result was to increase productivity, both per employee and per establishment, as is shown in Table 20.3.

The changes in the structure of the Kibbutz industry were greater than those which took place nationally: while the Kibbutzim lagged behind the national growth of output and exports they exceeded it in capital investment and industrial employment (Table 20.5). The result was a slight decrease in the share of the Kibbutz in national industrial output (Table 20.6) most of which occurred in traditional industries. This was not compensated for by the striking increase in the share they obtained of the plastics industry, which the Kibbutzim now dominate in Israel. This is the result of their early adoption of this industry and its also meeting their basic social needs. At the beginning of the 1960s KIA foresaw the growing worldwide demand for plastic products as substitutes for metal, wood and cement goods. The KIA stimulated their affiliated Kibbutzim to take advantage of the *Capital*

TABLE 20.2 Examples of product types by branch of industry, Kibbutz industry, Israel, 1980

Branch of industry	Product types
Metal products	Pressure gauges and regulators, irrigation electronic control systems, solar systems, air-conditioning systems, heat exchangers, automatic fire-extinguishing systems, optical microscopes, hydraulic power units, fertilizer spreaders, gas water-heaters
Electrical products	Magnetic cores for transformers, electrotherapy analgesic devices, electric motors, oscilloscopes, computerized monitor systems, television sets, micro-computer systems, communication devices, vacuum equipment, alarm systems, detectors for nuclear radiation
Plastics and rubber	Sprinkler and irrigation accessories, plastic netting, irrigation pipes, drip irrigation products, solar collectors, polyethylene and PVC products, pressure hoses, filters, fertilizer pumps
Optics	Optical lenses, safety lenses, optical sunglasses, photo-grey lenses, tinted lenses, ophthalmic plastic lenses
Foodstuffs	Spices, fermented products, glucose, starches for food, livestock feed
Building materials	Basalt and granolite aggregates, prepared concrete, bituminous concrete

Source: Kibbutz Industry Association, 1980.

TABLE 20.3 Changes in size and productivity by branch of industry, Israel, 1970 to 1979[a]

Branch of industry	Average size of plant			Production in $US000 (1979 values)					
				Per employee			Per establishment		
	1970	1979	$\frac{1979}{1970}$	1970	1979	$\frac{1979}{1970}$	1970	1979	$\frac{1979}{1970}$
Metal products	43	46	1.07	24.7	31.9	1.29	1062	1464	1.38
Plastics	38	38	1.00	33.6	64.6	1.92	1277	2429	1.90
Foodstuffs	84	65	0.77	25.0	56.6	2.26	2089	3642	1.74
Wood and furniture	138	126	0.91	26.5	25.2	0.95	3657	3178	0.87
Electronics	17	27	1.59	22.3	32.8	1.47	379	900	2.37
Others	27	28	1.04	31.6	27.2	0.86	853	763	0.89
Total industry	48	42	0.88	27.1	37.7	1.39	1300	1580	1.22

[a] Diamonds excluded.
Source: Kibbutz Industry Association, Annual Report, 1971, 1980.

TABLE 20.4 Size of plants and per cent of employed Kibbutz
members by year of establishment

Year of establishment	Number of plants	Employees	
		Average number	Per cent members
Up to 1950	50	87	49
1951–60	44	71	54
1961–65	35	61	70
1966–70	38	44	84
1971–75	76	25	91
1976–	33	21	88
Total	276	42	66

Source: Kibbutz Industry Association, *Annual Report,* 1980.

Investment Encouragement Law and move rapidly into this field. Plastics
factories provided indoor diversified job opportunities to the aging and
female unskilled members and, at the same time, created new employment
challenges for the young, who sought new technologies and managerial
activities. Other entrepreneurs have entered this field too late to override
the Kibbutzim's share in the production for local and foreign markets.

Thus Kibbutz industry has become further diversified and more balanced
through the addition of new branches of industry and by becoming less
labour-intensive and more capital and technology-intensive; these developments are mirrored in the number of factories per Kibbutz (Table 20.7). All
these changes reflect the growing awareness of Kibbutz institutions of the
special needs of both their aging and younger populations and the decline of
ideological rigidity as it relates to the role of the individual in the group and
to the centralized determination of labour mobilization.

The Kibbutz, a pluralistic democratic society, with multi-individual and
group initiatives, has always pursued mixed economic efforts and risk
distribution. Unlike agriculture, which has always complied with the goal of

TABLE 20.5 Percentage growth of industrial attributes,
Israel and Kibbutz, 1975 to 1979[a]

Area	Output	Exports	Investment	Employment
Israel	42	162	11	8
Kibbutz	32	132	28	26

[a] Diamonds excluded.
Source: Kibbutz Industry Association, *Annual Report,* 1976,
1980.

TABLE 20.6 Changes by branch of industry in the role of Kibbutz industry, Israel, 1975 to 1979[a]

Branch of industry	1975		1979		1979/1975	
	Production $US million	Per cent of Israel	Production $US million	Per cent of Israel	Kibbutz	Israel
Metal products	104.4	8.4	125.9	8.6	1.21	1.12
Plastics	85.6	46.6	157.9	68.6	1.84	1.28
Foodstuffs	54.7	3.7	69.2	3.4	1.27	1.37
Wood and furniture	63.0	19.9	57.2	15.5	0.91	1.15
Electronics	20.2	3.9	28.8	3.9	1.43	1.42
Others	68.6	1.9	85.5	1.5	1.25	1.58
Total	396.5	5.3	524.5	5.0	1.32	1.42

[a] Diamonds excluded.
Source: Kibbutz Industry Association, *Annual Report,* 1976, 1980.

diversity, industry initially evolved as a 'nucleus' branch in which a small core of highly motivated skilled workers dominated a wide periphery of unskilled labour, including many hired employees (Kupper, 1977). The hiring of labour was initiated as a desired natural regional process but later turned out to be an active threat to the Kibbutz way of life.

During the 1950s the Kibbutz economy grew rapidly. In part this was facilitated by the increasing number of new immigrants absorbed in the new

TABLE 20.7 Percentage distribution of Kibbutzim by number of industrial establishments, 1974 and 1978

Number of industrial establishments in a Kibbutz	Per cent of Kibbutzim		1978/1974
	1974	1978	
0	22.4	18.0	0.80
1	56.8	48.4	0.85
2	16.8	26.0	1.55
3	3.2	5.2	1.63
>4	0.8	2.4	3.00
Total	100.0	100.0	1.00
χ^2 values Ei = 1974[a]	11.61		

[a] χ^2 of α at 0.05 = 9.5 and α at 0.01 = 13.3.
Source: Kibbutz Industry Association, *Annual Report,* 1975, 1979.

towns of the long-established rural environment which were based on labour-intensive farm activities in their region (Kipnis, 1974). Later in the 1950s and during the 1960s, when the Kibbutz expanded its industry, it recruited labour from the less developed new towns. In so doing, the Kibbutz economy contributed to the national effort in absorbing new immigrants who had been settled, according to the Population Dispersal Policy, in peripheral regions. In turn, through participation in the national effort, the Kibbutz industry qualified for the *Capital Investment Encouragement Law* allowances which were designed as a key element of the Population Dispersal Policy (Zilberberg, 1973; Kipnis, 1976, 1977).

The increasing use of hired labour contradicted the essential of self-employment, a cornerstone of Kibbutz ideology. In the 1970s, hired labour in Kibbutz industry reached an alarming level of about one-third of the labour force which led to serious debate in some Kibbutzim. The opposition to external labour resources rapidly declined and it was decided to abolish, whenever possible, the hired labour system regardless of the economic costs to the Kibbutz and of the social consequences to the neighbouring new town. The recent return to the ideology of self-employment, along with greater opportunities for personal initiatives, has created the new phenomenon of several small capital-intensive advanced plants in a Kibbutz. In this respect, Kibbutz industry is returning to the traditional pattern of a multi-branch economy inherited from the long-established agriculture.

The process of Kibbutz industrialization is best summed up by an S-curve showing the increasing share of non-agricultural employment (mainly industry) in productive labour inputs (Figure 20.4). The curve facilitates the

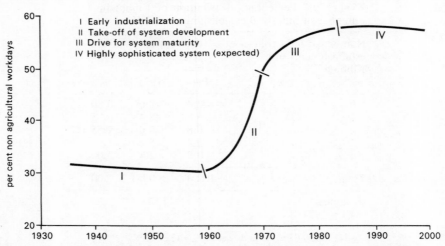

FIGURE 20.4 Stages in growth of non-agricultural employment in Kibbutzim, 1930 to 2000. [Sources: Barkai, 1971; Helman and Sonis, 1977]

delineation of 3 stages that the Kibbutz has already experienced in its 'industrial revolution', and speculation about a fourth, yet to come during the 1980s. Helman and Sonis (1977), employing Markov Chain analysis, suggest that non-agricultural employment will remain constant at a mid-1980s level of 57 per cent. Only extraordinary events in industrial development or agricultural technology might affect this. In the fourth stage the Kibbutz industrial system is assumed to use very sophisticated manufacturing methods to overcome labour shortages and the ideological constraints about hired labour. Some of the current issues, initial indicators of this future stage, have recently received increasing attention both within individual Kibbutzim and through KIA involvement.

THE ROLE OF THE KIBBUTZ INDUSTRY ASSOCIATION

To survive, given the small size and geographical isolation of its members, the Kibbutz movement has developed national and regional associations for planning, purchasing of inputs, marketing and extension services. Most were established by Kibbutzim affiliated to the same Federation framework, although some cooperation between Federations has occurred. Despite the centralized organization of the Kibbutz economy, the emergence of its industrial system has, on the whole, been a haphazard process. The penetration of domestic and foreign markets by the Kibbutz industry during the 'take-off' stage, stimulated the need for more controlled development. The establishment of the KIA in 1963 was a turning point towards planned industrialization; its role has increased and by the early 1970s its impact on the system, both internally and externally, was recognized and dominant.

The interfederative KIA organization enables the scattered, small independent Kibbutz industrial units to operate within a framework of scale economies. The KIA thus facilitates non-spatial 'organizational external economies', offering services as important as those provided in the context of locational externalities, which are missing from Kibbutz industry. It has had a significant influence in providing diversified operational services and in helping to adjust industry to the socio-economic needs of the Kibbutz. The KIA lacks any governing powers, its role being restricted to that of coordinator among Kibbutzim to promote competitive terms with the outside community and to reduce internal competition between them; the latter objective derives directly from the Kibbutz ideology which regards inter-Kibbutz social responsibility as one of its basic pillars.

The KIA furnishes advisory and developmental services. The first group includes production, judicial, investment, marketing and export advice as well as assistance in searching out sources of finance. These are aimed at proper selection of plant types, technological planning of production lines, mobilization of investment capital from government and other resources and the penetration of domestic and foreign markets. The developmental services consist of R & D, vocational training and socio-technology. All these services are solely advisory: the KIA does not assume any role in the actual production or distribution processes which remain the responsibility of the individual enterprise—the Kibbutz—though some Kibbutzim might join forces on a voluntary basis to establish mutual ventures for production and marketing.

Through the 1970s, when the Kibbutz industrial system grew rapidly towards maturity, the KIA was active in 2 directions: externally to attain economic growth through advanced technology, and internally to consolidate the productive entities in conformity with the Kibbutz ideology and way of life. These roles have raised a series of issues, the solution of which may have great impact on the future of the Kibbutz industrial system.

CURRENT ISSUES

The essence of the Kibbutz way of life is anchored in the principles of voluntary equality, mutuality, self-employment, and the distinction between the member-employee's contribution to his job and his actual personal gains. These principles seldom prevail in any other voluntary economic formation in the world. Yet the evolution of the Kibbutz industry has been a replica of the classical Western economy, in conflict with the host entity's ideology (Kibbutz Industry Association, 1979). The challenge, therefore, is to comprehend this conflict and to search for a way to turn back the existing industrial system to suit the nature of the Kibbutz.

One issue is how to motivate an industrial worker and a Kibbutz factory to maximize their production potential. Eden and Levitan (1974) reported that Kibbutz factory workers rated their job significantly below those employed in agriculture in terms of opportunities for self-realization even though all members of a Kibbutz, whether employed in agriculture or industry, enjoy the same economic rewards for their work. The KIA, in coping with this and other related questions, initiated a 'socio-technology' programme which has been implemented both in the plant and the whole industrial system. Rewards and self-realization are maintained through sequential modifications in job activity, a special physical working environment to induce collaboration and equality, equal sets of obligations and rights, and the abolition of any physical or abstract status symbols.

The socio-technology approach is costly and inefficient. For instance, the cost of maintaining inter-plant labour mobility or an inter-plant managerial cycle and responsibility—essential for the job enrichment programme—is considerable both in monetary and organizational terms. The continuity of this approach leads to the conclusion suggested by Barkai (1977) that the equality goal is a 'luxurious consumption good' for the Kibbutz.

In fact, 2 basic groups must be considered. The aging founders of the Kibbutz who have limited skills and need simple, physically suitable and routine jobs, are highly motivated and have been exposed to many work experiences during their lives (Kipnis and Salmon, 1972). In contrast, the young members desire advanced technology and efficiency and seek to avoid blue-collar jobs. This labour force structure has created the 'nucleus' indust-rial branch organization, and has led the Kibbutz industrial system to search for advanced, capital-intensive technology associated with a wide range of simple, easy-to-learn production processes. The abolition of the use of hired labour raises various social and economic problems which can be briefly discussed.

Shift work has been part of the Kibbutz economy from its early days, mainly on a seasonal or temporary basis. In advanced manufacturing, however, where more efficient use of capital is desired or where production processes demand continuous operations, shift work is essential. Shifts contravene both the biological and the social clocks, the latter of particular importance to the Kibbutz cultural and family way of life. To comprehend this issue, it should be remembered that a Kibbutz is an integrated social, cultural and economic entity. All social and cultural activities, like the economic ones, are essential segments of the sequential daily activities of a Kibbutz member. Active participation in community affairs and the late afternoon-early evening family gathering hours best illustrate the inherent conflict between the social clock and shift work. The latter is of great significance since the children, who in most Kibbutzim live in separated quarters and maintain a daily schedule of their own, 'visit' their parents during these hours. The conflict becomes more severe in the Kibbutz community which denies economic incentive for the extra effort of shift work (Shapira, 1980).

Employment of women in manufacturing is a common phenomenon throughout the world. Yet, despite the intensive drive for equal opportuni-ties, the status of the jobs open to women is generally inferior in practice or image. Recruitment of women to Kibbutz industry requires special provi-sions to secure a job image of sexual equality and to guarantee job responsibilities, rights and opportunities (Shapira, 1979).

Higher education and professional training are controversial issues on the Kibbutz. When related to industry, it raises questions like the nature of the proper know-how and its relationship to the member's own interest, and the stage of professional development most appropriate for acquiring industrial training. The new industrial technology introduced to the Kibbutz has augmented both the conflicts and the diversity of employment opportunities.

It has also produced favourable institutional and personal attitudes toward higher education in other sectors of the Kibbutz (Levitan, 1973; HaKibbutz HaArtzi, 1975).

Economic development constraints are imposed on the system with the increasing number of advanced-technology plants, with the gradual evolution of some production lines in one plant, or with the progressive establishment of new marketing channels. Each of these developments requires a core of skilled workers. If they occur quickly the local potential of innovative and skilled labour is exhausted, thus preventing further development of new economic activities in the Kibbutz. Another aspect of the new technology manufacturing relates to the R & D potential of the Kibbutz industrial system. Partial R & D activities have existed in the Kibbutz both in agriculture and in manufacturing: as a collective community and as a 'large economy business', Kibbutzim have been able to absorb and experiment with new ideas. These have been of 3 types: agricultural tools and implements, processed agricultural products, and consumer goods (mainly for children). Notable examples are irrigation systems and remote control devices for irrigation and other farm facilities; canned food, juices and syrups; and furniture, toys and educational devices. In all these the Kibbutz had a latent reputation as a 'choosy' user and consumer that it could employ in marketing its products.

The KIA has recently established an R & D institute to provide for scale economies in research on processes and product development. The Institute for Technology, Research and Development takes advantage of the accumulated know-how and experience of the various Kibbutzim and through concentrated R & D efforts devises products and production processes which suit the size and nature of Kibbutz industry (Kreiden, 1977). The cost of introducing modern technology into small establishments, essential for the Kibbutz social system and the successful implementation of sociotechnology programmes, is a crucial problem (Kupper, 1980). In some cases, the small plant might be economically valuable in competing for small-scale markets outside the sphere of influence of the larger plants. In others, the narrow economic base requires a development strategy that avoids uncertainty and risk, and aims for immediate rewards. Under this strategy, a small plant can become a profitable sub-contractor of a large firm, taking advantage of the latter's reputation and markets.

Three common sub-contracting arrangements might exist. First, the large firm can contract for a certain quantity of intermediate or final output which is then marketed as a product of the large firm. Second, the large firm can give the sub-contracting small plant a concession on a portion of its markets allowing it to use the name, reputation and advertisement services; this enables the large firm to devote more effort to the creation of new products, production lines and markets. Third, a Kibbutz plant can choose to purchase the rights to a new technology and product from a large firm or to join, for a reasonable commission, the distribution system of a large enterprise. All these strategies are very costly, harm the competitive capacity of the industry and risk its profitable operations.

Yet if the Kibbutz industrial system is to become an active force in world markets, it must seek ways to attain scale economies. One possibility is the extension of the R & D and other activities of the KIA; another is Kibbutz cooperation. More than 20 inter-Kibbutz partnerships existed in 1979, mainly involving a newly formed Kibbutz and a well-established industrial one. The latter seeks new labour resources to expand operations so that the partnership terms are based on labour allocation rather than financial arrangements. Six types of inter-Kibbutz industrial cooperations have evolved:

(a) full partnership in one plant;
(b) supplementary plants;
(c) allocation of one line of production;
(d) partnership in one production effort;
(e) regional division of the market;
(f) partnership in marketing efforts.

In most instances where 2 plants are involved, the tendency is to develop 1 plant on the premises of each Kibbutz to minimize commuting, mainly of the aged who constitute large segments of the labour force. Such arrangements can extend the opportunities for R & D, marketing research and other externalities. Moreover, they allow the splitting of high risk inherent in capital-intensive science-based industries.

Inter-Kibbutz cooperation may create both positive and negative regional development impacts. The evolution of regional specialization and complementary activities between 2 Kibbutzim may cause irreversible disparities between those Kibbutzim and other neighbouring settlements. The situation would affect most *Moshavim* (the cooperative type of rural settlements) and also neighbouring Kibbutzim possessing an inferior economic base. Furthermore, the joint ventures would stimulate new commuting flows, create new nodes of economic activity and could possibly generate a new social structure which may, in turn, alter the existing rural regional order. Cooperation in industrial ventures is a challenge for the Kibbutz industrial system and may come to dominate the course of events in the fourth stage of Kibbutz industrialization (Figure 20.4). These possibilities and the new regional order involve new potential as well as a hidden threat to the Kibbutz movement and to the balanced organization of the rural regions of the country.

THE KIBBUTZ INDUSTRIAL SYSTEM AT A CROSSROADS

The Kibbutz industrial system can take several possible directions to reach its last evolutionary phase of a highly sophisticated system (Figure 20.4). Each may entail substantial effects on the industrial system, the impact of which would be transmitted from the individual Kibbutz level to the entire Kibbutz movement, and further to the regional level and the nation at large.

The most obvious trend is towards the more technological and capital-intensive industries. In this situation, labour-capital ratios, the proportion of white-collar employees and the risk factor will increase, resulting in more diversified production lines both within the Kibbutz factory and through inter-Kibbutz cooperation. The diversification process will bring about more efficient use of labour and the reduction of risks. Cooperation between Kibbutzim will take advantage of wider labour and capital pools and geographical distribution of the impact of uncertainty. The dependence of the operating system on the KIA externalities will increase and the KIA will focus on capital mobilization and on the provision of R & D and marketing services to the few most promising growth industries, which will lead to large-scale cartelization of the Kibbutz industry. In cartelized operations the intimate social setting of the Kibbutz, which has been extended to absorb the cooperative principles, may demand more intensive KIA involvement in socio-technological projects: in turn, it will have to cope with a new set of social issues of a different geographical space, completely alien to Kibbutz ideology. At the Kibbutz level, the new trends will stimulate strong competition for capital and labour resources between manufacturing and agriculture. As in the past (Barkai, 1977), agriculture will lose its seniority in the Kibbutz economic structure, a change that will create a significant deviation from the initial philosophy which states that, regardless of quasi-urbanization processes leading to urban culture and behaviour (Kipnis and Salmon, 1972), the Kibbutz has been and will always be a rural-agricultural community.

The retreat from agriculture and the swift changes within the industrial sector will bring about a new social economic order in the Kibbutz, the attributes of which would be high labour mobility, changing patterns of employment and prestige, and a widening gap between the older untrained members and the highly trained white-collar younger generation. With the increasing spatial dimensions of industrial activity, large commuting distances will emerge, with both new regional images and increased personal mobility (already reflected in rising car ownership rates). These changes, initiated by industry, will require an extension of socio-technology methods to handle industry-ideology conflicts beyond the plant premises.

Capital accumulation has normally been directed into new economic investments with a very slight and gradual increase in standards of living, ideologically controlled by the Federations. The case might be completely different when capital is accumulated in an industrialized Kibbutz facing limited labour resources and imposing ideological restrictions on itself against hired labour. Such a Kibbutz might be in a dilemma analogous to that of a national economy approaching the mass-consumption stage (Rostow, 1971). Increased revenues could create local temptation for a higher standard of living and increasing consumption above declared and agreed norms. These trends might widen the gap between rich and poor Kibbutzim at the regional, federal and national levels. An alternative course of action—which would require intensive encouragement, support and initiative by the KIA— would be to allocate the excess capital into more inter-Kibbutz cooperation, programmed mutual support and induced R & D activities. The mass consumption option presents dangers to the future existence of the Kibbutz movement but the other, which might stimulate cartelization processes could create threats to regional and national economies.

Intensive industrialization of the Kibbutz would widen the gap already prevailing in most regions between the Kibbutzim and other types of neighbouring settlements, mainly Development Towns. The latter would experience increasing unemployment when more of their residents who have been hired by Kibbutz factories are declared redundant, a process already occurring for ideological or economic reasons. The new capital accumulation in the region is reinvested in new factories on the premises of the Kibbutzim or transferred through inter-Kibbutz cooperation to other regions. The Development Town would then continue to depend on out-of-region industrial capital. This issue is so pressing that a Kibbutz industry leader has suggested that the Kibbutzim should invest in the industrial establishments in the new towns within their region so as to create additional industrial employment for the residents of such places. Moreover, within a particular region industrialization may also create a growing gap between rich and poor Kibbutzim which could lead to a hierarchical status and economic dependency between the Kibbutzim there.

Industrialization of the Kibbutz, as envisaged here, may also have considerable impacts on the national economy. A strong industrial system, centrally controlled and coordinated by the KIA, would act as a unified dominating entity in a small Israeli economy. Similarly, the Kibbutzim control more than one-third of Israel's farm land and slightly less than two-thirds of its irrigated soils. Land and water are both limited resources. If Kibbutz industrialization results in less labour and capital allocated to agriculture, the farm product share in the GNP would decline. None the less the industrialization of the Kibbutz may, in the long run, have some positive effects. Induced industrial development could possibly alter the existing harsh inequality between the national core and peripheral regions. Since three-quarters of the Kibbutzim are peripherally located, industrialization would augment their contribution to GNP.

The Kibbutz industrial system has been a dynamic phenomenon in the

Israeli economy. During the last few decades it has spread geographically and functionally, with most Kibbutzim throughout the country having at least one factory and many having several. Moreover, industrialization has stimulated far-reaching modifications to the socio-economic structure of the Kibbutz. In striving towards advanced and growing industrial activities, the impact of the Kibbutz industrial system is likely to be felt outside the individual Kibbutz premises. Both the potential and the hazard of these new trends should be comprehensively evaluated by the institutions of the Kibbutz movement and by the government so that positive advantage can be taken of this unique and valuable economic activity.

Spatial Analysis, Industry and the Industrial Environment. Vol. 3 Regional Economies and Industrial Systems
Edited by F. E. I. Hamilton and G. J. R. Linge
© 1983 John Wiley & Sons Ltd.

Chapter 21

The Structure of Industrial Change: Regional Incentives to the Textile Industry of Northeast Brazil

ANTHONY EDWARDS

This chapter considers the structure of industrial change in a section of manufacturing industry which has undergone rapid expansion in Brazil, one of the newly industrializing countries (NICs). The textile industry of the Northeast Region there has been transformed from a stagnant traditional sector to a dynamic industry characterized by external ownership and modern technology. Strong industrial incentives have been granted to alleviate long-standing regional inequalities through successive policies of industrial restructuring, expansion and the encouragement of manufactured exports. The chapter examines the effect these have had on the indigenous textile sector.

INDUSTRY AND REGIONAL POLICY

The persistence of regional disparities in levels of development and regional income in economies of all types, seemingly irrespective of their economic integration or resource endowment, has meant that governments of all political ideologies have had to respond to pressures to equalize living standards between different regions of their territory (Brazil, 1974; Martin *et al.*, 1979; Centre for Urban and Regional Development Studies, 1979). Regional policy as such is hardly new but the intractability of regional problems has encouraged attention to be focused upon the dynamics of regional economies and their interaction within national and international frameworks (Holland, 1976; Massey, 1978). Such approaches have rejected 'regions' as autonomous, geographically defined analytical units but have attempted to uncover the processes which create spatially uneven development, through the analysis of exploitative elements which shape the pattern of economic development in each country at both national and regional levels. These relationships of power and dependency are continually evolving as the profitability of various forms of economic activity change (Massey and Meegan, 1978).

The power of governments to intervene in the mixed economy as both an agent of state expenditure and as a regulatory body is a critical force in shaping the form of such power and dependency relationships in pluralist democratic societies as well as in authoritarian regimes. Governments have formulated policies both as an expression of their political ideals and as an attempt to stave off criticism and unpopularity in regions adversely affected by chronic imbalances. These policy measures have generally included (Gonzales, 1980, p. 3):

(a) redistribution of public and private infrastructure investment;
(b) promotion of high productivity sectors to relocate in peripheral regions;
(c) creation of growth poles by concentrated investment in chosen sectors and areas;
(d) incentives for regional exports;
(e) manipulation of factor prices in peripheral regions.

Since industry has been a chief target for such measures, it is in industrial terms that the success or failure of regional policy has been judged. The basic units of industrial production are individual manufacturing establishments; change, if it is to occur, will have its impact at this level. However, to hold constant long and short-term variations between firms engaged in the production of fundamentally dissimilar goods has meant that the smallest comparable agglomerations for examining regional policy impacts have been specific industrial sectors. The problem of trying to evaluate the impacts of regional policy has been to surmount these barriers of spatial and industrial agglomeration to examine the mechanisms by which government policy has affected the individual establishment in terms of variations in the quantity and quality of output and hence to explain aggregate change measured at regional and sectoral levels.

Several studies have treated the establishment as the central unit to measure the effects of regional manufacturing and, where appropriate, the effects of regional policy. One such group of studies has attempted to provide an 'accounting framework' (Keeble, 1978) to look at each element of change at an aggregate level: expansion, decline, closure and creation of establishments and their consequent effect upon the local economy. Other workers have concentrated on the control and decision-making structures of complete enterprises; since they may be highly individual institutions, it may be inappropriate to compile a standardized framework of change without an analysis of corporate decision-making.

This chapter attempts to use techniques of establishment-based analysis to examine the effect of regional policy, which includes measures such as those already outlined, on industrial expansion in a peripheral region of Brazil. Regional disparities in Brazil have been particularly acute given the large size of the country and have been exacerbated by the rapid economic growth of the late 1960s and early 1970s, universally known as the Brazilian 'miracle'. Regional policy for the most depressed region, the Northeast, has tried to promote industrial expansion of traditionally important sectors as well as encourage the creation of new ones. The result has been a radical shift in the region's industrial structure as new establishments have been introduced. This chapter examines in detail how these changes have affected the textile industry.

THE GENESIS OF INDUSTRIAL POLICY

Regional imbalance within Brazil is closely related to structural differences in types of economic activity. Manufacturing is heavily concentrated in the southeastern states of São Paulo, Minas Gerais and Rio de Janeiro. Of the remaining regions, the South has a predominantly extensive agricultural system with some manufacturing in the larger urban areas, whilst the West and North Regions are still sparsely populated with very low levels of economic activity. The Northeast represents the most anomalous and problematic area: it has about a third of the population of Brazil but is characterized by inequality of land ownership in rural areas and low levels of industrial employment and periodically suffers catastrophic droughts (Figure 21.1 and Table 21.1).

The initial prosperity of the Northeast was based upon sugar cultivation using African slave labour, which created vast wealth for the land-owning élite but also an impoverished rural population. With the rise in importance of the coffee-producing areas of the southeastern states the Northeast suffered absolute and relative decline (Furtado, 1963). National concern over the moribund condition of the Northeast economy was articulated as early as the 1870s when a particularly severe drought killed 500,000 people (Hall, 1978). Government action was limited to creating workfronts and building dams for water storage, in the belief that these would be sufficient to overcome the droughts.

The region was not without some indigenous manufacturing industry even at this time, as poor communication with the rest of the country meant that the Northeast had to provide even the most basic requirements for its large population. The textile industry was one of these; at the end of the First World War the Northeast was producing about a quarter of the national output of textiles, which provided 95 per cent of internal consumption (Evans, 1979). This was the 'Golden Age' of textile production (Stein, 1957). Throughout the 1920s and 1930s the industry was granted high levels of protection to maintain internal demand and keep out cheap imports from industrialized countries. By 1939 the textile industry in Brazil employed

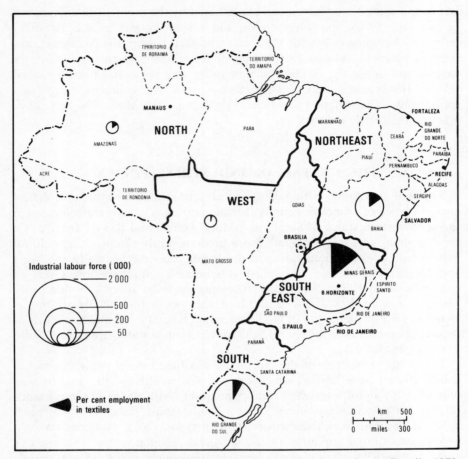

FIGURE 21.1 Regional distribution of the industrial labour force, Brazil, 1970.
[Source: Instituto Brasileiro de Geografia e Estatística, 1974]

about 235,000 people, of whom about 57,000 were employed in the Northeast, accounting for more than a quarter of that Region's industrial labour
force.

The Second World War opened new export markets to Brazilian producers, such as South Africa and the rest of Latin America, which were
normally supplied by the United Kingdom and the United States. Brazilian
mills dramatically increased production to unprecedented levels, working
machinery round the clock. Between 1942 and 1945 an average of 42,000
tonnes of cotton cloth was exported annually from Brazil. 'In 1946, the
Brazilian textile industry was one of the largest in the world supplying all

TABLE 21.1 Brazil: regional distribution of population and industry, 1973

Region	Total population[a]	Urban population[b]	Industrial workforce[c]	Industrial value added
North	4	3	2	1
Northeast	30	22	8	6
Southeast	42	56	72	78
South	18	14	17	14
West	6	5	1	1
Total	100	100	100	100

[a] Total 101,432,000.
[b] Total 59,033,000.
[c] Total 3,199,000.
Source: Instituto Brasileiro de Geografia e Estatística, 1978.

domestic needs and exporting to various countries' (Bergsman, 1970, p. 145). Unfortunately, little was done to capitalize on this situation: exports were temporarily forbidden in 1946 following complaints that home requirements were being neglected in favour of quick profits abroad (Stein, 1957) which were not reinvested in the industry to replace overworked and outdated machinery. By the beginning of the 1950s all exports had ceased.

The post-war years saw a turning point in government industrial and economic strategy. There was a strong nationalist movement towards greater intervention in the whole economy, evident in the foundation of a petroleum monopoly (Petrobrás) and the Volta Redonda Steelworks in Rio de Janeiro. Import restrictions on a wide range of consumer goods encouraged their domestic production which tended to be concentrated in the southeastern states, especially in the urban areas of São Paulo, Rio de Janeiro and Belo Horizonte. Other regions were forced by the import tariffs to purchase these manufactured goods from the Southeast with income obtained from the sale of primary products. The policy measures which were used to foster this form of industralization included a multiple exchange rate system which gave high levels of protection to certain industries while still allowing the import of capital goods, credits for industrial investment, and fiscal incentives to promote certain sectors (Baer 1965). Such incentives were weighted against agriculture in favour of 'dynamic' industries such as automobiles, metal working, chemicals and printing (Tyler, 1976). Older traditional industries like food processing and textiles, which had exhausted their import-substituting potentiality prior to the Second World War, were unable to participate in the expansion of the 1950s. By 1959 the textile industry had still not surpassed the peak output of 1943 (Versiani, 1972). The traditional industries were more important to the regions outside the Southeast, so that the sectoral policies pursued by the modernizing regimes of the 1950s had an implicit spatial impact.

THE MOST GRAVE PROBLEM

Specific regional initiatives were precipitated by a drought in the Northeast in 1958. New political and economic policies were necessary to overcome the chronic imbalance which existed between that region and the rest of Brazil, particularly the prosperous Southeast. A Working Party (Grupo do Trabalho do Desenvolvimento do Nordeste, 1959) was created to report on the situation and suggest remedial action. The starting point of its Report (p. 293) was unequivocal:

> The disparity of levels of income which exists between the Northeast and the Southeast of the country constitutes without doubt the most grave problem confronting the present stage of national economic development. This disparity is greater than that observed between the economy of the Southeast and the industrialized countries of Western Europe [author's translation].

The solutions recommended included the use of the more fertile areas of the Region for the production of food, colonization of the distant wetter areas, and the creation of a manufacturing base capable of absorbing the large pool of unemployed migrants who were forced into the cities. The means of carrying out the recommendations of the Working Party were achieved through the creation of a development agency charged with the task of formulating and implementing regional policy. The Superintendency for the Development of the Northeast (Superintêndencia do Desenvolvimento do Nordeste: SUDENE) was given power to draft comprehensive Master Plans and coordinate state and federal aid.

The textile industry was given a special place in the programme of industrialization because of its importance to the regional economy; its capital stock was in a disastrous condition and factories were in imminent danger of closure. A programme of modernization was put forward (SUDENE, 1962, p. 12), which sought to remedy the following problems:

(a) rigidity in the structure of production and participation in the least dynamic and profitable section of the market;
(b) obsolescence of equipment;
(c) loss of the relative advantages in the cost of labour aggravated by its excessive use in the process of production and by the lack of convenient labour training;
(d) administrative deficiencies leading to greater costs;
(e) lack of finance to replace obsolete equipment [author's translation].

The Northeast textile industry in 1959 consisted of 61 establishments, over 90 per cent being single plant independent firms: only 1 had an extensive chain of tied retail outlets. Only 7 Northeast mills had more than 25,000 spindles each before the Second World War (Stein, 1957) and, although precise figures for 1959 are not available, the post-war stagnation of the industry suggests that there would not have been any increase in capacity. In general the industry was small-scale, integrated and making low-quality cloth; and its position in relation to production in other regions was declining (Table 21.2).

The age and low output of the capital stock caused particularly acute problems of productivity. An investigation carried out by the SUDENE in 1961 revealed that more than 80 per cent of the 22,500 looms installed in the Northeast were at least 30 years old, as were more than 50 per cent of the 650,000 spindles. Over half the thread produced was classified as 'coarse', none as 'fine'. A subsequent report by the United Nations Economic Commission for Latin America (1963) on the whole Brazilian textile industry calculated a national labour productivity index of 46 against averages of 128 in Europe and 290 in North America. Given that the average age of spinning machinery was less in the Southeast Region (where 40 per cent of spindles were over 30 years old compared with more than 50 per cent in the Northeast), productivity in the Northeast was probably the lowest of any textile producing area of Latin America.

A programme of modernization, re-equipment and labour training was recommended by the Working Party. The replacement of machinery was to take place by negotiating individual projects between the SUDENE and each enterprise in the Region: the relative position of each firm would be maintained within the total output of the Region to avoid causing imbalance through some firms modernizing before others. None the less, the larger firms and those situated in the most depressed parts of the Northeast were

TABLE 21.2 Regional distribution of textile production by value, Brazil, 1919 to 1970 (per cent)

Region	1919	1939	1959	1970
North	—	0.4	1.0	1.1
Northeast	24.5	18.9	16.2	9.1
Southeast	66.2	77.7	77.1	78.6
South	4.5	3.0	5.7	10.8
West	—	—	—	0.4
Unspecified	4.8	—	—	—
Total	100.0	100.0	100.0	100.0

Source: Instituto Brasileiro de Geografia e Estatística, 1957, 1974.

given priority. The total cost of the programme was estimated at approximately $US37 million (1961 prices and exchange rates). Of this, 30 per cent was to be provided by the firms, 56 per cent by regional and national finance institutions, and the balance by the Inter-American Development Bank, as part of the post-Castro initiative to develop potentially revolutionary areas of Latin America. The regional multiplier effects of this initial investment were acknowledged to be low: the Southeast would provide the nationally produced machinery, estimated to account for nearly half the total planned investment; in addition foreign textile equipment would account for a further third of the investment.

The programme entailed the scrapping of 90 per cent of the 22,500 looms in the Northeast; the remaining ones were to be supplemented by purchasing 11,000 new looms, bringing the total to 14,000. Of 650,000 spindles, only 35 per cent were considered to be sufficiently productive; 115,000 were to be modernized and the remainder scrapped. A further 115,000 were to be purchased, which would have resulted in 455,000 operational spindles in the Northeast after modernization.

The programme, which was due to take place in the 1962–65 period, was hampered by severe political and economic conditions in Brazil. High levels of inflation, worker unrest and political turbulence culminated in the take-over by a military government in April 1964. These pressures resulted in the slow progress of textile projects in the Northeast. SUDENE records show that 46 firms formulated modernization plans and 94 projects were finalized (some firms had more than one stage in their modernization plans). Only 35 firms became actively involved in the programme, of which 27 had loans approved. Worse still, in only 2 cases were these loans actually made.

The difficulties which caused the failure of the modernization programme reflect the problems of constructing explicit regional policies in an adverse economic climate. The reasons which underlie the failure of the programme are almost entirely rooted in the problems of the national economy. The exchange rate rose in the 1960–64 period from 180 to 1200 cruzeiros per $US1, an increase which effectively raised the foreign exchange requirement of the programme from $US10 million to $US68 million. Simultaneously, interest rates soared, in line with the prevailing rate of inflation which reached more than 100 per cent in 1963.

The poor economic situation exacerbated the perennial problems of the Northeast textile industry: low profitability, problems of raw material supply and stocks, and lack of capital for expansion coupled with the absence of sophisticated management techniques. As a result the small independent entrepreneurs took a conservative position toward the sweeping changes involved in the modernization programme. The pressures placed on the industry did not allow it to stagnate: one element of change was the increase in the number of factory closures. No official figures exist, but a comparison of a list of establishments which existed in 1959 with subsequent records indicates that 14 out of 61 establishments closed during the 1960s. One estimate of job loss through closures was above 2600 (SUDENE, 1971), though this figure has been criticized as a substantial underestimate (Goodman, 1976). The spatial impact of these closures was very uneven: Maranhão State lost all its factories and there was a general tendency towards a greater concentration in the major urban areas. Small firms were also disproportionately affected.

CAPITAL SUBSIDIES AND RATIONALIZATION

The years after the military take-over in 1964 were characterized by policies designed to reduce inflation and encourage foreign investment. The economic model which emerged advocated low taxation and regulation of industry, irrespective of the social costs. Minimum wage rates fell by one-quarter in real terms between 1964 and 1970, while the share of income received by the top 10 per cent of the population increased from 40 to 48 per cent (Robock, 1975). Multinational companies increased their level of investment, particularly in the form of joint ventures with local Brazilian capital. However the poor economic performance during the 1964–67 deflationary period discredited pure economic liberalism. 'Despite the pro-*laissez-faire* convictions of many of the military's early supporters, the major impact of the military's takeover was the centralization of economic power' (Evans, 1979, p. 218).

This centralization brought about an increase in government intervention in economic planning at both national and regional levels. The SUDENE continued to supervise planning in the Northeast, though with a shift away from radical plans for the reorganization of agriculture towards proposals for tax incentives to industry. The system of tax incentives, known as 'Article 34/18' derived from laws passed in 1961, which were widened in 1963 to allow multinational companies to participate. Under this system companies could deduct 50 per cent of their corporate tax liability for deposit into a blocked account in the Banco do Nordeste do Brasil which was then invested in development projects approved by the SUDENE. Firms were allowed to invest these funds in their own factories or branch plants, or in other projects of their choice in return for preferential nonvoting shares (Hirschman, 1968; SUDENE, 1973; Goodman and Albuquerque, 1974).

The tax-credit system had the effect of lowering the relative factor price of capital in the Northeast. Companies located in other regions could use the facility to set up branch plants or to invest in other enterprises; for firms setting up in the Northeast, the tax credits reduced the capital requirements by 50 to 75 per cent. Initial problems arose with the monitoring and control of projects utilizing the funds; for several years more deposits were available than projects in which to invest. The SUDENE allowed higher rates of tax credits for projects in dynamic industries such as metal working, paper and chemicals, but all were included in the scheme. Similarly, extra tax credits were allowed to promote export-orientated and labour-intensive projects, or those located in the most underdeveloped parts of the Region. One sector which was introduced from the middle of the 1960s with the aid of Article 34/18 incentives was the production of artificial fibres and filaments. The SUDENE wished to found a 'petrochemical growth pole' in the city of Salvador: the production of artificial fibres complemented this aim by using chemical feedstocks and its output could be utilized as a raw material for a modernized textile industry. The large capital subsidies available under Article 34/18 regulations meant that, although the production of synthetic fibres is capital-intensive, existing producers with headquarters in the South-east were willing to establish large branch plants in the Northeast: thus the largest synthetic fibre company in Brazil, Rhodia (a subsidiary of the large French-owned Rhône-Poulenc), set up a Northeastern subsidiary, Rhodia do Nordeste, in 1967. Other, non-textile manufacturing groups from the Southeast formed joint ventures with multinational synthetic fibre producers such as Hoechst and the Japanese firm Toray (Evans, 1979). The control and decision-making of these branch plants were thus doubly removed from the regional economy. New firms were also founded in the spinning and weaving sectors at this time, being a mixture of branch plants (which were the largest) and new enterprises founded by local entrepreneurs. The subsidiary companies have continued to grow and have begun to overtake the indige-nous, long-established textile firms: 6 of the 10 largest textile plants now in the Northeast were established at this time (*Visão*, 29 August 1980).

The growth of new firms in the 1960s offset the dramatic losses of capacity and labour that occurred when the older firms shed antiquated machinery to achieve higher levels of productivity. Official figures published by the SUDENE are at variance with the industrial census as the latter also includes artisan workers; none the less, the latter recorded a 45 per cent fall in textile employment from 39,000 workers in 1959 to 21,000 in 1970 whereas research by SUDENE noted only a 6 per cent reduction from 32,500 to 30,600 during the same period. Without the 27 new establishments founded in this period which created nearly 7500 additional jobs the decrease in the SUDENE's figures would have been 28 per cent (Table 21.3).

The restructuring of the industry is also revealed in the changes of capital stock and productivity. Between 1959 and 1969 the number of working spindles fell by 33 per cent and of working looms by more than 50 per cent. By 1969 more than 36 per cent of the operating looms and spindles in the Northeast had been purchased since 1959, a substantial shift in the modern-ity of the capital stock, especially in the weaving sector (Table 21.4). The disproportionate distribution of new machinery among new and established

TABLE 21.3 Employment changes, Northeast Brazil textile industry, 1959 to 1979

States	Total employment 1959	Employment changes 1959–69		Total employment		Per cent change	
		New jobs created	Jobs lost— closures and modernization	1969	1979[a]	1959–69	1959–79
Maranhão	1,410	89	1,139	360	0	−74	−100
Piauí	0	0	0	0	471	0	—
Ceará	3,365	886	583	3,668	5,871	+9	+74
Rio Grande do Norte	141	250	29	362	3,407	+157	+2,316
Paraíba	4,108	586	2,113	2,581	3,448	−37	−16
Pernambuco	12,107	2,560	2,207	12,460	20,295	+3	+68
Alagoas	4,900	1,554	1,662	4,792	5,172	−2	+6
Sergipe	4,451	569	1,468	3,552	3,510	−20	−21
Bahia	2,091	877	133	2,835	4,850	+36	+132
Total	32,573	7,371	9,334	30,610	47,024	−6	+44

[a] Estimated.
Source: SUDENE, 1971, 1978.

TABLE 21.4 Changes in the composition of textile machinery, Northeast Brazil, 1959 to 1969

Age of equipment	1959		1969		Percentage change 1959–69
	Number	Per cent	Number	Per cent	
(a) Spindles					
More than 30 years	347,876	54.2	82,565	19.1	−76.3
Less than 30 years	294,430	45.8	350,619	80.9	+19.1
Total	642,306	100.0	433,184	100.0	−32.6
(b) Looms					
More than 30 years	18,259	81.2	3,468	31.5	−81.0
Less than 30 years	4,217	18.8	7,548	68.5	+79.0
Total	22,476	100.0	11,016	100.0	−51.0

Source: SUDENE, 1971, p. 46, Tables 5.1 and 5.2.

firms created a productivity differential. Calculations by the SUDENE in 1969, using the UN 1963 standard already mentioned, gave established firms a productivity index for spinning equipment of 71 compared with 113 for new firms. The index demonstrated that established firms had achieved some equipment productivity increases in the decade: the Brazilian average in 1961 had been 64. Labour shedding by established firms had increased their labour productivity even more sharply; against a Brazilian average in 1961 of 46 for spinning, in 1969 the labour productivity of established factories in the Northeast was 80 compared with 112 for the new firms. The index for established firms was calculated from a sub-sample of 12 firms (above average for their group) so that the differential between the new and established firms was even greater (SUDENE, 1971). The differential between the 2 groups also occurred in the quality of their production with the newest plants concentrated on the production of higher quality goods. The average spinning count of new plants was 39.6 compared with 17.1 in the older ones; looms in the new plants averaged 21.4 wefts per cm whereas existing factories averaged 16.2 wefts per cm.

The traditional factories were thus forced to produce for the lowest end of the market—itself showing less than average growth because of the unequal distribution of the effects of the economic 'miracle'. None the less, the market for textiles in the Northeast was growing and undergoing a radical transformation: economic growth in the Northeast had led to a rise of nearly 50 per cent in the per capita consumption of textiles. Coupled with rising population, annual usage in the region increased by some 75 per cent, from 265 million metres in 1958 to 465 million metres in 1969. Consumption grew at a faster rate than average increase in income (income elasticity for textiles was above unity); higher qualities were demanded, which neither new nor established mills in the Northeast were able to supply in full. Hence, the share of the Northeast textile consumption produced locally fell from 62 per cent in 1958 to 20 per cent in 1969; meanwhile imports from the Southeast increased by over 270 per cent (Brazil, Banco do Nordeste do Brasil, 1976). For the first time the Northeast had become a net importer of textiles. Southeastern firms were eager to penetrate these new markets; they had fulfilled all the import-substituting opportunities available in their home markets but because of their continuing low productivity were not internationally competitive. The Northeast represented a market without restrictions of quotas or tariffs but, like the rest of Brazil, was subject to severe restrictions on foreign competition. Indeed, tariffs on textiles had been among the highest on any industrial product during the 1960s (Bergsman, 1970). In part, the declining position of the Northeast in relation to the other textile producing areas, notably the Southeast, was the result of almost static output during the restructuring period. Increases in productivity had been offset by losses of equipment so that output rose by only 3 per cent during the 1960s, from 300 to 309 million metres. The increase in value added was even smaller—a mere 1.5 per cent. (The figures are distorted by the fact that many of the new plants installed with incentives granted through the SUDENE had yet to come into full production.) But the increases in production in the Northeast failed to match those elsewhere in Brazil, especially those of the specialized textile sector of the southern states which were producing knitted goods. The value added by the Brazilian textile industry as a whole (including the small increase of the Northeast) rose by 71.5 per cent in constant prices during the 1960s.

The relative share of the Northeast declined more rapidly during the 1960s than at any other time (see Table 21.2), though the small absolute increase is masked by the better performance of the South and Southeast Regions. These changes took place against a background of rapid industrial transformation in the economy as it gathered momentum during the high growth rates of the late 1960s. The regional policy administered by the SUDENE had to generate sufficient growth to ensure that the Northeast did not fall further behind the other regions of Brazil. The Brazilian government was firmly opposed to the policy of reducing regional inequalities through the restraint of high growth areas, for regional disparities could only be ameliorated if the lagging regions could attain higher growth rates than elsewhere. Since national growth rates were exceeding 10 per cent throughout the 'miracle' years, the task faced by regions like the Northeast was immense and was exacerbated when Article 34/18 provisions were progressively broadened to include other regions such as the Amazon and also sectors like tourism, forestry and fishing.

POLICIES OF NATIONAL INTEGRATION

The precariousness of the Northeastern economy, even after a decade of restructuring and regional incentives designed to create a base of manufacturing industry capable of absorbing large quantities of labour, was shown dramatically in 1970 when a further drought in the rural *sertão* (hinterland) again threw the whole regional economy into turmoil. At the peak of the drought in October 1970, 3.5 million people—nearly a fifth of the rural population—were totally dependent on drought relief. The cost of the drought was estimated at $US400 million (Hall, 1978) and acrimonious debate followed about the scope and priorities of the system of regional incentives operated by the SUDENE (Souza, 1979). Industrial projects were criticized as very capital-intensive, creating few regional multiplier effects and little direct employment; rural problems were still unsolved and remained the centre of instability in the regional economy.

New policy measures for the Northeast were announced in June 1970. The Programme of National Integration (PIN) was created, linking the problems of the rural population in the Northeast with the lack of development in the Amazon. The main proposal was to move rural population out of the worst affected area of the *sertão* towards the sparsely populated Amazon Basin along specially constructed highways which were to become axes of development. A further programme of land reform and irrigation (PROTERRA) was announced in June 1971 (Goodman and Albuquerque, 1974).

The role of industry in regional development was severely reduced, as was the authority of the SUDENE to decide regional priorities in the Northeast and constraints were imposed upon industrial expansion. The shift of policy represented a major loss of funds, the proportion of tax-credit revenues received by the SUDENE falling from 100 per cent in 1962 to 24.5 per cent in 1972, when in real terms their value was no greater than the level of 1965 (SUDENE, 1977). The PIN and PROTERRA programmes were allocated a statutory 30 and 20 per cent, respectively, of the tax-credit revenue. The abolition of the obligatory Drought Fund in 1967 had already led to the loss of the 1 per cent share of national tax revenue lodged with the Banco do Nordeste do Brasil (Souza, 1979). A further blow came with the subordination of policy-making within the Region to the national economic development plans formulated by the Brazilian government. Previously, the Directive Plans of the SUDENE had been drafted by its Executive Secretariat, then sent for approval by the Brazilian Congress, which was dominated by the Military Government. In 1972, the Brazilian government took control of policy-making in the Northeast and subordinated regional policy within the global targets of National Plans. In effect, the Fifth Directive Plan of the SUDENE became subsumed as a chapter in the First National Development Plan (1972–74). This was the culmination of the PIN strategy: the development of the Northeast was regarded as a necessary but not sufficient condition for the more important task of national economic integration, in which exploitation of the Amazon resources figured most prominently (Bourne, 1978). Whereas the regional policy of the Working Party on the Northeast in 1959 originated from an analysis of the interaction of the regional economy at a sub-regional level (in terms of rural to urban migration, land reform and industrial problems), the Second National Development Plan regarded 'the Northeast, Amazonia and the Centre-West as a unit within global policy' (Brazil, 1974, p. 60). The Plan (Brazil, 1974, pp. 61–2) envisaged that

> In order to reduce the economic gap between it and the rest of the country, the Northeast should grow at rates exceeding 10% annually. This is a difficult goal to achieve, but it may prove feasible, thanks to the maturing industrial investments made during the preceding period and if the agricultural sector reacts appropriately to the incentives given over the last two years.

The Second National Development Plan was a response to the changing situation of Brazil's foreign trade after the OPEC oil price rises: Brazil was a large importer of Middle Eastern oil and this dependency had been increasing because of the rapid growth of its industrial economy in the preceding 5 years. Brazil had little domestic oil production and faced a rapidly deteriorating balance of payments. The National Plan called for the reorientation of industrial policy to meet these challenges by increasing foreign earnings and decreasing non-essential imports. Industrial policy was geared to achieve these aims by

(a) attaining annual industrial growth of 12 per cent in the 1975–79 period;
(b) encouraging import substitution in basic sectors;
(c) using existing capacity to the full;
(d) exporting manufactured goods of greater complexity and value added;
(e) dispersing industry from overcrowded conurbations in the Southeast;
(f) taking advantage of economies of scale and of agglomeration in regional complexes of an industrial nature.

Industrial policy in the Northeast was no longer based on priorities within the Region, such as the need to absorb the massively underemployed urban population or to create extensive local linkages, but was subordinated to what were regarded as more pressing national needs.

While the operational ability of the SUDENE to dictate regional priorities was being restricted, there was also an increase in the level of economic planning activity by the individual states in the Northeast. These introduced various incentives to draw industry away from the 3 main metropolitan centres of the Region which together received 60 per cent of industrial investment: they included exemption from state taxes for fixed periods, purchase of shares in firms by state development agencies, technical assistance, subsidized land prices, credit facilities and the creation of industrial estates. For example, the State of Pernambuco in 1977 had 18 different types of industrial incentive (including those available from the SUDENE and the Banco do Nordeste do Brasil). Each state had its own package of incentives which were complex and competitive: the homogeneity of the Northeast as a policy unit was lost as the Region became internally differentiated in the scramble to attract available investment. The prestige and authority of the SUDENE was compromised by its inability to control investment decisions.

INDUSTRIAL EXPANSION IN THE 1970s

Although the years from 1970 to 1972 were marked by a substantial shift against industry in regional policy, by the time the Second National Development Plan was announced, investments made by the SUDENE through

Article 34/18 were coming to fruition. The textile industry featured prominently, ranking third among all sectors with 12 per cent of total investments approved—chemical and metal working being ahead with 17 and 14 per cent, respectively. In all, the SUDENE approved 581 industrial projects worth $US1369 million during the 1960s (Goodman and Albuquerque, 1974). Unfortunately not all the projects were successful, nor were all the investment plans carried through. None the less, by the early 1970s industrial growth rates in the Northeast were beginning to improve: the textile industry grew by 9.5 per cent in value-added terms between 1970 and 1973, whereas it had grown by only 1.5 per cent throughout the 1960s. Capital stock also increased: the number of spindles increased by 30 per cent from 435,000 in 1969 to 560,000 in 1973. But productivity still differed widely between firms, the poor performance of unmodernized factories being masked in the aggregate data. By 1973 only half the establishments over 10 years old had modernized in part or in full; of the 82 then working, 27 remained unmodernized, producing coarse yarn and cloth for agricultural use. The others were balanced evenly between modernized units (27 in 1973) and establishments created with Article 34/18 incentives (28).

The call for the development of 'regional complexes of an industrial nature' (Brazil, 1974 p. 41) in the Second National Development Plan formalized the *de facto* high concentrations of investments in the major metropolitan areas. Four states (Pernambuco, Ceará, Rio Grande do Norte and Paraíba) of the 9 in the Region received over three-quarters of Article 34/18 textile investment in the 1960s, a trend which intensified during the following decade. Since job loss through modernization was only being offset by new investment, those states not receiving such investment— including some traditionally important areas of textile production such as the State of Bahia—suffered higher than average employment loss. In 1973 the 4 states with the highest concentration of investment contained 21 of the 27 modernized establishments, 23 of the 28 establishments founded through Article 34/18 and 6 of the 7 establishments under foundation in 1973.

The industrial complexes called for by the Second National Development Plan were in petrochemical, fertilizer, engineering, textile and clothing industries. This narrow concentration of investment contrasted sharply with the broad spectrum of activities encouraged during the 1960s. The increase envisaged for the textile industry alone was massive: in 5 years the number of spindles was planned to increase from about 600,000 to 2,600,000. Part of the growth was to come from 700,000 spindles that were to be moved from the Southeast. An increase of this magnitude required a 50 per cent growth rate in the first year alone. The new capacity was to be concentrated in the states of Ceará, Rio Grande do Norte, and Piauí. The latter state was unusual in that, of all those in the Northeast, it had no textile industry whatsoever.

The level of investment necessary to meet the targets of the Plan required more stimulus than could be provided by the tax-credit scheme. Further incentives came from 2 sources. The first was the creation of special funds by the 3 states which were to set up the textile 'poles'. Tax revenues levied on textile production would be diverted into special accounts, supplemented by additional state funds, which would then be used to provide concessionary loans or to purchase shares in new or expanding textile enterprises. These incentives were in addition to the 75 per cent of total capital requirements already available through existing channels: in the most favoured cases new ventures needed to provide only 12.5 per cent of initial capital. The second source of funds came from a reorganization of the Article 34/18 tax-credit scheme. The previous system allowed independent brokers to bring together depositors and entrepreneurs; the role of the brokers had been criticized as inefficient and they were replaced in the new system by a central administration organized by the Banco do Nordeste do Brasil. A central fund administered by the Bank, known as the Northeast Investment Fund (FINOR), was set up into which all tax credits were deposited in return for general shares which could later be converted into equity in specific companies. The change to the Investment Fund did not increase the proportion of tax credits flowing into the Region, nor did it redress the imbalance between the excess demand and the supply of investment funds that had prevailed since the late 1960s. The decision to invest in any of the 5 competing investments funds (for the Northeast, the Amazon, fishing, forestry or tourism) was left to the depositor. Moreover, the statutory deductions of 50 per cent of all tax credits for PIN and PROTERRA reduced their net value. The Second National Development Plan may have called for an annual growth of 15 per cent in the industrial sector of the Northeast but the main financing mechanism was not given any statutory obligation to meet the increased requirement placed upon it.

The Second National Development Plan reaffirmed the commitment to private enterprise as the primary vehicle for industrial expansion. In contrast to the strategic petrochemical industries in which the Brazilian government investment was critical, the expansion of the textile and other chosen industries was placed in the private sector. The scale of growth was such that heavy demands were placed upon its financial resources since the capacity increase required not only new machinery but also new buildings and infrastructure. The resources needed to meet these expenditures increased the size of investment requirements: thus, the average estimated cost of textile projects rose from approximately $US2.5 million in 1970–72 to approximately $US12.6 million in 1976–78 (1977 prices and average exchange rates). The burden of higher investment requirements was met in part by the SUDENE. Incentives in total investment for approved textile projects rose from an average of 30 per cent in 1974 to 57 per cent in 1978. The reserves of the SUDENE were so depleted that in 1975 its expenditure exceeded its income for the first time. In the 1975–78 period the income from tax credits was 28 per cent below the expenditure on incentives; the deficit was covered only by direct contributions to the Northeast Investment Fund by the SUDENE.

The progress of individual projects was impeded by these difficulties. The rise in the percentage participation and absolute volume of the incentives, coupled with the growing size of projects and the difficulties of generating sufficient funds from tax-credit contributors, led to a failure to keep within the ambitious targets of the Second National Development Plan. In none of the first 3 years were the textile industry targets reached, and each year the accumulated deficit in the number of spindles approved grew. By the end of the third year of the Plan (1977), of a target of 990,000 new spindles for the Northeast, only 400,000 had been approved by the SUDENE. The cumulative deficit was greatly enlarged in 1978, when in the first 8 months only 10,000 spindles were approved from an annual target of 370,000. The momentum of the programme was lost. Yet the failure to meet the high (and what must be regarded as unrealistic) targets cannot obscure the impressive rate of growth of the textile industry throughout the 1970s: thus the number of spindles working in the Northeast had risen from 560,000 in 1972 to nearly 800,000 in August 1978 while a further 470,000 had been approved and contractual arrangements finalized. The growth in the weaving sector during this same period was more modest, from 10,800 to 12,300 looms, with 2100 more approved but not installed.

Other industries in the Northeast were also having problems maintaining growth; obstacles were occurring in the installation of industrial projects in virtually all sectors. The worst affected were the food processing and metal working industries, with 37 and 29 per cent respectively, of all investment in projects which were either paralysed or not working as planned. For textiles the figure was only 8 per cent against an average for all sectors of 17 per cent. Research by the SUDENE in 1978 revealed that the tax-credit incentives had created about 163,000 direct jobs since 1962, of which 33,500 had been in textiles, the largest single sector. Paralysed projects accounted for a further potential 50,000 jobs, 2000 of which were in textiles—a low figure given the size of the sector (Rebouças, 1979). Utilization of installed capacity was also high in textiles at 87 per cent, ranking third below the beverages and the plastics industries. Although the textile industry was unable to attain the targets of the Second National Development Plan, the efficiency and degree of success were among the highest of any industry in the Northeast.

AN ASSESSMENT OF STRUCTURAL CHANGE IN THE TEXTILE INDUSTRY

The past 2 decades have seen fundamental changes in the textile industry of Northeast Brazil: first, through the modernization of part of the indigenous industry; secondly, because major textile producers set up branch plants using tax-credit incentives; and, third, as the result of expansion under the Second National Development Plan. Although there has been a consistent tendency to set very ambitious targets which have not been attained, regional policy and incentives have acted as a spur to rationalization and growth. These changes have not been neutral in their effect upon the control and structure of output of the industry. The major criticisms of the policies used to promote industrial growth in the Northeast have been concerned with the effects upon industrial linkages, job creation, control of investment, the use of capital subsidies and the choice of the key sectors to which these policies would be directed. All these factors are interlinked, but 3 issues have emerged which synthesize the problems, namely, the choice of appropriate technology; the market orientation of the industries; and the control of the investments.

The use of Article 34/18 tax-credit incentives to stimulate external investment in the Northeast has encouraged a branch plant economy in all sectors, though textiles have been less dominated than most because a large indigenous industry existed before the start of industrial regional policy. Textile establishments that had taken advantage of Article 34/18 tax-credit incentives had 60 per cent of their capital originating from outside the Region in 1978, compared to an average 75 per cent for all industries. In fact, the real extent of external investment is higher because the tax credits forming the basis of the incentives, and which represented an average of 22 per cent of total investment in textiles, were predominantly of extra-regional origin. One estimate (Goodman, 1972) has put the proportion of tax-credit incentives originating from the Southeast at nearly 85 per cent.

The amount of external capital incorporated in the tax-credit and associated investment has shifted the balance of control between locally and externally controlled enterprises through the formation of green-field branch plants, without the need for take-over and merger activity. The number of new establishments founded since the inception of the SUDENE reached 48 by 1978, though not all of these had been successful: as many as 8 were paralysed (Brazil, Banco do Nordeste do Brasil, 1979). A further 37 indigenous firms had received Article 34/18 tax-credit incentives, many for modernization programmes in the late 1960s. The greatest share of investment under the Second National Development Plan was taken by the 20 establishments founded since the start of the Plan. The distribution of machinery installed under the Plan, divided into 3 groups of establishments, is given in Table 21.5. Clearly, the increase in capital equipment which formed a key part of the expansion programme was concentrated in new firms. Indigenous establishments acquired very few of the spindles around which the plans were formulated. Only 6 of 62 establishments existing in 1962 took part in the programme and only 1 of these increased its capacity

TABLE 21.5 Classification of establishments expanding capacity in
the Second National Development Plan, Brazil

Date of foundation	Number of establishments	Number of spindles/looms	Per cent distribution
(a) Spinning			
Pre-1962	6	43,000	7
1962–72	8	235,000	35
Post-1972	19	390,000	58
Total	33	668,000	100
(b) Weaving			
Pre-1962	5	732	20
1962–72	5	452	13
Post-1972	10	2,442	67
Total	20	3,626	100

Source: fieldwork.

by more than 10,000 spindles. Establishments founded in the first wave of Article 34/18 tax-credit investment projects also did not figure prominently in the expansion, their group being heavily weighted by 1 large project of over 130,000 spindles. In the new firms the average investment in machinery per plant has been greater than that in the other groups. However, among new firms there has been a greater preponderance of spinning-only plants, which account for 10 of the 19 plants in this category. Only 1 new firm planned to produce textiles alone. The distribution of new looms was skewed to the extent that this firm together with 2 others accounted for nearly half the looms going to new firms. The development of high-technology spinning plants contrasts with the low quality integrated production which predominated in the 1950s. The formation of these spinning plants marked the start of textile production in several established firms which had previously been engaged in cotton-ginning but which were undertaking yarn production as a first stage of vertical integration.

The expansion of the textile industry under the Second National Development Plan was based upon the use of home-grown cotton as a basic raw material. Consumption increased to such an extent during the Plan that raw cotton ceased to be a major export and indeed a shortage of cotton by 1979 became a real obstacle. The exodus of rural labourers to the cities and the continuing problems of the agricultural sector léd to stagnation in the production of cotton and the possibility that Brazil would become a net importer of this crop. The export of cotton as a primary product ceased, its place being taken by thread and fabrics with a higher added value.

The balance between the textile industry in the Northeast and that in other regions has been particularly affected by the development of large factories there. In 1970 the Northeast contained 10 of the 100 largest textile plants in Brazil (in terms of fixed capital stock) but by 1980 this figure had risen to 22. External control increased from half (5) of the establishments in 1970 to about two-thirds (14) in 1980. The large firms that had set up in the Northeast in the 1970s were predominantly branch plants of companies headquartered outside the Region. Of the other 78 establishments in the top 100 in 1980, the majority (43) were independent while some of the multi-plant establishments (35) were group headquarters. In short, large textile establishments were much more likely to be independent if they were located outside the Northeast. The concentration of branch plants in the Northeast was even higher among the very largest establishments. By 1980 the Northeast contained 7 of the top 20 establishments: 6 of the 7 were branch plants while the other was formed by the merger of 3 indigenous enterprises to use centralized finishing and warehouse facilities. The 6 branch plants had all received substantial investment through Article 34/18; only the independent firm had received no assistance.

The choice of technology has not been constant since the start of industrial regional policy. One of the principal reasons for including the textile industry as a key sector in the original plans of the SUDENE was the outdated and inefficient state of the capital equipment, resulting in high costs of production and low quality of output. The SUDENE originally called for re-equipment, using nationally produced weaving equipment together with some imported spinning equipment. Rapid technological change was not the aim—as demonstrated by the decision to use basic Brazilian-made equipment where possible. Rather the programme was to build a manufacturing base capable of creating jobs, for with the abundance of cheap labour new technology was not a primary consideration. Although some of the existing machinery was capable of increased productivity and quality of output, the failure of the modernization programme in its planned form affected these objectives. As already indicated, there was considerable job loss in the 1960s during the restructuring of the textile sector, while other industries had created insufficient jobs to ease the severe underemployment problems in the Region. Job creation was disadvantaged by the use of capital subsidy incentives and by policy designed to create regional poles of capital-intensive industry, such as artificial fibre production. The targets of the Second National Plan for the textile industry in the Northeast were set in terms of machinery not employment. Moreover, the concentration on spinning rather than on weaving showed a bias towards capital-intensive processes. Even so, the textile industry still provided the highest employment of all sectors in the Northeast—about 15 per cent of the total. The level of investment per job in textiles—approximately $US30,000 to $US35,000 (1977 prices and exchange rates)—was median for all manufacturing (Brazil, Banco do Nordeste do Brasil, 1979). This was 10 to 13 times greater than in the textile industries of countries such as Singapore, Thailand or Colombia (*Veja*, 21 December 1977). The low labour absorption of new spinning technology is shown by the fact that though the 3 states which have set up special textile funds will receive 40 per cent of planned spinning capacity, they will employ only 26 per cent of the labour force. Most capital goods have had to be imported into the Region because of the absence of local suppliers; only 1.8 per cent of textile equipment has been purchased locally, against an average of 4 per cent for all industries (Brazil, Banco do Nordeste do Brasil, 1979). Exemptions from import tax have encouraged the use of foreign machinery: since 1960 the SUDENE has granted import tax exemption licences for an estimated $US250 million of foreign textile machinery (SUDENE, 1978).

The policy of the Second National Development Plan switched the priority of industrial growth from creating 'an autonomous centre of manufacturing expansion in the Northeast' (Grupo do Trabalho do Desenvolvimento do Nordeste, 1959, p. 297) to integrating the Northeast into the national industrial economy with the aim of 'extensive programmes of exports of manufactured goods based on more complex technology' (Brazil, 1974, p. 77). This was necessary to support balance of payments deficits caused by the rising prices of oil imports while still allowing industrial expansion to continue at the level achieved during the economic boom. Exports of manufactured goods during the 1970s rose from $US420 million in 1970 (15 per cent of total exports) to $US6680 million in 1979 (44 per cent) as a result of these policy changes. Simultaneously the proportion of export earnings from coffee fell from 34 to 12 per cent (*Latin America Regional Reports: Brazil*, 14 March 1980, p. 8). Textile exports increased even more than manufactured goods in general, rising from $US14 million in 1969 to $US757 million in 1979 with confident predictions of annual export sales in excess of $US1000 million through the 1980s, provided that international textile agreements do not stem trade (*Latin America Regional Reports: Brazil*, 30 May 1980, p. 4). The annual growth rate in textile production as a whole was more than 5 per cent in 1978 and 1979 but the rise in exports was about 30 per cent as textile producers turned to foreign markets. Although data about the regional origin of exports for this period are few, it is clear that the Northeast was beginning to export textiles on a substantial scale by 1976, when it accounted for 13 per cent of Brazilian exports of cotton thread and 9 per cent of cotton textiles. Quality of output in the Northeast had been constantly improving and the most modern plants were easily capable of competing in international markets. In 1959 no thread produced in the Northeast was classified as above medium quality; by 1977, 40 per cent of production was estimated as fine quality, 40 per cent medium quality and 20 per cent coarse grade (Confederação Nacional da Indústria, 1978). The export of cotton yarn was itself becoming a major item, valued at $US155 million in 1979. The growth of the spinning sector in the Northeast and the transfer of equipment from factories in the Southeast indicate the probability that the Northeast will continue to produce an increasing proportion of Brazilian textile exports (*Latin America Regional Reports: Brazil*, 30 May 1980, p. 4).

The role of manufactured exports in the Brazilian economy is clearly different to that in other NICs. Brazilian exports are equivalent to only a small proportion of its GNP, being still equal to about only 8 per cent of GNP even after the jump in manufactured exports compared to 70 per cent for Hong Kong or 22 per cent for West Germany (Robock, 1975). The home market is still of overwhelming importance, accounting for 85 per cent of total textile production in 1978 and 75 per cent of cotton textiles (*Conjuntura Econômica*, 1979, pp. 102–3). The home market is still expanding at 6 to 7 per cent annually but cannot absorb the growth necessary for the industrial expansion of 12 per cent as set out in the Second National Development Plan. Brazil now supplies more than a third of Argentinian textile imports but the problems of political restrictions to trade are a constant threat, especially as Brazil's own tariffs are extremely high and may provide a reason for a backlash from importing countries. The Northeast is particularly vulnerable, without a secure regional market and with many branch plants liable to closure if the industry suffers severe recession: in 1978, 80 per cent of the output of mills aided through the Article 34/18 tax-credit scheme was destined for markets outside the Region, the fourth highest of any sector.

In terms of technology, market orientation and control of investment, the development of the textile industry in the Northeast has been conditioned by the activity of capital originating in the Southeast. Most of the policy measures noted at the beginning of the chapter have been applied to overcome long-standing regional disparities. The manipulation of factor prices through capital subsidies available in Article 34/18 incentives has encouraged the use of capital-intensive process technologies, even though the Northeast is a low-wage economy in need of job creation. The penetration of the textile market in the Northeast in the 1960s has reinforced the growth of regional exports, though international trade in textiles is very unstable and Brazil is vulnerable to protectionist measures. The promotion of high productivity sectors has taken place through the formation of a branch plant economy of sizeable proportions; autonomous industrial expansion has occurred only on a limited scale. The direction and type of industrial development permitted through regional policy has worked towards the 'substitution of a national economy formed by several regional economies in favour of a national economy localized into several parts of the national territory' (Oliveira and Reichstul, 1973, p. 148). Industrial expansion has taken place in the Northeast without threatening the industrial *status quo* while at the same time restructuring the unequal division of production which has maintained the Northeast as the poorest region of Brazil.

Spatial Analysis, Industry and the Industrial Environment. Vol. 3 Regional Economies and Industrial Systems
Edited by F. E. I. Hamilton and G. J. R. Linge
© 1983 John Wiley & Sons Ltd.

Chapter 22

Industrial Policy and Locational Dynamics of Small-scale Enterprises in India

S. K. SAHA

During the last 3 decades of economic planning in India (the first Five Year plan was launched in 1951) a persistent theme in the strategic thinking of Indian planners has been the need to include a programme of rapid industrialization as part of the overall national development policy. A common feature of all official documents and pronouncements on industrial progress under both the Congress and the Janata Parties has been a strong emphasis on the promotion of small-scale industries. The main economic reasoning has been that this would foster geographical decentralization of industries among India's small towns and villages, so diffusing the benefits of planned economic development to the whole population. This chapter examines the theoretical premises on which this thinking is based and enquires whether the reasoning corresponds with empirical reality.

India's First Five Year Plan was the first comprehensive national planning document in the world outside the centrally planned economies. Since then most Third World countries have adopted some form of national planning as an essential part of their development efforts (Mehmet, 1978, pp. 17, 35). India's experience with industrialization is, therefore, of considerable interest to theorists and planners studying Third World development problems.

The term 'small-scale industry' used here is identical with that specified in the last Census of Small Scale Industrial Units (Government of India, 1973, p. 34), i.e. an industry in which the original value of plant and machinery does not exceed Rs750,000 (£41,470) at 1973 prices. Household industries—those operated by family labour *and* located in the living premises of the proprietor—are excluded.

CHOTANAGPUR REGION, GROWTH INDUSTRIES AND SMALL-SCALE METAL-WORKING FIRMS

The empirical component of this study relates to the space-economy of the small-scale metal-working industry in the Chotanagpur region of India. This occupies the southern half of the populous eastern state of Bihar and forms the core of what is generally referred to as the industrial heartland of India—an elongated zone stretching 450 km from Raningunj coalfields in West Bengal to Sundargarh iron ore and manganese deposits in Orissa—which contains the bulk of India's basic, heavy and metallurgical industries. The Chotanagpur region itself, comprising 2 per cent both of India's area and of its population, accounts for 34 per cent of its steel ingot production and 26 per cent of the output of all heavy engineering goods (Government of India, 1974, p. 234; 1978a, p. 301). Studies in various parts of the world have shown that iron and steel and other metal-based industries are most effective among all standard industrial categories in generating regional growth through their greater linkage effects (Chenery and Watanabe, 1958), higher value-added rates (Taylor, 1978, p. 148) and higher overall growth rates (Klaassen, 1967, p. 36); indeed, Klaassen refers to them as 'growth industries'. Because of the large resource investments and high-technology-based production processes that such industries represent, they tend to be localized spatially, setting in motion a chain of agglomeration and other external economies which, in turn, promote regional convergence of industrial growth. The only way a theoretical premise for assuming a regional diffusion role for these industries can be established is by showing that they generate an intra-regional system of backward and forward linkages which act as channels of transfusion of the trickle-down effects into the regional economy. In operational terms, such a transfusion system can be seen as an array of small-scale industries which:

(a) absorb resource inputs from the regional economy;
(b) provide intermediate inputs to the regional growth industries;
(c) receive intermediate outputs from the regional growth industries as their own basic inputs; and
(d) combine local resource inputs and regional growth industries' intermediate outputs in further processing of new outputs for reabsorption in the regional economy, either in its final demand sector or as fresh supplies of intermediate inputs to other regional industries.

In such a theoretical scheme small-scale industries are analogous to transformer substations in an electricity distribution grid which, by stepping down the current to an appropriate voltage, facilitate the supply of electricity generated by large power stations (the regional growth industries) to a wide scatter of small consumers. If the electricity is to reach out to consumers distributed over a large area, these substations need to be widely dispersed. By the same analogy, any claim about the diffusive role of regional growth industries would need to be supported by the evidence of a wide dispersal of small-scale linkage industries all over the regional space.

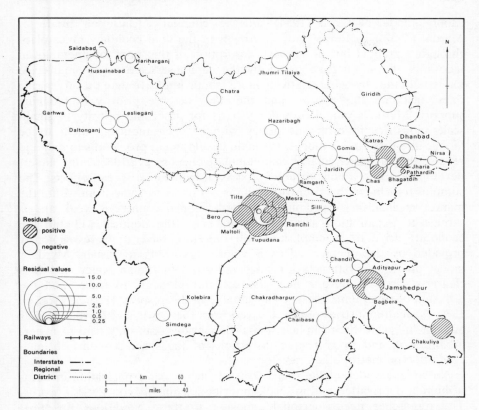

FIGURE 22.1 Distribution of small-scale metal-working production in the Chotanag-pur region of Bihar State, Eastern India, 1972. The proportional circles represent the values of metal-working production regressed against population

Chotanagpur region's growth industries comprise 2 large steel plants at Jamshedpur and Bokaro, a massive multi-plant heavy engineering complex employing 20,500 workers at Ranchi, and several metallurgy-based factories at Jamshedpur and Dhanbad. Given such a product base, the linkage effect would be expected to operate through a direct product processing line of metal-working firms. Hence the present enquiry is focused on small-scale metal-working firms only.

THEORETICAL APPROACHES TO SMALL-SCALE INDUSTRIES

Fisher (1968) in his seminal work on small-scale industries in India, draws theoretical support for promoting such activities as a policy instrument in the overall strategy of economic development, from the 'unlimited labour supply' model of Lewis (1954) and the 'cumulative causation' model of Myrdal (1957). In Lewis' model, growth in the dual economy takes place through a gradual but progressive absorption of the 'pool' of unemployed labour in the subsistence sector by the capitalist sector. The small-scale industrial units, by being relatively more labour-intensive than the large-scale ones, facilitate this process and therefore deserve priority in planning support. Myrdal's model provides a basis for according priority to small-scale industries in economic policy without even requiring them to be labour-intensive; in his model, the main development problem is to halt and reverse the vicious circularity and cumulativeness of ever-deepening under-development into a new virtuous process of cumulative spread effects. The stimulus to achieve this transformation is not likely to come from within the market mechanism, which in an underdeveloped country is weak and is subject to exploitation and corrupt practices: the political will and the economic drive to accomplish it will therefore have to be exogenously provided by the planners. This is where, according to Fisher, Myrdal's model provides a rationale for small industries in Indian policy, for 'it is clearly desired to have a new class of entrepreneurs in India, and the diffusion of small units is especially suitable in this respect' (Fisher, 1968, p. 137). A small-industries policy, derived from the Lewis and Myrdal models but not linked to their implicit spatial dimensions, can only lead to hyper-urbanization and to grotesque distortions of the space-economy through Calcutta-type metropolitan development.

An adequate idea of the social costs of such hyper-urbanization in terms of human deprivation and misery cannot be adequately conveyed in words. The researcher needs personal exposure to these conditions. In 1963, residential density in the Calcutta Municipal Corporation area was 726 people per ha, as against Delhi, 484; New York, 405; and Los Angeles, 58 (Calcutta Metropolitan Planning Organisation, 1966, p. 16). A recent source provides even more distressing figures: 86 per cent of the Calcutta Metropolitan District's 8.3 million inhabitants are not connected to any water-borne sewerage system; 200,000 people permanently live on the pavements and 44,000 of them depend on begging for a livelihood; 2.5 million people live in congested and insanitary slums (*bustees*) and the supply of filtered water has declined from 236 litres per person per day in 1931 to 127 in 1965 (Calcutta Metropolitan Development Authority, 1978, pp. 8–10).

Dhar and Lydall (1961, pp. 10–32) and Fisher (1968, pp. 138–48) base their support for encouraging the development of small enterprises in India on 4 broad groups of arguments:

(a) employment: small enterprises are essentially 'labour-intensive' and hence will generate more employment;

(b) decentralization: small enterprises can be more easily accommodated in small towns and villages;

(c) socio-political: small enterprises promote social justice, equitable income distribution and democracy;

(d) latency: small enterprises draw out hidden resources, especially those of entrepreneurship.

However, several points need to be borne in mind. First, 81 per cent of India's population live in 575,700 villages and 1790 small towns (fewer than 10,000 inhabitants) scattered all over the country, and these contain most of the pool of unemployed labour. Second, any socio-political process of achieving more equitable income distribution and greater democracy is meaningless without incorporating the population living in these places. Third, much of the latent human resources are also distributed accordingly and fourth, the urban infrastructure is not adequately coping even with the present rates of rural-urban migration. Thus, in the Indian context, any economic justification for a policy emphasizing small-scale industries resides in their ability to encourage decentralization.

Unlike Dhar and Lydall (1961) and Fisher (1968), Chandrashekar Shetty (1963, pp. 25–33) sees the spatial dimension of economic development in India as the most critical problem, arguing that unless economic development is adequately diffused through rural India, rural-to-urban migration would assume unmanageable proportions and many more Calcutta-type situations would appear. Between 1961 and 1971 the rate of growth of India's urban population was 46 per cent higher than that of the total population, which means that during the decade 10.7 million people moved from villages to towns. Thus Chandrashekar Shetty (1963, pp. 31–3) sees all other virtues of the small-scale enterprise, such as fuller employment, extension of democratic values and utilization of latent resources, as concomitant to, or resulting from, the decentralization process itself. He does not, however, examine 'the intimate relation between small-scale industries and the process of decentralization' and accepts without scrutiny that 'factors conducive to the growth and development of small-scale units are the same as those responsible for dispersal or decentralization of industrial organisation' and that the growth of small industrial units necessarily means 'the location of new industrial undertakings in rural areas' leading to the 'advantage of transmitting the benefits of urbanization' to such rural areas. This chapter questions the validity of these unexamined propositions.

OFFICIAL POLICY ON SMALL-SCALE INDUSTRIES IN INDIA

Even a quick scan of official policy documents shows that the small-scale sector has long occupied a high priority in the planning process from the very inception of planned economic development in India. A decentralized industrial pattern was the main theme of the Industrial Policy Resolution of 1948, and small-scale industries were seen as the main policy instruments of operationalizing that objective (Kurien, 1978a, p. 455). The resolution presented in the *Lok Sabha* [the Lower House of the Parliament] within 8 months of achieving independence was the first declaration by the government of India of its intention to pursue a vigorous programme of industrialization mainly through public sector operations. It also facilitated the *Industries (Development and Regulation) Act* of 1951 which imposed strict controls on private industry and the industrial strategy adopted in the First Five Year Plan (Government of India, 1952, pp. 422–4). This Plan discussed a 'common production programme' for the industrial sector as a whole. Small-scale industries were to play a prominent role: viable village craft-based industries would flourish without any protection and continue to provide decentralized mass employment in the rural areas. Other small industries would need to be 'integrated with and form a part of the production of the large-scale industry', and others again would need to be protected from the direct competition of their large-sector counterparts (Government of India, 1952, pp. 330–1).

The Second Five Year Plan (1956–57 to 1960–61) covered a period of massive expenditure on basic and heavy industries. It was hoped that such investments would generate greater demand for consumer goods. As the large-scale industry would be mainly engaged in the production of capital goods, much of the increased need for consumer items would have to be met by a huge expansion of small-scale industries which would rapidly soak up the vast pool of unemployed and underemployed labour in rural areas (Government of India, 1957). The Karve Committee, appointed by the Planning Commission to make a special study of the problems of small-scale industries, echoed a similar line. The creation of a decentralized production structure was regarded as an essential prerequisite for a democratic system wedded to the principles of social and economic justice, and the promotion of small-scale industries was seen as the only feasible policy instrument to achieve that paramount objective (Government of India, 1955, pp. 80–91). The economic argument stated in the Industrial Policy Resolution of 1956 for giving high priority to the small-scale industries in the overall economic policy also stems from a familiar, but untested frame of expectation:

> They provide immediate large-scale employment; they offer a method of ensuring a more equitable distribution of national income and they facilitate an effective mobilisation of resources of capital and skill which might otherwise remain unutilised. Some of the problems that unplanned urbanization tends to create will be avoided by the establishment of small centres of industrial production all over the country (Kurien, 1978a, p. 457).

The Third and Fourth Five Year Plan documents repeat, with renewed vigour, the assertion that small-scale industries promote, among other things, a progressive geographical decentralization of the production structure, which in turn ensures a 'more equitable distribution of the national income', avoids 'the problems of unplanned urbanisation' (Government of India, 1961, pp. 426–35), and leads to 'promotion of industries in semi-urban rural and backward areas' (Government of India, 1972, p. 291). The Third Plan document notes, with some amazement, that 'the development of small-scale industries has so far been, by and large, in or near the cities and larger towns', but then goes on to express the hope that further growth of these industries will take place 'in rural areas and in small towns as well as in less developed areas having a marked industrial potential' (Government of India, 1961, p. 435).

The Janata Government 1977–79, characterized by its continuous outpourings of strident rhetoric on rural development, vigorously reiterated its commitment to the promotion of small-scale industries. Its *Statement on Industrial Policy,* tabled in the Indian Parliament on 23 December 1977, commented 'The main thrust of the new industrial policy will be an effective promotion of cottage and small industries *widely dispersed in rural areas* and small towns' (Government of India, 1978b, p. iii [author's emphasis]). The new Five Year Plan document for the period 1978–83, introduced by the Janata Government in 1978 refers to the past deviations in implementing programmes for promoting small-scale industries which had led to development assistance being channelled mainly to the larger of the small-scale units, and especially to those located in towns and in large metropolitan urban areas. The new policy, it claimed, would remedy that and 'promote the growth of these industries in rural areas and small towns' (Government of India, 1979, pp. 118–19).

DECENTRALIZATION ARGUMENT: AN UNEXAMINED THEORETICAL PREMISE

There is no a priori theoretical reason why the smaller scale of production should indicate an intrinsic locational preference for rural areas or for smaller towns. External economies, by definition, are not in any way linked with the scale factor, and all non-primary production units, large as well as small, are subject to this pull towards the existing urban-industrial clusters. The locational preference of the small-scale industrial units, as indeed of the large-scale ones, is determined by the nature of their linkages with the rest of the economy and therefore by its overall structure. The Indian economy, like much of the Third World, is characterized by a 'structure of dualistic dependency' (Paauw and Fei, 1973; Friedmann and Douglass, 1978). This is a situation of extreme inequities in the rural-urban as well as interpersonal distribution of incomes and of productive assets leading to a marked discontinuity between the consumption patterns of mainly urban-based higher income groups and those of the rest of the population. The nature of discontinuity of consumption patterns between the affluent and the poor has been evocatively described in a succinct and true-to-life narrative by Hiro (1976). Recent figures on income distribution in India (Sinha *et al.*, 1979, pp. 32 and 35) present a more prosaic but factual description of the situation. The rural population spends 74 per cent of its income on food, 8 per cent on clothing and footwear and 3 per cent on other manufactured goods (corresponding figures for the urban population are 62, 8 and 6 per cent). The ratio between per capita consumption of the rural poor (Rs248) and that of the urban poor (Rs293) is 0.85, whereas the ratio of rural to urban consumption was only 0.73. Considering the poorest one-third of the population in rural and urban areas, the corresponding figures were, rural: 78, 4 and 3 per cent and urban: 71, 8 and 4 per cent. Whereas poverty levels between rural and urban areas are more or less comparable, affluent sections are considerably better off in urban areas than in rural ones, even though the affluent sections of the rural community are organically linked through the appropriation of value added, direct input-output, trade and social network relationships with the urban-based corporate sectors of the economy. The incidence of a truly 'modern' and Western type of consumption pattern is confined to a very thin social stratum comprising the higher-middle classes and above, which 'when translated into income distribution categories means from among the top two or three percent of households' (Kurien, 1978a, p. 459). This tip of the social pyramid is almost exclusively urban-based or urban-linked.

The locational preference of the small-scale industries would therefore depend upon the end of this fractured final demand sector to which their products eventually cater. If the market linkage of these industries is with the demand structure relating to the top of the social pyramid—highly concentrated in a few urban locations—a policy of promoting their development will obviously not lead to the decentralization of the production process. In the regional diffusion model elaborated earlier in this chapter regional growth industries were regarded as geographically localized in major urban centres, but the consumption-related regional final demand was equitably spread spatially. Only within this framework of areally concentrated regional growth industries and areally dispersed final demand can the backward and forward linkages be seen as integrating channels and, hence, as a means of geographically diffusing regional growth industry benefits. If the final demand becomes localized in the same urban centres as the regional growth industries the backward and forward production linkages become agents of centralization not decentralization.

The regional diffusion model will yield an a priori reason for the geographical dispersion of small-scale industries only if these forge linkages with the mass consumption-related final demand market and/or with the rural resource base. The mass consumption market, of course, embraces the whole national territory but, because of the existing low levels and the skewed patterns of income distribution in India, it is very thinly spread over much of this territory outside a few localized pockets of high consumerism. The product mix of this market is also very narrow, with essential items of food, clothing and footwear making up 82 per cent of it. The rural resource base is almost exclusively related to agriculture and, as Indian farming is mainly of subsistence type, it generates only a very limited supply of products for further processing. Thus small-scale industrial units having production linkages exclusively with the mass consumption market and/or the rural resource base will quickly run into severe cash limits. The logic of the market mechanism does not seem to provide much scope for the automatic expansion of small-scale industries with such linkages: it would in fact tend to dictate that entrepreneurs take advantage of the scale, external, and access economies provided by the concentrated upper income consumer market localized in a relatively few urban centres. Hence, if left to the market forces, the small-scale industries would expand in sectors labelled as 'luxury' and 'non-priority' and would be located in existing urban-industrial clusters. The only way the geographical decentralization of these industries could take place is through the deliberate forging of the appropriate production linkages with the mass consumption market and/or with the rural resource base through direct planning intervention. This would require strengthening the areal and social restructuring of the mass consumption market itself through an effective programme of redistribution of incomes and productive assets.

SMALL-SCALE METAL-WORKING INDUSTRY IN THE CHOTANAGPUR REGION: PRODUCT STRUCTURE AND REGIONAL LINKAGES

Given that the 2 main regional growth industries of the Chotanagpur region are iron and steel and metallurgy-based engineering, the small-scale metal-working units of the region which emerged in massive numbers immediately after the establishment of these regional growth industries would seem to represent a very tangible network of product and market linkages between them and the regional economy. The theoretical reasoning contained in the previous section would also suggest that one of the factors conditioning the locational pattern of these units within the region would be the nature of their product mix.

Basing the count on the 6-digit standard product classification adopted by the Government of India (1973), the region's metal-working units altogether make 375 separate products (Government of Bihar, 1976a). Mainly using the stages of processing (intermediate/final demand) and market linkage criteria, these products can be grouped into 10 broad categories (Table 22.1). The

TABLE 22.1 Product categories of the Chotanagpur region's small-scale metal-working industries

Product categories	Some of the products included in the specified categories	Number of products
1. Casting, rolling and forging of metal	Sluice valves, metal railway sleepers, cast-iron pipes, cast-iron pulleys, grey-iron pipe fittings, cane crusher rollers, cast-iron parts of sugar mills, grey-iron stay sets, axles of trucks and cars, steel metal sheets, rail anchors, grey-iron wire, copper wire, copper rods, brass wire, aluminium rods	56
2. Household and other final demand durables	Steel safes, steel vaults, meat safes, metal cabinets, iron buckets, ice boxes, school boxes, hurricane lanterns, miners' lamps, sieves	23
3. Builders' hardware	Steel doors and windows, rolling shutters, collapsible gates, metal fixtures, iron cots, angle rakes, steel files, hammers, clamps, axes	19
4. Agricultural implements	Persian wheels, chaff-cutter blades, plough shares, disc harrows, pick-axes, hoes, shovels, sickles, spades	24
5. General hardware	Wire nails, panel pins, machine screws, hooks and eyes, barbed wire	17
6. Household utensils	Spoons, forks, table knives, scissors, bell-metal utensils, stainless steel utensils, pressure cookers	32
7. General machinery	Road rollers, parts and accessories of construction and mining industries, diesel oil engines, oil engine trollies, equipment for flour-mills, oil crushers, oil expellers, air coolers, parts and accessories of industrial machines other than food and textile, concrete mixers, parts and accessories of conveying equipments, drilling machine parts, boring machines, crank shaft grinders, filtration and distillation equipment	63
8. Electrical machinery	Transformers, welding transformers, switch gears, electric motors and their parts and accessories, electric wire and cables, storage batteries, transistors, record players, amplifiers, switch-boards and control panels, transmission line accessories	46

TABLE 22.1 (*continued*)

Product categories	Some of the products included in the specified categories	Number of products
9. Transport machinery	Parts and accessories of railway coaches and wagons, parts and accessories of locomotives, grease guns, gun-metal bushes, auto hubs, king-pins, luggage carriers, pistons, silencers, starters, side-lamp assembly, tie rods, valves and cores for tyres and tubes, chassis parts, coil springs, bus and truck bodies, trailers, bicycle parts	72
10. Miscellaneous instruments	Clinical thermometers, distillation plants, hydrometer insulation testers, power lenses, timepieces	23

Source: compiled from Government of Bihar, 1976a.

production capacities (totalling Rs241 million), ex-factory gross value of output (totalling Rs103 million) and levels of capacity utilization of these industries are shown in Table 22.2.

The only category of metal-working units which has a clear direct market linkage with the rural resource base is that relating to agricultural implements, but that accounts for only 1 per cent of the region's total production

TABLE 22.2 Licensed capacity, ex-factory gross value of output and capacity utilization levels of the small-scale metal-working industries of Chotanagpur region, 1972

Product category	Capacity (per cent)	Output (per cent)	Capacity utilization (per cent)
1. Casting, rolling and forging of metal	32.4	27.5	34.8
2. Household and other final demand durables	16.6	24.9	61.5
3. Builders' hardware	16.9	16.2	39.2
4. Agricultural implements	1.0	1.0	41.2
5. General hardware	1.4	1.5	43.0
6. Household utensils	8.3	7.8	38.5
7. General machinery	16.4	12.8	31.8
8. Electrical machinery	1.7	1.3	33.0
9. Transport machinery	5.0	6.6	53.4
10. Miscellaneous instruments	0.3	0.4	45.5
Regional total	100.0	100.0	40.9

Source: compiled from Government of Bihar, 1976a.

capacity and the same proportion of the gross output there of all small-sector metal-working industries. The construction and modern housing industries in Bihar are almost exclusively urban enterprises in their ownership pattern and market linkages, and the builders' hardware and general hardware categories are mainly tied to them.

For most rural households in Bihar, housing means structures comprising mud or brick walls and thatched or clay-tiled roofs, and the inputs of hardware they require are negligible. In 1973 only 6 per cent of the region's villages had access to electricity, and even then only a minute percentage of households was connected to the supply (Government of Bihar, 1976b, p. 71). Thus the electrical machinery producing firms in the region are catering almost entirely for the urban, upper income demand markets. So, too, are the transport equipment plants because transport firms in Bihar are almost invariably urban based and owned by the affluent merchant classes. The category general machinery, which almost entirely consists of capital goods and intermediary products for supply to other modern sector industries (most of which are urban based), is also likely to have very limited rural diffusion propensity. A close examination of the product-mix of the miscellaneous instruments category also reveals an urban and higher income group orientation in its market linkage.

The only other activities which may possibly have some linkages with the mass consumption market and/or the rural resource base are casting, rolling and forging of metal, and making household and final demand durables and household implements.

The casting, rolling and forging units supply intermediate inputs to much of the rest of the manufacturing sector in the region and their market linkages and locational organization are therefore influenced by the social orientation and spatial patterns of other industries. If most manufacturing is clustered around major urban centres, these units will also tend to gravitate there. Among the 56 products in this category, only 2—sugar-cane crushers and rollers—could be directly related to the needs of the rural sector. In 1972, these 2 products represented barely 0.001 per cent of the region's metal-working capacity and of its gross output.

In the household durables category, the only item of mass consumption is iron buckets whose share of the region's metal-working capacity and output were about 0.005 per cent. All the other items, like steel safes and metal cabinets, are beyond the reach of all but a minute proportion of rural households. Among household utensils only 3 items, aluminium, copper and sheet-iron cooking utensils, have mass consumption linkages and their combined capacity and output shares were about 0.02 per cent.

Only 2 items of general machinery have links with the rural economy and these are spares for rice-milling plants and handloom equipment: their capacity and output shares were minuscule.

This analysis of the Chotanagpur region's small-scale metal-working industry shows that only 1.1 per cent of its capacity and a similar proportion of its output can be considered to have a linkage with the mass consumption market and/or the rural resource base. There is thus no a priori reason to expect that this industry will have a spatially diffused locational pattern. Therefore, the blanket hypothesis about small-scale production automatically leading to widespread geographical decentralization of industries is not tenable even in theory. In any event, hypothetical statements about the spatial decentralization of industrial production can only be formulated in terms of a given structure of the space-economy.

STRUCTURE OF CHOTANAGPUR REGION'S SPACE-ECONOMY: A PRIORI EXPECTATIONS ABOUT THE SPATIAL DISTRIBUTION OF SMALL-SCALE INDUSTRIAL PRODUCTION

The 1971 census classified only 2.1 million (19 per cent) of the region's 11 million people as urban (compared with 20 per cent for the whole of India). These people lived in 82 urban centres which were grouped in 10 urban agglomerations and 42 other individual towns (Table 22.3). Three of them—Dhanbad, Bokaro and Katras—form a conurbation and are treated here as a single entity.

With 61 per cent of its urban population concentrated in just 3 urban agglomerations, and with the smallest of these being nearly 4 times the size of the largest of its other urban locations (Bermo, 69,300), the region's urban hierarchy is distinctly primate in nature. The close correlation between the primacy of the urban hierarchy and dualism of the economy has been extensively documented in regional planning literature (Berry, 1971; El-Shakhs, 1972; Thompson, 1972; Saha, 1977, 1979). Economic dualism is

TABLE 22.3 Size distribution of Chotanagpur region's urban hierarchy, 1971

Urban agglomeration (UA)/ town	Number	Population	Per cent of region's urban population
Dhanbad-Bokaro-Katras UAs	3	565,800	27.0
Jamshedpur UA	1	456,200	21.8
Ranchi UA	1	255,600	12.2
Other UAs and towns			
50,000–100,000	2	124,100	5.9
25,000–50,000	9	338,500	16.2
10,000–25,000	16	228,000	10.9
Less than 10,000	20	126,000	6.0
Regional total	52	2,094,200	100.0

Source: compiled from 1971 population census data.

usually characterized by

(a) the organized, non-primary sectors of the economy operating more or less autonomously and independently of the rest of the economy, which is mainly based on subsistence production;

(b) acute disparities of income, market density and levels of production technology between the 2 parts of the economy; and

(c) the organized sector becoming spatialized in a few very large urban centres leaving the rest of the regional (or national) space as a vast undifferentiated rural expanse, sparsely dotted by 'central place' type small towns.

Given the conditions of primacy and dualism in the region's space-economy, and given the almost total orientation of the production and market linkages of the region's small-scale metal-working industry away from the mass consumption market and the rural economy, the a priori expectations about the locational pattern of this industry over the regional space would seem to be:

(a) production units will be mainly concentrated in the existing larger urban-industrial agglomerations;

(b) very limited regional diffusion of the units down the urban hierarchy (diffusion effect);

(c) any rural diffusion of the units would be limited to the villages contiguous to, or only a short distance from, the existing urban-industrial agglomerations (contagion effect).

The Empirical Evidence

Empirical verification of these a priori expectations was sought using data on manufacturing capacity, annual gross ex-factory value of production, capacity utilization and geographical location for the region's 567 metal-working firms obtained from the Directorate of Industries of the Government of Bihar. Some firms covered more than one product category as specified in Table 22.1 so that in the ensuing analysis 498 were treated as single, 51 as double, 15 as treble and 3 as quadruple product category units. The production units therefore total 657 distributed among the urban and rural areas of the region as shown in Table 22.4.

These production units are all privately owned and employ from 1 to about 100 workers. The oldest date back to 1953, though most came into existence in the late 1960s and early 1970s. Many are owned by Marwaries, a merchant class originating in the state of Rajasthan and having a stranglehold on trade and business in most parts of northern India. Most Bihar-born

TABLE 22.4 Spatial distribution of small-scale metal-working production units in the Chotanagpur region, 1972

Urban and rural distribution	Product categories[a]										
	1	2	3	4	5	6	7	8	9	10	Total
Urban agglomerations:											
Dhanbad-Bokaro-Katras UAs	20	54	37	3	2	3	5	11	3	2	140
Ranchi UA	21	32	37	6	6	10	7	13	16	7	155
Jamshedpur UA	17	16	42	3	3	3	48	4	13	0	149
Sub-total	*58*	*102*	*116*	*12*	*11*	*16*	*60*	*28*	*32*	*9*	*444*
Urban: 50,000–100,000	1	1	3	0	0	0	0	1	1	0	7
25,000–50,000	5	12	13	10	2	8	3	3	5	12	73
10,000–25,000	2	6	4	9	1	8	0	0	0	1	31
Less than 10,000	4	0	3	0	0	2	1	0	0	0	10
Sub-total	*12*	*19*	*23*	*19*	*3*	*18*	*4*	*4*	*6*	*13*	*121*
Total urban	70	121	139	31	14	34	64	32	38	22	565
Total rural	22	14	15	13	1	16	6	0	4	1	92
All production units	92	135	154	44	15	50	70	32	42	23	657

[a] As detailed in Table 22.1.
Source: compiled from Government of Bihar, 1976a.

owners are immigrants from the northern Gangetic plains who made their money from intermediary interests in land and now, because of the official abolition of these intermediary interests, are seeking alternative channels for the investment of their capital. Most of the production units are very small: only 22 had an annual value of production exceeding Rs1 million (£55,600) in 1973. In Dhanbad District (1 of the 6 administrative districts of the Chotanagpur region) for example, there were then 23 factories engaged in casting, forging and rolling of metal. Only 2 of these had an annual production valued at greater than Rs1 million; 1 produced between Rs500,000 and Rs1 million; 7 between Rs100,000 and Rs500,000; and the rest less than Rs100,000.

Most factories seem to have been set up in response to the new consumer demand created by the industrial and tertiary workforce in the 3 rapidly expanding urban agglomerations. A few have been directly sponsored by major industrial establishments. In 1978 the author found that 52 ancillary units in Ranchi depended entirely on the supply of parts and semi-manufactures to the Heavy Engineering Corporation's machine-building establishments located in the adjacent factory site. There were similar ancillary units at Adityapur (part of the Jamshedpur urban agglomeration) supplying the Tata Iron and Steel Company across the River Subarnarekha (which flows through the urban agglomeration) and also at Bokaro, supplying the nearby steelworks. These ancillary units mainly occupy sites provided by the 3 separate Industrial Area Development Authorities created recently by the Bihar state government in the 3 urban agglomerations. These Authorities, headed by senior civil servants, now act as liaising agencies to channel government and bank finance to new entrepreneurs.

Technology used in most of the production units is indigenous. Usually production is based on the adaptation of craft-based skills to new specifications of metal casting, forging, rolling and numerous fabrications. A few larger units are managed by foreign-trained metallurgy graduates but even so, all workmen are indigenously trained, having for the most part acquired the necessary skills through on-the-job apprenticeships. The 3 major industrial establishments in the region—Bokaro Steel, Tata Steel (at Jamshedpur) and the Heavy Engineering Corporation (at Ranchi)—run their own technical institutes where many of the workmen employed in the ancillary units sponsored by these establishments have been trained. There are also 2 higher institutes of technical education at Jamshedpur and Ranchi.

Locational Pattern and the Urban Hierarchy

While 81 per cent of Chotanagpur region's population lives in rural areas, these account for only 14 per cent of its metal-working factories. The 3 major urban agglomerations of the region, on the other hand, account for 12 per cent of the population and 68 per cent of the establishments. The corresponding figures for towns between 50,000 and 100,000 are 1 and 1 per cent; for those between 25,000 and 50,000, 3 and 11 per cent; for those between 10,000 and 25,000, 2 and 5 per cent; and for those below 10,000, 1 and 2 per cent. The clear urban orientation of small-scale metal-working production units and their very limited rural diffusion are clearly evident. The maximum spatial concentration of production units seems to be occurring in the 3 largest urban agglomerations which together constitute the apex of the area's urban hierarchy and which is where the regional growth industries are also localized. A second identifiable spatial clustering of these firms, though a much smaller one, has occurred in towns with 25,000 to 50,000 inhabitants, but there is a relative dearth of establishments in the 50,000 to 100,000 and below 10,000 categories. Thus the production units are very unevenly distributed within the urban hierarchy which does not seem to provide an effective mechanism for the regional diffusion of the industrialization process.

An analysis of the locational structure of the production units reveals that only in 2 of the 10 categories, agricultural implements and household utensils, do the rural areas account for more than a quarter of all production units; in another, casting, rolling and forging, the rural share is more than a fifth of the total. The rural share in each of the other 7 categories

SMALL-SCALE ENTERPRISES IN INDIA

varies between zero to one-tenth (Table 22.4). Even the limited rural diffusion of the industrialization process is thus very product specific.

Data about licensed capacity and actual production show that the region's 3 main urban agglomerations accounted for 71 per cent of each; corresponding figures for the rest of the urban hierarchy were 16 and 11 per cent; for the rural areas they were 13 and 18 per cent, respectively. (The term 'licensed capacity' refers to the annual production capacity of the industrial unit as certified by the Licensing Committee which was set up in September 1952 to operate within the framework of the *Industries (Development and Regulation) Act* of 1951: the techno-economic appreciation for specifying the capacity is done by the Directorate General of Technical Development (Bhagwati and Desai, 1979, pp. 249–52).) No product category has a rural share of more than a quarter, while only 3 (casting, rolling and forging of metal; household and other final demand durables; and agricultural implements) have more than a fifth. Three of the product categories (household and other final demand durables; agricultural implements and household implements) have rural shares of more than a quarter, and one (casting, rolling and forging of metal) of more than a fifth of the regional total. These data seem to fit the a priori reasoning presented in an earlier section of this chapter. Firms associated with the 6 categories—builders' hardware; general hardware; electrical machinery; transport machinery; general machinery; and miscellaneous instruments—did indeed prove to be nearly exclusively urban-orientated in their locational preference. These product categories were little diffused even within the urban hierarchy—between 76 to 94 per cent of the capacity and between 89 and 94 per cent of production were concentrated within the 3 major urban agglomerations. Even product categories earlier identified on a priori grounds as likely candidates for an areally diffuse production structure, had between 76 and 96 per cent of their capacity and between 70 and 78 per cent of their production concentrated within the hierarchy (45 to 76 per cent of their capacity and 39 to 67 per cent of their production located within the 3 urban agglomerations alone). The evidence thus strongly supports the first and second of the 3 a priori statements made previously; it also focuses attention on the need to examine closely theories about the rural diffusion of production which do not take adequate account of the nature of the rural market and rural resource base. These in turn are functions of the rural income distribution pattern and of the ownership structure of rural assets.

Technocratic Responses to the Empirical Evidence

One explanation of this concentration of small-scale production units in a few urban locations is to invoke arguments about the superior technical advantages and the better organized marketing facilities offered there.

Another relates to scale advantages: that is, urban areas attract small firms because they provide technical and market opportunities for a scale of production which permits them to be small but viable and hence remain cost-effective. The outgoing Janata Government's Five Year Plan document (1978–83) seems to attribute the excessive concentration of small-scale industrial units in urban areas to just such causes. This becomes obvious from the policy measures it prescribed to remedy the situation, namely, the provision of technical and marketing facilities in rural areas and an emphasis on the 'tiny' sector. These measures can only be adequate if the conceptualization of the problem from which they stem is shown to be based on sound premises.

In industrial production, a juxtaposition of the technological soundness of the manufacturing process and a satisfactory state of market linkages ought to be reflected in a high level of capacity utilization. If urban areas satisfy these conditions better than rural areas, production units in the former ought to show higher levels of capacity utilization. But this does not seem to be the case in this region: rural factories show a capacity utilization level of 55 per cent compared with 38 per cent by those in towns. The rural figure compares favourably even with the 41 per cent mean figure for the 3 largest urban agglomerations. Moreover, the rural production units register a better capacity utilization performance than their urban counterparts in all but 2 of the product categories. Even in such purely 'urban' activities as builders' hardware and general machinery, the rural units seem to perform better. Within the urban hierarchy itself, the larger towns do not seem to have an advantage over the smaller ones; urban agglomerations of over 100,000 show a mean capacity utilization figure of 41 per cent, while the corresponding figure for the size-category 10,000 to 25,000 is 52 per cent. Apparently, the urban preferences of the small-scale firms in this region do not stem from any intrinsic technocratic advantages offered by urban areas.

The mean size of a factory in both the urban and rural areas appears to be more or less the same—an average rural unit represents an annual production capacity of Rs362,000, whereas that for the urban unit is Rs386,000. Indeed, the rural units seem to be much larger than those in the towns having 10,000 to 50,000 inhabitants. As shown in Table 22.5, it is the smallest places that seem to have the largest mean size of the production units: concentration of the production units in the largest towns of the region thus cannot also be explained in terms of the scale economies of production.

The strong rebuttal of the decentralization argument by the empirical evidence thus cannot be rationalized away by invoking peripheral and technocratic reasons. For the small industries policy to initiate and sustain a regionwide diffusion of industrial production, it has to run parallel with fundamental changes in the structure of the economy itself.

TABLE 22.5 Mean size of licensed capacity of the small-scale metal-working units in the Chotanagpur region, 1972

Urban and rural distribution	Rupees	£
Urban: 3 agglomerations	402,200	22,300
50,000–100,000	1,220,300	67,800
25,000–50,000	201,200	11,200
10,000–25,000	20,900	1,200
Less than 10,000	1,577,300	87,600
Sub-total all urban	*386,300*	*21,500*
Rural	361,700	20,100
Regional average	382,800	21,300

Source: compiled from Government of Bihar, 1967a.

Rural Diffusion and the Contagion Effect

The region's rural areas account for 13 per cent of the capacity and 18 per cent of the production of its small-scale metal-working firms. The extent of the rural spread is very small, but what needs examination is whether even this limited spread represents a genuine integration of a part of the industrial production structure with the rural economy or merely a spillover of the urban-based production system into the adjacent villages. If the former it could be expected that rural-based production units would be sited in large villages or in main rural market centres, mainly supplying the local market and/or using local resources, and that such rural factories would be located largely independently of the spatial organization of the urban hierarchy.

In fact, however, over 93 per cent of these rural metal-working units operate within 20 km (13 miles) of the centres of the 3 main urban agglomerations (Table 22.6). Areas within such small peripheries around urban agglomerations which themselves are about 20 km across in places, would clearly include only those rural communities which nestle around the margins of these urban sprawls. Only 4.2 per cent of the rural production originates from units located 20 to 50 km from the centres of these agglomerations and only 2.5 per cent originates from units located more than 50 km. The only exception seems to be agricultural implements where 63 per cent of the production comes from units more than 100 km from the main urban agglomerations; it alone seems to show promise of real integration with the rural economy. The rest of the so-called 'rural diffusion' seems to be a mere spillover of urban-based production just across administrative boundaries. What appears in the raw statistics as the 'rural' share of industrial production, turns out to be in fact an additional component of the process of concentration of most non-primary economic activity in a few

TABLE 22.6 Spatial distribution of small-scale rural metal-working units in the Chotanagpur region, 1972 (per cent)

Distance from 3 major urban agglomerations (km)	Product categories[a]										
	1	2	3	4	5	6	7	8	9	10	Total
0–20	99.2	97.1	53.9	—	100.0	97.1	65.1	—	100.0	—	93.3
20–50	0.8	2.9	20.6	25.4	—	—	34.9	—	—	—	4.2
50–100	—	—	24.0	12.0	—	0.2	—	—	—	—	0.8
Over 100	—	—	1.5	62.6	—	2.7	—	—	—	100.0	1.7

[a] As detailed in Table 22.1.
Source: compiled from Government of Bihar, 1976a.

urban areas. This, surely, is not a 'diffusion effect': a 'contagion effect' would be a more apt description.

To understand better the overall locational structure of the small-scale metal-working firms in the Chotanagpur region and to further sharpen the distinction between the diffusion and contagion effects in the decentralization process, the percentage shares of production of all locations, urban and rural, were regressed against population and this produced a correlation coefficient of +0.782. With 52 degrees of freedom, this is a very strong relationship indeed: larger-sized locations in general tended to attract more industrial production. Residuals from this regression were also calculated for each of the 53 locations involved. If the diffusion effect prevailed, in which regional growth industries-generated impulses were to cascade down the urban hierarchy and into the rural areas, these residuals would be expected to be distributed in conformity with the size structure of the hierarchy of locations. The highest positive values should have occurred in the 3 urban agglomerations, the second highest values in the next tier of towns irrespective of their distance from the largest towns, and the negative values should have been shown up for the smallest towns and villages. The surest sign of the contagion effect would be high positive values clustering around major urban agglomerations, the agglomerations themselves having high positive values, and indifferent and negative values mostly spread out to distant locations, irrespective of size.

The spread of the residual values across the regional space seems to confirm that there is indeed a contagion effect. Places like Hazaribagh (54,800), Gomia (42,700) and Daltonganj (32,400), located respectively, 93, 101 and 175 km from their nearest urban agglomerations, show high negative residuals, whereas small villages around Ranchi urban agglomeration show high positive residuals. The empirical evidence thus also seems to confirm the third a priori proposition made earlier in this chapter.

SMALL-SCALE ENTERPRISES IN INDIA

POLICY IMPLICATIONS

The empirical analysis in this chapter shows that government policy to promote small-scale industry does not necessarily lead to a widespread geographical diffusion of manufacturing. The locational structure of the small-scale metal-working firms in the Chotanagpur region indicates that, even though 3 decades of official attempts to bring into being small-scale industrial enterprise succeeded in encouraging or sustaining 567 small firms, most were localized in the largest urban centres. Geographical decentralization down the urban hierarchy has been very limited and diffusion into rural areas has not taken place, apart from a few particular firms.

Failure of the small industries policy to achieve geographically decentralized production cannot be solely attributed to faulty policy implementation or to such technocratic reasons as inadequate extension of technical and organizational support into rural areas. More fundamentally the failure stems from basic conceptual inadequacies in the a priori reasoning on which the policy has been based. One major gap in the conceptualization process from which the policy emerged was an inadequate appreciation of the locational dynamics of industrial production units operating in a dualistic market situation.

Locational preferences of industrial units are subject, of course, to the nature of their linkages with the intermediate and final demand sectors of the market. The latter essentially caters for the consumption of goods and services by households and therefore its spatial and social dimensions are inextricably linked with inter-personal and rural-urban income distribution patterns. The extreme skewness of incomes (the overwhelming concentration of the higher income groups in urban areas, either through actual urban residence or through the urban linkages of the rural asset-owning groups, and the nearly absolute levels of poverty of the rest of the population) means that the final demand market for all commodities except food and basic clothing is almost totally confined to large and medium-size towns. This market concentration in a few urban locations inevitably also exerts a powerful locational pull on the intermediate-goods-producing industrial units. A mutually reinforcing process of urban-industrial agglomerative expansion is thus set in train and continually sustained. Small-scale industrial units are as much subject to this locational dynamic as the large-scale ones but it is this process that Indian small industries policy failed to appreciate.

The only way a process of widespread geographical diffusion of industrial production can be initiated and sustained in India is by spreading the spatial structure of the mass consumption or final demand market much more widely than it is now, and that, of course, would involve a far-reaching programme of redistribution of incomes and of productive assets. Short of such a programme, limited decentralization is still possible by encouraging industrial units which cater for a demand market of basic necessities which even the impoverished masses must buy, such as agricultural implements and essential household durables. This kind of product specificity does not, however, seem to have played any part in the small industries policy pursued in India so far.

The locational analysis presented here places the problems of the spatial distribution of India's small-scale industries within the central issue to which all economic processes must relate—the social organization of production. The locational dynamics, as indeed all spatial patterns, stem from the dynamics of social processes and it is to these processes that one must look for insight into the chain of causation. The spatial concentration of small-scale industries in India in and around larger cities is a problem derived from the spatial as well as social concentration of income and of the ownership of the means of production. It therefore follows that, in policy terms, the decentralization of these industries cannot be seen as an end in itself but only as a policy instrument to achieve the social objective of providing income to, and meeting the consumption needs of, the mass of the population which is spatially dispersed. Spatially dispersed population no doubt means dispersed needs, but as long as incomes are geographically concentrated, dispersion of needs cannot be translated into dispersion of demand. Private industry gravitates to demand and not to needs. An essential prerequisite for achieving the geographical decentralization of small-scale industry therefore has to be the creation of demand in the many thousands of villages and small towns in which the bulk of India's population lives.

What needs to be realized is that the planning for small-scale industries, as indeed for any sector, cannot be undertaken in isolation from the rest of the economy. In a country where the bulk of the non-subsistence production is geared to the needs of a small affluent section of the population which is either urban based or urban linked, the geographical decentralization of small-scale industries cannot make economic sense. But to accept the logic of economics within the framework of the present socio-economic structure is to accept defeat in the fight against poverty. Besides, as Kurien (1978b, p. 137) has recently pointed out 'there is no *economic* principle or historical law which says that the resources available in society must be used primarily to meet the basic needs of every member of that society just as there is no economic principle which can justify the use of resources to meet the growing wants of the few'. A decision of that kind is external to economics. In India, as in many other Third World countries, the officially proclaimed intent has been that of seeking a kind of development which is based on economic and social justice. The paradox is that within such a framework it is imperative that much of the intermediate level non-primary production is dispersed into rural areas, but that such dispersion is not possible without fundamental changes in the existing socio-economic structure.

Given a strong political and social will to back up the intent with action, there is no cause for despondency. There is indeed a strong social case for a programme of promoting geographically dispersed small-scale industries, which would have to be situated within a much broader programme of rural transformation. Effective land reform, income-generating rural works schemes and widespread availability of technical education are among the essential ingredients of this broader programme. Once incomes, skills, and command over means of production are more or less equitably distributed in the population, and as the bulk of the population is widely spread in the national territory anyway, the small towns and villages will increasingly assume the role of 'combiners and transformers of regional inputs' (Santos, 1979, p. 180). It is in that economic climate that a programme of promoting and geographically dispersing small-scale industries can be effectively pursued.

This chapter does not question the correctness of the policy of promoting small-scale industries or the desirability of having a geographically decentralized industrial production structure. Even with a more equitable income distribution between urban and rural areas and between the income-groups, generally low levels of income would mean that the mass consumption market will long remain thinly spread and spatially fragmented. In such a situation small scale of production would definitely have an advantage over large scale, because limited, localized markets would be able to sustain only small production units. What is argued here, however, is that a policy of promoting small-scale industries will not itself lead to geographical decentralization of industrial production. For that to occur, product specificity of an appropriate kind would have to be an essential part of that policy and a parallel programme of redistribution of incomes and assets would also need to be initiated.

Spatial Analysis, Industry and the Industrial Environment. Vol. 3 Regional Economies and Industrial Systems
Edited by F. E. I. Hamilton and G. J. R. Linge
© 1983 John Wiley & Sons Ltd.

Chapter 23

Rural Industrialization in Monsoonal and Equatorial Asia

ROBERT ORR WHYTE

It has become customary to embrace the mainland and island countries of South, South-East and East Asia within monsoonal and equatorial Asia. The differences between the ecology, biogeography, land use, crops, livestock, culture and history in this region and other parts of the developing world are far greater than those found between the relatively discrete parts of the Asian region itself. The latter relate primarily to the geographical distribution and seasonal variations in climate, with extreme types characteristic of western and eastern monsoon Asia, respectively, and many intermediate types between these and the humid tropical to equatorial bioclimates of South-East Asia and part of South Asia (Figure 23.1).

These ecological similarities and distinctions within Asia are reflected in characteristic types of land use and of crop and animal husbandry and in the resulting social and agrarian structure of diverse rural economies which have evolved over the centuries. Because of the growing imbalance between natural resources and the population that depends on them for their livelihood, planners and administrators are turning increasingly to other forms of employment off the land including rural industrialization.

There are 2 contrasting approaches to the planning and implementation of industrial enterprises in the smaller towns and their rural hinterlands of Asia: that of the urban industrialists and economists who wish to defend their existing or planned enterprises, especially at the medium and small-scale level, against competition from what they regard as less efficient and less economic rural enterprises, and that of the protagonists of integrated rural development who regard medium and small-scale industries as essential components of overall planning designed to improve the socio-economic status and way of life of the people for whom they are responsible. The swings of the pendulum are particularly noticeable in the People's Republic of China, depending on the relative success of the protagonists of large-scale metropolitan industry and of medium and small-scale rural industry in influencing economic policies at the national and provincial levels.

The major problems faced by planners of rural development relate to the provision of jobs and income for the surplus labour which is at present underemployed or unemployed. Although considerable reliance is placed on

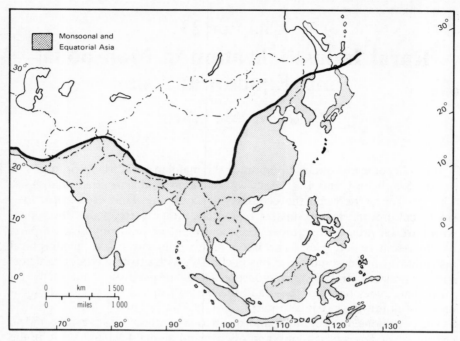

FIGURE 23.1 Monsoonal and Equatorial Asia

public works projects (construction of rural infrastructure such as roads and railways, dams for irrigation and power, and capital land reconstruction), these are essentially of a temporary, short-term nature. Planning authorities are therefore considering whether, and to what extent, the introduction of particular types of small and medium-scale industries into integrated rural development can provide significant employment opportunities off the land.

The objective is not primarily to raise the overall industrial production of a nation or a region, but to find ways of reducing the widespread poverty among the landless and those families whose holdings are too small to provide an acceptable living, even at a subsistence level. Increasingly it is being realized that the socio-economic status of these groups is unlikely to improve through the application of financial and technical assistance from international, bilateral and national agencies into agricultural development alone. Rather, the modernization of agriculture, animal husbandry and land use generally calls for a reduction in manpower per hectare or tonne of output. In the agriculturally more advanced parts of the region, such as Punjab (India), economists find that much of the labour employed on the land is 'surplus' in that it could be removed without affecting the present level of farm output at the existing level of technology (Bal *et al.*, 1979).

The need to assess the potential contribution of rural industrialization is likely to grow because of these factors along with the natural increase in population; the adoption of land policies leading to consolidation of holdings into larger, more productive units requiring fewer but more skilled workers; the mechanization of farm practices; and the greater availability of modern forms of energy.

The increased industrialization in urban centres of Asia following the Second World War is not at issue. At a seminar in Kyoto in October 1978, sponsored by the World Bank and the Agricultural Development Council, Louis Walinski asked:

> What was it that sent the teeming millions of impoverished and miserable landless labourers and cultivators streaming into the cities, where they could find neither employment, nor housing, nor schooling, nor health care for their children, nor escape from misery? Wasn't it the failure of governments to address the problems of the countryside, and their misguided overemphasis on industrialization? (Kearl and Weisblat, 1979).

To reduce the level of migration to the cities, planners and sociologists are trying to find ways of bringing specific types of industry to the rural people instead of bringing the rural people to factories in urban communities. In only one country of the region, Malaysia, does the latter process feature as part of official government policy.

INDUSTRIES ADAPTED TO RURAL ECONOMIES

Six main groups of small and medium-scale industry can be considered as potentially integral parts of rural development. These may be placed on a spatial gradient of population and functions, as well as the relative degrees of intensity of capital and labour inputs, nature of products, and standards of managerial and technological expertise of the operatives. Industries within these categories are:

(a) factories near major centres of population and industry, operating mainly on a sub-contracting basis;

(b) factories within the same or a lower range of population and functions, providing items for sale to larger urban centres or for export, or to smaller urban centres lower in the spatial hierarchy;

(c) factories and workshops in smaller rural towns, communes and larger villages, producing simple and inexpensive items for sale to similar settlements along the horizontal linkages or down the hierarchy to the level of the smaller communities and the rural hinterland in general;

(d) factories at the same spatial level designed for the partial or complete processing of produce from the land;

(e) service industries catering for the maintenance and repair of farm and transport equipment and machinery, electric power plants for irrigation pumps and other equipment;

(f) handicraft making in the home or in small village centres.

The categorization of this broad range of enterprises according to numbers employed differs from country to country but indicative statements can be made.

Large The well-planned enterprises of the primate cities and large urban centres, each with over 500 employees, operating with considerable technical efficiency and yielding an acceptable return on the investment.

Medium Factories with from 100 to 500 employees, frequently situated in the environs of major population centres or in the former market towns, now urbanized, with ready transport access to the cities.

Small The innumerable small-scale enterprises and service units employing from 5 to 100 workers, or operated on a family basis, located in major and minor urban centres, and in the small towns and larger villages which qualify as growth or service centres.

Criteria for Small-scale Industries

Examples of state recognition of small-scale industries, whether urban or rural, are given later (although the criteria are often changed).

India A small-scale industrial enterprise is defined as one with machinery and plant valued at 2 million rupees ($US183,000 as at March 1982) which will thus receive budget relief; ancillary units in rural areas are regarded as supplying at least half their production on sub-contract to one or more associated factories in urban centres. The smallest category is the 'tiny' units in towns and villages with fewer than 50,000 population. Industrial units established to export their entire output receive tax concessions no matter what they produce. Any industry set up in any of the country's export processing zones (EPZs) (at present Santa Cruz, near Bombay, and Kandla in Gujarat) qualifies for a 5-year tax exemption.

Bangladesh A small-scale industry is defined as having a fixed investment of 250,000 taka ($US16,500).

Malaysia Industries with a total fixed capital investment of $M250,000 ($US111,000) are regarded as small-scale.

Singapore The Small Industries Finance Scheme of the Economic Development Board applies to concerns that have less than $S2 million ($US968,000) in existing fixed assets.

Philippines Enterprises employing between 6 and 99 workers with a capitalization of not more than 1 million pesos ($US119,000).

Hong Kong Small industry includes establishments employing fewer than 50 people; medium-scale industry 50 to 499; large-scale industry over 500.

South Korea Manufacturing, mining or transport enterprises employing from 5 to 300 people or with total assets not exceeding 500 million won ($US704,000); construction businesses employing from 5 to 50 people with total assets up to 500 million won; commercial or service enterprises employing from 5 to 20 people with total assets not exceeding 50 million won (or not more than 200 million won for wholesale businesses); small industry cooperatives, their federations and members of the Korea Federation of Small Business, established in accordance with the *Small and Medium Industry Corporations Act,* and entities organized by small entrepreneurs.

COMPLEMENTARITY

Towards the top of the industrial system and of the urban to rural hierarchy of settlement, population and function are the factories in the former rural areas, now rapidly becoming urbanized, near metropolitan centres with their concentrations of people, expertise, capital and political power. A division of labour exists between the smaller factories in urban satellite communities which operate in complementarity systems similar to those in more advanced countries. The smaller concerns in this symbiosis with the major urban factories have lower overheads and lower labour costs, and require less capital. Thus the directors of large-scale industry find it profitable to equip their factories to make goods for export or of technologically complex nature, while relying on their medium and small-scale associate companies to provide components through sub-contracts.

The smaller enterprises gain from complementarity in the advanced technology, supported by some key technical staff and machine tools, which they may obtain from their larger partners. They also have a sound and stable guaranteed market. Rural entrepreneurs who establish factories on cheaper land in semi-rural and rural areas can draw on reserves of surplus labour, provided it is trainable. Satellite factories of urban concerns may be allocated some of the overall profits, which may then be used to improve the rural factory itself, or to contribute to the general catalytic effect of rural industry in improving agricultural technology and equipment and the general economic status of the peasant communities.

The extent to which large-scale urban industries can accept complementarity with medium and small-scale rural industries and rely on the quality of the components supplied differs greatly throughout the region. Thus at present sub-contracting can penetrate much deeper into the rural hinterlands of Japan and Taiwan than into other, less proficient rural communities.

Many of the urban and suburban satellite communities with medium and small-scale industries are former market towns that have become incorporated administratively within the parent metropolis, or are being developed as satellite urban centres around a core city which urban planners wish to limit in its ultimate size, as with Shanghai. The former market towns involved in these inevitable trends progressively lose whatever degree of rural character they may have once had; they are no longer attractive or comfortable places for rural people to visit to sell and purchase goods, or to make social contacts. Such conurbations now do not come within the ambit of rural planners, but the industrial population so created represents an important market for food products from the hinterland, and for items produced by less sophisticated factories in settlements lower in the spatial hierarchy.

RURAL INDUSTRIES

Medium and small-scale industries in smaller towns do, or could, produce items required by (and within the purchasing power of) people there and in the villages and hamlets even further down the spatial hierarchy. These activities do not call for a highly qualified workforce; they do not necessarily have to meet the standards required for items to be sent to urban markets, to other provinces or abroad. Until recently, such small-scale industries were extended down to the commune and brigade levels in the Chinese rural economy (see Sit's chapter in this volume). Now, on instructions from the central government, many such enterprises are being closed or amalgamated to ensure better production of reliable items for which a local market actually exists, and to economize in energy. Similar readjustments would appear to be called for in India. A Government of India survey conducted by the Planning Commission (*The Statesman* [New Delhi], 19 March 1982) found that in 1981 the numbers of medium and small-scale industrial units regarded as 'economically sick' were 1026 and 22,300 respectively; half the latter were regarded as non-viable. Although factors associated with supplies of coal, power and transport are the main causes of these failures, bad management is the most important.

Around the smaller rural towns and the larger villages being upgraded to growth centres emphasis is being placed on the processing and other plants of agriculture and forest-based industries. Moving these from larger urban centres to smaller rural towns reduces transport costs for non-processed commodities and provides employment for rural labour. Authorities in the People's Republic of China are stressing the economic desirability of this change. These plants represent the initial or complete stages of processing of farm and forest produce for transport and sale in urban markets or for disposal locally along horizontal linkages. Processing plants include cereal mills; oil crushers; works for processing plantation crops, canning and juicing fruit and vegetables, and collecting and processing milk; and ply-wood factories. Also in this agribusiness group should be included units assembling and packaging bulk inputs into the local agricultural economy such as animal-feed mixers; centres for bagging and distributing fertilizers and items for plant protection and veterinary purposes; and works for seed cleaning, packaging and distribution. All these provide off the land jobs for surplus labour, and represent important components of a typical rural growth centre in central place theory terms.

However, it is the maintenance and repair of equipment for farms and other forms of land use that provide the most important actual and potential source of rural employment. These activities are located in the smaller rural towns and larger villages and along the highways as a ribbon development (e.g. the Sikh motor workshops along the main roads of the Punjab) where they are readily accessible. They operate and service the local forms of motorized transport, and maintain and repair farm equipment characteristic of modern advanced agriculture, such as field machinery, irrigation pumps and electrical equipment.

Handicraft and cottage industries are regarded by planners of integrated rural development as being within the scope of rural industrialization. They represent an important source of off the land employment and income for women at the household or village level, especially in those communities where, for cultural reasons, it is not acceptable for women to work alongside men in the fields.

Hoselitz (1968) draws a distinction between cottage industries and handi-crafts. Chandrashekar Shetty (1963) gives 4 criteria for cottage industry—workplace, employment, use of motive power, and extent of market served. With special reference to Malaysia, Taib (1978) finds that handicrafts have 3 main characteristics: (a) the output is guided by social (including religious and ritual) needs; (b) there is a strong tradition of inherited techniques; and (c) there is extensive use of handpower, even where tools and machines are used in manufacturing. Some cottage industries may become upgraded to the level of industry in small-scale production units; others will remain a handicraft or, at best, a household industry because of the nature of their raw materials, their techniques of production and special attitudes towards them. Traditional technology in its present form has acquired various elements from modern technology leading to some evolution and change.

It will become increasingly necessary to protect the indigenous craft industries which are losing ground everywhere as improved communications open up rural markets to cheap, factory-made substitutes. Clearly, it is unrealistic to expect rural consumers to revert to more expensive and often less durable commodities made from resources available locally. But it seems to be agreed that some form of protection and guaranteed markets are necessary to preserve these sources of employment and to ensure that craftsmen can still find young apprentices. Taib (1978) suggests that the tourist industry should become involved and that the importance of the national heritage should be stressed so that more educated, wealthier urban people will continue to provide a market for craft products.

A SPATIAL BASIS FOR RURAL INDUSTRIALIZATION

It is desirable to consider and to plan for the introduction into rural economies of a new activity such as industry on the basis of an existing or planned spatial relation between the urban centres and their rural hinterlands. In this respect there is great variation between the individual countries of monsoonal and equatorial Asia. This may be expressed in terms of a hierarchy of settlements of graded population, degree of urbanization and range of functions, from primate centres or metropolises down to villages and hamlets (Whyte, 1981). Friedmann (1972) has classified an hypothetical developing country or territory into frontier regions, downward transitional regions, upward transitional regions, and core regions in relation to their socio-economic activities and the actual or potential rate of growth or decline in development (see Whyte, 1982[a], p. 33). It is difficult, however, to introduce guided change into such a static conception.

In this context, it is necessary to consider the relative merits of the 'top-down' versus 'bottom-up' approaches to introducing various kinds of rural development. Members of a colloquium on rural-urban relations and development planning held at the United Nations Centre for Regional Development at Nagoya in November 1977 stated that they

> reject the idea that the trickling-down process from urban-based industrialization alone will eliminate internal disparities in development . . .Recognizing that most Asian economies are basically agrarian, we advocate the transformation of their rural sectors to meet basic needs and a fairer share of development. In this reorientation, we also recognize ecological constraints on natural resources.

A document prepared by the United Nations Development Programme for a conference at Rome in August 1979 on agrarian reform and rural development noted that top-down paternalistic development processes are less effective than efforts which involve the community. Governments were urged to decentralize decision-making and to allow peasants to take a greater part in decisions affecting their lives and welfare.

It is possible to design an hypothetical hierarchy from urban to rural settlements on a spatial population and function gradient. Industries of varying size and sophistication of production methods may be placed on this hierarchy according to the relative degrees of intensity of inputs of capital and labour, the nature and complexity of products, and the standards of managerial and technological expertise among the operating personnel.

(a) *Special areas or science parks* Small to medium-scale industries in urban suburbs or rural areas, applying various high technologies; highly capital-intensive, using sophisticated equipment, offering limited employment to skilled workers and university graduates but employing little unskilled labour.

(b) *Metropolis, primate city, large city above 500,000 population* Large national or multinational enterprises, manufacturing for local sale or export to other provinces or abroad, or making bulk-produced items for sale lower in the spatial hierarchy, there to compete with produce of small industries. Receiving manufactured components from enterprises lower in the hierarchy operating under sub-contracts.

(c) *Towns, population 500,000 to 250,000* Relatively advanced technology, capital-intensive, experienced management and operatives, manufacturing for urban markets and for export, or sub-contracting for (b).

(d) *Towns, population 250,000 to 100,000* Similar to (c) but less capital-intensive, less experienced management and personnel; still some sub-contracting; manufacturing; advanced processing of agricultural products.

(e) *Small towns, population 100,000 to 25,000* Less capital-intensive, more labour-intensive, relatively simple manufacturing for sale mostly down the spatial scale; processing of agricultural products; receipt of bulk inputs (fertilizers, chemicals, seeds) for subdivision into smaller lots for distribution to (f) and (g); large-scale service industries for land operations.

(f) *Rural towns, population 25,000 and below* Labour-intensive; least skilled management by local entrepreneurs; less-skilled rural operatives; manufacture of items for sale to villages, hamlets, farms; initial collection and processing of farm and forest produce; assembly and distribution of inputs into farming and other land enterprises; servicing of agricultural machinery, transport, electrical equipment, irrigation pumps, etc.

(g) *Villages, communes, etc.* Rural people, finding employment and income on their own land or as casual labour on neighbours' land; or off the land in urban settlements (f) and (e) above, within daily or weekly commuting distance from their homes, or mobilized on a temporary basis for major public works projects or capital land reconstruction.

The potential for introducing industry into programmes of rural development varies greatly, from the People's Republic of China, where the present administration has inherited an almost ideal hierarchical system from the past in the more populous provinces (Skinner, 1964–65; Elvin, 1973), to the economies at present based on primate cities (Thailand, Indonesia and the Philippines), and to the situation in India, Pakistan and Bangladesh, where there is a great gap between the major metropolises and the small or rural towns and the villages or hamlets in their hinterlands.

It is in the lower segments, (d) to (g), of the hierarchy that by far the greater proportion of the people in the less developed Asian countries live, and in which planners following the bottom-up or grass-roots approach to development (Whyte, 1982a, p. 203) have to find ways of promoting and assisting the entrepreneurs who wish to establish industries at the rural level.

THE ENTREPRENEUR

The success of integrated rural development in general and of rural industrialization in particular largely depends on the initiative, energy and business acumen of the individual entrepreneur. This applies just as much in democratic and capitalist societies as in the centrally planned ones; in the latter, commune leaders are expected to follow central directives and guidance and then to take the initiative in establishing small industries at the commune and brigade level according to the available resources, manpower and managerial capacity.

Japan

Japan has seen the rise in recent decades of several outstanding entrepreneurs to international status in the business community: many of these began their careers in rural areas, employing local labour in the first instance (Whyte, 1982b, Chapter 8). For example, Matsushita moved from Osaka to Kadoma City in 1933 and succeeded on the basis of a subcontracting system and the availability of surplus rural labour. Hitachi City began in 1907 as an auxiliary machine-repair depot at a copper mine (village of 6000 population); this stimulated the growth of a manufacturing town employing local rural labour and also workers from elsewhere in Ibaraki

Prefecture (population 70,000 in 1938). Honda began in Hamamatsu City, Shizuoka Prefecture, first as an auto-repair shop, then manufacturing piston rings on sub-contract; in 1946 it established a small plant to equip bicycles with small engines (*bata-bata*). Kitayama established a factory for folk-craft manufacture in a remote valley in Kyushu flanked by Japanese cedars; he has now set up 350 cooperative factories to consolidate supplies elsewhere in Japan and in Thailand, Indonesia and the Philippines. The making of dolls from *Paulownia* wood began in Iwatsuki, Saitama Prefecture, during the Meiji period and as a result of the entrepreneurship of a number of producers it is now the doll capital of Japan.

Malaysia

A study by Chee *et al.* (1979) indicated that the government of Malaysia is not yet firmly committed to a policy of developing small-scale enterprises, although there is a Co-ordinating Council for Development of Small-Scale Industries. Small entrepreneurs need ready access to loans from commercial banks to remove the imbalance in a system which these authors regard as discriminatory. Industrial extension services comparable to those available for agriculture would disseminate knowledge of technical innovations and better management methods.

Philippines

The Commission on Small and Medium Industries provides functional assistance to entrepreneurs throughout the Philippines by preparing feasibility studies, negotiating with finance institutions and establishing pilot projects such as those in Aklan, Surigao del Norte and Palawan, as recommended by the joint Economic and Social Council for Asia and the Pacific/United Nations Industrial Development Organization Survey Team (Economic and Social Commission for Asia and the Pacific, 1979c). Twelve regional Small Business Advisory Centres provide managerial and technical assistance in cost analyses, plant layout, advertising, capital investment decision-making, applications for licensing or registration, and business organization. The Ministry of Industry has a National Cottage Industries Development Authority. The Philippines Institute of Small-Scale Industries conducts entrepreneurial development programmes in university and high school curricula. Entrepreneurs who have already established small industries are encouraged and assisted to progress from an owner-operator concern to a corporate enterprise having greater capacity to increase production of more diversified items, and to improve market penetration and growth.

Republic of South Korea

The authorities in South Korea recognize that many youngsters are keen to start small businesses but that, because of lack of support, many become frustrated and abandon the idea. Even those who do make a start amid great difficulties do not obtain matching support to sustain their venture, and many firms close each year (Soong Jun University, 1978). There is evidence of much risk-taking and of a marked entrepreneurial potential, but there is neglect of the 'golden business principle' that a new business should employ both borrowed and personal capital. A successful South Korean entrepreneur would take a maximum 60 per cent risk, be able to mobilize financial resources at least 2.6 times more than his personal capital, make a net profit of at least 15 per cent of the total assets, and reinvest at least 20 per cent of his net profit for expansion or diversification. The Asian Development Bank is lending the Korean Small and Medium Industry Promotion Corporation $US13 million towards the cost of establishing a Small and Medium Industry Management and Technology Institute with an annual training capacity for 4000 management and technical personnel and 960 extension service officers. Since small and medium-size establishments, admittedly primarily urban, account for 96 per cent of all industrial firms in South Korea, this programme should contribute to an overall increase in productivity and earnings of foreign exchange.

India

Prospective entrepreneurs are assisted in India by the Small Industries Development Organization (SIDO) of the Ministry of Industry in New Delhi and through the programme of the Rural Industries Project. SIDO provides extension services through its network of 16 small industries service institutes, 7 branch institutes, 41 extension centres and other facilities. The National Small Industries Corporation provides machines and equipment to entrepreneurs on hire purchase, assists enterprises in purchasing programmes, and provides training and facilities in the development of prototype equipment. The programme of the Rural Industries Project was essentially a federal extension scheme designed to assist entrepreneurs in selecting suitable product lines and appropriate technology, and in obtaining inputs like credit, raw materials and labour. As part of the emphasis on the development of small-scale and rural industries in India, the focal points for action have been moved from the large cities and state capitals to the district headquarters. District Industries Centres are sponsored by central government and implemented by state governments as part of their own promotion and assistance programmes. The development agencies identify the types of entrepreneurship which are thought to be latent in the rural areas, especially among the young, and to ensure that they act as agents for change in the modernization of rural communities. Development is seen to have a 3-tier basis: at the village level—rural artisans, male and female, and cottage industries; at the block level—simple processing industries; and at the district headquarters level—larger industries in the small-scale sector.

The best training and experience that a young entrepreneur can obtain is undoubtedly in the managerial offices and on the shop floors of established factories in urban centres higher up the spatial hierarchy. This applies especially to prospective plant managers who plan to enter into a sub-contracting arrangement with the larger concerns. The larger factories are only too willing to ensure that they can rely on the quality and regular supply from their associated small-scale industries.

CONCENTRATION OF RURAL INDUSTRY

The introduction of small and medium-scale industries into the rural spatial pattern on the scale visualized here would call for vast and generally unattainable expenditure of public funds to establish infrastructure that does not now exist. Hence, planners turn from the diffuse distribution of industrial estates or EPZs as in Thailand and the Philippines (see the chapter by Salita and Juanico in this volume). Land planners associated with such developments recommend that these schemes should be located on second or third-class land to reduce their effects on agricultural production. The state provides the water, power, access roads and other infrastructure, and may build simple factory buildings and godowns (warehouses) for rent to local entrepreneurs. The industrial estates are located near road or rail facilities for the inward movement of raw materials and the outward movement of semi-finished or finished products. In this way, access is provided for the daily movement of labour from the villages or small towns to be served by the estate, so that family structure will not be disrupted by wholesale emigration.

Indian experience with industrial estates (Government of India Ministry of Industry, n.d.) suggests that they should become part of the overall economic development plan for a region. They may develop into focal points of healthy industrial growth rather than as a cluster of inward-looking production units, and should be designed and managed so as to provide horizontal linkage in terms of common facilities, technical advice and guidance to other industrial units in the same area. In backward and rural areas, it is necessary to stimulate entrepreneurship among the local people, and to provide them with training and credit facilities: there such estates have a promotional role in the process of industrial development generally. There is a need for close and active involvement of local leadership and enterprise to obtain public support for a genuine people's programme because, when this has been lacking, estates have not had the desired impact.

When private initiative is ready, or the success of estates demonstrated by examples, the government's role may be confined to developing the site, providing roads and essential utilities, and prescribing minimum factory standards and leaving the construction and maintenance of buildings to private initiative. Entrepreneurs may be assisted in choosing the product to suit the crops and livestock characteristic of the region, to accommodate the market demand for mass consumption items, and to embrace development programmes (such as mechanization, electrification and irrigation). The state can also assist in marketing.

At these levels of productive skills planners see a significant place for intermediate or alternative technologies. Many simpler techniques are available, particularly for the first-stage processing of agricultural products. It is a matter of adapting each technique to the competence of rural labour and the capacity of simple machinery. All authorities stress the need to concentrate on resources available locally and on the demands created by improved farm technology—hence on the processing and service industries. The Chinese, in particular, stress the urgent need to economize on scarce sources of energy to operate plants at the commune and brigade level.

There will always be a tendency for secondary growth effects to manifest themselves around industrial estates in isolated rural sites. Haphazard growth of ancillary, service and transport industries, with their associated housing and other facilities and functions, is almost inevitable. It is in fact possible to visualize the development of the estate as the core of a new growth centre, whose further development may cause the progressive decay of older potential growth centres in the hinterland. EPZs will probably develop differently, since they will be established, manned and operated by larger national or multinational concerns to meet their particular export markets.

It is necessary to consider a third group of industrial concentration, namely the special development zones or science parks for research and production of high-technology items (see Barr's chapter in this volume). These represent the ultimate ambition and target of sophistication of developing countries in Asia. They provide employment for skilled graduate personnel but only a few jobs for unskilled maintenance staff. They will increasingly represent part of the evolving industrial systems in rural Asia, but will not make any marked contribution to off the land employment and income for rural people.

SOCIAL AND ENVIRONMENTAL FACTORS

The promotion of industrialization in rural Asia on the lines discussed here faces several powerful constraints.

(a) Urban sociologists and economists argue in favour of continued and increased support for the concentration of larger, medium and small-scale industries in the major urban centres and their suburbs or satellite towns where the political power, financial resources and technical expertise are concentrated in the hands of a small minority of the total population. This applies particularly to the Asian economies based on a primate city. Even in the People's Republic of China the Maoist attempts at rural small-scale industrialization were workable for some time, but it then became essential to shift to large-scale, capital-intensive, urban-based growth programmes. More recently, the emphasis has returned to light industry and to the encouragement of rural industrialization.

(b) Rural sociologists and anthropologists deplore the breakdown of traditional social structures of rural life which has occurred already over much of Japan and is thought to be almost inevitable elsewhere in Asia, even where every attempt is made to bring rural industries as near as possible to the villages and their hinterlands.

(c) The conservationists deplore, with even greater force, the destruction of an environment by introducing industrial estates and individual factories and their associated infrastructures into relatively unspoilt rural areas. They argue that these should be retained as country parks for recreational use by urban people, or as visual attractions for foreign tourists, ignoring the socio-economic status of people who subsist at or below the poverty threshold in the midst of natural beauty which they themselves are in no position to appreciate.

(d) Planners of rural small-scale industries have to realize that the introduction of their various types of off the land employment may not have the intended impact on the unemployed proportion of the rural population.

Thus a study by the Economic and Social Commission for Asia and the Pacific (1979d) lists 8 resource-based projects (e.g. rice-bran oil extraction, papermaking, tanning, and fruit and vegetable canning) and 8 demand-based projects (e.g. aluminium utensils, builders' hardware, plastic goods, and ready-made garments) proposed for the Khon Kaen Province of Thailand. Taken together, these projects will occupy 12,500 m^2 of factory space and require an investment in machinery and equipment of about 91 million bhat ($US4 million) but employ only 132 administrative and supervisory staff and 417 workers on the shop-floor itself.

The planner of integrated rural development has to consider these diverse factors in relation to the infinite variety of social, economic, spatial and political conditions to be found in the region. This necessarily brief account of a broad and evolving subject may be supplemented by a study of the community-based small industries in Japan (Yamazaki, 1980); the initiation and development of rural industries in the People's Republic of China (Sigurdson, 1977; American Rural Small-Scale Industries Delegation, 1977);

the report of the International Labour Office (1974) Mission to the Philippines which reviewed the role of rural industry in the overall context of employment, equity and growth; the report of the Mission sent to a number of Asian countries to work out a new alternative approach towards integrated industrialization in non-metropolitan areas (Economic and Social Commission for Asia and the Pacific, 1979a, b, c, d, e, f, g, h, i); and a comprehensive review of the industrial potential of rural Asia (Whyte, 1982b).

The main object is to transfer selected industries from their present urban locations to sites, probably industrial estates, as near as possible to the communities expected to supply the labour. A compromise has to be reached between the commuting distances which rural operatives can afford, and the lowest place in the spatial hierarchy to which qualified managers and engineers will come and still find the amenities (housing, health services, educational facilities) and other functions to which they and their families are accustomed. Enterprises introduced at the lower levels of the hierarchy are concerned with the manufacture of simple items for sale in the small towns and village stores. These items will have to be protected in some way from those imported into rural areas from major urban centres and which have attractive packaging and well-known brand names. At the same level will be promoted factories initially processing raw materials from farm, garden, plantation and forest. It is here also that support will need to be given to entrepreneurs providing repair and maintenance facilities for rural transport and for land machinery and equipment. Those engaged in production of raw materials from the land and the entrepreneurs starting small rural industries will tend to become disillusioned when they see considerable international and national aid going to more fortunate projects at higher levels in the hierarchy. As already noted, the trickle-down process has not worked satisfactorily, nor have successful methods of applying massive aid at the grass-roots level been evolved. To prevent this frustration from engendering some form of political unrest, it appears to be necessary to evolve an agro-industrial symbiosis at the rural level. The application of the usual inputs of integrated rural development to land enterprises will continue and lead to modernization of agriculture, horticulture, animal husbandry and other forms of rural production.

The evolution of rural industry will be initiated by limited state assistance providing accommodation in industrial estates, and credit, training and marketing assistance for entrepreneurs. It may be visualized that national and international agencies and foundations can supply the financial resources required to construct buildings and infrastructure, and also provide some of the credit required by entrepreneurs. Muslim countries and communities in the region may be able to apply to organizations in South-West Asia for loans according to Islamic financial customs but while these may be granted to entrepreneurs they will not be available for developing more permanent infrastructure.

The surplus labour recruited from the rural areas, the small farmers on unprofitable holdings, the landless and other casual labour will, with their purchasing power increased by employment in industry, represent a new market for the products from the land. Members of the farming community, such as the men who take up employment in urban factories and who leave their wives and parents to operate the farm in Japan, or girls and women who live on the family farm but work in nearby factories as in Japan and Taiwan, will increasingly tend to plough back some of their income into the family farm. It will thus be possible to increase the efficiency and productivity of the farming unit by the purchase of labour-saving machinery, the introduction of irrigation systems, the construction of modern buildings and the adoption of crop protection and veterinary treatment. Thus the rural people will maintain a type of self-regenerating revolving fund to increase that self-reliance so much stressed in the People's Republic of China. They will still need to depend on markets higher in the spatial hierarchy and along their horizontal linkages, but would be relatively independent from political and economic change in state policies at the centre, and on fluctuating forms of aid or charity from national or international agencies and foundations. Finally, industrial estates and other developments need not necessarily bring unacceptable ugliness into a rural setting, provided that landscape specialists are involved in their design and maintenance. The Republic of Singapore has demonstrated how the industrial environment may still be attractive in an urban community.

Spatial Analysis, Industry and the Industrial Environment. Vol. 3 Regional Economies and Industrial Systems
Edited by F. E. I. Hamilton and G. J. R. Linge
© 1983 John Wiley & Sons Ltd.

Chapter 24

The Informal Sector within a Communist Industrial Structure: The Case of the People's Republic of China

VICTOR F. S. SIT

THE SOCIALIST INDUSTRIAL STRUCTURE

The industrial systems of socialist countries share one common characteristic: a hierarchical arrangement. At the top are the various Ministries responsible for major branches of industry, though their activities may be coordinated partly by central planning organizations. In the People's Republic of China the central Ministries also operate local offices at the various administrative levels, i.e. the *xian* (county), *qu* (district), *shi* (municipal) and *sheng* (provincial) levels. Provincial and municipal administrations have some say in these local offices. However, the extent of 'decentralization' of industrial decisions varies between socialist countries but, in general, the central Ministries retain the bigger say even in local production matters. Thus these layered, bureaucratic and vertically arranged sub-systems of industrial branches produce a rigid national industrial system. This situation is not congenial to decentralization of decision-making nor conducive to inter-branch and inter-enterprise linkages. The bureaucratic structure hampers efficient and speedy transmission of market signals, not to mention the possibility of 'over-screening' them so that a delayed and greatly transformed image is presented to the decision-making body.

This description ignores the ownership of industrial enterprises, and relates largely to the state sector. Yet the collective sector is still a significant component of the socialist industrial system. There is even a private sector in East European countries (Table 24.1). Again, the non-state sectors vary in size between socialist countries. In Poland, in 1978, they were responsible for 13.3 per cent of the total value of industrial production, while the figure for China was 25.1 per cent (1979).

The various kinds of ownership in a socialist country not only have ideological connotations but have led to considerable differences between enterprises. In Hungary, for example, state industries (Ministerial industries) include the significant branches of 'large scale industries' and of 'mining, energy production, metallurgy, chemical industry and a great part of engineering', whereas local council and cooperative industries are mainly

TABLE 24.1 Relative significance of manufacturing enterprises by ownership sector in selected socialist countries, 1978/1979

Ownership	Poland	German Democratic Republic	People's Republic of China	
	Value of production	Employment	Value of production	Employment
State sector	86.7	84.0	54.4	74.9
Cooperative sector	11.5	13.6	45.6	25.1
Private sector	1.8	2.4	—	—

Sources: Kortus, 1980; Bora, 1980; Sit, unpublished data.

small to medium-scale activities which 'have mainly local supply functions in the domain of clothing products, food production and provision for repairs' (Bora, 1980).

There is strong evidence to support a 'dualistic' view of the Chinese economy, i.e. that the state and non-state sectors are not only qualitatively different but that the latter sector is sizeable, a situation almost comparable to the formal-informal sector split of the Third World (Sit, 1980a). Sigurdson (1977) terms these the Chinese dual 'planned' and 'non-planned' sectors. The former is the preferred one (Sit, 1980b), attracting the investment priority of the state as a result of direct control by central Ministries. The non-planned sector receives no state investment—indeed it is closely controlled mainly to maximize savings for the other sector—and such support as is given is mostly ideological to boost its morale, rather than material. This is evident in the concept of 'walking on two legs' and the urge for local self-sufficiency.

Little research has been conducted so far on the 'non-planned' collective or informal sector of the socialist industrial system, mainly perhaps because governments in socialist countries do not favour its development (a stance which is logical from a Marxist viewpoint), and because they generally regard the non-planned sector as a transitional element to be replaced by, or finally up-graded to become the state, planned sector. For these ideological reasons, too, official data and information on the non-planned sector are so scarce that many outside researchers may assume that it does not exist or is of very limited significance. Nevertheless, in a few instances—such as rural industrialization or the need to promote small industry to meet local market demands—the informal sector has commanded the attention of the media in socialist countries. The publicity, however, does not provide even the crudest understanding of the informal sector in these countries. Yet the outsider has extremely limited access to unpublished official data which must currently remain an important source in the People's Republic of China.

Since the 'Gang of Four' period, the Chinese government has reorientated planning goals towards more economic rationality and re-emphasized efficiency and cost-benefit considerations. As a result, some published reports are now available about the non-planned sector. Indeed, this sector is currently being upheld as the vanguard of the liberalization of industrial decision-making and of a shift towards profitability. Moreover, growing urban unemployment is forcing the government to pay more attention to the informal sector and to data collection in individual cities and communes.

These developments provide a basis, albeit inadequate, for a case study of the non-planned sector in China. Such a study is worthwhile because it may increase the understanding of the non-planned or informal industrial subsystem in a socialist country; inject new concepts and ideas and hence enrich the 'formal-informal' approach to the study of industrial systems; and improve the comprehensiveness of existing knowledge on the industrial system of socialist countries. Thus the chapter begins by defining the informal sector of China and then compares it with the formal sector by enterprise size, range of manufactures and regional patterns, and the linkages with the formal sector and overseas.

FORMAL AND INFORMAL SECTORS

Definitions

Although the Chinese industrial system assumes a hierarchical structure, division of ownership and control creates 2 discrete sub-systems of enterprises, one formal and the other informal. In addition, the formal sector is planned while the informal sector is largely left out of national and local plans.

The lowest order organizations within the formal sector are the 'enterprises', which are all state owned. Those using the same processes or producing related manufactures are grouped under industrial 'companies' which issue directives on production quantity and qualities. Industrial 'companies' of the same major branch are controlled and coordinated at the city or provincial level by an industrial bureau. The latter, in turn, looks towards its Ministry for directives and supervision (To, 1980). Some ministries have more than one type of local bureau: for instance, the Ministry for Light Industries (Figure 24.1) has a First Bureau for Light Industry and a Second Bureau for Light Industry which exist in parallel in all local administrative districts. The Second Bureau has under it all trades that were formerly defined as 'handicrafts' and the Bureau came into existence in 1957 when they were transformed into state enterprises or collective enterprises. The First Bureau includes all other trades under the label of light industries.

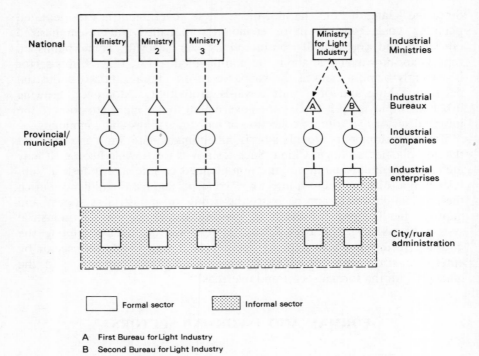

FIGURE 24.1 The industrial system of the People's Republic of China

The administrative structure of the informal sector is slightly different. Because it is generally a non-planned sector, the direction and supervision of enterprises are vested more with the local administrative authorities such as the city or *xian* (county) governments. Special offices for collective industrial enterprises are created within such local governments for carrying out coordinating and supervision functions. As Figure 24.1 shows, however, these local offices have no administrative link with the respective industrial Ministries, except in the case of light industries. The Second Bureau for Light Industry includes some collective enterprises. These Bureaux also provide management and supervisory advice to other collectives for a fee. Enterprises within the informal sector are all, of course, collectively owned and most of their production and supplies are excluded from official plans except for some enterprises under the Second Bureau for Light Industry. In aggregate about half the volume of production and supplies of this Bureau are covered under official plans.

Figure 24.2 indicates that enterprises of the 2 sub-systems may be further classified according to the level of their administrative control and their

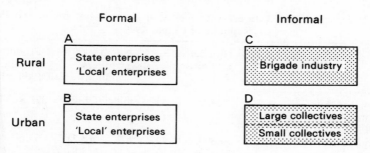

FIGURE 24.2 Composition of the 2 industrial sub-systems in the People's Republic of China

location in or outside urban places. The identification of these sub-types is important as the labels shown in Figure 24.2 are often used in Chinese publications. Moreover, the different labels connote substantial qualitative differences for the enterprises concerned, especially for those in the informal sector.

Within the formal sector, state enterprises are those directly controlled and supervised by central Ministries while the 'local' industries or enterprises are directly under local industrial bureaux. Enterprises owned and run by rural communes and their subordinate units, the production brigades, are collectively known as Brigade Industries and form the rural portion of the informal sector. In the cities, the informal sector consists of the 'large collectives' and the 'small collectives', the former mainly comprising urban collective enterprises directly under the Second Bureau for Light Industry and the latter generally denoting neighbourhood workshops.

Size

Data about the number of industrial enterprises, their employment and production values recently appeared in several journal and newspaper articles published in China. More comprehensive data can be found in the *1980 Chinese Encyclopedia* but their accuracy leaves much to be desired. For instance, most sources quoted a figure of 350,000 industrial enterprises in China in 1979. Some suggested that this included Brigade Industries but others made no such claim (Chuang *et al.*, 1980). In fact, the *1980 Chinese Encyclopedia* reported a total of more than 1 million small enterprises in the communes, so that the Brigade Industries alone exceeded this figure by more than double. Similarly, it can be assumed that the industrial production and employment figures both exclude Brigade Industries as they were probably incorporated into commune production and rural employment.

TABLE 24.2 The size of various components of the sub-systems in the People's Republic of China, 1979

Sector	Number of enterprises		Number of workers (million)		Production value (¥000 million)	
The formal sector	79,429	(7.1)	38.84	(54.4)	371.8	(74.9)
The informal sector						
Urban						
Large collectives[a]	56,800	(5.1)	6.22	(8.7)	33.6	(6.8)
Small collectives	214,378	(19.2)	11.30	(15.8)	53.7	(10.8)
Rural						
Brigade Industries	766,936	(68.6)	15.07	(21.1)	37.1	(7.5)
Total industrial system	1,117,543	(100.0)	71.43	(100.0)	496.2	(100.0)

[a] 1978 data.
Sources: based on *1980 Chinese Encyclopedia;* Sit, 1980a, Table 1.

Table 24.2 attempts to correlate the various available figures to provide a more complete picture of the Chinese industrial system.

Table 24.2 indicates, first, that the formal sector, which generated 75 per cent of the total value of industrial production, is undoubtedly the dominant one. Second, the informal sector, though only producing 25 per cent of the total value of industrial output, is still significant because it contains 93 per cent of all enterprises and 32.6 million workers, nearly 46 per cent of all industrial workers. Because of these attributes, the informal sector may be a better vehicle than the formal sector to assist in the decentralization of industry and in the generation of more jobs. Third, the size of the various sub-types differs within the informal sector although that based in the urban centres, comprising the large and small collectives, is more significant than its rural counterpart both by employment and production value. More precisely, in 1979 the urban informal sector of China included a quarter of all industrial enterprises and jobs and 17 per cent of the value of industrial production. It is a far more significant sub-system, therefore, than the collective industrial sector in some East European countries (Table 24.1).

Activities

The 2 Chinese sub-systems differ substantially in their functions. The formal sector comprises mostly large-scale enterprises in heavy industries, such as iron and steel, petrochemicals, cement, motor vehicles, shipbuilding and engineering. The informal sector is generally made up of small-scale operators producing light industrial goods to meet local consumer and producer needs. Table 24.3 illustrates the obvious orientation of Brigade

TABLE 24.3 Distribution of enterprises of Brigade
Industry by type of manufacture in the People's
Republic of China

Type of manufacture	Per cent of total Brigade Enterprises
Machine making	28.1
Construction materials	19.1
Others	52.8
Total	100.0

Source: based on *1980 Chinese Encyclopedia*, p. 355.

Industries towards rural needs in construction materials and light farm
machinery and tools. In the cities, both large and small collectives make
light consumer goods to serve local and export markets. In 1978, for
example, products from the Second Bureau for Light Industry, which are
mainly from large collectives, accounted for 37 per cent of the total value of
the nation's retail trade in daily consumer goods, and 35 per cent of the total
value of exports. Table 24.4 lists urban small collectives reported by Hong
Kong and Chinese newspapers and, though by no means complete, it does
point up the orientation of these workshops to light consumer goods for
daily consumption.

This division of labour between the formal and informal sectors has often
been viewed by the Chinese as rational and necessary. The long-standing
official policy has been that state and local enterprises are to produce
'high-price, high-technology and large-sized products', while collectives and
Brigade Industries concentrate on 'low, coarse and small products' (Sit,
1979, p. 93). Such specialization resembles that between state and collective
enterprises within the Polish industrial system.

Regional Pattern

The spatial pattern of Brigade Industries is still unknown outside, and
perhaps also inside, China. However, it is reported that the country's 5.2
million communes (the lowest level rural administrative unit, each having
10,000 to 100,000 population) have some industrial enterprises; at the lower
level administrative districts, 92 per cent of the Brigades (numbering 70
million) are running workshops. On average, there are 28 industrial enterprises in each commune (average population 50,000); together they
accounted for about 9 per cent of the country's rural labour force (*1980
Chinese Encyclopedia*). Apart from Shanghai and Xizang (Tibet), all the
provinces and municipalities have special offices for managing Brigade

TABLE 24.4 Regional distribution of state-owned and collectively owned industrial enterprises in the People's Republic of China, 1979

Province/ autonomous region/centrally administered city	State-owned (formal)			Collectively owned (informal, excluding Brigade Industries)			Total system (except Brigade Industries)		Significance of urban informal sector	
	Enterprises (number)	Persons employed (000)	Value of output (per cent of total)	Enterprises (number)	Persons employed (000)	Value of output (per cent of total)	Enterprises (number)	Persons employed (000)	Per cent of enterprises	Per cent of employment
Beijing	1,099	900	83.6	2,639	358	16.4	3,738	1,258	70.6	28.5
Shanghai	3,400	3,300	92.0	4,600	900	7.8	8,000	4,200	57.5	21.4
Tianjin	1,200	810	84.0	2,800	360	16.0	4,000	1,170	70.0	13.7
Hebei	3,977	1,626	80.4	10,743	910	19.6	14,720	2,536	73.0	35.9
Shanxi	2,327[a]	973[a]	n.a.	6,980[a]	487[a]	n.a.	9,307	1,460	75.0	33.4
Nei Mongol[b]	1,000	496	n.a.	3,000	251	n.a.	4,000	747	75.0	33.6
Liaoning	3,500	2,000	85.0	10,500	1,000	15.0	14,000	3,000	75.0	33.3
Jilin	2,500[a]	1,160[a]	n.a.	7,500[a]	580[a]	n.a.	10,000	1,740	75.0	33.3
Heilongjiang[b]	1,250	620	n.a.	3,750	314	n.a.	5,000	934	75.0	33.6
Shaanxi	2,447[a]	902[a]	n.a.	7,342[a]	451	n.a.	9,789	1,353	75.0	33.3
Gansu	1,327	590	93.5	3,379	90	6.5	4,706	680	71.8	13.2
Ningxia	374	143	87.7	698	26	12.3	1,072	169	65.1	15.4

Qinghai	517	140	n.a.	789	40	n.a.	1,306	180	60.4	22.2
Xinjiang	1,968	976[a]	n.a.	1,997	167[a]	n.a.	3,965	1,143	50.4	14.6
Shandong	3,672	1,598	n.a.	14,452	1,655	n.a.	18,124	3,253	79.7	58.9
Jiangsu	4,752	3,739	66.0	23,816	2,299	34.0	28,568	6,038	83.4	38.1
Zhejiang	3,199	1,968	64.5	20,878	1,431	35.5	24,077	3,399	86.7	42.1
Anhui	2,748	918	n.a.	10,953	409	n.a.	13,701	1,327	79.9	30.8
Jiangxi[b]	5,000	2,480	n.a.	15,000	1,257	n.a.	20,000	3,737	75.0	33.6
Fujian	2,500	585	78.0	7,100	378	20.0	9,600	963	74.0	39.2
Henan	3,783	3,626	81.5	11,176	776	18.5	14,959	4,402	74.7	17.6
Hubei	4,700	1,330	82.0	11,300	570	18.0	16,000	1,900	70.6	30.0
Hunan	3,564	1,184	78.7	16,622	497	21.3	20,186	1,681	82.3	29.6
Guangdong	4,000	1,370	73.2	18,000	900	26.8	22,000	2,270	81.8	39.6
Guangxi	3,244	2,015	n.a.	7,443	387	n.a.	10,687	2,402	69.6	16.1
Sichuan	6,500	2,200	83.0	37,800	700	17.0	44,300	2,900	85.3	24.1
Guizhou	2,000	530	86.5	5,000	160	13.5	7,000	690	71.4	23.2
Yunnan	2,666	644	85.7	4,906	161	14.3	7,572	795	64.7	20.2
Xizang	215	25	n.a.	15	5	n.a.	230	30	6.5	16.6
Total	79,429	38,839	81.0	271,178	17,519	19.0	350,607	56,357	77.3	31.1

[a] Estimated on the basis that three-quarters of all enterprises are collectively owned and one-third total industrial employment is within the collective sector.
[b] All figures based on estimation.
Source: computed from the 1980 Chinese Encyclopedia.

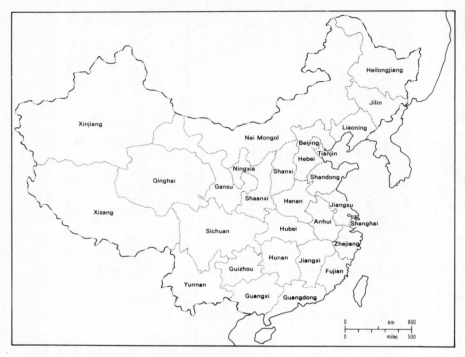

FIGURE 24.3 Administrative divisions of the People's Republic of China (based on boundaries in *Transport Atlas of China,* Shanxi, 1979, stated to be dated 31 July 1979)

Industries. It is reasonable to infer that Brigade Industries are spread throughout the country, although the more densely settled agricultural regions, such as the river basins, would have a higher concentration of them. Thus if it is assumed that Brigade Industries are widely spread and have no significant effect on the geographical pattern of Chinese industry, the spatial differentiation of the formal and informal sectors contained in Table 24.4 provides a basis for understanding the spatial parity of these sub-systems.

Figure 24.4 shows indices of industrialization by administrative regions (provinces and centrally administered municipalities). The more industrialized provinces lie in the east, Shanghai leading with 371 industrial workers per 1000 economically active population (eap) followed by Beijing (Peking) and Tianjin (Tiensin) with 144 and 158 eap, respectively. Regions with average industrialization (50 to 100 per 1000 eap) are, with the exception of Xinjiang, also located in eastern and northeastern China. Elsewhere industrialization is very limited (50 or fewer per 1000 eap).

The level of state ownership of industrial enterprises is comparatively

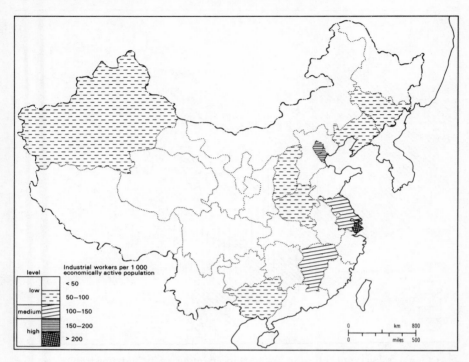

FIGURE 24.4 Levels of industrialization by administrative regions, People's Republic of China, 1979

higher in the less industrialized regions, underlining the national effort to locate manufacturing in these places which clearly lack a business environment conducive to the local establishment of collective industries. Figure 24.5 illustrates this: while 69 per cent of all Chinese industrial workers are in state-owned enterprises, most coastal provinces fall below this average, while those in western and central China register significantly higher levels of state ownership. By contrast, the urban informal sector is localized in the more industrialized coastal regions and Shanghai has a location quotient for the urban informal sector of 4.4, the highest of the country (Figure 24.6). Beijing, Tianjin, Jiangsu, Zhejiang and Jiangxi exhibit high quotients of 2 to 3 whereas most regions register quotients of less than 1. Four eastern provinces, however, have a more significant concentration of informal industry (Table 24.4) at least in terms of numbers of enterprises and employment: Shandong (79.7 and 58.9 per cent, respectively), Jiangsu (83.4 and 38.1 per cent), Zhejiang (86.7 and 42.1 per cent) and Guangdong (81.8 and 39.6 per cent). In 5 eastern provinces, one measure exceeds the national

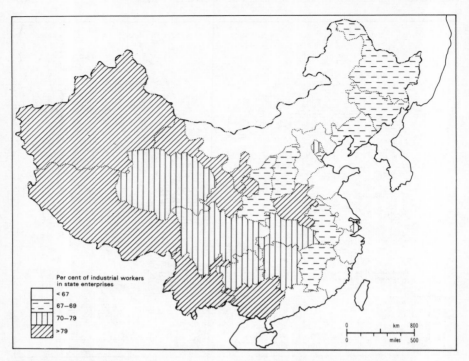

FIGURE 24.5 Per cent of state ownership in industry by administrative regions, People's Republic of China, 1979

average while the other measurement is less than 10 per cent short of the national average.

Thus, excluding Brigade Industries, the spatial patterns of the formal and the informal sectors are positively correlated with each other to a very large extent; the more industrialized areas also boast a greater concentration of informal activities.

URBAN INFORMAL INDUSTRIES

History of Development

Collective industrial enterprises in China have grown out of the handicraft industry which, even in 1949, was a substantial source of full and supplementary employment in the country. Collective industrial enterprises, or the urban informal sector, within Chinese cities are presently classified into 4 main types: the 'Cooperative factory', 'Fifty-eight factory', 'May-seventh

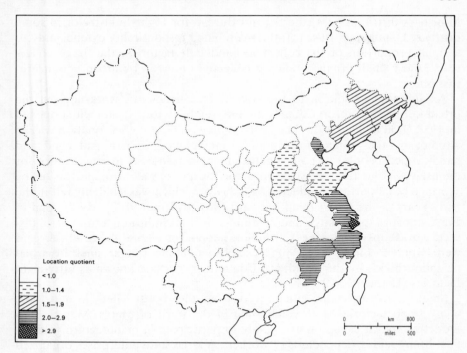

FIGURE 24.6 Location quotients for industrial employment by administrative regions, People's Republic of China, 1979

factory' and 'production-service cooperatives'. Each originated in a different period and political environment, yet they share similar features such as largely existing outside the system of central planning and allocation, and are thus forced to eke out a 'living' on local initiative and local resources. They are 'unprotected' and hence resemble the informal sector elsewhere in the Third World.

A national survey in 1954 (Economic Research Section Chinese Academy of Sciences, 1957) recorded 20 million people as being fully engaged in handicrafts and producing a gross value of 9300 million yuan ($US5314 million); these trades provided part-time jobs for 12 million rural dwellers. Between 1952 and 1957, handicrafts were subject to a crash programme of socialist transformation. By the end of 1956, 92 per cent of their labour and 93 per cent of their production value had been collectivized. Since 1957 handicrafts have ceased to be treated as a separate statistical category and are included in the figures for light industry, being administered by the Ministry for Light Industries. Although direct control operates through the

Ministry's district offices (the Second Bureau for Light Industry or in some districts, Handicrafts Bureau), their combined responsibility extends only to a small proportion of the collective handicraft factories, the 'large collectives'; most small urban handicraft collectives are run by urban administrative offices.

An important addition to the collectivized handicraft workshops in the urban informal sector in China is the Fifty-eight factories, which first opened in 1958 (Lou et al., 1980). The initial motive behind their formation was an attempt by the urban poor (mainly unemployed women and aged and handicapped people) to pool together meagre resources to create work for themselves. The rise of 'workshops for the poor' was also spurred on by shortage of labour in manufacturing industries which was suddenly felt in the early years of the Great Leap Forward (Sit, 1979, pp. 91–2). By the end of 1959, statistics for 43 large and medium-size cities indicated a total of 44,000 such workshops employing 1.4 million people, of whom about 80 per cent were women. Later, workshops established along similar lines in urban neighbourhoods by the Residents' Committees became known as Fifty-eight factories (Lou et al., 1980, p. 72).

Small industries in the cities received another boost when, in mid-1969, many small factories were established in the spirit of Mao's 'May-seventh Directive' which called on everybody to participate in manufacturing activities. Many family dependants of workers in large state enterprises organized themselves into small production units known as May-seventh brigades or May-seventh factories. Other unemployed hands, including housewives, within urban neighbourhoods joined in the movement to set up small workshops in residential areas. The movement was said to reach its peak in 1973 and was described by outside reports as symptomatic of yet another 'Great Leap Forward'.

The most recent stage in the development of the urban sector comprises the mushrooming of production-service co-ops since March, 1979 (Lou et al., 1980, p. 73). After the fall of the 'Gang of Four' in 1976, the Chinese searched for a new approach to economic development. Two previous policies which had had a considerable impact on urban employment were drastically altered. First, the shang-shan-xia-xiang (sending fresh graduates and other intellectuals to the countryside) policy was abandoned. Second, all state-owned enterprises were ordered to balance their books and given new freedom in handling their affairs, including the hiring of labour. The state enterprises responded by attempting to raise output (with bonuses payable to existing workers) through increased labour productivity, thus limiting labour recruitment. These changes combined to leave an estimated 7 million new graduates from secondary and tertiary institutions out of work (Ta Kung Pao [Hong Kong], 19 July 1979). Faced with mounting unemployment the Chinese government had to adopt quick remedial measures to encourage collective enterprises, many of which are engaged in manufacturing activities, as a 'sponge' to absorb people who would otherwise be unemployed. The *Nam Fang Daily* [Guangzhou] (3 July 1979, p. 4) reported that anything from 70 to 80 per cent of people seeking work had in recent years been finally placed in jobs in collective enterprises.

Composition and Administrative Allegiance

It is difficult to obtain accurate data about the exact size of each of the 4 components of the urban informal sector: that presented in Table 24.5, therefore, should be interpreted as only a rough guide. About a quarter of the workforce engaged in the urban informal manufacturing sector in China was employed in 'cooperative factories'. The May-seventh factories and the newly founded production-service co-ops are more significant in employment, together accounting for over 60 per cent of the reported jobs in this informal sector. Data for Beijing show that these 2 types of factories employ similar numbers of workers. If this is assumed to be the case nationally, each type employs roughly a third of all workers in the urban informal sector.

On average, cooperative factories employ more workers and achieve greater labour productivity, results that may also reflect differences between these and other types of enterprises.

Reports from China after 1976 gave urban collective industrial enterprises 2 new labels—'large' and 'small'. The former referred mainly to cooperative and Fifty-eight factories employing anything from 100 to upwards of 1000 people. 'Small' collectives embracing May-seventh factories and production-service co-ops (sometimes known as street industries or neighbourhood workshops) are generally smaller and owe their allegiance to non-industrial administrative units such as the Residents' Committees of urban neighbourhoods (Sit, 1979).

Differences between large and small collectives have been considered by Chu (1980). Investment in new large collectives stems mainly from the profits of existing ones. Official planned targets are the basis for up to half the output and raw material supplies of the large collectives. Within these a uniform wage system is practised: the remuneration of workers is not directly related to the business conditions of a particular enterprise. In these ways, therefore, large collectives are little different from state enterprises. Some large collectives which commenced as small collectives (such as the Fifty-eight factories) were later 'promoted' to large collective status; in reverse some state-owned factories—especially during the 1961–63 period—were demoted to large collectives. Many handicraft workshops that had been suddenly elevated to state factories in the Great Leap Forward were unable to sustain that status (Sit, 1980a, p. 2).

Small collectives, being largely outside the system of official plans in the purchasing of products and in the allocation of raw materials and other supplies, need to devise their own ways and means for marketing their products and for procuring materials. Their management thus demands initiative and flexibility. Mao's principles of 'self-reliance' and 'hard struggle' have often been exhorted as the appropriate ones for running such enterprises. Within these, the payment of wages relates to the sort of activities being undertaken and varies greatly between enterprises: in general, however, wage levels and worker benefits are lower than those in large collectives (Sit, 1980a, p. 2).

Economic and Social Roles

The contribution of the urban informal sector to China's industrial system has already been indicated in Table 24.2. In 1979, the value of production contributed by the urban informal sector amounted to ¥87,300 million ($US49,900 million) which was almost 4 times the total value of exports and nearly half (46 per cent) of the total value of the nation's retail trade in that year (*1980 Chinese Encyclopedia*, pp. 306 and 309). The urban informal sector also contributes directly to the supply of consumer goods and dominates the nation's exports. For example, in 1978, the large collectives within the Second Bureau for Light Industry alone accounted for 37 per cent by value of the total retail trade of China and for 35 per cent of the nation's total exports. These large collectives had thus earned foreign exchange worth $US1430 million.

Production has also been growing, and in 1977 was worth ¥73,400 million compared with ¥83,300 million in 1978 and ¥87,300 million in 1979 (Table 24.2). These increases do not seem to match the growth in the number of enterprises or in employment, especially for small collectives. The total number of enterprises in 1978 was estimated to be 148,043, with a workforce of 12.65 million (Sit, 1980a, p. 6): the figures at the end of 1979 were 271,178 enterprises (an increase of 83 per cent) and 17.52 million workers (39 per cent) (Table 24.2). Chinese sources indicate that in large collectives the number of enterprises and employment remained stable during those 2 years. What happened was a sudden leap in the number of small collectives from an estimated 91,243 in 1978 to 214,378 by the end of 1979, while employment rose from 6.4 million to 11.3 million during this year. It may reasonably be inferred that this expansion largely resulted from the mushrooming of production-service co-ops after March 1979. If the data for Beijing (Table 24.5) are indicative of the national position, the May-seventh factories had not changed to any noticeable extent though more than an equal number of enterprises and employment was added within the sub-sector of small collectives (Table 24.5). The 4.9 million new jobs so created represent a major advance towards solving the nation's unemployment

TABLE 24.5 Types of collective industrial enterprises, Beijing and the People's Republic of China, 1980

Type and nature of enterprise	Beijing			People's Republic of China					
	Enterprises	Persons employed		Enterprises		Persons employed		Value of output	
	Number	Number (000)	Per cent	Number	Per cent	Number (000)	Per cent	¥ (million)	Per cent
Cooperative factory (large collective)	n.a.	46	12.8	33,700	12.4	4,620	26.4	27,256	31.3
Fifty-eight factory (large collective)	700	50	14.0	23,100	8.5	1,600	9.1	6,329	7.2
May-seventh factory (small collective)	n.a.	122	34.1 }	214,378	79.1	11,300	64.5	53,715	61.5
Production-service co-ops (small collectives)	n.a.	140	39.1 }						
Total	2,639	358	100.0	271,178	100.0	17,520	100.0	87,300	100.0

Sources: calculated from Lou, *et al.*, 1980; *1980 Chinese Encyclopedia.*

problem in the cities: 9 million people out of work at the beginning of 1979 and reportedly 26 million in 1981 (*Sing Tao Yat Po* [Hong Kong], 16 February 1981, p. 2). The production-service co-ops of the urban informal sector thus provided a quick means to absorb the unemployed.

Other than the obvious economic roles in providing urban employment and in supplying the country with the much needed foreign exchange earnings and daily consumables, a recent editorial of the *People's Daily* [Beijing] (4 August 1979, p. 1) laid great emphasis on the urban collective industrial enterprise as a means of speeding up the pace of modernization and of helping to promote small to medium-size towns to narrow the gap between city and countryside—a greatly desired goal of the Chinese Communists. The modernization strategy of the People's Republic of China, according to this editorial, must be one which upholds the principles of the simultaneous development of large and small enterprises; mechanization and semi-mechanization; and automation and semi-automation to suit the present circumstances of the nation. By such a strategy, it is said that China could effectively mobilize its vast manpower resources and could maximize the diverse forms of technology which already exist within the country.

The 'socialist' role of the urban collective sector has also been explicitly defined in the same editorial:

> To achieve socialism in a country with such an extensive territory as our own, we need a network of thousands of small towns, not just one or two hundred large and medium-sized cities. We must develop more small towns . . . We have to gradually develop a range of collective enterprises in manufacturing, services and commerce within a large number of small towns to meet the needs of the rural populace. By such means, we may gradually shift our manufacturing industry towards the locations of the market and raw materials. Such a situation would be advantageous as industry could then serve agriculture better, and a more rational distribution of productive activities could be realised. It can further promote rural industrialization and narrow the gap between the city and the countryside.

The non-economic ideals expressed, however, are not as radical as the political role entrusted to the Fifty-eight factories and May-seventh factories during the Great Leap Forward (1957 to 1959) and the Cultural Revolution (1966 to 1970). Then, the collective enterprises, especially the small ones, were not regarded as mere production units. They had to function as a political tool to mobilize the urban populace. Besides serving as assistants to state enterprises and producing consumables to satisfy the needs of the people, they were being entrusted 'to transform the city and its residents' and 'to free the millions of women who had been traditionally tied to the narrow confine of the household by household work' (Sit, 1979, pp. 94–6).

Two cases studies based on fieldwork and published and unpublished sources are reported on here to illustrate the operation of the administrative hierarchy and to elaborate the functions and linkages of informal sector enterprises. One is devoted to the large collectives of Guangzhou and the other to the small collectives of Shanghai.

LARGE COLLECTIVES IN GUANGZHOU

Large collectives form most of the industrial enterprises of the Second Bureau for Light Industry of Guangzhou. The Bureau administers 68 state enterprises and 215 collectives; of the latter only 10 are small and 5 of these are located in rural counties. By the end of 1978, the collectives (except the 5 in the rural counties) employed 74,621 persons and yielded a gross output of ¥670 million ($US383 million) representing 77 and 63 per cent of the respective totals for all enterprises of the Bureau. The Bureau's gross output value in 1978 was ¥1062 million ($US607 million) or about 7.1 per cent of the value of the city's total manufacturing output. It also contributed 41 per cent of its total exports (¥323 million). The products included an array of 4100 items, 70 per cent of which were small daily consumables, though some were small farm implements or components for larger-scale state industries. The collectives and state enterprises within the Bureau are organized into 19 'companies', each representing an industrial activity like the manufacture of metal tools, fabricated metal utensils, plastic products, domestic electrical appliances, handicrafts and garments. The role of the company is to coordinate activities within a particular industrial sub-branch.

The Bureau has experienced 3 stages of development. First, handicraft workshop collectivization was initiated in the immediate post-Liberation years; 1455 handicraft cooperatives were formed in 1950 with 78,400 workers. Cooperatives were then diffused through a sequence of lower grade cooperatives to higher grade cooperatives, until the handicraft industry was completely collectivized in 1958. Second, 1958 to 1960 was a period of transformation and consolidation which led to amalgamation of some smaller workshops into larger enterprises to improve management. Third, this was followed by a gradual process of promotion into collective factories which are the present-day large collectives. Throughout these stages the number of enterprises declined and their size increased: for example, 563 collectives employed 57,447 persons in 1965, an average of 102 workers each, while by 1978 the average was 355 each.

The collective sector of the Bureau receives no subsidy or investment from the state. Its capital for expansion and for setting up new enterprises comes from a fund derived in a form of 'tax', or submission (i.e. the Bureau's proportionate share) on the profits of existing collectives. Between 1965 and 1978 the collectives generated ¥116 million ($US66 million) for these purposes. Such 'tax' was equivalent to 31.5 per cent of the gross profits of a collective (Table 24.6). During the same period, the value of fixed assets

TABLE 24.6 Distribution of gross profits in large collectives, People's Republic of China (per cent), 1979

Category of use	Guangzhou	Harbin
State profit tax	55.0	55.0
Urban tax	4.5⎫	
Submissions to superior organizations	31.5⎭	41.4
Retained profits	9.0	3.6

Sources: Sit, 1980b, p. 12; Chuang *et al.*, 1980, p. 15.

of the collectives rose from ¥30 million to ¥160 million ($US17 million to $US91 million), the increase stemming almost entirely from this source.

Table 24.6 shows the distribution of gross profits of some large collectives in Guangzhou and Harbin. Although there are differences in the amount of retained profits in the 2 places, the state takes the lion's share. Out of the total remittances to superior organizations, the company takes one-third as its operating budget and as the source of capital for new investments and expansion of capacity of existing collectives. The Bureau's headquarters receives the other two-thirds for similar purposes.

Of the many products made under the aegis of the Bureau, only 64 (less than 2 per cent) are included in central and local plans. These items, however, are the popular ones most in demand and hence represent about half the total value of output of the bureau. A fair proportion is made by state enterprises, leaving about 80 per cent of the products of collective enterprises not covered by any plan.

Despite receiving few production targets from state and local plans, the collectives face an increasing demand for their activities which are normally geared to market requirements. Their orders arise in several ways. Some jobs, with materials supplied, come from foreign trade and trade institutions; others may be sudden and rush purchases by various wholesale agents to meet short-term market demands. The Bureau also has its own retail outlets and sends salesmen to other cities and provinces to solicit orders for the collectives.

Since most production activities lie outside official plans in the Chinese system of state-regulated material distribution, the collectives suffer greatly from a lack of guaranteed supplies: some institutes do supply the collectives with materials to enable them to fulfil orders but most are unable to do so. For example, electricity is an essential production factor that is allocated by the state: being on the margin of the planned economy, the Bureau is low on the list of priorities. Often the supplies it can obtain are channelled to state enterprises or to production activities of those collectives that happen to be within official plans. For example, in 1978 the Bureau obtained only about 48 per cent of the steel, 40 per cent of the pig-iron and 50 to 60 per cent of the electricity required. The collectives, therefore, have had to use their initiatives to find alternative supplies, such as odds and ends or scrap, and to economize on consumption. Obviously, these alternatives can adversely affect the quality of products produced, and any supply-demand margin after such efforts would represent a forced cut in their efficiency or under-utilization of capacity.

The large collectives follow fairly closely the principles concerning wages and worker benefits that are applied in state enterprises. The wage rate for any given type of job or level of skill is uniform and thus, although large collectives are independent accounting units, worker remuneration and benefits bear little relation to the business operations of an individual collective. Other benefits—sick leave, medical care, pension and welfare subsidies (such as canteen and nursery facilities)—come out of a central fund allocated from the enterprise's revenue at a standard rate of 11 per cent of the total wage bill.

SMALL COLLECTIVES IN SHANGHAI

The urban core of Shanghai (with an area of 156 km^2) is a crowded centre in a metropolis which in 1978 accommodated about 6 million people and contained 2700 state factories and 3300 small collectives. This core is subdivided administratively into 10 urban districts which in turn are subdivided into 120 streets that further contain 1000 neighbourhoods. Small collectives operate within each of the neighbourhoods. Employment per collective ranges from a few workers to 400 or 500, though the average is about 50. A survey in 1978 of one of these urban districts, Jing An, indicated that of the 251 small collectives there, 45.4 per cent were employing fewer than 50 persons, 53 per cent 50 to 300 persons, and only 1.6 per cent more than 300 persons.

Some collectives are owned collectively by local residents and run by their representative body, the Residents' Committee. Higher up the urban administrative hierarchy are the Street Committees, the District Committees and finally the municipal office. At these higher levels, there are special offices responsible for coordinating and supervising the running of small collectives. However, management supervision and advice of a technical nature comes from the various industrial bureaux, often the Second Bureau for Light Industry. In return, these bureaux charge the collectives a fee amounting to about 1.5 per cent of a collective's revenue.

The initial capital usually comes from meagre contributions by local residents, in the form of money, equipment (such as a sewing-machine) and the factory premises; or it may come from nearby factories or the institutions where the husbands of the women organizers are working. The donation is usually in the form of old machines or scrap materials or, on rare occasions, loans of money. The borrowed part of the initial capital is usually paid back quickly.

As many as 9 out of every 10 small collectives depend on sub-contract work—mostly processing—which creates 80 per cent of their income. Only 6 per cent of the collectives produce finished articles and only 3 per cent engage in repairing services. Since the materials needed for processing jobs mainly come from the contractor's factory, there is no raw material supply problem. Dependence on sub-contracting underlines the difficulty of the small collectives in expanding their activities since limited material sources effectively constrain the types of business activities that they can pursue. Yet that dependence is a means for survival and longevity of the enterprise: a survey in Jing An district indicated that 56 per cent of the small collectives had had such ties for over 10 years, 20 per cent for 6 to 10 years and 24 per cent for up to 5 years. The maintenance of orders seemingly correlates with the length of their relationship with contractors because 54 per cent of the collectives were said to be stable and 30 per cent unstable while 16 per cent claimed that they had insufficient orders.

The contractors are usually other industrial enterprises—both state concerns and large collectives. In Shanghai, the small collectives are linked with 2700 enterprises, half of which are administered by the Bureau for Handicrafts (the equivalent of the Second Bureau for Light Industry). Their production involved 60 'companies' and 25 bureaux, including in particular, the Bureau for Textiles (or First Bureau for Light Industry), the Bureau for Electrical Engineering and the Bureau for Electronics. The Bureau for Commerce, which is not an industrial bureau, ranks third according to the number of enterprises linked up with small collectives. Its less significant position underlines the fact that small collectives seldom produce finished goods or have a direct relation with wholesale and retailing outlets. This situation is somewhat different from that of the large collectives. It could mean that small collectives are less capable of initiating business because they are even further away from the planned economy, such that their material supplies are much worse than that of the large collectives.

Attempts have been made since 1978 to diversify the activities of small collectives which are being encouraged to market their own products. For example, in Jing An district, the small collectives directly marketed 23.3 per cent (by value) of their 1977 output and 32.6 per cent in 1978. Three other channels are also being tested.

(a) Joint ventures with state enterprise, a partnership between small collectives and those nearby state enterprises that are currently finding it difficult to meet state or local production targets. The small collective is invited to participate on a profit sharing basis while the state enterprise undertakes to give assistance in the form of equipment, technology and advice.

(b) Official purchase of materials; by using go-between bureau companies, a small collective may acquire official material supplies which can be included in the formal system of purchases and supplies.

(c) Compensation trade with foreign firms, a practice that started in about 1979 when the People's Republic of China began to open its doors to foreign participation in economic ventures. The foreign partner provides the raw materials and some of the equipment (usually imported). The small collective charges a fee for the job to pay for this while the products are exported through arrangements made by the contractor. In one case in Shanghai (a wrist-watch band producer), 10 per cent of the fees for one year's work done was said to be sufficient to pay for imported new equipment.

The new channels, however, are only in an experimental stage. Most small collectives still conduct business in the usual, restricted way, being constrained by lack of access to official orders and supplies. Since 1979, an entirely different sort of organization has appeared in Chinese cities—the production-service co-ops—which during the first half of 1979 created jobs for 70,000 unemployed youths in Shanghai alone. But, so far, little is known about the way these are being run, although it is assumed that they operate like other small collectives.

PROSPECTS AND PROBLEMS

Small collectives are financially independent, but each must remit a substantial portion of its gross profits to the administrative offices that oversee it and also contribute money and labour for various urban services (Chuang *et al.,* 1980, p. 15). Table 24.7 indicates that a small collective retains only about a fifth of its gross profits although the proportion seems to vary from place to place.

The Chinese authorities have long considered that small collectives are lower order enterprises within a socialist system and that they should be gradually transformed from collective into state ownership. The 3-stage transition from small collectives to large collectives and to state enterprises is currently a major source of controversy (Chu, 1980, pp. 6–8; *People's Daily* [Beijing], 28 April 1980, p. 5). It is not yet clear within China whether this formula of transformation, together with its several implications for the character of the various enterprises and worker benefits, conforms ideologically with socialism. There has long been a promotion system that helps small

TABLE 24.7 Percentage distribution of gross profits in small collectives, Guangzhou and Hebei, People's Republic of China, 1979

Items	Guangzhou		Hebei
	Factory A	Factory B	
State tax[a]	50	52	55
Remittances to superior organizations	14	16 ⎫	26
Bonus and welfare funds	14	12 ⎭	
Retained for reinvestment	22	20	19
Total gross profits	100	100	100

[a] Maximum is 55 per cent.
Sources: Sit, 1980b, Table 2; Chuang *et al.*, 1980, p. 15.

collectives to become large collectives and thence state enterprises. Thus, in Shanghai in 1963, for example, several small collectives were promoted to cooperative factory status, a reorganization that involved 30,000 jobs (*Wen Wei Pao* [Shanghai], 2 August 1979, p. 2). Or again in Beijing in 1978, 700 'Fifty-eight' style small collectives, with 50,000 employees, were promoted to large collective status (Lou *et al.*, 1980, p. 72), while between 1975 and 1978, 400 small collectives in Guangzhou were raised in status to large collectives (Sit, 1979, p. 94). A set of criteria was applied to judge small collectives before the promotion decision was made.

At present this process seems to have been temporarily halted. The emphasis now is on economic efficiency, enterprise independence and management freedom. The addition of numerous new small collectives to solve the urban employment problem should also add a new dimension to the business environment.

The spatial pattern of small collectives within the city can best be described as spread out and chaotic. There are at least some small collectives in every neighbourhood, mostly located centrally near the office of the Residents' Committee and other community establishments such as the library or the television room, so forming a multi-functional neighbourhood core (discussed, with Guangzhou as the example, by Sit, 1980c). Such an arrangement, however, often appears to be chaotic in terms of industrial linkages and production efficiency.

Orders received by small collectives usually result from personal contacts, their physical locations being related to the availability of empty or usable structures within the neighbourhood. Thus, some jobs for collectives come from very distant urban districts through personal connections, whereas similar jobs may be turned down by a neighbourhood near the source of orders because of a lack of suitable accommodation.

Currently 70 to 80 per cent of the floor space of small collectives in the core of Shanghai are in domestic premises. Space per worker ranges from 1.3 to 4.1 m^2 (14 to 44 square feet). Accommodation problems create inefficiency because operations are scattered between many production units. The juxtaposition of activities that generate excessive heat, noise, smell and smoke among residential uses has led to complaints about the detailed spatial organization of small collectives within Shanghai: it has been urged that neighbourhoods should come to cooperative agreements to eliminate conflicts so that vacant houses in neighbourhoods close to sources of orders could be made available for expanding operations.

COLLECTIVE ENTERPRISES AND THE INFORMAL SECTOR

The Informal Sector Concept

The dualistic view of economic activities as a formal-informal dichotomy grew out of a series of reports published in the early 1970s by the International Labour Office and the United Nations Employment Programme (Thorbecke, 1973; Moser, 1978) which concluded that the problem of urban employment in developing countries is not merely statistics of the unemployed. Rather, the crux of the matter lies in what the reports called the 'working poor' (International Labour Office, 1972) who avoid unemployment by engaging in 'informal' economic activities such as small industries, handicrafts and hawking or as trishaw-drivers, domestic servants, beggars and prostitutes. These activities are not formally recognized by the governments, are thus not officially recorded and registered and, of course, are not regulated or supervised. These 'informal sector' activities are variously characterized as the 'bazaar-type economy', 'the lower circuit activities', 'the unorganized sector' and the 'unprotected sector' (McGee, 1978).

Some economists in developing countries are now demanding that the informal sector of the national industrial system should be duly recognized by governments, as is the formal sector, and allocated resources and assistance. They contend that the informal sector not only contributes to economic growth but that it also plays an important role in generating job opportunities in cities teeming with unemployed rural migrants. This view was supported during a seminar in Djakarta (Human Resources Development Centre, 1978, p. 1):

> One characteristic the ASEAN countries [have] in common is the openness of their economies. They are also essentially primary commodity producing countries. This has tended to place them in a somewhat economically disadvantageous position in the competitive world market. In order to solve this problem

the ASEAN countries have in the past adopted economic policies designed to accelerate industrialization through import-substitution. This has indeed led to growth in GNP in the region, but this growth has consisted essentially of value-added emanating from economic enterprises in the formal sector, i.e. economic enterprises that have acquired "formal economic protection" from their governments. Left out in the process were a high percentage of economic units or enterprises located in the urban as well as in the rural areas. These enterprises, though receiving no "formal economic protection" from their governments, have nevertheless survived on their own. Today they have come to be known as participants in the informal sector. The high rate of growth of the population, the movement of people from rural to urban areas and the inability of the urban formal sector to provide adequate employment opportunities have led to the persistence of the urban informal sector. In the last three or four years, it has been realized that these enterprises have considerable value-added creating as well as employment generating potential.

The Urban Informal Sector in China

Like other developing countries, the People's Republic of China has, since the first Five-Year Plan (1953–58), focused attention on the development and planning of the formal sector (i.e. state enterprises). Nevertheless, circumstances also required the continuation of an informal sector to generate sufficient employment quickly and yet inexpensively. As a result of differences in the political-economic system of China and that of most other developing countries, the informal sector in China largely consists of urban collective industrial enterprises. Other sorts are insignificant, although since 1979 hawkers, individual handicraftsmen and sole proprietor private businesses offering various services have been allowed (*Ta Kung Pao* [Hong Kong], 13 August 1980, p. 11); these form only an insignificant and undocumented part of the urban informal sector. Urban collective industrial enterprises closely parallel the informal sector of the developing countries, in that they have little or no 'formal' economic protection.

Tables 24.8 and 24.9 indicate differences between urban collectives and the state enterprises. Collective enterprises are fairly easy to start (Table 24.9); no official permission is required and, very often, local initiatives and contributions of money and materials are all that are required. Thus they receive no central or official investment allocation but depend entirely on meagre local resources. The markets for goods made by the collectives are also 'unprotected', since they are off the state's list of suppliers: hence they eke out a living by filling gaps, such as by providing a service to larger industrial enterprises or by meeting rush and small orders from trade departments. Thus such enterprises exist precariously, and depend very much on the formal sector for supplies and for jobs. These features of subservience to the formal sector closely resemble those of the informal sector in developing countries generally.

TABLE 24.8 Characteristics of enterprises within the formal and informal sectors

Formal sector enterprises	Informal sector enterprises
1. Difficult entry	1. Ease of entry
2. Frequent reliance on overseas resources	2. Reliance on indigenous resources
3. Corporate ownership	3. Family ownership
4. Large-scale operation	4. Small-scale operation
5. Capital-intensive and often imported technology	5. Labour-intensive and adapted technology
6. Formally acquired skills often expatriates	6. Skills acquired outside the formal school system
7. Protected markets (through tariffs, quotas and trade licences)	7. Unregulated and competitive markets

Sources: modified from International Labour Office, 1972; Sethuraman, 1976.

There are also disparities between state and collective industries in wages, welfare benefits, labour-hiring and the distribution of enterprise profits. For many years, the rule that 'collectives must be lower than state enterprises' has been rigidly applied and is still true in many cities even today (Chu, 1980, p. 10). Thus in Beijing the monthly wage rate for a grade 2 worker is ¥35.5 ($US20.3) in collectives and ¥41.5 ($US23.7) in state enterprises

TABLE 24.9 Characteristics of industrial enterprises within the state and collective sectors in the People's Republic of China

State enterprises	Collective enterprises
1. Difficult entry, decided by central government	1. Ease of entry
2. State owned	2. Collectively owned
3. Dependent on national or provincial resources (allocated by official plans)	3. Dependent on meagre local resources (no state allocation)
4. Large-scale operation	4. Small-scale operation
5. Capital-intensive, even use imported technology	5. Labour-intensive and adapted technology
6. Formally acquired skills	6. Skills acquired outside the formal school system
7. Protected markets (all within official plans)	7. Unregulated and competitive markets
8. No financial responsibility (loss will be made good by state)	8. Financially independent
9. Higher worker remuneration and welfare benefits	9. Lower worker remuneration and welfare benefits

Source: compiled by author.

(Chuang *et al.*, 1980, p. 10). Workers in collectives cannot enjoy the same standard as those in state enterprises in the amounts and quality of food allocations and subsidies for hazardous jobs. In some collectives in Beijing workers are not entitled to pensions or to compensation when fired because many collectives have fluctuating levels of activity and may close altogether when work is lacking. In such cases people are simply laid off whereas workers in state enterprises have guaranteed jobs even if this means transferring to other enterprises (Chuang *et al.*, 1980, p. 14).

Collectives, such as those in Beijing, are confined, as a matter of policy, to a limited labour market in that they can only employ housewives, the unemployed and the sick or partially handicapped. They have no access to, and are being given no assistance by, the Labour Bureau which controls the allocation of young graduates and school-leavers. Such a practice not only deprives collectives of a vigorous labour force but also artificially holds down their technical competence. The proportion of labour force in collectives classifiable as trained technicians is therefore very small, being only 1.04 per cent in Shanghai and 0.35 per cent in Shandong (Li and Hwang, 1979). Most of these are in the large collectives under the Second Bureau for Light Industry; technicians are almost non-existent in small collectives.

In the People's Republic of China an exploitative relationship also exists between state and collective enterprises, and this is underlined by the complaints of the latter of the unreasonably low level of sub-contracting fees paid by the former. In Shanghai, it is reported that 70 per cent of the sub-contracting work of small collectives in 1977 was paid at a rate of less than ¥80 ($US45.7) per worker per month (Li and Hwang, 1979, p. 30) which is said only to cover depreciation charges, outlays on water, electricity and tools, and direct wages. It omits an element of reasonable profit for the collective, an element that has invariably been exploited by contractor factories, that is the state enterprises. Though the latter have to submit all their profits to the state, the lack of a 'reasonable profit' allowance for the small collectives has enlarged the gross profit of state enterprises and hence their claim for larger bonuses. Moreover, the state has already taken the lion's share of the profit (Tables 24.6 and 24.7) and spends most of it on the development of the formal sector. The collectives gain little substantive advantage in return, except for some of the larger ones which may enjoy inclusion of their operations and products in official plans. The comparatively larger proportion of profit retained by small collectives (Table 24.7) is only superficially true because some of this has to be used to meet various claims from the Residents' Committees responsible for their operation. Among these are salaries of cadres of the Committee, fees for road repairs and minor public works and sanitary services within the neighbourhood (Li and Hwang, 1979, p. 29). In any case the lower profitability of small collectives makes them less viable than the larger ones.

COLLECTIVES: PRINCIPLES AND PRACTICES

Any dualistic concept is defective because in the real world divisions are seldom very rigid, a point well put in the case of the formal-informal dichotomy by McGee (1978, p. 13). It equally applies to the division of industrial enterprises in China into state and collective enterprises: instead of 2 discrete ownership types there is a continuum. Large collectives share some features with both the state enterprises and the small collectives. Yet the formal-informal division is a useful tool for exposing the true essence of the industrial system of the People's Republic of China.

The investigation into the informal sub-system has led, of course, logically and unavoidably to a tempting comparison between the urban collectives and the informal sector of developing countries because the state and collective enterprises of China do, in many ways, appear to be similar to the dual systems described by Santos (1973), Barratt-Brown (1974) and Sethuraman (1976). Indeed, collective enterprises are, in general, outside what Weeks (1975) called 'the system of benefits and regulations'. But in China the socialist system does make the collective enterprises markedly different from the informal sector of developing countries in several ways.

First, there is much more official involvement in collective industries in China. The street residents' offices, although urban administrative agents, are official institutes. Their role in promoting, supervising and having a substantial share in the achievements of the small collectives is fairly obvious. Even the small collectives are better recorded, regulated and protected (at least administratively) than the informal sector in most developing countries. Although their activities are much constrained by the absence of a largely free market from where they could procure supplies and sell products, none the less they have all been banded together—either under the District Neighbourhood Workshops Management Committee or various companies of the industrial bureaux—so that they have access to a larger pool of capital and management expertise than the informal sector of developing countries.

Second, since much of the 'surplus' produced by the 'exploitative' process of sub-contracting cannot be largely held within any individual enterprise, a redistributive process occurs which leads to a flow of the major part of such surplus back to the general populace through reinvestment in industry and in urban and social infrastructure. This indicates, therefore, that there is no need for an antagonistic relationship to exist between the formal and informal sectors: the state, through regulations and taxes, can always effect a transfer of resources from the 'haves' to the 'have-nots' for the benefit of the entire nation.

Two factors have been suggested to explain the rationale of the informal element of the Chinese industrial system: the dysfunction of the rigid planning system and the conflict between modern large-scale production processes and widespread urban unemployment. Mounting unemployment in Chinese cities makes it obvious that the informal sub-system will persist and continue to expand. Indeed, in a situation of capital scarcity, growth of collective enterprises would not only contribute to solving unemployment but also, if handled well, be a good adjunct to state enterprises through a system of sub-contracting.

Yet conditions within the sub-system and its relations with the formal sector need to be improved. Artificial constraints that stifle growth and expansion of collectives and transfer excess proportions of their 'profits' to the state or superior offices have to be carefully reconsidered. Suggestions made at a recent seminar (Human Resources Development Centre, 1978, p. 5) about ways in which members of the Association of South-East Asian Nations might promote the growth of their informal sectors seem, in principle, to have some applicability to the People's Republic of China. Among these were:

(a) to overcome unreasonable obstacles which constrain their growth;
(b) to raise their productivity and enhance the employment opportunities they provide;
(c) to use them as a mechanism for improving living standards in both rural and urban areas.

Differences in political systems may lead to different ways and means of putting these principles into practice. Yet, whether in China or in the developing countries, the informal elements of their industrial systems, in the context of their present economic development and current unemployment and underemployment situations, certainly merit a hard and critical re-evaluation.

References

Acheson, T. W., 1971, 'The social origins of Canadian industrialism: a study in the structure of entrepreneurship', unpublished Ph.D. dissertation (Toronto: University of Toronto).

Acheson, T. W., 1972, 'The social origins of the Canadian industrial élite, 1880–1885', in D. S. Macmillan (Ed.), *Canadian Business History: Selected Studies, 1497–1971* (Toronto: McClelland and Stewart), 144–74.

Ádám, G., 1975, 'Multinational corporations and worldwide sourcing', in H. Radice (Ed.), *International Firms and Modern Imperialism* (Harmondsworth: Penguin Education), 89–103.

Aglietta, M., 1979, *A Theory of Capitalist Regulation: the U.S. Experience* (London: New Left Books).

Aharoni, Y., 1966, *The Foreign Investment Decision Process* (Boston: Harvard University Press).

Aharoni, Y., 1978, 'SMR Forum: a comment on multinationals from small countries', *Sloan Management Review*, **19**, 83–8.

Ahn, M., 1974, *Industrial Bibliography* (Washington, DC: Urban Land Institute Research Report No. 22).

Alchian, A. A., 1950, 'Uncertainty, evolution, and economic theory', *The Journal of Political Economy*, **58**, 211–21.

Aliber, R. Z., 1970, 'A theory of direct foreign investment', in C. P. Kindleberger (Ed.), *The International Corporation* (Cambridge, Mass.: MIT Press), 42–56.

Allen, G. C., 1929, *The Industrial Development of Birmingham and the Black Country, 1860–1927* (London: Allen and Unwin).

Allen, K. and Yuill, D., 1979, *Regional Incentives in the European Community: A Comparative Study* (Brussels: Commission of EC Regional Policy Series No. 15).

Alonso, W., 1964, *Location and Land Use: Toward a General Theory of Land Rent* (Cambridge, Mass.: Harvard University Press).

Ambrose, P. and Colenutt, B., 1975, *The Property Machine* (Harmondsworth: Penguin).

American Rural Small-Scale Industry Delegation, 1977, *Rural Small-Scale Industry in the People's Republic of China* (Berkeley: University of California Press).

Amin, S., 1976, *Unequal Development: An Essay on the Social Formations of Peripheral Capitalism*, translated by B. Pearce (New York: Monthly Review Press).

Andreff, W., 1976, *Profits et Structures du Capitalisme Mondial* [*Profits and Structures of World Capitalism*] (Paris: Calmann-Levy).

Andrews, H. F., 1978, 'Journey to work considerations in the labour force participation of married women', *Regional Studies*, **12**, 11–20.

Angel, J. L., 1978, *Directory of Foreign Firms Operating in the United States* (New York: World Trade Academy Press).

Anonymous, 1976, 'A site seeker's guide to industrial parks', *Business Management*, **32**(5), 57–76.

Anonymous, 1980, 'Low cost labor topnotchers', *The WEPZA News*, **2**(3), 1.

Arora, S. S. and Brown, M., 1977, 'Alternative approaches to spatial autocorrelation: an improvement over current practice', *International Regional Science Review*, **2**, 67–78.

Arpan, J. S. and Ricks, D. A., 1974, 'Foreign direct investments in the U.S. and some attendant research problems', *Journal of International Business Studies*, **5**, 1–7.

Association of Independent Businesses, 1980, 'Comments on enterprise zones policy proposals' [mimeo] (London: AIB).

Australia, Commonwealth Bureau of Census and Statistics, 1947, *Census of the Commonwealth of Australia 1947*, Vol. 1 (Canberra: CBCS).

Australia, Commonwealth Bureau of Census and Statistics, 1970, *Official Year Book of the Commonwealth of Australia No. 55, 1969* (Canberra: CBCS).

Australia, Commonwealth Bureau of Census and Statistics, 1971, *Census of Population and Housing: Characteristics of Population and Housing*, Bulletin Nos. 1–7 (Canberra: CBCS).

Australia, Department of Industry and Commerce, 1979a, *The Australian Aluminium Industry: Supply Potential* (Canberra: Australian Government Publishing Service).

Australia, Department of Industry and Commerce, 1979b, 'Aluminum expansion and its impact on the Australian economy', *Journal of Industry and Commerce*, No. 21, December 1979, 13–15.

Australian Bureau of Statistics, 1974, *Official Year Book Australia No. 59, 1973* (Canberra: ABS).

Australian Bureau of Statistics, 1975, *Manufacturing Establishments: Summary of Operations by Industry Class 1972–73* (Canberra: ABS, ref. 12.23).

Australian Bureau of Statistics, 1980a, *Manufacturing Establishments: Summary of Operations by Industry Class 1978–79* (Canberra: ABS, ref. 8202.0).

Australian Bureau of Statistics, 1980b, *Year Book Australia No. 64, 1980* (Canberra: ABS, ref. 1301.0).

Austrin, T. and Beynon, H., 1979, *Global Outpost: The Working Class Experience of Big Business in the North East of England, 1964–79* (Durham: University of Durham).

Averitt, R. T., 1968, *The Dual Economy: The Dynamics of American Industry Structure* (New York: Norton).

Ayeni, B., 1979, *Concepts and Techniques in Urban Analysis* (London: Croom Helm).

Backman, J. and Bloch, E. (Eds.), 1974, *Multinational Corporations, Trade and the Dollar in the Seventies* (New York: New York University Press).

Baer, W., 1965, *Industrialization and Economic Development in Brazil* (Homewood, Illinois: Irwin).

Bal, H. S., Bant Singh and Bal, H. K., 1979, 'Surplus farm labour in Punjab', *Agricultural Situation in India*, **33**, 795–801.

Balassa, B., 1965, 'Trade liberalisation and "revealed" comparative advantage', *Manchester School of Economic and Social Studies*, **33**, 99–124.

Baldwin, R. E., 1979, 'Determinants of trade and foreign investment: further evidence', *The Review of Economics and Statistics*, **61**, 40–8.

Baldwin, W. L., 1958, *A Report on the Dartmouth College Conference on Industrial Parks* (Cambridge, Mass.: Arthur D. Little Inc.).

Bale, J. R., 1972, 'The development of industrial estates with special reference to South Wales, 1936–1969', unpublished M.Phil. dissertation (London: University of London).

Bale, J. R., 1974a, 'Towards a definition of the industrial estate: a note on a neglected aspect of urban geography', *Geography*, **59**, 31–4.

Bale, J. R., 1974b, 'Toward a geography of the industrial estate', *The Professional Geographer*, **26**, 291–7.

Bale, J. R., 1976, *Industrial Estates: A Bibliography and Geographical Introduction* (Monticello: Council of Planning Librarians Exchange Bibliography No. 1022).

Balogh, T., 1950, *Studies in Financial Organization* (Cambridge: Cambridge University Press).

Bandman, M. K., 1980, *Territorial Industrial Complexes: Optimisation Models and General Aspects* (Moscow: Progress Publishers).

Bannister, G., 1976, 'Towards a model of impulse transmissions for an urban system', *Environment and Planning A, 8*, 385–94.

Barclays Bank Ltd, 1979a, 'Barclays bank briefing: Eurobonds' (in *The Economist*, 20 October 1979).

Barclays Bank Ltd, 1979b, 'Barclays bank briefing: removing the mystique of the currency swap' (in *The Economist*, 21 April 1979).

Barkai, H., 1971, 'The industrial revolution on the Kibbutz [in Hebrew]', (paper presented at the Van Leer Symposium, Tel-Aviv, Israel).

Barkai, H., 1977, *Growth Patterns of the Kibbutz Economy* (Amsterdam: North-Holland).

Barlow, E. R. and Wender, I., 1955, *Foreign Investment and Taxation* (Englewood Cliffs: Prentice-Hall).

Barr, B. M. and Matthews, A. S., 1980, 'Agglomeration economies in public and private metropolitan industrial parks' (paper presented to the Conference of the IGU Commission on Industrial Systems, Chuo University, Tokyo, August 1980).

Barras, R. and Broadbent, T. A., 1979, 'The analysis in English structure plans', *Urban Studies, 16*, 1–18.

Barratt-Brown, M., 1974, *The Economics of Imperialism* (Harmondsworth: Penguin).

Barron, I. and Curnow, R., 1979, *The Future with Microelectronics: Forecasting the Effects of Information Technology* (London: Frances Pinter).

Barrows, D. S. and Bookbinder, J. H., 1975, 'Land use', in F. L. Cross and J. L. S. Simons (Eds.), *Industrial Plant Siting* (Westport, Conn.: Technomic Publication Co.), 31–40.

Bassett, K. and Haggett, P., 1971, 'Towards short-term forecasting for cyclic behaviour in a regional system of cities', in M. Chisholm, A. E. Frey and P. Haggett (Eds.), *Regional Forecasting* (London: Butterworth).

Batty, M., 1976, *Urban Modelling: Algorithms, Calibrations, Predictions* (Cambridge: Cambridge University Press).

Batty, M., 1978, 'Urban models in the planning process', in D. T. Herbert and R. J. Johnston (Eds.), *Geography and the Urban Environment*, Vol. 1 (Chichester: Wiley), 63–134.

Baxter, R., Echenique, M. and Owers, J. (Eds.), 1975, *Urban Development Models* (Hornby: Construction Press, LUBFS Conference Proceedings No. 3).

Beal, G. M. and Rogers, E. M., 1960, *The Adoption of Two Farm Practices in a Central Iowa Community* (Ames: Iowa State University, Agricultural and Home Economics Experiment Station Special Report No. 26).

Benson, J. K., 1975, 'The interorganizational network as a political economy', *Administrative Science Quarterly, 20*, 229–49.

Benwell Community Development Project, 1978, *Permanent Unemployment* (Newcastle upon Tyne: BCDP).

Bergsman, J., 1970, *Brazil: Industrialization and Trade Policies* (London: Published on behalf of the OECD Development Centre by Oxford University Press).

Berry, B. J. L., 1969, 'Relationship between regional economic development and the urban system: the case of Chile', *Tijdschrift voor Economische en Sociale Geografie*, **60**, 283–307.

Berry, B. J. L., 1971, 'City size and economic development: conceptual synthesis and policy problems, with special reference to South and Southeast Asia', in L. Jakobson and V. Prakash (Eds.), *Urbanization and National Development: South and Southeast Asia Urban Affairs Annual* (Beverly Hills: Sage Publications), 111–55.

Berry, B. J. L. and Horton, F., 1970, *Geographic Perspectives on Urban Systems; With Integrated Readings* (Englewood Cliffs: Prentice-Hall).

Beyers, W. B., 1973, 'Growth centers and interindustry linkages', *Proceedings, Association of American Geographers*, **5**, 16–21.

Beyers, W. B., 1974, 'On geographical properties of growth center linkage systems', *Economic Geography*, **50**, 203–18.

Beyers, W. B., 1976, 'Empirical identification of key sectors: some further evidence', *Environment and Planning A*, **8**, 231–6.

Beyers, W. B., 1978, 'On the structure and development of multiregional economic systems', *Regional Science Association, Papers*, **40**, 109–33.

Bhagwati, J. N. and Desai, P., 1979, *India, Planning for Industrialization: Industrialization and Trade Policies Since 1951* (Delhi: Oxford University Press).

Biehl, D., Hussmann, E. and Schnyder, S., 1972, 'Zur regionalen Einkommensverteilung in der Europäischen Wirtschaftsgemeinschaft [Towards a regional income distribution in the European Economic Community]', *Die Weltwirtschaft*, No. 1, 64–78.

Blackaby, F. (Ed.), 1979, *De-Industrialisation* (London: Heinemann).

Blake, P., 1964, *God's Own Junkyard: The Planned Deterioration of America's Landscape* (New York: Holt, Rinehart and Winston).

Blauner, R., 1969, 'Internal colonialism and ghetto revolt', *Social Problems*, **16**, 393–408.

Blaut, J. M., 1977, 'Two views of diffusion', *Annals of the Association of American Geographers*, **67**, 343–59.

Blin, J. M., 1973, 'A further procedure for ordering an input-output matrix: some empirical evidence', *Economics of Planning*, **13**, 121–9.

Bliss, M., 1974, *A Living Profit: Studies in the Social History of Canadian Business, 1883–1911* (Toronto: McClelland and Stewart).

Bluestone, B. and Harrison, B., 1979, 'Capital mobility and economic dislocation' [mimeo] (Chestnut Hill, Mass.: Boston College, Social Welfare Research Institute).

Bluestone, B. and Harrison, B., 1980, *Capital and Communities: The Causes and Consequences of Private Disinvestment* (Washington, DC: Progressive Alliance).

Blumberg, P., 1975, *The Megacorporation in American Society: The Scope of Corporate Power* (Englewood Cliffs: Prentice-Hall).

Boarman, P. M. and Schollhammer, H. (Eds.), 1975, *Multinational Corporations and Governments: Business-Government Relations in an International Context* (New York: Praeger).

Boddy, M., 1979, 'Investment by financi_l institutions in commercial property', in M. Boddy (Ed.), *Land Property and Finance* (Bristol: University of Bristol, School for Advanced Urban Studies Working Paper 2), 17–34.

Boley, R. E., 1961, *Industrial Districts Restudied: An Analysis of Characteristics*

Based on Surveys and Projects (Washington, DC: Urban Land Institute Technical Bulletin No. 41).

Boley, R. E., 1962, *Industrial Districts: Principles in Practice* (Washington, DC: Urban Land Institute Technical Bulletin No. 44).

Boley, R. E., 1967, 'Rx for successful industrial park development', *Urban land,* **26**(6), 3–11.

Bolin, R. L., 1978, 'WIFZA—Association for production sharing', *Journal of Proceedings of the Inaugural Meeting of the World Export Processing Zones Association, Manila and Bataan, 31 January to 4 February 1978* (Manila: WEPZA Secretariat), 77–9.

Bora, G., 1980, 'The spatial structure and dynamics of the socialist industrial system based on the Hungarian case' (paper presented to the Conference of the IGU Commission on Industrial Systems, Chuo University, Tokyo, August 1980).

Borrie, W. D., 1975, *Population and Australia: A Demographic Analysis and Projection* (First report of the National Population Inquiry) (2 vols.) (Canberra: Australian Government Publishing Service).

Bourne, L. S., 1975, *Urban Systems: Strategies for Regulation: A Comparison of Policies in Britain, Sweden, Australia and Canada* (Oxford: Clarendon Press).

Bourne, R., 1978, *Assault on the Amazon* (London: Goilancz).

Bowden, P. J., 1965, 'Regional problems and policies in the North-East of England', in T. Wilson (Ed.), *Papers on Regional Development* (Oxford: Blackwell), 20–39.

Boyce, D. E., Day, N. D. and McDonald, C., 1970, *Metropolitan Plan Making: An Analysis of Experience with the Preparation and Evaluation of Alternative Land Use and Transportation Plans* (Philadelphia: Regional Science Research Institute Monograph 4).

Boykin, J. H., 1969, *Industrial Real Estate: An Annotated Bibliography* (Washington, DC: Society of Industrial Realtors).

Braverman, H., 1974, *Labor and Monopoly Capital; The Degradation of Work in the Twentieth Century* (New York: Monthly Review Press).

Brazil, 1974, *IIPND: II National Development Plan, 1975–1979* (Rio de Janeiro: Printing Service of Instituto Brasileiro de Geografia e Estatística).

Brazil, Banco do Nordeste do Brasil, 1976, *Opportunidades de Investimentos no Nordeste: Indústria Têxtíl* [*Opportunities for Investment in the Northeast: The Textile Industry*] (Fortaleza: Banco do Nordeste do Brasil Press).

Brazil, Banco do Nordeste do Brasil, 1979, 'Desafios e alternativas do desenvolvimento da indústria [Challenges and alternatives of development in industry]' (paper presented to a meeting of the Governors of the Northeast States, Fortaleza, January 1979).

Bredo, W., 1960, *Industrial Estates: Tool for Industrialization* (Glencoe, Illinois: The Free Press).

Bredo, W., 1970, 'The industrial estate spreads the development risk', *Columbia Journal of World Business,* **5**(2), 19–25.

Britton, J. N. H., 1980, 'Industrial dependence and technological underdevelopment: Canadian consequences of foreign direct investment', *Regional Studies,* **14,** 181–200.

Broadbent, T. A., 1977, *Planning and Profit in the Urban Economy* (London: Methuen).

Brown, A. J. and Burrows, E. M., 1977, *Regional Economic Problems: Comparative Experiences of Some Market Economies* (London: Allen and Unwin).

Brown, H. J., Ginn, J. R., James, F. J., Kain, J. F. and Straszkein, M. R., 1972, *Empirical Models of Urban Land Use: Suggestions on Research Objectives and*

Organization (New York: National Bureau of Economic Research, distributed by Columbia University Press).

Bruton, M. J. (Ed.), 1974a, *The Spirit and Purpose of Planning* (London: Hutchinson).

Bruton, M. J., 1974b, 'Introduction: general planning and physical planning', in M. J. Bruton (Ed.), *The Spirit and Purpose of Planning* (London: Hutchinson) 7–22.

Buck, T. W. and Atkins, M. H., 1976, 'The impact of British regional policies on employment growth', *Oxford Economic Papers,* **28,** New Series, 118–32.

Bundgaard-Nielsen, M. and Fiehn, P., 1974, 'The diffusion of new technology in the U.S. petroleum refining industry', *Technological Forecasting and Social Change,* **6,** 33–9.

Burns, W., 1967, *Newcastle: A Study in Replanning at Newcastle upon Tyne* (Newcastle: Leonard Hill).

Business International SA (Ed.), 1971, *European Business Strategies in the United States: Meeting the Challenge of the World's Largest Market,* based on research by L. G. Franko (Geneva: Business International SA Research Report 71–2).

Buswell, R. J. and Lewis, E. W., 1970, 'The geographical distribution of industrial research activity in the United Kingdom', *Regional Studies,* **4,** 297–306.

Cable, V., 1977a, 'British protectionism and ldc imports', *ODI Review,* No. 2, 29–48.

Cable, V., 1977b, *Import Controls: The Case Against* (London: Fabian Society Research Series 335).

Cable, V., 1979, *World Textile Trade and Production* (London: The Economist Intelligence Unit Special Report No. 63).

Calcutta Metropolitan Development Authority, 1978, *Calcutta Metropolitan District: Some Facts and Figures* (Calcutta: Directorate of Planning, CMDA).

Calcutta Metropolitan Planning Organisation, 1966, *Basic Development Plan: Calcutta Metropolitan District: 1966–1986* (Calcutta: Planning Department).

Cameron, G. C., 1973, 'Intraurban location and the new plant', *Regional Science Association, Papers,* **31,** 125–43.

Cameron, G. C., 1979, 'The national industrial strategy and regional policy', in D. Maclennan and J. B. Parr (Eds.), *Regional Policy: Past Experience and New Directions* (Oxford: Martin Robertson), 297–322.

Cameron, G. C. and Clark, B. D., 1966, *Industrial Movement and the Regional Problem* (University of Glasgow, Social and Economic Studies Occasional Paper No. 5).

Cameron, G. C. and Johnson, K. M., 1969, 'Comprehensive urban renewal and industrial relocation: the Glasgow case', in J. B. Cullingworth and S. C. Orr (Eds.), *Regional and Urban Studies* (London: Allen and Unwin), 242–80.

Cameron, R., 1967a, 'England 1750–1844', in R. Cameron (Ed.), *Banking in the Early Stages of Industrialisation; A Study in Comparative Economic History* (New York: Oxford University Press), 15–59.

Cameron, R., 1976b, 'France 1800–1870', in R. Cameron (Ed.), *Banking in the Early Stages of Industrialisation; A Study in Comparative Economic History* (New York: Oxford University Press), 60–99.

Cameron, R. (Ed.), 1967c, *Banking in the Early Stages of Industrialisation; A Study in Comparative Economic History* (New York: Oxford University Press).

Cameron, R. (Ed.), 1972, *Banking and Economic Development: Some Lessons of History* (New York: Oxford University Press).

Campbell, M. F., 1966, *A Mountain and a City; The Story of Hamilton* (Toronto: McClelland and Stewart).

Carney, J., 1980, 'Regions in crisis: accumulation, regional problems and crisis formation', in J. Carney, R. Hudson and J. Lewis (Eds.), *Regions in Crisis: New Perspectives in European Regional Theory* (London: Croom Helm), 28–59.

Carney, J. and Hudson, R., 1974, *Ideology, Public Policy and Underdevelopment in the North East* (Durham: University of Durham, North East Area Study Working Paper No. 6).

Carney, J. and Hudson, R., 1978, 'Capital, politics and ideology: the North East of England, 1870–1946', *Antipode*, **10**(2), 64–78.

Carney, J., Hudson, R., Ive, G. and Lewis, J., 1976, 'Regional underdevelopment in late capitalism: a study of the North East of England', in I. Masser (Ed.), *Theory and Practice in Regional Science* (London: Pion, London Papers in Regional Science 6), 11–29.

Carney, J., Hudson, R. and Lewis, J., 1977, 'Coal combines and interregional uneven development in the UK', in D. Massey and P. W. J. Batey (Eds.), *Alternative Frameworks for Analysis* (London: Pion, London Papers in Regional Science 7), 52–67.

Carney, J., Hudson, R. and Lewis, J. (Eds.), 1980, *Regions in Crisis: New Perspectives in European Regional Theory* (London: Croom Helm).

Casetti, E., King, L. J. and Jeffrey, D., 1971, 'Structural imbalance in the US urban economic system', *Geographical Analysis, 3*, 238–55.

Castells, M., 1972, *La Question Urbaine [The Urban Question]* (Paris: F. Maspero).

Castells, M. (Ed.), 1974, *Estructura de Clases y Politica urbana en America Latina [Class Structure and Urban Policy in Latin America]* (Buenos Aires: Ediciones SIAP).

Castells, M. and Godard, F., 1974, *Monopolville: L'Entreprise, l'Etat, l'Urbain [Monopolville: the Enterprise, the State, the Urban System]* (Paris: Mouton).

Catsambas, T., 1978, *Regional Impacts of Federal Fiscal Policy: Theory and Estimation of Economic Incidence* [Lexington, Mass.: D. C. Heath].

Caves, R. E., 1971, 'International corporations: the industrial economics of foreign investment', *Economica*, **38**, 1–27.

Centre for Urban and Regional Development Studies, 1979, *The Mobilisation of Indigenous Potential in the U.K.: A Report to the Regional Policy Directorate of the European Community* (Newcastle: CURDS).

Cha, S. M., 1977, 'The costs and effects of establishing the Masan Free Export Zone', in N. Vittal (Ed.), *Export Processing Zones in Asia: Some Dimensions* (Tokyo: Asian Productivity Organization), 87–92.

Chalkley, B. S., 1978, 'The relocation decisions of small displaced firms', unpublished Ph.D. dissertation (Southampton: University of Southampton).

Chandler, A. D., 1959, 'The beginnings of "Big Business" in American industry', *Business History Review*, **33**, 1–31.

Chandrashekar Shetty, M., 1963, *Small-Scale and Household Industries in a Developing Economy: A Study of their Rationale, Structure, and Operative Conditions* (Bombay: Asia Publishing House).

Chee, P. L., Puthucheary, M. C. and Lee, D., 1979, *A Study of Small Entrepreneurs and Entrepreneurial Development Programmes in Malaysia* (Kuala Lumpur: University of Malaya Press).

Chenery, H. B. and Watanabe, T., 1958, 'International comparisons of the structure of production', *Econometrica*, **26**, 487–521.

Cho, D. W. and McDougall, G. S., 1978, 'Regional cyclical patterns and structure, 1954–1975', *Economic Geography*, **54**, 66–74.

Christelow, D. B., 1979–80, 'National policies toward foreign direct investment', *Quarterly Review* (New York: Federal Reserve Board of New York), 21–32.

Chu, T., 1980, 'A few policy issues on urban collective economic activities [in Chinese]', *Economic Studies* (Beijing), No. 2, 3–11.

Chuang, K. T., Sun, K. Y. and Wu, Y., 1980, 'Urban collective economic enterprises must be vigorously promoted [in Chinese]', *Economic Studies* (Beijing), No. 4, 10–16.

Churchill, B. C., 1955, 'Age and life expectancy of business firms', *Survey of Current Business,* **35** (December), 15–19.

Clark,` C., 1982, *Regional and Urban Location* (St Lucia: Queensland University Press).

Clark, C., Wilson, F. and Bradley, J., 1969, 'Industrial location and economic potential in Western Europe', *Regional Studies,* **3,** 197–212.

Clark, G., 1978, 'Regional labour supply and national fluctuations: Canadian evidence for 1969–1975', *Environment and Planning A,* **10,** 621–32.

Clayton, G. and Osborn, W. T., 1965, *Insurance Company Investment: Principles and Policy* (London: Allen and Unwin).

Cleary, E. J., 1965, *The Building Society Movement* (London: Elek).

Clothing Economic Development Council, 1979, *Industrial Strategy, Progress Report* (London: HMSO).

Clothing Economic Development Council, 1980, *Clothing '80: Fight for Success* (London: HMSO).

Cockburn, C., 1977, *The Local State: Management of Cities and People* (London: Pluto).

Cockerill, A. and Silbertson, A., 1974, *The Steel Industry: International Comparisons of Industrial Structure and Performance* (Cambridge: Cambridge University Press).

Cohen, R. B., 1977, 'Multinational corporations, international finance and the sunbelt', in D. C. Perry and A. J. Watkins (Eds.), *The Rise of the Sunbelt Cities* (Beverly Hills: Sage Publishing, Urban Affairs Annual Reviews 14), 211–26.

Comalco Limited, 1980, 'Making energy work', *Aluminium,* No. 25, 11–15.

Commission of the European Communities, 1971, *The Regional Development in the European Economic Community, Analytical Balance* (Luxembourg: Commission of EC).

Committee of Inquiry on Small Firms (the Bolton Committee), 1971, *Report* (London: HMSO, Cmnd 4811).

Committee on Finance and Industry (the Macmillan Committee), 1931, *Report* (London: HMSO, Cmnd 3897).

Committee on Industry and Trade (the Balfour Committee), 1927, *Final Report: Factors in Industrial and Commercial Efficiency* (London: HMSO, Cmnd 3282).

Committee to Review the Functioning of Financial Institutions (the Wilson Committee), 1980, *Report* (2 parts) (London: HMSO, Cmnd 7937).

Confederação Nacional da Indústria, 1978, *III Encontro de Investidores no Nordeste* [*Third Meeting of Investors in the Northeast*] (Rio de Janeiro: Ediçáo do Gruder).

Confederation of British Industry, 1970, *Problems of Small Firms* (London: CBI).

Conference of the Socialist Economists Microelectronics Group, 1980, *Microelectronics: Capitalist Technology and the Working Class* (London: CSE Books).

Connell, S., 1974, *Report of the 1973 Office Communications Survey* (London: University College, Communications Studies Group Paper No. P/74067/CN).

Connell, S. and Sokoloff, S., 1972, *Report on the Pilot Office Communications Survey Contract* (London: University College, Communications Studies Group, Joint Unit for Planning Research).

CONSAD, 1967, *Regional Federal Procurement Study* (Washington DC: Government Printing Office).

Conway, H. M., Liston, L. L. and Saul, R. J., 1979, *Industrial Park Growth: An Environmental Success Story* (Atlanta: Conway Publications).

Conway Publications Inc., 1976, *Site Selection Handbook. Office and Industrial Parks Index*, **21**(4), 292–8.

Conway Publications Inc., 1977, *Site Selection Handbook. Office and Industrial Parks Index/77*, **22**(4), 344–8.

Cooke, T. W., 1978, 'Causality reconsidered: a note', *Journal of Urban Economics*, **5**, 538–42.

Coraggio, J. L., 1977, 'On the possibilities and difficulties of "radical spatial analysis"' (paper presented to the Conference of the IGU Commission on Industrial Systems, Uniwersytet Jagielloński, Kraków, September 1977).

Corden, W. M., 1975, 'The costs and consequences of protection: a survey of empirical work, in P. B. Kenen (Ed.), *International Trade and Finance: Frontiers for Research* (London: Cambridge University Press), 51–91.

Cottrell, P. L., 1975, *British Overseas Investment in the Nineteenth Century* (London: Macmillan).

Cottrell, P. L., 1980, *Industrial Finance, 1830–1914: The Finance and Organization of English Manufacturing Industry* (London: Methuen).

Courbis, R., 1975, 'Le modèle REGINA, modèle du développement national, régional et urbain de l'économie française [REGINA, a model of national, regional and urban development of the French economy]', *Economie Appliquée*, **28**(2–3), 569–600.

Court, W. H. B., 1953, *The Rise of the Midland Industries, 1600–1838* (London: Oxford University Press).

Cousins, J. and Brown, R., 1970, 'Shipbuilding in the North-East', in J. C. Dewdney (Ed.), *Durham County and City with Teesside* (Durham: British Association for the Advancement of Science), 313–29.

Crossman, R., 1976, *The Diaries of a Cabinet Minister*, Vol. 2 (London: Hamish Hamilton).

Crum, R. E. and Gudgin, G., 1978, *Non-Production Activities in U.K. Manufacturing Industry*, a report by the School of Social Studies of the University of East Anglia (Norwich) to the UK Department of Industry and the EEC (Brussels: Commission of EC Regional Policy Series No. 3).

Currie, J., 1979, *Investment: The Growing Role of Export Processing Zones* (London: The Economist Intelligence Unit Ltd, Special Report No. 64).

Cutajar, M. Z. and Franks, A., 1967, *The Less Developed Countries in World Trade* (London: Overseas Development Institute).

Cyert, R. M. and March, J. G., 1963, *A Behavioral Theory of the Firm* (Englewood Cliffs: Prentice-Hall).

Czamanski, S., 1971, 'Some empirical evidence on the strength of linkages between groups of related industries in urban-regional complexes', *Regional Science Association, Papers*, **27**, 137–60.

Czamanski, S., 1973, 'Linkages between industries in urban-regional complexes', in G. G. Judge and T. Takayama (Eds.), *Studies in Economic Planning Over Space and Time* (Amsterdam: North-Holland), 180–204.

Czamanski, S., 1974, *Study of Clustering of Industries* (Halifax: Dalhousie University, Institute of Public Affairs).

Czamanski, S., 1976, *Study of Spatial Industrial Complexes* (Halifax: Dalhousie University, Institute of Public Affairs).

Daly, M. T., Fagan, R. H., Rowling, J. H. and Brown, J. M., 1974, *A Study of Migrational Potential* (Canberra: Cities Commission).

Damette, F., 1980, 'The regional framework of monopoly exploitation; new problems and trends', in J. Carney, R. Hudson and J. Lewis (Eds.), *Regions in Crisis: New Perspectives in European Regional Theory* (London: Croom Helm), 76–92.

Daniels, J. D., 1971, *Recent Foreign Direct Manufacturing Investment in the United States; An Interview Study of the Decision Process* (New York: Praeger).

Danielsson, A., 1964, 'The location decision from the point of view of the individual company', *Swedish Journal of Economics,* **66,** 47–87.

Davies, J. R. and Kelly, M., 1972, 'Small firms in the manufacturing sector', *Committee of Inquiry on Small Firms Research Report No. 3* (London: HMSO).

Davis, E. W. and Yeomans, K. A., 1974, *Company Finance and the Capital Market: A Study of the Effects of Firm Size* (London: Cambridge University Press).

Davis, S. I., 1976, *The Euro-bank: Its Origins, Management and Outlook* (London: Macmillan).

Dear, M. J. and Scott, A. J., 1981, 'An analytical perspective on urbanization and urban planning in capitalist society', in M. J. Dear and A. J. Scott (Eds.), *Urbanization and Urban Planning in Capitalist Society* (New York: Methuen).

Denison, E. F., 1962, *The Sources of Economic Growth in the United States and the Alternatives Before Us* (New York: Committee for Economic Development).

Dennis, R., 1978, 'The decline of manufacturing employment in Greater London: 1966–1974', *Urban Studies,* **15,** 63–73.

Deutermann, E. P., 1966, 'Seeding science based industry', *New England Business Review,* 7–15.

Devine, P. J., Lee, N., Jones, R. M. and Tyson, W. J., 1979, *An Introduction to Industrial Economics* [3rd edn.] (London: Allen and Unwin).

Dhar, P. N. and Lydall, H. F., 1961, *The Role of Small Enterprises in Indian Economic Development* (New York: Asia Publishing House).

Diamond, D. (Ed.), 1982, 'Regional disparities and regional policies: case studies of industrial, transitional and developing countries', *Geoforum,* **13**(2), 69–192.

Dicken, P., 1968, 'The location of the clothing industry in the Manchester conurbation', unpublished M.A. dissertation (Manchester: University of Manchester).

Dicken, P., 1971, 'Some aspects of the decision making behavior of business organizations', *Economic Geography,* **47,** 426–37.

Dicken, P., 1976, 'The multiplant business enterprise and geographical space: some issues in the study of external control and regional development', *Regional Studies,* **10,** 401–12.

Dicken, P., 1977, 'A note on location theory and the large business enterprise', *Area,* **9,** 138–43.

Dicken, P. and Lloyd, P. E., 1978, 'Inner metropolitan industrial change, enterprise structures and policy issues: case studies of Manchester and Merseyside', *Regional Studies,* **12,** 181–97.

Dobb, M., 1937, *Political Economy and Capitalism: Some Essays in Economic Tradition* (London: G. Routledge and Sons).

Dobb, M., 1970, 'The Sraffa system and critique of the neo-classical theory of distribution', *De Economist,* **118,** 347–62.

Don, Y., 1976, 'Industrialization in advanced rural communities (the Israeli Kibbutz)' (paper presented at the Fourth World Congress of Rural Sociology, Turon, Poland).

Drakakis-Smith, D., 1981, 'Advance Australia fair: internal colonialism in the Antipodes' (paper presented to the Workshop on Internal Colonialism organized by the Developing Areas Study Group, Institute of British Geographers, University of Keele).

Dun and Bradstreet, 1981, *Key British Enterprises, Volume 1* (London: Dun and Bradstreet).

Dunford, M. F., 1979a, *Regional Policy and the Restructuring of Capital* (Brighton: University of Sussex, Urban and Regional Studies Working Paper 4).

Dunford, M. F., 1979b, 'Capital accumulation and regional development in France', *Geoforum*, **10**(1), 81–108.

Dunn, E. S., 1956, 'The market potential concept and the analysis of location', *Regional Science Association, Papers*, **2**, 183–94.

Dunning, J. H., 1971, *Insurance in the Economy* (London: Institute of Economic Affairs Occasional Paper 34).

Dunning, J. H., 1973, 'The determinants of international production', *Oxford Economic Papers*, **25**, New Series, 289–336.

Dunning, J. H., 1980, 'Towards an eclectic theory of international production: some empirical tests', *Journal of International Business Studies*, **11**(1), 9–31.

Durham County Council, 1951, *County Development Plan: Draft Written Analysis* (Durham: DCC).

Dziewonski, K., 1973, 'Presidential address', *Regional Science Association, Papers*, **30**, 7–13.

Echenique, M., Crowther, D., Lindsay, W. and Stibbs, R., 1969a, *Model of a Town: Reading* (Cambridge: University of Cambridge Land Use and Built Form Studies Working Paper 12).

Echenique, M., Crowther, D. and Lindsay, W., 1969b, *Development of a Model of a Town* (Cambridge: University of Cambridge Land Use and Built Form Studies Working Paper 26).

Economic and Social Commission for Asia and the Pacific, 1979a, *New Alternative Approach towards Integrated Industrialization in Non-Metropolitan Areas in the ESCAP Member Countries*, Vol. 1 (Bangkok: ESCAP).

Economic and Social Commission for Asia and the Pacific, 1979b, *Indonesia: Establishment of Pilot Projects in Central Java in Support of Integrated Industrialization in Non-Metropolitan Areas*, Vol. 2 (Bangkok: ESCAP).

Economic and Social Commission for Asia and the Pacific, 1979c, *The Philippines: Establishment of Pilot Projects in Aklan, Palawan and Surigao del Norte in Support of Integrated Industrialization in Non-Metropolitan Areas*, Vol. 3 (Bangkok: ESCAP).

Economic and Social Commission for Asia and the Pacific, 1979d, *Thailand: Establishment of Pilot Projects in Khon Kaen and Songkhla Provinces in Support of Integrated Industrialization in Non-Metropolitan Areas*, Vol. 4 (Bangkok: ESCAP).

Economic and Social Commission for Asia and the Pacific, 1979e, *Malaysia: Establishment of Pilot Projects in the State of Kedah in Support of Integrated Industrialization in Non-Metropolitan Areas*, Vol. 5 (Bangkok: ESCAP).

Economic and Social Commission for Asia and the Pacific, 1979f, *Sri Lanka: Establishment of Pilot Projects in Trincomalee and Polonnaruwa in Support of Integrated Industrialization in Non-Metropolitan Areas*, Vol. 6 (Bangkok: ESCAP).

Economic and Social Commission for Asia and the Pacific, 1979g, *Bangladesh: Establishment of Pilot Projects in the Rajshahi Division in Support of Integrated Industrialization in Non-Metropolitan Areas*, Vol. 7 (Bangkok: ESCAP).

Economic and Social Commission for Asia and the Pacific, 1979h, *India: Establishment of Pilot Projects in the Districts of Durg, Kangra, Nalanda, Nalgonda, Mirzapur and Sabarkanta in Support of Integrated Industrialization in Non-Metropolitan Areas*, Vol. 8 (Bangkok: ESCAP).

Economic and Social Commission for Asia and the Pacific, 1979i, *Summary Report of the ESCAP INA Missions to Bangladesh, India, Indonesia, Malaysia, the Philippines, Sri Lanka and Thailand,* Vol. 9 (Bangkok: ESCAP).

Economic Research Section Chinese Academy of Sciences, 1957, *Handicraft Industries of the Whole Country, 1954* (Peking: Handicrafts Group).

Eden, D. and Levitan, U., 1974, 'Farm and Factory in the Kibbutz: a study in agrico-industrial psychology', *Journal of Applied Psychology,* **59,** 596–602.

Eiteman, D. K. and Stonehill, A. I., 1973, *Multinational Business Finance* (Reading, Mass.: Addison-Wesley).

Ellinger, B., 1933, *This Money Business; A Simple Account of the Institutions and Working of the Banking and Financial World* (London: P. S. King).

Elsaid, H. H. and Darling, J. R., 1978, 'Techniques used by business firms in analyzing investment decisions in the developed countries', *Liiketaloudellinen Aikahauskirja,* **27,** 225–34.

El-Shakhs, S., 1972, 'Development, primacy and systems of cities', *The Journal of Developing Areas,* **7,** 11–36.

Elvin, M., 1973, *The Pattern of the Chinese Past* (London: Eyre Methuen).

Erickson, R. and Leinbach, T. R., 1979, 'Characteristics of branch plants attracted to nonmetropolitan areas', in R. F. Lonsdale and W. L. Seyler (Eds.), *Nonmetropolitan Industrialization* (New York: Halstead Press), 57–78.

Erritt, M. J. and Alexander, J. C. D., 1977, 'Ownership of company shares: a new survey', *Economic Trends,* No. 287, 96–107.

Evans, P., 1979, *Dependent Development: the Alliance of Multinational, State, and Local Capital in Brazil* (Princeton: Princeton University Press).

Evans, S., 1972a, 'Industrial parks restudied: what is an industrial park? How has the concept changed over the years? Where is the industrial park headed?', *Urban Land,* **31,** 14–21.

Evans, S., 1972b, 'Industrial park developments', *The Appraisal Journal,* **40,** 235–45.

Ewers, H.-J. and Wettmann, R. W., 1980, 'Innovation-oriented regional policy', *Regional Studies,* **14,** 161–79.

Fagg, J. J., 1978, 'A re-examination of the incubator hypothesis; a case study of the location of new manufacturing firms in Greater Leicester, 1957–1970' (paper presented to the Annual Conference of the Institute of British Geographers, Manchester, January 1978).

Faith, N., 1972, *The Infiltrators: The European Business Invasion of America* (New York: Dutton).

Fales, R. L. and Moses, L. N., 1972, 'Thünen, Weber and the spatial structure of the nineteenth century city', in M. Perlman, C. Leven and B. Chinitz (Eds.), *Spatial, Regional and Population Economics* (New York: Gordon and Breech), 137–68.

Falk, N. and Martinos, H., 1975, *Inner City: Local Government and Economic Renewal* (London: Fabian Society Research Series 320, Initiatives in Local Government 2).

Feller, I., 1975, 'Invention, diffusion and industrial location' in L. Collins and D. F. Walker (Eds.), *Locational Dynamics of Manufacturing Activity* (London: Wiley), 83–107.

Ferguson, C. E., 1960, 'The relationship of business size to stability: an empirical approach', *The Journal of Industrial Economics,* **9,** 43–62.

Findlay, R., 1978, 'Some aspects of technology transfer and direct foreign investment', *American Economic Review,* **68**(2), 275–9.

Firn, J. R., 1975, 'External control and regional development: the case of Scotland', *Environment and Planning A,* **7,** 393–414.

Firn, J. R. and Hughes, J. T., 1973, 'Employment growth and decentralisation of manufacturing industry: some paradoxes', *Papers from Urban Economics Conference* (London: Centre for Environmental Studies), 485–518.

Firn, J. R. and Swales, J. K., 1978, 'The formation of new manufacturing establishments in the Central Clydeside and West Midlands conurbations, 1963–72: a comparative analysis', *Regional Studies*, **12**, 199–214.

Fisher, D., 1968, 'A survey of the literature on small-sized industrial undertakings in India', in B. T. Hoselitz (Ed.), *The Role of Small Industry in the Process of Economic Growth* (The Hague: Mouton), 115–218.

Fisher, J. S., Hanink, D. M. and Wheeler, J. O., 1979, *Industrial Location Analysis: A Bibliography 1966–1979* (Athens: University of Georgia, Department of Geography).

Fisher, L., 1966, 'Airport industrial parks: who should develop them?', *Urban Land*, **25**, 3–6.

Fisher, W. D. and Fisher, M. C. L., 1975, 'The spatial allocation of employment and residence within a metropolitan area', *Journal of Regional Science*, **15**, 261–76.

Flowers, E. B., 1976, 'Oligopolistic reactions in European and Canadian direct investment in the United States', *Journal of International Business Studies*, **7**(2), 43–55.

Fogarty, F., 1959, 'Industrial parks—city style', *Architectural Forum*, **111**(6), 94–7.

Foley, D. L., 1964, 'An approach to metropolitan spatial structure', in M. M. Webber, J. W. Dyckman, D. L. Foley, A. Z. Guttenberg, W. L. C. Wheaton and C. B. Wurster, *Explorations into Urban Structure* (Philadelphia: University of Pennsylvania Press), 21–78.

Foreman-Peck, J. S. and Gripaios, P. A., 1977, 'Inner city problems and inner city policies', *Regional Studies*, **11**, 401–12.

Fothergill, S. and Gudgin, G., 1978, *Regional Employment Statistics on a Comparable Basis, 1952–75* (London: Centre for Environmental Studies Occasional Paper No. 5).

Francis, A., 1980, 'Families, firms and finance capital: the development of UK industrial firms with particular reference to their ownership and control', *Sociology*, **14**, 1–28.

Frank, A. G., 1969, *Capitalism and Underdevelopment in Latin America* (New York: Monthly Review Press).

Frank, R. H. and Freeman, R. T., 1978, *The Distributional Consequences of Direct Foreign Investment* (New York: Academic Press).

Franklin, P. J. and Woodhead, C., 1980, *The U.K. Life Assurance Industry: A Study in Applied Economics* (London: Croom Helm).

Frazer, P., 1976, 'The clearing banks move to medium-term finance', *The Banker*, **126**, 1451–56.

Fredriksson, G. C. and Lindmark, L. G., 1979, 'From firms to systems of firms: a study of interregional dependence in a dynamic society', in F. E. I. Hamilton and G. J. R. Linge (Eds.), *Spatial Analysis, Industry and the Industrial Environment: Progress in Research and Applications*, Vol. 1 (Chichester: Wiley), 155–86.

Freeman, C., 1974, *The Economics of Industrial Innovation* (Harmondsworth: Penguin).

Freeman, C., 1977a, 'The Kondratiev long-wave technical change and unemployment' [mimeo] (paper prepared for the OECD conference, University of Sussex Science Policy Research Unit).

Freeman, C., 1977b, 'Innovation in the long cycle' [mimeo] (paper presented to OECD conference, University of Sussex Science Policy Research Unit).

Freeman, C., 1978, 'Government policies for industrial innovation', (J. D. Bernal Memorial Lecture, Birkbeck College, London).

Freeman, C., 1979a, 'Unemployment, inequality and technical change' (paper presented to the Sociology Conference on Perspectives in Industrial Society, Vienna, October 1979).

Freeman, C., 1979b, 'Unemployment and technical change', (Thomas McLoughlin Memorial Lecture, Dublin, November 1979).

Freeman, C., 1979c, 'Microelectronics and unemployment', in *Automation and Unemployment* (papers presented at an Australian and New Zealand Association for the Advancement of Science Symposium, Sydney, 28 July 1979) (Sydney: The Law Book Co.), 99–113.

Freeman, C., 1979d, 'Technical innovation and British trade performance', in F. Blackaby (Ed.), *De-industrialisation,* National Institute of Economic and Social Research, Economic Policy Papers 2 (London: Heinemann Educational), 56–73.

French, R. A. and Hamilton, F. E. I., 1979, *The Socialist City* (Chichester: Wiley).

Friedmann, J., 1972, 'A general theory of polarized development', in N. M. Hansen (Ed.), *Growth Centers in Regional Economic Development* (New York: The Free Press), 82–107.

Friedmann, J., 1973, *Urbanization Planning and National Development* (Beverly Hills: Sage Publications).

Friedmann, J. and Douglass, M., 1978, 'Agropolitan development: towards a new strategy for regional planning in Asia', in Fu-Chen Lo and K. Salih (Eds.), *Growth Pole Strategy and Regional Development Policy: Asian Experiences and Alternative Approaches* (Oxford: Pergamon Press), 163–92.

Fröbel, F., Heinrichs, J. and Kreye, O., 1980, *The New International Division of Labour: Structural Unemployment in Industrialised Countries and Industrialisation in Developing Countries* (Cambridge: Cambridge University Press).

Frost, R., 1954, 'The Macmillan gap, 1931–53', *Oxford Economic Papers,* **6,** New Series, 181–201.

Fujimori, H., 1980a, 'Economic and social impacts of EPZs in the Third World', *The WEPZA News,* **2**(3), 3.

Fujimori, H., 1980b, 'Japanese industrialist cites EPZs in Third World countries', *The WEPZA News,* **2**(4), 3 and 8.

Fujimori, H., 1980c, 'Country paper', presented to Asian Productivity Organization Symposium on Economic and Social Impacts of Export Processing Zones (Sri Lanka, 5–9 August 1980, and Taiwan, 10–14 August 1980).

Furtado, C., 1963, *The Economic Growth of Brazil: A Survey from Colonial to Modern Times* (translated by R. W. de Aguiar and E. C. Drysdale) (Berkeley: University of California Press).

Galbraith, J. K., 1954, *The Great Crash, 1929* (Harmondsworth: Penguin).

Garegnani, P., 1970, 'Heterogeneous capital, the production function and the theory of distribution', *Review of Economic Studies,* **37,** 407–36.

Garin, R. A., 1966, 'A matrix formulation of the Lowry Model for intrametropolitan activity allocation', *Journal of the American Institute of Planners,* **32,** 361–64.

Geddes, M., 1978, 'Regional policy and crisis and the cuts' (paper presented to a meeting of the Conference of Socialist Economists Regionalism Group, London).

George, R. E., 1970, *A Leader and a Laggard: Manufacturing Industry in Nova Scotia, Quebec and Ontario* (Toronto: University of Toronto Press).

Gershuny, J. I., 1978, *After Industrial Society?: The Emerging Self-Service Economy* (London: Macmillan).

Ghosh, A. and Sarkar, H., 1970, 'An input-output matrix as a spatial configuration', *Economics of Planning,* **10,** 133–42.

Gibson, K. D., Graham, J. and Shakow, D., forthcoming, 'A theoretical approach to capital and labor restructuring', in J. Carney (Ed.), *Regions in Crisis: Strategies for Classes* (London: Croom Helm).

Gibson, L. J., 1970, 'An analysis of the location of instrument manufacturers in the United States', *Annals of the Association of American Geographers*, **60**, 352–67.

Gilmore, J. S., 1976, 'Boom towns may hinder energy resource development', *Science*, **191**, 535–40.

Goddard, J. B., 1971, 'Office communications and office location: a review of current research', *Regional Studies*, **5**, 263–80.

Goddard, J. B., 1975, 'Organisational information flows and the urban system', *Economie Appliquée*, **28**, 125–64.

Goddard, J. B., 1977, 'Urban geography: city and regional systems', *Progress in Human Geography*, **1**, 296–303.

Goddard, J. B., 1978, 'The location of non-manufacturing activities within manufacturing industries', in F. E. I. Hamilton (Ed.), *Contemporary Industrialization: Spatial Analysis and Regional Development* (London: Longman), 62–85.

Goddard, J. B., 1979, 'Office development and urban and regional development in Britain', in P. W. Daniels (Ed.), *Spatial Patterns of Office Growth and Location* (Chichester: Wiley), 29–60.

Goddard, J. B., 1980, 'Technology forecasting in a spatial context', *Futures*, **12**, 90–105.

Goddard, J. B. and Morris, D., 1976, 'The communications factor in office decentralization', *Progress in Planning*, **6**(1), 1–80.

Goddard, J. B. and Smith, I. J., 1978, 'Changes in corporate control in the British urban system, 1972–77', *Environment and Planning A*, **10**, 1073–84.

Goldberg, M. A., 1967, 'An industrial location model for the San Francisco Bay area', *Annals of Regional Science*, **1**(1), 60–73.

Goldner, W., 1971, 'The Lowry model heritage', *Journal of the American Institute of Planners*, **37**, 100-10.

Gonzales, G. M. de, 1980, *Regional Planning under the Transition to Socialism* (Swansea: University College of Swansea, Centre for Development Studies Monograph 11).

Goodman, D. E., 1972, 'Industrial development in the Brazilian Northeast: an interim assessment of the tax credit scheme of Article 34/18', in R. Roett (Ed.), *Brazil in the Sixties* (Nashville: Vanderbilt University Press), 231–72.

Goodman, D. E., 1976, 'The Brazilian economic "miracle" and regional policy: some evidence from the urban Northeast', *Journal of Latin American Studies*, **8**, 1–27.

Goodman, D. E. and Albuquerque, R. C. de, 1974, *Incentivos a Industrialização e Desenvolvimento do Nordeste* [*Incentives to Industrialization and Development in the Northeast*] (Rio de Janeiro: Instituto de Planejamento Econômico e Social).

Gordon, P. and Ledent, J., 1980, 'Modelling the dynamics of a system of metropolitan areas: a demoeconomic approach', *Environment and Planning A*, **12**, 125–33.

Gottlieb, J. R., 1972, 'Industrial park appraisal in the 1970s', *The Appraisal Journal*, **40**, 600–10.

Gottmann, J., 1980, *Centre and Periphery: Spatial Variation in Politics* (Beverly Hills: Sage Publications).

Government of Bihar, 1976a, *An Industrial Directory of Bihar: Products, Procedures and Production* (Patna: Directorate of Industries, Bihar).

Government of Bihar, 1976b, *Selected Plan Statistics: Bihar* (Patna; Bihar State Planning Board).

Government of India, 1952, *The First Five Year Plan* (New Delhi: Planning Commission).

Government of India, 1955, *Report of the Village and Small-Scale Industries (Second Five Year Plan) Committee* (New Delhi: Planning Commission).

Government of India, 1957, *The Second Five Year Plan* (New Delhi: Planning Commission).

Government of India, 1961, *The Third Five Year Plan* (New Delhi: Planning Commission).

Government of India, 1972, *The Fourth Five Year Plan* (New Delhi: Planning Commission).

Government of India, 1973, *Census of Small Scale Industrial Units: Guidebook for Census Staff, Development Commissioner (Small Scale Industries)* (New Delhi: Ministry of Industrial Development).

Government of India, 1974, *India: A Reference Annual: 1974* (New Delhi: Publications Division, Ministry of Information and Broadcasting).

Government of India, 1978a, *A Reference Annual: 1977 and 1978* (New Delhi: Publications Division, Ministry of Information and Broadcasting).

Government of India, 1978b, *Annual Report of the Ministry of Industry: 1977–78* (New Delhi: Ministry of Industry), III–VI.

Government of India, 1979, *Draft Five Year Plan: 1978–83, Vols. 1–3* (New Delhi: Planning Commission).

Government of India Ministry of Industry, n.d., *Establishment of Small-Scale Industries and Industrial Estates: the Indian Experience* (New Delhi: Ministry of Industry, Development Commissioner).

Gradus, Y. and Krakover, S., 1977, 'The effect of government policy on the spatial structure of manufacturing in Israel', *The Journal of Developing Areas*, **11**, 393–409.

Graham, E. M., 1978, 'Transatlantic investment by multinational firms: a rivalistic phenomenon', *Journal of Post Keynesian Economics*, **1**, 82–99.

Grant, A. T. K., 1937, *A Study of the Capital Market in Post-War Britain* (London: Macmillan).

Green, F. and Nore, P. (Eds.), 1977, *Economics, An Anti-Text* (London: Macmillan).

Greenhut, M. L., 1956, *Plant Location in Theory and in Practice: The Economics of Space* (Chapel Hill: University of North Carolina Press).

Gregory, D., 1978, 'The process of industrial change, 1730–1900', in R. A. Dodgshon and R. A. Butlin (Eds.), *An Historical Geography of England and Wales* (London: Academic Press), 291–311.

Gregory, R., 1975, 'The cow green reservoir', in P. J. Smith (Ed.), *The Politics of Physical Resources* (Harmondsworth: Penguin), 144–201.

Griefen, R. J., 1970, 'The impact of the industrial park', *The Appraisal Journal*, **38**, 83–91.

Grigg, D. B., 1965, 'The logic of regional systems', *Annals of the Association of American Geographers*, **55**, 465–91.

Grigg, D. B., 1967, 'Regions, models and classes', in R. J. Chorley and P. Haggett (Eds.), *Models in Geography* (London: Methuen), 461–509.

Gripaios, P., 1977a, 'The closure of firms in the inner city: the south east London case 1970–75', *Regional Studies*, **11**, 1–6.

Gripaios, P., 1977b, 'Industrial decline in London: an examination of its causes', *Urban Studies*, **14**, 181–9.

Grønhaug, K. and Fredrikesen, T., 1978, *Resources, Environmental Contact and*

Organisational Innovation (Bergen, Norway: Institute for Industrial Economics Research Note No. 23).

Grupo do Trabalho para o Desenvolvimento do Nordeste [Working Party for the Development of the Northeast], 1959, 'Uma politica de desenvolvimento economico para o Nordeste [A policy of economic development for the Northeast]' [2nd edn.] reprinted in F. R. Versiani and J. M. R. de Barros, 1977, *Formação Econômica do Brasil* (São Paulo: Saraiva), 293–338.

Gudgin, G., 1978, *Industrial Location Processes and Regional Employment Growth* (Farnborough: Saxon House).

Guglielmo, R., 1981, 'Le redéploiement industriel: discours et réalités', *Non! Repères pour le Socialisme,* No. 8 (July–August).

Habermas, J., 1976, *Legitimation Crisis* (London: Heinemann).

Habermas, J., 1979, 'Conservatism and capitalist crisis', *New Left Review,* **115,** 73–84.

Hague, D. C. and Newman, R. K., 1952, *Costs in Alternative Locations: The Clothing Industry* (Cambridge: National Institute of Economic and Social Research Occasional Paper No. 15).

Håkanson, L., 1979, 'Towards a theory of location and corporate growth', in F. E. I. Hamilton and G. J. R. Linge (Eds.), *Spatial Analysis, Industry and the Industrial Environment: Progress in Research and Applications,* Vol. 1 (Chichester: Wiley), 115–38.

HaKibbutz HaArtzi, 1975, 'Science-intensive employment in the Kibbutz: a discussion' [mimeo in Hebrew] (Givat-Haviva: The Institute of Kibbutz Society Studies).

Hall, A. L., 1978, *Drought and Irrigation in North-East Brazil* (Cambridge: Cambridge University Press).

Hall, M. (Ed.), 1959, *Made in New York: Case Studies in Metropolitan Manufacturing* (Cambridge, Mass.: Harvard University Press).

Hall, P., 1975, *Urban and Regional Planning* (Newton Abbot: David and Charles).

Hall, P., Gracey, H., Drewett, R. and Thomas, R., 1973, *The Containment of Urban England, Vol. 2: The Planning System* (London: Allen and Unwin).

Hall, W., 1976, 'The fashionable world of project finance', *The Banker,* **126,** 71–7.

Hamilton, F. E. I., 1967, 'Models of industrial location', in R. J. Chorley and P. Haggett (Eds.), *Models in Geography* (London: Methuen), 361–424.

Hamilton, F. E. I., 1968, *Yugoslavia: Patterns of Economic Activity* (London: Bell and Sons).

Hamilton, F. E. I. (Ed.), 1974, *Spatial Perspectives on Industrial Organization and Decision-making* (London: Wiley).

Hamilton, F. E. I., 1976, *The Moscow City Region* (Oxford: Oxford University Press).

Hamilton, F. E. I., 1978, 'The changing milieu of spatial industrial research', in F. E. I. Hamilton (Ed.), *Contemporary Industrialization: Spatial Analysis and Regional Development* (London: Longman), 1–19.

Hamilton, F. E. I., 1979, *Planned Economies* (London: Macmillan Educational).

Hamilton, F. E. I. and Linge, G. J. R., 1979, 'Industrial systems', in F. E. I. Hamilton and G. J. R. Linge (Eds.), *Spatial Analysis, Industry and the Industrial Environment: Progress in Research and Applications,* Vol. 1 (Chichester: Wiley), 1–23.

Harris, B., 1965, 'New tools for planning', *Journal of the American Institute of Planners,* **31,** 90–5.

Harris, C. C., 1974, *Regional Economic Effects of Alternative Highway Systems* (Cambridge, Mass.: Ballinger).

Harris, C. D., 1954, 'The market as a factor in the localization of industry in the United States', *Annals of the Association of American Geographers*, **44**, 315–48.

Harrison, B., 1974, *Urban Economic Development: Suburbanization, Minority Opportunity and the Condition of the Central City* (Washington, DC: Urban Institute).

Harrison, R. T., 1982, 'Assisted industry, employment stability and industrial decline: some evidence from Northern Ireland', *Regional Studies*, **16**(4), 267–85.

Hartshorn, T. A., 1973, 'Industrial/office parks: a new look for the city', *Journal of Geography*, **72**(3), 33–46.

Hartwig, M., 1978, 'Capitalism and Aborigines: the theory of internal colonialism and its rivals', in E. L. Wheelwright and K. Buckley (Eds.), *Essays in the Political Economy of Australian Capitalism*, Vol. 3 (Sydney: Australia and New Zealand Book Company), 119–41.

Harvey, D., 1975a, 'The geography of capitalist accumulation, a reconstruction of the Marxian theory', *Antipode*, **7**(2), 9–21.

Harvey, D., 1975b, 'The political economy of urbanization in advanced capitalist societies: the case of the United States', in G. Gappert and H. M. Rose (Eds.), *The Social Economy of Cities* (Beverly Hills: Sage Publications), 119–64.

Harvey, D., 1978, 'Labor, capital and class struggle around the built environment in advanced capitalist societies', in K. Cox (Ed.), *Urbanization and Conflict in Market Societies* (London: Methuen), 9–37.

Hayes, R. H. and Abernathy, W. J., 1980, 'Managing our way to economic decline', *Harvard Business Review*, **58** (July–August), 67–77.

Hayter, R. and Watts, H. D., forthcoming, 'The geography of enterprise: a re-appraisal', *Progress in Human Geography*.

Headey, B., 1978, *Housing Policy in the Developed Economy: the United Kingdom, Sweden and the United States* (London: Croom Helm).

Heap, D., 1978, *An Outline of Planning Law* (London: Sweet and Maxwell).

Hechter, M., 1975, *Internal Colonialism: The Celtic Fringe in British National Development, 1536–1966* (Berkeley: University of California Press).

Helfgott, R. B., 1959, 'Women's and children's apparel', in M. Hall (Ed.), *Made in New York: Case Studies in Metropolitan Manufacturing* (Cambridge, Mass.: Harvard University Press), 19–134.

Helleiner, G. K., 1973, 'Manufactured exports from less-developed countries and multinational firms', *The Economic Journal*, **83**, 21–47.

Helman, A. and Sonis M., 1977, 'The position of agriculture in Kibbutz economy—an attempt at quantitative projection', *Socio-Economic Planning Sciences*, **11**, 319–21.

Henderson, J., 1979, 'An analysis of closures amongst Scottish manufacturing plants' [mimeo] (Edinburgh: Scottish Economic Planning Department).

Henderson, R. F., 1951, *The New Issue Market and the Finance of Industry* (Cambridge: Bowes & Bowes).

Herbert, J. D. and Stevens, B. H., 1960, 'A model for the distribution of residential activity in urban areas', *Journal of Regional Science*, **2**, 21–36.

Hewings, G. J. D., 1974, 'The effect of aggregation on the empirical identification of key sectors in a regional economy: a partial evaluation of alternative techniques', *Environment and Planning A*, **6**, 439–53.

Hewings, G. J. D., 1977, *Regional Industrial Analysis and Development* (London: Methuen).

Hewings, G. J. D., 1978, 'The trade-off between aggregate national efficiency and interregional equity: some recent empirical evidence', *Economic Geography*, **54**, 254–63.

Higgins, B., 1977, 'Development poles: do they exist?', *Economie Appliquée,* **30**(2), 241–58.

Hilferding, R., 1981, *Finance Capital: A Study of the Latest Phase of Capitalist Development* (London: Routledge and Kegan Paul).

Hill, D. M., 1965, 'A growth allocation model for the Boston region', *Journal of the American Institute of Planners,* **31,** 111–20.

Hill, D. M., Brand, D. and Hansen, W. B., 1966, 'Prototype development of statistical land-use prediction model for Greater Boston region', *Highway Research Record,* **114,** 51–70.

Hines, C. and Searle, G., 1979, *Automatic Unemployment: Discussion of the Impact of Microelectronic Technology on U.K. Unemployment and the Responses this Demands* (London: Earth Resources Research).

Hiro, D., 1976, *Inside India Today* (London: Routledge and Kegan Paul).

Hirschman, A. O., 1968, 'Industrial development in the Brazilian Northeast and the tax-credit scheme of Article 34/18', *Journal of Development Studies,* **5,** 5–28.

Hjern, B. and Hull, C., 1980, *Helping Small Manufacturing Firms Grow: Proposals for a Study of Experience in Great Britain, Sweden and Germany* (Berlin: International Institute of Management).

Hoare, A. G., 1975, 'Linkage flows, locational evaluation and industrial geography: a case study of Greater London', *Environment and Planning A,* **7,** 41–58.

Hobson, A., 1969, 'A new theorem of information theory', *Journal of Statistical Physics,* **1,** 383–91.

Hobson, A. and Cheng, B., 1973, 'A comparison of the Shannon and Kullback information measures', *Journal of Statistical Physics,* **7,** 301–10.

Hodge, G., 1978, 'Second thoughts on the relation between urban systems and economic development' (paper presented to the Fourth Advanced Studies Institute in Regional Science, University of Siegen).

Holborn, P. R. M. and Edwards, E. C. N., 1971, 'Development of the UK venture capital market', *The Banker,* **121,** 488–92.

Holland, S., 1976, *Capital versus the Regions* (London: Macmillan).

Hoover, E. M. and Vernon, R., 1962, *Anatomy of a Metropolis; The Changing Distribution of People and Jobs Within the New York Metropolitan Region* (New York: Doubleday).

Horst, T. O., 1972, 'Firm and industry determinants of the decision to invest abroad: an empirical study', *The Review of Economics and Statistics,* **54,** 258–66.

Hoselitz, B. F. (Ed.), 1968, *The Role of Small Industry in the Process of Economic Growth* (M. Shinohara, 'Japan' and D. Fisher, 'India') (The Hague: Mouton).

House, J. and Fullerton, B., 1960, *Tees-side at Mid-Century: An Industrial and Economic Survey* (London: Macmillan).

Howard, M. C. and King, J. E., 1975, *The Political Economy of Marx* (Harlow: Longman).

Hudson, E. A. and Jorgenson, D. W., 1976, 'US energy policy and economic growth, 1975–2000', *Bell Journal of Economics and Land Management Science,* **5,** 461–514.

Hudson, J. C., 1972, *Geographical Diffusion Theory* (Evanston, Illinois.: North Western University, Department of Geography, Studies in Geography No. 19).

Hudson, R., 1976a, *New Towns in North East England* (London: Social Science Research Council, Report No. HR1734).

Hudson, R., 1976b, *Preliminary Notes on Restructuring Production in the Northern Region* (Durham: University of Durham).

Hudson, R., 1980a, 'New towns and spatial policy: the case of Washington New Town', in G. Geddes and T. Lobstein (Eds.), *Production of the Built Environment*

(London: University College, Proceedings of the Bartlett Summer School 1979), 142–61.

Hudson, R., 1980b, 'Regional development, state policies and the growth of female employment: a study of Washington New Town', *Area*, **12**(3), 229–34.

Hudson, R., 1980c, *Women and Work: A Study of Washington New Town* (Durham: University of Durham, Department of Geography Occasional Publications, New Series No. 16).

Hudson, R., 1981a, 'The development of the chemicals industry on Teesside', *North East England* (Roskilde: Roskilde Universitetscenter, Institut for Geografi, Samfundsanalyse og Datalogie), 54–94.

Hudson, R., 1981b, 'The development of chemicals production in Western Europe in the post-war period' (paper presented to the XXI European Congress of the Regional Science Association, Barcelona, 25–28 August).

Hughes, D., 1979, 'Economic-environment trade-off in regional development—an input-output study', in N. D. Karunaratne (Ed.), *Proceedings of the Input-Output Workshop, Fourth Meeting of the Australian and New Zealand Section of the Regional Science Association, Wodonga, December* (St Lucia: University of Queensland, Department of Economics).

Hughes, J. W. (Ed.), 1974, *Suburbanization Dynamics and the Future of the City* (New Brunswick: Rutgers University Center for Urban Policy Research).

Human Resources Development Centre, 1978, 'Recommendations and conclusions', *ASEAN Seminar on Informal Sector, 11–16 December 1978* (Djakarta).

Hunt, E. K. and Schwartz, J. G. (Eds.), 1972, *A Critique of Economic Theory* (Harmondsworth: Penguin).

Hymer, S. H., 1976, *The International Operations of National Firms: A Study of Direct Foreign Investment* (Cambridge, Mass.: MIT Press).

Hymer, S., 1979a, 'The efficiency (contradictions) of multinational corporations', in R. B. Cohen *et al.* (Eds.), *The Multinational Corporation* (Cambridge: Cambridge University Press); 40–53.

Hymer, S., 1979b, 'The multinational corporation and the international division of labour', in R. B. Cohen *et al.* (Eds.), *The Multinational Corporation* (Cambridge: Cambridge University Press), 140–64.

Institut National d'Etudes Démographiques, 1972, 'Les migrations intérieures 1954–1968', *Population et Sociétés*, No. 50 (September).

Institut National d'Etudes Démographiques, 1975, 'Variations intercensitaires', *Population et Sociétés*, No. 86 (December).

Institut National de la Statistique et des Etudes Economiques, 1979, *Statistiques et Indicateurs des Régions Françaises* (Paris: INSEE, Series R, Nos. 34–5).

Instituto Brasileiro de Geografia e Estatística, 1957, *Censo Industrial, Brasil, VI Recenseamento Geral 1950, Série Nacional* [*Industrial Census, Brazil, VI General Poll 1950, National Series*], Vol. 3 (1), (Rio de Janeiro: IBGE, Conselho Nacional de Estatística).

Instituto Brasileiro de Geografia e Estatística, 1974, *Censo Industrial, Brasil, VIII Recenseamento Geral 1970, Série Nacional* [*Industrial Census, Brazil, VIII General Poll, National Series*], Vol. 1 (Rio de Janeiro: IBGE, Ministério de Planejamento).

Instituto Brasileiro de Geografia e Estatística, 1978, *Anuário Estatístico do Brasil 1978* [*Statistical Yearbook of Brazil 1978*] (Rio de Janeiro: IBGE).

International Labour Office, 1962, 'Aspects of labour and management on industrial estates with special reference to small industries in Asian countries', in *Industrial*

Estates in Asia and the Far East (New York: United Nations, Sales No. 62.II.B.5), 61–84.

International Labour Office, 1972 *Employment, Incomes and Equality: A Strategy for Increasing Productive Employment in Kenya* (Geneva: ILO).

International Labour Office, 1974, *Sharing in Development: A Programme of Employment, Equity and Growth for the Philippines* (Geneva: ILO; and Manila: Economic and Development Authority).

Ironside, R. G., 1977, 'Growth centres, entrepreneurship, and social engineering', *The Canadian Geographer,* **21,** 175–82.

Isard, W., 1956, *Location and Space-Economy: A General Theory Relating to Industrial Location, Market Areas, Land Use, Trade and Urban Structure* (Cambridge, Mass.: MIT Press).

Isard, W. and Liossatos, P., 1979, *Spatial Dynamics and Optimal Space-Time Development* (Amsterdam: North-Holland).

James, F. J. and Hughes, J. W., 1973, 'The process of employment location change: an empirical analysis', *Land Economics,* **49,** 404–13.

James, V. Z., 1978, *Office Employment in the Northern Regions: its National, Regional and Organisational Context* (Newcastle: University of Newcastle upon Tyne, Centre for Urban and Regional Development Studies).

James, V. Z., Marshall, J. N. and Waters, N., 1979, *Telecommunications and Office Location* (Newcastle: University of Newcastle upon Tyne, Centre for Urban and Regional Development Studies, Final Report to the Department of the Environment).

Jansen, A. C. M., De Smidt, M. and Wever, E., 1979, *Industrie en Ruimte: Die Industriële Ontwikkeling van Nederland in Een veranderend Sociaal-Ruimtelijk Bestel [Industry and Space: The Industrial Development of the Netherlands in a Changing Social-Spatial Environment]* (Assen: Van Gorcum).

Jaynes, E. T., 1957, 'Information theory and statistical mechanics', *Physical Review,* **106,** 620–30.

Jensen, R. C., Mandeville, T. D. and Karunaratne, N. D., 1979, *Regional Economic Planning: Generation of Regional Input-Output Analysis* (London: Croom Helm).

Johansen, L., 1963, 'Labour theory of value and marginal utilities', *Economics of Planning,* **3,** 89–103.

Johanson, J. and Vahlne, J-E., 1978, 'A model for the decision making process affecting the pattern and pace of the internationalization of the firm', in M. Ghertman and J. Leontiades (Eds.), *European Research in International Business* (Amsterdam: North-Holland), 9–27.

John, A. H., 1950, *Industrial Development in South Wales, 1750–1850; An Essay* (Cardiff: University of Wales Press).

Johnson, H. G., 1963, 'Effects of changes in comparative costs as influenced by technical change', in R. Harrod and D. Hague (Eds.), *International Trade in a Developing World* (London: Macmillan).

Joint Textile Committee, 1976, *Textile Trends, 1966–75* (London: HMSO).

Joint Textile Committee, 1977, *Textile Trends, 1970–76* (London: HMSO).

Joyce, P., 1980, *Work, Society and Politics: The Culture of the Factory in Later Victorian England* (Brighton: Harvester Press).

Juanico, M. B., 1977, 'O desenvolvimento de pequenas cidades no terceiro mundo [Developing small towns in the Third World]', *Boletim Geografico,* No. 252, 25–6.

Jumper, S. R., Bell, T. L. and Ralston, B. A., 1980, *Economic Growth and Disparities* (Englewood Cliffs: Prentice-Hall).

Karl, K. F., 1968, *Industrial Parks and Districts: An Annotated Bibliography* (Monticello: Council of Planning Librarians Exchange Bibliography No. 63).

Kearl, B. E. and Weisblat, A. M., 1979, 'Institutional innovational reform: the Ladejinsky legacy' (New York: Agricultural Development Council Inc. Seminar Report No. 19).

Keats, J., 1957, *The Crack in the Picture Window* (Boston: Houghton Mifflin).

Keeble, D., 1968, 'Industrial decentralization and the metropolis: the north-west London case', *Transactions of the Institute of British Geographers*, **44**, 1–54.

Keeble, D., 1971, 'Employment mobility in Britain', in M. Chisholm and G. Manners (Eds.), *Spatial Policy Problems of the British Economy* (London: Cambridge University Press), 24–68.

Keeble, D., 1976, *Industrial Location and Planning in the United Kingdom* (London: Methuen).

Keeble, D., 1978, 'Industrial geography', *Progress in Human Geography*, **2**, 318–23.

Keeble, D. and Owens, P. L., 1980, *The Influence of Peripheral and Central Locations on the Relative Development of Regions,* Third Interim Report [to the EEC Commission on Regional Policy] (Cambridge: Cambridge University, Department of Geography).

Kelleher, T., 1976, *Handbook on Export Free Zones* (Vienna: United Nations Industrial Development Organization, Distr. Restricted, UNIDO/10D.31, 22 July 1976, id. 76.3699).

Kendrick, J. W., 1961, *Productivity Trends in the United States* (Princeton: Princeton University Press).

Khrushchev, A. T., 1970, 'Industrial nodes of the USSR and principles for a typology', translated in *Soviet Geography: Review and Translation,* **12**(1971), 91–103.

Kibbutz Industry Association, 1979, 'It is possible in different manners: socio-technology in pleasant applications' [mimeo in Hebrew] (Tel Aviv: KIA).

Kibbutz Industry Association, 1980, *List of Factories* [in Hebrew] (Tel-Aviv: KIA).

Kilbourn, W., 1960, *The Elements Combined: A History of the Steel Company of Canada* (Toronto: Clarke, Irwin).

Kilby, P., 1971, *Entrepreneurship and Economic Development* (New York: Free Press).

Kindleberger, C. P., 1969, *American Business Abroad; Six Lectures on Direct Investment* (New Haven: Yale University Press).

King, L. J., Casetti, E. and Jeffrey, D., 1969, 'Economic impulses in a regional system of cities: a study of spatial interaction', *Regional Studies*, **3**, 213–18.

King, L. J., Casetti, E., Jeffrey, D. and Odland, J., 1972, 'Classifying US cities: spatial-temporal patterns in employment growth', *Growth and Change*, **3**, 37–42.

King, M., 1977, *Public Policy and the Corporation* (London: Chapman and Hall).

Kinnard, W. N. and Messner, S. D., 1971, *Industrial Real Estate,* [2nd edn.] (Washington, DC: Society of Industrial Realtors of the National Association of Real Estate Boards).

Kipnis, B. A., 1974, 'Interrelationships between a new town and its region as a basis for urban development, a case study: Oiryat-Shemona', unpublished Ph.D. dissertation (Jerusalem: Hebrew University).

Kipnis, B. A., 1976, 'Industry as employer in new towns [in Hebrew]', *Economic Quarterly* No. 91, 3–9.

Kipnis, B. A., 1977, 'The impact of factory size on urban growth and development', *Economic Geography*, **53**, 295–302.

Kipnis, B. A. and Salmon, S., 1972, 'Indicators for urbanization processes in the

Kibbutz [in Hebrew]', *Environmental Planning Association Quarterly*, No. 21–22, 9–21.

Klaassen, L. H., 1967, *Methods of Selecting Industries for Depressed Areas: An Introduction to Feasibility Studies* (Paris: OECD, Developing Job Opportunities Series No. 2).

Klaassen, L. H., 1972, 'Growth poles in economic theory and policy', in A. Kuklinski and R. Petrella (Eds.), *Growth Poles and Regional Policies* (The Hague: Mouton), 1–40.

Knickerbocker, F. T., 1973, *Oligopolistic Reaction and Multinational Enterprise* (Boston: Harvard University Graduate School of Administration).

Kobe, Y., 1980, 'An investor's view of the FTZ concept', *The WEPZA News*, **2**(3), 1, 6, 8.

Kolosovskiy, N. N., 1947, 'The territorial-production combination (complex) in Soviet economic geography', translated in *Journal of Regional Science*, **3**(1961), 1–25.

Kortus, B., 1980, 'The dynamics and structure of the Polish industrial system' (paper presented to the Conference of the IGU Commission on Industrial Systems, Chuo University, Tokyo, August 1980).

Kotz, D. M., 1978, *Bank Control of Large Corporations in the United States* (Berkeley: University of California Press).

Kreiden, J., 1977, 'The contribution of research to the Kibbutz industry [in Hebrew]' *The Kibbutz and Industry*, No. 2, 25–6.

Krieger, J., 1979, 'British colliery closure programmes in the North East: from paradox to contradiction', in I. G. Cullen (Ed.), *Analysis and Decision in Regional Policy* (London: Pion, London Papers in Regional Science 9), 219–32.

Kruijt, B., 1979, 'The changing spatial pattern of firms in Amsterdam: empirical evidence', *Tijdschrift voor Economische en Sociale Geografie*, **70**, 144–56.

Krumme, G., 1969a, 'Notes on locational adjustment patterns in industrial geography', *Geografiska Annaler*, Series B, **51**, 15–19.

Krumme, G,. 1969b, 'Towards a geography of enterprise', *Economic Geography*, **45**, 30–40.

Kuehn, J. A. and Bender, L. D., 1969, 'An empirical identification of growth centers', *Land Economics*, **45**, 435–43.

Kullback, S., 1959, *Information Theory and Statistics* (New York: Wiley).

Kumar, K., 1978, *Prophecy and Progress: The Sociology of Industrial and Post-Industrial Society* (Harmondsworth: Penguin).

Kupper, A., 1977, 'Selection of an industrial plant for a Kibbutz [in Hebrew]', *The Kibbutz and Industry*, No. 2, 7–11.

Kupper, A., 1980, 'A strategy for the search of industrial project [in Hebrew]', *The Kibbutz and Industry*, No. 3, 21–28.

Kurien, C. T., 1978a, 'Small sector in new industrial policy', *Economic and Political Weekly*, **13**, 455–61.

Kurien, C. T., 1978b, *Poverty, Planning and Social Transformation* (Bombay: Allied Publishers Private Limited).

Lamberton, D. M. (Ed.), 1971, *Economics of Information and Knowledge: Selected Readings* (Harmondsworth: Penguin).

Langdon, S., 1975, 'Multinational corporations, taste transfer and underdevelopment: a case study from Kenya', *Review of African Political Economy*, **2**, 12–35.

Langrish, J., Gibbons, M., Evans, W. G. and Jevons, F. R., 1972, *Wealth from Knowledge: Studies of Innovation in Industry* (London: Macmillan).

Läpple, D. and van Hoogstraten, P., 1980, 'Remarks on the spatial structure of capitalist development: the case of the Netherlands', in J. Carney, R. Hudson and J. Lewis (Eds.), *Regions in Crisis: New Perspectives in European Regional Theory* (London: Croom Helm), 117–66.

Launhardt, W., 1882, 'Die Bestimmung des zweckmässigsten Standorts einer gewerblichen Anlage [The selection of the most efficient location for an industrial plant]', *Zeitschrift des Vereins Deutscher Ingenieure,* 106–15.

Lavington, F., 1921, *The English Capital Market* (London: Methuen).

Leftwich, R. B., 1973, 'Foreign direct investments in the United States, 1962–71', *Survey of Current Business,* **53** (2), 29–40.

Le Heron, R. B., 1980, 'The diversified corporation and development policy: New Zealand's experience', *Regional Studies,* **14,** 201–17.

Leigh, R. and North, D. J., 1978, 'Regional aspects of acquisition activity in British manufacturing industry', *Regional Studies,* **12,** 227–45.

Lenin, V. I., 1952, *Razvitie Kapitalizma v Rossii* [*The Development of Capitalism in Russia*] (Moscow: Gosudarstvennoe Izdatel'stvo Politicheskoi Literatury).

Léo, P-Y., 1978, *L'Analyse Dynamique des Systèmes Industriels Régionaux* [*The Dynamic Analysis of Regional Industrial Systems*] (Aix-en-Provence: Centre d'Economie Régionale de l'Université de Droit, D'Economie et des Sciences d'Aix-Marseille).

Leone, R. A., 1972, 'The role of data availability in intrametropolitan workplace location studies', *Annals of Economic and Social Measurement,* **1,** 171–82.

Leone, R. A. and Struyk, R., 1976, 'The incubator hypothesis evidence from five SMSAs', *Urban Studies,* **13,** 325–31.

Leontief, W. [in collaboration with] Strout, A., 1963, 'Multiregional input-output analysis', in T. Barna (Ed.), *Structure Interdependence and Economic Development* (London: Macmillan), 119–50.

Leroy, G., 1976, *Multinational Product Strategy: A Typology for Analysis of World-wide Product Innovation and Diffusion* (New York: Praeger).

Levitan, U., 1973, 'Science intensity—the future core of Kibbutz employment' [mimeo in Hebrew] (Givat-Haviva: The Institute of Kibbutz Society Studies).

Lewis, W. A., 1954, 'Economic development with unlimited supplies of labour', *The Manchester School of Economic and Social Studies,* **22,** 139–91.

Leys, C., 1975, *Underdevelopment in Kenya: The Political Economy of Neo-Colonialism, 1964–1971* (London: Heinemann).

Li, C. Y. and Hwang, Y. C., 1979, 'Certain issues in the development of urban collective industries [in Chinese]', *Economic Studies* (Beijing), No. 1, 27–32.

Lichtenberg, R. M., 1960, *One-Tenth of a Nation; National Forces in the Economic Growth of the New York Region* (Cambridge, Mass.: Harvard University Press).

Lindberg, J. and McCarty, H. H., 1966, *A Preface to Economic Geography* (Englewood Cliffs: Prentice-Hall).

Linge, G. J. R., 1979, 'Australian manufacturing in recession: a review of the spatial implications', *Environment and Planning A,* **11,** 1405–30.

Linge, G. J. R., Karaska, G. J. and Hamilton, F. E. I., 1978, 'An appraisal of the Soviet concept of the territorial production complex', *Soviet Geography: Review and Translation,* **19,** 681–97.

Linge, G. J. R. and Hamilton, F. E. I., 1981, 'International industrial systems', in F.E.I. Hamilton and G. J. R. Linge (Eds.), *Spatial Analysis, Industry and The Industrial Environment: Progress in Research and Applications,* Vol. 2 (Chichester: Wiley), 1–117.

Linn, J., 1978, 'Urbanization trends, polarization reversal and spatial policy in Colombia', *Fourth Advanced Studies Institute in Regional Science* (Siegen: University of Siegen).

Lipietz, A., 1977, *Le Capital et son Espace* [*Capital and its Space*] (Paris: F. Maspero, séries 'Economie et socialisme' No. 34).

Lipietz, A., 1980a, 'Inter-regional polarisation and the tertiarisation of society', *Regional Science Association, Papers,* **44,** 3–17.

Lipietz, A., 1980b, 'The structuration of space, the problem of land, and spatial policy', in J. Carney, R. Hudson and J. Lewis (Eds.), *Regions in Crisis: New Perspectives in European Regional Theory* (London: Croom Helm), 60–75.

Little, A. D., Inc., 1976, 'The reasons and outlook for foreign direct investment in the United States', in United States Department of Commerce, *Foreign Direct Investment in the United States,* Vol. 5 (Washington, DC: Government Printing Office), 1–339.

Little, J. S., 1978, 'Locational decisions of foreign direct investors in the United States', *New England Economic Review,* July–August, 43–63.

Lloyd, P. E., 1979, 'The components of industrial change for Merseyside Inner Area: 1966–1975', *Urban Studies,* **16,** 45–60.

Lloyd, P. E. and Dicken, P., 1977, *Location in Space: A Theoretical Approach to Economic Geography* (New York: Harper & Row).

Lloyd, P. E. and Mason, C. M., 1976, *Establishment-based Data for the Study of Intra-Urban and Sub-Regional Industrial Change, the Manchester Industrial Data-Bank* (University of Glasgow, Urban and Regional Studies Discussion Paper No. 22).

Lloyd, P. E. and Mason, C. M., 1978, 'Manufacturing industry in the inner city: a case study of Greater Manchester', *Transactions of the Institute of British Geographers,* **3,** New Series, 66–90.

Lo, F. and Salih, K., 1978, 'Introduction', in Fu-Chen Lo and K. Salih (Eds.), *Growth Pole Strategy and Regional Development Policy: Asian Experiences and Alternative Approaches* (Oxford: Pergamon), xi–xvi.

Logan, M. I., 1966, 'Locational behavior of manufacturing firms in urban areas', *Annals of the Association of American Geographers,* **56,** 451–66.

Lösch, A., 1954, *The Economics of Location,* translated by W. H. Woglom assisted by W. F. Stolper [from *Die räumliche Ordnung der Wirtschaft* (1940)] (New Haven: Yale University Press).

Lou, K. B., Li, Y. C. and Pun, T. L., 1980, 'A preliminary survey on collective industries of Beijing [in Chinese]', *Economic Studies* (Beijing), No. 3, 72–3.

Lowry, I. S., 1964, *A Model of Metropolis* (Santa Monica: Rand Corporation, Research Memorandum RM-4035-RC).

Lowry, I. S., 1968, 'Seven models of urban development: a structural comparison', in G. C. Hemmens (Ed.), *Urban Development Models* (Washington, DC: Highway Research Board), 126–46.

Lucas, R., 1976, 'The conflict over public power in Hamilton, Ontario, 1906–1914', *Ontario History',* **68,** 236–46.

Luttrell, W. F., 1962, *Factory Location and Industrial Movement: A Study of Recent Experience in Great Britain,* Vol. 1 (London: National Institute of Economic and Social Research).

McConnell, J. E., 1980, 'Foreign direct investment in the United States', *Annals of the Association of American Geographers,* **70,** 259–70.

McConnell, J. E., 1981, 'Foreign ownership and trade of U.S. high-technology manufacturing', *The Professional Geographer,* **33,** 63–71.

McDermott, P. J., 1976, 'Ownership, organization and regional dependence in the Scottish electronics industry', *Regional Studies,* **10,** 319–35.

McDermott, P. J., 1977a, 'Overseas investment and the industrial geography of the United Kingdom', *Area,* **9,** 200–7.

McDermott, P., 1977b, 'Regional variations in enterprise: electronics firms in Scotland, London and the Outer Metropolitan Area', unpublished Ph.D. dissertation (Cambridge: University of Cambridge).

MacElwee, R. S., 1926, *Port Development,* [2nd edn.] (New York: McGraw-Hill).

McEwen, A. and Barr, B. M., 1975, 'Some aspects of Calgary's role in the intra-industry manufacturing linkages of Southern Alberta: the case of the mobile-home industry', in B. M. Barr (Ed.), *Calgary: Metropolitan Structure and Influence* (Victoria, BC: University of Victoria, Western Geographical Series Vol. 11), 52–76.

McEwen, A. and Barr, B. M., 1977, 'The replacement process in economic development: transformation of deactivated military bases into industrial estates', in B. M. Barr (Ed.), *Research Studies by Western Canadian Geographers: The Edmonton Papers* (Vancouver: Tantalus Research Ltd, BC, Geographical Series, Occasional Papers in Geography No. 24), 49–65.

McGee, T. G., 1978, 'An invitation to the 'ball': dress formal or informal', in P. J. Rimmer, D. W. Drakakis-Smith and T. G. McGee (Eds.), *Food, Shelter and Transport in Southeast Asia and the Pacific: Challenging the 'Unconventional Wisdom' of Development Studies in the Third World* (Canberra: The Australian National University, Department of Human Geography Publication No. HG/12 (1978)), 3–27.

Macgill, S. M., 1977, 'Theoretical properties of biproportional matrix adjustments', *Environment and Planning A,* **9,** 687–701.

McKean, R., 1975, *The Impact of Comprehensive Development Area Policies on Industry in Glasgow* (University of Glasgow, Urban and Regional Studies Discussion Paper No. 15).

McKee, L., 1967, *Income and Employment in the Southeast: A Study in Cyclical Behavior* (Lexington: University of Kentucky Press).

Mackett, R. L. and Mountcastle, G. D., 1977, 'Developments of the Lowry model', in A. G. Wilson, P. H. Rees and C. M. Leigh (Eds.), *Models of Cities and Regions: Theoretical and Empirical Developments* (Chichester: Wiley), 209–82.

McNee, R. B., 1958, 'Functional geography of the firm, with an illustrative case study from the petroleum industry', *Economic Geography,* **34,** 321–37.

McNee, R. B., 1974, 'A systems approach to understanding the geographic behaviour of organisations, especially large corporations', in F. E. I. Hamilton (Ed.), *Spatial Perspectives on Industrial Organization and Decision-making* (London: Wiley), 47–76.

Malecki, E. J., 1979a, 'Agglomeration and intra-firm linkage in R & D location in the United States', *Tijdschrift voor Economische en Sociale Geografie,* **70,** 322–32.

Malecki, E. J., 1979b, 'Locational trends in R & D by large U.S. corporations, 1965–1977', *Economic Geography,* **55,** 309–23.

Malecki, E. J., 1980, 'Corporate organization of R and D and the location of technological activities', *Regional Studies,* **14,** 219–34.

Malinowski, Z. S. and Kinnard Jr, W. N., 1963, *The Place of Small Business in Planned Industrial Districts* (Storrs: University of Connecticut).

Manchester City Planning Department, 1970, *Industry and Wholesale Distribution in Manchester* (Manchester: City and County Borough of Manchester).

Mandel, E., 1963, 'The dialectic of class and region in Belgium', *New Left Review,* **20,** 5–31.

Mandel, E., 1968, *Marxist Economic Theory,* 2 vols. (New York: Monthly Review Press).

Mandel, E., 1975, *Late Capitalism,* translated by Joris De Bres [rev. edn.] (London: New Left Books).

Mandel, E., 1978, *The Second Slump: A Marxist Analysis of Recession in the Seventies* (London: New Left Books).

Mandeville, T. D., 1978, 'The impact of the proposed Gladstone aluminium smelter on the subregion, region, state and national economies' (paper presented to the Input-Output Workshop of the Third Annual Meeting, Regional Science Association, Australian and New Zealand Section, Melbourne, December 1978).

Mandeville, T. D., 1979, 'Some recent developments in the construction and use of regional input-output tables' (paper presented to the Australia and New Zealand Association for the Advancement of Science 49th Congress, Section 24, Economics, Auckland, January 1979).

Mandeville, T. D. and Jensen, R. C., 1978a, *The Impact of Major Development Projects on the Gladstone/Calliope Fitzroy, Queensland, and Australian Economies: An Application of Input-Output Analysis, Report to the Department of Commercial and Industrial Development and Comalco Limited* (St Lucia: University of Queensland, Department of Economics).

Mandeville, T. D. and Jensen, R. C., 1978b, *The Economic Impact of Industrial Developments in the Gladstone Area of Central Queensland, Report to the Department of Commercial and Industrial Development and the Co-ordinator General's Department* (St Lucia: University of Queensland, Department of Economics).

Mandeville, T., Macdonald, S. and Lamberton, D., 1980, 'The fortuneteller's new clothes: a critical appraisal of IMPACT's technological change projections to 1990–91', *Search,* **11**(1–2), 14–17.

Manners, G., Keeble, D., Rodgers, B. and Warren, K., 1972, *Regional Development in Britain* (London: Wiley).

Manpower Services Commission, 1979, *Annual Report, 1978–9* (London: MSC).

Manpower Services Commission, 1981, *Regional Employment Market Intelligence Trends,* No. 10 (Newcastle: MSC).

Mansfield, E., Rapoport, J., Schnee, J., Wagner, S. and Hamburger, M., 1971, *Research and Innovation in the Modern Corporation* (New York: Norton).

March, L. and Batty, M., 1975, 'Generalized measures of information, Bayes' likelihood ratio and Jaynes' formalism', *Environment and Planning B,* **2**, 99–105.

Marquand, J., 1980, *Measuring the Effects and Costs of Regional Incentives* (London: Department of Industry, Government Economic Service Working Paper No. 32).

Marris, R., 1964, *The Economic Theory of 'Managerial' Capitalism* (London: Macmillan).

Marshall, J. N., 1979a, 'Corporate organisation and regional office employment', *Environment and Planning A,* **11**, 553–63.

Marshall, J. N., 1979b, 'Ownership, organisation and industrial linkage: a case study of the Northern Region of England', *Regional Studies,* **13**, 531–57.

Martin, F., Swan, N., Banks, I., Barker, G. and Beaudry, R., 1979, *The Interregional Diffusion of Innovation in Canada* (Ottawa: Economic Council of Canada).

Martin, J. E., 1966, *Greater London: An Industrial Geography* (London: Bell).

Martin, J. E., 1981, 'La desindustrialisation de la Grande Bretagne [The deindustrialization of Great Britain]', *Revue d'Economie Régionale et Urbaine,* No. 3, 283–9.

Mason, C. M., 1978, 'Manufacturing change in metropolitan areas: a case study of Greater Manchester', unpublished Ph.D. dissertation (Manchester: University of Manchester).

608   REFERENCES

Masser, I., Coleman, A. and Wynn, R. F., 1971, 'Estimation of a growth allocation model for North-west England', *Environment and Planning A,* **3,** 451–63.

Massey, D. B., 1971, *The Basic Service Categorisation in Planning* (London: Centre for Environmental Studies Working Paper 63).

Massey, D. B., 1973, 'A critique of industrial location theory', *Antipode,* **5**(3), 33–9.

Massey, D. B., 1978, 'Survey: regionalism: some current issues', *Capital and Class,* **6,** 106–25.

Massey, D. B., 1979a, 'A critical evaluation of industrial-location theory', in F.E.I. Hamilton and G. J. R. Linge (Eds.), *Spatial Analysis, Industry and the Industrial Environment: Progress in Research and Applications,* Vol. 1 (Chichester: Wiley), 57–72.

Massey, D. B., 1979b, 'In what sense a regional problem?', *Regional Studies,* **13,** 233–43.

Massey, D. B., 1980, 'Industrial location in context: a proposal' (paper presented to Institute of British Geographers Study Group on Industrial Activity and Area Development, London School of Economics, May 1980).

Massey, D. B. and Meegan, R. A., 1978, 'Industrial restructuring versus the cities', *Urban Studies,* **15,** 273–88.

Massey, D. B. and Meegan, R. A., 1979, 'The geography of industrial reorganisation: the spatial effects of the restructuring of the electrical engineering sector under the Industrial Reorganisation Corporation', *Progress in Planning,* **10**(3), 155–237.

Matthews, A. S., 1979, 'A comparison of the forces of agglomeration within Calgary's industrial parks', unpublished M.A. dissertation (Calgary: University of Calgary).

Medio, A., 1972, 'Profits and surplus-value: appearance and reality in capitalist production', in E. K. Hunt and J. G. Schwartz (Eds.), *A Critique of Economic Theory* (Harmondsworth: Penguin), 312–46.

Meek, R., 1956, *Studies in the Labour Theory of Value* (London: Lawrence and Wishart).

Meeks, G., 1977, *Disappointing Marriage: A Study of the Gains from Merger* (Cambridge: Cambridge University Press, Cambridge University, Department of Applied Economics Occasional Paper No. 51).

Mehmet, O., 1978, *Economic Planning and Social Justice in Developing Countries* (London: Croom Helm).

Meir, A., 1977, 'Diffusion, spread and spatial innovation transmission processes: the adoption of industrialization by the Kibbutzim in Israel as a case study', unpublished Ph.D. dissertation (Cincinnati: University of Cincinnati).

Meir, A., 1979a, 'A disparity-based diffusion model', *The Professional Geographer,* **31,** 382–7.

Meir, A., 1979b, 'A dynamic spatial diffusion model: an application to the Kibbutz industry in Israel', *GeoJournal,* **3**(1), 81–7.

Meir, A., 1980, 'The diffusion of industry adoption by Kibbutz rural settlements in Israel', *The Journal of Developing Areas,* **14,** 539–52.

Meir, A., (1982), 'Growth, nature and determinants of the industrialization of Kibbutz rural settlements in Israel', in I. Volgyes and G. Enyedi (Eds.), *The Effect of Modern Agriculture on Rural Development* (New York: Pergamon), 259–80.

Mensch, G., 1979, *Stalemate in Technology: Innovations Overcome the Depression* (Cambridge, Mass.: Ballinger).

Middleton, D. J. and Walker, D. F., 1980, 'Manufacturers and industrial development policy in Hamilton, 1890–1910', *Urban History Review,* **8**(3), 20–46.

Miernyk, W. H., Shellhammer, K. L., Brown, D. M., Coccari, R. L., Gallagher, C. J. and Wineman, W. H., 1970, *Simulating Regional Economic Development: An Interindustry Analysis of the West Virginia Economy* (Lexington, Mass.: Heath Lexington Books).

Mihailović, K., 1972, *Regional Development: Experiences and Prospects in Eastern Europe* (The Hague: Mouton).

Miller, E. W. and Miller, R. M., 1978, *Industrial Location: A Bibliography* (Worcester, Mass.: Clark University Press).

Miller, R. R. and Weigel, D. R., 1973, 'Factors affecting resource transfer through direct investment', in C. G. Alexandrides (Ed.), *International Business Systems Perspectives* (Atlanta: Georgia State University School of Business Administration), 129–44.

Mills, E. S., 1972, *Studies in the Structure of the Urban Economy* (Baltimore: Johns Hopkins Press).

Minns, R., 1979, *Pension Funds and the Ownership of Shares in U.K. Companies* (London: Centre for Environmental Studies Research Series 27).

Minns, R., 1980, *Pension Funds and British Capitalism: The Ownership and Control of Shareholdings* (London: Heinemann).

Minns, R., 1981, 'A comment on "Finance capital and the crisis in Britain"', *Capital and Class*, **14,** 98–110.

Mok, V., 1980, 'Trade barriers and industrial diversification: Hong Kong's new experience', *The WEPZA News*, **2**(4), 5–7.

Moore, B. and Rhodes, J., 1973, 'Evaluating the effects of British regional economic policy', *The Economic Journal*, **83,** 87–110.

Moore, B. and Rhodes, J., 1982, 'A second Great Depression in the UK regions: can anything be done?', *Regional Studies*, **16**(5), 323–33.

Moore, B., Rhodes, J. and Tyler, P., 1977, 'The impact of regional policy in the 1970s', *Centre for Environmental Studies Review*, No. 1, 67–77.

Moore, C. L., Karaska, G. J. and Bickford, D. J., 1981, 'Banking and the regional income multiplier' [mimeo] (Amherst: University of Massachusetts).

Morgan, K., 1979, *State Regional Intervention and Industrial Reconstruction in Post-War Britain: The Case of Wales* (Brighton: University of Sussex, Urban and Regional Studies Working Paper 16).

Morgan, K., 1980. *The Reformulation of the Regional Question, Regional Policy and the British State* (Brighton: University of Sussex, Urban and Regional Studies Working Paper 18).

Moseley, M. J., 1974, *Growth Centres in Spatial Planning* (Oxford: Pergamon).

Moseley, M. J. and Townroe, P. M., 1973, 'Linkage adjustment following industrial movement', *Tijdschrift voor Economische en Sociale Geografie*, **64,** 137–44.

Moser, C. O. N., 1978, 'Informal sector or petty commodity production: dualism or dependence in urban development', *World Development*, **6,** 1041–64.

Moses, L. N., 1962, 'Towards a theory of intra-urban wage differentials and their influence on travel patterns', *Regional Science Association, Papers*, **9,** 53–63.

Moses, L. and Williamson, H. F., 1967, 'The location of economic activity in cities', *American Economic Review*, **57,** Pt. 2, 211–22.

Mukherjee, S., 1974, *Free Trade is Good, But What About the Workers?* (London: Political and Economic Planning).

Mumford, L., 1961, *The City in History: Its Origins, Its Transformations and Its Prospects* (New York: Harcourt Brace and World).

Murata, K. (Ed.), 1980, *An Industrial Geography of Japan* (London: Bell & Hyman).

Murray, R., 1972, 'Underdevelopment, the international firm and the international division of labour', *Towards a New World Economy* (papers and proceedings of the 5th European Conference of the Society for International Development, The Hague, October 1971) (Rotterdam: Rotterdam University Press).

Myrdal, G., 1957, *Economic Theory and Under-developed Regions* (London: Duckworth).

Naipaul, S., 1978, *North of South: An African Journey* (London: Andre Deutsch).

Nairn, T., 1977, *The Break-up of Britain: Crisis and Neo-nationalism* (London: New Left Books).

National Economic Development Office, 1971, *Technology and the Garment Industry* (London: HMSO).

National Economic Development Office, 1974, *Clothing: Industrial Review to 1977* (London: HMSO).

National Union of Tailors and Garment Workers, 1978, *Employment in Clothing—A Struggle for Survival* (Milton Keynes: NUTGW).

Naylor, R. T., 1975, *The History of Canadian Business, 1867–1914*, Vol. 2 (Toronto: James Lorimer).

Nelson, R. L., 1959, *Merger Movements in American Industry, 1895–1956* (Princeton: Princeton University Press).

New South Wales, Department of Decentralisation and Development, 1973, *Annual Report 1972–73* (Sydney: NSW Government Publisher).

New South Wales, State Planning Authority, 1968, *Sydney Region—Outline Plan 1970–2000 A.D.* (Sydney: SPA).

North, D. C., 1955, 'Location theory and regional economic growth', *The Journal of Political Economy*, **63**, 243–58.

North, D. C., 1956, 'A reply', *The Journal of Political Economy*, **64**, 165–8.

North East Area Study, 1975, *Social Consequences and Implications of the Teesside Structure Plan* (Durham: University of Durham).

North East Trades Union Studies Information Unit, 1976, *The Crisis Facing the UK Power Plant Manufacturing Industry* (Newcastle: NETUSIU).

North East Trades Union Studies Information Unit, 1977, *Multinationals in Tyne and Wear* (Newcastle: NETUSIU).

North Tyneside Community Development Project, 1978a, *North Shields, Living with Industrial Change* (London: Home Office).

North Tyneside Community Development Project, 1978b, *North Shields, Women's Work* (London: Home Office).

North Tyneside Trades Council, 1979, *Shipbuilding—The Cost of Redundancy* (Newcastle: NTTC).

Northern Region Strategy Team, 1975, *Change and Efficiency in the Northern Region, 1948–73* (Newcastle, NRST Technical Report No. 3).

Northern Region Strategy Team, 1976a, *Linkages in the Northern Region* (Newcastle, NRST Working Paper No. 6).

Northern Region Strategy Team, 1976b, *Public Expenditure in the Northern Region* (Newcastle: NRST Technical Report No. 12).

Northern Region Strategy Team, 1977, *Strategic Plan for the Northern Region* (5 vols.) (Newcastle: NRST).

Norton, R. D. and Rees, J., 1979, 'The product cycle and the spatial decentralization of American manufacturing', *Regional Studies*, **13**, 141–51.

Nunnally, N. and Pollina, R., 1973, 'Recent trends in industrial park location in the Chicago Metropolitan Area', *Land Economics*, **49**, 356–61.

Oakey, R. P., 1978, 'The British scientific and industrial instruments industry', unpublished Ph.D. dissertation (London: University of London).

Oakey, R. P., 1979a, 'The effects of technical contacts with local research establishments on the British instruments industry', *Area*, **11**, 146–50.

Oakey, R. P., 1979b, 'Technological change and regional development: a note on policy implications', *Area*, **11**, 340–4.

Oakey, R. P., Thwaites, A. T. and Nash, P. A., 1980, 'The regional distribution of innovative manufacturing establishments in Britain', *Regional Studies*, **14**, 235–53.

O'Connor, J., 1973, *The Fiscal Crisis of the State* (New York: St Martins Press).

O'Farrell, P. N., 1976, 'An analysis of industrial closures: Irish experience 1960–1973', *Regional Studies*, **10**, 433–48.

Offe, C., 1975a, 'The theory of the capitalist state and the problem of policy formation', in L. N. Lindberg, R. Alford, C. Crouch and C. Offe (Eds.), *Stress and Contradiction in Modern Capitalism* (Lexington, Mass.: Lexington Books), 125–44.

Offe, C., 1975b, 'Introduction to Part III', in L. N. Lindberg, R. Alford, C. Crouch and C. Offe (Eds.), *Stress and Contradiction in Modern Capitalism* (Lexington, Mass.: Lexington Books), 245–59.

Ohlsson, L., 1977a, *Regionernas Specialisering och Internationella Beroende, Val av Regionindelning* [*The International Dependence and Specialisation of Swedish Regions, Choice of Regional Delineation*] (Stockholm: Ministry of Industry, Expert Group on Regional Studies Underlagsmaterial No. U20).

Ohlsson, L., 1977b, 'Patterns of engineering trade specialization, 1960–1970, and Sweden's factor abundance', *The Journal of Political Economy*, **85**, 361–78.

Ohlsson, L., 1977c, *Regionernas Specialisering och Internationella Beroende, Val av Branschindelning* [*The International Dependence and Specialisation of Swedish Regions, Choice of Industrial Classification and Aggregation*] (Stockholm: Ministry of Industry, Expert Group on Regional Studies Underlagsmaterial No. U19).

Ohlsson, L., 1979a, *Components of Urban Industrial Employment Change in a Small Open Economy: Sweden* (Laxenberg, Austria: International Institute for Applied Systems Analysis Working Paper No. 79–32).

Ohlsson, L., 1979b, *Tracing Regional Patterns of Industrial Specialisation Trends in Sweden* (Laxenburg, Austria: International Institute for Applied Systems Analysis Working Paper No. 79–33).

Ohlsson, L., 1979c, 'Regional arbetsfordelning i svensk industri [Regional development of labour in Swedish industry]', in *Regional Arbetsfordelning inom Industrin*, ERU [Swedish Expert Group on Regional Studies] series No. 1979:90 (Stockholm: SOU).

Ohlsson, L., 1980a, *Engineering Trade Specialisation of Sweden and Other Industrial Countries*, Studies in International Economics Vol. 6 (Amsterdam: North-Holland).

Ohlsson, L., 1980b, 'Industrial structure and possible industrial futures of the Malmoehus county' [mimeo] (Stockholm: Stockholm School of Economics, Economic Research Institute).

Ohlsson, L., 1980c, 'Regional industrial policies in a small, open economy: a retrospective study of means, effects and limitations of Swedish regional policies 1965–75' [mimeo] (Laxenburg, Austria: International Institute for Applied Systems Analysis).

Oliveira, F. de, and Reichstul, H. P., 1973, 'Mudanças na divisão interregional do trabalho no Brasil [Changes in the interregional division of labour in Brazil]', *Estudos Cebrap*, **4**, 131–68.

Onofri, P. and Stagni, A., 1979, 'Saggio di profito e rendimento della attivita finanziare nell industria italiana, 1957–1977 [Essay on profit and interpretation of the financial activity of Italian industry, 1957–1977]', *Rivista di Politica Economica*, **10**, 1087–125.

Ontario Industrial Innovation Centre, 1980, *Implementation Plan* (Waterloo: OIIC).

Organisation for Economic Co-operation and Development, 1976, *The 1974–5 Recession and the Employment of Women* (Paris: OECD).

Overbeek, H., 1980, 'Finance capital and the crisis in Britain', *Capital and Class*, **11**, 99–120.

Owen, W., 1968, *Distance and Development: Transport and Communications in India* (Washington, DC: The Brookings Institution).

Ozawa, T., 1979a, 'International investment and industrial structure: new theoretical implications from the Japanese experience', *Oxford Economic Papers*, **31**, New Series, 72–92.

Ozawa, T., 1979b, *Multinationalism, Japanese Style: The Political Economy of Outward Dependency* (Princeton: Princeton University Press).

Paauw, D. S. and Fei, J. C. H., 1973, *The Transition in Open Dualistic Economies: Theory and South East Asian Experience* (New Haven: Yale University Press).

Pack, J. R., 1978, *Urban Models: Diffusion and Policy Application* (Philadelphia: Regional Science Research Institute Monograph 7).

Page, W. L., Gilmore, D. J. and Hewings, G. J. D., 1979, *Energy Demand Forecasting in the Ohio River Basin Energy Study Region* (Urbana: University of Illinois).

Palander, T., 1935, *Beitrage zur Standortstheorie* (Uppsala: Almqvist & Wiksell).

Palloix, C., 1973, *Les Firmes Multinationales et le Procès d'Internationalisation* [*Multinational Firms and the Process of Internationalization*] (Paris: F. Maspero, séries 'Economie et socialisme' No. 19).

Papa, R. J., 1980, 'Regional income and foreign direct investment in the United States', *Proceedings of the Middle States Division of the Association of American Geographers*, **14**, 41–7.

Parr, J. B., 1973, 'Growth poles, regional development and central place theory', *Regional Science Association, Papers*, **31**, 173–212.

Parsons, G. F., 1972, 'The giant manufacturing corporations and balanced regional growth in Britain', *Area*, **4**, 99–103.

Paterno, V., 1978, 'Keynote speech', *Journal of Proceedings of the Inaugural Meeting of the World Export Processing Zones Association, Manila and Bataan, 31 January to 4 February 1978*, 35–7.

Pepler, G. and MacFarlane, P. W., 1949, 'The North East Area Development Plan' (unpublished Interim Report presented to the Minister of Town and Country Planning).

Perrons, D., 1979, *The Role of Ireland in the New International Division of Labour* (Brighton: University of Sussex, Urban and Regional Studies Working Paper 15).

Perroux, F., 1955, 'Note sur la notion de "pôle de croissance" [Note on the concept of "growth pole"]', *Matériaux pour une analyse de la croissance économique* (Paris: Cahiers de l'Institut de Science Economique Appliquée, Série D, No. 8), 307–20.

Perroux, F., 1964, 'Economic space: theory and applications', in J. Friedmann and W. Alonso (Eds.), *Regional Development and Planning* (Cambridge, Mass.: MIT Press), 21–36.

Peschel, K., 1975, 'Integration and the spatial distribution of economic activity', *Regional Science Association, Papers*, **34**, 27–42.

Peseh, N., 1979, *Economic, Social and Normative Impact of Hired-Labor in the Kibbutz Industry* (Tel-Aviv: Kibbutz Industry Association).

Peterson, R., 1977, *Small Business: Building a Balanced Economy* (Erin, Ontario: Porcépic).

Petrella, R., 1972, 'Some notes on growth poles', in A. Kuklinski and R. Petrella (Eds.), *Growth Poles and Regional Policies* (The Hague: Mouton), 187–211.

Pfeffer, J., 1972a, 'Size and composition of corporate boards of directors: the organisation and its environment', *Administrative Science Quarterly*, **17**, 218–28.

Pfeffer, J., 1972b, 'Merger as a response to organizational interdependence', *Administrative Science Quarterly*, **17**, 382–94.

Pfeffer, J. and Salancik, G. R., 1974, 'Organizational decision making as a political process: the case of a university budget', *Administrative Science Quarterly*, **19**, 135–51.

Pfeffer, J. and Salancik, G. R., 1978, *The External Control of Organisations: A Resource Dependence Perspective* (New York: Harper & Row).

Philippines Investment Coordination Committee, 1980, *Report of the Subcommittee to Review BEPZ Enterprises* (Manila: National Economic and Development Authority).

Piercy, Lord, 1955, 'The Macmillan gap and the shortage of risk capital', *Journal of the Royal Statistical Society*, **118**, 1–7.

Poche, B., 1975, 'Mode de production et structures urbaines [Mode of production and urban structures]', *Espace et Société*, No. 16(November), 15–30.

Polenske, K. R., 1972, 'The implementation of a multiregional input-output model for the United States', in A. Bródy and A. P. Carter (Eds.), *Input-Output Techniques* (Amsterdam: North-Holland), 171–89.

Pollard, S., 1981, *Peaceful Conquest: The Industrialization of Europe, 1760–1970* (Oxford: Oxford University Press).

Pollina, R. R., 1974, 'Industrial parks in the Chicago Metropolitan Area: criteria for successful developments', unpublished Ph.D. dissertation (Urbana: University of Illinois at Urbana-Champaign).

Pollina, R. R., 1975, 'Industrial parks: tool for community development', *Geographical Perspectives*, **35**, 31–42.

Prais, S. J., 1976, *The Evolution of Giant Firms in Britain: A Study of the Growth of Concentration in Manufacturing Industry in Britain, 1909–70* (Cambridge: Cambridge University Press).

Pred, A. R., 1965, 'The concentration of high-value-added manufacturing', *Economic Geography*, **41**, 108–32.

Pred, A. R., 1966, *The Spatial Dynamics of U.S. Urban-industrial Growth, 1800–1914: Interpretive and Theoretical Essays* (Cambridge, Mass.: MIT Press).

Pred, A. R., 1973, 'Urbanization, domestic planning problems and Swedish geographic research', *Progress in Geography*, **5**, 3–76.

Pred, A. R., 1974, *Major Job-Providing Organizations and Systems of Cities* (Washington, DC: Association of American Geographers, Commission on College Geography Resource Paper No. 27).

Pred, A. R., 1977, *City-Systems in Advanced Economies: Past Growth, Present Processes and Future Development Options* (London: Hutchinson).

Pred, A. R. and Törnqvist, G., 1973, *Systems of Cities and Information Flows, Two Essays* (Lund: Gleerup, Lund Studies in Geography, Series B, No. 38).

Pressnell, L., 1956, *Country Banking in the Industrial Revolution* (Oxford: Clarendon Press).

Putman, S. H., 1972, 'Intraurban employment forecasting models: a review and a suggested new model construct', *Journal of the American Institute of Planners*, **38**, 216–30.

Putman, S. H., 1976, 'Laboratory testing of predictive land use models: some comparisons', in S. H. Putman (Ed.), *Urban Residential Location Models* (Boston: Martinus Nijhoff), 19–29.

Pye, R. and Williams, E., 1977, 'Teleconferencing: is video valuable or is audio adequate?', *Telecommunications Policy*, **1**, 230–41.

Rama, R., 1979, 'El proteccionismo de México y su modelo de desarrollo economicó de 1960 à 1970 [Mexican protectionism and its model for economic development from 1960 to 1970]', *Cuadernos de Economia*, **7**(18), 87–108.

Rappaport, A., 1979, 'Strategic analysis for more profitable acquisitions', *Harvard Business Review*, **57**(4), 99–110.

Ray, E. J., 1977, 'Foreign direct investment in manufacturing', *The Journal of Political Economy*, **85**, 283–97.

Ray, G. F., 1980, 'Innovation in the long cycle', *Lloyds Bank Review*, No. 135, 14–28.

Rebouças, O. E., 1979, 'Desenvolvimento do Nordeste: diagnóstico e sugestões de políticas [Development of the Northeast: diagnosis and policy suggestions]', *Revista Econômica do Nordeste*, **10**, 189–430.

Redman, A. E., 1967, 'What is an industrial park?', *Industrial Development*, **136**, 22–4.

Reed, M. C., 1975, *Investment in Railways in Britain, 1820–1844: A Study in the Development of the Capital Market* (Oxford: Oxford University Press).

Rees, G. and Rees, T., 1980, *Poverty and Social Inequality in Wales* (London: Croom Helm).

Rees, J., 1972, 'The industrial corporation and location decision analysis', *Area*, **4**, 199–205.

Rees, J., 1974, 'Decision-making, the growth of the firm and the business environment', in F. E. I. Hamilton (Ed.), *Spatial Perspectives on Industrial Organization and Decision-making* (London: Wiley), 189–211.

Rees, J., 1979a, 'Technological change and regional shifts in American manufacturing', *The Professional Geographer*, **31**, 45–54.

Rees, J., 1979b, 'Manufacturing change, internal control and government spending in a growth region of the USA' in F. E. I. Hamilton (Ed.), *Industrial Change: International Experience and Public Policy* (London: Longman), 155–74.

Rees, J., Hewings, G. J. D. and Stafford, H. A. (Eds.), 1981, *Industrial Location and Regional Systems: Spatial Organization in the Economic Sector* (London: Croom Helm).

Regional Policy Research Unit, 1979, *State Regional Policies and Uneven Development: the Case of North East England* (London: Centre for Environmental Studies, Final Report No. RP270).

Research Triangle Institute, 1977, *An Analysis of the National Science Foundation's Innovation Centres Experiment* (Research Triangle Park: RTI).

Richards, S. F., 1981, 'Industrial activities in the periphery: Hong Kong', in F. E. I. Hamilton and G. J. R. Linge (Eds.), *Spatial Analysis, Industry and the Industrial Environment: Progress in Research and Applications*, Vol. 2 (Chichester: Wiley), 465–80.

Richardson, H. W., 1972, *Input-Output and Regional Economics* (London: Weidenfeld and Nicolson).

Richardson, H. W., Vipond, J. and Furbey, R., 1975, *Housing and Urban Spatial Structure: A Case Study* (Farnborough: Saxon House).

Richter, C. E., 1969, 'The impact of industrial linkages on geographic association', *Journal of Regional Science*, **9**, 19–28.

Robinson, J. F. F. and Storey, D., 1979, 'Employment change in manufacturing industry in Cleveland, 1965–76', (paper presented to a meeting of the Conference of Socialist Economists Regionalism Group, Durham).

Robock, S. H., 1975, *Brazil, a Study in Development Progress* (Lexington, Mass.: Lexington Books).

Rodgers, A., 1979, *Economic Development in Retrospect: The Italian Model and its Significance for Regional Planning in Market-Oriented Economies* (Washington, DC: Winston and Sons).

Roepke, H., Adams, D. and Wiseman, R., 1974, 'A new approach to the identification of industrial complexes using input-output data', *Journal of Regional Science*, **14**, 15–29.

Rogers, E. M. and Agawala-Rogers, R., 1976, *Communication in Organizations* (New York: The Free Press).

Rogers, E. M. and Shoemaker, F. F., 1971, *Communication of Innovations: A Cross Cultural Approach* (New York: The Free Press).

Rogerson, C. M., 1980, 'Internal colonialism, transnationalization and spatial inequality', *The South African Geographical Journal*, **62**, 103–20.

Rogerson, C. M., 1981, 'Industrialization in the shadows of apartheid: a world-systems analysis', in F. E. I. Hamilton and G. J. R. Linge (Eds.), *Spatial Analysis, Industry and The Industrial Environment: Progress in Research and Applications*, Vol. 2 (Chichester: Wiley), 395–421.

Root, F. R., 1978, *International Trade and Investment* (Cincinnati: Southwestern Publishing Company).

Rose, E. A., 1974, 'Philosophy and purpose of planning', in M. J. Bruton (Ed.), *The Spirit and Purpose of Planning* (London: Hutchinson), 23–65.

Rose, S., 1977, 'Why the multinational tide is ebbing', *Fortune*, **96**(2), 111–20.

Rostow, W. W., 1971, *The Stages of Economic Growth: A Non-Communist Manifesto* [2nd edn.] (Cambridge: Cambridge University Press).

Rothschild, K. W., 1947, 'Price theory and oligopoly', *The Economic Journal*, **57**, 299–320.

Rothwell, R. and Zegveld, W., 1979, *Technical Change and Employment* (London: Frances Pinter).

Roweis, S. and Scott, A. J., 1978, 'The urban land question', in K. Cox (Ed.), *Urbanization and Conflict in Market Societies* (London: Methuen), 38–75.

Roy, M. K., 1971, 'A note on the computation of an optimal ordering for an input-output matrix', *Economics of Planning*, **11**, 95–7.

Royal Commission on the Distribution of the Industrial Population (the Barlow Report), 1940, *Report* (London: HMSO, Cmnd 6153).

Sachs, I., 1981, 'Whither industrial societies?' in D. Soen (Ed.), *Industrial Development and Technology Transfer* (London: George Godwin, International Forum Series), 7–14.

Sack, R. D., 1974, 'The spatial separatist theme in geography', *Economic Geography*, **50**, 1–19.

Sadler, P. G., Archer, B. H. and Owen, C. B., 1973, *Regional Income Multipliers: The Anglesey Study* (Cardiff: University of Wales, Bangor Occasional Papers in Economics No. 1).

Saha, S. K., 1977, 'Spatial impact of growth poles in the regional planning context: a case study in the Ranchi Region (Bihar), India', unpublished Ph.D. dissertation (Cardiff: University of Wales).

Saha, S. K., 1979, 'River-basin planning in the Damodar Valley of India', *The Geographical Review*, **69**, 273–87.

Salancik, G. R. and Pfeffer, J., 1974, 'The bases and use of power in organizational decision making: the case of a university', *Administrative Science Quarterly*, **19**, 453–73.

Salih, M., Pakkasem, P., Prantilla, E. B. and Soegijoko, S., 1978, 'Decentralization policy, growth pole approach, and resource frontier development: a synthesis of the response in four Southeast Asian countries', in Fu-Chen Lo and K. Salih (Eds.), *Growth Pole Strategy and Regional Development Policy: Asian Experiences and Alternative Approaches* (Oxford: Pergamon), 79–146.

Sallez, A., 1975, 'Sous-traitance, productivité économique et croissance régionale [Sub-contracting, economic productivity and regional growth]', *Economie Appliquée*, **28**(2–3), 459–96.

Samuel, R., 1977, 'Workshop of the world: steam power and hand technology in mid-Victorian Britain', *History Workshop*, No. 3, 6–72.

Santos, M., 1973, 'Economic development and urbanization in underdeveloped countries: the two circuits of the urban economy and their spatial implications', unpublished manuscript (Toronto: University of Toronto).

Santos, M., 1979, *The Shared Space: The Two Circuits of the Urban Economy in Underdeveloped Countries* (London: Methuen).

Sappho, 1972, *Success and Failure in Industrial Innovation: Report on Project Sappho* (Brighton: University of Sussex, Science Policy Research Unit).

Saushkin, Yu. G., 1967, 'Energoproizvodstvennie tsikly [Energy production cycles]', *Vestnik Moskovskogo Universiteta: Serya Geografiya*, **4**, 211–32.

Sauvant, K. P., 1976, 'The potential of multinational enterprises as vehicles for the transmission of business culture', in K. P. Sauvant and F. G. Lavipour (Eds.), *Controlling Multinational Enterprises: Problems, Strategies, Counter-strategies* (Boulder, Colorado: Westview Press), 39–78.

Save Scotswood Campaign Committee, 1979, *Economic Audit on Vickers Scotswood*, (Newcastle: SSCC).

Savey, S., 1981, 'Pechiney Ugine Kuhlmann: a French multinational corporation', in F. E. I. Hamilton and G. J. R. Linge (Eds.), *Spatial Analysis, Industry and the Industrial Environment: Progress in Research and Applications*, Vol. 2 (Chichester: Wiley), 305–27.

Sayer, R. A., 1976, 'A critique of urban modelling: from regional science to urban and regional political economy', *Progress in Planning*, **6**(3), 187–254.

Sayer, R. A., 1979, 'Understanding urban models versus understanding cities', *Environment and Planning A*, **11**, 853–62.

Sayer, R. A., 1980, 'Some methodological problems in industrial location studies' (paper presented to the Conference of the Industrial Activity and Area Development Group of the Institute of British Geographers, May 1980).

Sayer, R. A., 1982, 'Explanation in economic geography: abstraction versus generalization', *Progress in Human Geography*, **6**(1), 68–88.

Schnore, L. F. and Klaff, V. Z., 1972, 'Suburbanization in the sixties: a preliminary analysis', *Land Economics*, **48**, 23–33.

Schoeppler, O., 1976, 'Merchant banking: the new look', *The Banker*, **126**, 953–7.

Schofield, R. E., 1963, *The Lunar Society of Birmingham: A Social History of Provincial Science and Industry in Eighteenth-century England* (Oxford: Clarendon Press).

Schollhammer, H., 1974, *Locational Strategies of Multinational Firms* (Los Angeles: Pepperdine University, Center for International Business).

Schon, D. A., 1964, 'Innovation by invasion', *International Science Technology*, **10**, 52–60.

Schumacher, E. F., 1973, *Small is Beautiful: A Study of Economics as if People Mattered* (London: Blond and Briggs).

Schumpeter, J. A., 1934, *The Theory of Economic Development: An Inquiry into Profits, Capital, Credit, Interest and the Business Cycle,* translated by R. Opie (Cambridge, Mass.: Harvard University Press).

Science Council of Canada, 1979, *Forging the Links—A Technological Policy for Canada* (Ottawa: SCC Report No. 29).

Scott, A. J., 1976, 'Urban transport and the economic surplus: notes towards a distributional theory', in A. Karlqvist, L. Lundqvist, F. Snickars and J. W. Weibull (Eds.), *Spatial Interaction Theory and Planning Models* (Amsterdam: North-Holland), 335–60.

Scott, A. J., 1979, 'Commodity production and the dynamics of land-use differentiation', *Urban Studies,* **16,** 95–104.

Scott, A. J., 1980, *The Urban Land Nexus and the State* (London: Pion).

Scott, A. J. and Roweis, S. T., 1977, 'Urban planning in theory and practice; a reappraisal', *Environment and Planning A,* **9,** 1097–119.

Scott, J., 1979, *Corporations, Classes and Capitalism* (London: Hutchinson).

Seers, D., 1978, *The Congruence of Marxism and Other Neo-classical Doctrines* (Brighton: University of Sussex, Institute of Development Studies Discussion Paper 136).

Segal, M., 1960, *Wages in the Metropolis: Their Influence on the Location of Industries in the New York Region* (Cambridge, Mass.: Harvard University Press).

Segal, N., 1979, 'The limits and means of "self-reliant" regional economic growth', in D. Maclennan and J. B. Parr (Eds.), *Regional Policy: Past Experience and New Directions* (Oxford: Martin Robertson), 211–24.

Seidman, N., n.d., *The Construction of an Urban Growth Model* (Delaware Valley: Regional Planning Commission Report No. 1, Technical Supplement, Vol. A).

Semmens, P., 1970, 'The chemical industry (of Teesside and South Durham)', in J. C. Dewdney (Ed.), *Durham County and City with Teesside* (Durham: British Association for the Advancement of Science), 330–40.

Semple, R. K., Gauthier, H. L. and Youngmann, C. E., 1972, 'Growth poles in São Paulo, Brazil', *Annals of the Association of American Geographers,* **62,** 591–8.

Sethuraman, S. V., 1976, 'The informal sector: concept, measurement and policy', *International Labour Review,* **114,** 69–81.

Shanks, M., 1977, *Planning and Politics: the British Experience, 1960–76* (London: Allen and Unwin).

Shannon, C. E., 1948, 'A mathematical theory of communication', *Bell System Technical Journal,* **27,** 379–423 and 623–56.

Shapira, R., 1979, 'Women employment in Kibbutz industry' [mimeo in Hebrew] (Tel-Aviv: Kibbutz Industry Association).

Shapira, R., 1980, 'Shift employment in the Kibbutz industry [in Hebrew]', *The Kibbutz and Industry,* No. 3, 32–44.

Shapiro, D. M., 1977, 'A migration model of U.S. direct investment flows', *Economia Internazionale,* **30,** 295–304.

Sharpston, M., 1975, 'International sub-contracting', *Oxford Economic Papers,* **27,** New Series, 94–135.

Sheppard, E. S., 1976, 'Entropy, theory construction and spatial analysis', *Environment and Planning A,* **8,** 741–52.

Short, J., 1981, *Public Expenditure and Taxation in the UK Regions* [Farnborough: Gower].

Siegal, R. A., 1966, 'Do regional business cycles exist', *Western Economic Journal*, **5,** 44–57.

Sigurdson, J., 1977, *Rural Industrialization in China* (Cambridge, Mass.: Council on East Asian Studies, distributed by Harvard University Press).

Sinha, R., Pearson, P., Kadekodi, G. and Gregory, M., 1979, *Income Distribution, Growth and Basic Needs in India* (London: Croom Helm).

Sit, V. F. S., 1979, 'Neighbourhood workshops in the socialist transformation of Chinese cities', in S. S. K. Chin (Ed.), *Modernization in China* (Hong Kong: University of Hong Kong, Centre of Asian Studies), 91–102.

Sit, V. F. S., 1980a, 'Urban collectives in China [in Chinese]', *Dou Sau*, No. 37, 1–10.

Sit, V. F. S., 1980b, 'Collective industrial enterprises in the People's Republic of China' (paper presented to the conference of the IGU Commission on Industrial Systems, Chuo University, Tokyo, August 1980).

Sit, V. F. S., 1980c, 'Neighbourhood workshops in Guangzhou', *Canton Companion* (Hong Kong), No. 2, 22–6.

Skinner, G. W., 1964–5, 'Marketing and social structure in rural China', *Journal of Asian Studies,* **24,** Part 1: 3–43; Part 2: 195–228; Part 3: 363–99.

Smith, D. M., 1966, 'A theoretical framework for geographical studies of industrial location', *Economic Geography,* **42,** 95–113.

Smith, D. M., 1971, *Industrial Location: An Economic Geographical Analysis* (New York: Wiley).

Smith, D. M., 1981, *Industrial Location: An Economic Geographical Analysis* [2nd edn.] (Chichester: Wiley).

Smith, I. J., 1979, 'The effect of external takeovers on manufacturing employment change in the Northern Region between 1963 and 1973', *Regional Studies,* **13,** 421–37.

Smith, I. J., 1980, *Some Aspects of Direct Inward Investment in the United Kingdom, with Particular Reference to the Northern Region* (Newcastle: University of Newcastle upon Tyne, Centre for Urban and Regional Development Studies Discussion Paper No. 31).

Snickars, F. and Weibull, J. W., 1977, 'A minimum information principle: theory and practice', *Regional Science and Urban Economics,* **5,** 137–68.

Society of Industrial Realtors of the National Association of Real Estate Boards, n.d., *Industrial Parks: Their Growth and Impact on the Industrial Real Estate Market* (Washington, DC: The Society).

Society of Industrial Realtors of the National Association of Realtors and the National Association of Industrial and Office Parks, 1979, *A Guide to Industrial Site Selection* (Washington, DC: The Society).

Soong Jun University, 1978, *International Research Project on Korean Small Industry Development* (Seoul: Soong Jun University, Integrated Development Center).

Sørlie, J. E., 1978, *The Access of Small Industrial Enterprises to Capital from the Norwegian Regional Development Fund* (Bergen, Norway: Institute for Industrial Economics Working Paper No. 5).

Soshani, E., 1973, *The Kibbutz in Israel* [In Hebrew] (Tel-Aviv: HaKibbutz HaMenchas).

Souza, J. G. de, 1979, *O Nordeste Brasileiro: Uma Experiênca de Desenvolvimento Regional [The Northeast Brazilian: an Experience of Regional Development]* (Fortaleza: Banco do Nordeste do Brasil Press).

Springate, D., 1972, 'Regional development, incentive grants and private investment in Canada', unpublished Ph.D. dissertation (Cambridge, Mass.: Harvard University).

Sraffa, P., 1960, *Production of Commodities by Means of Commodities: Prelude to a Critique of Economic Theory* (Cambridge: Cambridge University Press).

Stafford, H. A., 1979, *Principles of Industrial Facility Location* (Atlanta: Conway Publications).

Starbuck, J. C., 1976, *Recent Articles on Office and Industrial Parks* (Monticello: Council of Planning Librarians Exchange Bibliography No. 1101).

Stavenhagen, R., 1965, 'Classes, colonialism and acculturation: essay on a system of inter-ethnic relations in Mesoamerica', *Studies in Comparative International Development*, **1**(6), 53–77.

Stedman, M. B. and Wood, P. A., 1965, 'Urban renewal in Birmingham', *Geography*, **50**, 1–17.

Steed, G. P. F., 1968, 'The changing milieu of a firm: a case study of a shipbuilding concern', *Annals of the Association of American Geographers,* **58**, 506–25.

Steed, G. P. F., 1971a, 'Internal organization, firm integration, and locational change: the Northern Ireland linen complex, 1954–64', *Economic Geography,* **47**, 371–83.

Steed, G. P. F., 1971b, 'Plant adaptation, firm environments and location analysis', *The Professional Geographer,* **23**, 324–8.

Steed, G. P. F., 1971c, 'Forms of corporate-environmental adaptation', *Tijdschrift voor Economische en Sociale Geografie,* **62**, 90–4.

Steed, G. P. F., 1971d, 'Locational implications of corporate organization of industry', *The Canadian Geographer,* **15**, 54–7.

Steed, G. P. F., 1971e, 'Changing processes of corporate environment relations', *Area,* **3**, 207–11.

Steed, G. P. F., 1976, 'Centrality and locational change printing, publishing, and clothing in Montreal and Toronto', *Economic Geography,* **52**, 193–205.

Steed, G. P. F., 1978a, 'Global industrial systems—a case study of the clothing industry', *Geoforum,* **9**, 35–47.

Steed, G. P. F., 1978b, 'Product differentiation, locational protection and economic integration: Western Europe's clothing industries', *Geoforum,* **9**, 307–18.

Steed, G. P. F., 1981, 'International location and comparative advantage: the clothing industries and developing countries', in F. E. I. Hamilton and G. J. R. Linge (Eds.), *Spatial Analysis, Industry and the Industrial Environment: Progress in Research and Applications,* Vol. 2 (Chichester: Wiley), 265–303.

Steele, F. E., 1926, *The Banker as a Lender* (London: Pitman).

Stein, S. J., 1957, *The Brazilian Cotton Manufacture: Textile Enterprise in an Underdeveloped Area, 1850–1950* (Cambridge, Mass.: Harvard University Press).

Steinnes, D. N., 1977, 'Causality and intraurban location', *Journal of Urban Economics,* **4**, 69–79.

Steinnes, D. N. and Fisher, W. D., 1974, 'An econometric model of intraurban location', *Journal of Regional Science,* **14**, 65–80.

Stevens, B. H. and Brackett, C. A., 1967, *Industrial Location: A Review and Annotated Bibliography of Theoretical, Empirical and Case Studies* (Philadelphia: Regional Science Research Institute Bibliography Series No. 3).

Stevens, G. V. G., 1974, 'The determinants of investment', in J. H. Dunning (Ed.), *Economic Analysis and the Multinational Enterprise* (London: Allen and Unwin), 47–88.

Stewart, J. Q., 1947, 'Empirical mathematical rules concerning the distribution and equilibrium of population', *The Geographical Review,* **37**, 461–85.

Stilwell, F. J. B., 1974, *Australian Urban and Regional Development* (Sydney: ANZ Book Co.).

Stone, T., 1973, *Analysing the Regional Aspect of Defence Spending: A Survey*

(Aberdeen: University of Aberdeen, Defence Economics Research Unit, Aberdeen Studies in Defence Economics No. 3).

Storper, M., 1981, 'Toward a structural theory of industrial location', in J. Rees, G. J. D. Hewings and H. A. Stafford (Eds.), *Industrial Location and Regional Systems: Spatial Organization in the Economic Sector* (London: Croom Helm), 17–40.

Streit, M. E., 1969, 'Spatial associations and economic linkages between industries', *Journal of Regional Science*, **9**, 177–88.

Struyk, R. J. and James, F. J., 1975, *Intrametropolitan Industrial Location: The Pattern and Process of Change* (Lexington, Mass.: Lexington Books).

Stubenitsky, F., 1970, *American Direct Investment in the Netherlands Industry; A Survey of the Year 1966* (Rotterdam: Rotterdam University Press).

Stuckey, J. A., 1979, 'Vertical integration in aluminium: theory, evidence, and implications for Australia' (paper presented to Eighth Conference of Economists, Melbourne, August 1979).

Study Group on Structural Adjustment (the Crawford Report), 1979, *Report* (Canberra: Australian Government Publishing Service).

Superintêndencia do Desenvolvimento do Nordeste, 1962, *Sumário do Programa do Reequipamento da Indústria Têxtil Regional* [*Summary of a Programme of Re-equipment for the Regional Textile Industry*] (Recife: SUDENE).

Superintêndencia do Desenvolvimento do Nordeste, 1971, *Pesquisa Sobre a Indústria Têxtil do Nordeste* [*Research on the Textile Industry of the Northeast*] (Recife: SUDENE).

Superintêndencia do Desenvolvimento do Nordeste, 1977, *Posição dos Projetos Aprovados: Situação em 31/12/1977* [*Position of Approved Projects: Situation at 31/12/1977*] (Recife: SUDENE).

Superintêndencia do Desenvolvimento do Nordeste, 1978, *A Indústria Têxtil no Nordeste* [*The Textile Industry in the Northeast*] (Recife: SUDENE).

Superintendency for the Development of the Northeast, 1973, *Incentives to Industry and Farming in Northeast Brazil* (Recife: SUDENE).

Susman, P., 1979, 'Problems of regional decline in advanced capitalist countries: the case of northeast England', unpublished Ph.D. dissertation (Worcester, Mass.: Clark University).

Swales, J. R., 1976, 'The formation of new manufacturing enterprises in the West Midlands conurbation, 1963–72' (paper presented to Social Science Research Council Industrial Economics Study Group, University of Newcastle upon Tyne).

Sweezy, P. M., 1942, *The Theory of Capitalist Development: Principles of Marxian Political Economy* (New York: Oxford University Press).

Sykes, J., 1926, *The Amalgamation Movement in English Banking, 1825–1924* (London: P. S. King).

Sylla, R., 1969, 'Federal policy, banking market structure and capital mobilization in the United States, 1863–1913', *Journal of Economic History*, **29**, 657–86.

Sylla, R., 1972, 'The United States, 1863–1913', in R. Cameron (Ed.), *Banking and Economic Development: Some Lessons of History* (New York: Oxford University Press), 232–62.

Taib, M. bin Osman, 1978, 'A place for traditional technology in industrialization planning, Peninsular Malaysia', *Malaysian Geographer*, **1**, 37–58.

Taylor, G., 1979, 'The restructuring of capital in the Teesside chemical and steel industries' (paper presented to a meeting of the Conference of Socialist Economists Regionalism Group, Durham).

Taylor, M. J., 1969, 'Industrial linkage, seedbed growth and the location of firms' (London: University College, Department of Geography Occasional Paper No. 3).

Taylor, M. J., 1975, 'Organisational growth, spatial interaction and location decision-making', *Regional Studies*, **9**, 313–23.

Taylor, M. J., 1977, 'Spatial dimensions of inventiveness in New Zealand: the role of individuals and institutions', *Tijdschrift voor Economische en Sociale Geografie*, **68**, 330–40.

Taylor, M. J., 1978, 'Spatial competition and the sales linkages of Auckland manufacturers', in F. E. I. Hamilton (Ed.), *Contemporary Industrialization: Spatial Analysis and Regional Development* (London: Longman), 144–57.

Taylor, M. J. and Thrift, N. J., 1980, 'Finance and organisations: towards a dualistic interpretation of the geography of enterprise' (paper presented at the Association of American Geographers meeting, Louisville, May 1980).

Taylor, M. J. and Thrift, N. J., 1981, 'The historical geography of financial and industrial organisation: a submodal approach' (paper presented at Association of American Geographers meeting, Los Angeles, May 1981).

Terpstra, V., 1972, *International Marketing* (Hinsdale, Illinois: Dryden Press).

Tew, B., 1977, *The Evolution of the International Monetary System 1945–77* (London: Hutchinson).

The Conference Board, 1974, *Foreign Investment in the United States: Policy, Problems and Obstacles* (New York: The Conference Board).

The Conference Board, 1977–79, *Announcements of Foreign Investment in U.S. Manufacturing Industries* (New York: The Conference Board).

The Economist Newspaper Ltd, 1978, 'The new leviathans: property and financial institutions, a survey' (in *The Economist*, 10 June 1978).

The Economist Newspaper Ltd, 1979, 'Schools brief: the borrowing boom' (in *The Economist*, 24 March 1979, 25–6).

The Economist Newspaper Ltd, 1981, 'No longer a business apart: a survey of Wall Street' (in *The Economist*, 20 June 1981).

Thirlwall, A. P., 1973, 'Forecasting regional unemployment in Great Britain', *Regional Science and Urban Economics*, **5**, 357–74.

Thomas, M. D., 1964, 'The export base and development stages theories of regional economic growth: an appraisal', *Land Economics*, **40**, 421–32.

Thomas, M. D., 1972, 'Growth pole theory: an examination of some of its basic concepts', in N. M. Hansen (Ed.), *Growth Centers in Regional Economic Development* (New York: Free Press), 50–81.

Thomas, M. D., 1980, 'Explanatory frameworks for growth and change in multi-regional firms', *Economic Geography*, **56**, 1–17.

Thomas, M. D. and Le Heron, R. B., 1975, 'Perspectives in technological change and the process of diffusion in the manufacturing sector', *Economic Geography*, **51**, 231–51.

Thomas, W. A., 1978, *The Finance of British Industry, 1918–1976* (London: Methuen).

Thompson, G., 1977, 'The relationship between the financial and industrial sector in the United Kingdom', *Economy and Society*, **6**, 235–83.

Thompson, W. R., 1965, *A Preface to Urban Economics* (Baltimore: Johns Hopkins Press).

Thompson, W. R., 1966, 'Urban economic development', in W. Z. Hirsch (Ed.), *Regional Accounts for Policy Decisions* (Baltimore: Johns Hopkins Press), 81–121.

Thompson, W. R., 1968, 'Internal and external factors in the development of urban economies', in H. S. Perloff and L. Wingo (Eds.), *Issues in Urban Economics* (Baltimore: Johns Hopkins Press), 43–62.

Thompson, W. R., 1972, 'The national system of cities as an object of public policy', *Urban Studies,* **9,** 99–116.

Thorbecke, E., 1973, 'The employment problem: a critical evaluation of four ILO comprehensive country reports', *International Labour Review,* **107,** 393–424.

Thorngren, B., 1970, 'How do contact systems affect regional development', *Environment and Planning A,* **2,** 409–27.

Thoss, R., 1977, *Regional Concentration in the Countries of the European Community* (Brussels: Commission of EC, Regional Policy Series No. 4).

Thwaites, A. T., 1977, *The Industrial Entrepreneur: A Definitional Problem* (Newcastle: University of Newcastle upon Tyne, Centre for Urban and Regional Development Studies Discussion Paper No. 4).

Thwaites, A. T., 1978a, *The Future Development of R. & D. Activity in the Northern Region: A Comment* (Newcastle Upon Tyne: University of Newcastle Upon Tyne, Centre for Urban and Regional Development Studies Discussion Paper No. 12).

Thwaites, A. T., 1978b, 'Technological change, mobile plants and regional development', *Regional Studies,* **12,** 445–61.

Thwaites, A. T., Oakey, R. P. and Nash, P. A., 1981, *Industrial Innovation and Regional Development: Final Report to the Department of the Environment* (2 vols.) (Newcastle: University of Newcastle upon Tyne, Centre for Urban and Regional Development Studies).

Tiebout, C. M., 1956, 'Exports and regional economic growth' and 'Rejoinder', *The Journal of Political Economy,* **64,** 160–4, 169.

Tiebout, C. M., 1957, 'Location theory, empirical evidence and economic evolution', *Regional Science Association, Papers,* **3,** 74–86.

Tiebout, C. M., 1962, *The Community Economic Base Study* (New York: Committee for Economic Development, Supplementary Paper No. 16).

Tiebout, C. M., 1967, 'Input-output and the firm: a technique for using national and regional tables', *Review of Economics and Statistics,* **49,** 260–2.

Tiebout, C. M. and Lane, T., 1966, 'The local service sector in relation to economic growth', in *Research and Education for Regional and Area Development* (Ames: Iowa State University Press), 95–109.

Tilly, R., 1967, 'Germany 1815–1870', in R. Cameron (Ed.), *Banking in the Early Stages of Industrialisation; A Study in Comparative Economic History* (New York: Oxford University Press), 151–82.

Time Incorporated, 1978, *The Fortune Double 500 Directory* (New York: Time Inc.).

Timmins, S. (Ed.), 1967, *Birmingham and the Midland Hardware District: A Series of Reports . . .* (London: F. Cass) (First published 1866 under title *The Resources, Products, and Industrial History of Birmingham).*

To, Y. L., 1980, *Basic Knowledge on the Management of Industrial Enterprises* [in Chinese] (Honan: Honan People's Publication Company).

Todd, D., 1978, *Polarization and the Regional Problem: Manufacturing in Nova Scotia 1960–1973* (Winnipeg: University of Manitoba, Department of Geography Manitoba Geographical Studies No. 6).

Törnqvist, G. E., 1968, 'Flows of information and the location of economic activities', *Geografiska Annaler,* Series B, **50,** 99–107.

Törnqvist, G. E., 1973, 'Contact requirements and travel facilities', in A. R. Pred and G. E. Törnqvist (Eds.), *Systems of Cities and Information Flows: Two Essays* (Lund: Gleerup, Lund Studies in Geography, Series B, No. 38).

Törnqvist, G. E., 1977, 'The geography of economic activities: some critical viewpoints on theory and application', *Economic Geography,* **53,** 153–62.

Townroe, P. M., 1969, 'Locational choice and the individual firm', *Regional Studies*, **3**, 15–24.

Townroe, P. M., 1970, 'Industrial linkage, agglomeration and external economies', *Journal of the Town Planning Institute*, **56**, 18–20.

Townroe, P. M., 1971, *Industrial Location Decisions: A Study in Management Behaviour* (Birmingham: University of Birmingham, Centre for Urban and Regional Studies Occasional Paper No. 15).

Townroe, P. M., 1972, 'Some behavioural considerations in the industrial location decision', *Regional Studies*, **6**, 261–72.

Townroe, P. M., 1976, 'Settling-in costs in mobile plants', *Urban Studies*, **13**, 67–70.

Townsend, A., 1980a, 'Closures and redundancies in Britain' (paper presented to Institute of British Geographers Social Geography Conference on the Impact of the Recession, King's College, London, July 1980).

Townsend, A., 1980b, 'Unemployment, geography and the new government's "regional" aid', *Area*, **12**, 9–18.

Trescott, P. B., 1963, *Financing American Enterprise; The Story of Commercial Banking* (New York: Harper & Row).

Trigge, A. St. L., 1934, *A History of the Canadian Bank of Commerce*, Vol. 3 (Toronto: The Canadian Bank of Commerce).

Tyler, M., 1973, *Interactions between Telecommunications and Face to Face Contact: Prospects for Teleconference Systems* (Cambridge: UK Post Office, Telecommunications Systems Strategy Department Long Range Intelligence Bulletin No. 9).

Tyler, W. G., 1976, *Manufactured Export Expansion and Industrialization in Brazil* (Tübingen: Mohr).

Union Carbide Canada Ltd, n.d., *Saga of a Canadian Inventor: 'Carbide'* (Canada: Union Carbide Canada Ltd).

United Kingdom, Board of Trade, 1963, *The North East: a Programme for Regional Development and Growth* (London: HMSO, Cmnd 2206).

United Kingdom, Central Statistical Office, 1975–80, *Regional Statistics*, Nos. 11–15 (London: HMSO).

United Kingdom, Central Statistical Office, 1981, *Regional Trends* (London: HMSO).

United Kingdom, Department of Employment, 1976–81, *Department of Employment Gazette* (London: HMSO).

United Kingdom, Department of Employment and Productivity, 1971, *British Labour Statistics, Historical Abstract, 1886–1968* (London: HMSO).

United Kingdom, Department of Industry Business Statistics Office, 1974, *Business Monitor: Reports on the Census of Production* (London: HMSO, PA 254).

United Kingdom, Department of Industry Business Statistics Office, 1975a, *Business Monitor Quarterly Series* (London: HMSO, PQ 354).

United Kingdom, Department of Industry Business Statistics Office, 1975b, *Business Monitor: Reports on the Census of Production* (London: HMSO, PA 354).

United Kingdom, Foreign and Commonwealth Office, 1979, *The Newly Industrialising Countries and the Adjustment Problem* (London: Foreign and Commonwealth Office, Government Economic Service Working Paper No. 18).

United Kingdom, Ministry of Labour, 1967, *Ministry of Labour Gazette*, **74**, (London: HMSO).

United Kingdom, Office of Population Censuses and Surveys, 1975, *Census of England and Wales, 1971: Greater Manchester* (London: HMSO).

United Nations Economic Commission for Latin America, 1963, *The Textile Industry in Latin America. Vol, 2: Brazil* (New York: United Nations, Sales no. 64.II.G.2).

United Nations Economic and Social Commission for Asia and the Far East, 1969, *Foreign Trade Statistics of Asia and the Far East, 1966, Volume V, Series A, No. 2, Exports* (New York: United Nations, Sales no. E.70.II.F.5).

United Nations Economic and Social Commission for Asia and the Pacific, 1977, *Statistical Yearbook for Asia and the Pacific* (Bangkok: United Nations, Sales no. E/F.78.II.F.14).

United Nations Economic and Social Commission for Asia and the Pacific, 1978, *Foreign Trade Statistics of Asia and the Pacific, 1975, Volume XIV, Series A, No. 1, Exports* (New York: United Nations, Sales no. E/S.78.II.F.15).

United Nations Economic and Social Council, 1978, *Transnational Corporations in World Development: A Re-examination* (New York: United Nations, Sales no. E.78.II.A.5).

United Nations Industrial Development Organization, 1968, 'Policies and programs for the establishment of industrial estates', *Ekistics*, **25**(148), 177–80.

United Nations Industrial Development Organization, 1977, 'Export Processing Zones in non-APO regions', in N. Vittal (Ed.), *Export Processing Zones in Asia: Some Dimensions* (Tokyo: Asian Productivity Association), 75–80.

United Nations Industrial Development Organization, 1978, *The Effectiveness of Industrial Estates in Developing Countries* (New York: United Nations, Sales no. E.78.II.B.11).

United Nations Industrial Development Organization, 1980, 'Export Processing Zones in developing countries', prepared by the Global and Conceptual Studies Section, International Centre for Industrial Studies (UNIDO Working Papers on Structural Change, No. 19, August 1980).

United States, Bureau of Economic Analysis, Department of Commerce, 1977, *BEA Economic Areas* (Washington, DC: Government Printing Office).

United States, Bureau of Economic Analysis, Department of Commerce, 1980, *Survey of Current Business* (Washington, DC: Government Printing Office).

United States Department of Commerce, 1967, *Regional Effects of Government Procurement and Related Policies* (Washington DC: Government Printing Office).

United States Department of Commerce, 1976, *Foreign Direct Investment in the United States* (Washington, DC: Government Printing Office).

United States Department of Commerce, Office of Foreign Investment in the United States, 1977–79, *The Impact of Foreign Direct Investment on U.S. Cities and Regions* (Washington, DC: Government Printing Office).

United States Department of Commerce, Office of Foreign Investment in the United States, 1980, *Canadian Direct Investment in the United States* (Washington, DC: Government Printing Office).

United States Economic Development Administration, 1972, *Program Evaluation: The EDA Growth Center Strategy* (Washington DC: Government Printing Office).

United States, National Science Foundation, National Science Board, 1977, *Science Indicators, 1976* (Washington, DC: Government Printing Office).

United States, Office of Community Planning and Development, 1979, *The Impact of Foreign Direct Investment on U.S. Cities and Regions* (Washington, DC: US Department of Housing and Urban Development).

United States, President, 1978, *Economic Report of the President* (Washington, DC: Government Printing Office).

University of Waterloo, 1978, *Proposal for the Establishment of the Waterloo Innovation Centre* (Waterloo: University of Waterloo).

Urban Land Institute, 1975, *Industrial Development Handbook* (Washington, DC: The Institute, Community Builders' Handbook Series).

Van, B. G., 1975, 'Survey on duty-free export processing zones in APO member countries', unpublished report to Asian Productivity Organization, July 1975.

Vance, M., 1961, *Planned Industrial Districts* (Monticello: Committee of Planning Librarians Exchange Bibliography No. 17).

Van Driel, G. J., Hartog, J. A. and Van Ravenzwaaij, C., 1975, *On the International Comparison of Technology Matrices* (Rotterdam: Erasmus Universiteit, Department of Economics).

Vernon, R., 1966, 'International investment and international trade in the product cycle', *The Quarterly Journal of Economics*, **80**, 190–207.

Vernon, R., 1971, *Sovereignty at Bay: The Multinational Spread of U.S. Enterprises* (New York: Basic Books).

Vernon, R., 1974, 'The location of economic activity', in J. H. Dunning (Ed.), *Economic Analysis and the Multinational Enterprise* (London: Allen and Unwin), 89–114.

Versiani, F. R., 1972, 'Industrialização e emprego: o problema da reposição de equipamentos [Industrialization and employment: the problem of equipment replacement]', *Pesquisa e Planejamento Econômico*, **2**, 3–54.

Vittal, N., 1977a, 'Summary of discussions of the symposium', in N. Vittal (Ed.), *Export Processing Zones in Asia: Some Dimensions* (Tokyo: Asian Productivity Organization), 38–47.

Vittal, N., 1977b, 'Export Processing Zones—some conceptual aspects', in N. Vittal (Ed.), *Export Processing Zones in Asia: Some Dimensions* (Tokyo: Asian Productivity Organization), 1–13.

Vittal, N., 1977c, 'The economics of Export Processing Zones', in N. Vittal (Ed.), *Export Processing Zones in Asia: Some Dimensions* (Tokyo: Asian Productivity Organization), 24–33.

Von Weber, P., 1977, 'Industrieparks in Portugal', *Geographische Zeitschrift*, **65**, 124–35.

Walker, R. A., 1978, 'The transformation of urban structure in the nineteenth century and the beginnings of suburbanization', in K. Cox (Ed.), *Urbanization and Conflict in Market Societies* (London: Methuen), 165–212.

Wang, K. J., 1977, 'Critical review of costs and benefits of establishing and operating Export Processing Zones in the Republic of China', in N. Vittal (Ed.), *Export Processing Zones in Asia: Some Dimensions* (Tokyo: Asian Productivity Organization), 81–6.

Warnes, A. M., 1977, 'The decentralization of employment from the large English cities' (London: University of London, King's College, Department of Geography Occasional Paper No. 5).

Warntz, W., 1956, 'Measuring spatial association with special consideration of the case of market orientation of production', *Journal of the American Statistical Association*, **51**, 597–604.

Watkins, A. J. and Perry, D. C., 1977, 'Regional change and the impact of uneven urban development', in D. C. Perry and A. J. Watkins (Eds.), *The Rise of the Sunbelt Cities* (Beverly Hills: Sage Publications, Urban Affairs Annual Reviews 14), 19–54.

Watts, H. D., 1980, *The Large Industrial Enterprise: Some Spatial Perspectives* (London: Croom Helm).

Watts, H. D., 1981, *The Branch Plant Economy: A Study of External Control* (Harlow: Longman).

Webber, M. J., 1968, 'Sub-optimal behaviour and the concept of maximum profits in location theory', *Australian Geographical Studies*, **7**, 1–8.

Webber, M. J., 1972, *Impact of Uncertainty on Location* (Cambridge, Mass.: MIT Press).

Webber, M. J., 1980a, *Information Theory and Urban Spatial Structure* (London: Croom Helm).

Webber, M. J., 1980b, 'A theoretical analysis of aggregation in spatial interaction models', *Geographical Analysis*, **12**, 129–41.

Webber, M. J., forthcoming, 'Life cycle stages, mobility and metropolitan change: 1—Theoretical issues; 2—A model of migration', *Environment and Planning A*.

Webber, M. J. and Daly, M. T., 1971a, 'Location of manufacturing growth within cities: a predictive model for Sydney, 1954–1966', *Royal Australian Planning Institute Journal*, **9**, 130–6.

Webber, M. J. and Daly, M. T., 1971b, 'Spatial and temporal variations in short term industrial change within cities', *Australian Geographical Studies*, **9**, 15–32.

Weber, A., 1909, *Uber den Standort der Industrien*, translated by C. J. Friedrich as *Theory of the Location of Industries* (1929) (Chicago: University of Chicago Press).

Webley, S., 1974, *Foreign Direct Investment in the United States: Opportunities and Impediments* (London: British-North American Committee).

Weeks, J., 1975, 'Policies for expanding employment in the informal urban sector of developing economies', *International Labour Review*, **111**, 1–13.

Wells, L. T. (Ed.), 1972, *The Product Life Cycle and International Trade* (Boston: Harvard University, Graduate School of Business Administration).

Wells, L. T., 1977, 'The internationalization of firms from developing countries', in T. Agmon and C. P. Kindleberger (Eds.), *Multinationals from Small Countries* (Cambridge, Mass.: MIT Press), 133–56.

West, G. R., Wilkinson, J. T. and Jensen, R. C., 1979, *Generation of Regional Input-Output Tables for the State and Regions of South Australia, Report to the Treasury Department, the Department of Urban and Regional Affairs, and the Department of Trade and Industry* (St Lucia: University of Queensland, Department of Economics).

West, G. R., Wilkinson, J. T. and Jensen, R. C., 1980, *Generation of Regional Input-Output Tables for the Northern Territory, Report to the Northern Territory Department of the Chief Minister* (St Lucia: University of Queensland, Department of Economics).

Weston, W. J., 1931, *Economics of the English Banking System* (London: Pitman).

Wheaton, W. L. C., 1964, 'Public and private agents of change in urban expansion', in M. M. Webber, J. W. Dyckman, D. L. Foley, A. Z. Guttenberg, W. L. C. Wheaton and C. B. Wurster, *Explorations into Urban Structure* (Philadelphia: University of Pennsylvania Press), 154–96.

Wheelwright, T., 1980, 'The new international division of labour in the age of the transnational corporation', in J. Friedmann, T. Wheelwright and J. Connell (Eds.), *Development Strategies in the Eighties* (Sydney: University of Sydney, Department of Town and Country Planning, The Development Studies Colloquium), 43–58.

White, E. and Hewings, G. J. D., 1979, 'Space-time employment estimation using seemingly unrelated regression analysis' [mimeo] (Urbana: University of Illinois at Urbana-Champaign, Department of Geography).

Whyte, R. O., 1981, 'Employment for Asia's rural labour', *SPAN*, **24**, 57–9.

Whyte, R. O., 1982a, *The Spatial Geography of Rural Economies* (Delhi: Oxford University Press).

Whyte, R. O., 1982b, *The Industrial Potential of Rural Asia* (Hong Kong: University of Hong Kong, Centre of Asian Studies).

Wilbur, C. K. (Ed.), 1979, *The Political Economy of Development and Underdevelopment* (New York: Random House).

Williams, S., 1981, 'Internal colonialism: a theoretical examination' (paper presented to the Workshop on Internal Colonialism organized by the Developing Areas Study Group, Institute of British Geographers, University of Keele).

Wilson, A. G., 1967, 'A statistical theory of spatial distribution models', *Transportation Research*, **1**, 253–69.

Wilson, A. G., 1970a, *Entropy in Urban and Regional Modelling* (London: Pion).

Wilson, A. G., 1970b, *Generalizing the Lowry Model* (London: Centre for Environmental Studies Working Paper 56).

Wilson, A. G., 1974, *Urban and Regional Models in Geography and Planning* (Chichester: Wiley).

Wilson, A. G., 1977, 'Research methods for urban and regional modelling', in A. G. Wilson, P. H. Rees and C. M. Leigh (Eds.), *Models of Cities and Regions: Theoretical and Empirical Developments* (Chichester: Wiley), 1–21.

Wilson, A. G., Rees, P. H. and Leigh, C. M. (Eds.), 1977, *Models of Cities and Regions: Theoretical and Empirical Developments* (Chichester: Wiley).

Winternitz, J., 1948, 'Values and prices: a solution of the so-called transformation problem', *The Economic Journal*, **58**, 276–80.

Wolpe, H., 1975, 'The theory of internal colonialism: the South African case', in I. Oxaal, T. Barnett and D. Booth (Eds.), *Beyond the Sociology of Development: Economy and Society in Latin America and Africa* (London: Routledge and Kegan Paul), 229–52.

Wood, P. A., 1978, *Priorities in Industrial Location Research, A Report to the Human Geography Committee* (London: Social Science Research Council).

Wood, P. A., 1981, 'Industrial geography', *Progress in Human Geography*, **5**, 414–19.

Woodward, R. S., 1974, 'The capital bias of DREE incentives', *Canadian Journal of Economics*, **7**, 161–73.

Wurster, C. B., 1964, 'Introduction', in M. M. Webber, J. W. Dyckman, D. L. Foley, A. Z. Guttenberg, W. L. C. Wheaton and C. B. Wurster, *Explorations into Urban Structure* (Philadelphia: University of Pennsylvania Press), 9–13.

Yamamura, N., 1979, 'Asia's new economic giant in the 1980s', *The World Economy*, **2**, 79–89.

Yamazaki, M., 1980, *Japan's Community-Based Industries: A Case Study of Small Industry* (Tokyo: Asian Productivity Organization).

Yannopoulos, G. N. and Dunning, J. H., 1976, 'Multinational enterprises and regional development: an exploratory paper', *Regional Studies*, **10**, 389–99.

Yeates, M. H. and Lloyd, P. E., 1970, *Impact of Industrial Incentives: Southern Georgian Bay Region, Ontario* (Ottawa: Department of Energy, Mines and Resources).

Zilberberg, R., 1973, *Population Distribution in Israel 1948–1972, Economic Analysis of the Population Dispersal Policy* [in Hebrew] (Jerusalem: Ministry of the Treasury, Economic Planning Authority).

Index

References to countries and geographic names are italicized (e.g. *Aberdeen*) while the titles or names of decision-making economic organizations directly managing productive and service activities are presented in small capitals (e.g. ALCAN ALUMINIUM).

Unit trusts, 370–371, 377–378
UNITED DOMINIONS TRUST (UDT), 374
United Kingdom, xxi–xxii, 9, 12, 16–17,
21, 26, 29, 30, 31–32, 33–35, 42–43,
54, 61, 67, 70–72, 83–85, 122,
126–139, 147, 150, 152–154, 169, 176,
181, 190, 242–252, 255–295, 337, 342,
344–347, 351–355, 360–385, 415, 417–
419, 423, 432, 488
United Kingdom Committee of Inquiry
on Small Firms (Bolton Committee),
266
United Kingdom New Development
Act, 153
United Kingdom New Towns Act, 153
United Kingdom Royal Commission on
the Distribution of the Industrial
Population (the Barlow Report),
42–43
United Kingdom Town and Country
Planning Acts, 153, 249–250
United Nations, 399–400, 430, 442,
540–542, 575
United Nations Industrial Development
Organization (UNIDO), 442, 444,
459, 461
United States, xxi–xxii, 12, 14, 21–22,
29, 35, 43, 45, 47, 48, 52, 117, 150,
152–153, 162, 170, 176, 180–182,
187–188, 206, 226–227, 242, 257, 260,
287, 337–358, 360–385, 387, 391, 399,
413, 416–417, 429–430, 432–433, 435,
488
United States Bureau of Economic
Analysis, 348–351
United States Department of Com-
merce, 55, 348–349
United States Economic Development
Administration, 54–55
United States National Science Foundation, 226
United States Office for Foreign Investment, 348
Unskilled labour, xix, 92–94, 103, 113,
137, 294–295, 302–303, 319, 394–396,
450, 452, 467, 541, 546
Upper Silesian Industrial District, 30
Urban planning, 60, 149–155, 249–252,
404–406, 423–439
Urban redevelopment, 90, 94, 230,
249–252, 418–419, 431, 435, 437–438

Urbanization 128–135, 301, 351, 399,
401–402, 405, 414, 450, 504–505,
512–513, 540–541, 576

Value/Value added, 61–62, 75, 81, 100,
124, 174, 295, 303, 320–322, 342,
345–347, 390–391, 427, 434, 450, 452,
489, 497, 499, 505, 510, 516, 522, 552–
553, 566–570, 576
Vehicles, 12, 16, 24, 70, 207, 267, 284,
295, 312, 333, 375, 405, 410, 416–417,
445, 489, 542–543, 556
Venezuela, 205, 399
Venture capital, 227, 229–232, 374–375
VENTURE FOUNDERS CORPORATION,
229–232
Vertical disintegration, 172, 416
Vertical integration, 21–25, 32–33, 87,
96, 204, 414, 416, 418, 539
Victoria, 204, 216, 401, 403–404, 407
VINIDEC-TUBEMAKERS, 215
VOLKSWAGENWERK AG, xvii–xix
VOLVO AB, 312

Wages, 50, 77, 79–80, 84, 88, 109, 112,
113, 114–115, 120, 148, 173, 177, 180,
185–186, 194, 196, 198–199, 241–242,
253, 319, 344, 390–391, 395–398, 403,
435, 441, 449–450, 452, 456, 458–459,
460–461, 565–566, 571, 577–578
Wales, 9, 15–17, 32, 35–36, 71, 99, 259,
285, 376
Wallonia, 16–17
WALT DISNEY PRODUCTIONS LTD., 381
Waltham (Mass.), 229–230
Warehousing, 230, 361–362, 434–435,
442, 505, 539, 545
Warsaw, 30
Washington(UK), 76, 90, 93
Washington (USA), 50
Water supply, 91, 95, 171, 219, 466, 545,
578
Wearside, 76, 84
Weberian analysis (see also: Classical
concepts; Theory), 19, 122, 125, 170–
173, 454–456
Weipa, 211
Welfare, 18, 19, 20, 23–24, 29, 30,
34–36, 72, 84, 118, 120, 129–135, 143,
148, 150–153, 253, 395–397, 401, 455,
463–464, 535, 548, 571, 574, 577